MORAL ISSUES IN BUSINESS

MORAL ISSUES IN BUSINESS
Fourth Edition

William H. Shaw
San Jose State University
Vincent Barry
Bakersfield College

Wadsworth Publishing Company
Belmont, California
A Division of Wadsworth, Inc.

Philosophy Editor: Kenneth King
Production: Del Mar Associates
Print Buyer: Randy Hurst
Designer: Cynthia Bassett
Copy Editor: Dave Estrada
Compositor: TypeLink, Inc.
Cover: Al Burkhardt

Printed in the United States of America

1 2 3 4 5 6 7 8 9 10---93 92 91 90 89

Library of Congress Cataloging-in-Publication Data

Shaw, William H., 1948–
    Moral issues in business / William Shaw, Vincent Barry. — 4th ed.
        p. cm.
    Rev. ed. of: Moral issues in business / Vincent Barry. 3rd ed.
        c1986.
    Includes bibliographies and index.
    ISBN 0-534-09786-3
    1. Business ethics. 2. Business ethics—Case studies. I. Barry, Vincent E.
II. Barry, Vincent E. Moral issues in business. III. Title.
HF5387.B35 1989   174′.4—dc19   88-20444

PREFACE

This new edition of *Moral Issues in Business* pursues four main objectives of the previous editions: (1) to expose readers to the important moral issues that arise in various business contexts; (2) to provide them with an understanding of the moral, social, and economic environments within which those problems occur; (3) to introduce them to the ethical concepts that are relevant for resolving those moral problems; and (4) to assist them in developing the necessary reasoning and analytical skills for doing so. Although the book's primary emphasis remains on business, its scope has been broadened to include related moral issues in other organizational contexts and in the professions.

Moral Issues in Business has four parts: Part I, "Moral Philosophy and Business," examines the nature of morality and presents the main theories of normative ethics and the leading approaches to questions of economic justice. Part II, "American Business and Its Basis," discusses the institutional foundations of business, focusing on capitalism as an economic system and the nature and role of corporations in our society. Part III, "The Organization and the People in It," identifies a variety of ethical issues and moral challenges that arise out of the interplay of employers and employees within an organization, including the problem of discrimination. Part IV, "Business and Society," concerns moral problems involving consumers, the environment, and the professions.

Although instructors who have used the previous edition will find the organization and structure of the book familiar, there have been substantial changes throughout. The chapter on justice and economic distribution has been moved to Part I; previous chapters on the workplace and on privacy have been merged; and Chapter 11, "The Professions," is entirely new. The text itself has been completely rewritten. In doing so, we have tried to enhance the philosophical depth and accuracy of our treatment of issues, while at the same time retaining our commitment to providing students with a text that they will find clear, understandable, and engaging. We have updated material wherever necessary, and the book now discusses many new topics, including ethical relativism, the nature of conscience, *prima facie* principles, civil liberties in the corporation, day care and maternity leave, the legal context of affirmative action, sexual harassment, the debate over the social desirability of advertising, and our obligations to future generations and to animals, among many more.

The case studies in our book are intended to provide a springboard for lively discussions in class and for applying ethical concepts. We have retained, and where necessary updated, cases that (according to previous users) performed this function well. But we have also added a variety of new cases, increasing the total to forty. The book's carefully edited readings are intended to supplement the text by permitting topics to be pursued in more detail and by exposing students to alternative perspectives and analyses. The readings have increased in number to twenty-six, two-thirds of which are new. In selecting the readings, we have sought to provide philosophically interesting essays that will engage students and lend themselves well to class discussion.

Because of the three types of material in the book—text, cases, and readings—and because of the amount of material we have provided and the range of topics covered, teachers have great flexibility in how they use *Moral Issues in Business* and in how they organize their courses. Naturally, the book can be taught from cover to cover just as it is, but in a semester course this will require a fairly brisk pace. Many instructors will wish to linger on certain topics, touch briefly on others, and skip some altogether.

Assigning all the cases and extra readings as well as the text of a chapter obviously provides for the greatest depth of coverage, but the text can easily be taught by itself or with only some of the cases or readings. The book readily permits topics to be dealt with briefly by assigning only selections from the case studies, the readings, or the text itself, instead of the chapter as a whole. Depending on the instructor's approach and classroom style, it is even possible that the focus of the course could be the case studies themselves or the readings, with the text assigned only as recommended background.

The chapters themselves are surprisingly self-contained, permitting them to be taught in various orders. Instructors eager to get to the more specific moral issues discussed in later chapters could skip Parts I and II (perhaps assigning only Solomon and Hanson's "It's Good Business") and begin with the topics that interest them. Other instructors might wish to start with the analysis of capitalism in Chapter 5 or with the discussion of corporate social responsibility in Chapter 6, then spend the bulk of the term on the chapters discussing particular moral topics in business, returning later to some of the issues of Part I. Yet other teachers may wish to devote much of a semester to the foundational concerns of Parts I and II and deal more briefly and selectively with later matters.

We wish to acknowledge our great debt to the many people whose ideas and writings have influenced us over the years. Philosophy is widely acknowledged to involve a process of ongoing dialogue. This is nowhere more evident than in the writing and rewriting of philosophy textbooks, whose authors can rarely claim that the ideas being synthesized, organized, and presented are theirs alone. Without our colleagues, without our students, and without a larger philosophical community concerned with business and ethics, this book would not be possible. We also thank our reviewers for their suggestions and criticisms: George E. Derfer, California State Polytechnic University at Pomona; Salvatore DeSimone,

Salem State College; Robert Winslow Faaborg, University of Cincinnati; Frank Fair, Sam Houston State University; Leslie Francis, University of Utah; Samuel Gomez, North Adams State College; Michael Harrington, University of Mississippi; and Robert M. Johnson, Castleton State College.

William H. Shaw
Vincent Barry

BRIEF CONTENTS

CONTENTS

Chapter 7: Moral Choices Facing Employees   296

Chapter 8: Job Discrimination   347

PART IV: BUSINESS AND SOCIETY   389

Chapter 9: Consumers   389

Chapter 10: The Environment   440

Chapter 11: The Professions   480

MORAL ISSUES IN BUSINESS

PART I
MORAL PHILOSOPHY AND BUSINESS

CHAPTER 1
THE NATURE OF MORALITY

Sometimes the rich and mighty fall. Ivan F. Boesky's world began crumbling in the last months of 1986. On April 23, 1987, he formally pleaded guilty in federal court to a felony charge of stock manipulation. Although everyone in the courtroom realized that he had been involved in a wide range of criminal activity, Boesky was not charged on any further counts because he was cooperating with the authorities in their investigations. But a brilliant career had nose-dived and crashed.

Boesky had been Wall Street's best-known speculator in corporate takeovers. During the recent boom months in the stock market, as various corporate wars of merger and acquisition were fought, Boesky was often behind the scenes as the institutional fates of billion-dollar organizations were decided. He became rich in the process, but he was also a symbol of the new breed of corporate raiders and Wall Street financiers. *Time* had put him on its cover. Now everybody knew that he was crooked.

When word of Boesky's impending indictment was first made public, Wall Street was awash in rumors. Boesky was a big fish; if he did time for illegal insider trading, it seemed clear that other giants of commerce would, too. And Boesky was soon telling authorities shocking tales of corruption on Wall Street and disclosing wrongdoing by a number of major securities firms. When the ex-

traordinarily sustained bull market led to an equally spectacular crash in October 1987, some business writers drew historical comparisons with the shady characters who had dominated the stock market before the great crash of 1929 and who were later jailed for their illegal activities. Nor was Wall Street's reputation helped much earlier in 1987 by the well-publicized drug bust of some of its top brokers, caught by a federal sting operation offering cocaine to their clients along with the usual array of stock options.

Against this backdrop, Federal Judge Morris Lasker decided that Boesky should go to jail as a warning to others, despite his having cooperated with authorities. On December 18, 1987, Lasker sentenced the former arbitrageur to three years in jail. This was in addition to the $100 million civil penalty that Boesky had already paid and to the scores of lawsuits that still faced him.

Although the topic of business ethics has been a recurrent theme in the popular media, the Boesky and other Wall Street scandals have now made it virtually impossible for a person to avoid hearing some discussion of it. In the newspapers and on television, commentators worry that greed is running rampant in the business world—that its leaders are more interested in fast profits through corporate takeovers and stock maneuvers than in making money through the more

member making money by manipulation rather than by producing something

1

time-honored practice of actually producing
goods and competing with them in the marketplace. The nation's recent crop of MBAs
have also come in for a drubbing, with various
pundits alleging that our future captains of
finance and industry are devoid of any sense
of social responsibility and uniquely single
minded in their pursuit of personal gain.

Although "business ethics" makes good
copy for the media, not all moral issues in
business involve the giants of Wall Street or
cocaine sales, and few cases of business ethics
gain wide publicity. The vast majority of them
involve the mundane, uncelebrated moral
challenges that working men and women
meet daily and suffer silently. The topic of
business ethics includes not just the question
of the moral or immoral motivations of businesspeople, but also a whole range of problems that arise in the context of business.
These issues are too numerous to compile,
but consider these typical questions:

Is passing a lie-detector test a justifiable pre-employment condition? Are
personality and honesty tests? What, if
anything, must business do to improve
work conditions?

Should manufacturers reveal product
defects? At what point does "acceptable
exaggeration" become lying about a
product?

Is a corporation obliged to help remedy social problems such as poverty,
pollution, and urban decay? Must business help fight sexism and racism?

May a worker ever use privileged information to advance his or her own
interests? Is insider trading immoral? Is a
ban on it enforceable?

What, if anything, does a worker owe
outside parties, such as customers, competitors, or society generally?

When, if ever, is an act of "whistle
blowing" defensible (that is, going public with information about organizational
wrongdoing)?

These questions typify business issues
with *moral* significance. The answers we give

to them will be determined largely by our
moral standards, principles, and values.
What these standards and principles are,
where they come from, and how they can be
assessed are some of the concerns of this
opening chapter in our study of business
ethics. In particular we shall examine the following topics:

1. The definition of "ethics" and "morality,"
   and the scope and purpose of business
   ethics.

2. The distinguishing features of morality,
   and how it differs from etiquette, law, and
   professional codes of conduct.

3. The relation between morality and
   religion.

4. The doctrine of "ethical relativism" and
   its difficulties.

5. What it means to have moral principles,
   the nature of conscience, and the relationship between morality and self-interest.

6. The place of values and ideals in a person's life.

7. The social and psychological factors that
   sometimes jeopardize an individual's
   integrity.

8. The characteristics of sound moral
   reasoning.

ETHICS

"The word 'ethics' comes from the Greek
word *ethos*, meaning character or custom,"
writes philosophy professor Robert C. Solomon.[1] Today we use the word "ethos" to refer
to the distinguishing disposition, character,
or attitude of a specific people, culture, or
group (as in, for example, "the American
ethos" or "the business ethos"). According to
Solomon, the etymology of "ethics" suggests
its basic concerns: (1) individual character, including what it means to be "a good person,"
and (2) the social rules that govern and limit
our conduct, especially the ultimate rules con-

cerning right and wrong, which we call *morality*.[2]

Some philosophers like to distinguish ethics from morality, such that "morality" refers to human conduct and values and "ethics" refers to the study of those areas. By this account, "morals" and "moral" refer to the conduct itself, whereas "ethics" and "ethical" refer to the study of moral conduct or to the code of conduct one follows. In everyday parlance, however, we interchange "ethical" and "moral" to describe people we consider "good" and actions we consider "right." And we interchange "unethical" and "immoral" to describe "bad" people and "wrong" actions. We will follow this convention throughout this text.

The study of ethics concerns questions of moral right and wrong, duty and obligation, and moral responsibility. For example, is an act of abortion or euthanasia ever morally permissible? Are we always morally obliged to tell the truth, or may we lie sometimes? Under what conditions am I morally responsible for my actions?

Business and Organizational Ethics

The primary focus of this book is ethics as it applies to business. *Business ethics is the study of what constitutes right and wrong, or good and bad, human conduct in a business context.* For example, is a worker ever *right* in "blowing the whistle"? Under what conditions, if any, can such an act be justified? Is a worker ever morally *obliged* to blow the whistle?

One difficulty in talking about business ethics is that "business" and "businessperson" have various meanings. "Business" may denote a corner hamburger stand or a corporation that does business in several nations. A "businessperson" may be a gardener engaged in a one-person operation or a corporation president responsible for thousands of workers and enormous corporate investments. We will simply use the word "business" to mean *any organization whose objective is to provide goods or services for profit.* "Businesspeople" are *those who participate in planning, organizing, or directing the work of business.*

But this text takes a broader view as well. It is concerned with moral issues that arise *anywhere* that employers and employees come together. Thus, it is as much about "organizational" as "business" ethics.

An organization is a group of people working together to achieve a common purpose. The purpose may be to offer a product or service primarily for profit, as in business. But the purpose may be health care, as in medical organizations, public safety and order, as in law-enforcement organizations, education, as in academic organizations, and so on. A number of the cases and illustrations you will come across in this text, therefore, deal with moral issues and dilemmas in nonbusiness organizational settings, with what constitutes right and wrong human conduct within organizational practice, policy, and relationships.

In addition, many questions explored in this book concern topics that are also relevant to "professional ethics," that is, to the ethical problems that professionals—like lawyers, nurses, engineers, and many others—face in various contexts. All the major professions have a significant business aspect to them; moreover, many business people view themselves as "professionals." (Harvard Business School, for example, sees itself as "making business a profession.") So, it should not be surprising that there is a large overlap between professional ethics and business ethics. Some moral dilemmas that arise specifically in professional practice—for example, client confidentiality and the idea of loyalty to the profession—are discussed in Chapter 11, along with the difficult question of what it means to be a "professional" in the first place.

People occasionally poke fun at the idea of "business ethics," declaring that the term is a contradiction or that business has no ethics. Such people take themselves to be worldly and realistic. They think that they have a down-to-earth idea of how things really work. In fact, this attitude, despite its pretense of sophistication, is embarrassingly naive. People who express it have little grasp of the nature of ethics and only a superficial understanding of the real world of business, organizations, and the professions. The authors hope that after you have read this book, you will see the truth of this judgment.

Because the study of business, organizational, and professional ethics is part of the general study of ethics, this book discusses general ethical concepts. For example, if we are to discover the guidelines for moral decision making within any organization, we must first explore guidelines for making moral decisions generally. One way to do this is to investigate general ethical theories.

The intimacy between general ethical theory and ethics as applied to business contexts implies that one's personal ethics cannot be neatly divorced from one's organizational ethics. In fact, it is safe to say that those who have studied and thought seriously about ethics in general have a more useful basis for making moral decisions in an organizational setting than those who have not.

Perhaps recognition of the intimacy between personal and organizational ethics was what prompted a number of chief executive officers (CEOs) of top American companies and the deans and alumni of prestigious business schools to suggest in a recent study that the ideal graduate program in business administration should include a sound grounding in ethics. In the words of Roger L. Jenkins, dean for graduate business programs at the University of Tennessee and the study's conductor: "Today's marketplace calls for a business executive who is bold enough to build his [or her] reputation on integrity and who has a keen sensitivity to the ethical ramifications of his [or her] decision making."[3]

If people within business and nonbusiness organizations are to have the "keen sensitivity to the ethical ramifications" of their decision making that the dean refers to, they must have moral standards. Moral standards are the basis for moral behavior and differ significantly from nonmoral standards.

MORAL VERSUS NONMORAL STANDARDS

What falls outside the sphere of moral concern is termed "nonmoral." Whether your new sports car will "top out" at 120 or 130 mph is a nonmoral question. Whether you should top it out on Main Street on a Wednesday at high noon (or even at 3 A.M., for that matter!) would be a moral question. To see why requires an understanding of the difference between moral standards and other kinds of standards.

Wearing shorts to a formal dinner party would be boorish behavior. Murdering the "King's English" with grammatical solecisms violates the basic conventions of proper language usage. Photographing the finish of a horse race with low-speed film is poor photographic technique. In each case a standard is violated—fashion, grammatical, artistic—but the violation does not pose a serious threat to human well-being.

One characteristic of moral standards that distinguishes them from others is that they concern behavior that can be of serious consequence to human welfare, that can profoundly injure or benefit people.[4] Driving at breakneck speed down Main Street can result in injury to someone, whereas driving cautiously minimizes that risk. Unsafe or unhealthful products, dangerous work conditions, invasions of privacy, and environmental pollution all threaten human well-being. On the other hand, safe and healthful products, safe work conditions, respect for privacy, and environmental stewardship generally benefit people. The conventional moral norms against lying, stealing, and murder deal with actions that can hurt people. And the moral principle that human beings should be treated with dignity and respect uplifts the human personality.

A second characteristic of moral standards is that their soundness depends on the adequacy of the reasons that support or justify them. For the most part, fashion standards are set by clothing designers, merchandisers, and consumers; grammatical standards by grammarians and students of language; artistic standards by art critics and academics. Legislators make laws, boards of directors make organizational policy, and licensing boards establish standards for professionals. In every case, some authoritative body is the ultimate validating source of the standards and thus can change the standards if it wishes. Moral standards are not made by such bodies, although they are often endorsed or rejected by them. More precisely, the validity of moral standards depends not on authoritative fiat but on the adequacy of the reasons that support or justify them. Precisely what constitutes "adequate reasons" for moral standards is problematic and, as we will see, lies at the base of abundant disagreement about the legitimacy of specific moral principles.

Although these two features set moral standards apart from others, it is useful to distinguish morality more specifically from three areas with which it is sometimes confused: etiquette, law, and so-called professional codes of ethics.

Morality and Etiquette

Etiquette refers to any special code of behavior or courtesy. In our society, for example, it is usually considered bad etiquette to eat with one's fingers or to use obscene language in public; it is considered good etiquette to say "please" when requesting and "thank you" when receiving and to hold a door open for someone entering immediately behind us. Good business etiquette typically calls for follow-up letters to meetings, returning phone calls, and appropriate dress. It is commonplace to judge people's manners as "good" or "bad" and the conduct that reflects them as "right" or "wrong." Thus, "The treasurer was wrong to use vulgar language at the board meeting," "Jane was right to introduce her friend to her parents," "It's bad to slurp your soup," "It's good to wear dark clothes to a funeral." "Good," "bad," "right," and "wrong" here simply mean "socially appropriate" or "socially inappropriate." In these contexts, such words express judgments about manners, not ethics; about matters of taste, not morality.

So-called rules of etiquette that you might learn in an etiquette book are prescriptions for socially acceptable behavior. If you want to "fit in," get along with others, and be thought well of by them, you should observe common rules of etiquette. If you violate the rules, then you're rightly considered ill-mannered or uncivilized, but not necessarily immoral.

Rules of etiquette are generally nonmoral assertions: "Give the groom your 'congratulations,' but the bride your 'best wishes'"; "Push your chair back into place upon leaving a dinner table." But what is considered bad taste can also raise a moral question. The male boss who refers to female subordinates as "honey" and "doll" shows bad manners. If such epithets diminish the worth of female employees or perpetuate sexism, then they also raise moral issues concerning equal treatment and denial of dignity to human beings.

Scrupulous observance of rules of etiquette does not make one moral. In fact, it can camouflage moral issues that only etiquette rule-breaking can expose. Not too long ago in some parts of the United States it was thought "bad manners" for blacks and whites to eat together. Those who obeyed the convention and were thus judged "well-mannered" certainly had no grounds for feeling moral. The only way to dramatize the injustice underlying this practice was to violate the rule and be judged "ill mannered." For those in the 1960s who conducted "sit-ins," being considered boorish was a small price to pay for exposing the unequal treatment and human degradation that underlay this rule of etiquette.

Morality and Law

Before distinguishing between morality and law, let's clarify the term *law*. Basically, there are four kinds of law: statutes, regulations, common law, and constitutional law.

1. *Statutes* are laws enacted by legislative bodies. The law that prohibits theft is a statute. Congress and state legislatures enact statutes. (Laws enacted by local governing bodies like city councils usually are termed *ordinances*.) Statutes comprise a large part of the law and are what many of us mean when we speak of "laws."

Limited in their knowledge, legislatures often set up boards or agencies whose functions include issuing detailed regulations of certain kinds of conduct—*administrative regulations.* For example, state legislatures establish license boards to formulate regulations for the licensing of physicians and nurses. As long as these regulations do not exceed the board's statutory powers and do not conflict with other kinds of law, they are legally binding.

3. *Common law* refers to laws applied in the English-speaking world before there were any statutes. Courts frequently wrote opinions explaining the bases of their decisions in specific cases, including the legal principles they deemed appropriate. Each of these opinions became a precedent for later decisions in similar cases. Over the years, a massive body of legal principles accumulated that is collectively referred to as common law. Like administrative regulations, common law is valid if it harmonizes with statutory law and with still another kind, constitutional law.

4. *Constitutional law* refers to court rulings on the constitutionality of any law. The courts are empowered under the U.S. Constitution to decide whether laws are compatible with the Constitution. State courts may also rule on the constitutionality of state laws under state constitutions. Although the courts cannot make laws, they have far-reaching powers to rule on the constitutionality of laws and to declare them invalid. The U.S. Supreme Court has the greatest judiciary power and rules on an array of cases, some of which bear directly on our study of ethics.

Is the law, whatever its source, always a reliable standard for determining moral conduct? It is, if and only if: (1) what is legal is always moral, and (2) what is not prohibited by law is always moral. Both these propositions, however, are untrue.

Regarding the first—that what is legal is necessarily moral—consider an actual case of a four-month-old baby suffering from diarrhea and fever.[5] The family physician prescribed medication on the second day of the child's illness and saw him during office hours on the third day. On the fourth day, the child's condition worsened. Knowing that the doctor was not in the office that day, the parents whisked the child to the emergency room of a nearby hospital, where they were told that hospital policy forbade treating anyone already under a doctor's care without first contacting the doctor. Unable to reach the doctor and thus denied emergency treatment, the parents took their child home, where he died later that day of what turned out to be bronchial pneumonia.

There was a time when hospitals had a legal right to accept for emergency treatment only those they chose to accept. Under such a rule, then, the hospital would have been exercising its legal right. But would the hospital have been morally justified in exercising that right, when by so doing it would deny the child life-saving care? Philosophers might disagree in their answers. But they would agree that the issue cannot be satisfactorily resolved by appeal to law alone. The hospital may have acted legally but immorally. (As it happened, the case went to court and set a precedent of repudiation of the traditional discretionary powers given a hospital in operating its emergency facility. But if the court had upheld the institution's legal right, profound moral questions of injury and fairness would have still remained.)

What about the second proposition—that what is not expressly prohibited by law is always moral? Let's suppose that you're driving to work one day and see an accident victim on the side of the road, blood oozing from his leg. He is clearly in need of immediate medical attention, which you can provide since you just completed a first aid course. *Should* (not *would*) you stop?

Legally speaking, you have no obligation to stop and offer aid. Under the common law, the prudent thing would be to drive on, since by stopping you would bind yourself to use reasonable care and thus incur legal liability if you fail to do so and the victim thereby suffers injury.

Most states have enacted so-called "Good Samaritan laws" to provide immunity from damages to those rendering aid (except for gross negligence or serious misconduct). But the law does not oblige people to render such aid or even (in most states) to call an ambulance. Moral theorists would agree, however, that if you sped away without rendering aid or even calling for help, your action might be perfectly legal, but it would be morally suspect. Regardless of the law, such conduct would raise serious moral questions of beneficence, noninjury, and justice.

Again, most businesses are permitted to price products and services at whatever level the market will bear. Within the constraints of minimum wage law, they can pay workers whatever they choose. In many states, employers may use polygraph (lie detector) tests as pre-employment screens. Although perfectly legal, these practices raise moral concerns about fairness, noninjury, privacy, autonomy, and respect for persons—all matters of critical importance to human well-being.

What then may we say of the relationship between law and morality? (In theory and practice, law codifies customs, ideals, beliefs, and a society's moral values. Law undoubtedly reflects changes in a society's outlooks, its views of right and wrong, good and bad. But it is a mistake to view law as sufficiently establishing the moral standards of an individual, a profession, an organization, or society. Law simply cannot cover the variety of individual and group conduct. The law does prohibit egregious affronts to a society's moral standards and in that sense is the "floor" of moral conduct. But countless cases of less-than-wanton breaches of moral conduct fall through the cracks in that floor.

Although useful in alerting us to moral issues and informing us of our rights and responsibilities, law cannot be taken as an adequate standard of moral conduct. Conformity with law is neither requisite nor sufficient for determining moral conduct any more than conformity to rule of etiquette is. By the same token, nonconformity with law is not necessarily immoral, for the law disobeyed may be unjust. Probably no one in the modern era has expressed this point more eloquently than the inspirational president of the Southern Christian Leadership Conference, Reverend Martin Luther King, Jr. Confined in the Birmingham, Alabama, city jail on charges of "parading without a permit," King penned his now famous "Letter From Birmingham Jail" to eight of his fellow clergymen who had published a statement attacking King's unauthorized protest of racial segregation as unwise and untimely. King wrote:

> All segregation statutes are unjust because segregation distorts the soul and damages the personality. It gives the segregator a false sense of superiority and the segregated a false sense of inferiority. Segregation, to use the terminology of the Jewish philosopher Martin Buber, substitutes an "I-it" relationship for an "I-thou" relationship and ends up relegating persons to the status

of things. Hence segregation is not only politically, economically, and sociologically unsound, it is morally wrong and sinful. Paul Tillich has said that sin is separation. Is not segregation an existential expression of man's tragic separation, his awful estrangement, his terrible sinfulness? Thus it is that I can urge men to obey the 1954 decision of the Supreme Court,[6] for it is morally right; and I can urge them to disobey segregation ordinances, for they are morally wrong.[7]

Professional Codes

Somewhere between etiquette and law lie professional codes of ethics. These are the rules that are supposed to govern the conduct of members of a given profession. Generally speaking, the members of a profession are understood to have agreed to abide by those rules as a condition of their engaging in that profession. Violation of the professional code may result in the disapproval of one's professional peers and, in serious cases, loss of one's license to practice that profession. Sometimes these codes are unwritten and are part of the common understanding of members of a profession as to what constitutes proper professional conduct—for example, that professors should not date students in their classes. In other instances, these codes, or portions of them, may be written down by various authoritative bodies in order that they may be better taught and more efficiently enforced.

These written rules are sometimes so vague and general as to be of little value, and often they amount to little more than self-promotion by the professional organization. The same is frequently true when industries or corporations publish statements of their ethical standards. In other cases, for example with attorneys, professional codes can be very specific and detailed. It is hard to generalize about the content of professional codes of ethics, however, since they frequently involve a mix of purely moral rules (e.g., concerning client confidentiality), of professional etiquette (e.g., concerning the billing of services to other professionals), and of restrictions intended to benefit the group's economic interests (e.g., prohibition of price competition).

Given their nature, professional codes of ethics are neither a complete nor a completely reliable guide to one's moral obligations. First, not all the rules of a professional code are purely moral in character, and even where they are, the fact that a rule is officially enshrined as part of the code of a profession does not guarantee that it is a sound moral principle. As a professional, you must take seriously the injunctions of your profession, but you still have the responsibility to critically assess those rules for yourself.

Regarding those parts of the code that concern etiquette or financial matters, bear in mind that by joining a profession, you are probably agreeing, explicitly or implicitly, to abide by those standards. Assuming that those rules don't require morally impermissible conduct, then consenting to them gives you some moral obligation to follow them. In addition, for many, living up to the standards of a chosen profession is an important source of personal satisfaction. Still, you must be alert to situations in which professional standards or customary professional practice conflicts with the ordinary demands of morality. Adherence to a professional code does not exempt one's conduct from scrutiny from the broader perspective of morality.

Where Do Moral Standards Come From?

So far we have distinguished moral standards from various nonmoral standards, but you are probably concerned to know the source of those moral standards. As we shall discuss later, most, if not all, people have certain moral principles, or a moral code, which they explicitly or implicitly accept.

Since the moral principles of different people in the same society overlap, at least in part, we can also talk about the moral code of a society, meaning the moral standards shared in common by its members. How do we come to have certain moral principles and not others? Obviously, many things influence us in the moral principles we accept: our early upbringing, the behavior of those around us, the explicit and implicit standards of our culture, our own experiences, and our critical reflections on those experiences.

For philosophers, though, the important question is not how in fact we come to have the particular principles we have. The philosophical issue is whether the principles we have can be justified. Do we simply take for granted the values of those around us, or, like Martin Luther King, Jr., are we able to think independently about moral matters? By analogy, we pick up our nonmoral beliefs from all sorts of sources: textbooks, conversations with friends, movies, various experiences we've had. The philosopher's concern is not so much with how we actually get the beliefs we have, but whether, or to what extent, those beliefs—for example, that women are more emotional than men or that telekinesis is possible—can withstand critical scrutiny. Likewise, ethical theories attempt to justify moral standards and ethical beliefs. In the next chapter, we examine some of the major theories of normative ethics. That is, we will be looking at what some of the major thinkers in human history have argued to be the best-justified standards of right and wrong.

But first we need to look at the relation between morality and religion on the one hand, and morality and society on the other. Some people maintain that morality just boils down to religion. Others have argued for the doctrine of *ethical relativism*, which says that right and wrong are only a function of what your particular society takes to be right and wrong. The authors of this text maintain that both these views are mistaken.

RELIGION AND MORALITY

Any religion provides its believers with a world view, part of which involves certain moral instructions, values, and commitments. The Jewish and Christian traditions, to name just two, offer a view of humans as unique products of a divine intervention that has endowed them with consciousness and an ability to love. Both these traditions posit creatures who stand midway between nature and spirit. On the one hand, we are finite, bound to earth, and capable of sin. On the other, we can transcend nature and realize infinite possibilities.

Primarily because of the influence of Western religion, many Americans and others view themselves as beings with a supernatural destiny, as possessing a life after death, as being immortal. One's purpose in life is found in serving and loving God. For the Christian, the way to serve and love God is by emulating the life of Jesus of Nazareth. In the life of Jesus, Christians find an expression of the highest virtue—love. They love when they perform selfless acts, develop a keen social conscience, and realize that human beings are creatures of God and therefore intrinsically worthwhile. For the Jew, one serves and loves God chiefly through expressions of justice and righteousness. Jews also develop a sense of honor derived from a commitment to truth, humility, fidelity, and kindness. This commitment hones their sense of responsibility to family and community.

Religion, then, involves not only a formal system of worship but prescriptions for social relationships. One example is the mandate "Do unto others as you would have them do unto you." Termed "the Golden Rule," this injunction represents one of humankind's highest moral ideals and can be found in essence in all the great religions of the world.

Good people proceed while considering that what is best for others is best for themselves. (*Hitopadesa*, Hinduism)

Thou shalt love thy neighbor as thyself. (*Leviticus* 19:18, Judaism)

Therefore all things whatsoever ye would that men should do to you, do ye even so to them. (*Matthew* 7:12, Christianity)

Hurt not others with that which pains yourself. (*Udanavarga* 5:18, Buddhism)

What you do not want done to yourself, do not do to others. (*Analects* 15:23, Confucianism)

No one of you is a believer until he loves for his brother what he loves for himself. (*Traditions*, Islam)

Although inspiring, such religious ideals are very general and can be difficult to translate into precise policy injunctions. Religious bodies, nevertheless, occasionally articulate positions on more specific political, educational, economic, and medical issues, which help mold public opinion on matters as diverse as abortion, euthanasia, nuclear weapons, and national defense. Roman Catholicism has a rich tradition of formally applying its core values to the moral aspects of industrial relations. The National Conference of Catholic Bishops' recent pastoral letter, *Economic Justice for All*, on Catholic social teaching and the U.S. economy, stands in this tradition. Having gone through several drafts over more than two years before its final approval by the Conference in November 1986, the pastoral letter is really a book-length reflection on the moral dimensions and human consequences of American economic life. It examines specific policy questions and is intended to help shape a national discussion of these issues.

Morality Needn't Rest on Religion

Many people believe that morality must be based on religion, either in the sense that without religion people would have no incentive to be moral or in the sense that only religion can provide us guidance. Others contend that morality is based on the commands of God. None of these claims is very plausible.

First, although a desire to avoid hell and to go to heaven may prompt some people to act morally, this is not the only reason, or even the most common reason, that people behave morally. Often, we act morally out of habit or simply because that is the kind of person we are. It would just not occur to us to swipe that elderly lady's purse. And if the idea did occur to us, we wouldn't do it because it simply doesn't fit with our personal standards or with our concept of ourselves. We are often motivated to do what is morally right out of concern for others or just because it is right. In addition, the approval of our peers, the need to appease our consciences, as well as the desire to avoid earthly punishment, all may motivate us to behave morally. And it is worth noting that many atheists—like the philosopher Bertrand Russell—have led morally admirable lives.

Second, the moral instructions of the world's great religions are general and somewhat vague: they do not relieve one of the necessity to engage in moral reasoning oneself. For example, the Bible says, "Thou shall not kill." Yet, Christians disagree among themselves over the morality of fighting in wars, of capital punishment, of killing in self-defense, of slaughtering animals, of abortion and euthanasia, and of allowing foreigners to die from famine because we have not provided them with as much food as we might have. The Bible does not give unambiguous answers to these moral problems. So, even a believer is led to engage in moral philosophy if he or she is to have an intelligent answer to them. On the other hand, there are lots of reasons for believing that, say, a cold-blooded murder motivated by greed is immoral; one does not have to believe in a religion to figure that out.

Third, although some theologians have

advocated the *Divine Command Theory*—that if something is wrong (like killing an innocent person for fun), then the only reason it is wrong is that God commands us not to do it—many theologians and certainly most philosophers would reject this view. They would contend that if God commands human beings not to do something, like commit rape, it is because God sees that rape is wrong. God forbids rape because rape is wrong, but it is not God's forbidding rape that makes it wrong. The fact that rape is wrong is independent of God's decrees.

Most believers think not only that God gives us moral instructions or rules, but also that God has moral reasons for giving them to us. According to the Divine Command Theory, this would make no sense. In this view, there is no reason that something is right or wrong, other than it being God's will. All believers, of course, believe that God is good and that He commands us to do what is right and forbids us to do what is wrong. But this doesn't mean, say the critics of the Divine Command Theory, that it is God's saying so that makes it wrong, anymore than it is your mother's telling you not to steal that makes it wrong to steal.

All this is simply to argue that morality is not necessarily based on religion in any of the three senses distinguished above. That religion influences the moral standards and values of most of us is beyond doubt. But given that religions differ in their moral principles, and that even members of the same faith often disagree among themselves on moral matters, practically speaking you cannot justify a moral principle simply by appealing to religion—for that will only persuade those who already agree with your particular interpretation of your particular religion. Besides, most religions hold that human reason is capable of understanding what is right and wrong, so it is human reason to which you will have to appeal in order to support your ethical principle.

ETHICAL RELATIVISM

Some people do not believe that morality boils down to religion, but rather that it is just a function of what a particular society happens to believe. This view is called *ethical relativism*. It is the theory that what is right is determined by what a culture or society says is right. What is right in one place may be wrong in another, because the only criterion for distinguishing right from wrong—and so the only ethical standard for judging an action—is the moral system of the society in which the act occurs.

Abortion, for example, is condemned as immoral in Catholic Spain but is practiced as a morally neutral form of birth control in Japan. According to the ethical relativist, then, abortion is wrong in Spain but morally permissible in Japan. The relativist is not saying merely that the Spanish believe abortion is abominable and the Japanese do not; that is acknowledged by everyone. Rather, the ethical relativist contends that abortion is immoral in Spain because the Spanish believe it to be immoral and morally permissible in Japan because the Japanese believe it to be so. Thus, for the ethical relativist there is no absolute ethical standard independent of cultural context, no criterion of right and wrong by which to judge other than that of particular societies. In short, what morality requires is relative to society.

Those who endorse ethical relativism point to the apparent diverseness of human values and the multiformity of moral codes to support their case. From our own cultural perspective, some seemingly "immoral" moralities have been adopted; polygamy, homosexuality, stealing, slavery, infanticide, and the eating of strangers have all been tolerated or even encouraged by the moral system of one society or another. In light of this, the ethical relativist believes that there can be no nonethnocentric standard by which to judge actions.

Contrary to the relativist, some argue that

the moral differences between societies are not as great or as significant as they appear. They contend that variations in moral standards reflect differing factual beliefs and differing circumstances rather than fundamental differences in values. But suppose the relativist is right about this matter. His conclusion still does not follow. As Allan Bloom writes, "The fact that there have been different opinions about good and bad in different times and places in no way proves that none is true or superior to others. To say that it does so prove is as absurd as to say that the diversity of points of view expressed in a college bull session proves there is no truth."[8] Disagreement in ethical matters does not imply that all opinions are equally correct.

Moreover, ethical relativism has some unpleasant implications. First, it undermines any moral criticism of the practices of other societies as long as their actions conform to their own standards. We cannot say that slavery in a slave society like that of the American South of the last century was immoral and unjust as long as that society held it to be morally permissible.

Second, and closely related, is the fact that for the relativist there is no such thing as ethical progress. While moralities may change, they cannot not get better or worse. Thus, we cannot say that our moral standards today are any more enlightened than they were in the Middle Ages.

Third, it makes no sense from the relativist's point of view to criticize some of the principles or practices accepted by our own society. People can be censured for not living up to their society's moral code, but that is all; the moral code itself cannot be criticized. Whatever a society takes to be right really is right for it. Reformers who campaign against the "injustices" of their society are only encouraging people to be immoral—that is, to depart from the moral standards of their society—unless or until the majority of the society agrees with the reformers. The minority can never be right in moral matters; to be right it must become the majority.

The ethical relativist is right to emphasize that in viewing other cultures we should keep an open mind and not simply dismiss alien social practices on the basis of our own cultural prejudices. But the relativist's theory of morality doesn't hold up. The more carefully we examine it, the less plausible it becomes. There is no good reason for saying that the majority view on moral issues is automatically right, and the belief that it is automatically right has unacceptable consequences.

Relativism and the "Game" of Business

In his well-known and influential essay "Is Business Bluffing Ethical?" Albert Carr argues that business, as practiced by individuals as well as by corporations, has the impersonal character of a game—a game that demands both special strategy and an understanding of its special ethical standards.[9] Business has its own norms and rules, differing from the rest of society. Thus, according to Carr, a number of things that we normally think of as wrong are really permissible in a business context. His examples include: conscious misstatement and concealment of pertinent facts in negotiation, lying about your age on a résumé, deceptive packaging, automobile companies neglecting car safety, and utility companies eluding regulators and overcharging the users of electricity. He draws an analogy with poker:

> Poker's own brand of ethics is different from the ethical ideals of civilized human relationships. The game calls for distrust of the other fellow. It ignores the claim of friendship. Cunning deception and concealment of one's strength and intentions, not kindness and openheartedness, are vital in poker. No one thinks any the worse of poker on that account. And no one should think any the worse

of the game of business because its standards of right and wrong differ from the prevailing traditions or morality in our society.

What Carr is defending here is a kind of ethical relativism: Business has its own moral standards and business actions should be evaluated only by those standards.

One can argue whether Carr has accurately identified the implicit rules of the business world (for example, is misrepresentation on one's résumé really a permissible move in the business game?), but let's put that issue aside. The basic question is whether business is a separate world to which ordinary moral standards don't apply. Carr's thesis implies that any special activity following its own rules is exempt from external moral evaluation, but as a general thesis this is unacceptable. The Mafia, for example, has an elaborate code of conduct, accepted by the members of the rival "families." For them, gunning down a competitor or terrorizing a local shopkeeper may be strategic moves in a competitive environment. Yet we rightly refuse to say that gangsters cannot be criticized for following their own standards. Normal business activity is a world away from gangsterism, but the point still holds. Any specialized activity or practice will have its own distinctive rules and procedures, but this does not mean that those rules and procedures cannot be morally evaluated.

Moreover, Carr's poker analogy is itself weak. For one thing, business activity can affect those—like consumers—who have not consciously and freely chosen to play the "game." Business is indeed an activity involving distinctive rules and customary ways of doing things, but it is not really a game. It is the economic basis of our society, and we all have an interest in the goals of business (in productivity and consumer satisfaction, for instance) and in the rules business follows. Why should these be exempt from public evaluation and assessment? Later chapters return to the question of what these goals and rules should be. But to take one simple point, notice that a business/economic system that permits, encourages, or tolerates deception will be less efficient (that is, work less well) than one in which the participants have fuller knowledge about the goods and services being exchanged.

In sum, by divorcing business from morality, Carr misrepresents both. He incorrectly treats the standards and rules of everyday business activity as if they had nothing to do with the standards and rules of ordinary morality. And he treats morality as something that we give lip service to on Sundays, but which otherwise has no influence on our lives.

HAVING MORAL PRINCIPLES

Most people at some time in their lives pause to reflect on what moral principles they have or should have and on what moral standards are the best justified. (Moral philosophers themselves have defended different moral standards, and Chapter 2 discusses these various theories.) When a person accepts a moral principle, when that principle is part of his or her personal moral code, then naturally the person believes the principle is important and that it is well justified. But there is more to it than that, as Professor Richard Brandt of the University of Michigan has emphasized. When a principle is part of a person's moral code, the person is strongly motivated toward the conduct required by the principle and against behavior that conflicts with that principle. The person will tend to feel guilty when his or her own conduct violates that principle and (perhaps to a lesser extent) to disapprove of others whose behavior conflicts with it. Likewise, the person will tend to hold in esteem those whose conduct shows an abundance of the motivation required by the principle.[10]

Other philosophers have, in different ways, reinforced Brandt's point. To accept a moral principle is not a purely intellectual act like accepting a scientific hypothesis or a mathematical theorem. Rather, it involves also a desire to follow that principle for its own sake, the likelihood of feeling guilty about not doing so, and a tendency to evaluate the conduct of others according to the principle in question. We would find it very strange, for example, if Sally claimed to be morally opposed to cruelty to animals yet abused her own pets and felt no inclination to protest when some ruffians down the street lit a cat on fire.

Conscience

People can and, unfortunately, sometimes do go against their moral principles. But we would doubt that they sincerely held the principle in question if violating it did not bother their conscience. We have all felt the pangs of conscience, but what exactly is conscience and how reliable a guide is it? Our conscience, of course, is not literally a little voice inside of us. To oversimplify a complex story in developmental psychology, our conscience reflects our internalizing the moral instructions of the parents or other authority figures who raised us as children.

When we were very young we were probably told to tell the truth and to return something we liked to its proper owner. If we were caught lying or being dishonest, we were probably punished—scolded, spanked, sent to bed without dinner, denied a privilege. On the other hand, truth telling and honesty were probably rewarded—with approval, praise, maybe even hugs or candy. Seeking reward and avoiding punishment motivate small children to do what is expected of them. Gradually, children come to internalize those parental commands. Thus, they feel vaguely that their parents know what they are doing even when the parents are not around. When a child does something forbidden, he or she experiences the same feelings as when scolded by the parents—the first stirrings of guilt. On the other hand, even in the absence of explicit parental reward, the child feels a sense of self-approval about having done what he or she was supposed to have done. As we grow older, of course, our motivations are not so simple and our self-understanding is greater. We are able to reflect on and understand the moral lessons we were taught, as well as to refine and modify those principles. As adults we are morally independent agents. Yet however much our consciences have evolved and however much our adult moral code differs from the moral perspective of our childhood, those pangs of guilt we occasionally feel still stem from that early internalization of parental demands.

The Limits of Conscience

Something like this is the psychological story of conscience, but how reliable a guide is it? People often say, "Follow your conscience" or "You should never go against your conscience," but not only is such advice not very helpful, it may sometimes be bad advice. First, when we are genuinely perplexed over what we ought morally to do, we are trying to figure out what our conscience ought to be saying to us. When it is not possible to do both, should we keep our promise to a colleague or come to the aid of an old friend? To be told that we should follow our conscience is no help at all.

Second, it may not always be good for us to follow our conscience. It all depends on what our conscience says. Our conscience might reflect moral motivations that cannot withstand critical scrutiny. Consider an episode in chapter 16 of Mark Twain's *The Adventures of Huckleberry Finn*. Huck has taken off down the Mississippi on a raft with his friend, the runaway slave Jim. But, as they get nearer to the place where Jim will become legally free, Huck starts feeling guilty about helping him run away:

It hadn't ever come home to me, before, what this thing was that I was doing. But now it did; and it stayed with me, and scorched me more and more. I tried to make out to myself that *I* warn't to blame, because I didn't run Jim off from his rightful owner; but it warn't no use, conscience up and say, every time: "But you knowed he was running for his freedom, and you could a paddled ashore and told somebody." That was so—I couldn't get around that, no way. That was where it pinched. Conscience says to me: "What had poor Miss Watson done to you, that you could see her nigger go off right under your eyes and never say one single word? What did that poor old woman do to you, that you could treat her so mean? . . ." I got to feeling so mean and so miserable I most wished I was dead.

Here Huck is feeling guilty about doing what we would all agree is the morally right thing to do. But Huck is only a boy, and his pangs of conscience reflect the principles that he has picked up uncritically from the slave-owning society around him. Unable to think independently about matters of right and wrong, Huck in the end decides to disregard his conscience. He follows his instincts and sticks by his friend Jim.

The point here is not that we should ignore our consciences, but that the voice of conscience is itself something that can be critically examined. A pang of conscience is like a warning. When we feel one, we should definitely stop and reflect on the rightness of what we are doing. On the other hand, we cannot justify our actions simply by saying that we were "following our conscience." Terrible crimes have occasionally been committed in the name of "conscience."

Moral Principles and Self-Interest

Sometimes doing what you believe would be morally right and doing what would best satisfy your own interests may be two different things. Imagine that you are in your car hurrying home along a quiet road, trying hard to get there in time to see the kickoff of an important football game. You pass an acquaintance who is having car trouble. He doesn't recognize you. As a dedicated fan, you would much prefer to keep on going than to stop and help him, thus missing at least part of the game. You might rationalize that someone else will eventually come along and help him if you don't, but deep down you know that you really ought to stop. On the other hand, self-interest seems to say, "Keep going."

Or consider an example suggested by Baruch Brody.[11] You have applied for a new job, and if you land it, it will be an enormous break for you: it is exactly the kind of position you want and have been trying to get for some time. It pays well and will settle you into a desirable career for the rest of your life. The competition has come down to just you and one other person, and you believe correctly that she has a slight edge on you. Now imagine that you could spread a nasty rumor about her that would guarantee that she wouldn't get the job and that you could do this in a way that wouldn't come back to you. We are assuming that it would violate your moral code to circulate this lie; on the other hand, doing it would clearly benefit old "Number One."

Some people argue that moral action and self-interest can never genuinely be in conflict, and some philosophers have gone to great lengths to try to prove this, but they are almost certainly mistaken. They maintain that if you do the wrong thing, then you will be caught, your conscience will bother you, or, in some way, "what goes around comes around," so that your misdeed will come back to haunt you. This is often correct. But, unfortunate as it may be, sometimes—viewed just in terms of personal self-interest—it may pay off for a person to do what he or she knows to be wrong. People sometimes get away with their wrongdoings, and if their conscience bothers them at all, it may not bother them that much. To believe otherwise is not only wishful thinking, but also shows a lack of understanding of morality.

Morality serves to restrain the purely self-interested desires of each of us in order to make it possible for us all to live together. The moral standards of a society provide the basic guidelines for cooperative social existence and allow conflicts to be resolved by appeal to shared principles of justification. If people's interests never came into conflict—that is, if it were never advantageous for one person to deceive or cheat another—then there would be little need for morality. We would already be in heaven. Both a system of law that punishes people for hurting others and a system of morality that encourages people to refrain from pursuing their self-interest at great expense to others help to make social existence possible.

Usually, following our moral principles will be in our best interest. This is particularly worth noting in the business context. Several recent writers have argued persuasively not only that moral behavior is consistent with profitability, but also that the companies that are the most morally responsible are among the most profitable.[12] Apparently, when a company respects the rights of its employees, treats its suppliers fairly, and is straightforward with its customers, it pays off.

But notice one thing. If one does the right thing only because he or she thinks it will pay off, one is not really motivated by moral concerns. Having a moral principle involves having a desire to follow the principle for its own sake—just because it is the right thing to do. If one only does the right thing because of the belief that it will pay off, he or she might just as easily not do it if it looks like it is not going to pay off.

In addition, there is no guarantee that moral behavior will always pay off in strictly selfish terms. As argued above, there will be exceptions. From the moral point of view, one ought to stop and help his or her colleague,

and one shouldn't lie about competitors. From the selfish point of view, one should do exactly the opposite. Should one follow one's self-interest or one's moral principles? There's no final answer to this. From the moral point of view, one should, of course, follow one's moral principles. From the selfish point of view, on the other hand, one should look out solely for "Number One."

What *you* in fact do in a situation like this will depend upon the relative strength of your self-interested or "self-regarding" desires in comparison with the strength of your "other-regarding" desires (that is, your moral motivations and your concern for others). In other words, it will depend upon what kind of person you are, and that goes back in large part to how you were raised. A person who is basically selfish will pass by the acquaintance in distress and will spread the rumor, while a person who has a stronger concern for others, or a stronger desire to do what is right just because it is right, will not.

While it may be impossible to prove to selfish persons that they should not do the thing that best advances their self-interest (since, if they are selfish, then that is all they care about), there are considerations that suggest that it is not in a person's overall self-interest to be a selfish person. People who are exclusively concerned with their own interests tend to have less happy and less satisfying lives than do those whose desires extend beyond themselves. This is sometimes called the "paradox of hedonism." Individuals who care only about their own happiness will generally be less happy than those who care about others. And people often find greater satisfaction in a life lived according to moral principle, and in being the kind of person which that entails, than in a life devoted solely to immediate self-interest. Thus, or so many philosophers have argued, people have self-interested reasons not to be so self-interested. How do selfish people make themselves less so? Not overnight, obviously, but by involving themselves in the concerns and cares of others, they can in time come to care sincerely about those persons.

MORALITY AND PERSONAL VALUES

Some philosophers distinguish between morality in a narrow sense and morality in a broad sense. In a narrow sense morality refers to the moral code of an individual or of a society (insofar as the moral codes of the individuals making up that society overlap). While the principles that comprise these codes may not be explicitly formulated like laws, they do guide us in our conduct. They are internal monitors of our own behavior as well as the basis to which we appeal in assessing the actions of others. Morality in the narrow sense concerns the principles that do or should regulate people's conduct and relations with others. These principles can be debated, however. Take, for example, John Stuart Mill's contention that people's liberty ought not to be interfered with when their actions affect only themselves. And a large part of moral philosophy involves assessing rival moral principles. This discussion is part of the ongoing development of our moral culture. What is at stake are the basic standards that ought to govern our behavior—that is, the basic framework or ground rules that make coexistence possible. If there were not already fairly widespread agreement about these principles, our social order would not be possible.

But, in addition, we can talk about our morality in a broader sense, meaning not just the principles of conduct that we embrace, but also the values, ideals, and aspirations that shape our lives. There are many different ways of living our lives that would meet our basic moral obligations. The type of life each of us seeks to live reflects our individual values—whether following a profession, devoting ourselves to community service, raising a family, seeking solitude, pursuing scientific truth, striving for athletic excellence, amassing political power, cultivating glamorous people as friends, or some combination of these and many other possible ways of living. The life that each of us forges and the way we understand that life are part of our morality in the broad sense of the term.

It is important to bear this in mind throughout our study of business ethics. While our usual concern is with the principles that ought to govern conduct in certain situations—for example, whether a hiring officer may take the race of applicants into account, whether employees may be forced to take an AIDS test, or whether corporate bribery is permissible in countries where people turn a blind eye to it—our choices in the business, organizational, or professional worlds will also reflect our other values and ideals—or, in other words, the kind of person each of us is striving to be. What sort of ideal do *you* have of yourself as a businessperson? How much weight do you put on profitability, for instance, as against the quality of your product or the socially beneficial character of your service?

Many of the decisions we make in our careers and much of the way we shape our working lives depends not just on our moral code, but also on the self-understanding we have of ourselves in certain roles and relationships. Our "morality" in the sense of our ideals, values, and aspirations involves, among other things, our understanding of human nature, tradition, and society; our proper relationship to the natural environment; and our place in the cosmos. Professionals, for example, will invariably be guided not just by rules, but also by their understanding of what "being a professional" involves. Their conception of the ideal or model relationship between professional and client will greatly influence their day-to-day conduct. Is the ideal to be a friend to clients, to be the "hired gun" who simply carries out the client's commands, to be a neutral and objective third party, or something else altogether?

But there is more to living a morally good

life than being a good professional or a good businessperson, as Aristotle (384–322 B.C.) argued long ago. He underscored the necessity of our trying to achieve virtue or excellence, not just in some particular field of endeavor, but as human beings. Aristotle thought that things have functions. The function of a piano, for instance, is to make certain sounds, and a piano that performs this function well is a good or excellent piano. Likewise, we have an idea of what it is for a person to be an excellent athlete, an excellent manager, or an excellent professor—it is to do well the types of things that athletes, managers, or professors are supposed to do.

But Aristotle also thought that, just as there was an ideal of excellence for any particular craft or occupation, similarly there must be an excellence that we can achieve simply as human beings. That is, he thought that we can live our lives as a whole in such a way that they can be judged not just as excellent in this respect or in that occupation, but as excellent, period. Aristotle thought that only when we develop our truly human capacities sufficiently to achieve this human excellence would we have lives blessed with happiness. Philosophers since Aristotle's time have been skeptical of his apparent belief that this human excellence would come in just one form, but many would underscore the importance of developing our various potential capacities and of striving to achieve a kind of excellence in our lives. How we understand this excellence will be a function of our values, ideals, and world view—our morality in a broad sense.

INDIVIDUAL INTEGRITY AND RESPONSIBILITY

We have discussed what it is for a person to have a moral code, as well as the sometimes conflicting pulls of moral conscience and self-interest. In addition, we have seen that people have values and ideals above and beyond their moral principles, narrowly understood,

that also influence the lives they lead. And we have stressed the importance of reflecting critically on both our moral principles and our moral ideals and values as we seek to live morally good and worthwhile lives. None of us, however, lives in a vacuum, and there are always social pressures of various sorts on us. Sometimes these pressures make it difficult to stick with our principles and to be the kind of person we wish to be. Corporations are a particularly relevant, though not necessarily the worst, example of an environment that can potentially damage individual integrity and responsibility.

The Individual Inside the Corporation

Corporations exact a price for the many benefits they offer their members—jobs, status, money, friendships, personal fulfillment. Sometimes the price of corporate membership amounts to individual conscience, as the experience of David A. Frew, professor of behavioral science, indicates.[13]

As a case-working theorist, Frew interviewed a number of workers at various levels of a corporation known to be a substantial polluter. Frew discovered that, although each of the persons recognized and deplored the organization's pollution activities, each was willing to continue his or her daily activities that contributed to the very problem they found so appalling. One respondent even volunteered that it wouldn't be long before the company despoiled the surrounding area. When pressed further about his feelings, he said that he could do nothing but move to a cleaner environment.

Frew was frightened by the "ecologically schizophrenic" behavior he witnessed. But this schizophrenia goes beyond ecological issues. On many fronts—marketing, pricing, competition, contract fulfillment, management practices—the man or woman inside the organization can find it difficult, at times perhaps impossible, to reconcile the dictates of conscience with organizational policy and philosophy.

One need not study the corporate scene long before observing the double bind that people can experience from trying to reconcile two basic roles. The first role is that of the private individual: a decent, responsible person who readily admits the need for moral principles. The second role is that of the organizational member: a human being who rarely exhibits, or is expected and encouraged to exhibit, any of the moral sensitivity of the private person. These Jekyll-and-Hyde personalities share little moral ground, and Hyde can often brutalize Jekyll when personal and organizational values collide.

Take, for example, the case of Tex Harris, a big, friendly Texan, who was sent to Argentina in 1976 by the U.S. State Department to investigate complaints of human rights violations by the governing junta. Harris's approach was rather unorthodox. He believed that the only way to find out what was happening was to open the door of the U.S. Embassy and invite in victims and their families. Hundreds of people showed up with shocking revelations of junta atrocities. In one instance, a mother reported that her teenage son had been arrested en route to a social function. The boy's "offense"? Being in the vicinity of an antigovernment protest and thus judged to be a subversive. The woman begged Harris to get her son released.

Touched by the stories he heard, Harris undertook a personal campaign to publicize the inhumanities of the ruling junta and gain the release of as many political prisoners as possible. His superiors at the embassy did more than blanch at the prospects of such individual initiative. They toned down Harris's shockingly honest reports and insisted that he drop his personal crusade for human rights in Argentina. Harris persisted and straightaway became a heroic freedom fighter for Argentina's oppressed. Argentinian newspaper editor Jacob Timerman, a celebrated target of the junta's wrath, reported that

while in prison the news of Harris's efforts buoyed up him and other prisoners with hope of deliverance.

Harris's efforts had mixed results. He by no means gained the release of all or even most of the political prisoners. But some, like the teenager, owe their freedom directly to Harris's campaign. And American and world opinion were better informed of what was happening in Argentina, as a result of the foreign service officer's actions. As for Harris himself, he paid a heavy price for "bucking the system." A sheaf of poor performance evaluations and promotion denials dogged him back to the United States, where he currently occupies a seemingly dead-end job with the State Department. Had he acted more conventionally—that is, suppressed his righteous indignation or at least not have been so publicly demonstrative—Harris presumably would have enriched his career. As it is, since he has not received the promotion requisite for continuance as a foreign service officer, he faces job termination within a few years. And what do those say who were in charge of the American Embassy in Argentina during all this? Invited to tell their side of the story on the CBS television program "Crossroads" (August 7, 1984), Harris's immediate superiors declined to be interviewed.

It's easy and incorrect to write off the preceding as another tussle between individual and bureaucracy in government institutions. In fact, similar kinds of inherent tensions exist between individuals and the corporate organizations that employ them. And when members meet corporations at the intersection of individual conscience and corporate expectations, members are generally expected to yield—or seize the right of way at their own peril.

About a century ago, Dan Drew, church builder and founder of Drew Theological Seminary, made a distinction between one's private life and one's business life that can be viewed as a philosophical basis for the subordination of the individual to organizational interests. Addressing a group of businessmen in the late nineteenth century, Drew said:

> Sentiment is all right up in that part of the city where your home is. But downtown, no. Down there the dog that snaps the quickest gets the bone. Friendship is very nice for a Sunday afternoon when you're sitting around the dinner table with your relations, talking about the sermon that morning. But nine o'clock Monday morning, notions should be brushed aside like cobwebs from a machine. I never took any stock in a man who mixed up business with anything else. He can go into other things outside of business hours, but when he's in the office he ought not to have a relation in the world—and least of all a poor relation.[14]

The many recent cases of corporate misconduct suggest that corporate organizations have enthusiastically embraced Drew's exhortation, thereby encouraging a kind of Jekyll-Hyde personality. "Downtown" the dominant businessperson personality, Mr. Hyde, often is expected to repress the values that the private individual, Dr. Jekyll, lives by at home. In conflicts, the decent personality is to be sacrificed on the altar of expedience with a prayerful "That's business."

But don't assume that members of corporations would not prefer it otherwise. A basic assumption of the authors is that they would prefer Dr. Jekyll to Mr. Hyde, Tex Harris to a conscienceless "team player." And yet the structure and function of organizations in general, and corporate organizations in particular, require that their members adhere to organizational norms and, in fact, force commitment and conformity to them.

Organizational Norms

One of the major characteristics of an organization, indeed any group, is the shared acceptance of organizational rules by its members. The acceptance may be conscious or un-

conscious, take one form or another, be overt or subtle, but it is almost always present.

The corporation's goal is profit. To achieve this goal top management sets a return on equity, sales quotas, market shares, and so forth. For the most part, the norms or rules that govern corporate existence are derived from these goals. But clearly there's nothing in either the norms or goals that encourages moral behavior, and in fact they may have the effect of discouraging it.

There is mounting evidence that managers at every level experience role conflicts between what is expected of them as efficient, profit-minded managers and what is expected of them as ethical persons. Managers' role conflicts that are most frequently experienced today center around honesty in communication; gifts, entertainment, and kickbacks; fairness and discrimination; contract honesty; and firings and layoffs.[15] In a survey conducted in 1975, Archie Carroll discovered that managers at all levels experience such role conflicts primarily because of "pressure from the top" to meet corporate goals and comply with corporate norms. Of the managers interviewed, 50 percent of top managers, 65 percent of middle managers, and 84 percent of lower managers agreed that "managers today feel under pressure to compromise personal standards to achieve company goals."[16]

At the very least, this and other studies show that although corporate goals and norms may not be objectionable, they frequently put in a moral pressure cooker corporate members who must implement them. Meeting corporate objectives and playing by the "rules of the game" may call for unethical behavior.

Commitment

Like any group, an organization can survive only if it holds its members together. Organizations accomplish group cohesiveness by getting members to "commit" themselves—that is, to relinquish some of their own personal freedom to work toward organizational goals. One's degree of commitment—the extent to which one will subordinate self to organizational goals—is a measure of one's loyalty to "the team."

In most instances, the freedom one surrenders is trivial. I must wear a jacket and tie rather than my own preference, jeans and an open-neck shirt; or I must accept periodic reassignment rather than stay in one place, which I'd prefer. But in some cases, the freedom lost may amount to freedom of conscience. Acting on moral principle may be viewed as lack of commitment—disloyalty.

Professor Albert Carr recounts the experience of an executive who wrote several memoranda to superiors detailing instances of the company's environmental pollution.[17] Rather than being lauded for his sense of social responsibility, the executive was reprimanded for a "negative attitude."

Another executive of Carr's acquaintance realized his company was involved in political corruption. As far as he could determine, he had only three choices: (1) argue for nonprofitable change and thus jeopardize his job by being labeled "unrealistic" or "idealistic"; (2) remain silent and lose self-respect; or (3) move to another company and swap one set of moral misgivings for another. It's safe to assume that many more men and women silently suffer such intrapsychic conflict—conflict that results from being forced to choose between two incompatible goals, for example fidelity to one's own conscience and loyalty to organization. Taken collectively, these experiences suggest that the commitment organizations exact for self-maintenance can so constrain choice as to make individual acts of moral responsibility within the organization exceedingly difficult.

Conformity

It is no secret that organizations exert pressures on their members to conform to norms and goals. What may not be so widely known is how easily individuals can be induced to behave similarly to others. A dramatic example is provided in the early conformity studies by social psychologist Solomon Asch.[18]

In the classic experiment, Asch asked a group of seven to nine college students to say which of three lines on a card (right below) matched the length of a standard line on a second card (left below).

 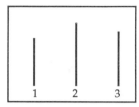

Only one of the subjects in each group was "naive," or unaware of the nature of the experiment. The others were stooges of the experimenter, who had instructed them to make incorrect judgments in about two-thirds of the cases and in this way to pressure the dissenting naive subjects to alter their correct judgments.

The results were intriguing, to say the least. When subjects were not exposed to pressure, they inevitably judged correctly. But when the stooges gave false answers, the subjects changed their responses to conform with the unanimous majority judgments. When one stooge always gave the correct answers, naive subjects maintained their position three-fourths of the time. But when the honest confederate switched to the majority view in later trials, the errors made by naive subjects rose to about the same level as that of subjects who stood alone against a unanimous majority.

Why did they yield? Some respondents said they didn't want to seem different, even though they continued to believe their judgments were correct. Others said that, although their perceptions seemed correct, the majority couldn't be wrong. Still other subjects didn't even seem aware that they had caved in to group pressure. Even those who held their ground tended to be profoundly disturbed by being out of step with the majority and confessed to being sorely tempted to alter their judgments. Indeed, a later study found that students who stood firm in their judgments suffered more anxiety than those who switched. One student with the strength of his correct conviction literally was dripping with perspiration by the end of the experiment.[19]

It's worthwhile to remark that in these experiments, which cumulatively included several hundred students, the subjects were not exposed to the arch authority symbols that organization members face: bosses, boards, presidents, peer groups, established policy, and so on. Nor would their responses entail the serious long-range impact that "bucking the system" can carry for organizational members: being transferred, dismissed, "frozen" in a position, or made an organizational pariah. And, of course, the students did not bring to these experiments the financial, educational, and other personal investments that individuals bring with them into jobs, which they can jeopardize by not "going along." In short, men and women within the organization are under greater pressures to conform than the students. Conformity can mean the surrender of moral autonomy. It can also result in what social psychologists term "bystander apathy."

Bystander Apathy.   Back in the 1960s a tragic event leaped off the front pages of our newspapers. A young woman named Kitty Genovese was stabbed to death in New York City. The murder was not in itself so unusual. What was particularly distressing was that thirty-eight of Kitty Genovese's neighbors witnessed her brutal slaying. In answer to her pitiful screams of terror, they came to their windows at 3 A.M., where they remained for

the 30 minutes it took her assailant to brutalize her. Of the thirty-eight, not one attempted to intervene in any way; no one even phoned the police.

So distressed by this shocking behavior were scientists John M. Darley and Bibb Latané that they began a study to find out why people refuse to help others in similar situations. Darley and Latané believe that their findings support the conclusion that the individual's sense of personal responsibility is inversely proportional to the number of people witnessing the event.[20] Thus, the more people who are observing an event with me, the less likely I am to feel obliged to do anything. In emergency situations, then, we seem naturally to let the behavior of those around us dictate our response. Conflicted between what we believe is the right thing to do and fear of violating group norms and expectations, most of us—about two-thirds, according to researchers—will yield to the group.

Bystander apathy appears to result in part from diffusion of responsibility. Submerged in the group, the individual can lose any sense of individuality. Deindividuation can occur in a group of strangers or large crowds, when pursuing a "greater cause" or following orders. In such situations, the individual may not only feel anonymous, and thus not responsible, but in fact may not even question the morality of his or her actions.

Is there anything about the corporate organization that encourages diffusion of responsibility and thus bystander apathy? Viewed as a massive group, corporations certainly encourage these phenomena as much as, and perhaps more than, most groups. Moreover, organizational pressure to produce, make profit, and conform can cultivate, or at least do nothing to inhibit, these propensities. Beyond this, few corporations institutionalize ethics. They don't articulate or communicate ethical standards to their members, nor do they actively enforce them. As a result, economic goals and norms can become the sole compass for charting any and all behavior within the corporation.

Why People Conform. Why do people conform? Social psychologists tell us that one potent determinant of conformity is the extent to which an individual understands and accepts the group's norms and goals. The more the individual does, the greater the pressure to conform.

Certainly corporate members are fully aware of the corporation's primary interest in survival and growth and know that they are expected to do everything within the law to advance those interests. In fact, individuals are schooled in such matters even before they go to work for the corporation.

If by no other way than through osmosis, college business majors certainly ingest the self-maintenance priorities of the business community that they will soon enter. Most of the required courses are geared to make them reasonably proficient in various aspects of business enterprise: accounting, finance, management, business policy, strategic planning, computer science. Even to the slowest learner, the message is clear: "I must master these skills to get and keep a job." What may be less clear, however, is another implied message: Businesses place a priority on these skills because through them they survive and prosper. Business education, therefore, is not just a matter of skill learning but is the absorption of an ideology, mastery of the rules of the business and corporate game.

Conspicuously absent from the typical business curriculum until very recently have been courses designed to offer alternative goals and norms within business and corporate organization. Rarely have students been required to think about the broad social and moral ramifications of their business specializations, such as courses in the ethics of accounting or marketing would encourage. Only now, and still rarely, are they being ex-

posed to values that include the perspectives and insights of the humanities. By orienting students largely to the narrow goals and norms of business enterprise, business curricula have, in effect, encouraged conformity to them.

Once inside the organization, members quickly are apprised of organizational objectives and standards in the context of the individual's area of specialization. Although what is expected of them sometimes clashes with their own moral values, they are rarely encouraged to deal with the conflict in an open, mature way. In fact, the more one suppresses individual moral urges in the cause of organizational interests, the more "mature," committed, and loyal one is considered to be. Conversely, the less willing the individual, the less "mature" and the more suspect.

The profit-making goals of corporations and the behavioral norms those goals spawn do little if anything to require moral accountability at any level of corporate operation. Even where codes of conduct exist, they are often vague and general or function only as window dressing. When such codes amount to little more than another handout in the thick packet of employee orientation material, it's no wonder workers often respond apathetically. And it should come as little surprise that once they recognize the true corporate agenda, employees have to fight hard to maintain their moral integrity in a showdown with organizational priorities.

Often, of course, the problem facing us is not that of doing what we know to be right, but rather that of deciding what the right thing to do is. In business, organizational, and professional contexts, there are many difficult and puzzling moral questions that need to be answered. How do we go about doing that? Is there a single "right way" or method for answering moral questions, as, for example, there is a right way to do science? As philosophy professor Tom Regan observes, if we want scientific answers to questions, we should use scientific method—a method of investigating a phenomenon that is based on collecting, analyzing, and interpreting evidence to determine the most probable explanations.[21] Scientific method does not contain answers to specific scientific questions—for example, whether saccharin causes cancer. It provides a method of approach for those wanting to give scientific answers as opposed to nonscientific ones. There is no comparable "moral method" for engaging moral questions. But there is general agreement about what constitutes good moral reasoning. Before identifying the main criteria of good moral reasoning, we must first find out what moral reasoning involves.

MORAL REASONING

It is useful to view moral reasoning at first in the context of *argument.* An argument is a group of statements one of which (called the *conclusion*) is claimed to follow from the others (called the *premises*). Here's an example of an argument:

Argument 1:

If a person is a mother, the person is a female.

Fran is a mother.

———————————

Therefore, Fran is a female.

The first two statements (the premises) of this argument happen to entail the third (the conclusion), which means that if I accept the first two as true, then I must accept the third as also true. Not to accept the conclusion while accepting the premises would result in a contradiction—holding two beliefs that cannot both be true at the same time. In other words, if I believe that all mothers are females and Fran is a mother (the premises), I cannot deny that Fran is a female (the conclusion) without contradicting myself. An argument

like this one, whose premises logically entail its conclusion, is termed *valid.*

An *invalid* argument is one whose premises do *not* entail its conclusion. In an invalid argument, I can accept the premises as true *and* reject the conclusion *without any contradiction.* Thus:

Argument 2:

If a person is a mother, the person is a female.

Fran is a female.

———————————

Therefore, Fran is a mother.

The conclusion of this argument does not necessarily follow from the true premises. I can believe that every mother is a female and that Fran is a female and deny that Fran is a mother without contradicting myself.

One way to show this is by means of a *counterexample,* an example that is consistent with the premises but is inconsistent with the conclusion. Thus, let's suppose Fran is a two-year-old, a premise that is perfectly consistent with the two stated premises. If she is, she can't possibly be a mother. Or let's suppose Fran is an adult female who happens to be childless, another premise that is perfectly consistent with the stated premises but obviously at odds with the conclusion. In a valid argument, such as Argument 1, no counterexamples are possible.

A valid argument can have untrue premises, as in the following:

Argument 3:

If a person is a female, she must be a mother.

Fran is a female.

———————————

Therefore, Fran must be a mother.

Like Argument 1, this one is *valid*. If I accept its premises as true, I must accept its conclusion as true; otherwise I will contradict myself. Although valid, this argument is unsound, because one of its premises is false—namely, "If a person is a female, she must be a mother." Realizing the patent absurdity of one of its premises, no sensible person would accept this argument's conclusion. But notice why the argument is unsound—not because the reasoning procedure is invalid but because one of the premises is false. *Sound arguments*, like Argument 1, have *true premises* and *valid reasoning*. *Unsound arguments* have at least one false premise, as in Argument 3, or invalid reasoning, as in Argument 2.

Now let's consider some *moral arguments*, which we can define simply as arguments whose conclusions are moral judgments, assertions about the moral worth of a person, action, activity, policy, or organization. Here are some examples that deal with affirmative action for women and minorities in the workplace.

Argument 4:

If an action violates the law, it is morally wrong.

Affirmative action on behalf of women and minorities in personnel matters violates the law.

Therefore, affirmative action on behalf of women and minorities in personnel matters is morally wrong.

Argument 5:

If an action violates the will of the majority, it is morally wrong.

Affirmative action on behalf of women and minorities in personnel matters violates the will of the majority.

Therefore, affirmative action on behalf of women and minorities in personnel matters is morally wrong.

Argument 6:

If an action redresses past injuries to special groups, it is morally permissible.

Affirmative action on behalf of women and minorities in personnel matters redresses injuries done to special groups.

Therefore, affirmative action on behalf of women and minorities in personnel matters is morally permissible.

Argument 7:

If an action is the only practical way to remedy a social problem, then it is morally permissible.

Affirmative action on behalf of women and minorities in personnel matters is the only practical way to remedy the social problem of unequal employment opportunity.

Therefore, affirmative action on behalf of women and minorities in personnel matters is morally permissible.

The first premise in each of these arguments is a moral standard, the second an alleged fact, and the conclusion a moral judgment. *Moral reasoning or argument typically moves from a moral standard, through one or more factual judgments about some person, action, or policy related to that standard, to a moral judgment about that person, action, or policy.* Good moral reasoning will frequently be more complicated than the examples above; often it will involve an appeal to more than one standard as well as to various appropriate factual claims. But in its most basic form, moral argument looks like this:

Premise 1: Moral standard

Premise 2: Fact

Conclusion: Moral judgment

Defensible Moral Judgments

If a moral judgment or conclusion is defensible, then it must be supportable by a defensible moral standard, together with relevant facts. A moral standard supports a moral judgment if the standard, taken together with the relevant facts, logically entails the moral judgment and if the moral standard itself is a sound standard. If someone argues that affirmative action for minorities and women is right (or wrong) but cannot produce a supporting principle when asked, then the person's position is considerably weakened. And if the person does not see any need to support the judgment by appeal to a moral standard, then he or she simply does not understand how moral concepts are used or is using moral words like "right" or "wrong" much different from the way they are commonly used.

Keeping this in mind—that moral judgments must be supportable by moral standards and facts—will aid your understanding of moral discourse, which can be highly complex and sophisticated. It will also sharpen your own critical faculties and improve your moral reasoning and ability to formulate relevant moral arguments.

Patterns of Defense and Challenge

In assessing arguments, one must be careful to clarify the meanings of their key terms and phrases. Often premises can be understood in more than one way, and this ambiguity may lead people to accept (or reject) arguments that they shouldn't. For example, "affirmative action" seems to mean different things to different people (see Chapter 8 on Job Discrimination). Before we can profitably assess Arguments 4 through 7, we have to agree on how we understand "affirmative action." Similarly, Argument 5 relies on the idea of "violating the will of the majority," but this has to be clarified before we can evaluate either the moral principle that it is

wrong to violate the will of the majority or the factual claim that affirmative action does violate the majority's will.

Assuming that the arguments are logically valid in their form (as Arguments 4 through 7 are) and that their terms have been clarified and possible ambiguities eliminated, then we must turn our attention to assessing the premises of the arguments. Should we accept or reject their premises? Remember that if an argument is valid, then if you accept the premises, you must accept the conclusion. Let's look at some further aspects of this assessment process.

1. *Evaluating the Factual Claims*. If parties are willing to accept the moral standard (or standards) in question, then they will concentrate on the factual claims. Thus, for example, in Argument 4: is affirmative action on behalf of women and minorities in fact illegal? Or in Argument 7: is affirmative action really the only practical way to remedy the social problem of unequal employment opportunity? Analogous questions can be asked about the factual claims of Arguments 5 and 6. Answering them in the affirmative would require considerable supporting data.

2. *Challenging the Moral Standard*. Moral arguments generally involve more than factual disputes. The moral standards they appeal to may be controversial. One party might challenge the moral standard upon which the argument relies, contending that it is not a plausible one and that we should not accept it. The critic might do this in several different ways, for example, by showing that there are exceptions to the standard, that the standard leads to unacceptable consequences, or that it is inconsistent with the arguer's other moral beliefs.

In the following dialogue, for example, Lynn is attacking Sam's advocacy of the standard "If an action redresses past injuries to special groups, it is morally permissible."

Lynn: What would you think of affirmative action for Jews in the workplace?

Sam: I'd be against it.

Lynn: What about Catholics?

Sam: No.

Lynn: People of Irish extraction?

Sam: They should be treated the same as anybody else.

Lynn: But each of these groups and more I could mention were victimized in the past by unfair discrimination, and probably in some cases continue to be.

Sam: So?

Lynn: So the standard you're defending leads to a judgment you reject—Jews, Catholics, and Irish, while wronged in the past, should not be compensated. How do you account for this inconsistency?

At this point Sam, or any rational person in a similar position, has three alternatives: abandon or modify the standard, alter the judgment, or show how women and minorities fit the principle, whereas the other groups do not.

3. *Defending the Moral Standard.* When the standard is criticized, then its advocate must defend it. Often this requires invoking an even more general principle. A defender of Argument 6, for example, might defend the redress principle by appealing to some more general conception of social justice. Or defenders might try to show how the standard in question entails other moral judgments that the critic accepts, thereby pointing out contradictions in the critic's moral reasoning. In the following exchange, Lynn is defending the standard of Argument 5: "If an action violates the will of the majority, it's wrong":

Lynn: Okay, do you think the government should impose a national religion on all Americans?

Sam: Of course not.

Lynn: What about requiring people to register their hand guns?

Sam: I'm all for it.

Lynn: And using kids in pornography?

Sam: There rightly are laws against it.

Lynn: But the principle you're objecting to leads to these judgments that you accept.

Of course, Lynn's argument is by no means a conclusive defense for her moral standard. Other moral standards could just as easily entail the judgments she cites, as Sam is quick to point out:

Sam: Now wait a minute. I oppose a state religion on constitutional grounds, not because it violates majority will. As for gun control, I'm for it because I think it will reduce violent crimes. And using kids in pornography is wrong because it exploits and endangers children.

Although Lynn's strategy for defending the standard about majority rule proved inconclusive, it did serve to shift the burden of argument to Sam. It forced him to counter with alternative standards that at least equally well supported the moral judgments raised.

4. *Revision and Modification.* Our affirmative action examples are illustrations, and all the moral principles they mention are very simple—too simple for one to accept any of them without qualification. (The principle that it is immoral to break the law in all circumstances, for example, is implausible. Nazi Germany furnishes an obvious counterexample to it.) But once the standard has been effectively challenged, the defender of the argument, rather than abandon the argument altogether, might try to reformulate it. That is, the defender might replace the original, contested premise with a better and more plausible one that still supports the conclusion. For example, Premise 1 of Argument 4 might be replaced by: "If an action violates a law that is democratically decided and that law is not itself morally unjust, then the action is immoral."

In this way, the discussion continues, the

arguments on both sides of an issue improve, and we make progress in the analysis and resolution of ethical issues. In general, in philosophy we study logic and criticize arguments not in order to be able to score quick debating points, but rather to be able to think better and more deeply about moral and other problems. Our goal as moral philosophers is not to "win" arguments, but to arrive at the truth—or, put less grandly, to find that answer to an ethical question that is the most reasonable one to accept.

Although we have outlined some basic features of moral reasoning and argumentation, moral discussion and the analysis of ethical issues can take various, often complicated, paths. Nevertheless, the preceding discussion implies certain minimum adequacy requirements for moral judgments. Let's make these requirements explicit.

Minimum Adequacy Requirements for Moral Judgments

Having spoken of moral reasoning and defensible moral judgments, we can now identify what criteria moral judgments should meet to be considered adequate.[22]

Although there is no complete list of adequacy criteria for moral judgments, moral judgments should be (1) logical, (2) based on facts, and (3) based on sound or defensible moral principles. Lacking any of these features, a moral judgment is less than ideal.

Moral Judgments Should Be Logical. To say that moral judgments should be logical implies several things. First, as indicated in the discussion of moral reasoning, our moral judgments should follow logically from their premises. The connection between (1) the standard, (2) the conduct or policy, and (3) the moral judgment should be such that 1 and 2 logically entail 3. Our goal is to be able to support our moral judgments with reasons

and evidence, rather than basing them solely on emotion, sentiment, or social or personal preference.

Forming logical moral judgments also means ensuring that any particular moral judgment of ours is compatible with our other moral and nonmoral beliefs. We must avoid inconsistency. George Brenkert relies on this point in "Privacy, Polygraphs, and Work" (pp. 278–286), when he calls the corporate defense of polygraphs one-sided. He contends that the same employers who condone lie-detector tests for corporate job applicants as necessary measures would probably object to them if the government, for similar security reasons, required them to take polygraphs in order to qualify for a government contract.

Moral Judgments Should Be Based on the Facts. Adequate moral judgments cannot be made in a vacuum. We must gather as much relevant information as possible before making them. Thus, D. W. Haslett in "Is Inheritance Justified?" (pp. 128–136) documents the fact that estate and gift taxes do virtually nothing at present to reduce inequalities of wealth due to inheritance before going on to argue that the practice of inheritance should be abolished. And in "Rich and Poor" (pp. 122–128) Peter Singer reviews the seriousness of world poverty and the paucity of assistance being given by Western nations, before turning to a discussion of our moral obligations.

The information supporting the moral judgment, the facts, should be relevant—that is, the information should actually relate to the judgment; it should be complete, or inclusive of all significant data; and it should be accurate or true.

Moral Judgments Should Be Based on Acceptable Moral Principles. We know that moral judgments are based on moral standards. At the highest level of moral reasoning, these standards embody and express very general moral principles. Reliable moral judgments must be based on sound moral principles—principles that can withstand critical scrutiny and rational criticism. But what precisely makes a moral principle sound or acceptable is one of the most difficult questions that the study of ethics raises and is beyond the scope of this book. But one criterion is worth mentioning, what professor of philosophy Tom Regan calls "considered beliefs."

Regan contrasts considered beliefs with beliefs we just happen to hold, perhaps because of ignorance or prejudice. "Our considered beliefs," he writes, "are those we hold *only after* we have made a conscientious effort (a) to attain maximum conceptual clarity, (b) to acquire all relevant information, (c) to think about the belief and its implications rationally, (d) impartially, and with the benefit of reflection, (e) coolly."[23] We have grounds to doubt a moral principle when it clashes with not one but many such beliefs. Conversely, conformity with not one but many considered beliefs is good reason for regarding it as provisionally established.

This does not mean that conformity with our considered beliefs is the sole or even basic test of a moral principle, any more than conformity with well-established beliefs is the exclusive or even fundamental test of a scientific hypothesis. (Copernicus's heliocentric hypothesis, for example, did not conform with what passed in the Medieval world as a well-considered belief, the Ptolemaic view.) But conformity with our considered beliefs seemingly must play some part in evaluating the many alternative moral principles that we will explore in the next chapter.

SUMMARY

1. Ethics deals with (1) individual character and (2) the moral rules that govern and limit our conduct. It investigates questions of moral right and wrong, duty and obligation, and moral responsibility.

2. Business ethics is the study of what constitutes right and wrong, good and bad human conduct in a business context. Closely related moral questions arise in other organizational contexts and in the professions.

3. Moral standards, as opposed to nonmoral standards, concern behavior that has serious consequences for human well-being. Their soundness depends on the adequacy of the reasons that support or justify them.

4. Morality must be distinguished from etiquette (which concerns rules for well-mannered behavior), from law (statutes, regulations, common law, and constitutional law), and from professional codes of ethics (which are the special rules governing the members of a profession).

5. Morality is not necessarily based on religion. Although we draw our moral beliefs from many sources, for philosophers the issue is whether those beliefs can be justified.

6. Ethical relativism is the theory that right and wrong are determined by what your society says is right and wrong. There are many problems with this theory. Also dubious is the theory that business has its own morality, divorced from ordinary ideas of right and wrong.

7. Accepting a moral principle involves a motivation to conform one's conduct to that principle. Violating the principle will bother one's conscience. But conscience is not a perfectly reliable guide to right and wrong.

8. Part of the point of morality is to make social existence possible by restraining self-interested behavior. Sometimes doing what is morally right can conflict with our personal interests. In general, though, following your moral principles will enable you to live a more satisfying life.

9. Morality as a code of conduct can be distinguished from morality in the broader sense of the various values, ideals, and aspirations that shape a person's life.

10. Several aspects of corporate structure and function work against individual morality. Organizational norms, group commitment, pressure to conform, and diffusion of responsibility (sometimes leading to bystander apathy) can all make the exercise of individual integrity difficult.

11. Moral reasoning consists of forming moral judgments, assessments of the moral worth of persons, actions, activities, policies, or organizations. Moral reasoning and argument typically appeal both to moral standards and to relevant facts. Moral judgments should be entailed by the relevant moral standards and the facts, and they should not contradict our other beliefs. Both standards and facts must be assessed when moral arguments are being evaluated.

12. Philosophical discussion generally involves the revision and modification of arguments; in this way progress is made in the analysis and resolution of moral and other issues.

13. Conformity with "considered beliefs" is an important consideration in the evaluation of moral principles. A considered moral belief is one held only after we have made a conscientious effort to be conceptually clear, to acquire all relevant information, and to think rationally, impartially, and dispassionately about the belief and its implications. We should doubt any moral principle that clashes with many of our considered beliefs.

CASE 1.1

Made in the U.S.A.—"Dumped" in Brazil, Belize, Iraq . . .

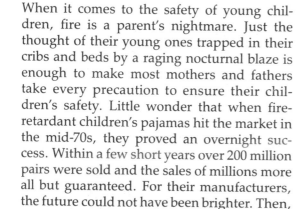

When it comes to the safety of young children, fire is a parent's nightmare. Just the thought of their young ones trapped in their cribs and beds by a raging nocturnal blaze is enough to make most mothers and fathers take every precaution to ensure their children's safety. Little wonder that when fire-retardant children's pajamas hit the market in the mid-70s, they proved an overnight success. Within a few short years over 200 million pairs were sold and the sales of millions more all but guaranteed. For their manufacturers, the future could not have been brighter. Then, like a bolt from the blue, came word that the pajamas were killers.

In June 1977, the U.S. Consumer Product Safety Commission (CPSC) banned the sale of these pajamas and ordered the recall of millions of pairs. Reason: The pajamas contained the flame-retardant chemical Tris (2,3-dibromopropyl) phosphate, which had been found to cause kidney cancer in children.

Whereas just months earlier the 100 medium- and small-garment manufacturers of the Tris-impregnated pajamas couldn't fill orders fast enough, suddenly they were worrying about how to get rid of the millions of pairs now sitting in warehouses. Because of its toxicity, the sleepwear couldn't even be thrown away, let alone sold. Indeed, the CPSC left no doubt about how the pajamas were to be disposed of—buried or burned, or used as industrial wiping cloths. Either way meant millions of dollars in losses for manufacturers.

The companies affected—mostly small,

family-run operations employing fewer than 100 workers—immediately attempted to shift blame to the mills that made the cloth. When that attempt failed, they tried to get the big department stores that sold the pajamas and the chemical companies that produced Tris to share the financial losses. Again, no sale. Finally, in desperation, the companies lobbied in Washington for a bill making the federal government partially responsible for the losses. It was the government, they argued, that originally had required the companies to add Tris to pajamas and then had prohibited their sale. Congress was sympathetic; it passed a bill granting companies relief. But President Carter vetoed it.

While the small firms were waging their political battle in the halls of Congress, ads began appearing in the classified pages of *Women's Wear Daily*. "Tris-Tris-Tris . . . We will buy any fabric containing Tris," read one. Another said, "Tris—we will purchase any large quantities of garments containing Tris."[24] The ads had been placed by exporters, who began buying up the pajamas at fire-sale prices, usually at 10 percent to 30 percent of the normal wholesale price.[25] Their intent was clear: to dump[26] the carcinogenic pajamas on overseas markets.

When CPSC chairperson S. John Byington learned of the plot, he wrote Secretary of Commerce Juanita Kreps, whose department administered the Commodity Control List of prohibited exports. Under the law, the president is empowered to place on the list, and thus prohibit the exportation of, any product that is deemed scarce, potentially threatening to national security, or potentially harmful to foreign relations. In his letter to Kreps, Byington argued that the exportation of the cancer-causing garments would have "serious implications for foreign policy."[27] Four months later, in a reply to Byington, Kreps wrote that she had been informed by the State Department that "the controls of Tris and Tris-treated garments are not . . . ' necessary to fur-

ther significantly the foreign policy of the U.S. to fulfill its international responsibilities.'"[28]

Nevertheless, on June 14, 1978, the CPSC, acting on its own, banned the export of Tris-treated pajamas. It is estimated that tens of millions of pairs of the carcinogenic sleepwear were exported to South America, the Caribbean, and Europe in the year between the domestic ban and the export bans.[29]

While Tris brought dumping into the political arena, it was by no means the only example of dumping. In the months following its ban, reports of numerous dumpings began to surface. In 1972, 400 Iraqis died and 5,000 were hospitalized after eating wheat and barley treated with a U.S.-banned organic mercury fungicide. Winstrol, a synthetic male hormone that had been found to stunt the growth of American children, was made available in Brazil as an appetite stimulant for children. Depro-Provera, an injectible contraceptive known to cause malignant tumors in animals, was shipped overseas to seventy countries where it was used in U.S.-sponsored population control programs. And 450,000 baby pacifiers, of the type known to have caused choking deaths, were exported for sale overseas.

Manufacturers that dump products abroad clearly are motivated by profit or at least by the hope of avoiding massive financial losses resulting from having to withdraw a product from the market. For government and health agencies that cooperate in the exporting of dangerous products, the motives are more complex.[30]

For example, as early as 1971 the dangers of the Dalkon Shield intrauterine device were well documented.[31] Among the adverse reactions were pelvic inflammation, blood poisoning, pregnancies resulting in spontaneous abortions, tubal pregnancies, and uterine perforations. A number of deaths were even attributed to the device. Faced with losing its domestic market, A. H. Robbins Co., manufacturer of the Dalkon Shield, worked out a deal with the Office of Population within the U.S. Agency for International Development (AID) whereby AID bought thousands of the devices at a reduced price for use in population-control programs in forty-two countries.

Why do governmental and population-control agencies approve for sale and use overseas birth control devices proved dangerous in the United States? They say their motives are humanitarian. Since the rate of dying in childbirth is high in Third World countries, almost any birth control device is preferable to none. Third World scientists and government officials frequently support this argument. They insist that denying their countries access to the contraceptives of their choice is tantamount to violating their countries' national sovereignty.

Apparently this argument has found a sympathetic ear in Washington, for it turns up in the "notification" system that regulates the export of banned or dangerous products overseas. Based on the principles of national sovereignty, self-determination, and free trade, the notification system requires that foreign governments be notified whenever a product is banned, deregulated, suspended, or canceled by an American regulatory agency. The State Department, which implements the system, has a policy statement on the subject that reads, in part: "No country should establish itself as the arbiter of others' health and safety standards. Individual governments are generally in the best position to establish standards of public health and safety."[32]

Critics of the system claim that notifying foreign health officials is virtually useless. For one thing, other governments rarely can establish health standards or even control imports into their countries. Indeed, most of the Third World countries where banned or dangerous products are dumped lack regulatory agencies, adequate testing facilities, and well-staffed customs departments.

Then there's the problem of "getting the word out" about hazardous products. In the-

ory, when a government agency such as the Environmental Protection Agency or the Food and Drug Administration finds a product hazardous, it is supposed to inform the State Department, which is to notify local health officials. But agencies often fail to inform the State Department of the product they have banned or found harmful. And when it is notified, its communiqués typically go no further than the U.S. embassies abroad. One embassy official even told the General Accounting Office that he "did not routinely forward notification of chemicals not registered in the host country because it may adversely affect U.S. exporting."[33] When foreign officials are notified by U.S. embassies, they sometimes find the communiqués vague or ambiguous or too technical to understand.

But even if the communication procedure works perfectly, there are ways that companies can circumvent the potential adverse effects of the notification system—for example, simply changing the name of the product or exporting the individual ingredients of a product separately via different routes to a recombining plant in the foreign country. Once there the ingredients can be reassembled and the product dumped.[34]

Discussion Questions

1. Do you think dumping involves any moral issues?

2. Complete the following statements by filling in the blanks with either "moral" or "nonmoral":

   a. That the Dalkon Shield was dumped overseas is a _____ issue.

   b. Whether or not dumping should be permitted is a _____ question.

   c. "Are dangerous products of any use in the Third World?" is a _____ question.

   d. "Is it proper for the U.S. government to sponsor the export of dangerous products overseas?'' That is a _____ question.

e. Whether or not the notification system will protect the health and safety of people in foreign lands is a _____ _____ matter.

3. Explain why you do or do not object to dumping. Identify the principles and values embedded in your explanation.

4. Defend or challenge the notification system by appeal to moral principle and facts.

CASE 1.2
The A7D Affair

Kermit Vandivier could not have predicted the impact on his life of purchase order P-23718, issued on June 18, 1967, by LTV Aerospace Corporation. The order was for 202 brake assemblies for a new Air Force light attack plane, the A7D, a project Vandivier didn't become personally involved in until April 11, 1968, the day of the thirteenth test on the brakes—and the thirteenth failure. Six months later, on October 25, Vandivier was told by his boss, H. C. Sunderman, to clean out his desk and immediately leave the B. F. Goodrich Plant at Troy, Ohio, where he'd worked for six years.

Back in June of '67, news of the LTV contract had been cause for uncorking the champagne at the Troy plant. Everyone agreed, including Vandivier, that Goodrich had carried off a real coup. Although the LTV order was a small one—the total price for the 202 assemblies was $69,417, a paltry sum in an industry where brake contracts can run into the millions—it signaled that Goodrich was back in LTV's good graces, after ten years of living under a cloud of disrepute. Back in the mid-50s Goodrich had built a brake for LTV that, to put it kindly, hadn't cut the mustard. As a result, LTV had written off Goodrich as a reliable source of brakes. So, while modest,

The material for this case has been drawn from Kermit Vandivier, "Why Should My Conscience Bother Me?" in Robert Heilbronner, ed., *In The Name of Profit* (New York: Doubleday, 1972). Quotations are from source.

the LTV contract was a chance for Goodrich to redeem itself, one that the people at the Troy plant were determined to make good.

LTV's unexpected change of heart after ten years was easily explained. Goodrich made LTV an offer it couldn't refuse—a ridiculously low bid for making the four-disk brake. Had Goodrich taken leave of its financial senses? Hardly. Since aircraft brakes are custom-made for a particular aircraft, only the brakes' manufacturer has replacement parts. Thus, even if it took a loss on the job, Goodrich figured it could more than make up for it in the sale of replacement parts. Of course, if Goodrich bungled the job, there wouldn't be a third chance.

John Warren, a seven-year veteran and one of Goodrich's most capable engineers, was made project engineer and lost no time in working up a preliminary design for the brake. Perhaps because the design was faultless or perhaps because Warren was given to temper tantrums when criticized, coworkers accepted the engineer's plan without question. So there was no reason to suspect that young Searle Lawson, one year out of college and six months with Goodrich, would think otherwise.

Lawson was assigned by Warren to produce the final production design. He had to determine the best materials for brake linings and any needed adjustments in the brake design. This process called for extensive testing to meet military specifications. If the brakes passed the grueling tests, they would then be flight-tested by the Air Force.

Lawson was under pressure to meet LTV's target date for flight tests, the last two weeks of June 1968; so he lost no time in getting down to work. Since he hadn't received the brake housing and some other parts yet, he used housing from a brake similar to the A7D's and built a prototype of the four-disk design. What Lawson particularly wanted to learn was whether the brake could withstand the extreme internal temperatures, in excess of 1,000 degrees, when the aircraft landed.

When the brake linings disintegrated in the first test, Lawson thought the problem might be defective parts or an unsuitable lining. But after two more consecutive failures, he decided the problem lay in the design: The four-disk design was simply too small to stop the aircraft without generating heat enough to melt the brake linings. In Lawson's view, a larger, five-disk brake was needed.

Lawson well knew the implications of his conclusion. The four-disk brake assemblies that finally had begun to arrive at the plant would have to be junked, and more tests would have to be conducted. The accompanying delays would preclude delivery of the first production brakes in the few short weeks that LTV anticipated.

Lawson reported his findings and recommendations to John Warren. Going to a five-disk design was impossible, Warren told him. Officials at Goodrich, he said, were already boasting to LTV about how well the tests were going. Besides, Warren was confident that the problem lay not in the four-disk design but in the brake linings themselves.

Unconvinced, Lawson went to Robert Sink, who was in charge of supervising engineers on projects. Sink was, to say the least, in a tight spot. If he agreed with Lawson, he would be indicting his own professional judg-

ment—he was the man who had assigned Warren to the job. What's more, he had accepted Warren's design without reservation and had assured LTV more than once that there was little left to do but ship them the brakes. To recant now would mean explaining the reversal not only to LTV but also to the Goodrich hierarchy. In the end, Sink, who was not an engineer, deferred to the seasoned judgment of Warren and instructed Lawson to continue the tests.

His own professional judgment overriden, Lawson could do little but bash on with the tests. Since all the parts for the brake had by this time arrived, he was able to build up a production model of the brake with new linings and subject it to the rigorous qualification tests. Thirteen more tests were conducted, and thirteen more failures resulted. It was at this point that data analyst and technical writer Kermit Vandivier entered the picture.

On April 11, Vandivier was looking over the data of the latest A7D test when he noticed an irregularity: The instrument recording some of the stops had been deliberately miscalibrated to indicate that less pressure was required to stop the aircraft than actually was the case. Vandivier immediately showed the test logs to test lab supervisor Ralph Gretzinger. Gretzinger said he'd learned from the technician who had miscalibrated the instrument that Lawson had requested that he miscalibrate it. Later, while confirming this account, Lawson said he was simply following the orders of Sink and Russell Van Horn, manager of the design engineering section, who according to Lawson were intent on qualifying the brakes at whatever cost. For his part, Gretzinger vowed he would never permit deliberately falsified data or reports to leave his lab.

On May 24, the brake was again tested, and again it failed. Nevertheless, Lawson asked Vandivier to start preparing the various graph and chart displays for qualification.

Vandivier refused and told Gretzinger what he'd been asked to do. Gretzinger was livid. He again vowed that his lab would not be part of a conspiracy to defraud. Then, bent on getting to the bottom of the matter, Gretzinger rushed off to see Russell Line, manager of the Goodrich Technical Services Section.

An hour later, Gretzinger returned to his desk looking like a beaten man. He knew he had only two choices: defy his superiors or do their bidding.

"You know," he said to Vandivier, "I've been an engineer for a long time, and I've always believed that ethics and integrity were every bit as important as theorems and formulas, and never once has anything happened to change my beliefs. Now this. . . . Hell, I've got two sons I've got to put through school and I just. . . ." When his voice trailed off, it was clear that he would in fact knuckle under. He and Vandivier would prepare the qualifying data, then someone "upstairs" would actually write the report. Their part, Gretzinger rationalized, wasn't really so bad. "After all," he said, "we're just drawing some curves, and what happens to them after they leave here, well, we're not responsible for that." Vandivier knew Gretzinger didn't believe what he was saying about not being responsible. Both of them knew that they were about to become principal characters in a plot to defraud.

Unwilling to play his part, Vandivier decided that he, too, would confer with Line. Line was sympathetic; he said he understood what Vandivier was going through. But in the end he said he would not refer the matter to chief engineer, H. C. "Bud" Sunderman, as Vandivier had suggested. Why not? Vandivier wanted to know.

"Because it's none of my business, and it's none of yours," Line told him. "I learned a long time ago not to worry about things over which I had no control. I have no control over this."

Vandivier pressed the point. What about the test pilots who might get injured because of the faulty brakes? Didn't their uncertain fate prick Line's conscience?

"Look," said Line, growing impatient with Vandivier's moral needling. "I just told you I have no control over this thing. Why should my conscience bother me?" Then he added, "You're just getting all upset over this thing for nothing. I just do what I'm told, and I'd advise you to do the same."

Vandivier made his decision that night. He knew, of course, he was on the horns of a dilemma. If he wrote the report, he would save his job at the expense of his conscience. If he refused, he would honor his moral code and, he was convinced, lose his job—an ugly prospect for anyone, let alone a forty-two-year-old man with a wife and seven children. The next day Vandivier phoned Lawson and told him he was ready to begin on the qualification report.

Lawson shot over to Vandivier's office with all the speed of one who knows that, swallowed fast, a bitter pill doesn't taste so bad. Before they started on the report, though, Vandivier, still uneasy with his decision, asked Lawson if he fully understood what they were about to do.

"Yeah," Lawson said acidly, "we're going to screw LTV. And speaking of screwing," he continued, "I know now how a whore feels, because that's exactly what I've become, an engineering whore. I've sold myself. It's all I can do to look at myself in the mirror when I shave. I make me sick."

For someone like Vandivier who had written dozens of them, the qualification report was a snap. It took about a month, during which time the brake failed still another final qualification test and the two men talked almost exclusively about the enormity of what they were doing. In the Nuremberg trials they found a historical analogy to their own complicity and culpability in the A7D affair. More than once, Lawson opined that the brakes were downright dangerous, that anything could happen during the flight tests. His opinion proved prophetic.

On June 5, 1968, the report was published and copies went to the Air Force and LTV. Within a week test flights were begun at Edwards Air Force Base in California. Goodrich dispatched Lawson to Edwards as its representative, but he wasn't there long. Several ''unusual incidents'' brought the flight tests literally to a screeching halt. Lawson returned to the Troy plant, full of talk about several near crashes during landings caused by brake trouble. That was enough to send Vandivier to his attorney, to whom he told the whole sorry tale.

Although the attorney didn't think Vandivier was guilty of fraud, he was convinced that the analyst/writer was guilty of participating in a conspiracy to defraud. Vandivier's only hope, the attorney counseled, was to make a clear breast of the matter to the FBI. Vandivier did.

Evidently the FBI informed the Air Force of Vandivier's disclosure, for within days the Air Force, which had previously accepted the qualification report, demanded to see some of the raw data compiled during the tests.

Lawson resigned from Goodrich in October. Vandivier submitted his own resignation on October 18, to take effect November 1. In his letter of resignation, addressed to Russell Line, Vandivier cited the A7D report and stated: ''As you are aware, this report contained numerous deliberate and willful misrepresentations which, according to legal counsel, constitute fraud and expose both myself and others to criminal charges of conspiracy to defraud. . . . The events of the past seven months have created an atmosphere of deceit and distrust in which it is impossible to work. . . .''

On October 25, Vandivier was summoned to the office of ''Bud'' Sunderman who bawled him out. Among other things, Sunderman accused Vandivier of making irresponsible charges and of arch disloyalty. It would be best, said Sunderman, if Vandivier cleared out immediately.

Within minutes, Vandivier had cleaned out his desk and left the plant. Two days later Goodrich announced it was recalling the qualification report and replacing the old brake with a new five-disk brake at no cost to LTV.

Aftermath:
On August 13, 1969, a Congressional committee reviewed the A7D affair. Vandivier and Lawson testified as government witnesses, together with Air Force officers and a General Accounting Office team. All testified that the brake was dangerous.

Robert Sink, representing the Troy plant, depicted Vandivier as a mere high-school graduate with no technical training, who preferred to follow his own lights rather than organizational guidance. R. G. Jeter, vice-president and general counsel of Goodrich, dismissed as ludicrous even the possibility that some thirty engineers at the Troy plant would stand idly by and see reports changed and falsified. The committee adjourned after four hours with no real conclusion. The following day the Department of Defense, citing the A7D episode, made major changes in its inspection, testing, and reporting procedures.

The A7D eventually went into service with the Goodrich-made five-disk brake.

Searle Lawson went to work as an engineer for LTV assigned to the A7D project.

Russell Line was promoted to production superintendent.

Robert Sink moved up into Line's old job.

Kermit Vandivier became a newspaper reporter for the *Daily News* in Troy, Ohio.

Discussion Questions

1. Identify and discuss the pressure to conform evident in the A7D episode.

2. Discuss the diffusion of responsibility aspects of the case.

3. Do you think that the existence of a corporate ethical code, a high-ranking ethics committee, and in-house ethical training might have altered events?

4. Do you think that Vandivier was wrong to work up the qualification report? Justify your judgment by appeal to moral principles.

5. Do you think that Vandivier was right in "blowing the whistle"? Again, justify your judgment by appeal to moral principles.

6. There is enough circumstantial evidence to infer that both Vandivier and Gretzinger considered moral ideals, obligations, and effects before deciding to participate in the fraud and even while they were implementing their decision. Where specifically did they place the emphasis that led them to participate? Would it be fair to infer that Vandivier's subsequent decision to seek legal counsel and then to be a government witness reflect the same point of emphasis?

7. Given later events, would you say that Goodrich took steps to ensure more ethical behavior within the organization?

8. In your opinion, can Goodrich Corporation in any way be held morally responsible for the A7D affair, or does the responsibility fall solely on individuals?

NOTES

1. Robert C. Solomon, *Morality & the Good Life* (New York: McGraw-Hill, 1984), 3.

2. Ibid.

3. Beverly T. Watkins, "Business Schools Told They Should Produce Generalists, Not Specialists," *The Chronicle of Higher Education*, April 25, 1984, 13.

4. See Manuel G. Velasquez, *Business Ethics* (Englewood Cliffs, N.J.: Prentice-Hall, 1982), 10.

5. *Wilmington General Hospital* v. *Manlove*, 54, Delaware 15, 174A 2nd 135, 1961.

6. Ed. note: In *Brown* v. *Board of Education of Topeka* (1954), the Supreme Court struck down the half-century-old "separate but equal doctrine," which permitted racially segregated schools so long as comparable quality was maintained.

7. Martin Luther King, Jr., "Letter from Birmingham Jail," in *Why We Can't Wait* (New York: Harper & Row, 1963), 85.

8. Allen Bloom, *The Closing of the American Mind* (New York: Simon & Schuster, 1987), 39.

9. Albert Carr, "Is Business Bluffing Ethical?" *Harvard Business Review*, January–February 1968.

10. Richard B. Brandt, *A Theory of the Good and the Right* (New York: Oxford University Press, 1979).

11. Baruch Brady, *Beginning Philosophy* (Englewood Cliffs, N.J.: Prentice-Hall, 1977).

12. See, in particular, Tad Tuleja, *Beyond the Bottom Line* (New York: Penguin Books, 1987).

13. See David A. Frew, "Pollution: Can the People Be Innocent While Their Systems Are Guilty?" *Academy of Management Review*, March 1973.

14. Quoted in Robert Bartels, ed., *Ethics in Business* (Columbus: Ohio State University Press, 1963), 35.

15. See Milton Snoeyenbos, Robert Almeder, and James Humber, eds. *Business Ethics* (Buffalo, N.Y.: Prometheus Books, 1983), 99.

16. Archie B. Carroll, "Managerial Ethics: A Post-Watergate View," *Business Horizons* 18 (April 1975): 75–80. Reported in Snoeyenbos et al., *Business Ethics*, 99.

17. Albert Z. Carr, "Can an Executive Afford a Conscience?" *Harvard Business Review*, July–August 1970.

18. See Solomon E. Asch, "Opinion and Social Pressure," *Scientific American*, November 1955, 31–35.

19. M. D. Bogdanoff et al., "The Modifying Effect of Conforming Behavior Upon Lipid Responses Accompanying CNS Arousal," *Clinical Research* 9 (1961): 135.

20. J. Darley and B. Latané, "When Will People Help in a Crisis?" In *Readings in Psychology Today* (Del Mar, Calif.: CRM Books, 1969).

21. Tom Regan, in *Just Business: New Introductory Essays in Business Ethics*, ed. Tom Regan (New York: Random House, 1984), 9.

22. For additional criteria, see Regan, *Just Business*, 13–18.
23. Ibid., 17.
24. Mark Hosenball, "Karl Marx and the Pajama Game," *Mother Jones*, November 1979, 47.
25. Ibid.
26. "Dumping" is a term apparently coined by *Mother Jones* magazine to refer to the practice of exporting to overseas countries products that have been banned or declared hazardous in the United States.
27. Mark Dowie, "The Corporate Crime of the Century," *Mother Jones*, November 1979, 38. The facts reported in this case are based largely on this article.
28. Ibid.
29. Hosenball, "Karl Marx," 47.
30. Dowie, "Corporate Crime," 24.
31. See Mark Dowie and Tracy Johnston, "A Case of Corporate Malpractice," *Mother Jones*, November 1976.
32. Dowie, "Corporate Crime," 38.
33. Ibid.
34. Mark Dowie, "A Dumper's Guide to Tricks of the Trade," *Mother Jones*, November 1979, 25.

It's Good Business

Robert C. Solomon and Kristine Hanson

Solomon and Hanson argue for the immediate, practical relevance of ethics for our business lives. They debunk the idea that business is fundamentally amoral or immoral. Business is not a blind scramble for profits and survival. It is an established practice with firmly fixed rules and expectations, and people in business are professionals. Although unethical business, like crime, sometimes pays, there is no conflict between ethical business behavior and success. Solomon and Hanson conclude with eight crucial rules for ethical thinking in business.

Why Ethics?

Our seminars in business ethics are typically sandwiched in between sessions on financial analysis and production planning. Not unreasonably, business people expect similarly hard-headed, decisive, pragmatic, issue-oriented, goal-directed, job-defined, bottom-line-minded, and imminently useful information. Not surprisingly, then, our seminars almost always begin with and are periodically brought back around to such practical questions as "What does this have to do with my job?" or "Will understanding ethics help me do my job better?"

Such questions deserve and demand three immediate, practical answers.

1. Ethical errors end careers more quickly and more definitively than any other mistake in judgment or ac-counting. To err is human, perhaps, but to be caught lying, cheating, stealing, or reneging on contracts is not easily forgotten or forgiven in the business world. And for good reason: Such actions undermine the ethical foundation on which the business world thrives. Almost everyone can have compassion for someone caught in an ethical dilemma. No one can excuse immorality.

For every glaring case of known unethical conduct that goes unpunished, a dozen once-promising careers silently hit a dead end or quietly go down the tubes. On relatively rare occasions, an unhappy executive or employee is singled out and forced to pay public penance for conduct that everyone knows—he or she and the attorney will loudly protest—"goes on all the time." But much more often, unethical behavior, though unearthed, will go unannounced; indeed, the executive or employee in question will keep his or her job and may not even find out that he or she has been found out—may never even realize the unethical nature of his or her behavior. A career will just go nowhere. Responsibilities will remain routine, promotions elusive.

What makes such career calamities so pathetic is that they are not the product of greed or immorality or wickedness. They are the result of ethical naiveté.

They happen because an employee unthinkingly "did what he was told to do"—and became the scapegoat as well.

They happen because a casual public comment was ill-considered and had clearly unethical implications—though nothing of the kind may have been intended.

They happen because a middle manager, pressed from above for results, tragically believed the adolescent clichés that pervade the mid-regions of the business world, such as "In business, you do whatever you have to do to survive." (It is both revealing and instructive that although we often hear such sentiments expressed in seminars for middle managers, we virtually never hear them in similar seminars for upper-level executives.)

They happen because upper management wasn't clear about standards, priorities, and limits, or wasn't reasonable in its expectations, or wasn't available for appeal at the critical moment.

They happen because an anonymous employee or middle manager hidden in the complexity of a large organization foolishly believed that such safe anonymity would continue, whatever his or her behavior.

They happen, most of all, because a person in business is typically trained and pressured to "think business," without regard for the larger context in which business decisions are made and legitimized.

Unethical thinking isn't just "bad business"; it is an invitation to disaster in business, however rarely (it might sometimes seem) unethical behavior is actually found out and punished.

2. *Ethics provides the broader framework within which business life must be understood.* There may be a few people for whom business is all of life, for whom family and friendship are irrelevant, for whom money means only more investment potential and has nothing to do with respect or status or enjoying the good life. But most successful executives understand that *business is part of life.* Corporations are part of a society that consists of something more than a market. Executives and employees do not disappear into their jobs as if into a well, only

to reappear in "real life" at the end of the business day.

Successful managers, we now all know, stay close to their subordinates—and not just as subordinates. The best corporations in their "search for excellence" begin and remain close to their customers, and not just in their narrowest role as consumers. Money may be a scorecard, a measure of status and accomplishment, but it is not the ultimate end. Business success, like happiness, often comes most readily to those who do not aim at it directly.

Executives are most effective and successful when they retain their "real life" view of themselves, their position, and the human world outside as well as inside the corporation. Business ethics, ultimately, is just business in its larger human context.

> A corporation's responsibilities include how the whole business is conducted every day. It must be a thoughtful institution which rises above the bottom line to consider the impact of its action on all, from shareholders to the society at large. Its business activities must make business sense.
> Andrew Siglér, "The Business Roundtable,"
> *New York Times*, February 1981

3. *Nothing is more dangerous to a business—or to business in general—than a tarnished public image.* A few years ago, *Business and Society Review* reported the results of a Harris Poll—one among many—that showed that public confidence in the executives running major corporations had declined "drastically" from 55% in 1966 to 16% in 1976; 87% of the respondents in a parallel poll agreed that most businessmen were more interested in profits than in the public interest. Whether or not such suspicions seriously affect sales, they indisputably hurt the bottom line in a dozen other hurtful ways—not least among them the pressure for government regulation. The fact is that a tarnished image has direct consequences, for sales, for profits, for morale, for the day-to-day running of the business. Distrust of an industry ("big oil," "the insurance racket") can hurt every company, and distrust of an individual company can quickly drive it to bankruptcy.

The editors of the *Review* tried to find the reason for the "falling image of private enterprise" and the flawed image of the men and women who devote their lives to business. They surveyed the chief executives of some of the nation's large corporations, asking for their opinions about what had happened and what could be done. As one would expect, there was vast disagreement on causes—from blaming the press to blaming the universities to expressing the view that since Watergate, all people and institutions in power are inevitably suffering from a more general loss of confidence. But what all of the respondents agreed about was the need to correct the image of business and free enterprise as essentially antagonistic or indifferent to the public good and morality. That correction, in turn, depends on the ability of business people to speak out for themselves, to express in their own terms the ethics and economics of their work without depending on the press to do it for them. Indeed, business ethics is not so much a subject matter as an alternative language in which business people must articulate their own awareness and aims of the work that they do. (The alternative assumption: "If they won't even tell us what they're doing, they must be doing something wrong.")

The Myth of Amoral Business

Business people have not always been their own best friends. John D. Rockefeller once boasted that he was quite willing to pay a man an annual salary of a million dollars, if the man had certain qualities:

> [He] must know how to glide over every moral restraint with almost childlike disregard . . . [and have], besides other positive qualities, no scruples whatsoever, and [be] ready to kill off thousands of victims—without a murmur.
>
> Robert Warshow, *Jay Gould* (1928)

Such talk is unusually ruthless, but it exemplifies horribly a myth that has often clouded business thinking—what University of Kansas business ethicist Richard deGeorge calls the "myth of amoral business." According to the myth, business and ethics don't mix. People in business are concerned with profits, with producing goods and services, with buying and selling. They may not be immoral, but they are amoral—that is, not concerned with morals. Moralizing is out of place in

business. Indeed, even good acts are to be praised not in moral terms but only in the cost/benefit language of "good business."

The myth of amoral business has a macho, mock-heroic corollary that makes ethical paralysis almost inevitable. It is the dog-eat-dog rhetoric of the Darwinian jungle—"survival of the fittest." In fact, almost everybody and most companies manage to survive without being the "fittest." The anxiety of switching jobs, of not getting promotions, of losing an investment, or of going bankrupt, however upsetting, is rarely a "matter of life and death." In *The Right Stuff*, Tom Wolfe sympathetically quotes the wife of one of the Air Force test pilots. She mentions a friend's complaint about her husband's dog-eat-dog existence on Madison Avenue and reflects, "What if her husband went into a meeting with a one-in-four chance of survival?"

If the myth of amoral business and its Darwinian corollary were nothing but a way of talking on the way to the office, it would not be worth attention or criticism. But the fact is that it does enter into business thinking, and often at exactly the critical moment when an ethical decision is to be made. Worse, the amoral rhetoric of business quickly feeds public suspicion of business and easily becomes part of the condemnation of business. A handful of scandals and accidents that might otherwise be viewed as the unfortunate by-products of any enterprise become "proof" of what the businessmen themselves have been saying all along—that there is no interest in ethics in business, only the pursuit of profits.

What has become apparent is that there is too much theoretical agreement between those who attack business and those who practice it. It is as if both business people and their harshest critics agree that business is amoral and self-serving, but whereas the critics say so in the persuasive language of justice and fairness, business people damn themselves in the language of "cost effectiveness," thus demonstrating in linguistic form if not in content just the accusation being leveled against them.

Business people who do not talk about ethics often complain a great deal about "regulation" without realizing that the two are intimately connected. Legal regulation is the natural response of both society and government to the practice of amorality, however nobly that practice is couched in the rhetoric of "free enterprise." If a business scandal or tragedy is quickly and convincingly chastized by business people, there is neither time nor pressure for regulation. But when scandal and tragedy are at the same time surrounded by ethical neglect or silence or, worse, yet another appeal to "the market" as the long-term corrective, government regulation becomes inevitable. In case anyone still wants to ask why ethics should be relevant to the bottom line, one might simply reply that regulation is the price business pays for bad ethical strategy.

The Three Cs of Business Ethics

Writing in the *Wall Street Journal* in 1979, Irving Kristol commented:

> Once again, modern business is paying the price for conceiving of itself as representing an abstract species of "economic man," rather than as men and women engaged in a fully human activity. It is this self-delusion that has helped so significantly to create the divorce between the business communities and academic-intellectual communities—a divorce that leaves the business community so defenseless when ideas (about morality or anything else) are used unscrupulously as weapons against it.

Business ethics is not an attack on business but rather its first line of defense. Adam Smith knew this well enough: Business has prospered because business has dramatically improved the quality of life for all of us. Moreover, the emphasis on freedom and individuality in a business society has done more than any conceivable socialist revolution to break down traditional inequities in power and wealth, even if it inevitably creates some inequities of its own. Business ethics begins with consumer demand and productivity, with the freedom to engage in business as one wishes, and with the hope—inconceivable in most parts of the world— that one can better one's life considerably through one's own hard work and intelligence. These are the values of business ethics, and the whole point of business ethics is to define and defend the basic goals of prosperity, freedom, fairness, and individual dignity.

Many critics of business are trained in the rhetoric of ethics, but most business people are not. Those in business naturally prefer to stick with what they know and sidestep the ethical issues— which is ruinous. It is one thing to know that product Z costs $.14 to make and retails for $1.59, that raising the price to $1.79 would increase profits and not dampen demand, that cheaper materials or foreign labor could lower the cost of manufacturing to $.09, although sales would eventually diminish as consumer expectations went unsatisfied. But it is something more to think about the quality of product Z, the contribution it makes to American life (even if only by way of amusement or novelty). Not incidentally, these ethical virtues may be essential to the bottom line as well.

Business ethics is nothing less than the full awareness of what one is doing, its consequences and complications. Thinking about ethics in business is no more than acknowledging that one has taken these into account and is willing to be responsible for them. It is being aware of

1. the need for *compliance* with the rules, including the laws of the land, the principles of morality, the customs and expectations of the community, the policies of the company, and such general concerns as fairness;

2. the *contributions* business can make to society, through the value and quality of one's products or services, by way of the jobs one provides for workers and managers, through the prosperity and usefulness of one's activities to the surrounding community;

3. the *consequences* of business activity, both inside and outside the company, both intended and unintended, including the reputation of one's own company and industry. . . .

Part of the problem for business ethics is the image of business as "big" business, as a world of impersonal corporations in which the individual is submerged and ethics is inevitably sacrificed to bureaucratic objectives. To set the image straight, therefore, let us remind ourselves of a single vital statistic: Half of American business is family business; 50% of the GNP; 50% of the employees. Some of these family businesses are among the Fortune 500. Others are Mom and Pop groceries and Sally and Lou's Restaurant. But it is essential to remember that however much our focus may be on corporations and corporate life, business in America is not a monolithic, inhuman enterprise. As the great French philosopher Rousseau once said of society, we might say of American business life that its origins are in the family, that its "natural" model *is* the family. Business is ultimately about relationships between people—our compliance with the rules we all form together, our contributions to the well-being of others as well as to our own, the consequences of our activities, for good and otherwise. There is nothing amoral or unethical about it.

Business Scum

The most powerful argument for ethics in business is success. Ethical businesses are successful businesses; excellence is also ethical. But ethics is no guarantee of success. To say so on our part would be—unethical. The fact is that there are, as we all know, business scum—those shifty, snatch-a-buck operations that give business a bad name. And some of them, ethics be damned, are profitable.

Brake Breakers, Inc., is a small franchise in the Midwest that specializes in brake, suspension, and wheel repairs. Company policy includes hiring men with little education and working them long hours at a single semiskilled job. Wages are accordingly minimal, and employee turnover is more often a matter of burn out than of leaving for another job. (This saves a lot on fringe benefits and pensions; no one has ever collected on them.) Foremost among the employee's skills, however, is the delivery of a prepackaged sermon designed to convince all but the most cautious customer that the $149.25 brake-rebuilding special is far preferable to the mere replacement of the brake shoes, which is all that is usually required (and often all that is actually done).

Managers are rewarded on the basis of the success of these little speeches by their employees. Their job is first and foremost to make sure that the minimum is never enough—not hard given the level of mechanical know-how of most of the customers. But even with the $149.25 special, extra costs are almost always included, sometimes for some other (unnecessary) part but more often than not because of the "unexpected difficulty" of this particular repair. When a customer insists on the minimum repair, it is up to the manager to see to it that more absolutely necessary work is "discovered" in the middle of the job. (This is called the "step method.") Few customers are in a position to do more than complain and curse for the moment, but no one ever expects them to come back anyway.

Managers are expected to keep actual costs down. Used parts are sold in place of new parts. (Sometimes, the car's original part is cleaned or polished and simply reinstalled.) A few miles down the road, who can tell?

Within the company, employees are reminded daily, "There are fifty people waiting for your job." Everyone is hired with the promise "Within three years, you can work up to a managerial position." In fact, managers are always hired from outside— typically friends of the boss. (It is understood that they will supplement their salaries by skimming within the shop.) Managerial turnover, accordingly, is low. Brake Breakers is not the sort of company that can afford to have a disgruntled manager quit in disgust, although any charges he might bring against the company could dependably be turned against him as well.

Brake Breakers, Inc., is everyone's stereotypical image of unethical business in action. Its people sell a shoddy product to customers who don't need it, and they don't always sell what they say they are selling. Employees are treated like serfs, and accounting procedures at every level of the company are, to put it politely, suspect. The customer is virtually never satisfied, but it is the nature of the business that people who need brake repairs need them fast and do not know what has to be done or how much it should cost. They are ripe for the taking, and they are taken. The price is still low enough and the job near enough adequate that no one sues. The "lifetime guarantee" isn't worth the paper it's printed on, but it is a fact about brake jobs that there is only so much that can go wrong, and a disgruntled customer usually doesn't bother coming back anyway. It's a perfect setup. At least half of the profits, even on a modest system of objective ethical accounting, are obtained by cheating the customer and the employees.

How does Brake Breakers, Inc., stack up according to our three Cs of business ethics? Not very well.

Compliance: Minimal; just enough to avoid legal penalties and major lawsuits but far below the level of concern for ethics that we all expect of every business.

Contributions: Well, they do fix brakes, even if some of them aren't broken. But a dozen more dependable businesses— both national franchises and local service stations—would do a better job with less flimflam. To provide a service is not in itself a contribution. We also want to know if it is a service that would otherwise be performed as well and as cheaply by other firms.

Consequences: Disgruntled customers, hesitation among motorists to have their brakes checked when they ought to, occasional accidents, a notoriously bad reputation for car-repair shops in general (hurting those that do good, honest work), and an exemplary case of unethical business to turn consumers and congressional investigators against business in general.

It is too often supposed that the business of business ethics is to prove to the management of such unethical enterprises as Brake Breakers, Inc., that crime does not pay. That is too much to ask for.

Show them, perhaps, that they are setting themselves up for lawsuits.

In fact, it just hasn't happened.

Show them, then, that they are losing customers.

In fact, it is a business with a regular supply of customers, no repeat customers in any case and little dependence on word of mouth. (In fact, they depend on the absence of word of mouth, since people are often too ashamed at having been "taken" to tell their friends about it.)

Show them how well Midas and Meineke have been doing because of their reputation for dependability.

But, the manager at Brake Breakers tells us with a laugh, "We ain't Midas."

Argue, then, that unethical business practices cannot possibly pay off in the long run.

"In the long run," the amused manager tells us, unknowingly echoing the economist John Maynard Keynes, "we're all dead."

The fact—sad, perhaps—is that unethical business, like crime, sometimes pays. In any system based on trust, a few deceivers will prosper. There is no guarantee that ethics is good for the bottom line. There is no guarantee that those who do wrong will get caught or feel guilty. There is no guarantee—in business or elsewhere—that the wicked will suffer and the virtuous will be rewarded (at least, not in this life). But, that said, we can nonetheless insist without apology that good ethics is good business. Where immorality is so easily identified, we can be sure that morality is the general rule, not merely an accessory or an exception. The *point* of doing business is to do well by providing the best service or product at a reasonable cost. Those businesses that exploit the *possibility* of getting away with less are merely parasitic on the overwhelming number of businesses that are doing what they are supposed to.

Practices Make Perfect: A Better Way to Look at Business

A practice is any association of definitely patterned human behavior wherein the description and meaning of kinds of behavior involved and the kinds of expectations involved are dependent upon those rules which define the practice.

John Rawls
(professor of philosophy, Harvard University)

Business is not a scramble for profits and survival. It is a way of life, an established and proven *practice* whose prosperity and survival depend on the participation of its practitioners. Business ethics is not ethics applied to business. It is the foundation of business. Business life thrives on competition, but it survives on the basis of its ethics.

Business is first of all a cooperative enterprise with firmly fixed rules and expectations. A view from the visitor's gallery down to the floor of the New York Stock Exchange may not look very much like a cooperative enterprise with fixed rules and expectations, but beneath the apparent chaos is a carefully orchestrated set of agreements and rituals without which the Exchange could not operate at all. There can be no bogus orders, and bid ranges are carefully controlled. The use of information is restricted, but traders trade information as well as securities. The rules of the exchange, contrary to superficial appearances, are uncompromising. Break them and you're off the floor for good. Right there at the busy heart of capitalism, there is no question that *business is a practice*, and people in business are *professionals*.

In business ethics, it is often profitable to compare business with a game. Games are also practices. Baseball, for instance, is a practice. It has its own language, its own gestures with their own meanings, its own way of giving significance to activities that, apart from the game, might very well mean nothing at all. (Imagine a person who suddenly runs and slides into a canvas bag filled with sand on the sidewalk, declaring himself "safe" as he does so.) The practice is defined by certain sorts of behavior—"pitching" the ball in a certain way (if, that is, the practice designates you as the "pitcher"), trying to hit the ball with a certain well-defined implement (the "bat"), running a certain sequence of "bases" in a certain order subject to certain complex restrictions (one of which is that one not be "tagged" by another person holding the ball). Anyone who has tried to explain what is happening in a baseball game to a visitor from another country with a different "national pastime" can attest to the complexity of these rules and definitions, though most Americans feel quite familiar with them and can focus their attention—as players or as spectators—on such simple-sounding concerns as "Who's up?" and "Who's on first?"

Business is like baseball in that it is a practice. A day at the stock exchange makes it quite clear just how many rituals, rules, and restrictions are involved in every buy-and-sell transaction. The implements of doing business (like "base," "bat," and "ball" in baseball) are also defined within business. What constitutes a contract and fulfillment of a contract is an essential part of the language of business—and often of the contract itself. Consider the not uncommon misunderstanding when a statement of casual intention is misconstrued as a promise (or when "I love you" is mistaken for a statement of commitment instead of an imprudent outburst of passion). The business world is far more open to extra "players" and to alternative courses of action than is baseball, but within the institutions that make up the practice of business, roles and alternatives are clearly specified—as "jobs" and "positions," as obligations and options. Strategic ethics begins by emphasizing business as a practice with strict rules and expectations that

acceptable players honor implicitly—*or they are out of the game*. To throw out players who cheat is as important to a healthy enterprise as is the inevitable exit of players who can't play well. Bad business is much more damaging to business than are badly run businesses.

Business, like baseball, is defined by its rules. Some of these have to do with the nature of contracts. Many have to do with *fairness* in dealing with employees, customers, and government agents (hence the existence of such policing bodies as the IRS, the SEC, the FDA, etc., etc.). Indeed, the notion of fairness in exchanges is more central to business than to any other practice—whether in terms of work and salary, price and product, or public services and subsidies. Without fairness as the central expectation, there are few people who would enter into the market at all. (Consider the chill on the market following dramatic "insider trading" cases.) Without the recognition of fair play, the phrase "free enterprise" would be something of a joke. The rules of business, accordingly, have mainly to do with fairness. Some of these rules ensure that the market will remain open to everyone. Some of the rules protect those who are not players in the practice but whose health, jobs, or careers are affected by it. Some of the rules have to do with serving the needs or wishes of the community (the law of supply and demand can be interpreted not only as an economic mechanism but as an ethical imperative). Some have to do with "impact"—the effects of a business on its surrounding communities and environment. If business had no effects on the surrounding community but was rather a self-enclosed game, there would be no more public cry for business ethics than for "hopscotch ethics" (which is not to say that there is no ethics to hopscotch).

It is within this description of a practice that we can also define the terms "virtue" and "vice" in business ethics. Some virtues and vices go far beyond the bounds of business, of course; they are matters of morality (honesty, for instance). But in business ethics there are virtues and vices that are particular to business and to certain business roles. Close accounting and "watching every penny" are virtues in a shipping clerk but not in someone who is entertaining a client. Keeping a police distance is a virtue in a stockholder but not in a general manager. Tenaciousness may be a virtue in a salesman but not in a consultant. Outspokenness may be a virtue in a board member but not in the assistant to the president. Being tough-minded is a virtue in some managerial roles but not in others.

In general, we can say this: A virtue sustains and improves a practice. A virtue in business is an ethical trait that makes business in general possible, and this necessarily includes such virtues as respect for contracts as well as concern for product quality, consumer satisfaction, and the bottom line. A vice, on the other hand, degrades and undermines the practice. Shady dealing and reneging on contracts are vices and unethical not because of an absolute moral law but because they undermine the very practice that makes doing business possible.

Thinking about business as a practice and business people as professionals gives us a set of persuasive responses to the Brake Breakers case:

1. Business in general depends on the acceptance of rules and expectations, on mutual trust and a sense of fairness, even if—as in any such practice—a few unscrupulous participants can take advantage of that trust and betray that concern for fairness.

2. Brake Breakers, Inc., can continue to prosper in their scummy ways only so long as they remain relatively insignificant, with a small enough market share not to bring down the wrath of major competitors and sufficiently little publicity not to inspire a class-action suit. Unethical behavior may bring profits, but only limited profits.

3. It is clearly in the interest of business in general and other firms in that particular industry to warn consumers about Brake Breakers, even to put them out of business. The success and strength of a profession and its independence from externally imposed regulations depends on the internal "policing" of unethical behavior. Doctors have never doubted this; lawyers are learning. But so long as business thinks of itself as unregulated competition where "anything goes" rather than as a profession to be protected from abuse, this vital policing for survival will go unattended, or it will be attended to by the government.

4. The practice of business is a small world. Fly-by-Night Enterprises Ltd. and Brake Breakers, Inc., may succeed for a while, but, in general, people catch on—fast. Irate customers tell their

friends—and their lawyers. They also get even. They sue, for triple damages. They write the newspapers, or *60 Minutes*. They drop a note to the IRS, or they call the Better Business Bureau. The banker's kid who was cheated on the job complains to his father the month before the lease has to be renewed. Or the victim happens to be a litigious lawyer with time on his hands. But the effects of unethical business practices are not always so obvious as a dip in the bottom line or a subpoena waiting at the office. They are often slow and insidious, the bottom of a career eaten out from under, or a company that is doing "OK" but could and should be doing much better. There are no guarantees that unethical behavior will be punished, but the odds are pretty impressive.

5. In any profession, it's hard to get clean again. Suppliers tighten their terms; priority status disappears. The hardheaded businessman is supposed to say "Who cares?" But if so, there are few hardheaded businessmen, only a small number of bottom-line-minded sociopaths. Character is who you are, the thing you are trying to prove by making money in the first place. One of the classic movie lines is "My money's as good as anyone else's." Perhaps. But are *you* as good? That isn't just a matter of money.

Why should Brake Breakers, Inc., get ethical? Let's ask another question: How would you feel about yourself if you spent your working days as a manager of Brake Breakers? What would you tell your kids? . . .

Thinking Ethics: The Rules of the Game

Ethics is, first of all, a way of thinking.

Being ethical is also—of course—*doing* the right thing, but what one does is hardly separable from how one thinks. Most people in business who do wrong do so not because they are wicked but because they think they are trapped and do not even consider the ethical significance or implications of their actions.

What is thinking ethically? It is thinking in terms of *compliance* with the rules, implicit as well as explicit, thinking in terms of the *contributions* one can make as well as one's own possible gains, thinking in terms of avoiding harmful *consequences* to others as well as to oneself. Accordingly, we have constructed eight crucial rules for ethical thinking in business.

Rule No. 1: Consider other people's well-being, including the well-being of nonparticipants. In virtually every major religion this is the golden rule: "Do unto others as you would have them do unto you"; or, negatively, "Do not do unto others as you would not have them do unto you." Ideally, this might mean that one should try to maximize everyone's interests, but this is unreasonable. First of all, no one really expects that a businessman (or anyone else) would or should sacrifice his own interests for everyone else's. Second, it is impossible to take everyone into account; indeed, for any major transaction, the number of people who will be affected—some unpredictably—may run into the tens or hundreds of thousands. But we can readily accept a minimum version of this rule, which is to make a *contribution* where it is reasonable to do so and to avoid *consequences* that are harmful to others. There is nothing in the golden rule that demands that one deny one's own interests or make sacrifices to the public good. It says only that one must take into account human effects beyond one's own bottom line and weigh one's own gain against the losses of others.

Rule No. 2: Think as a member of the business community and not as an isolated individual. Business has its own rules of propriety and fairness. These are not just matters of courtesy and protocol; they are the conditions that make business possible. Respect for contracts, paying one's debts, and selling decent products at a reasonable price are not only to one's own advantage; they are necessary for the very existence of the business community.

Rule No. 3: Obey, but do not depend solely on, the law. It goes without saying, as a matter of prudence if not of morality, that businesses and business people ought to obey the law—the most obvious meaning of *compliance.* But what needs to be added is that ethical thinking is not limited to legal obedience. There is much unethical behavior that is not illegal, and the question of what is right is not always defined by the law. The fact is that many things that are not immoral or illegal are repulsive,

disgusting, unfair, and unethical—belching aloud in elevators, throwing a disappointing dish at one's host at dinner, paying debts only after the "final notice" and the threat of a lawsuit arrives, fleecing the feebleminded, taking advantage of trust and good faith, selling faulty if not dangerous merchandise under the rubric "Buyer beware." Check the law—but don't stop there.

Rule No. 4: Think of yourself—and your company—as part of society. Business people and businesses are citizens in society. They share the fabric of feelings that make up society and, in fact, contribute much of that feeling themselves. Business is not a closed community. It exists and thrives because it serves and does not harm society. It is sometimes suggested that business has its own ethical rules and that they are decidedly different from those of the larger society. Several years ago business writer Alfred Carr raised a major storm in the *Harvard Business Review* by arguing that business, like poker, had its own rules and that these were not to be confused with the moral rules of the larger society. The comparison with poker has its own problems, but, leaving those aside for now, we can see how such a view not only invites but *demands* the most rigorous regulation of business. Business is subject to the same ethical rules as everyone else because businessmen do *not* think of themselves as separate from society. A few years ago, the then chairman of the Ford Foundation put it bluntly: "Either we have a social fabric that embraces us all, or we're in real trouble." So too with ethics.

Rule No. 5: Obey moral rules. This is the most obvious and unavoidable rule of ethical thinking and the most important single sense of *compliance.* There may be room for debate about whether a moral rule applies. There may be questions of interpretation. But there can be no excuse of ignorance ("Oh, I didn't know that one isn't supposed to lie and cheat"), and there can be no unexcused exceptions ("Well, it would be all right to steal in *this* case"). The German philosopher Immanuel Kant called moral rules "categorical imperatives," meaning that they are absolute and unqualified commands for everyone, in every walk of life, without exception, not even for harried executives. This is, perhaps, too extreme to be practical, but moral rules are the heart of ethics, and there can be no ethics—and no business—without them.

Rule No. 6: Think objectively. Ethics is not a science, but it does have one feature in common with science: The rules apply equally to everyone, and being able to be "disinterested"—that is, to think for a moment from other people's perspectives—is essential. Whether an action is *right* is a matter quite distinct from whether or not it is in *your* interest. For that matter, it is quite independent of your personal opinions as well.

Rule No. 7: Ask the question "What sort of person would do such a thing?" Our word "ethics" comes from the Greek word *ethos*, meaning "character." Accordingly, ethics is not just obedience to rules so much as it is the concern for your personal (and company) character—your reputation and "good name"—and, more important, how you feel about yourself. Peter Drucker summarizes the whole of business ethics as "being able to look at your face in the mirror in the morning."

Rule No. 8: Respect the customs of others, but not at the expense of your own ethics. The most difficult kind of ethical thinking that people in business have to do concerns not a conflict between ethics and profits but rather the conflict between two ethical systems. In general, it is an apt rule of thumb that one should follow the customs and ethics of the community. But suppose there is a conflict not only of mores but of morals, as in the apartheid policies of South Africa. Then the rule to obey (and support) one's own moral principles takes priority. What is even more difficult is what one should do when the moral issue is not clear and moral categories vary from culture to culture. A much debated example is the question of giving money to expedite a transaction in many third-world countries. It is "bribery" in our system, "supporting public servants" in theirs. Bribery is illegal and unethical here because it contradicts our notion of a free and open market. But does the same apply in the third world, where business (and social life) have very different presuppositions? . . .

Ethical thinking is ultimately no more than

considering oneself and one's company as citizens of the business community and of the larger society, with some concern for the well-being of others and—the mirror image of this—respect for oneself and one's character. Nothing in ethics excludes financially sound thinking, and there is nothing about ethics that requires sacrificing the bottom line. In both the long and the short run, ethical thinking is essential to strategic planning. There is nothing unethical about making money, but money is not the currency of ethical thinking in business.

Review and Discussion Questions

1. Solomon and Hanson describe the view that business and ethics don't mix as the "myth of amoral business." Why do they think it is a myth? Do you agree?

2. Do most business people respect the "Three Cs"? In your opinion, how much unethical behavior is there in business today? What happens to companies like Brake Breakers? Can they be successful?

3. Does the existence of "business scum" undermine Solomon and Hanson's claim that business people are professionals and that business is a practice with definite rules?

4. What are the "rules of the game" in business today? Should those rules be changed in any way?

For Further Reading

On Ethics

James Rachels, *Elements of Moral Philosophy* (New York: Random House, 1986) is an excellent, clear introduction.

Robert C. Solomon, *Ethics: A Brief Introduction* (New York: McGraw-Hill, 1984) is a brief, useful guide.

John Arthur, ed., *Morality and Moral Controversies,* 2nd ed. (Englewood Cliffs, N.J.: Prentice-Hall,

1986) contains essays in both theoretical and applied ethics.

George Sher, ed., *Moral Philosophy* (San Diego, Calif.: Harcourt Brace Jovanovich, 1986) is a more advanced collection of readings on various topics in moral philosophy.

Moral Reasoning

Vincent Barry, *Invitation to Critical Thinking* (New York: Holt, Rinehart & Winston, 1984), especially Chapter 7, provides a guide to argument assessment.

Patrick Hurley, *A Concise Introduction to Logic*, 3rd ed. (Belmont, Calif.: Wadsworth, 1988) is a good introduction to all the main areas of logic.

Business and Morality

Both **Richard T. George,** *Business Ethics*, 2nd ed. (New York: Macmillan, 1986) and **Manuel G. Velasquez,** *Business Ethics* (Englewood Cliffs, N.J.: Prentice-Hall, 1982) contain useful introductions to moral philosophy in relation to business.

CHAPTER 2

NORMATIVE THEORIES OF ETHICS

Captain Frank Furillo, in an Emmy-award-winning episode of the television drama *Hill Street Blues*, firmly believes that the two toughs just brought in by his officers are guilty of the rape-murder earlier that morning of a nun inside the parish church. But the evidence is only circumstantial. As word of the crime spreads, the community is aghast and angry. From all sides—the press, the local citizens, city hall, the police commissioner—pressure mounts on Furillo and his department for a speedy resolution of the matter. Outside the Hill Street station, a mob is growing frenzied, hoping to get their hands on the two young men and administrate "street justice" to them. One of its members has even taken a shot at the suspects inside the police station!

The police, however, have only enough evidence to arraign the suspects on the relatively minor charge of being in possession of goods stolen from the church. Furillo and his colleagues could demand a high bail, thus keeping the defendants in custody, while the police try to turn up evidence that will convict the men of murder. But in a surprise move at the arraignment, the district attorney, acting in conjunction with Furillo, declines to ask the judge for bail. The men are free to go. But they and their outraged public defender, Joyce Davenport, know that their lives would be worthless once they hit the streets: Community members have sworn to revenge the much-loved sister if the police are unable to do their job. To remain in police custody, and thus safe, their only choice is to confess to the murder. So the two men confess.

Davenport argues passionately, but unsuccessfully, against what she considers to be a police-state tactic. Anyone in that circumstance, guilty or innocent, would confess. It is an affront to the very idea of the rule of law, she contends: police coercion by way of mob pressure. No system of justice can permit such conduct from its public officials. Yet, the confession allows the police to locate the murder weapon, thus bringing independent confirmation of the culprits' guilt. Furillo's tactic, nevertheless, does not rest easily on his own conscience, and the screenplay closes with him entering the church confessional later that night: "Forgive me Father, for I have sinned . . ."

We can understand why Furillo is worried about whether he did the morally right thing. His action was successful, and it was for a good cause. But does the end always justify the means? Did the police and district attorney behave in a way that accords with due process and the rights of defendants? Should community pressure influence one's professional decisions? Did Furillo act in accordance with some principle that he could defend publicly? In a tough and controversial situation like this, the issue does not concern the moral sincerity of either Furillo or Davenport. Both can be assumed to want to do what is right, but what exactly is the morally justified thing to do? How are we to judge Furillo's tactics? These are the questions.

In the preceding chapter we noted that if a moral judgment is defensible, it must be supportable by a sound moral principle. Moral principles provide the confirmatory standard for moral judgments. The use of these principles, however, is not a mechanical process in which one cranks in data and out pops an automatic moral judgment. Rather, the principles provide a conceptual framework that guides us in the making of moral decisions. Careful thought and open-minded reflection are always necessary to work from one's moral principles to a considered moral judgment.

But what are the appropriate principles to rely on when making moral judgments? The truth is that there is no consensus among people who have studied ethics and reflected on these matters. Different theories exist as to the proper standard of right and wrong. As Professor Bernard Williams has put it, we are heirs to a rich and complex ethical tradition, in which a variety of different moral principles and ethical considerations intertwine and sometimes compete.[1] In this chapter we discuss the different normative perspectives and rival ethical principles that are our heritage. After distinguishing between what are called consequentialist and nonconsequentialist normative theories, we shall look in detail at several ethical approaches, discussing their pros and cons and their relevance to moral decision making in an organizational context:

1. Egoism, both as an ethical theory and as a psychological theory.

2. Utilitarianism, the theory that the morally right action is the one that promotes the greatest happiness for the greatest number of people.

3. Kant's ethics, with his *Categorical Imperative* and his emphasis on moral motivation and respecting persons.

4. Other nonconsequentialist normative themes: duties, moral rights, and *prima facie* principles.

We conclude with an attempt to tie together the major concerns of the different normative theories and suggest a general way of approaching moral decision making.

CONSEQUENTIALIST AND NONCONSEQUENTIALIST THEORIES

In ethics, normative theories are theories that propose some principle or principles for distinguishing right actions from wrong actions. These theories can, for convenience of exposition, be divided into consequentialist and nonconsequentialist approaches.

Many philosophers have argued that the moral rightness of an action is determined solely by its results. If its consequences are good, then the act is right; if they are bad, the act is wrong. Moral theorists who adopt this approach are therefore called *consequentialists*. They determine what is right by weighing the ratio of good to bad that an action is likely to produce. The right act is the one that produces, will probably produce, or is intended to produce at least as great a ratio of good to evil as any other course of action.

One question that arises here is: consequences for whom? Should one consider the consequences only for oneself? Or the consequences for everyone affected? The two most important consequentialist theories, *egoism* and *utilitarianism*, are distinguished by their different answers to this question. Egoism advocates individual self-interest as its guiding principle, while utilitarianism holds that one must take into account everyone affected by the action. But both theorists agree that rightness and wrongness are solely a function of an action's results.

By contrast, *nonconsequentialist* (or, alternatively, *deontological*) theories contend that there is more to the determination of right and wrong than the likely consequences of an action. Nonconsequentialists do not necessarily deny that consequences are morally significant, but they believe that other factors are also relevant to the moral assessment of an action. For example, a nonconsequentialist would hold that for Tom to break his promise to Fred is wrong not simply because it has bad results (Fred's hurt feelings, Tom's damaged reputation, and so on) but because of the inherent character of the act itself. Even if more good than bad were to come from Tom's breaking the promise, a nonconsequentialist might still view it as wrong. What matters is the nature of the act in question, not just its results. This will become clearer later in the chapter as we examine some specific nonconsequentialist theories.

EGOISM

In January 1977, the Firestone Tire and Rubber Company announced that it was discontinuing its controversial "500" steel-belted radial, which according to a House subcommittee had been associated with fifteen deaths and thirty-one injuries. Newspapers interpreted the Firestone announcement as an immediate removal of the tires from the market, whereas Firestone intended a "rolling phase-out."

In the spring of 1978, a House subcommittee found that Firestone had in fact continued making the steel-belted "500" radial, despite earlier media reports to the contrary. Immediately thereafter, newspapers reported a Firestone spokesperson as denying that Firestone had misled the public. Asked why Firestone had not corrected the media misinterpretation of the company's intent, the spokesperson said that Firestone's policy was to ask for corrections only when it was beneficial to the company to do so—in other words, when it was in the company's self-interest.

The view that associates morality with self-interest ordinarily is referred to as *egoism*. Egoism contends that *an act is moral when it promotes the individual's best long-term interests*. ("Individual" here refers to a single person or a particular group, organization, society, or nation.) Egoists use their best long-term advantage to measure an action's rightness. If an action produces, will probably produce, or is intended to produce a greater ratio of good to evil for the individual in the long run than any other alternative, then that action is the right

one to perform, and the individual should take that course to be moral.

Moral philosophers distinguish between two kinds of egoism: personal and impersonal. Personal egoists claim they should pursue their own best long-term interests, but they do not say what others should do. Impersonal egoists claim that everyone should follow his or her best long-term interests.

Misconceptions About Egoism

Several misconceptions haunt both versions of egoism. One is that egoists only do what they like, that they are believers of "eat, drink, and be merry." Not so. Undergoing unpleasant, even painful experience meshes with egoism, provided such temporary sacrifice is consistent with the advancement of long-term happiness.

Another misconception is that egoists cannot act honestly or generously or be helpful to others. But whatever is compatible with one's best interests is compatible with egoism. For example, to shield themselves against increasingly harsh criticism from political activists, U.S. companies doing business in racist South Africa feverishly seek the approval of black Minister Leon H. Sullivan and management consultant D. Reid Weedon. These two men, who want corporations to fight racial discrimination in South Africa, administer the "Sullivan Code," a system for grading corporate conduct there. Some companies resent the interference; others believe it is ineffectual. And many complain about the criteria of the code. Nevertheless, most companies try to comply out of pragmatic self-interest—to fend off oppressive legislation, to improve public relations, to blunt emotional stockholder resolutions.

Still another misconception is that all egoists endorse hedonism, the view that only pleasure (or happiness) is of intrinsic value, the only good in life worth pursuing. Although some egoists are hedonistic—as was the ancient Greek philosopher Epicurus (341–

270 B.C.)—others identify the good with knowledge, power, rational self-interest, or what some modern psychologists call self-actualization. In fact, ethical egoists may hold any theory of what is good.

Perhaps the chief misconception about egoism, however, is that it disallows acts intended to benefit someone else. In fact, there are two sorts of cases in which egoism seemingly would *require* such acts. The first is where we expect our "generosity" to be reciprocated. Thus, those American companies in South Africa that annually scramble to sponsor "socially responsible" programs in that country want something in return: passing scores from Weedon and Sullivan. The other sort of case in which egoism calls for actions that benefit others is when the act would bring pleasure (or in some other way promote the good) of the egoist himself. Egoism might recommend to the chair of the board that she hire as a vice-president her nephew, who is not the best candidate for the job, but whom the chair is very fond of. Hiring the nephew might bring more satisfaction to her than any other course of action, even if the nephew doesn't perform his job as well as someone else might.

Psychological Egoism

So, egoism does *not* preach that we should never act generously but that there is no *moral duty* requiring us to act in the interests of others. Egoism does not bind Ford, Coca-Cola, and Monsanto to institute policies of political and social reform in South Africa, if they otherwise would not want to. According to egoism, these companies have no obligations toward others. If they do have a moral duty, it is to themselves. The same applies, of course, to individual persons. You and I are not *required* to act in the interests of others, but we should if that is the only way to promote our own self-interest. In short: Always "look out for Number One."

Proponents of the ethical theory of egoism generally attempt to derive their basic moral principle from the alleged fact that humans are, by nature, selfish creatures. According to this doctrine, termed *psychological egoism*, human beings are, as a matter of *fact*, so constructed that they must behave selfishly. Psychological egoists claim that all actions are in fact selfishly motivated and that unselfish actions are therefore impossible. This would include even such apparently self-sacrificial acts as parents giving up their own lives in order to save the lives of their children or workers "blowing the whistle" on organizational misdeeds even at great personal expense. Such acts, say psychological egoists, are selfishly motivated. They are done to satisfy the parents' desires to benefit themselves—for example, to perpetuate their family line or avoid unbearable guilt—or the workers' desires for celebrity or revenge or, again, to blunt guilt feelings.

Egoism in an Organizational Context

Two features in particular make ethical egoism somewhat appealing in an organizational setting.

First, egoism provides a basis for formulating and testing policies. Regardless of size, all organizations have aims and regulate their practices accordingly. Regulation usually takes the form of directives, guidelines, explicit policies, and codes of conduct. The purpose of such injunctions is to ease individual decision making by discouraging certain kinds of actions and encouraging others. But how are the actions to be evaluated?

Egoism provides one answer. A policy is legitimate when it promotes the organization's best long-term interest. To test the efficacy of existing policies, one need only determine whether they are advancing or retarding the firm's best interests. Should a company institute an antipollution policy?

Yes, if it serves the company's best interest; no, if it doesn't. Recall the Firestone defense. Only when it is in its own best interests does Firestone correct media errors relative to its policies.

A second strength of egoism is that it *provides moral decision making the flexibility that organizations find appealing.* Egoism does not acknowledge any action such as truth telling as always being the right action, because all actions and rules for actions must be evaluated in terms of best long-term self-interest. As a result, egoism allows organizations to sculpt codes of conduct to suit the complexities of their dealings. It allows them to say—if they choose to—that in some instances concealing facts about products is right but in other cases it's wrong, that bribery is all right in parts of Asia but not in the United States.

Egoism provides this apparent flexibility in moral decision making without arbitrariness, for the principle of best long-term self-interest serves as the governing principle. Thus, had it been in Firestone's interest to correct the media misrepresentation, it would have done so. If it is not in the interest of U.S. multinationals to fight racism in South Africa, they shouldn't.

Critical Inquiries

Despite its immediate appeal, egoism invites several critical inquiries:

1. *How sound is psychological egoism?* Of course, everyone is motivated to some extent by self-interest, and we all know of situations in which someone pretended to be acting altruistically or morally but was really only motivated by self-interest. The theory of psychological egoism maintains more than this, however; it contends that people are always motivated only by self-interested concerns.

Now this claim seems open to counterexamples. Take the actual case of a man who, while driving eastbound in a company truck, spotted smoke coming from inside a parked car and a child trying to escape from the vehicle. The man quickly made a U-turn, drove over to the burning vehicle, and found a one-year-old girl trapped in the back seat, restrained by a seat belt. Flames raged in the front seat as heavy smoke billowed from the car. Disregarding his own safety, the man entered the car and removed the infant, who authorities said would otherwise have died from the poisonous fumes and the flames.

Or take a more mundane example. It's Saturday, and you feel like having a beer with a couple of pals and watching the ball game. On the other hand, you believe you ought to take your two children to the zoo, as you had earlier suggested to them that you might. It would bring them a lot of pleasure and, besides, you haven't done much with them recently. Of course, you love your children and it will bring you some pleasure to go to the zoo with them, but—let's face it—they've been rather cranky lately and you'd prefer to watch the ball game. Nonetheless, you feel an obligation and so you go to the zoo.

These appear to be cases in which people are acting for reasons other than self-interested ones. Of course, the reasons that lead you to take your children to the zoo—a sense of obligation, a desire to promote their happiness—are *your* reasons, but that by itself does not make them self-interested reasons. Still less does it show that you are selfish. Anything that you do is a result of your various desires, but that doesn't establish what the believer in psychological egoism claims—namely, that the only desires you have, or the only desires that ultimately move you, are desires that advance your self-interest.

Now psychological egoists (that is, advocates of the theory of psychological egoism) will claim that "deep down" both the heroic man who saved the girl and the unheroic parent taking the children to the zoo were really motivated by self-interest in some way or another. Maybe the hero was hoping to win praise, or the parent to advance his or her own pleasure by enhancing the children's affection for the parent. Or maybe some other self-interested consideration motivated them. Psychological egoists can always claim that some yet-to-be-identified subconscious egoistic motivation is the main impulse behind any action.

At this point, though, the psychological egoists' claims sound a little farfetched. And we may suspect them of trying to make their theory true by definition. Whatever example we come up with, they will simply claim that the person is "really" motivated by self-interest. One may well wonder how scientific this theory is, or how much content it has, when both the hero and the coward, both the parent who goes to the zoo and the parent who stays home, are equally selfish in their motivations.

An egoist could concede that people are not fully egoistic by nature, and yet continue to maintain egoism as an ethical doctrine— that is, to insist that people *ought* morally to pursue their interests. Yet, without the doctrine of psychological egoism, the ethical thesis of egoism loses a lot of its plausibility. Other types of ethical principles are possible. We all care about ourselves, but how much sense does it make to see self-interest as the basis of right and wrong? If someone does an altruistic act, do we really want to say he is behaving immorally?

2. *Does egoism provide a means for settling conflicts?* To understand this inquiry, consider the case of Peter Faulkner.[2] In 1974, five years before the near-disaster at the nuclear power station at Three Mile Island,[3] Faulkner was warning of the inevitable accidents in nuclear power stations due to mechanical and design deficiencies. At the time, Faulkner was working as a systems application engineer for Nuclear Services Corporation (NSC), a nuclear engineering firm. While in that position, he began collecting evidence that he believed showed that nuclear power station systems were being sold before potential safety problems had been worked out. Moreover, he and several others designed a management information system that they believed would identify defects prior to sales. But NSC, says Faulkner, wasn't interested.

Thwarted within the firm, Faulkner went public with the matter. He wrote his senator detailing myriad alleged design flaws in nuclear reactors. The paper became part of the proceedings of a Senate subcommittee. When the president of NSC learned of Faulkner's action, he allegedly pressured Faulkner not to circulate the paper further.

Now, for argument's sake, let's assume that for some reason it was in Faulkner's best long-term interest to "blow the whistle" and in the president's to silence him. Presumably, ethical egoists would have each man do whatever was necessary to promote his own best long-term self-interest. But what Faulkner should do is incompatible with what the president supposedly should do (and the president's self-interest might even be opposed to NSC's). Which of the apparently two opposing ethical obligations is right? Egoists insist that the self-interest principle is not intended to arbitrate ethical conflicts like these. Nevertheless, critics claim that a valid moral principle must be able to do precisely that.

3. *Is egoism really a moral principle?* Almost all moral theorists maintain that moral principles apply equally to the conduct of all persons and that their application requires us to be objective and impartial. Moral agents are seen as those who, despite their own involvement in an issue, can be reasonably disinterested and objective—those who try to see all sides of an issue without being committed to the interests of a particular individual or group, including themselves. If we accept this attitude of detachment and impartiality as at least part of what it means to take a moral point of view, then we must look for it in any proposed moral principle.

Ethical egoists are anything but objective,

for they are always influenced by their own best interests, regardless of the issue or circumstances. Neither Faulkner nor the president should even attempt to be impartial except insofar as impartiality furthers his own interests. And any third person offering advice must advise Faulkner and the president *not* in their own best interests but in the third party's own interest. Thus, Faulkner, the president, and their advisor must be committed to the narrowest form of moral provincialism.

4. *Does egoism ignore blatant wrongs?* The most common objection to egoism is that by reducing everything to the standard of best long-term self-interest, egoism takes no stand against seemingly outrageous acts like stealing, murder, racial and sexual discrimination, deliberately false advertising, and wanton pollution. All such actions are morally neutral until the test of self-interest is applied.

Of course, the egoist might call this objection a case of question begging—*assuming* that the aforementioned acts are immoral as grounds for repudiating egoism when, in fact, their morality is the very issue that moral principles such as egoism are meant to evaluate. Still, egoism must respond to the widely observed human desire to be fair or just, a desire that at least sometimes seems stronger than competing selfish desires. A moral principle that allows in theory the possibility of murder in the cause of self-interest offends our basic moral intuitions about justice and noninjury; it clashes with many of our "considered beliefs."

UTILITARIANISM

Utilitarianism is the moral doctrine that we should always act so as to produce the greatest possible balance of good over bad for everyone affected by our action. By "good," utilitarians understand happiness or pleasure. Thus, they answer the question "What makes a moral act right?" by asserting: the greatest happiness of all. Although the basic theme of utilitarianism is

present in the writings of many earlier thinkers, Jeremy Bentham (1748–1832) and John Stuart Mill (1806–1873) were the first to develop the theory explicitly and in detail. Both Bentham and Mill were philosophers with a strong interest in legal and social reform. They used the utilitarian standard to evaluate and criticize the social and political institutions of their day—for example, the prison system. As a result, utilitarianism has long been associated with social improvement.

Bentham viewed the community as no more than the individual persons who composed it. The interests of the community were simply the sum of the interests of its members. An action promoted the interests of an individual when it added to the sum total of the individual's pleasure or diminished the sum total of the person's pain. Correspondingly, an action augmented the happiness of a community only insofar as it increased the total amount of individual happiness. In this way, Bentham argued for the utilitarian principle that actions are right if they promote the greatest human welfare, wrong if they do not.

For Bentham pleasure and pain were merely types of sensations, which differed only in number, intensity, and duration. He offered a "hedonic calculus" of six criteria for evaluating pleasure and pain by measurement alone, exclusively by their quantitative differences. This calculus, he believed, made possible an objective determination of the morality of anyone's conduct, individual or collective, on any occasion.

Bentham rejected any distinctions based on quality of pleasure except insofar as they might indicate differences in quantity. Thus, where equal amounts of pleasure are involved, throwing darts is as good as writing poetry and baking a cake as good as composing a symphony; reading Mickey Spillane is of no less value than reading Shakespeare. Although he himself was an intelligent, cultivated man, Bentham maintained there was nothing intrinsically better about cultivated and intellectual pleasures than about crude and prosaic ones, except insofar as either might yield a greater amount of enjoyment than the other.

John Stuart Mill thought Bentham's concept of pleasure was too simple. He viewed human beings as having elevated faculties that allow them to pursue various kinds of pleasure. The pleasures of the intellect and imagination, in particular, have a higher value than those of mere sensation. Thus for Mill the utility principle allowed consideration of the relative *quality* of pleasure and pain.

Although Bentham and Mill offered different conceptions of pleasure or happiness, they agreed in thinking happiness to be the ultimate value. In this sense they are *hedonists*: Happiness, in their view, is the one thing that is intrinsically good or worthwhile. Anything that is good is good only because it brings about happiness (or pleasure), directly or indirectly. Take education, for example. The learning process itself might be pleasurable to us; reflecting on, or working with, what we have learned might bring us satisfaction at some later time; or, by making possible a career and life that we could not have had otherwise, education might bring us happiness indirectly. By contrast, critics of Bentham and Mill have contended that things other than happiness are or can be also inherently good—for example, knowledge, friendship, or aesthetic satisfaction. This implies that these things would be valuable even if they did not lead to happiness.

Some moral theorists have modified utilitarianism so that it aims at other consequences in addition to happiness. Other utilitarians, wary of how to compare one person's happiness with another, have interpreted their theory as requiring us not to maximize happiness, but rather to maximize the satisfaction of people's preferences (or desires). But we will focus on utilitarianism in its standard form, in which the good to be aimed at is human happiness or welfare. But what we shall say about standard or classical utilitarianism applies, with the appropriate modifications, to other versions as well.

Although we shall later introduce and discuss another form of utilitarianism, known as *rule utilitarianism*, utilitarianism in its most basic version, often called *act utilitarianism*, states that in performing an action we must ask ourselves what the consequences of this particular act in this particular situation will be for all those affected. If its consequences bring more total good than those of any alternative course of action, then this action is the right one and the one we should perform. Thus, a utilitarian could defend Frank Furillo's decision not to request bail, thereby coercing a confession from the suspects.

Consider another example: In 1956, medical researchers initiated a long-range study of viral hepatitis at Willowbrook State Hospital, a New York institution for mentally retarded children. The researchers were interested in determining the natural history of viral hepatitis and the effectiveness of gamma globulin as an agent for inoculating against hepatitis. Willowbrook seemed like a good choice for investigation because the disease was rampant there. In order to get the kind of precise data they considered most useful, the researchers decided to deliberately infect some of the incoming children with the strain of hepatitis virus epidemic at the institution.

The value of the Willowbrook research is well documented. As a direct result, we have increased our scientific understanding of viral hepatitis and how to treat it. But nagging moral questions persist. Should retarded children have been used as experimental subjects in experiments that were not directly therapeutic? Was the free and informed consent of the children's parents obtained? Supporters of the research answer both questions in the affirmative. But even if the facts warranted another conclusion, some people would still defend the Willowbrook experiments on the grounds that they produced the greatest good for the greatest number. In other words, the suffering of some individuals was justified because it maximized the total good produced.

Six Points About Utilitarianism

Before evaluating utilitarianism, let's clear up some points that might lead to confusion and misapplication. First, when a utilitarian like Bentham advocates "the greatest happiness for the greatest number," we must consider unhappiness or pain as well as happiness. Suppose, for example, an action produces eight units of happiness and four units of unhappiness. Its net worth is four units of happiness. An opposed action produces ten units of happiness and seven units of unhappiness; its net worth is three units. In this case we should choose the first action over the second. In the event that both lead not to happiness but to unhappiness, and there is no third option, we should choose the one that brings fewer units of unhappiness.

Second, actions affect people to different degrees. Your playing your radio loudly might enhance two persons' pleasure a little, cause significant discomfort to two others, and leave a fifth person indifferent. The utilitarian theory is not that each person votes on the basis of his or her pleasure or pain, with the majority ruling, but that we add up the various pleasures and pains, however large or small, and go with the action that brings about the greatest total amount of happiness.

Third, since utilitarians evaluate actions according to their consequences, and actions produce different results in different circumstances, then according to the utilitarian theory almost anything might, in principle, be morally right in some particular circumstance. For example, while breaking a promise generally produces unhappiness, there can be circumstances in which, on balance, more

happiness would be produced by breaking the promise than by keeping it. In those circumstances, utilitarianism would require us to break the promise.

Fourth, utilitarians wish to maximize happiness, not simply immediately, but in the long run as well. All the indirect ramifications of an act have to be taken into account. Lying might seem a good way out of a tough situation, but if and when the people we deceive find out, not only will they be unhappy, but our reputations and our relationships with them will be damaged. This is a serious risk that a utilitarian cannot ignore.

Fifth, utilitarians acknowledge that we often do not know with certainty what the future consequences of our actions will be. Accordingly, we must act so that the expected or likely happiness is as great as possible. If I take my friend's money, unbeknownst to him, and buy lottery tickets with it, there is a chance that we will end up millionaires and that my action will have maximized happiness all around. But the odds are definitely against it; the most likely result is loss of money (and probably of a friendship, too). Therefore, no utilitarian could justify gambling with purloined funds on the grounds that it "might" maximize happiness.

Sometimes it may seem hard to know the likely results of alternative actions, and no modern utilitarian really believes that we can assign precise units of happiness and unhappiness to people. But, as Mill reminds us, we really do have quite a lot of experience as to what typically makes people happy or unhappy. In any case, as utilitarians, our duty is to strive to maximize total happiness, even where it may seem difficult to know what action is likely to promote the good effectively.

Finally, when choosing among possible actions, utilitarianism does not require us to disregard our own pleasure. Nor should we give it added weight. Rather, our own pleasure and pain enter into the calculus equally with the pleasures and pains of others. Even if we are sincere in our utilitarianism, we must guard against the possibility of being biased in our calculations when our own interests are at stake. For this reason, and because it would be time consuming to do a utilitarian calculation before every action, utilitarians encourage us to rely on "rules of thumb" in ordinary moral circumstances. We can make it a rule of thumb, for example, to tell the truth and keep our promises, rather than to calculate possible pleasures and pains in every routine case, because we know that in general telling the truth and keeping promises results in more happiness than lying and breaking promises.

Utilitarianism in an Organizational Context

Several features about utilitarianism make it appealing as a standard for moral decisions in business and nonbusiness organizations.

First, like egoism, utilitarianism provides a basis for formulating and testing policies. By utilitarian standards, an organizational policy decision or action is good if it promotes the general welfare more than any other alternative. To show that a policy is wrong (or needs modification) requires only that it not promote total utility as well as some alternative would. Utilitarians do not ask us to accept rules, policies, or principles blindly. Rather, they require us to test their worth against the standard of utility.

Second, utilitarianism provides an objective way of resolving conflicts of self-interest. This feature of utilitarianism dramatically contrasts with egoism, which seemed incapable of resolving conflicts of self-interest between organizations, between individuals and organizations, and between individuals and individuals. By proposing a standard outside self-interest, utilitarianism greatly minimizes and may actually eliminate such disputes. Thus, individuals within organizations make moral decisions and evaluate their actions by ap-

pealing to a uniform standard: the general good.

Third, utilitarianism recognizes the four primary claimant groups in organizational activity: owners, employees, customers (clients), and society. This feature follows from utilitarianism's concern with the greatest happiness for the greatest number of people. Organizational activity inevitably involves complex transactions that involve multiple interests. This is especially true because today's economy is characterized by interdependent economic and social interests. An ethical standard that does not address this network of interdependency seems woefully lacking. The principle of utility, however, broadens the scope of organizational decisions, policies, and actions. It requires that people in business, for example, make moral decisions against the background of collective interest.

Fourth, like egoism, utilitarianism provides the latitude in moral decision making that organizations seem to need. By recognizing no actions of a general kind as inherently right or wrong, utilitarianism allows organizations to tailor policies and allows individuals to make personal decisions to suit the complexities of the situation. This facet of utilitarianism provides organizations the moral elasticity they need to make realistic judgments.

Critical Inquiries

1. *Is utilitarianism really workable?* Utilitarianism instructs us always to maximize happiness, but in hard cases we may be very uncertain about the likely results of the alternative courses of action open to us. Further, comparing your level of happiness or unhappiness with mine is at best tricky, at worst—impossible, and when many people are involved, the matter may get hopelessly complex. Even if we assume that it is possible to make comparisons and to calculate the various possible consequences (and the odds of each happening) of each course of action that

a person might take, is it realistic to expect people to take the time to make those calculations and, if they do, to make them accurately? Some critics of act utilitarianism have contended that it would not in fact promote happiness to teach people to follow the basic utilitarian principle because of the difficulties in applying it accurately.

2. *Are some actions wrong, even if they produce good?* Like egoism, utilitarianism focuses on the end of actions, not the means used to achieve them. (*End* refers to the consequences or results, *means* to the action itself—its nature and characteristics.) For utilitarians the end justifies the means. No action is in itself objectionable. It is objectionable only when it leads to a lesser amount of total good than could otherwise have been brought about. Critics of utilitarianism, by contrast, contend that some actions can be immoral, and thus something we must not do, even if doing them would maximize happiness.

Consider the example of the death-bed promise, in which a dying woman has asked you to promise to send the $25,000 under her bed to her nephew in another part of the country. She dies without anyone else knowing of the money or of the promise that you made. Now suppose, too, that you know that the nephew is a spendthrift and a drunkard and that, were the money delivered to him, it would be wasted in a week of outrageous partying. On the other hand, a very fine orphanage in your town needs such a sum to improve and expand its recreational facilities, something that would provide happiness to many children for years to come. Admittedly, this is not an everyday decision, but if we assume these are the facts, then it seems clear that on utilitarian grounds you should give the money to the orphanage because this would result in more total happiness.

On the other hand, many people will balk at this utilitarian conclusion, contending that it would be wrong to break your promise, even if doing so would bring about more good

than keeping it. Having made a promise, we have an obligation to keep it, and a death-bed promise is a particularly serious promise. Furthermore, the deceased woman had a right to do with her money as she wished; it is not for you to decide how to spend it. Likewise, having been bequeathed the money, the nephew has a right to it, regardless of how wisely or foolishly he might spend it. Defenders of utilitarianism, however, will stick to their guns, insisting that promoting happiness is all that really matters and warning us not to be blinded by moral prejudice.

Critics of utilitarianism, on the other hand, maintain that it is utilitarianism that is morally blind in not just permitting, but requiring, immoral actions in order to maximize happiness. Philosopher Richard Brandt states the case against act utilitarianism this way:

> Act utilitarianism implies that if you have employed a boy to mow your lawn and he has finished the job and asks for his pay, you should pay him what you promised only if you cannot find a better use for your money. . . . It implies that if your father is ill and has no prospect of good in his life, and maintaining him is a drain on the energy and enjoyment of others, then, if you can end his life without provoking any public scandal or setting a bad example, it is your positive duty to take matters into your own hands and bring his life to a close.[4]

In the same vein, ethicist A. C. Ewing concludes that "act utilitarian principles, logically carried, would result in far more cheating, lying and unfair action than any good person would tolerate."[5]

Defenders of act utilitarianism would reply that these charges are exaggerated. While theoretically possible, for example, that it might maximize happiness *not* to pay the boy for his work, this is extremely unlikely. Utilitarians will contend that only in very unusual circumstances will pursuit of the good conflict with our ordinary ideas of right and wrong, and in those cases—like the death-bed promise—we should put aside those ordinary ideas. The antiutilitarian contends that the theoretical possibility alone of utilitarianism requiring immoral conduct shows it to be an unsatisfactory moral theory.

3. *Is utilitarianism unjust?* Utilitarianism concerns itself with the total sum of happiness produced, not with how that happiness is distributed. If policy X brings two units of happiness to each of five people, and policy Y brings four units of happiness to one person, one unit each to two others, and none to the remaining two, then Y is to be preferred (eleven units of happiness versus ten) even though it distributes that happiness very unequally.

Worse still from the critic's point of view, utilitarianism may even require that some people's happiness be sacrificed in order to achieve the greatest overall amount of happiness. Sometimes the general utility may be served only at the expense of a single individual or group. Under the right of eminent domain, for example, the government may appropriate private property for public use, usually with compensation to the owner. Thus the government may legally purchase your house from you in order to widen a highway—even though you don't want to sell the house or want more money than the government is willing to pay. The public interest is served at your private expense. Is this just?

Or consider the Dan River experiment, which is a recent entry in the long-term controversy over the cause of brown lung disease, bynninesis. Claiming that the disease is caused by the inhalation of microscopic fibers in cotton dust, textile unions have fought for tough regulations to protect their workers. The Occupational Safety and Health Administration (OSHA) responded by proposing cotton dust standards, which would require firms to install expensive new equipment. A few months before the March 27, 1984, deadline for installing the equipment, officials at Dan River, Inc., textile plants in Virginia asked the state to waive the requirements for six months so that they could conduct an experiment to determine the precise cause of brown lung. Both the state and the Department of Labor allowed the extension. In response, the Amalgamated Clothing and Textile Workers Unions asked OSHA to stop the proposed project, charging "It is simply unconscionable to allow hundreds of cotton mill workers to continue to face a high risk of developing brown lung disease."[6]

Now let's suppose that the Dan River project in fact does expose workers to a "high risk" of contracting lung disease. If so, then a small group of individuals—633 textile workers at ten locations in Danville, Virginia—are being compelled to carry the burden of isolating the cause of brown lung. Is this just?

It is, utilitarians would respond, if it's expedient. Is it expedient? It may be. If the project succeeded in identifying the exact cause of the disease, then thousands of textile workers across the country and perhaps around the world will benefit. Also researchers might discover a more economical way to ensure worker safety, which in turn would yield a consumer benefit: more economic textiles than the ones produced after the industry had to install expensive new equipment. Certainly, utilitarians would introduce the potential negative impact on workers at Dan River, but merely as one effect among many others. If, after the interests of all the affected parties are equally weighed, the extension would likely yield the greatest net utility, then it is just to make workers at Dan River carry the main burden of isolating the cause of brown lung disease—even if by so doing those workers may be injured. (It should be noted that this sketchy analysis is not intended to justify the project or to foreclose a fuller utilitarian analysis of this case, but merely to illustrate generally the utilitarian approach.)

The Interplay between Self-Interest and Utility

Both self-interest and utility play important roles in organizational decisions, and the views of many businesspersons blend these two theories. To the extent that each business pursues its own interests and each businessperson tries to maximize personal success, business practice can be called egoistic. But business practice is also utilitarian in that pursuing self-interest is thought to maximize the total good and playing by the established rules of the competitive game is seen as advancing the good of society as a whole. The classical capitalist economist Adam Smith (1723–1790) held such a view. He argued that if business is left to pursue its self-interest, the good of society will be served. Indeed, Smith believed that only through egoistic pursuits could the greatest happiness for the greatest number be produced. The essence of Smith's position can be seen in the following passage from *The Wealth of Nations* (1776). Notice that while discussing the need to restrict imports, Smith underscores the interplay between self-interest and the social good and between egoism and utilitarianism.

> Every individual is continually exerting himself to find out the most advantageous employment for whatever capital he can command. It is his own advantage, indeed, and not that of the society, which he has in view. But the study of his own advantage, naturally, or rather necessarily, leads him to prefer that employment which is most advantageous to the society. . . .
>
> As every individual, therefore, endeavours as much as he can both to employ his capital in the support of domestic industry, and so to direct that industry that its produce may be of the greatest value, every individual necessarily labors to render the annual revenue of the society as great as he can.

> He generally, indeed, neither intends to promote the public interest, nor knows how much he is promoting it. By preferring the support of domestic to that of foreign industry, he intends only his own security; and by directing that industry in such a manner as its produce may be of the greatest value, he intends only his own gain, and he is in this, as in many other cases, led by an invisible hand to promote an end which was no part of his intention. Nor is it always the worse for the society that it was no part of it. By pursuing his own interest he frequently promotes that of the society more effectually than when he really intends to promote it. I have never known much good done by those who affected to trade for the public good. It is an affectation, indeed, not very common among merchants, and very few words need be employed in dissuading them from it.[7]

Many today would agree with Smith, conceding that business is part of a social system, that cooperation is necessary, and that certain competitive ground rules are needed and should be followed. At the same time they would argue that the social system is best served by the active pursuit of self-interest within the context of established rules. Thus, within the rules of business practice these individuals might view business ethics as the ethics of a "restrained egoist." It is egoistic because it is an ethic based on the pursuit of self-interest; it is restrained because it permits pursuit of self-interest only within the rules of business practice.[8]

In Chapter 4 we will examine Smith's position in more detail.

KANT'S ETHICS

Most of us find the ideal of promoting human happiness and well-being an attractive one and, as a result, admire greatly a woman like

Mother Theresa, who has devoted her life to working with the poor. Despite the attractiveness of this ideal, many moral philosophers are, as we have seen, critical of utilitarianism —in particular because, like egoism, it reduces all of morality to a concern with consequences. Although nonconsequentialist (or deontological) normative theories vary significantly among themselves, adopting different approaches and stressing different themes, the writings of the preeminent German philosopher Immanuel Kant (1724–1804) provide an excellent example of a thoroughgoing nonconsequentialist approach in ethics. Perhaps few thinkers today would endorse Kant's theory on every point, but his work has not only greatly influenced philosophers, it has also helped to shape our general moral culture. We shall therefore look at his thinking in some detail.

Kant sought moral principles that do not rest on contingencies and that define actions as inherently right or wrong apart from any particular circumstances. He believed that moral rules can, in principle, be known as a result of *reason* alone, and are not based on observation (as are, for example, scientific judgments). In contrast to utilitarianism or other consequentialist theories, Kant would contend that we do not have to know anything about the likely results of, say, my telling a lie to my boss in order to know that it is immoral. "The basis of obligation," Kant writes, "must not be sought in human nature, [nor] in the circumstances of the world." Rather it is *a priori*, by which he meant that reason by itself can reveal to us the basic moral principles and that moral reasoning is not based on factual knowledge.

As a rational being, I not only ask "What shall I do?" but "What *should* I do?" I can assume, said Kant, that all rational beings are conscious of being under an obligation to act in particular ways. Thus when I answer the question "What should I do?" I am also considering what *all* rational beings must do, for if the moral law is valid for me as a rational being, it must be valid for you and all other rational beings. *A major test of a morally right act, therefore, is whether its principle can be applied to all rational beings and be applied consistently.*

Good Will

We referred elsewhere to Good Samaritan laws, which protect those rendering emergency aid from lawsuits. Such laws, in effect, give legal status to the humanitarian impulses behind emergency interventions. They formally recognize that the interventionist's heart was in the right place, that the person's intention was irreproachable. And because the person acted from right intention, he or she should not be held culpable, except for grievous negligence. The widely observable human tendency to introduce a person's intentions in assigning blame or praise is a good springboard for engaging Kant's ethics.

Nothing, said Kant, is good in itself except a good will. This does not mean that many facets of the human personality are not good and desirable—intelligence, sensitivity, talent, virtue, rational development, and so on. But Kant believed that their goodness resides in the will that makes use of them.

By "will" Kant meant the uniquely human capacity to act from principle. Contained in the good will is the concept of duty: Only when we act from duty does our action have moral worth. When we act only out of feeling, inclination, or self-interest, our actions—though they may be otherwise identical with ones that spring from the sense of duty—have no true moral worth.

To illustrate, let's suppose that you're a clerk in a small stop-and-go store. Late one night a customer pays for his five-dollar purchase with a twenty-dollar bill, which you mistake for a ten. It's only after the customer leaves that you realize you shortchanged him. You race out the front door and find him lingering by a vending machine. You give him the ten dollars with your apologies, and he thanks you profusely.

Now, can we say with certainty that you acted from a good will? Not necessarily. You may have acted from a desire to promote business or to avoid legal entanglement. If so, you would have acted *in accordance with* but not *from* duty. Your apparently virtuous gesture just happened to coincide with duty. According to Kant, if you did not will the action from a sense of duty to be fair and honest, your action does not have true moral worth. Actions have true moral worth only when they spring from a recognition of duty and a choice to discharge it.

But then what determines our duty? How do we know what morality requires of us? Kant answered these questions by formulating what he called the *Categorical Imperative*. This extraordinarily significant moral concept provides Kant's answer to the question, "What makes a moral act right?"

The Categorical Imperative

We have seen that egoists and utilitarians allow factual circumstances or empirical data to determine moral judgments. In contrast, Kant believed that reason alone could yield a moral law. We do not have to rely on empirical evidence relating to similar situations or to consequences or to any religious injunctions. Just as we know, seemingly through reason alone, certain abstract truths like "Every change must have a cause," so we can arrive at absolute moral truth through the same kind of reasoning. And we can thereby discover our duty.

For Kant, an absolute moral truth must be logically consistent, free from internal contradiction. For example, it is a contradiction to say that an effect does not have a cause. Kant aimed to ensure that his absolute moral law would avoid such contradictions. If he could formulate such a rule, he maintained, it would oblige everyone to follow it without exception.

Kant believed that there is just one command (imperative) that is categorical—that is, presents an action as of itself necessary, regardless of any other considerations. From this one categorical imperative, this universal command, we can derive all commands of duty. *Kant's Categorical Imperative says that we should act in such a way that we can will the maxim of our action to become a universal law.* So Kant's answer to the question "What makes a moral act right?" is that we can will it to become a universal law of conduct. We will see that this answer has two other formulations.

The obvious and crucial question that arises here is: "When are we justified in saying that the maxim of our action can become a universal law of conduct?" Let's explore Kant's answer by first defining and illustrating "maxim."

By maxim, Kant meant the subjective principle of an action, the principle (or rule) that people in effect formulate in determining their conduct. For example, suppose building contractor John Martin promises to install a sprinkling system in a project but is willing to break that promise if it suits his purposes. His maxim can be expressed: "I'll make promises that I'll break whenever keeping them no longer suits my purposes." This is the subjective principle, the maxim, that directs his action. Kant insisted that the morality of any maxim depends on whether we can logically will it to become a universal law. Could Martin's maxim be universally acted upon?

That depends on whether the maxim as law would involve a contradiction. The maxim "I'll make promises that I'll break whenever keeping them no longer suits my purposes" could not be universally acted upon because it involves a contradiction of will. On the one hand, Martin is willing that it be possible to make promises and have them honored. On the other, if everyone intended to break promises when they so desired, then promises could not be honored in the first place, because it is in the nature of promises that they be believed. A law that allowed promise breaking would contradict the very nature of a promise. Similarly, a law that allowed lying would contradict the very nature of serious communication, for the activity of serious communication (as opposed to joking), by definition, requires that participants intend to speak the truth. I cannot without contradiction *will* both serious conversation and lying.

Consider, as another example, Kant's account of a man who, in despair after suffering a series of major setbacks, contemplates suicide. While still rational, the man asks whether it would be contrary to his duty to take his own life. Could the maxim of his action become a universal law of nature? Kant thinks not:

> His maxim . . . is: For love of myself, I make it my principle to shorten my life when by a longer duration it threatens more evils than satisfaction. But it is questionable whether this principle of self-love could become a universal law of nature. One immediately sees a contradiction in a system of nature whose law would be to destroy life by the feeling whose special office is to impel the improvement of life. In this case, it would not exist as nature: hence the maxim cannot obtain as a law of nature, and thus it wholly contradicts the supreme principle of all duty.[9]

When Kant insists that a moral rule be consistently universalizable, he is saying that moral rules prescribe categorically, not hypothetically. A hypothetical prescription tells us what to do if we desire a particular outcome. Thus, "If I want people to like me, I should be nice to them" and "If you want to go to medical school, you must take biology" are hypothetical imperatives. They tell us what we must do on the assumption that we have some particular goal. If that is what we want, then this is what we must do. On the other hand, if we don't want to go to medical school, then the command to take biology does not apply to us.

In contrast, Kant's imperative is categorical—it commands unconditionally. That is, it is binding on everyone, regardless of their specific goals or desires, regardless of consequences. A categorical imperative takes the form of "Do this" or "Don't do that"—no ifs, ands, or buts. Such a command must be universalizable, because if it were not its worth would be based upon consequential grounds. Put another way, if a person did not follow a moral rule solely on the grounds that it was a universal law of moral conduct, that person would allow results to determine whether to follow the rule. But, according to Kant, the rule would then lose its inherent necessity and universality and thus its moral character.

A closer look at examples like the preceding reveals two other formulations of the Categorical Imperative besides universalization. One embodies the *principle of humanity as an end*, never as merely a means; the other incorporates the *principle of universal acceptability*.

The Principle of Humanity as an End, Never as Merely a Means. The second formulation of the Categorical Imperative is that *rational creatures should always treat other rational creatures as ends in themselves and never as only means to ends*. This formulation underscores Kant's belief that every rational creature has an inherent worth that results from the sheer possession of rationality. As rational beings, humans would act inconsistently if they did not treat everyone else the way they themselves would want to be treated. Here we see shades of the Golden Rule. Indeed, Kant's moral philosophy can be viewed as a profound philosophical reconsideration of this basic nonconsequential principle. Because rational beings recognize their own inner worth, they would never wish to be used as entities possessing worth only as means to an end.

Thus, Kant would object to the practice of *compelling* prisoners to be subjects in medical experiments to yield a cure for cancer—even though great social benefit might result. The reason is that researchers would be intentionally using the prisoners as means to an end against their will. No matter how desirable that end, Kant would nevertheless oppose this practice. At the very least, he would require the subjects' informed consent.

The Principle of Universal Acceptability.   A third formulation of the Categorical Imperative stems from the *autonomy* or self-determination of the will. Kant believed that the moral law must be universally acceptable. This is because each person, through his or her own act of will, legislates the moral law. He distinguished autonomy from heteronomy, the determination of a law or action by someone or something other than the self. The heteronomous will is influenced, even determined, by desires or inclinations shaped by outside forces. In contrast, the autonomous will is free and independent. It is the supreme arbiter of morality. The moral laws that we obey are not imposed on us from the outside. They are self-imposed and self-recognized, fully internalized principles. The sense of duty that we obey comes from within; it is an expression of our own higher selves.

Moral beings give themselves the moral law and accept its demands on themselves. As ends in themselves, they are not subservient to anyone else. That does not mean we can prescribe anything we want, for we are bound by reason and its demands. Since reason is the same for all rational beings, we give ourselves the *same* moral law.

The universal acceptability of the moral law is a function of the fact that each moral being gives himself or herself the moral law. To see whether a rule or principle is a moral law, said Kant, we should ask if what the rule commands would be acceptable to *all* rational beings acting rationally. In considering lying, theft, or murder, for example, I must consider the act not only from my own viewpoint but from the perspective of the person lied to, robbed, or murdered. Presumably rational beings will see that they do not want to be lied to, robbed, or murdered. They will reach this determination not merely from considering their own good, but because as rational beings they accept the limits of what they permit themselves to do as members of a community. *The test of the morality of a rule, then, is* not whether people in fact accept it, but *whether all rational beings thinking rationally would accept it regardless of whether they are the doers or the receivers of the actions.*

Professor of philosophy George Brenkert uses this point to argue against the use of polygraphs as a pre-employment screen (see "Privacy, Polygraphs and Work," p. 278). He says that the corporate defense of polygraphs seems "one sided." On the one hand, corporate managers say polygraph tests are needed as pre-employment screens to protect corporate property from potential employee thieves. On the other hand, they themselves would object if the government, for comparable security reasons, made them submit to a polygraph test as a condition for a government contract.

A similar application can be made to workplace sexism. Suppose a man were to advocate discriminatory hiring policies against women. If this rule were to be universally acceptable, the man would have to allow sexism directed at himself were he a woman, something he presumably would be unwilling to allow.

Again, suppose manufacturers of a product advocated its marketing even though they knew the product was dangerous to the health and safety of consumers and that consumers were ignorant of this fact. Applying the universal acceptability principle, the manufacturers would have to advocate marketing the product even if they were in the position of uninformed consumers. Presumably they would be unwilling to do this. So the rule that would allow such activity would fail the test of universal acceptability: It would not be acceptable to rational beings acting rationally.

We said earlier that Kant's answer to the

question of what makes a moral act right is that it can be willed to become a universal law. Now we can give two reformulations that are more easily grasped and applied:

> *First Reformulation:* What makes a moral act right is that it (that is, the doer) treats human beings as ends in themselves.
> *Second Reformulation:* What makes a moral act right is that the doer would be willing to be so treated were the positions of the parties reversed.

Kant in an Organizational Context

Like egoism and utilitarianism, Kant's ethics has application for organizations.

First, the Categorical Imperative takes much of the guess work out of moral decision making. Business people rightly complain that professional codes of conduct are often so vague as to be useless. Worse, these codes of conduct leave much up to individual interpretation, making morality into a kind of guessing game or exercise in public relations. Kant's ethics remove much of this uncertainty and subjectivity. No matter what the consequences may be, some actions are always wrong. Lying is an example; no matter how much good may come from misrepresenting a product, such deliberate misrepresentation is always wrong. Similarly, exposing workers to the risk of lung disease could not be justified in order to advance medical knowledge.

Second, Kant's ethics introduce a needed humanistic dimension into business decisions. We saw that one of the principal objections to egoism and utilitarianism is that they intentionally treat humans as means to ends. Kant's ethics clearly forbids this. Many would say that respect for the inherent worth and dignity of human beings is much needed today in business, where encroaching technology and computerization tend to dehumanize people under the guise of efficiency. Kant's ethics also puts the emphasis of organizational deci-

sion making where it belongs: on individuals. Organizations, after all, involve individuals working in concert to provide goods and services for other individuals. The primacy Kant gives the individual reflects this essential function of business.

Third, Kant stresses the importance of motivation and of acting on principle. According to Kant, it is not just enough to do the right thing; an action has moral worth only if it is done from a sense of duty, that is, from a desire to do the right thing for its own sake. The importance of this is too often forgotten. Sometimes when individuals and organizations believe that an action promotes not only their own interests but those of others as well, they are actually rationalizing—doing what is best for themselves and only imagining that somehow or other it will promote happiness in general. Worse still, they may defend their actions as morally praiseworthy when, in fact, they are only behaving egoistically. They wouldn't do the morally justifiable thing if they didn't think that it would pay off for them. By stressing the importance of motivation, a Kantian approach serves as a corrective to this. Even an action that helps others has moral value for Kant only if the person doing it is morally motivated, that is, acting on principle or out of moral conviction.

Critical Inquiries

1. *What has moral worth?* According to Kant, the clerk who returned the ten dollars to the customer did the right thing, but if his action was motivated by self-interest (perhaps he wanted to get a reputation for honesty), then it did not have moral worth. That seems plausible. But Kant also held that if the clerk did the right thing out of instinct, habit, or a feeling of human sympathy for the other person, then the act still does not have moral worth. Only if it is done out of a sense of duty will the clerk's action have moral value. Many moral theorists have felt that Kant was too

severe on this point. Do we really want to say of people who give to famine relief because they are moved by pictures of starving children, that their action has no moral worth? We might, to the contrary, find a person with strong human sympathies better than someone who gave solely out of an abstract sense of duty.

2. *Is the Categorical Imperative an adequate test of right?* Kant says that a moral rule must function without exception. Critics wonder why the prohibition against actions such as lying, promise breaking, suicide, and so on must be exceptionless. They say that Kant failed to distinguish between saying that a person should not except himself or herself from a rule and that the rule itself has no exceptions.

If stealing is wrong, it's wrong for me as well as for you. "Stealing is wrong, except if I do it" is not universalizable, for then stealing would be right for all to do, which contradicts the assertion that stealing is wrong. But because no one may make of oneself an exception to a rule, it does not follow that the rule itself has no exceptions.

Suppose, for example, we decide that stealing is sometimes right, perhaps in the case of a person who is starving. Thus the rule becomes "Never steal except when starving." This rule seems just as universalizable as "Never steal." The phrase "except . . ." can be viewed not as an *exception* to the rule but as a *qualification* of it. Critics in effect are asking why a qualified rule is not just as good as an unqualified one. If it is, then we no longer need to state rules in the simple, direct, unqualified manner that Kant did.

In fairness to Kant, it could be argued that his universalization formula, in fact, can be interpreted flexibly enough to meet commonsense objections. For example, perhaps we could universalize the principle that individuals should steal rather than starve to death or that it is permissible to take one's own life to extinguish unspeakable pain. And yet to qual-

ify the rules against stealing, lying, and taking one's life seems to invite a non-Kantian empirical analysis to morally justify the exceptions. One could, it seems, universalize more than one moral rule in a given situation: "Do not lie unless a life is at stake" versus "Lying is wrong unless necessary to avoid the suffering of innocent people." If so, then the categorical imperative would supply at best a necessary, but not a sufficient, test of right. But once we start choosing among various alternative rules, then we are adopting an approach to ethics that Kant would reject.

3. *What does it mean to treat people as means?* Kant's mandate that individuals must always be considered as ends in themselves and never as means expresses our sense of the intrinsic value of the human spirit and has profound moral appeal. Yet it is not always clear when people are being treated as ends and when as means. For example, Kant believed that prostitution was immoral because, by selling their sexual services, prostitutes allow themselves to be treated as means. Prostitutes, however, are not the only ones to sell their services. Anyone who works for a wage does so. Does that mean that we are all being treated immorally, since our employers are presumably hiring us as a means to advance their own ends? Perhaps not, because we freely agreed to do the work. But then the prostitute might have freely chosen that line of work, too.

OTHER NONCONSEQUENTIALIST PERSPECTIVES

For Kant the Categorical Imperative provides the basic test of right and wrong, and he is resolutely nonconsequentialist in his application of it. We know now what he would say about the case of the death-bed promise: The maxim permitting you to break your promise cannot be universalized and, hence, it would be immoral of you to give the money to the orphanage, despite the happiness that doing so would bring. But nonconsequentialists are not necessarily Kantians, and when we discussed the death-bed promise example several different nonutilitarian moral concerns emerged. We now need to examine some emphases and themes of other nonconsequentialist perspectives.

Critics of act utilitarianism believe that utilitarianism is faulty for maintaining that we have one and only one moral duty. A utilitarian might follow various principles as rules of thumb, but they are only calculation substitutes. All that matters morally is the maximization of happiness. Yet this, many philosophers think, fails to do justice to the richness and complexity of our moral lives.

Prima Facie Principles

One influential philosopher who argued this way was the British scholar W. D. Ross (1877–1971).[10] Ross complained that utilitarianism is too simple and is untrue to the way in which we ordinarily think about morality and about our moral obligations. For we see ourselves, Ross and others contend, as being under various moral obligations that cannot be reduced to the single obligation of maximizing happiness. Often these obligations grow out of special relations that we enter or out of determinate roles that we undertake.

For example, having decided to raise children, I have moral responsibilities to them, responsibilities unique to me. Likewise, as friend, student, teacher, coworker, or spouse I am intertwined with other people in very specific contexts and have, as a result, certain moral obligations. As a professor, Jones is obligated to assist her students in the learning process, evaluate their work in a fair and educationally productive way, and so on—obligations to the specific people in her classroom that she does not have to other people. As a spouse, Jones must maintain a certain emotional and sexual fidelity to her partner. As a

parent, she must provide for the specific human beings who are her children. As a friend to Smith, she may have a moral responsibility to help him out in a time of crisis. Having borrowed money from Brown, Smith has a moral obligation to pay it back. And so on: Different relations and different circumstances generate a variety of specific moral obligations.

In addition, there are certain moral obligations which we have that do not arise from our unique interactions and relations with other people. For example, we ought morally to treat people justly, to remedy injustices, and to promote human welfare. The latter obligation is important, but it is, for the nonconsequentialist, one among many obligations that we may have. At any given time, we are likely to be under more than one obligation, and sometimes, unfortunately, these obligations may conflict. That is, we may have an obligation to do *A* and a distinct obligation to do *B*, where it is not possible to do both *A* and *B*. For example, I promised to meet a friend on an urgent matter and now, as I am hurrying there, I pass an injured person who is obviously in need of some assistance. Yet stopping to aid him will make it impossible for me to fulfill my promise. What should I do?

For moral philosophers like Ross, there is no single answer for all cases. What I ought to do will depend on the circumstances and the relative importance of the conflicting obligations. I have an obligation to keep my promise, and I have an obligation to assist people in distress. What I must decide is, in the given circumstance, which of these obligations is the more important. I must weigh the moral significance of the promise against the comparative moral urgency of assisting the injured person.

Philosophers like Ross believe that most, or even all, of our moral obligations are *prima facie* ones. A *prima facie* obligation is simply an obligation that can be overridden by a more important obligation. For example, we take promise keeping seriously, but almost everyone would agree that in some circumstances, for example, when a life is at stake, it would not only be permissible but morally required of us to break a promise. Our obligation to keep our promise is a real one, and if there were no conflicting obligation, then we must keep our promise. But that obligation is not absolute or categorical; it could in principle be outweighed by a more stringent moral obligation. That is foreign to Kant's way of looking at things.

Let's take an example that Kant himself discusses. Imagine that a murderer comes to your door, wanting to know where your friend is, so that he can kill him. Your friend is in fact hiding in your attic. Most people would probably agree that your obligation to your friend outweighs your general obligation to tell the truth: You should lie in order to throw the murderer off your friend's trail. You have a genuine obligation to tell the truth, but it is a *prima facie* obligation, one that can be outweighed by other moral factors. Kant disagrees. He maintains that you must tell the truth in all circumstances without exception—come hell or high water. For him it is an absolute or categorical obligation, not a *prima facie* one.

A perspective like Ross's is pluralistic in recognizing, unlike utilitarianism, a variety of genuine moral obligations. But contrary to Kant, these obligations are not seen as absolute and exceptionless. On both points, Ross contends that his view of morality fits more closely our actual moral experience and the way in which we view our moral obligations. Take promises. We feel that we have an obligation to keep a promise simply because we made it, Ross argues, and not because keeping it will promote happiness. On the other hand, we acknowledge that this obligation may conflict with other obligations and even sometimes be outweighed by these other moral considerations.

Ross maintains that moral philosophers need to stick closely to the way in which peo-

ple actually think about morality. When a neat and tidy theory like utilitarianism conflicts with the more complicated way in which we actually experience our moral obligations, we should give up the theory as being untrue to the very phenomena it is trying to account for. In this way, Ross sides with commonsense morality.

Ross also sides with commonsense morality in that he thinks it is obvious what our *prima facie* obligations actually are. What we should do, all things considered, when two or more *prima facie* obligations conflict is often a difficult matter of judgment. But that we ought morally to tell the truth, keep our promises, and aid people in distress—these are truths that any person who has reached the age of reason can see. We can no more deny, Ross thinks, that it is wrong to injure people needlessly than that $2 + 2 = 4$.

Assisting Others

Nonconsequentialists believe that utilitarianism presents too simple a picture of our moral world. In addition, they worry that utilitarianism risks making us all slaves to the maximization of total happiness. Stop and think about it: Isn't there something that you could be doing—for instance, volunteering at the local hospital or orphanage, collecting money for third-world development, helping the homeless—that would do more for the general good than what you are doing now or are planning to do tonight or tomorrow? Sure, working with the homeless might not bring you quite as much pleasure as what you would otherwise be doing, but if it would nonetheless maximize total happiness, then you are morally required to do it. However, by following this reasoning, you could end up working around the clock, sacrificing yourself for the greater good. This seems mistaken.

Most nonutilitarian philosophers like Ross believe that we have some obligation to promote the general welfare, but they typically view this obligation as less stringent than, for example, the obligation not to injure people. They see us as having a much stronger obligation to refrain from violating people's rights than we do to promote their happiness or well-being. Consider an example of this distinction from an organizational context.

Cate School in Carpinteria, California, may be the only private school in the country with access to one computer for every two students. Such bounty is the result of an unusual business-academic arrangement. In exchange for the use of the school's facility for a summer computer camp, Cate is provided with fifty-nine Apple II and sixty Commodore 64 microcomputers and their maintenance during the school year.

About the same time Cate was receiving its first computers, an explosion occurred 100 miles to the south in a plant that makes refrigeration units. One section of a coil being lowered into 840-degree zinc did not have a vent. Apparently pressure on a substance, possibly water, inside the coil built up and caused the explosion. One man was killed; two others were burned enough to require hospitalization in a nearby burn unit. Shortly thereafter, a California OSHA filed charges of safety violations against the firm.

Most people would agree that companies always have a duty to provide workers a reasonably safe work environment. They would thus deplore the refrigeration company's apparent negligence and applaud OSHA's action. On the other hand, we would not be as certain that companies have duties to underwrite academic programs. While applauding the computer industry's generosity toward Cate School, we might at the same time deny that they were duty-bound to provide the school with computers. It was, to be sure, a grand gesture that could serve as an example for other joint business-academic ventures, though not an obligatory one. Or if we do

think the computer industry, or other business, has a duty to assist schools in these times of tight academic budgets, we would probably view that duty as different in kind from the duty to provide reasonably safe work conditions.

Many moral philosophers would distinguish actions that we are morally *required* to take from *supererogatory* acts—that is, actions that would be good to take, but not immoral *not* to take. Act utilitarianism does not make this distinction. Yet, by contrast, while we admire a Mother Theresa or an Albert Schweitzer for devoting their lives to doing good works among the poor, we see them as acting above and beyond the call of duty. Ordinary people who are not moral heroes or who fall short of sainthood may nonetheless be living morally satisfactory lives.

Nonutilitarian theorists see the distinction between morally obligatory actions and supererogatory actions not so much as a realistic concession to human weakness, but as a necessary demarcation if we are to avoid becoming enslaved to the maximization of the general welfare. The idea here is that each of us should have a sphere in which to pursue our own plans and goals, to carve out a distinctive life plan. These plans and goals are limited by various moral obligations, in particular by various rights that other people have, but the demands of morality are not all-encompassing.

Moral Rights

What, then, are rights and what rights do people have? Broadly defined, a *right* is an entitlement to act or have others act in a certain way. The connection between rights and duties is that, generally speaking, if you have a right to do something, then some other party or parties have a correlative duty to act in a certain way. For example, if you claim a "right" to drive, you mean that you are entitled to drive or that others should—that is, have a duty to—permit you to drive. The right to drive under certain specified conditions is derived from a legal system and is thus considered a *legal right*.

In addition to rights that are derived from some specific legal system, we also have *moral rights*. Some of these moral rights derive from special relationships, roles, or circumstances in which we happen to be. For example, if Tom has an obligation to return Bob's car to him on Saturday morning, then Bob has a right that Tom return his car. Having agreed to water your plants while you are on vacation, you now have a right that I look after them in your absence. As a student, you have a right that your instructor grade your work fairly, and so on. In these cases, the rights in question derive not from legal rules, but from moral rules or from the moral obligations that we have.

Even more important are rights that do *not* rest on special relationships, roles, or situations. For example, the rights to life, free speech, and unhampered religious affiliation are widely accepted, not just as the entitlements of some specific political or legal system, but as fundamental moral rights. More controversial, but often championed as moral rights, are the "rights" to medical care, decent housing, education, and work. Moral rights that are not the result of particular roles, special relationships, or specific circumstances are called *human rights*. They have several important characteristics.

First, human rights are universal. Everyone has human rights, just by virtue of their being human, not because they live in a certain legal system and not because they have done something special. If the right to life is a human right, as most of us believe it is, then everyone, everywhere and at all times, has that right. By contrast, there is nothing universal about your right that I keep my promise to you or about my right to drive 65 mph on certain roads.

Second, and closely related, human rights are equal rights. If the right to free speech is a human right, then everyone has this right equally. No one has a greater right to free speech than anyone else. By contrast, your daughter has a greater right than do the daughters of other people to your emotional and financial support.

Third, human rights are not transferable. If we do have a fundamental human right, we cannot give, lend, or sell it to someone else. That is what is meant in the Declaration of Independence when certain rights—namely life, liberty, and the pursuit of happiness—are described as "inalienable." By contrast, legal rights can be transferred, as when one party sells another a house or a business.

Fourth, human rights are "natural" rights, not in the sense that they can be derived from a study of human nature, but in the sense that they are not dependent on particular human institutions in the way that statutory rights are. If people have human rights, they have them simply because they are human beings and not because some authoritative body has assigned them these rights. The law may attempt to protect human rights, to make them safe and explicit, but law is not their source. Human rights derive from the assumption that all human beings, merely by virtue of their being human beings, have certain entitlements.

Rights, and in particular human rights, can be divided into two broad categories: *negative* rights and *positive* rights. Negative rights are vital interests that human beings have in being free from outside interference. The rights guaranteed in the Bill of Rights—freedom of speech, assembly, religion, and so on—fall within this category, as do the right of freedom from injury and the right to privacy. Correlating with these are duties that we all have not to interfere with others' pursuits of these interests and activities. Positive rights are vital interests that human beings have in receiving certain benefits. They are rights that others act to provide us with certain goods, services, or opportunities. Today, positive rights often are taken to include: the rights to education, medical care, decent neighborhood, equal job opportunity, comparable pay, and so on. Correlating with these are positive duties that appropriate parties have to assist individuals in their pursuit of these interests.

Thus, a child's right to education implies not just that no one should interfere with the child's education, but also that the necessary resources for that education ought morally to be provided. In the case of some positive rights—for example, the right to a decent standard of living as proclaimed by the United Nations' 1948 Human Rights Charter—it is unclear on whom exactly the duty to fulfill that right falls. Also, it is sometimes controversial whether a right should be interpreted as a negative right or as a positive right. For example, is my right to liberty simply the right not to be interfered with as I live my own life, or is it also the right that I be provided with the means to make the exercise of that liberty meaningful?

The significance of positing moral rights is that they provide grounds for making moral judgments that radically differ from utilitarianism's grounds. Once moral rights are asserted, the locus of moral judgment becomes the individual, not society. For example, if every potential human subject has a moral right to be fully informed about the nature of a medical experiment and the moral right to decide freely for himself or herself whether to participate, then it is wrong to violate these rights—even if, by so doing, the common good will be served. Again, if workers have a right to compensation equal to what others receive for doing comparable work, then they cannot be paid less on grounds of the greatest good for the greatest number. And if every-

one has a right to equal consideration for a job regardless of color or sex, then sex and color cannot be introduced merely because so doing will result in the greatest net utility.

Utilitarianism, in effect, treats all such "entitlements" as subordinate to the general welfare. Thus, individuals are "entitled" to act in a certain way and entitled to have others allow or even aid them to so act only insofar as the greatest good is effected. The assertion of moral rights, therefore, decisively sets nonconsequentialists apart from utilitarians.

Nonconsequentialism in an Organizational Context

We have already looked at Kant's ethics in an organization context, but the themes of the other nonconsequentialist approaches that we have been discussing also have important implications for moral decision making in business and nonbusiness organizations.

First, in its non-Kantian forms *nonconsequentialism stresses that moral decision making involves the weighing of various different moral factors and considerations.* Unlike utilitarianism and egoism, nonconsequentialism does not reduce morality solely to the calculation of consequences, but recognizes that an organization must usually take into account other equally important moral concerns. Theorists like Ross emphasize that, contrary to Kant, there can often be rival and even conflicting obligations on an organization. For example, obligations to employees, stockholders, and consumers may pull the corporation in different directions, and determining the organization's proper moral course may not be easy.

Second, *nonconsequentialism acknowledges that the organization has its own legitimate goals to pursue.* There are limits to the demands of morality, and an organization that fulfills its moral obligations and respects the relevant rights of individuals is morally free to advance whatever (morally permissible) ends it has—public service, profit, government administration, and so on. Contrary to utilitarianism, organizations and the people in them need not see themselves as under an overarching obligation to seek continually to enhance the general welfare.

Third, *nonconsequentialism stresses the importance of moral rights*. Moral rights, and in particular human rights, are a crucial factor in most moral deliberations, including those of organizations. Before it acts, any morally responsible business or nonbusiness organization must consider carefully how its actions will impinge on the rights of individuals—not just the rights of its members, such as stockholders and employees, but also the rights of others, such as consumers. Moral rights place distinct and firm constraints on what sorts of things an organization can do to fulfill its own ends.

Critical Inquiries

A critical assessment of the nonconsequentialist points we have been examining would involve a comparison with the strong and weak points of the major theoretical alternatives that we have surveyed so far, in particular Kant's ethics and utilitarianism. We shall not repeat our discussion of those theories, but rather limit ourselves to two lines of critical inquiry.

1. How well justified are these nonconsequentialist principles and moral rights? Ross's theory, as we have seen, maintains that we have immediate intuitive knowledge of the basic *prima facie* moral principles, and indeed it would seem absurd for someone to try to deny that it was wrong to cause needless suffering or that making a promise imposes upon one some obligation to keep it. Only someone who was the moral equivalent of color-blind could fail to see the truth of these statements; to reject them would seem as preposterous to us as denying some obvious fact of arithmetic—for example, that $12 + 4 = 16$. Likewise, it appears obvious—indeed, as Thomas Jefferson

wrote, "self-evident"—that human beings have certain basic and inalienable moral rights, unconditional rights that do not depend on the decrees of any particular government.

Yet, we must be careful. What seems obvious, even self-evident, to one culture or at one time in human history may turn out to be not only not self-evident, but actually false. That the earth was flat and that heavier objects fall faster than lighter ones were two "truths" taken as obvious in former centuries. Likewise, the inferiority of women and of various nonwhite races was long taken for granted as something anyone with the slightest degree of common sense could see; it was so "obvious" that it was hardly even commented on. The idea that people have a right to practice a religion that the majority "knows" to be false—or, indeed, to practice no religion whatsoever—would have seemed morally scandalous to many of our forebears, and is still not embraced in all countries today. Today, many vegetarians eschew meat eating on moral grounds and contend that future generations will think our treatment of animals, factory farming in particular, was as morally benighted as slavery. So what seems "obvious," "self-evident," or simple "common sense" may not be the most reliable guide to morally sound principles.

2. Can nonconsequentialists satisfactorily handle conflicting rights and principles? People today disagree among themselves about the correctness of certain moral principles. Claims of right, as we have seen, are often controversial. For example, do employees have a moral right to their jobs—an entitlement not to be fired without just cause? To some of us, it may seem obvious that they do. To others, perhaps not. And how are we to settle various conflicting claims of right? Jones, for instance, claims a right to her property, which she has acquired honestly through her labors; that is, she claims a right to do with it as she wishes. Smith is ill and claims adequate medical care as a human right. Since he cannot afford the care himself, acknowledging his right will involve infringing Jones's property right.

To sum up these two critical points: first, even the deliverances of moral common sense have to be examined critically, and, second, nonconsequentialists ought not to rest content until they find a way of resolving disputes among conflicting *prima facie* principles or rights. We do not intend to suggest, however, that nonconsequentialists cannot find deeper and theoretically more satisfactory ways of grounding moral claims and of handling disputes between them. We underscore only the necessity of doing so.

UTILITARIANISM ONCE MORE

Until now, we have discussed utilitarianism in its most straightforward form, called act utilitarianism. According to act utilitarianism, we have one and only one moral obligation, the maximization of happiness for everyone concerned, and every action is to be judged according to how well it lives up to this principle. But there is a different utilitarian approach, called *rule utilitarianism*, that is relevant to our discussion of the moral concerns characteristic of nonconsequentialism, in particular, to the nonconsequentialist's criticisms of act utilitarianism. The rule utilitarian would, in fact, agree with many of these criticisms. (Since rule utilitarianism has itself been formulated in different ways, we shall follow the version defended by Professor Richard Brandt of the University of Michigan.)

Rule utilitarianism maintains that the utilitarian standard should be applied not to individual actions, but to moral codes as a whole. The rule utilitarian asks what moral code (that is, what set of moral rules) a society should adopt in order to maximize happiness. The principles that make up that code would then be the basis for distinguishing right actions from wrong actions. As Brandt explains:

A rule-utilitarian thinks that right actions are the kind permitted by the moral code optimal for the society of which the agent is a member. An optimal code is one designed to maximize welfare or what is good (thus, utility). This leaves open the possibility that a particular right action may not maximize benefit. . . . On the rule-utilitarian view, then, to find what is morally right or wrong we need to find which actions would be permitted by a moral system that is "optimal" for the agent's society.[11]

The "optimal" moral code does not refer to a set of rules that would do the most good if everyone conformed to them all the time. The meaning is more complex. The "optimal" moral code must take into account what rules can reasonably be taught to, and obeyed by, people, as well as the costs of inculcating those rules in them. Recall from Chapter 1 that if a principle or rule is part of a person's moral code, then it will influence the person's behavior. The person will tend to follow that principle, to feel guilty when he or she does not follow it, and to disapprove of others who fail to conform to it. Rule utilitarians must consider not just the benefits of having people motivated to act in certain ways, but also the costs of instilling those motivations in them. As Brandt writes:

The more intense and widespread an aversion to a certain sort of behavior, the less frequent the behavior is apt to be. But the more intense and widespread, the greater the cost of teaching the rule and keeping it alive, the greater the burden on the individual, and so on.[12]

Thus, the "optimality" of a moral code encompasses both the benefits of reduced objectionable behavior and the long-term costs. Perfect compliance is not a realistic goal. "Like the law," Brandt continues, "the optimal moral code will not produce 100 percent compliance with all its rules; that would be too costly."

Elements of the rule-utilitarian approach were clearly suggested by Mill himself, although he did not draw the distinction between act and rule utilitarianism. According to the rule-utilitarian perspective, we should apply the utilitarian standard only to the assessment of alternative moral codes; we should not try to apply it to individual actions. We should seek, that is, to determine the specific set of principles that would in fact best promote total happiness for society to promulgate, for us to instill in ourselves, and for the next generation to be taught.

What Will the Ideal Code Look Like?

Rule utilitarians like Brandt argue strenuously that the ideal moral code would not be the single act-utilitarian command to maximize happiness. They contend that it would not in fact maximize happiness to teach people that their only obligation was to maximize happiness.

First, people will make mistakes if they always try to do that which promotes total happiness. Second, if everyone were an act utilitarian, such practices as keeping promises and telling the truth would be rather shaky, since people would only expect others to keep promises or tell the truth when those others believed that their doing so would maximize happiness. Third, the act-utilitarian principle is too demanding, since it seems to imply that each person should continually be striving to promote total well-being.

For these reasons, rule utilitarians believe that more happiness will come from instilling in people a pluralistic moral code, one with a number of different principles. By analogy, we can imagine a traffic system that contains just one rule: Drive your car in such a way that you maximize happiness. Such a system would be counterproductive; we do much better in terms of total human well-being to have a variety of traffic regulations—for example, obey stop signs and pass only on the left. In such a pluralistic system we could not justify cruising through a red light with the argument that doing so maximized total happiness by getting us home more quickly.

The principles of the ideal code would presumably be *prima facie* in Ross's sense—that is, capable of being overridden by other principles. Different principles would also have different moral weights. It would make sense, for example, that an aversion to killing be more strongly instilled in people than an aversion to telling "white lies." In addition, the ideal code would acknowledge moral rights. Teaching people to respect moral rights will maximize human welfare in the long run.

The rules of the ideal code provide the sole basis for determining right and wrong. An action is not necessarily wrong if it fails to maximize happiness; it is wrong only if it conflicts with the ideal moral code. Rule utilitarianism thus gets around many of the problems that plague act utilitarianism. At the same time, it provides a plausible basis for deciding which moral principles and rights we should acknowledge and how much weight we should attach to them. We try to determine those principles and rights that, generally adhered to, would best promote human happiness.

Still, rule utilitarianism has its critics. Let's consider two possible objections to it. First, act utilitarians will maintain that if one is a utilitarian and cares about happiness, one should be willing to violate the rule utilitarian's rules in order to maximize happiness. Why make a fetish out of the rules?

Second, nonconsequentialists, while presumably viewing rule utilitarianism more favorably than act utilitarianism, will still balk at seeing moral principles determined by their consequences. They will contend, in particular, that rule utilitarians, by ultimately subordinating rights to utilitarian calculation, fail to treat rights as fundamental and independent moral factors.

MORAL DECISION MAKING: TOWARD A SYNTHESIS

Theoretical controversies permeate the subject of ethics and, as we have seen, philosophers have proposed rival ways of understanding right and wrong. These philosophical differences of perspective, emphasis, and theory are significant and can have profound practical consequences. We have surveyed some of these issues, but obviously we cannot attempt here to resolve all of the questions that divide moral philosophers. Fortunately, however, many problems of business, professional, and organizational ethics can be intelligently discussed and even resolved by people whose fundamental moral theories differ (or who have not yet worked out their own moral ideas in some systematic way). In this section, we discuss some important points to keep in mind when engaging in moral analysis and discussion and offer, as a kind of model, one possible procedure for making moral decisions.

In the abstract, it might seem impossible for people to reach agreement on controversial ethical issues, given that ethical theories differ so much and that people themselves place moral value on different things. Yet, in practice moral problems are rarely so intractable that open-minded and thoughtful people cannot, by discussing matters calmly, rationally, and thoroughly, make significant progress toward resolving them. In Chapter 1 we stressed that moral judgments should be logical, should be based on facts, and should appeal to valid moral principles. Bearing this in mind can often help, especially when various people are discussing an issue and proposing rival answers.

First, in any moral discussion, make sure that there is agreement among the partici-

pants about the relevant facts. Often moral disputes hinge not on matters of moral principle, but on differing assessments of what the facts of the situation are, what alternatives are open, and what the probable results of different courses of action will be. For instance, the directors of an international firm might acrimoniously dispute the moral permissibility of a new overseas investment. The conflict might appear to involve some fundamental clash of moral principles and perspectives and yet, in fact, be the result of some underlying disagreement as to what effects the proposed investment will have on the lives of the local population. Until this factual disagreement is acknowledged and dealt with, little is apt to be resolved.

Second, once there is general agreement on factual matters, try to spell out the moral principles to which different people are, at least implicitly, appealing. Seeking to determine these principles will often help people clarify their own thinking enough that a solution can be reached. Sometimes there will be agreement on what moral principles are relevant, and yet disagreement over how to balance them. But determining this can itself be useful. Bear in mind, too, that skepticism is in order when someone's moral stance on an issue appears to rest simply on a hunch or intuition and cannot be related to some more general moral principle. As moral decision makers we are seeking not just an "answer" to a moral issue, but an answer that can be publicly defended. And the public defense of a moral judgment will usually require an appeal to general principle. (By analogy, judges do not hand down judgments simply based on what strikes them as fair in a particular case. They must relate their decisions to general legal principles or statutes.)

A reluctance to defend our moral decisions in public is almost always a warning signal. If we are unwilling to account for our actions publicly, the chances are that we are doing something we cannot really justify morally. In addition, Kant's point that we must be willing to universalize our moral judgments is relevant here. This means that we cannot sincerely endorse a principle if we are not willing to see it applied generally. Unfortunately, we occasionally do make judgments—for example, that Alfred's being late to work is a satisfactory reason for firing him—that rest on a principle that we would be unwilling to see applied to our own situations. Hence, the moral relevance of the familiar question, "How would you like it if . . . ?" Looking at an issue from the other person's point of view can cure moral myopia.

Obligations, Ideals, Effects

As a practical basis for discussing moral issues in organizations, it is useful to try to approach those issues in a way that is acceptable to individuals of diverse moral viewpoints. We want to avoid as much as possible presupposing the truth of one particular theoretical perspective. By emphasizing factors that are relevant to various theories, both consequentialist and nonconsequentialist, we can find some common ground on which moral decision making can proceed in practice. In this way moral dialogue can take place in an objective and analytical way, even if there is not full agreement among the participants on all philosophical issues.

What concerns, then, seem common to most ethical systems? Following Professor V. R. Ruggiero, three common concerns suggest themselves.[13] A first concern is with *obligations*. Every significant human action—personal and professional—arises in the context of human relationships. As we have already seen, these relationships can be the source of quite specific duties and rights. Obligations bind us. In their presence, morality requires us, at least *prima facie*, to do certain things and to avoid doing others.

A second concern common to most ethical systems is the impact of our actions on

important *ideals*. An ideal is some morally important goal, some virtue, or notion of excellence worth striving for. Clearly, different cultures impart different ideals and, equally important, different ways of pursuing them. Our culture respects virtues like tolerance, compassion, loyalty, forgiveness, brotherhood, as well as such more abstract ideals as peace, justice, fairness, and respect for persons. In addition to these moral ideals there are institutional or organizational ones: efficiency, productivity, quality, stability, and so forth. Does a particular act serve or violate these ideals? Certainly, both consequentialists and nonconsequentialists can agree that this is an important concern in determining the moral quality of actions.

A third common consideration regards the *effects* of actions. Although nonconsequentialists maintain that things other than consequences or effects determine the rightness or wrongness of actions, few if any of them would ignore consequences entirely. Concern with consequences generally finds a place in ethical theories and certainly in business.

Ruggiero has isolated, then, three concerns common to almost all ethical systems: *obligations*, *ideals*, and *effects*. In so doing he provides a kind of practical synthesis of consequentialist and nonconsequentialist thought, which seems appropriate for our concerns. *A useful approach to moral questions in an organizational context will reflect these considerations: the obligations that derive from organizational relationships, the ideals involved, and the effects or consequences of alternative actions.* Any action that honors obligations while advancing ideals and benefiting people can be presumed to be moral. An action that does not pass scrutiny in these respects will be morally suspect.

This synthetic view leads to what is essentially a two-step procedure for evaluating actions and choices. The first step is to identify the important considerations involved: obligations, ideals, and effects. Accordingly, we should ask: Are there any basic obligations involved? If so, what are they and who has them? What ideals does the action respect or promote? What ideals does it neglect or thwart? Who is affected by the action, and how? How do these effects compare to those of the alternatives open to us? The second step is to decide where the emphasis should lie among the three considerations. Sometimes the issue may be largely a matter of obligations; other times some ideal may predominate; still other times, consideration of effects may be the overriding concern.

The following rough guidelines should be kept in mind when handling cases of conflicts and mixed effects:

1. When two or more moral obligations conflict, choose the stronger one.

2. When two or more ideals conflict, or when ideals conflict with obligations, honor the more important one.

3. When the effects are mixed, choose the action that produces the greater good or the lesser harm.

These guidelines suggest that we know (1) which one of the conflicting obligations is greater, (2) which of the conflicting ideals is higher, and (3) which of the actions will achieve the greater good or the lesser harm. They also presuppose that we have some definite way of balancing obligations, ideals, and effects when these considerations pull in different directions.

The fact is that we have no sure procedure for making such comparative determinations, which involve assessing worth and assigning relative priorities to our assessments. In large part, the chapters ahead attempt to flush out the values and principles that are embedded in the tangled web of frequently subtle, ill-defined problems we meet in business and organizational life. It is hoped that an examination of these issues will help you to (1) identify the obligations, ideals, and effects involved in various specific moral issues, and (2) decide where the emphasis should lie among the competing considerations.

SUMMARY

1. Consequentialist moral theories see the moral rightness or wrongness of actions as a function of their results. If the consequences are good, the action is right; if they are bad, the action is wrong. Nonconsequentialist theories see other factors as also relevant to the determination of right and wrong.

2. Egoism is the consequentialist theory that an action is right when it promotes the individual's best interests. Proponents of this theory base their view on the alleged fact that human beings are, by nature, selfish (the doctrine of psychological egoism). Egoism helps formulate and test organizational policies and allows organizations flexibility in moral decision making. But critics of egoism wonder (1) whether psychological egoism is plausible, (2) whether ethical egoism can settle conflicts, (3) whether egoism is really a moral principle, and (4) whether egoism ignores blatant wrongs.

3. Utilitarianism, another consequentialist theory, maintains that the morally right action is the one that provides the greatest happiness for all those affected. In an organizational context, utilitarianism provides an objective way to resolve conflicts of self-interest and gives organizations latitude in moral decision making. But critics contend (1) that utilitarianism is not really workable, (2) that some actions are wrong even if they produce good results, and (3) that utilitarianism incorrectly overlooks considerations of justice and the distribution of happiness.

4. Kant's theory is an important example of a purely nonconsequentialist approach to

ethics. Kant holds that only when we act from duty does our action have moral worth. Good will is the only thing that is good in itself.

5. Kant's Categorical Imperative states that an action is morally right only if we can will that the maxim (or principle) represented by the action be a universal law. For example, a person making a promise with no intention of keeping it cannot universalize the maxim governing his action because if everyone followed this principle, promising would make no sense. Kant's Categorical Imperative is binding on all rational creatures, regardless of their specific goals or desires, and regardless of the consequences.

6. There are two alternative formulations of the Categorical Imperative. The first is that one must always act so as to treat other people as ends, not means. The second is that an act is right only if the actor would be willing to be so treated if the positions of the parties were reversed.

7. Kant's ethics takes much of the guesswork out of moral decision making; it injects a humanistic element and stresses the importance of acting on principle and from a sense of duty. Critics, however, worry (1) that Kant's view of moral worth is too restrictive, (2) that the Categorical Imperative is not a sufficient test of right and wrong, and (3) that the distinction between treating people as means and respecting them as ends in themselves may be hard to identify in practice.

8. Other nonconsequentialist theories stress other moral themes. Philosophers like Ross argue, against both Kant and consequentialists, that we are under a variety of distinct moral obligations. These are *prima facie*, meaning that it is possible for any one of them to be outweighed in some circumstances by other, more important moral considerations. Nonconsequential-

ists believe that a duty to assist others and to promote total happiness is only one of a number of duties incumbent on us.

9. Nonconsequentialists typically emphasize moral rights—entitlements to act in a certain way or to have others act in a certain way. These rights can rest on special relationships and roles, or they can be general human rights. Rights can be negative, protecting us from outside interference, or they can be positive, requiring others to provide us with certain benefits or opportunities.

10. In an organizational context, nonconsequentialism (in its non-Kantian forms) stresses the plurality of moral considerations to be weighed. While emphasizing the importance of respecting moral rights, it acknowledges that morality has limits and that organizations have legitimate goals to pursue. Critics question (1) whether nonconsequentialist principles are adequately justified, and (2) whether nonconsequentialism can handle satisfactorily conflicting rights and principles.

11. Rule utilitarianism is a hybrid theory. It maintains that the proper principles of right and wrong are those that it would maximize happiness for society to adopt. Thus, the utilitarian standard does not apply directly to individual actions, but rather to the adoption of the moral principles which are then to guide individual action. Rule utilitarianism avoids many of the standard criticisms of act utilitarianism.

12. Despite disagreements on controversial theoretical issues, people can make significant progress in resolving practical moral problems through open-minded and reflective discussion. One useful approach is to identify the (possibly conflicting) obligations, ideals, and values in a given situation and then to identify where the emphasis should lie among these different considerations.

CASE 2.1
Baby M

In 1985 Mary Beth Whitehead of Brick Town, New Jersey, agreed to be impregnated by artificial insemination with the sperm of a stranger and to carry his child. In other words, she agreed, like hundreds of other women in the past decade, to be a "surrogate mother." She was twenty-nine years old, happily married, with a son and a daughter of her own. Why did she decide to do it? Mary Beth called it "the most loving gift of happiness," but she also saw the practical side. The $10,000 she would earn would help to pay for her children's education.[14]

The man who was to become the sperm-donating father of Mary Beth's child was William Stern, a forty-year-old biochemist. Both he and his wife, Elizabeth, a pediatrician, longed to have children of their own. But Elizabeth was diagnosed as having a mild form of multiple sclerosis, and pregnancy was felt to be risky for her. Not only is there a shortage of healthy, white babies available for adoption, but also the couple was too old to be acceptable to most adoption agencies. In any case, Stern wanted a child that was his own flesh and blood. Noel Keane, a Dearborn, Michigan, lawyer who specializes in surrogacy cases, brought the Sterns together with Whitehead and her husband. They signed a contract, which Keane had drawn up.

The six-page contract was strictly business. In addition to Whitehead's fee, which was put in escrow until Stern received the baby, the Sterns paid over $10,000 in nonrefundable fees and expenses to Keane. In the contract Stern agreed to assume all legal responsibility for the baby, even if it was born with serious defects. On the other hand, Whitehead was required to undergo amniocentesis; if the test indicated problems, she agreed to have an abortion if Stern requested it. In the contract Mary Beth Whitehead acknowledged that the child would be conceived "for the sole purpose of giving said child to William Stern."

Noel Keane's law firm and the Infertility Center of New York (which he partly owns) have arranged over 150 commercial surrogate births since 1976. Whitehead later claimed that Keane did not give her proper counseling, while he maintains that the standard psychological tests she took gave little reason to anticipate any special problems. In only two cases handled by Keane had the surrogate mothers changed their minds. This was to be the third time.

On March 27, 1987, Mary Beth Whitehead gave birth to a healthy, blond, blue-eyed little girl—called Sara by her, Melissa by the Sterns, and "Baby M" by the courts. Mary Beth's first moments with the baby were intensely emotional. "Seeing her, holding her. She was my child," Whitehead remembers. "It overpowered me. I had no control. I had to keep her."

Whitehead gave the child to the Sterns as agreed, but her first night without the baby was miserable. The next day she begged the Sterns to let her have the child for just one week. They agreed, but at the end of the week, Whitehead didn't want to return the child. She asked if the Sterns would agree to let her have the child one weekend a month and two weeks during the summer. They insisted on the original contract and went to court to enforce it. The money due Whitehead was still in the escrow account. On May 5, a family court judge awarded them temporary custody. But the next day the Whiteheads ran off with the baby. The Sterns paid more than $20,000 for a private investigator, who spent three months tracing the Whiteheads to the home of Mary Beth's mother in Florida. He and the FBI visited the home, grabbed the baby, and took her away, returning her to the Sterns.

Four days after Baby M's first birthday, New Jersey Judge Harvey R. Sorkow awarded her to her father, William Stern. A three-judge panel upheld his decision, but Whitehead promised to continue the legal battle. Months went by. Finally, on February 3, 1988, the New Jersey State Supreme Court ruled that the surrogacy agreement was "illegal, perhaps criminal, and potentially degrading to women." Custody was granted to Stern, but Whitehead won visitation rights, and adoption by Mrs. Stern (who has no parental rights) was voided. But the moral and legal controversy won't end here. The decision is binding only in New Jersey, and even there, legislative change could render the ruling obsolete.

Discussion Questions

1. Is there a case of "baby selling," as critics charge, or are surrogate agencies correct to claim that they are simply selling a woman's services? Under either description is there anything morally questionable about surrogate-mother agreements? How would such agreements be analyzed from the point of view of each of the major theories discussed in this chapter?

2. In the case of Baby M, Mary Beth Whitehead was the genetic mother. But there have been successful cases of so-called "full surrogacy." If this had been the procedure, then an egg from Elizabeth Stern would have been fertilized in a laboratory with sperm from William and then placed in Whitehead's womb. How would this affect your moral analysis of the case?

3. Discuss the motivations of the various parties to this dispute. To what moral principle(s) could Mary Beth Whitehead appeal to justify her subsequent actions? How could the Sterns defend their response?

4. Lawyers like Noel Keane are in the business of arranging surrogate births. How should their role be morally evaluated?

5. Who should keep Baby M? In your opinion did the New Jersey State Supreme Court make the right decision? Identify and weigh the relevant moral principles.

6. Should surrogate motherhood be legal? If so, how (if at all) should the law regulate it? What legislative provisions would be best?

CASE 2.2
Ford's Pinto

There was a time when the "made in Japan" label brought a predictable smirk of superiority to the face of most Americans. The quality of most Japanese products usually was as low as their price. In fact, few imports could match their domestic counterparts, the proud products of "Yankee know-how." But by the late 1960s, an invasion of foreign-made goods chiseled a few worry lines into the countenance of American industry. And in Detroit, worry was fast fading to panic as the Japa-

nese, not to mention the Germans, began to gobble up more and more of the subcompact auto market.

Never one to take a back seat to the competition, Ford Motor Company decided to meet the threat from abroad head-on. In 1968, Ford executives decided to produce the Pinto.

Eager to have its own subcompact ready for the 1971 model year, Ford decided to compress the normal from-drafting-board-to-showroom time of about three-and-a-half years into two. The compressed schedule meant that any design changes typically made before production-line tooling would have to be made during it.

Prior to producing the Pinto, Ford crash-tested eleven of them, in part to learn if they met the National Highway Traffic Safety Administration (NHTSA) proposed safety standard that all autos be able to withstand a fixed-barrier impact of 20 mph without fuel loss. Eight standardly designed Pintos failed the tests, which were conducted at an average speed of 31 mph. The three cars that passed the test all had some kind of gas-tank modification. One had a plastic baffle between the front of the tank and the differential housing; the second had a piece of steel between the tank and the rear bumper; and the third had a rubber-lined gas tank.

Ford officials faced a tough decision. Should they go ahead with the standard design, thereby meeting the production timetable, but possibly jeopardize consumer safety? Or should they delay production of the Pinto by redesigning the gas tank to make it safer and thus concede another year of subcompact dominance to foreign companies?

In order to determine whether to proceed with the original design of the Pinto fuel tank, Ford decided to do a cost benefit study, which is an analysis of the expected costs and the social benefits of doing something. Would the social benefits of a new tank design outweigh design costs, or would they not?

To find the answer, Ford would have to assign specific values to the variables involved. For some factors in the equation, this posed no problem. The costs of design improvement, for example, could be estimated at eleven dollars per vehicle. But what about human life? Could a dollar-and-cents figure be assigned to a human being?

NHTSA thought it could. It had estimated that society loses $200,725 every time a person is killed in an auto accident. It broke down the costs as follows:

Future Productivity Losses	
Direct	$132,000
Indirect	41,300
Medical Costs	
Hospital	700
Other	425
Property Damage	1,500
Insurance Administration	4,700
Legal and Court	3,000
Employer Losses	1,000
Victim's Pain and Suffering	10,000
Funeral	900
Assets (Lost Consumption)	5,000
Miscellaneous Accident Cost	200
Total per Fatality	$200,725[15]

Ford used NHTSA and other statistical studies in its cost benefit analysis, which yielded the following estimates:

Benefits

Savings: 180 burn deaths, 180 serious burn injuries, 2,100 burned vehicles

Unit Cost: $200,000 per death, $67,000 per injury, $700 per vehicle

Total Benefit: 180 × ($200,000) + 180 × ($67,000) + 2,100 × ($700) = $49.5 million

Costs

Sales: 11 million cars, 1.5 million light trucks

Unit Cost: $11 per car, $11 per truck

Total Costs: 12.5 million × ($11) = $137.5 million[16]

Since the costs of the safety improvement outweighed its benefits, Ford decided to push ahead with the original design. Here is what happened after it made this decision:

More than fifty persons died in accidents involving Pinto fires and many more were burned.

NHTSA's standard was adopted in 1977. The Pinto then acquired a rupture-proof fuel tank.

Between 1971 and 1978 approximately fifty lawsuits were brought against Ford in connection with rear-end accidents in the Pinto.

On August 10, 1978, 18-year-old Judy Ulrich and her 16-year-old sister, Lynn, and 18-year-old cousin, Donna, were struck from the rear in their 1973 Ford Pinto by a van. The gas tank of the Pinto exploded on impact. In the fire that resulted, the three teenagers were burned to death. Ford was charged with criminal homicide. The judge presiding over the twenty-week trial advised jurors that Ford should be convicted if it had clearly disregarded the harm that might result from its actions and that that disregard represented a substantial deviation from acceptable standards of conduct. On March 13, 1980, the jury found Ford not guilty of criminal homicide.

Discussion Questions

1. Suppose Ford officials were asked: "What makes your moral decision right?" What moral principles do you think they would invoke? Explain.

2. Do you think Ford officials practiced "restrained egoism"?

3. Utilitarians would say that jeopardizing motorists by itself does not make Ford's action morally objectionable. The only morally relevant matter is whether Ford gave each affected party equal consideration and gave their pleasures and preferences equal weighting in reaching its decision. Do you think Ford did this?

4. Could Ford's cost-benefit analysis have been improved upon? How legitimate are such analyses in general? What role should they play in moral deliberation?

5. Speculate about Kant's response to the NHTSA's placing a financial value on a human life.

6. What responsibilities to its customers do you think Ford had? What would you say are the most important moral rights, if any, operating in this case?

7. The maxim of Ford's action might be stated: "When it would cost more to make a safety improvement than not, it's all right not to make it." Can this maxim be universalized? Does it treat humans as ends in themselves? Would manufacturers likely be willing to abide by it were the positions reversed, if they were in the role of unsuspecting consumers?

8. What obligations, ideals, and effects are apparent in the Pinto case? Where do you think the weight should lie? Why?

CASE 2.3
Blood for Sale

Sol Levin was a successful stockbroker in Tampa, Florida, when, recognizing the potentially profitable market for safe and uncontaminated blood, he and some colleagues founded Plasma International. Not everybody is willing to make money by selling their own blood, and in the beginning Plasma International bought it from men and women who were addicted to wine. Although innovative marketing increased Plasma International's sales dramatically, several cases of hepatitis were reported in recipients. The company then began looking for new sources of blood.[17]

Plasma International searched worldwide and, with the advice of a qualified team of medical consultants, did extensive testing. Eventually, they found that the blood profiles of several rural West African tribes made them ideal prospective donors. After negotiations with the local government, Plasma International signed an agreement with several tribal chieftains to purchase blood.

Business went smoothly and profitably for Plasma International until a local Tampa paper charged that Plasma was purchasing blood for as little as fifteen cents a pint and then reselling it to hospitals in the United States and South America for twenty-five dollars per pint. In one recent disaster, the newspaper alleged, Plasma International had sold ten thousand pints, netting nearly a quarter of a million dollars.

The newspaper story stirred up controversy in Tampa, but the existence of commercialized blood market systems in the United States is nothing new. Approximately half the blood and plasma obtained in the United States is bought and sold like any other commodity. About 40 percent is given to avoid having to pay for blood received or to build up credit so that blood will be available without charge if needed. By contrast, the National Health Service in Britain relies entirely on a voluntary system of blood donation. Blood is neither bought nor sold. It is available to anyone who needs it without charge or obligation, and donors gain no preference over nondonors.

In an important study, economist Richard Titmuss has shown that the British system works better than the American in terms of (a) economic efficiency, (b) administrative efficiency, (c) price, and (d) blood quality. Hemophiliacs, in particular, are disadvantaged by the American system and have enormous bills to pay. Titmuss also argues that the existence of a commercialized system discourages voluntary donors. People are less likely to give blood if they know that others are selling theirs.

Philosopher Peter Singer has elaborated on this point:

If blood is a commodity with a price, to give blood means merely to save someone money. Blood has a cash value of a certain number of dollars, and the importance of the gift will vary with the wealth of the recipient. If blood cannot be bought, however, the gift's value depends upon the need of the recipient. Often, it will be worth life itself. Under these circumstances blood becomes a very special kind of gift, and giving it means providing for strangers, without hope of reward, something they cannot buy and without which they may die. The gift relates strangers in a manner that is not possible when blood is a commodity.

This may sound like a philosopher's abstraction, far removed from the thoughts of ordinary people. On the contrary, it is an idea spontaneously expressed by British donors in response to Titmuss's questionnaire. As one woman, a machine operator, wrote in reply to the question why she first decided to become a blood donor: "You can't get blood from supermarkets and chain stores. People themselves must come forward; sick people can't get out of bed to ask you for a pint to save their life, so I came forward in hopes to help somebody who needs blood."

The implication of this answer, and others like it, is that even if the formal right to give blood can coexist with commercialized blood banks, the respondent's action would have lost much of its significance to her, and the blood would probably not have been given at all. When blood is a commodity, and can be purchased if it is not given, altruism becomes unnecessary, and so loosens the bonds that can otherwise exist between strangers in a community. The existence of a market in blood does not threaten the formal right to give blood, but it does away with the right to give blood which cannot be bought, has no cash value, and must be given freely if it is to be obtained at all. If there is such a right, it is incompatible with the right to sell blood, and we cannot avoid violating one of these rights when we grant the other.[18]

Both Titmuss and Singer believe that the weakening of the spirit of altruism in this sphere has important repercussions. It marks, they think, the increasing commercialization of our lives and makes similar changes in attitude, motive, and relationships more likely in other fields.

Discussion Questions

1. Is Sol Levin running a business "just like any other business," or is his company open to moral criticism? Defend your answer by appeal to moral principle.

2. What are the contrasting ideals of the British and American blood systems? Which system in your opinion best promotes human freedom and respect for persons?

3. Examine the pros and cons of commercial transactions in blood from the egoistic, the utilitarian, and the Kantian perspectives.

4. Are Titmuss and Singer right to suggest that the buying and selling of blood reduces altruism? Does knowing that you can sell your blood (and that others are selling theirs) make *you* less inclined to donate your blood? Do we have a right to give blood that cannot be bought?

5. Many believe that commercialization is increasing in all areas of modern life. If this is so, is it something to be applauded or condemned? Are there certain things—like human organs—that it is wrong to treat as commodities?

6. Did Plasma International strike a fair bar-

gain with the West Africans who supplied their blood to the company? Or is Plasma guilty of exploiting them in some way? Explain your answer.

7. Do you believe that we have a moral duty to donate blood? If so, why and under what circumstances? If not, why not?

NOTES

1. Bernard Williams, *Ethics and the Limits of Philosophy* (Cambridge, Mass.: Harvard University Press, 1985), 16.

2. See David Clutterbuck, "Blowing the Whistle on Corporate Misconduct," *International Management* (January 1980).

3. See Case 10.3: "Paying the Bill for Cleaning Up Three Mile Island," on page 460.

4. Richard B. Brandt, "Toward a Credible Form of Utilitarianism," in *Morality and the Language of Conduct*, Hector-Neri Castaneda and George Naknikian, eds. (Detroit: Wayne State University, 1965), 109–110.

5. A. C. Ewing, *Ethics* (New York: Free Press, 1965), 41.

6. Molly Moore, "Did the Experts Really Approve the 'Brown Lung' Experiment?" *The Washington Post National Weekly Edition*, June 4, 1984, 31.

7. Adam Smith, *The Wealth of Nations* (New York: The Modern Library, 1937), 421–423.

8. Tom L. Beauchamp and Norman E. Bowie, eds., *Ethical Theory and Business* (Englewood Cliffs, N.J.: Prentice-Hall, 1977), 11.

9. Immanuel Kant, *Foundations of the Metaphysics of Morals*, 6th ed., trans. T. K. Abbott (London: Longman's Green, 1909), 15.

10. See, in particular, W. D. Ross, *The Right and the Good* (London: Oxford University Press, 1930).

11. Richard B. Brandt, "The Real and Alleged Problems of Utilitarianism," *The Hastings Center Report* (April 1983): 38.

12. Ibid., 42.

13. Vincent Ryan Ruggiero, *The Moral Imperative* (Port Washington, N.Y.: Alfred Publishers, 1973).

14. The facts of this case are based on articles from *Newsweek*, January 19 and April 13, 1987, and from *The Economist*, March 21, 1987.

15. Ralph Drayton, "One Manufacturer's Approach to Automobile Safety Standards," *CTLA News*, VIII (February 1968): 11.

16. Mark Dowie, "Pinto Madness," *Mother Jones*, September–October 1977, 20.

17. The following four paragraphs are based on a case prepared by T. W. Zimmerer and P. L. Preston in R. D. Hay, E. R. Gray, and J. E. Gates, eds., *Business and Society* (Cincinnati: South-Western, 1976). The remainder of the case draws on Peter Singer,

"Rights and the Market," in J. Arthur and W. H. Shaw, eds., *Justice and Economic Distribution* (Englewood Cliffs, N.J.: Prentice-Hall, 1978), and Richard M. Titmuss, *The Gift Relationship* (London: George Allen & Unwin, 1972).

18. Singer, "Rights and the Market," 213. Reprinted by permission of Prentice-Hall, Inc.

What Would a Satisfactory Moral Theory Be Like? _____

James Rachels

After studying various moral theories, one is bound to be left wondering what to believe. In this selection from The Elements of Moral Theory, *James Rachels sketches what he thinks would be a satisfactory ethical theory. Although his theory has much in common with utilitarianism, it takes seriously people's right to choose and the moral importance of treating people as they deserve to be treated. In this way Rachels follows Kant's emphasis on respect for persons.*

> Some people believe that there cannot be progress in Ethics, since everything has already been said. . . . I believe the opposite. . . . Compared with the other sciences, Non-Religious Ethics is the youngest and least advanced.
>
> Derek Parfit, *Reasons and Persons* (1984)

Morality Without Hubris

Moral philosophy has a rich and fascinating history. A great many thinkers have approached the subject from a wide variety of perspectives and have produced theories that both attract and repel the thoughtful reader. Almost all the classical theories contain plausible elements, which is hardly surprising, considering that they were devised by philosophers of undoubted genius. Yet the various theories are not consistent with one another, and most are vulnerable to crippling objections. After reviewing them, one is left wondering what to believe. What, in the final analysis, is the truth? Of course, different philosophers would answer this question in different ways. Some might refuse to answer at all, on the grounds that we do not yet know enough to have reached the "final analysis." (In this, moral philosophy is not much worse off

than any other subject of human inquiry—we do not know the final truth about almost anything.) But we do know a lot, and it may not be unduly rash to venture a guess as to what a satisfactory moral theory might be like.

A satisfactory theory would, first of all, be sensitive to the facts about human nature, and it would be appropriately modest about the place of human beings in the scheme of things. The universe is some 18 billion years old—that is the time elapsed since the "big bang"—and the earth itself was formed about 4.6 billion years ago. The evolution of life on the planet was a slow process, guided not by design but (largely) by random mutation and natural selection. The first humans appeared quite recently. The extinction of the great dinosaurs 65 million years ago (possibly as the result of a catastrophic collision between the earth and an asteroid) left ecological room for the evolution of the few little mammals that were about, and after 63 or 64 million *more* years, one line of that evolution finally produced us. In geological time, we arrived only yesterday.

But no sooner did our ancestors arrive than they began to think of themselves as the most important things in all creation. Some of them even imagined that the whole universe had been made for their benefit. Thus, when they began to develop theories of right and wrong, they held that the protection of their own interests had a kind of ultimate and objective value. The rest of creation, they reasoned, was intended for their use. We now know better. We now know that we exist by evolutionary accident, as one species among many, on a small and insignificant world in one little corner of the cosmos.

Hume, who knew only a little of this story, nevertheless realized that human *hubris* is largely unjustified. "The life of a man," he wrote, "is of no greater importance to the universe than that of an oyster." But he also recognized that our lives are important to *us*. We are creatures with desires, needs, plans, and hopes; and even if "the universe" does not care about those things, we do. Our theory of morality may begin from this point. In order to have a convenient name for it, let us call this theory *Morality Without Hubris*—or *MWH* for short. MWH incorporates some elements of the various classical theories while rejecting others.

Human *hubris* is largely unjustified, but it is not *entirely* unjustified. Compared to the other creatures on earth, we do have impressive intellectual capacities. We have evolved as rational beings. This fact gives some point to our inflated opinion of ourselves; and, as it turns out, it is also what makes us capable of having a morality. Because we are rational, we are able to take some facts as *reasons* for behaving one way rather than another. We can articulate those reasons and think about them. Thus we take the fact that an action would help satisfy our desires, needs, and so on—in short, the fact that an action would *promote our interests*—as a reason in favor of doing that action. And of course we take the fact that an action would frustrate our interests as a reason against doing it.

The origin of our concept of "ought" may be found in these facts. If we were not capable of considering reasons for and against actions, we would have no use for such a notion. Like the lower animals, we would simply act from impulse or habit, or as Kant put it, from "inclination." But the consideration of reasons introduces a new factor. Now we find ourselves impelled to act in certain ways as a result of deliberation, as a result of thinking about our behavior and its consequences. We use the word "ought" to mark this new element of the situation: we *ought* to do the act supported by the weightiest reasons.

Once we consider morality as a matter of acting on reason, another important point emerges. In reasoning about what to do, we can be consistent or inconsistent. One way of being inconsistent is to accept a fact as a reason for action on one occasion, while refusing to accept a similar fact as a reason on another occasion, even though there is no difference between the two occasions that would justify distinguishing them. (This is the legitimate point made by Kant's Categorical Imperative. . . .) This happens, for example, when a person unjustifiably places the interests of his own race or social group above the comparable interests of other races and social groups. Racism means counting the interests of the members of other races as less important than the interests of the members of one's own race, despite the fact that there is no general difference between the races that would justify it. It is an offense against morality because it is first an offense against reason. Similar remarks could be made about other doctrines that divide humanity into the morally favored and disfavored, such as egoism, sexism, and (some forms of) nationalism. The upshot is that reason requires impartiality: we ought to act so as to promote the interests of everyone alike.

If Psychological Egoism were true, this would mean that reason demands more of us than we can manage. But Psychological Egoism is not true; it gives an altogether false picture of human nature and the human condition. We have evolved as social creatures, living together in groups, wanting one another's company, needing one another's cooperation, and capable of caring about one another's welfare. So there is a pleasing theoretical "fit" between (a) what reason requires, namely impartiality; (b) the requirements of social living, namely adherence to a set of rules that, if fairly applied, would serve everyone's interests; and (c) our natural inclination to care about others, at least to a modest degree. All three work together to make morality not only possible, but in an important sense natural, for us.

So far, MWH sounds very much like Utilitarianism. However, there is one other fact about human beings that must be taken into account, and doing so will give the theory a decidedly nonutilitarian twist. As rational agents, humans have the power of choice: they may choose to do what they see to be right, or they may choose to do wrong. Thus they are *responsible* for their freely chosen actions, and they are judged morally good if they choose well or wicked if they choose badly. This, I think, has two consequences. First, it helps to explain why freedom is among the most cherished human values. A person who is denied the right to choose his or her own actions is thereby denied the possibility of achieving any kind of personal moral worth. Second, the way a person may be treated by others depends, to some extent, on the way he or she has chosen to treat them. One who treats others well deserves to be treated well in return, while one who treats others badly deserves to be treated badly in return.

This last point is liable to sound a little strange, so let me elaborate it just a bit. Suppose Smith has always been generous to others, helping them whenever he could; now he is in trouble and needs help in return. There is now a *special* reason *he* should be helped, above the general obligation we have to promote the interests of everyone alike. He is not just another member of the crowd. He is a particular person who, by his own previous conduct, has *earned* our respect and gratitude. But now consider someone with the opposite history: suppose Jones is your neighbor, and he has always *refused* to help you when you needed it. One day your car wouldn't start, for example, and Jones wouldn't give you a lift to work—he had no particular excuse, he just wouldn't be bothered. Imagine that, after this episode, Jones has car trouble and he has the nerve to ask you for a ride. Perhaps you think you should help him anyway, despite his own lack of helpfulness. (You might think that this will teach him generosity.) Nevertheless, if we concentrate on what he *deserves*, we must conclude that he deserves to be left to fend for himself.

Adjusting our treatment of individuals to match how they themselves have chosen to treat others is not just a matter of rewarding friends and holding grudges against enemies. It is a matter of treating people as *responsible agents*, who by their own choices show themselves to be deserving of particular responses, and toward whom such emotions as gratitude and resentment are appropriate. There is an important difference between Smith and Jones; why shouldn't that be reflected in the way we respond to them? What would it be like if we did *not* tailor our responses to people in this way? For one thing, we would be denying people (including ourselves) the ability to earn good treatment at the hands of others. Morally speaking, we would all become simply members of the great crowd of humanity, rather than individuals with particular personalities and deserts. Respecting people's right to choose their own conduct, and then adjusting our treatment of them according to how they choose, is ultimately a matter of "respect for persons" in a sense somewhat like Kant's.

We are now in a position to summarize the outline of what, in my judgment, a satisfactory moral theory would be like. Such a theory would see morality as based on facts about our nature and interests, rather than on some exaggerated conception of our "importance." As for the principles on which we ought to act, the theory is a combination of two ideas: first, that *we ought to act so as to promote the interests of everyone alike*; and second, that *we should treat people as they deserve to be treated, considering how they have themselves chosen to behave.*

But now the key question is: How are these two ideas related? How do they fit together to form a unified principle of conduct? They are not to be understood as entirely independent of one another. The first establishes a general presumption in favor of promoting everyone's interests, impartially; and the second specifies grounds on which this presumption may be overridden. Thus the second thought functions as a qualification to the first; it specifies that we may sometimes *depart from* a policy of "equal treatment" on the grounds that a person has shown by his past behavior that he deserves some particular response. We may therefore combine them into a single principle. The primary rule of morality, according to MWH, is:

> We ought to act so as to promote impartially the interests of everyone alike, except when individuals deserve particular responses as a result of their own past behavior.

This principle combines the best elements of both Utilitarianism and Kantian "respect for persons," but it is not produced simply by stitching those two philosophies together. Rather, it springs naturally from a consideration of the main facts of the human condition—that we are perishable beings with interests that may be promoted or frustrated, and that we are rational beings responsible for our conduct. Although more needs to be said about the theoretical basis of this view, I will say no more about it here. Instead I will turn to some of its practical implications. Like every moral theory, MWH implies that we should behave in certain ways; and in some cases, it implies that commonly accepted patterns of behavior are wrong and should be changed. The plausibility of the theory will depend in part on how successful it is in convincing us that our behavior should conform to its directives.

The Moral Community

When we are deciding what to do, whose interests should we take into account? People have answered this question in different ways at different times: egoists have said that one's own interests are all-important; racists have restricted moral concern to their own race; and nationalists have held that moral concern stops at the borders of one's country. The answer given by MWH is that *we ought to give equal consideration to the interests of everyone who will be affected by our conduct.* In principle, the community with which we should be concerned is limited only by the number of individuals who have interests, and that, as we shall see, is a very large number indeed.

This may seem a pious platitude, but in reality it can be a hard doctrine. As this is being written, for example, there is famine in Ethiopia and millions of people are starving. People in the affluent countries have not responded very well. There has been some aid given, but relatively few people have felt personally obligated to help by sending contributions to famine-relief agencies. People would no doubt feel a greater sense of obligation if it were their neighbors starving, rather than strangers in a foreign country. But on the theory we are considering, the location of the starving people makes no difference; *everyone* is included in the community of moral concern. This has radical consequences: for example, when a person is faced with the choice between spending ten dollars on a trip to the movies or contributing it for famine relief, he should ask himself which action would most effectively promote human welfare, with each person's interests counted as equally important. Would he benefit more from seeing the movie than a starving person would from getting food? Clearly, he would not. So he should contribute the money for famine relief. If this sort of reasoning were taken seriously, it would make an enormous difference in our responses to such emergencies.

If the moral community is not limited to people in one place, neither is it limited to people at any one *time.* Whether people will be affected by our actions now or in the distant future makes no difference. Our obligation is to consider all their interests equally. This is an important point because, with the development of nuclear weapons, we now have the capacity to alter the course of history in an especially dramatic way. Some argue that a full-scale nuclear exchange between the superpowers would result in the extinction of the human race. The prediction of "nuclear winter" supports this conclusion. The idea is that the detonation of so many nuclear devices would send millions of tons of dust and ash into the stratosphere, where it would block the sun's rays. The surface of the earth would become cold. This condition would persist for years, and the ecology would collapse. Those who were "lucky" enough to escape death earlier would nevertheless perish in the nuclear winter. Other theorists contend that this estimate is too pessimistic. Civilization might come to an end, they say, and most people might die, but a few will survive, and the long upward struggle will begin again.

Considering this, it is difficult to imagine *any* circumstances in which the large-scale use of nuclear weapons would be morally justified. Some political analysts seem to think that *our* interests are served by policies that run the risk of nuclear war. Let us suppose this is so. To make the best possible case, let us grant that (a) the United States has vital interests that can be protected only by maintaining a nuclear arsenal as a balance against Soviet threats; (b) it is in the best interests of the rest of the world for the United States to pursue this course; and (c) the United States is "in the right" in its conflict with the Soviet Union. In other words, we will grant every point the defenders of our nuclear policy want to make. But then suppose a situation arises in which the Soviet Union, despite America's nuclear strength, acts against the very interests our arsenal is supposed to protect. Would we then be justified in using our strategic weapons? Suppose we did. In executing a policy designed to protect our interests, we would not only have destroyed ourselves; we would have violated the interests of all the people yet to come (assuming, of course, that there were at least some survivors who could try to rebuild civilization). In the larger historical context, our interests are of only passing importance, certainly not worth the price of condemning countless future generations to the miseries of a post–nuclear war age. History would not judge the Nazis to have been the pre-eminent villains of our time. That distinction would be reserved for us.

There is one other way in which our conception of the moral community must be expanded. Humans, as we have noted, are only one species of animal inhabiting this planet. Like humans, the other animals also have interests that are affected by what we do. When we kill or torture them, they are harmed, just as humans are harmed when treated in those ways. The utilitarians were right to insist that the interests of nonhuman animals must be given weight in our moral calculations. As Bentham pointed out, excluding creatures from moral consideration because of their species is no more justified than excluding them because of race, nationality, or sex. . . . Impartiality requires the expansion of the moral community—not only across space and time but across the boundaries of species as well.

Justice and Fairness

MWH has much in common with Utilitarianism, especially in what I called MWH's "first idea." But . . . Utilitarianism has been severely criticized for failing to account for the values of justice and fairness. Can MWH do any better in this regard? It does, because it makes a person's past behavior relevant to how he or she should be treated. This introduces into the theory an acknowledgment of personal merit that is lacking in unqualified Utilitarianism.

One specific criticism of Utilitarianism [has] to do with its implications for the institution of punishment. We can imagine cases in which it promotes the general welfare to frame an innocent person, which is blatantly unjust; and taking the Principle of Utility as our ultimate standard, it is hard to explain why this is so. More generally, as Kant pointed out, the basic utilitarian "justification" of punishment is in terms of treating individuals as mere "means." MWH provides a different view of the matter. In punishing someone, we are

treating him differently from the way we treat others—punishment involves a failure of impartiality. But this is justified, on our account, by the person's own past deeds. It is a response to what he has done. That is why it is not right to frame an innocent person; the innocent person has not done anything to deserve being singled out for such treatment. The account of punishment suggested by MWH is very close to Kant's.

The theory of punishment, however, is only one small part of the subject of justice. Questions of justice arise any time one person is treated differently from another. Suppose an employer must choose which of two employees to promote, when he can promote only one of them. The first candidate has worked hard for the company, taking on extra work when it was needed, giving up her vacation to help out, and so on. The second candidate, on the other hand, has always done only the minimum required of him. (And we will assume he has no excuse; he has simply *chosen* not to work very hard for the company.) Obviously, the two employees will be treated very differently: one will get the promotion; the other will not. But this is all right, according to our theory, because the first employee deserves to be advanced over the second, considering the past performance of each. The first employee has earned the promotion, the second has not.

This is an easy case, in that it is obvious what the employer should do. But it illustrates an important difference between our theory and Utilitarianism. Utilitarians might argue that their theory also yields the right decision in this case. They might observe that it promotes the general welfare for companies to reward hard work; therefore the Principle of Utility, unsupplemented by any further consideration, would also say that the first employee, but not the second, should be promoted. Perhaps this is so. Nevertheless, this is unsatisfactory because it has the first employee being promoted for the *wrong reason*. She has a claim on the promotion because of her own hard work, and not simply because promoting her would be better for us all. MWH accommodates this vital point, whereas Utilitarianism does not.

MWH holds that a person's voluntary actions can justify departures from the basic policy of "equal treatment," but *nothing else can*. This goes against a common view of the matter. Often, people think it is right for individuals to be rewarded for physical beauty, superior intelligence, or other native endowments. (In practice, people often get better jobs and a greater share of life's good things just because they were born with greater natural gifts.) But on reflection, this does not seem right. People do not deserve their native endowments; they have them as a result of what John Rawls has called "the natural lottery." Suppose the first employee in our example was passed over for the promotion, despite her hard work, because the second employee had some native talent that was more useful in the new position. Even if the employer could justify this decision in terms of the company's needs, the first employee would rightly feel that there is something unfair going on. She has worked harder, yet he is now getting the promotion, and the benefits that go with it, because of something he did nothing to merit. That is not fair. A just society, according to MWH, would be one in which people may improve their positions through work (with the opportunity for work available to everyone), but they would not enjoy superior positions simply because they were born lucky. . . .

As I said at the outset, MWH represents my best guess about what an ultimately satisfactory moral theory might be like. I say "guess" not to indicate any lack of confidence; in my opinion, MWH *is* a satisfactory moral theory. However, it is instructive to remember that a great many thinkers have tried to devise such a theory, and history has judged them to have been only partially successful. This suggests that it would be wise not to make too grandiose a claim for one's own view. Moreover, as the Oxford philosopher Derek Parfit has observed, the earth will remain habitable for another billion years, and civilization is now only a few thousand years old. If we do not destroy ourselves, moral philosophy, along with all the other human inquiries, may yet have a long way to go.

Review and Discussion Questions

1. Why does Rachels call his theory "morality without hubris"?

2. According to him, what important implications does the fact of human rationality have for ethics?

3. How and why does Rachels modify the utilitarian approach? Would you agree that Rachels successfully combines the best elements of utilitarianism and Kantianism?

4. According to Rachels, who is in "the moral community"? How would adopting his perspective cause people to change their moral attitudes and conduct?

For Further Reading

Tom L. Beauchamp, *Philosophical Ethics* (New York: McGraw-Hill, 1982) is an introductory text with selected readings covering classical ethical theories, rights, and the nature of morality.

Richard Norman, *The Moral Philosophers* (New York: Oxford University Press, 1983) discusses the thought of several key thinkers in the history of ethics.

J. J. C. Smart and B. Williams, *Utilitarianism: For and Against* (New York: Cambridge University Press, 1973) debates the merits of act utilitarianism in clear and accessible essays.

C. H. Sommers, ed., *Right and Wrong* (New York: Harcourt Brace Jovanovich, 1986) provides a good selection of readings on egoism, utilitarianism, and Kantianism.

(Consult also the readings suggested at the end of Chapter 1.)

CHAPTER 3

JUSTICE AND ECONOMIC DISTRIBUTION

NO INCOME TAX until 1913

It seems strange to recall that until the early years of this century, there was no federal tax on personal income, and only with the passing of the Nineteenth Amendment to the United States Constitution in 1913 was Congress granted the right to collect tax on the income of its citizens. Since then, the income tax laws have grown enormously in complexity. Lawyers study for years to master the intricacies of the system, and most people with middle incomes or better require professional assistance in order to file their annual IRS forms. Over the years, the tax rules have encouraged our economy to develop in specific directions by rewarding investment in some areas but not in others. Most of us have heard stories of wealthy individuals who manage, legally, to pay little or no income tax, and many of us doubt the fairness of the tax rules. Yet, the exemptions and supposed loopholes in the tax laws, which have done so much to shape the exact character of our economy as well as the distribution of income across the land, do not affect just so-called special interests. For instance, millions of American families are home owners, a fact of profound sociological and economic importance, and one that has been encouraged by decades of tax deductions for home-mortgage payments.

In 1986 President Ronald Reagan achieved what most Washington pundits had long said was an impossibility: He managed to coax, goad, and pressure Congress into a comprehensive overhaul of the federal income tax code. Traditionally, our income tax has been "progressive" in the sense that wealthy people paid taxes at a higher rate than poor people. President Reagan had already slashed the top rates substantially during his first term in office, and the new law further lowered the percentage rate of taxation for the wealthiest income group to well under half of what it had once been. On the other hand, by eliminating many pet exemptions and closing numerous loopholes in the previous tax system, the overall result may not favor the rich as much as the percentages alone suggest. It is hard to predict the exact economic and distributive effects of the recent changes, which are to be phased in over several years. Only as people adjust themselves to the new system will we be able to see who the winners and losers are and how much they have won or lost. But whatever the results, the principle of "progressivity," namely, that fairness requires that the wealthy pay more tax than others, has suffered a heavy blow.

This comes at a time when economists are reporting "a surge in inequality" in the distribution of income in the U.S.[1] To be sure, our nation has long had significant income inequalities. To use a metaphor employed some years ago by the Nobel prize winning economist Paul Samuelson: If we were to make an income pyramid out of child's blocks, with each layer representing $1000 of income, the peak would be far higher than the Eiffel Tower, but most of us would be within a yard of the ground. Since the 1970s, however, inequality in the distribution of income in the U.S. has, disturbingly, increased even further. Put briefly, the rich are getting richer, the poor are increasing in number, and the middle class is having trouble holding its own.

According to the U.S. Bureau of the Census, in 1985 the families that make up the top 20 percent income group took home 43.5 percent of the total national income, their highest level since figures were first collected in 1947. The income share of the bottom 60 percent, on the other hand, fell to its lowest ever: 32.4 percent. The data of the Federal Reserve Board on income distribution, which include items, such as capital gains, that are not counted in the Census Bureau's definition of income, show that between 1969 and 1982 people in the top 10 percent of the population raised their income share from 29 percent to 33 percent of the national total. Meanwhile, the bottom 60 percent's income slumped from 32 percent to 28 percent.

In this chapter we will not speculate on the causes of this income shift, but we can see the evidence of it all around us. Our economy has created millions of new jobs in the last decade, but these have been predominantly in low-income sectors of the economy, like the fast-food industry. Good, well-paying middle-income jobs—especially in industries like steel, automotives, and machine tools—are scarcer than ever. More and more families require two incomes just to get by; those with only one income frequently find themselves unable to sustain a middle-class lifestyle. Discount department stores like K Mart prosper, as do upscale department stores like Bloomingdale's, while stores in the middle, like Gimbel's, go out of business.

These shifts of income distribution are more dramatic when set against the background of an even more unequal distribution of wealth in this country. While the top 2 percent of the population receives 14 percent of the total income, they already own 28 percent of the nation's total net worth. The top 10 percent has 57 percent of the nation's wealth in its hands, leaving the bottom 50 percent of the population with 4.5 percent. If one leaves out homes and real estate, the top 2 percent of all families owns 54 percent of the nation's net

financial assets (stocks, bonds, pension funds, and so on). The top 10 percent controls 86 percent, while those making up the bottom 55 percent have zero or negative financial assets. About half of the country's top wealth holders inherited their wealth; half got to the top through their own efforts. Ninety-eight percent of the top wealth group are white.

There is nothing inevitable about such great inequalities in income and wealth. The distribution of income in Japan is far more equal than that in the U.S., and Japan is just as thoroughly a capitalist nation as we are. Likewise, in West Germany, before taxes and transfers, the income of 28 percent of the population is less than half the national median; in the U.S. the figure is 27 percent. After taxes and transfers, however, the West German figure drops to 6 percent, while in the U.S. it drops only to 17 percent. Inequality of income is not some brute fact of nature, even in market-oriented societies. Rather, political choices determine how income is ultimately distributed. How much inequality a society is willing to accept reflects both its moral values and the relative strength of its contending social and political forces.

Arguments can be made for and against different degrees of income inequality, for and against progressivity in taxation, and for and against more specific tax regulations. But whatever one's position on these issues, it probably relies on some theory of economic justice in terms of which a particular tax regulation, the tax system as a whole, or even the type of economic system that a society has can be evaluated. The topic of economic justice deals with that constellation of moral issues raised by a society's distribution of wealth, income, status, and power.

Ethical dilemmas, problems, and questions arise daily about how wealth and goods should be allocated. Given the relative scarcity of a society's resources, deciding how these resources should be distributed is an important moral task. Should everyone receive roughly the same amount? Or should people be rewarded according to how hard they work or how much they contribute to society? To what extent should economic distribution take need into account? For example, with modern technology at their disposal, today's hospitals are able to perform life-prolonging feats of medicine that were undreamed of only a couple of decades ago. But these services are often extraordinarily costly. Who, then, should have access to them? Those who can afford it? Any who need it? Those who are most likely to benefit?

In Chapter 2 we discussed several basic moral theories and the general principles of right and wrong associated with them. In this chapter we will focus on the more specific topic of justice and economic distribution, that is, on the principles that are relevant to the moral assessment of society's distribution of economic goods and services. Although the topic is an abstract one, it is particularly relevant to our study of business ethics, because it concerns the moral standards to be used in evaluating the institutional frameworks within which both business and nonbusiness organizations, as well as the professions, operate. Specifically, in this chapter we will examine:

1. The concept of justice in general and some basic principles that have been proposed as standards of economic distribution.

2. The utilitarian approach to justice in general and economic justice in particular.

3. The libertarian theory that places a moral priority on liberty and free exchange.

4. The contractarian and egalitarian theory of John Rawls.

THE NATURE OF JUSTICE

Justice is an old concept with a rich history, a concept that is fundamental to any discussion of how society ought to be organized. Philo-sophical concern with justice goes back at least to ancient Greece. For Plato and some of his contemporaries, justice seems to have been the paramount virtue or, more precisely, the sum of virtue with regard to our relations with others. Philosophers today, however, generally distinguish justice from the whole of morality. To claim something is "unjust" is a more specific complaint than to say it is "bad" or "immoral."

What, then, makes an act unjust? Talk of justice or injustice focuses on at least one of several related ideas. First, a claim that one is treated unjustly often suggests that one's moral *rights* have been violated—in particular, that one has been made to suffer some burden that one had a right to avoid or that one has been denied some benefit that one had a right to possess. If, for example, we agree to go into business together and you back out without justification, costing me time and money, then you have violated a right of mine, and I may well claim that you have treated me unjustly.

Second, justice is often used to mean *fairness*. Justice frequently concerns the fair treatment of members of groups of people or else looks backward to the fair compensation of prior injuries. Exactly what fairness requires is hard to say, and different standards may well be applied to the same case. If corporate manager Smith commits bribery, he is justly punished under our laws. If other managers commit equally serious crimes but escape punishment, then Smith suffers a comparative injustice, since he was singled out. On the other hand, our treatment of Smith and other white-collar lawbreakers is unjust, although this time for the opposite reason, when compared to the stiffer sentences meted out to "common" criminals for less grave offenses.

Injustice in one sense of unfairness occurs when like cases are not treated in the same fashion. Following Aristotle, many philosophers believe that we are required, as a formal principle of justice, to treat similar cases alike except where there is some relevant difference. This principle emphasizes the role of impartiality and consistency in justice, but it is a purely formal principle because it does not tell us which differences are relevant and which are not. Satisfying this formal requirement, furthermore, does not guarantee that justice is done. For example, by treating like cases similarly, a judge can nonarbitrarily administer a law (like an apartheid regulation in South Africa) that is itself unjust. (Similarly, a fair procedure can lead to unjust results, as when a guilty man is mistakenly acquitted by an honest jury.)

Related to Aristotle's fairness requirement is a third idea commonly bound up with the concept of justice, namely that of *equality*. Justice is frequently held to require that our treatment of people reflects their fundamental moral equality. While Aristotle's formal principle of justice does not say whether we are to assume equality of treatment until some difference between cases is shown or to assume the opposite until some relevant similarities are demonstrated, a claim of injustice based on equality is meant to place the burden of proof on those who would endorse unequal treatment. Still, to claim that all persons are equal is not to establish a direct relationship between justice and economic distribution. We all believe that *some* differences in the treatment of persons are consistent with equality (punishment, for example), and neither respect for equality nor the requirement of equal treatment necessarily implies an equal distribution of economic goods.

Despite equality, then, individual circumstances—in particular, what a person has done—make a difference. We think it is unjust, for example, when a guilty person goes free or an innocent person hangs, regardless of how others have been treated. This suggests that justice sometimes involves, as a fourth aspect, something beyond equal or even impartial treatment. Justice also requires that people get what they *deserve*.

Rival Principles of Distribution

Justice, then, is an important subclass of morality in general, a subclass that generally involves appeals to the overlapping notions of rights, fairness, equality, or desert. Justice is not the only virtue an individual or social institution can pursue, and many of the most difficult moral dilemmas arise when the requirements of justice conflict with other goods or obligations.

When we turn to the topic of distributive justice, that is, to the proper distribution of social benefits and burdens (in particular, of economic benefits and burdens), we find several possible principles that might be used as a basis for distribution. Let's look at five.

The first principle states: *Each person should receive an equal share.* Accordingly, when a company distributes end-of-year bonuses it should insure that each eligible party receives a share equal to every other eligible party. A second possible principle is: *To each according to individual need.* Thus, in assigning overtime the company should distribute work on the basis of the individual needs of the workers, with the more needy getting priority. A third candidate for a principle of distributive justice states: *To each according to individual effort.* Using this guideline, the company should promote workers according to the effort put forth by each party eligible for the promotion. A fourth possible principle is: *To each according to societal contribution.* If the company is making a particularly valuable contribution to the welfare of society (e.g., locating in the inner city and training the hard-core unemployed), it should get tax incentives denied a company that is not making a comparable contribution. Finally, a fifth possible principle is: *To each according to merit.* This would mean that the company should hire, promote, and distribute bonuses strictly on the basis of individual merit.

Each of these five possible principles of economic distribution—pure equality, need,

[handwritten margin notes: "Marxist idea", "if you try you get it", "Fact of Nature"]

effort, social contribution, merit—has its advocates, and, to be sure, each seems plausible in some circumstances. But only in some. There are problems with each. For example, if equality of income were guaranteed, then the lazy would receive as much as the industrious. On the other hand, effort is hard to measure and compare, while what one is able to contribute to society may depend on being at the right place at the right time. And so on: none of the principles seems to work in enough circumstances to be defended successfully as *the* principle of justice in distribution.

It seems, in fact, that we simply apply different principles of justice at different times. For example, the opportunity to vote is distributed *equally* to all citizens above a certain age; each has one vote, and nobody more than one. Welfare programs like those providing food stamps or aiding poor people with children operate on the basis of *need*. At the lower levels of schooling, teachers commonly give grades, in part, on the basis of student *effort*. Corporations in certain industries may be given tax breaks on the basis of *social contribution*. And jobs and promotions are usually awarded (distributed) on the basis of *merit*.

Multiple principles, however, may often be relevant to a single situation. Sometimes they may pull in the same direction, as when wealthy professionals like doctors defend their high incomes simultaneously on grounds of superior effort, merit, social contribution, and even (because of the high cost of malpractice insurance) need. Or the principles may pull in different directions, as when a teacher must balance effort against merit in assigning grades to pupils. Many philosophers are content to leave the situation here. They say simply that there are various *prima facie* principles of just distribution and one must find that which best applies to the given situation. If several principles seem to apply, then one must simply weigh them the best one can.

This need not be done uncritically, of course. For example, we can discuss intelligently whether effort or merit (or even need) is the most appropriate basis for assigning grades, and why, and we can examine whether doctors really do, as they allege, make a greater social contribution than nurses. But many writers have found themselves discontent philosophically with this sort of situation, in which a great many different commonsense principles seem to be floating about without precise guidelines for balancing them against one another or employing them in specific cases. These moral philosophers have undertaken, instead, to develop more fully some theory of justice, from the perspective of which these principles, especially insofar as they apply to economic distribution, can be assessed and then modified, discarded, or defended. We will look at three such approaches: the utilitarian, the libertarian, and the Rawlsian (egalitarian).

THE UTILITARIAN VIEW

Just as one would expect, utilitarianism approaches the concept of justice in general and the question of economic distribution in particular in a way that reflects its overall theoretical orientation. For utilitarians, as we have seen in the previous chapter, happiness is the overarching value. Whether one assesses the rightness and wrongness of individual actions in terms of how much happiness they produce, as an act utilitarian does, or whether one uses happiness as the standard for deciding what moral principles a society should accept as the basis for determining right and wrong, as a rule utilitarian does, happiness is the only thing that is good, in and of itself. On that utilitarians are agreed.

For utilitarians, justice is not an independent moral standard, distinct from their general principle. Rather, the maximization of happiness ultimately determines what is just and unjust. Critics of utilitarianism contend that knowing what will promote happiness is always difficult. People are bound to estimate consequences differently, thus making the standard of utility an inexact and unreliable principle for determining what is just. John Stuart Mill, however, did not see much merit in this criticism. For one thing, it presupposes that we all agree about what the principles of justice are and how to apply them. This is far from the case, argues Mill in his famous work *Utilitarianism*. Indeed, without utilitarianism to provide a determinate standard of justice, one is always left with a plethora of competing principles, all of which seem to have some plausibility, but which are mutually incompatible.

As an example Mill considers the conflict of principles of justice that occurs in the realm of economic distribution.[2] Is it just or not, he asks, that more talented workers should receive a greater remuneration? There are two possible answers to this question:

> On the negative side of the question it is argued that whoever does the best he can deserves equally well, and ought not in justice be put in a position of inferiority for no fault of his own; that superior abilities have already advantages more than enough . . . without adding to these a superior share of the world's goods; and that society is bound in justice rather to make compensation to the less favored for this unmerited inequality of advantages than to aggravate it.

This sounds plausible, but then so does the alternative answer:

> On the contrary side it is contended that society receives more from the more efficient laborer; that, his services being more useful, society owes him a larger return for them; that a greater share of the joint result is actually his work, and not to allow his claim to it is a kind of robbery; that, if he is only to receive as

much as others, he can only be justly required to produce as much.

Here we have two conflicting principles of justice. How are we to decide between them? The problem, Mill says, is that both principles seem plausible:

> Justice has in this case two sides to it, which it is impossible to bring into harmony, and the two disputants have chosen opposite sides; the one looks to what it is just that the individual should receive, the other to what it is just that the community should give.

Each disputant is, from his or her own point of view, unanswerable. "Any choice between them on grounds of justice," Mill continues, "must be perfectly arbitrary." What then is the solution? For Mill, the utilitarian, it is straightforward: "Social utility alone can decide the preference." The utilitarian standard must be the ultimate court of appeal in such cases. Only the utilitarian standard can provide an intelligent and satisfactory way of handling controversial questions of justice and of resolving conflicts between competing principles of justice. To understand this better we must look at exactly what Mill understands justice to be.

Mill's Theory of Justice

Most moral theorists agree that the demands of justice are only a subset of the general class of moral obligations. What then is the relation between justice and other moral obligations? Mill's answer is that injustice involves the violation of the rights of some identifiable individual. This distinguishes it from other types of immoral behavior.

> Whether the injustice consists in depriving a person of a possession, or in breaking faith with him, or in treating him worse than he deserves, or worse than other people who have no greater

claims—in each case the supposition implies two things: a wrong done, and some assignable person who is wronged. . . . It seems to me that this feature in the case—a right in some person, correlative to the moral obligation—constitutes the specific difference between justice and generosity or beneficence. Justice implies something which is not only right to do, and wrong not to do, but which some individual person can claim from us as his moral right.[3]

But if injustice involves the violation of moral rights, the question arises of how a utilitarian like Mill understands talk of rights. Mill's position is that to say I have a right to something is to say that I have a valid claim on society to protect me in the possession of that thing, either by the force of law or through education and opinion. And I have that valid claim in the first place because society's protection of my possession of that thing is warranted on utilitarian grounds. "To have a right, then, is . . . to have something which society ought to defend me in the possession of. If the objector goes on to ask why it ought, I can give him no other reason than general utility."[4] What utilitarianism identifies as "rights" are certain moral rules whose observance is of the utmost importance for the long-run, overall maximization of happiness.

Accordingly, Mill sums up his view of justice as follows:

> Justice is the name for certain classes of moral rules which concern the essentials of human well-being more nearly, and are therefore of more absolute obligation, than any other rules for the guidance of life; and the notion that we have found to be of the essence of the idea of justice—that of a right residing in an individual—implies and testifies to this more binding obligation.
>
> The moral rules which forbid mankind to hurt one another (in which we must never forget to include wrongful interference with each other's freedom) are

more vital to human well being than any maxims, however important, which only point out the best mode of managing some department of human affairs.[5]

Thus, while justice for Mill is ultimately a matter of promoting social well-being (or of "expediency," as he sometimes puts it), not every issue of social utility is a matter of justice. The concept of justice identifies certain very important social utilities, on which society puts great stake. The importance of these social utilities is marked by the very strong feelings that typically attach to them. A perception of injustice causes feelings of resentment, Mill believes, feelings that are absent (or at least much weaker) in other cases where someone has failed to maximize human happiness.

Utilitarianism and Economic Distribution

The utilitarian theory of justice ties the question of economic distribution to the promotion of social well-being or happiness. Utilitarians want that economic system which will bring more good to society than any other system. What system is that? Utilitarianism itself, as a normative theory, provides no answer. The answer depends on the relevant social, economic, and political facts. A utilitarian must understand the various possibilities, determine their consequences, and assess the available options. Obviously, this is not a simple task. Deciding what sort of economic arrangements would best promote human happiness will require the utilitarian to consider many things. Among these are: (1) the type of economic ownership (private, public, mixed); (2) the way of organizing production and distribution in general (pure laissez-faire, markets with government planning and regulation, fully centralized planning); (3) the type of authority arrangements within the units of production (worker control versus managerial prerogative); (4) the range and character of material incentives; and (5) the nature and extent of social security and welfare provisions.

As a matter of historical fact, utilitarians in the early nineteenth century were advocates of laissez-faire capitalism, endorsing the view of Adam Smith that unregulated market relations and free competition best promote the total social good.[6] Today it is probably fair to say that few, if any, utilitarians believe happiness would be maximized by a pure nineteenth-century-style capitalism, without any welfare arrangements. But they are not in agreement on the question of what economic arrangements would in fact maximize happiness. Nonetheless, many utilitarians would view favorably (1) an increase of worker participation in industrial life and (2) a more equal distribution of income.

Worker Participation. In his *Principles of Political Economy*, originally published in 1848, Mill argued for the desirability of breaking down the sharp and hostile division between the producers or workers, on the one hand, and the capitalists or owners, on the other hand.[7] Not only would this be a good thing, it is also something that the advance of civilization was tending naturally to bring about: "The relation of masters and workpeople will be gradually superseded by partnership, in one or two forms: in some cases, association of the labourers with the capitalist; in others, and perhaps finally in all, association of labourers among themselves." These developments would not only enhance productiveness, but—more importantly—they would promote the fuller development and well-being of the human beings involved. The aim, Mill thought, should be to enable people "to work with or for one another in relations not involving dependence."

By the association of labor and capital, Mill has in mind different schemes of profit sharing. For example, "in the American ships trading to China, it has long been the custom for every sailor to have an interest in the profits of the voyage; and to this has been ascribed the general good conduct of those seamen." This sort of association, however, would eventually give way to a more complete system of worker cooperatives:

> The form of association, however, which if mankind continue to improve, must be expected in the end to predominate, is not that which can exist between a capitalist as chief, and work-people without a voice in management, but the association of the labourers themselves on terms of equality, collectively owning the capital with which they carry on their operations, and working under managers elected and removable by themselves.[8]

In *Principles* Mill discusses several examples of successful cooperative associations and viewed optimistically the future of the cooperative movement.

> Eventually, and in perhaps a less remote future than may be supposed, we may, through the co-operative principle, see our way to a change in society, which would combine the freedom and independence of the individual, with the moral, intellectual, and economical advantages of aggregate production; and which . . . would realize, at least in the industrial department, the best aspirations of the democratic spirit.

What that transformation implied for Mill was nothing less than "the nearest approach to social justice, and the most beneficial ordering of industrial affairs for the universal good, which it is possible at present to foresee."[9]

Greater Equality of Income. Utilitarians are likely to be sympathetic to the argument that steps should be taken to reduce the great disparities in income that characterize our society. That is, they are likely to believe that making the distribution of income more equal is a good strategy for maximizing happiness. The reason for this goes back to what economists would call "the declining marginal utility of money." This simply means that successive additions to one's income produce, on average, less happiness or welfare than did earlier additions.

The declining utility of money follows from the fact, as Professor Richard Brandt explains it, that the outcomes we want are preferentially ordered, some being more strongly wanted than others:

> So a person, when deciding how to spend his resources, picks a basket of groceries which is at least as appealing as any other he can purchase with the money he has. The things he does not buy are omitted because other things are wanted more. If we double a person's income, he will spend the extra money on items he wants less (some special cases aside), and which will give less enjoyment than will the original income. The more one's income, the fewer preferred items one buys and the more preferred items one already has. On the whole, then, when the necessities of life have been purchased and the individual is spending on luxury items, he is buying items which will give less enjoyment. . . . This conclusion corresponds well with common-sense reflection and practice.[10]

The obvious implication is that the allocation of income in a more egalitarian direction, that is, in a way that increases the income of those who now earn less, would be happiness maximizing. This leads Brandt, for one, to defend equality of after-tax income on utilitarian grounds, subject to the following exceptions: (a) supplements to meet special needs, (b) supplementary payments necessary for incentives or to allocate resources efficiently, and (c) variations to achieve other socially desirable ends such as population control.[11] Brandt states that this guiding principle of distribution is of only *prima facie* force

and may have to be balanced against other principles and considerations. But it illustrates the point that utilitarians today are likely to advocate increased economic equality.

THE LIBERTARIAN APPROACH

While utilitarians, as we have seen, associate justice with social utility, philosophers who endorse what is called *libertarianism* identify justice with an ideal of liberty. For them, liberty is the prime value, and justice consists in permitting each to live as he or she pleases, free from the interference of others. Accordingly, one libertarian asserts: "We are concerned with the condition of men in which coercion of some by others is reduced as much as possible in society."[12] Another maintains that libertarianism is "a philosophy of personal liberty—the liberty of each person to live according to his own choices, provided he does not attempt to coerce others and thus prevent them from living according to their choices."[13] Such views show clearly the libertarian's association of justice with liberty and of liberty itself with the absence of interference by other persons.

Libertarians firmly reject utilitarianism's concern for total social well-being. Utilitarians are willing to restrict the liberty of some, to interfere with their choices, if doing so will promote greater net happiness than not doing so. Libertarians cannot stomach this. As long as you are not doing something that interferes with anyone else's liberty, then no person, group, or government should disturb you in living the life you choose—not even if their doing so would maximize social happiness.

Although the ideal of individual liberty is one that almost all of us value, it may not be the only thing we value. For the libertarian, however, liberty takes priority over other moral concerns. In particular, justice consists solely in respecting individual liberty. A libertarian world in which there were a complete commitment to individual liberty would be a very different world from the one in which we now live. Consider the following: In 1986, in the case of *Bowers v. Hardwick*, the Supreme Court upheld a Georgia law forbidding sodomy between consenting male homosexuals; the government registers young men for military service and can, if it chooses, draft them; the state imposes taxes on our income to, among many other things, support needy citizens, provide loans to college students, and fund various projects for the common good. None of these policies is just from a libertarian perspective.

Given the assumption that liberty means noninterference, libertarians generally agree that liberty allows only a minimal or "night-watchman" state. Such a state is limited to the narrow functions of protecting against force, theft, and fraud; to the enforcement of contracts; and to other such basic maintenance functions. In this view, a more extensive state—in particular, one that taxes its better-off citizens to support the less fortunate ones—cannot be justified because it violates the liberty of individuals by forcing them to support projects, policies, or persons they have not freely chosen to support.

Nozick's Theory of Justice

Although libertarians differ in how they formulate their theory, Harvard professor Robert Nozick's *Anarchy, State, and Utopia*[14] is a very influential statement of the libertarian case. Nozick's challenging and powerful advocacy of libertarianism has stimulated much debate, obliging philosophers of all political persuasions to take the libertarian theory seriously. His views are, thus, worth presenting in detail.

Nozick begins from the premise that we have certain basic moral rights (e.g., life and liberty). He calls these "Lockean rights," referring to the famous seventeenth-century British philosopher, John Locke (1632–1704). By alluding to Locke's political philosophy,

Nozick wishes to underscore that these rights are (a) negative and (b) natural. They are *negative* because they require only that we refrain from acting in certain ways—in particular, that we refrain from interfering with others. Beyond this, we are not obliged to do anything positive for anyone else, nor is anyone else obliged to do anything positive for us. We have no right, for example, to be provided with satisfying work or with any material goods we might need. These negative rights, according to Nozick, are *natural* in the sense that we possess them independently of any social or political institutions.

These individual rights impose firm, virtually absolute restrictions (or, in Nozick's phrase, "side constraints") on how we may act. That is, we cannot morally infringe someone's rights for any purpose. Not only may we not interfere with a person's liberty in order to promote the general welfare, we are forbidden to do so even if violating that individual's rights would reduce the total number of rights violations. Each individual is autonomous and responsible, and should be left to fashion his or her own life free from the interference of others—as long as this is compatible with the rights of others to do the same. Only the acknowledgment of this almost absolute right to be free from coercion, Nozick argues, fully respects the distinctiveness of persons, each with a unique life to lead.

A belief in these rights shapes Nozick's specific theory of economic justice, which he calls the "entitlement theory." Essentially, Nozick believes that we are entitled to our holdings (i.e., goods, money, and property) so long as we have acquired them fairly. Stated another way, if you have acquired your possessions without violating anyone's Lockean rights, then you are entitled to them and may dispose of them however *you* choose. No one else has a legitimate claim on them. If you have obtained a vast fortune without injuring anyone else, violating their rights, or defrauding them, then you are entitled to do with your fortune whatever you wish—bequeath it to a relative, endow a university, invest it wisely or foolishly, or squander it in riotous living. Even though other people may be going hungry, justice imposes no obligation on you to assist.

Nozick presents his entitlement theory as a function of three basic principles, but he doesn't attempt to specify them in detail. The first of these principles concerns the original acquisition of holdings—that is, the appropriation of unheld goods or the creation of new rights to goods. If a person has acquired a holding in accordance with this principle, then he or she is entitled to that holding. If, for example, you retrieve minerals from the wilderness or make something out of materials you already possess, then you have acquired justly this new holding. Nozick does not spell out this principle or specify fully what constitutes a just original acquisition, but the basic idea is clear, and reflects again the thinking of John Locke.

Property is a moral right, said Locke, by virtue of a human's labor. Individuals are morally entitled to the products of their labor. When they mix their labor with the natural world, they are entitled to the resulting product. Thus if a man works the land, then he is entitled to the land and its products because through his labor he has put something of himself into them. This investment of self through labor is the moral basis of ownership. Locke expressed the case for the moral right to property this way:

> In the beginning . . . Men had a Right to appropriate, by their Labour, each one to himself, as much of the things of Nature, as he could use. . . . The same *measures* governed the *Possession of Land* too: Whatsoever he tilled and reaped, laid up and made use of, before it spoiled, that was his peculiar Right; whatsoever he enclosed, and could feed, and make use of, the Cattle and Product was also his. But if either the Grass of

> his Inclosures rotted on the Ground, or the Fruit of his planting perished without gathering, and laying up, this part of the Earth, notwithstanding his Inclosure, was still to be looked on as Waste, and might be the Possession of any other.[15]

In this early state of nature, property rights are limited not just by the requirement that one not waste what one has claimed, but also by the restriction that "enough and as good" be left for others—that is, others must not be made worse off by one's appropriation. Later, however, with the introduction of money, Locke thinks that both these restrictions are overcome. You can, for example, pile up money beyond your needs without it spoiling; and by using your property productively and offering the proceeds for sale, others are not made worse off by your appropriation.

Nozick's second principle concerns transfers of already-owned goods from one person to another: how people may legitimately transfer holdings and how they may legitimately acquire holdings from others. If a person comes into possession of a holding legitimately, then he or she is entitled to it. Again, Nozick does not formulate the guidelines in detail, but it is clear that acquiring something by purchase, as a gift, or through an exchange would constitute a legitimate acquisition. Acquiring it through theft, force, or fraud would violate the principle of justice in transfer.

The third principle rectifies injustice—that is, violations of a person's rights. Nozick holds that a person who has come by a holding in any way other than by applying the first two principles simply is not entitled to it.

In sum, Nozick believes that if the world were wholly just, the following three principles would completely cover the subject of distributive justice:

1. A person who acquires a holding in accordance with the principle of justice in acquisition is entitled to that holding.

2. A person who acquires a holding in accordance with the principle of justice in transfer, from someone else entitled to the holding, is entitled to the holding.

3. No one is entitled to a holding except by (repeated) applications of 1 and 2.[16]

The complete principle of distributive justice, then, would say: *A distribution is just if persons are entitled to the holdings they possess under the distribution.*

Nozick believes that his entitlement principles have decided advantages over other formulations of distributive justice. Other theories hold that justice is determined by the structure of the present distribution of goods (Is it equal? Does it maximize social utility?), or they require that distribution fit some formula like "To each according to his _____," where the blank is filled in with something like "need," "merit," or "effort." While what counts for these theories is the shape or pattern of economic distribution, what matters for Nozick is how people came to have what they have. If people are entitled to their possessions, then the distribution of economic holdings is just, regardless of what the actual distribution happens to look like (for instance, how many people are above or below the average income). The entitlement theory is historical: Whether a distribution is just depends on how it came about; aside from that, the actual nature of the distribution is irrelevant.

The Wilt Chamberlain Story

In arguing his case for an entitlement approach, Nozick offers some ingenious examples, the most memorable of which concerns Wilt Chamberlain. In the following very famous passage,* he argues that a respect for liberty will inevitably lead one to repudiate

*From *Anarchy, State, and Utopia* by Robert Nozick. Copyright © 1974 by Basic Books, Inc. Reprinted by permission of the publisher.

other conceptions of economic justice in favor of his entitlement approach.

It is not clear how those holding alternative conceptions of distributive justice can reject the entitlement conception of justice in holdings. For suppose a distribution favored by one of these nonentitlement conceptions is realized. Let us suppose it is your favorite one and let us call this distribution D_1; perhaps everyone has an equal share, perhaps shares vary in accordance with some dimension you treasure. Now suppose that Wilt Chamberlain is greatly in demand by basketball teams, being a great gate attraction. . . . He signs the following sort of contract with a team: In each home game, twenty-five cents from the price of each ticket of admission goes to him. . . . The season starts, and people cheerfully attend his team's games; they buy their tickets, each time dropping a separate twenty-five cents of their admission price into a special box with Chamberlain's name on it. They are excited about seeing him play; it is worth the total admission price to them. Let us suppose that in one season one million persons attend his home games, and Wilt Chamberlain winds up with $250,000, a much larger sum than the average income and larger even than anyone else has.

So Wilt Chamberlain has become wealthy and the initial distributional pattern (D_1) has been upset. Can the proponent of D_1 complain about this? Nozick thinks not.

Is [Chamberlain] entitled to this income? Is this new distribution D_2, unjust? If so, why? There is *no* question about whether each of the people was entitled to the control over the resources they held in D_1, because that was the distribution (your favorite) that (for the purposes of argument) we assumed was acceptable. Each of these persons *chose* to give twenty-five cents of their money to

Chamberlain. They could have spent it on going to the movies, or on candy bars, or on copies of *Dissent* magazine, or of *Monthly Review*. But they all, at least one million of them, converged on giving it to Wilt Chamberlain in exchange for watching him play basketball. If D_1 was a just distribution, and people voluntarily moved from it to D_2 transferring parts of their shares they were given under D_1 (what was it for if not to do something with?), isn't D_2 also just? If people were entitled to dispose of the resources to which they were entitled (under D_1), didn't this include their being entitled to give it to, or exchange it with, Wilt Chamberlain? Can anyone else complain on grounds of justice? . . . To cut off objections irrelevant here, we might imagine the exchanges occurring in a socialist society, after hours: After playing whatever basketball he does in his daily work, or doing whatever other daily work he does, Wilt Chamberlain decides to put in *overtime* to earn additional money. (First his work quota is set; he works time over that.) Or imagine it is a skilled juggler people like to see, who puts on shows after hours.

Having defended the legitimacy of Chamberlain's new wealth, Nozick pursues his case further, arguing that any effort to maintain some initial distributional arrangement like D_1 will interfere with people's liberty to use their resources (to which they are entitled under D_1) as they wish. To preserve this original distribution, society would have to "forbid capitalist acts between consenting adults."

Why might someone work overtime in a society in which it is assumed their needs are satisfied? Perhaps because they care about things other than needs. I like to write in books that I read, and to have easy access to books for browsing at odd hours. It would be very pleasant and convenient to have the resources of Widener Library in my back yard. No society, I assume, will provide such

resources close to each person who would like them as part of his regular allotment (under D_1). Thus, persons either must do without some extra things that they want, or be allowed to do something extra to get some of these things. On what basis could the inequalities that would eventuate be forbidden? Notice also that small factories would spring up in a socialist society, unless forbidden. I melt down some of my personal possessions (under D_1) and build a machine out of the material. I offer you, and others, a philosophy lecture once a week in exchange for your cranking the handle on my machine, whose products I exchange for yet other things, and so on. . . . I wish merely to note how private property even in means of production would occur in a socialist society that did not forbid people to use as they wished some of the resources they are given under the socialist distribution D_1. The socialist society would have to forbid capitalist acts between consenting adults.

Nozick argues that any theory of justice other than his will inevitably fail to respect people's liberty. The effort to maintain any specific structure of economic distribution will involve a sacrifice of liberty that Nozick finds unacceptable.

The general point illustrated by the Wilt Chamberlain example and the example of the entrepreneur in a socialist society is that no end-state principle or distributional patterned principle of justice can be continuously realized without continuous interference with people's lives. Any favored pattern would be transformed into one unfavored by the principle, by people choosing to act in various ways; for example, by people exchanging goods and services with other people, or giving things to other people, things the transferrers are entitled to under the favored distributional pattern. To maintain a pattern one must either continually interfere to stop people from transferring resources as they wish to, or continually (or periodically) interfere to take from some persons resources that others for some reason chose to transfer to them.

The Libertarian View of Liberty

In the next chapter we examine the nature of market economies in general and capitalism in particular, but it is clear from what Nozick has said that libertarianism involves a commitment to leaving market relations—buying, selling, and other exchanges—totally unrestricted. Force and fraud are forbidden, of course. But there should be no interference with the uncoerced exchanges of consenting individuals. Not only is the market morally legitimate, but any attempt to interfere with consenting and nonfraudulent transactions between adults will be unacceptable. Thus, libertarians are for economic laissez-faire and against any governmental economic activity that interferes with the marketplace, even if the point of the interference is to enhance the performance of the economy.

It is important to emphasize that libertarianism's enthusiasm for the market rests upon this commitment to liberty. By contrast, utilitarian defenders of the market defend it on the ground that an unregulated market works better than either a planned, socialist economy or the sort of regulated capitalism with some welfare benefits that we in fact have in the United States. That is, if a utilitarian defends laissez-faire, he or she does so because of its consequences. Convince a utilitarian that some other form of economic organization better promotes human well-being, and the utilitarian will advocate that instead. With libertarians this is definitely not the case. As a matter of fact, libertarians typically agree with Adam Smith that unregulated capitalist behavior best promotes everyone's interests. But even if, hypothetically, someone like Nozick were convinced that some

sort of socialism or welfare capitalism outperforms laissez-faire capitalism economically—greater productivity, shorter working day, higher standard of living—he or she would still reject this alternative as morally unacceptable. To tinker with the market, however beneficial it might be, would involve violating someone's liberty.

This libertarian conviction reflects, of course, the priority that the theory puts on liberty over all other values. In addition, it reflects the way in which the theory understands liberty. As we have seen, libertarians believe that we have certain natural, Lockean rights not to be interfered with. But we have no basic rights to assistance from others or to be provided with anything by society, not even an equal opportunity to compete with others. Libertarians understand liberty in terms of their conception of rights and thus operate with a distinctive and controversial definition of liberty. Let's consider a couple of examples.

Suppose, first, that Horace lives in a poor country and has fallen into desperate financial circumstances, perhaps because a natural disaster has destroyed his small farm. His only alternative is to accept your offer of long, hard work on your plantation in return for just enough food to keep him alive. Normally, one might say that Horace was coerced by circumstances and even that your wage offer was exploitative, but a libertarian would disagree on both counts. No one has violated Horace's rights; therefore, he has been neither coerced nor exploited. The agreement was a free and voluntary one.

Or suppose that I want to take a boat out for a spin on the lake. Having none, I attempt to take yours, which is sitting moored and idle. If the harbor police stop me, they have prevented me from doing what I want to do. But according to libertarianism, they have not interfered with my liberty. Why not? Because my "borrowing" the boat would have violated your rights, as the owner of the boat.

In both cases, libertarians seem driven to an unusual and controversial use of familiar terminology, but they have no choice. Libertarianism does not value liberty simply in the sense of people doing what they want. One has liberty only to do that which does not violate someone else's Lockean rights; likewise, one is coerced only when one's rights are violated. If libertarians admit that Horace has been coerced or that allowing me to use the boat would expand my liberty, then their theory would be in jeopardy. They would have to acknowledge that restricting some people's liberty could enhance the liberty of others. In other words, if their theory committed them simply to promoting as much as possible people doing what they want to do, then libertarians would be in the position of balancing the freedom of one against the freedom of another. For instance, restrictions on the market behavior of some might make it possible for others to do more effectively the things they want to do. But this sort of balancing and trading off is just what libertarians dislike about utilitarianism and want to avoid at all costs.

Markets and Free Exchange

Libertarians defend market relations, then, as necessary to respect human liberty (as their theory defines liberty). But they do not maintain that, morally speaking, people *deserve* what they receive from others through gift or exchange, only that they are *entitled* to that which they receive. The market tends generally, libertarians believe, to reward people for skill, diligence, and successful performance. Yet luck plays a role, too. Hank makes a fortune from having been in the right place at the right time with his Hula Hoops, while Karen loses her investment because the market for designer jeans collapses. Nozick is quite clear that the libertarian position is not that Tom deserves to be wealthy (and Karen does not). Rather, it is that Tom is entitled to his holdings

if he has acquired them in accordance with the principles of justice.

The same point comes up with regard to gifts in general and inheritance in particular. Critics of libertarianism sometimes contend that inheritance is patently unfair. Is it just, they ask, that one child at birth should inherit a vast fortune, the best schooling, and social, political, and business connections that will insure its future, while another child inherits indigence, inferior schooling, and connections with crime? At birth neither baby *deserves* anything—a fact suggesting that an equal division of holdings and opportunities is the only fair allocation.

For his part, Nozick contends that deserving has no bearing on the justice of inherited wealth; people are simply entitled to it as long as it was not ill-gotten. Or looking at it the other way, if one is entitled to one's holdings, then one is permitted to do with them what one wishes, including using them to benefit one's children. (The justice of inheritance is explored in more detail by D. W. Haslett in "Is Inheritance Justified?" which begins on page 128.)

According to libertarians, totally free market relations are necessary if people are to be allowed to exercise their fundamental rights. In certain circumstances, however, market relations can lead to disastrous results. Unfortunately, this is not just a theoretical possibility. In an important recent study of several of this century's worst famines, Professor Amartya Sen of Oxford University has shown how, in certain circumstances, changing market entitlements, the economic dynamics of which he attempts to unravel, have led to mass starvation.[17] Although the average person thinks of famine as caused simply by a shortage of food, Sen and other experts have pointed out that famines are frequently accompanied by no shortfall of food in absolute terms. Indeed, even more food may be available during a famine than in nonfamine years—if one has the money to buy it. Famine occurs because large numbers of people lack the financial wherewithal to obtain the necessary food.

For example, given the interconnectedness of nations, people in underdeveloped countries can be seriously hurt through fluctuation in commodity prices. So reliant are some of these countries on one or another commodity (for example, tobacco, coffee, cocoa, sugar) that a sharp drop in its prices can result in mass starvation. Plummeting prices are not always the result of acts of nature, such as floods or droughts. At least sometimes they result from the profit-motivated manipulation of investors and brokers—case in point: the 1974 famine in the Sahelian region of Africa and the Indian subcontinent.

Experts attribute the famine partly to climatic shifts and partly to increased oil prices that raised the price of human necessities: fertilizer and grains such as wheat. Here is how two agronomists accounted for the human loss: "The recent doubling in international prices of essential foodstuffs will, of necessity, be reflected in high death rates among the world's lowest income groups, who lack the income to increase their food expenditures proportionately, but live on diets near the subsistence level to begin with."[18] Philosopher Onora O'Neill has called the resulting deaths "killings." "To the extent that the raising of oil prices is an achievement of Arab diplomacy and oil company management rather than a windfall," she writes, "the consequent deaths are killings."[19]

Libertarians would find it immoral and unjust to coerce people to give food or money to the starving. Nor does justice require that a wealthy merchant assist the hungry children in his community in order to save their lives. And it would certainly violate the merchant's property rights for the children to help themselves to his excess food. Nevertheless, while justice does not require that one assist those in need, libertarians would generally acknowledge that we have some humanitarian

obligations toward others. Accordingly, they would not only permit, but also presumably encourage, people to assist others in various voluntary ways. Justice does not require the merchant to donate, and it forbids us from forcing him to do so, but charity on his part would be a good thing. This reflects the libertarian's firm commitment to property rights: What you have legitimately acquired is yours to do with as you will.

Property Rights

Nozick's theory, as we have seen, makes property rights virtually sacrosanct. From the perspective of libertarianism, property rights grow out of one's basic moral rights, either reflecting one's initial creation or appropriation of the product, some sort of exchange or transfer between consenting persons, or a combination of these. Property rights exist prior to any social arrangements and are morally antecedent to any legislative decisions that a society might make. Because of this, Nozick believes, for instance, that justice forbids taxation for redistributive purposes. "Taxation of earnings from labor," he writes, "is on a par with forced labor."

In speaking of ownership and of property rights, however, we must avoid oversimplification. We must not assume that property is merely a physical object. In the popular mind, "property" is synonymous with some *thing*: a car, a watch, a house, a piece of land.

But property is also a bundle of rights and interests. According to professor of philosophy Virginia Held, the set of rights implied in the concept of property comprises the rights to possess, use, manage, dispose of, and restrict others' access to things.[20] And property implies a set of interests in the sense that if our ownings become worthless we no longer have property.

It is true, of course, that property rights and interests often relate to physical objects. But in developed societies, as Held notes, property rights and interests can be more complicated. Thus we have rights to pay our debts with the balances in our bank accounts and interests that the currency they represent not be devalued; rights to dividends from our corporate investments and interests in the company's paying as big a dividend as possible; rights to a pension plan we have joined and interests in the plan's solvency; rights to social security when we satisfy specific conditions and interests in the integrity of the social security system. In identifying property with things, then, we may overlook that the aforementioned rights and interests are all aspects of property.

Thus, it is wrong to think of property ownership as some simple relationship. Rather, ownership involves all the rules and regulations governing the legal acquisition and transfer of various goods, interests, and claims. Accordingly, many nonlibertarian social and political theorists maintain that property rights are a function of the particular institutions of a given society. Ownership involves a bundle of different rights, and the nature of this bundle differs, as do the types of things that can be owned, between societies. The nature of ownership can also change over time in any given society. As a general trend, the social restrictions on property ownership in the United States have increased dramatically during our history (much to the displeasure of libertarians). This is not to say a society's property arrangements cannot be criticized. On the contrary, they can be morally assessed just as any other institution can.

RAWLS'S THEORY OF JUSTICE

A Theory of Justice[21] by Harvard University's John Rawls is generally thought to be the single most influential work of the postwar period in social and political philosophy, at least in the English language. Not only has Rawls's elegant theory touched a responsive chord in many readers, but also, since its appearance in 1971, his book has helped to rejuvenate serious work in normative theory. Even those who are not persuaded by Rawls find themselves obliged to come to terms with his thinking. Although Rawls's basic approach is not difficult to explain (and Rawls himself had sketched out his key concepts in earlier articles), *A Theory of Justice* elaborates Rawls's ideas with such painstaking care and philosophical thoroughness that even vigorous critics of the book (like his colleague Robert Nozick) pay sincere tribute to its many virtues.

By his own account, Rawls presents his theory as a modern alternative to utilitarianism, one that he hopes will be compatible with the belief that justice must be associated with fairness and the moral equality of persons. Rawls firmly wishes to avoid reducing justice to a matter of social utility. At the same time, his approach differs fundamentally from that of Nozick. Rawls conceives of society as a cooperative venture among its members, and he elaborates a conception of justice that is thoroughly social. He does not base his theory, as Nozick does, on the postulate that individuals possess certain natural rights prior to any political or social organization.

There are two main features of Rawls's theory that are particularly important for our purposes: (1) his hypothetical contract approach, and (2) the principles of justice that he derives with it. Rawls's strategy is to ask what we would choose as the fundamental principles to govern society if, hypothetically, we were to meet for this purpose in what he calls the "original position." He then elaborates the nature of this original position, the constraints on the choice facing us, and the reasoning that he thinks people in the original position would follow. In this way, Rawls offers a modern variant of *social contract* theory, in the tradition of Hobbes, Locke, Rousseau, and other earlier philosophers. Rawls argues that people in the original position would agree on two principles as the basic governing principles of their society, and that these principles are, accordingly, the principles of justice. We will examine these principles at some length in a later section, but briefly, the first is a guarantee of certain familiar and fundamental liberties to each person, and the second—more controversial—holds in part that social and economic inequalities are justified only if those inequalities benefit the least advantaged members of society.

The Original Position

Theorists have, as we have seen, proposed various principles of economic justice, but an important question for philosophers is whether, and how, any such principles can be justified. Thinking of possible principles of economic distribution is not all that difficult, but proving the soundness of such a principle, or at least showing it to be more plausible than its rivals, is a challenging task. After all, people seem to differ in their intuitions about what is just and unjust, and their sentiments are bound to be influenced by their social position. Nozick's entitlement theory, for example, with its priority on property rights, is bound to seem more plausible to a corporate executive than to a migrant farm worker. The justice of some children being born into wealth, while other children struggle by on welfare, will not seem as obvious to the poor as it may to the well-to-do.

The strategy Rawls employs to identify and justify some foundational principle or principles of justice is to imagine that people come together for the purpose of deciding on the ground rules for their society, in particular on the rules governing economic distribution. While groups of people have in the past written down constitutions and similar political documents, never have the members of a society decided from scratch on the basic principles of justice that should govern them. Nor is it even remotely likely that people will do this in the future. What Rawls imagines is a *thought experiment*. The question is hypothetical: What principles *would* people choose if they were in this sort of original position? If we can identify these principles, Rawls contends, then we will have identified the principles of justice just because they are the principles that we would all have agreed to.

The Nature of the Choice. On what basis are we to choose these principles? The most obvious answer is that we should select those principles that strike us as just. But this won't work. Even if we are all agreed on what is just and unjust, we simply would be relying on our already existing ideas about justice as a basis for choosing the principles to govern our society. Philosophically, this doesn't accomplish anything. We would simply be going in a circle, using our existing conception of justice to "prove" the principles of justice.

Rawls suggests instead that we imagine that people in the original position choose solely on the basis of self-interest. That is, each individual is concerned to choose that set of principles for governing society that will be best for himself or herself (and his or her loved ones). We don't have to imagine that people are antagonistic to each other or that outside of the original position they are selfish; we just imagine that they hope to get the group to choose those principles that will, more than any other possible principles, benefit them. If people in the original position can agree on some governing principles on the basis of mutual self-interest, then these principles will be, Rawls thinks, the principles of justice. Why? Because the principles are agreed to under conditions of equality and free choice. By analogy, if we make up a game, nobody can later complain that the rules were unfair if we all agreed ahead of time, freely and equally, on how the game was to be played.

The Veil of Ignorance. If people in the original position are supposed to choose principles on the basis of self-interest, agreement seems unlikely. If Carolyn has vast real estate holdings, she will certainly want rules that guarantee her extensive property rights, while her tenants are likely to advocate rules that permit, say, rent control. Likewise, the wealthy will tend to advocate rules rather like Nozick's entitlement theory, while those without property will, on the basis of their self-interest, desire a redistribution of property. Conflicts of self-interest seem bound to create totally irreconcilable demands. For instance, artists may contend that they should be rewarded more than professional people, men that they should earn more than women, and laborers that they merit more than people with desk jobs.

Agreement seems unlikely, given that some rules would benefit one group while other rules would benefit another. As a way around this problem, Rawls asks us to imagine that the people in the original position do not know what social position or status they hold in society. They do not know whether they are rich or poor, and they do not know their personal talents and characteristics—whether, for example, they are athletic or sedentary, artistic or tone-deaf, intelligent or not very bright, physically sound or handicapped in some way. Behind what Rawls calls "the veil of ignorance," the people in the original position know nothing about themselves personally or about what their individual situation will be once the rules are chosen and the veil is lifted. They do not know their race or even their sex. They do, however, have a general knowledge of history, sociology, and psychology—although no specific information about the society they will be in once the veil is lifted.

Under the veil of ignorance, the people in Rawls's original position have no knowledge about themselves or their situation that would lead them to argue from a partial or biased point of view. No individual is likely to argue that some particular group—such as white men, property owners, star athletes, philoso-

phers—should receive special social and economic privileges when, for all that individual knows, he or she will be nonwhite, propertyless, unathletic, and bored by philosophy when the veil is lifted. Because individuals in the original position are all equally ignorant of their personal predicament and they are all trying to advance their self-interest, agreement is possible. The reasoning of any one person will be the same as the reasoning of each of the others, for each is in identical circumstances and each has the same motivation. As a result, no actual group has to perform Rawls's thought experiment. People who read Rawls's theory can imagine that they are in the original position and then decide whether they would choose the principles Rawls thinks they would.

The veil of ignorance, in effect, forces people in the original position to be objective and impartial and makes agreement possible. Also, according to Rawls, the fact that people have no special knowledge that would allow them to argue in a biased way accords with our sense of fairness. The circumstances of the original position are genuinely equal and fair, and because of this, the principles agreed to under these conditions have a good claim to be considered the principles of justice.

Choosing the Principles

Although people in the original position are ignorant of their individual circumstances, they know that whatever their particular goals, interests, and talents turn out to be, they will want more, rather than less, of what Rawls calls the "primary social goods." These include not just income and wealth, but rights, liberties, opportunities, status, and self-respect, as well. Of course, once people are outside of the veil of ignorance, they will have more specific ideas about what is good for them—they may choose a life built around religion, or one spent in commerce and industry, or one devoted to academic study. But whatever these particular individual goals, interests, and plans turn out to be, they will almost certainly be furthered, and definitely never limited, by the fact that people in the original position secured for themselves more rather than less in the way of primary goods.

How, then, will people in the original position choose their principles? *A Theory of Justice* explores in depth the reasoning that Rawls thinks would guide their choice. At the heart of Rawls's argument is the contention that people in the original position will be conservative, in the sense that they will not wish to gamble with their futures. In setting up the ground rules for their society, they are determining their own fate and that of their children. This is not something to be taken lightly, a game to be played and replayed. Rather, with so much at stake, people will reason cautiously.

Consider, for example, the possibility of setting up a feudal-type society: 10 percent of the population will be nobles, living a life of incredible wealth, privilege, and leisure; the other 90 percent will be serfs, toiling away long hours to support the extravagant lifestyles of the aristocracy. Perhaps we can imagine some people thinking that the joy of being a pampered noble would be so great that they would vote for such an arrangement behind the veil of ignorance. But they would be banking on a long shot. When the veil of ignorance is lifted, the odds are nine-to-one that they will be poor and miserable serfs, not lords. Rawls thinks that people in the original position will not, in fact, look at things this way. They will not wish to gamble with their futures, and they will shy away from such risks. They will not agree to rules that make it overwhelmingly likely that they will have to face a grim life of hardship.

Rawls argues that for similar reasons people in the original position will not adopt the utilitarian standard to govern their society, though this might seem like a good idea, since the utilitarian principle would guarantee that society is organized in a way that would maximize the happiness of its members. However, as we have seen in Chapter 2, the utilitarian standard is concerned with *total* happiness and not, or at least not directly, with how that happiness is distributed. Thus, it is possible that under the utilitarian standard the well-being of some might be sacrificed in order to enhance the overall total happiness of society. People in the original position, Rawls argues, will not be willing to chance this. They will not relish running the risk that, once the veil of ignorance is lifted, it is their own happiness that has to be sacrificed for the greater good.

What people in the original position would actually do, Rawls believes, is follow what game strategists call the *maximin* rule for making decisions under certain particular circumstances. This rule says that you should elect the alternative under which the worst that could happen to you is better than the worst that could happen to you under any other alternative. That is, you should try to *maxi*mize the *min*imum that you will receive; hence the term *maximin*. This rule makes sense when you care much more about avoiding an unacceptable or disastrous result (such as being a serf) than about getting the best possible result (say, being a noble), and when you have no real idea what odds you are facing. It is a conservative decision principle, but Rawls thinks that people in the original position will find it a rational and appropriate guideline for their deliberations.

Rawls's Two Principles

Rawls argues that as people in the original position consider various alternatives, they will eventually be led to endorse two principles as the most basic governing principles of their society. As we have noted, these principles, because they would be agreed to in an initial situation of equality and fairness, are the principles of justice. In *A Theory of Justice* Rawls imagines that once these two principles of justice are decided, the people in the original position are gradually given more and more information about their specific society. With this information, and guided by these principles, they go on to design their basic social and political institutions in more detail. Rawls states these two basic principles of justice as follows:

> 1. Each person has an equal right to the most extensive scheme of equal basic liberties compatible with a similar scheme of liberties for all.
> 2. Social and economic inequalities are to meet two conditions: they must be (a) to the greatest expected benefit of the least advantaged; and (b) attached to offices and positions open to all under conditions of fair opportunity.[22]

According to Rawls, the first principle takes priority over the second, at least for societies that have attained a moderate level of affluence. The liberties Rawls has in mind are the traditional democratic ones of freedom of thought, conscience, and religious worship, as well as freedom of the person and political liberty. Explicitly absent are "the right to own certain kinds of property (e.g., means of production), and freedom of contract as understood by the doctrine of laissez-faire."[23] The first principle guarantees not only equal liberty to individuals, but also that each person have as much liberty as possible, compatible with others having the same amount of liberty. There is no reason why people in the original position would settle for anything less than this.

All regulations could be seen as infringing on personal liberty, since they limit what a person may do. The law that requires you to drive on the right-hand side of the road denies you the freedom to drive on either side whenever you wish. Some would argue that justice requires only an *equal* liberty. For example, as long as every motorist is required to drive on the right-hand side of the road, justice is being served; or if everyone in a dictatorial society is forbidden to criticize the leader's decisions, then all are equal in their liberty. But Rawls argues that if a more extensive liberty were possible, without inhibiting the liberty of others, then it would be irrational to settle for a lesser degree of liberty. In the case of driving, permitting me to drive on either side of the road would only interfere with the liberty of others to drive efficiently to their various destinations, while introducing right-turn-on-red laws would enhance everyone's liberty. In the dictatorship example, free speech could be more extensive without limiting anyone's liberty.

The second principle concerns social and economic inequalities. Regarding inequalities, Rawls writes,

> it is best to understand not *any* differences between offices and positions, but differences in the benefits and burdens attached to them either directly or indirectly, such as prestige and wealth, or liability to taxation and compulsory services. Players in a game do not protest against there being different positions, such as batter, pitcher, catcher, and the like, nor to there being various privileges and powers as specified by the rules; nor do the citizens of a country object to there being the different offices of government such as president, senator, governor, judge, and so on, each with their special rights and duties.[24]

Rather, at issue are differences in wealth and power, honors and rewards, privileges and salaries, that attach to different roles in society.

Part (b) of Rawls's second principle states that insofar as inequalities are permitted—that is, insofar as it is compatible with justice for some jobs or positions to bring greater rewards than others—these positions must be open to all. In other words, there must be meaningful equality of opportunity in the competition among individuals for those positions in society that bring greater economic and social rewards. This, of course, is a familiar principle, and few in our society would defend a policy of reserving to special groups the opportunity to pursue certain careers.

Part (a) of the second principle, sometimes called the *Difference Principle*, is less familiar and more controversial. It is, however, the distinctive core of Rawls's theory. It states that inequalities are justified only if they work to the benefit of the least advantaged group in society. By "least advantaged" Rawls simply means the group that is the least well off group in society. But what does it mean to require that inequalities work to the benefit of this group?

Imagine that we are back in the original position. People there wish to make sure that under the principles they choose the worst that happens to them once the veil of ignorance is lifted is still better than the worst that might have happened to them under some alternative arrangement. One might, therefore, figure that they would choose strict social and economic equality. With an equal division of goods, there's no risk of doing worse than anyone else, no danger of being sacrificed to the greatest total happiness. And in the case of liberty, people in the original position do insist on full equality. But with social and economic inequality, the matter is a little different.

Suppose, for instance, that as a result of dividing things up equally, people lacked an incentive to undertake some of the more difficult work that society needs done. It might then be the case that allowing certain inequalities, for example, paying people more for being particularly productive or for undertaking the necessary training to perform some socially useful task, would work to everyone's benefit, including those who would now be earning less than the others. If so, then why not permit those inequalities? Compare the following two diagrams:

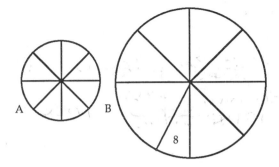

Each pie represents a possible social and economic distribution among eight basic groups (the number eight is arbitrary) in society. In Figure A, things are divided equally; in Figure B, unequally. Now what we are trying to imagine is that, if a society permits inequalities as an incentive to get people to work harder or to do work that they would not have wanted to do otherwise, then the overall amount to be distributed among the members of society will be greater. That is, the economic pie will increase in size from A to B, and the person with the thinnest slice of B will be better off than they would have been with an equal slice of A.

Which society will people in the original position prefer? Obviously the one represented by Figure B, because the minimum they can attain in B (slice #8) is more than any of the eight equal slices in A. People in the original position do not care about equality of distribution as a value in and of itself; they want the social and economic arrangement that will provide them with the highest minimum. Rawls is not trying to prove that economic inequalities will always, or even usually, "trickle down" to the least advantaged (though, of course, some people believe that). Rather, his point is simply that people in the original position would not insist on social and economic equality at all costs. *If* permitting some people to be better off than the average resulted in the least well off segment of society being better off than it would have been otherwise (under a strictly equal division), then this is what people in the original position will want. Rawls's Difference Principle is intended to capture this idea. While Rawls's principles permit economic inequalities, these inequalities are justified only if they do in fact benefit the least advantaged.

In 1986 Congress raised the pay of various federal employees, including federal judges. Federal judges were, from one perspective, already paid well, with salaries (around $100,000 per year) several times the national income average. But their annual pay was nonetheless boosted by about $30,000. Administration officials defended this handsome raise on the grounds that it was necessary to get talented people, who might otherwise remain in the lucrative world of corporate law, to take up judgeships. Critics like Ralph Nader countered that there were many highly qualified lawyers for whom the original salary would have meant a pay raise (for example, law professors), or who would be willing to accept a judgeship, even if it meant a pay cut, for the professional prestige and challenge as well as out of a sense of public service.

Applying Rawls's Difference Principle to this case, the crucial question is whether increasing the pay of federal judges works to the advantage of everyone, including those who are least advantaged. That is, does the expenditure of tax money to increase the salaries of federal judges benefit the disadvantaged members of our society more than any other way of spending that money? The answer, in this case, is probably no.

This is only an illustration, however, and we must remember that Rawls intends his principles to be used, not as a guide to day-to-day policy decisions, but rather as the basis for determining what form society's primary social, political, and economic institutions should take in the first place. What will these institutions look like? More specifically, what sort of economic system will best satisfy Rawls's Difference Principle? Rawls himself does not answer this question. He sees it as primarily a question for economists and other social scientists, while the task of philosophers like himself is the preliminary one of working out a satisfactory conception of justice. Rawls does appear to believe, however, that a liberal form of capitalism, with sufficient welfare provisions, would satisfy his principles, but he does not rule out the possibility that a democratic socialist system could as well.

Fairness and the Basic Structure

We have seen that Rawls intends his theory as a fundamental alternative to utilitarianism, which he rejects on the grounds that, in order to maximize the total well-being of society, it could permit an unfair and unequal distribution of burdens and benefits among the different members of society. Utilitarianism, in Rawls's view, treats people's pleasures and pains as completely interchangeable—a decrease of happiness *here* is justified by greater happiness *there*. Within a person's own life, such trade-offs are sensible. An increase of pain now (as the dentist fills a cavity in my tooth) is justified in terms of greater happiness later (no painful, rotted tooth). But between individuals, as when Jack's happiness is decreased in order to provide Jill with a more-than-compensating gain, such trade-offs are morally problematic.

Thus, Rawls stresses that, in his view,

> each person possesses an inviolability founded on justice that even the welfare of society as a whole cannot override. . . . Therefore, . . . the rights secured by justice are not subject to political bargaining or to the calculus of social interests.[25]

And he emphasizes that the Difference Principle

> excludes, therefore, the justification of inequalities on the grounds that the disadvantages of those in one position are outweighed by the greater advantages of those in another position. This rather simple restriction is the main modifica-

tion I wish to make in the utilitarian principle as usually understood.[26]

On the other hand, Rawls is equally unsympathetic to the approach adopted by Nozick. Contrary to the entitlement theory, he argues that the primary subject of justice is not, in the first instance, transactions between individuals, but rather "the basic structure, the fundamental social institutions and their arrangement into one scheme." Why?

> First of all, any discussion of social justice must take the nature of the basic structure into account. Suppose we begin with the initially attractive idea that the social process should be allowed to develop over time as free agreements fairly arrived at and fully honored require. Straightaway we need an account of when agreements are free and the conditions under which they are reached are fair. In addition, while these conditions may be satisfied at an earlier time, the accumulated results of agreements in conjunction with social and historical contingencies are likely to change institutions and opportunities so that the conditions for free and fair agreements no longer hold. The basic structure specifies the background conditions against which the actions of individuals, groups, and associations take place. Unless this structure is regulated and corrected so as to be just over time, the social process with its procedures and outcomes is no longer just, however free and fair particular transactions may look to us when viewed by themselves. We recognise this principle when we say that the distribution resulting from voluntary market transactions will not in general be fair unless the antecedent distribution of income and wealth and the structure of the market is fair. Thus we seem forced to start with an account of a just basic structure.[27]

Additional considerations support taking the basic structure of society as the primary subject of justice, in particular the fact that the basic structure shapes the wants, desires, hopes, and ambitions of individuals. Thus, Rawls continues,

> it has always been recognised that the social system shapes the desires and aspirations of its members; it determines in large part the kind of persons they want to be as well as the kind of persons they are. Thus an economic system is not only an institutional device for satisfying existing wants and desires but a way of fashioning wants and desires in the future.

Rawls concludes his discussion by stressing that because the basic structure is the proper focus of a theory of justice, we cannot expect that the principles that apply to it are simply an extension of the principles that govern everyday individual transactions.

> The justice of the basic structure is, then, of predominant importance. The first problem of justice is to determine the principles to regulate inequalities and to adjust the profound and long-lasting effects of social, natural, and historical contingencies, particularly since these contingencies combined with inequalities generate tendencies that, when left to themselves, are sharply at odds with the freedom and equality appropriate for a well-ordered society. In view of the special role of the basic structure, we cannot assume that the principles suitable to it are natural applications, or even extensions, of the familiar principles governing the actions of individuals and associations in everyday life which take place within its framework. Most likely we shall have to loosen ourselves from our ordinary perspective and take a more comprehensive viewpoint.

Benefits and Burdens

The passages we have quoted touch on a theme that is central to Rawls's theory: Inevitably, there will be natural differences between human beings—in terms of physical prowess, mental agility, and so on. But there is nothing natural or inevitable about the weight attached by society to those differences. For Rawls, a desirable feature of any account of justice is that it strive to minimize the social consequences of purely arbitrary, natural differences. He stresses that no one deserves his or her particular natural characteristics. We cannot say that Robert Redford deserves to be handsome or that Albert Einstein deserved to be blessed with an excellent mind anymore than we can say that Fred merits his shortness or Pamela her nearsightedness. Their attributes are simply the result of a genetic lottery. But Rawls goes beyond this to argue that even personal characteristics like diligence and perseverance reflect the environment in which one was raised:

> It seems to be one of the fixed points of our considered judgments that no one deserves his place in the distribution of native endowments, any more than one deserves one's initial starting place in society. The assertion that a man deserves the superior character that enables him to make the effort to cultivate his abilities is equally problematic; for his character depends in large part upon fortunate family and social circumstances for which he can claim no credit. The notion of desert seems not to apply to these cases.[28]

Accordingly, Rawls thinks we cannot really claim moral credit for our special talents or even our virtuous character. In Rawls's view, then, if our personal characteristics are not something that we deserve, we have no strong claim to the economic rewards they might bring. On the contrary, justice requires that the social and economic consequences of these arbitrarily distributed assets be minimized.

> We see then that the difference principle represents, in effect, an agreement to regard the distribution of natural talents as a common asset and to share in the benefits of this distribution whatever it turns out to be. Those who have been favored by nature, whoever they are, may gain from their good fortune only on terms that improve the situation of those who have lost out. The naturally advantaged are not to gain merely because they are more gifted, but only to cover the costs of training and education and for using their endowments in ways that help the less fortunate as well. No one deserves his greater natural capacity nor merits a more favorable starting place in society. But it does not follow that one should eliminate these distinctions. There is another way to deal with them. The basic structure can be arranged so that these contingencies work for the good of the least fortunate. Thus we are led to the difference principle if we wish to set up the social system so that no one gains or loses from his arbitrary place in the distribution of natural assets or his initial position in society without giving or receiving compensating advantages in return.[29]

This important passage from *A Theory of Justice* reflects well Rawls's vision of society as a cooperative project for mutual benefit.

SUMMARY

1. Justice is one important aspect of morality. Talk of justice and injustice generally involves appeals to the related notions of rights, fairness, equality, or desert. Economic or distributive justice concerns the principles appropriate for assessing society's distribution of social benefits and burdens, in particular, wealth, income, status, and power.

2. Economic distribution might be based on pure equality, need, effort, social contribution, or merit. Each of these principles

is plausible in some circumstances but not in others. In some situations the principles pull us in different directions. Dissatisfied with this fact, some moral philosophers have sought to develop more general theories of justice.

3. Utilitarianism holds that the maximization of happiness ultimately determines what is just and unjust. Mill contends, more specifically, that the concept of justice identifies certain very important social utilities and that injustice involves the violation of the rights of some specific individual.

4. Utilitarians must examine a number of factual issues in order to determine for themselves which economic system and principles will best promote social well-being or happiness. Many utilitarians view favorably (1) an increase of worker participation and (2) a more equal distribution of income.

5. The libertarian theory identifies justice with liberty, which libertarians understand as living according to our own choices, free from the interference of others. They reject utilitarianism's concern for total social well-being.

6. The libertarian philosopher Robert Nozick defends the "entitlement theory." His theory holds that the distribution of goods, money, and property is just if people are entitled to what they have; that is, if they have acquired their possessions without violating the rights of anyone else.

7. In the story of Wilt Chamberlain, Nozick argues that theories of economic justice not in accord with his will inevitably fail to respect people's liberty.

8. Libertarians operate with a distinctive concept of liberty, they defend free exchange and laissez-faire markets without regard to results, they put a priority on liberty over all other values, and they see property rights as existing prior to any social arrangements. Critics contest each of these features of libertarianism.

9. John Rawls's approach lies within the social contract tradition. He asks us to imagine people meeting in the "original position" to choose the basic principles that are to govern their society. Although in this original position people choose on the basis of self-interest, we are to imagine that they are behind a "veil of ignorance." This means that they do not have any personal information about themselves. Rawls contends that any principles agreed to under these circumstances have a strong claim to be considered the principles of justice.

10. Rawls argues that people in the original position would follow the *maximin* rule for making decisions. They would choose principles that would guarantee that the worst that could happen to them is better than the worst that could happen to them under any rival principles. Rawls argues that they would agree on two principles. The first principle states that each person has a right to the most extensive scheme of liberties compatible with others having the same amount of liberty. The second principle states that any inequalities must be (1) to the greatest expected benefit of the least advantaged and (2) open to all under conditions of fair opportunity.

11. Rawls rejects utilitarianism because it might permit an unfair distribution of burdens and benefits. Contrary to the entitlement theory, he argues that the primary focus of justice should be the basic social structure, not transactions between individuals. He contends that society is a cooperative project for mutual benefit and that justice requires that the social and economic consequences of arbitrary natural differences among people be minimized.

CASE 3.1

Whatever Happened to the Steel Industry?

Steel was the core of American industry—the heavy metal basis for a productive system that was the envy of the world. Pittsburgh, Youngstown, and other communities in our industrial heartland symbolized that productive system. Built around the steel industry, they were hard-working, tough, proud, and patriotic—the home turf of athletes like Joe Namath and Stan Musial. Steel was good for those cities, for the people who made it, and for the country.

For generations, an implicit social contract had existed in those steel towns. Since the early 1940s, the companies had recognized the union; the union had left investment decisions to the companies; and steelworker families had bought homes, sent children to college for the first time, and retired on pensions.[30] But now, sadly, that world has come to an end. The steel industry has collapsed.

While as recently as the 1970s Youngstown, Ohio, and neighboring Pittsburgh were employing more than 100,000 steelworkers, by the late 1980s little or no steel was being made in either community. (Nationwide, there were 400,000 workers in basic steel in 1980, but only 155,000 in 1987.)[31] The steel communities were traumatized; their life support had been ripped out. As one local union president remarked, "You felt as if the mill would always be there." But now it was all over. The vice-president of another local union said: "Most people couldn't believe it. It was so huge and had operated so long and so many people depended on it for their livelihood." More than one steelworker in Youngstown indicated that the only thing they had experienced like it was Pearl Harbor.

From 1977 to 1986, the steel companies presented an unchanging public message: They were anxious to modernize their mills and to continue making steel. But they lacked capital. Through no fault of their own, the steel companies claimed, but as the result of restrictive environmental regulation, high union wages and benefits, and the unfair dumping in American markets of foreign, government-subsidized steel, they found themselves unable to make steel profitably and were therefore unable to accumulate the necessary capital for updating American steel mills technologically.

Initially, communities like Youngstown and Pittsburgh accepted this message and threw their political support behind the companies. When the first major mill closing occurred in 1977, union leaders petitioned Congress to impose emergency quotas on foreign steel. Yet, the attitude of the communities and the workers gradually changed. A string of broken promises led them to doubt the sincerity of the steel industry's claim that it sought to invest in steel. As lawyer and community activist Staughton Lynd reports,

> Painfully it was learned that the problem went beyond the companies' lack of commitment to existing mills. The companies were not even committed to steel. They would "flow" investment capital to whatever investment opportunity was most profitable. They would take money created by steelworkers and use it to buy real estate, chemical companies, savings and loan associations, insurance companies and oil fields.

The steel companies were disinvesting from steel. Symbolically, U.S. Steel changed its name to USX. They were getting out of the steel business.

In the fight against the plant shutdowns that were destroying their communities, local activists and union members were led to two conclusions. First, because the steel industry bases its investment decisions on the effort to maximize profits in the short run, steel companies were postponing needed modernization in order to invest outside the steel industry where the rate of profit is higher. Second, because of its capital-intensive character, steel will probably continue to yield a lower rate of profit than other investment opportunities. Tinkering with external factors (environmental regulation, depreciation allowances, import quotas, currency exchange rates, and so on) in order to induce the steel companies to make a socially desirable investment in steel is a policy that has failed.

In light of the shutdowns and the above conclusions, lots of new, even radical, ideas began to circulate in the traditionally conservative steel towns. One response was the emergence of the idea of "eminent domain," championed by Lynd and others. Legally, eminent domain is the sovereign's power to take private property for public use against the owner's will, subject to the constitutional requirement that "just compensation" be paid. Applied to the crisis in steel, eminent domain is something a community can consider. When authorized by state law, a state or local government can take, or threaten to take, a closed or closing plant from the company that owns it and then operate the plant or sell it to a new owner. In effect, the community says, "If USX (or whatever company) still wants to run the Homestead Works (or whatever facility is threatened with closure), God bless it. But if it refuses to run it any longer, then we, the people, will have to find another way."

In 1985 nine municipalities in the Monongahela Valley joined to incorporate the Steel Valley Authority (SVA), a regional development authority organized under the Pennsylvania Municipal Authorities Act. Under the act the SVA has the power to take property by eminent domain for the purpose of retaining and developing existing industries. Armed with eminent domain power, a community could acquire an abandoned steel mill without the consent of its owner and so bring about its reutilization. Underlying this, Lynd suggests,

is the concept of a generalized trust that a community extends to enterprises within its border to operate for the common good. So long as the enterprise exercises such stewardship it can, and should, remain in private hands. But if the enterprise is permitted to stand idle, or if capital earned there is taken out of the community for other purposes, then the community can rightfully intervene by eminent domain.

Discussion Questions

1. The steel companies blame the decline of their industry on restrictive environmental regulations, high wages, and unfair foreign competition. Steelworkers argue that the companies are too absorbed with short-run profits, that they failed to anticipate and respond to foreign competition, and that they lack a sense of social responsibility. Evaluate these claims and counterclaims.

2. What social obligation, if any, does a company have to continue producing an important commodity when it can invest more profitably elsewhere? Union members and activists believe that renewed investment in steel is socially desirable. Assess that assumption.

3. Can the steel companies be accused of acting unjustly? What responsibilities, if any, does a company have to the community and to its work force to continue operating?

4. Does justice require that companies exercise a kind of "stewardship" for the common good, as Lynd suggests?

5. Assess the idea of eminent domain as a response to the crisis in the steel industry. Is it morally defensible?

6. How would the utilitarian, libertarian, and Rawlsian theories of justice evaluate the use of eminent domain, both in general and in this particular case?

CASE 3.2
Poverty in America

According to our government's official definition, thirty-three million Americans—about one in every seven people in our nation—live below the poverty level. Since 1973 the poverty rate has increased by a third; it stands at a level higher than any time in the past two decades. One out of every four Americans lives in substandard housing. One out of every five adults is functionally illiterate. In the United States today one can see people roaming the streets in tattered clothing, picking their food out of garbage cans. Homeless people—many of them former mental patients released from state hospitals—live in abandoned cars and shacks or simply sleep in doorways and on subway grates.[32]

Most people think that those described as "poor" in the United States are pretty well off by world standards. One study, however, found that twelve million Americans suffered from an acute hunger comparable to that found in poorer nations. In Philadelphia alone an investigator found "tens of thousands" of men, women, and children "desperate for food." Another study found that 50 percent of children from the poorest families grow up with impaired learning ability, while 5 percent are born mentally retarded because of prenatal malnourishment. Malnutrition from extreme poverty has caused brain damage in an estimated one million babies and young children. Yet, less than half of the American poor receives either food stamps or free food, and in New York State alone an estimated one million people who need food stamps are not getting them.

People in different walks of life and in different circumstances experience poverty. Some work but are unable to pull themselves out of poverty. Others live on the edge of poverty; though not officially classified as poor, they are continually in danger of falling into poverty. Many are unable to work and depend on outside assistance. Investigation shows, however, that most people do not stay for years on the welfare rolls. They move on and off, and less than 1 percent obtain welfare for ten years. Contrary to popular mythology, the majority of AFDC recipients (Aid to Families with Dependent Children) are young children, whose mothers must remain at home. They are not able-bodied adults, unwilling to work. Seventy percent of AFDC families have only one or two children, and there is little financial incentive to have more. Half of the families who receive AFDC have an adult who works full- or part-time, and research consistently demonstrates that poor people have the same strong desire to work that the rest of the population does.

Poverty is not an isolated problem, nor is it limited to specific groups. Still, poverty strikes some groups more severely than others. Children are one example. Today one in every four children under six, and one in every two black children under six, are poor. Millions of children live in poverty, and their ranks are steadily growing. The problem is particularly serious among female-headed families, where half of all children are poor.

The past twenty years have also seen a dramatic increase in the number of women in poverty. This includes women with inadequate income following divorce, widowhood, or retirement, as well as women raising children alone. Wage discrimination against women is one factor. Women who work full-time, year-around earn only 61 percent of what men earn. Hundreds of thousands of women who hold full-time jobs are still poor. Women's responsibilities for child rearing are another important factor. Despite many changes in recent years, women continue to have primary responsibility in this area. When marriages break up, mothers typically take custody and bear the major financial burden. Less than half of the women raising children alone are awarded child support, and less than half of those entitled to it receive the full amount.

Most poor people in our nation are white—about two-thirds of them. But blacks are about three times more likely to be poor than whites. While one out of every nine white Americans is poor, one of every three blacks and Native Americans and more than one of every four Hispanics are below the poverty line. Many members of the minority communities have succeeded in moving up the economic ladder, but the overall picture is bleak. Black family income, for instance, is only 55 percent that of white family income— a gap that is wider than any time in the last fifteen years.

Discussion Questions

1. Does the existence of poverty imply that our socioeconomic system is unjust? Does the concentration of poverty in certain groups make it more unjust than it would be otherwise?

2. What moral obligation, if any, do we have, individually and as a society, to reduce poverty? What steps could be taken? What role should business play?

3. How would a utilitarian view the facts presented above? What are the implications in this case of the concept of the "declining marginal utility of money"?

4. How would a libertarian like Nozick view poverty in the U.S.? How plausible do you find the libertarian's preference for private charity over public welfare?

5. How would our economy be assessed from the point of view of Rawls's Difference Principle? Can it be plausibly maintained that, despite poverty, our system

works to "the greatest expected benefit of the least advantaged"? Is this an appropriate standard?

NOTES

1. See Lester C. Thurow, "A Surge in Inequality," *Scientific American* 256 (May 1987), from which the figures in the following paragraphs are drawn.

2. John Stuart Mill, *Utilitarianism* (New York: Bobbs-Merrill, 1957), 71.

3. Ibid., 62.

4. Ibid., 66.

5. Ibid., 73.

6. Smith's ideas are discussed further in Chapter 4.

7. John Stuart Mill, *Principles of Political Economy*, ed. Donald Winch (Harmondsworth, Middlesex: Penguin, 1970), 129–141.

8. Ibid., 133.

9. Ibid., 140–141.

10. *A Theory of the Good and the Right* (New York: Oxford University Press, 1979), 312–313.

11. Ibid., 310.

12. F. A. Hayek, *The Constitution of Liberty* (Chicago: University of Chicago Press, 1960), 11.

13. John Hospers, *Libertarianism* (Los Angeles: Nash, 1971), 5.

14. New York: Basic Books, 1974.

15. John Locke, *Two Treatises on Government*, 2nd ed., Peter Laslett, ed. (Cambridge, England: Cambridge University Press, 1967).

16. *Anarchy, State, and Utopia*, 150.

17. A. K. Sen, *Poverty and Famines* (New York: Oxford University Press, 1981).

18. Lester R. Brown and Erik P. Eckhol, "The Empty Breadbasket," *Ceres*, March–April 1974, 59.

19. Onora O'Neill, "Lifeboat Earth," *Philosophy and Public Affairs* 4 (1975): 288.

20. Virginia Held, ed. *Property, Profits, and Economic Justice* (Belmont, Calif.: Wadsworth, 1980), 1–3.

21. Harvard University Press, 1971.

22. John Rawls, "A Kantian Conception of Justice," *Cambridge Review* 96 (February 1975).

23. Ibid.

24. John Rawls, "Justice as Fairness," *Philosophical Review* 67 (April 1958).

25. Rawls, *A Theory of Justice*, 4.

26. Rawls, "Justice as Fairness."

27. Rawls, "A Kantian Conception of Equality," 94.
28. Rawls, *A Theory of Justice*, 104.
29. Ibid., 101–102.
30. See Staughton Lynd, "Towards a Not-For-Profit Economy: Public Development Authorities for Acquisition and Use of Industrial Property," *Harvard Civil Rights Civil Liberties Law Review* 22 (Winter 1987), from which this case study is drawn.
31. "Pricing Yourself into a Job," *The Economist*, April 16, 1988, 49–50.
32. See Michael Parenti, *Democracy for the Few*, 4th ed. (New York: St. Martin's, 1983), 28–32, and National Conference of Catholic Bishops, *Economic Justice for All* (Washington, D.C.: U.S. Catholic Conference, 1986), 83–106, for these figures and those that follow, as well as for further references.

Rich and Poor

Peter Singer

After reviewing the seriousness and extensiveness of world poverty, Singer argues that we have a duty to provide far more aid to those in need than we now give. The principle to which he appeals is one that, he argues, we already implicitly acknowledge in everyday life. Singer rejects Nozick's theory of rights and argues against the view that we should simply write certain countries off as "hopeless" and allow famine, disease, and natural disaster to reduce their populations.

Consider these facts: by the most cautious estimates, 400 million people lack the calories, protein, vitamins and minerals needed for a normally healthy life. Millions are constantly hungry; others suffer from deficiency diseases and from infections they would be able to resist on a better diet. Children are worst affected. According to one estimate, 15 million children under five die every year from the combined effects of malnutrition and infection. In some areas, half the children born can be expected to die before their fifth birthday.

Nor is lack of food the only hardship of the poor. To give a broader picture, Robert McNamara, President of the World Bank, has suggested the term 'absolute poverty'. The poverty we are familiar with in industrialized nations is relative poverty—meaning that some citizens are poor, relative to the wealth enjoyed by their neighbours. People living in relative poverty in Australia might be quite comfortably off by comparison with old-age pensioners in Britain, and British old-age pensioners are not poor in comparison with the poverty that exists in Mali or Ethiopia. Absolute poverty, on the other hand, is poverty by any standard. In McNamara's words:

Poverty at the absolute level . . . is life at the very margin of existence.

The absolute poor are severely deprived human beings struggling to survive in a set of squalid and degraded circumstances almost beyond the power of our sophisticated imaginations and privileged circumstances to conceive.

Compared to those fortunate enough to live in developed countries, individuals in the poorest nations have:

An infant mortality rate eight times higher
A life expectancy one-third lower
An adult literacy rate 60% less
A nutritional level, for one out of every two in the population, below acceptable standards; and for millions of infants, less protein than is sufficient to permit optimum development of the brain.

And McNamara has summed up absolute poverty as:

a condition of life so characterized by malnutrition, illiteracy, disease, squalid surroundings, high infant mortality and low life expectancy as to be beneath any reasonable definition of human decency. . . .

Death and disease apart, absolute poverty remains a miserable condition of life, with inadequate food, shelter, clothing, sanitation, health services and education. According to World Bank estimates which define absolute poverty in terms of income levels insufficient to provide adequate nutrition, something like 800 million people—almost 40% of the people of developing countries—

live in absolute poverty. Absolute poverty is probably the principal cause of human misery today. . . .

The problem is not that the world cannot produce enough to feed and shelter its people. People in the poor countries consume, on average, 400 lbs of grain a year, while North Americans average more than 2000 lbs. The difference is caused by the fact that in the rich countries we feed most of our grain to animals, converting it into meat, milk and eggs. Because this is an inefficient process, wasting up to 95% of the food value of the animal feed, people in rich countries are responsible for the consumption of far more food than those in poor countries who eat few animal products. If we stopped feeding animals on grains, soybeans and fishmeal the amount of food saved would—if distributed to those who need it—be more than enough to end hunger throughout the world.

These facts about animal food do not mean that we can easily solve the world food problem by cutting down on animal products, but they show that the problem is essentially one of distribution rather than production. The world does produce enough food. Moreover the poorer nations themselves could produce far more if they made more use of improved agricultural techniques.

So why are people hungry? Poor people cannot afford to buy grain grown by American farmers. Poor farmers cannot afford to buy improved seeds, or fertilizers, or the machinery needed for drilling wells and pumping water. Only by transferring some of the wealth of the developed nations to the poor of the undeveloped nations can the situation be changed.

That this wealth exists is clear. Against the picture of absolute poverty that McNamara has painted, one might pose a picture of 'absolute affluence'. Those who are absolutely affluent are not necessarily affluent by comparison with their neighbours, but they are affluent by any reasonable definition of human needs. This means that they have more income than they need to provide themselves adequately with all the basic necessities of life. After buying food, shelter, clothing, necessary health services and education, the absolutely affluent are still able to spend money on luxuries. The absolutely affluent choose their food for the pleasures of the palate, not to stop hunger; they buy new clothes to look fashionable, not to keep warm; they move house to be in a better neigh-

bourhood or have a play room for the children, not to keep out the rain; and after all this there is still money to spend on books and records, colour television, and overseas holidays.

At this stage I am making no ethical judgments about absolute affluence, merely pointing out that it exists. Its defining characteristic is a significant amount of income above the level necessary to provide for the basic human needs of oneself and one's dependents. By this standard Western Europe, North America, Japan, Australia, New Zealand and the oil-rich Middle Eastern states are all absolutely affluent, and so are many, if not all, of their citizens. The USSR and Eastern Europe might also be included on this list. To quote McNamara once more:

> The average citizen of a developed country enjoys wealth beyond the wildest dreams of the one billion people in countries with per capita incomes under $200 . . .

These, therefore, are the countries—and individuals—who have wealth which they could, without threatening their own basic welfare, transfer to the absolutely poor.

At present, very little is being transferred. Members of the Organization of Petroleum Exporting Countries lead the way, giving an average of 2.1% of their Gross National Product. Apart from them, only Sweden, The Netherlands and Norway have reached the modest UN target of 0.7% of GNP. Britain gives 0.38% of its GNP in official development assistance and a small additional amount in unofficial aid from voluntary organizations. The total comes to less than £1 per month per person, and compares with 5.5% of GNP spent on alcohol, and 3% on tobacco. Other, even wealthier nations, give still less: Germany gives 0.27%, the United States 0.22% and Japan 0.21%. . .

The Obligation to Assist

The Argument for an Obligation to Assist

The path from the library at my university to the Humanities lecture theatre passes a shallow ornamental pond. Suppose that on my way to give a lecture I notice that a small child has fallen in and is in danger of drowning. Would anyone deny that I ought to wade in and pull the child out? This will mean getting my clothes muddy, and either cancelling my lecture or delaying it until I can find something dry to change into; but compared with the avoidable death of a child this is insignificant.

A plausible principle that would support the judgment that I ought to pull the child out is this: if it is in our power to prevent something very bad happening, without thereby sacrificing anything of comparable moral significance, we ought to do it. This principle seems uncontroversial. It will obviously win the assent of consequentialists; but non-consequentialists should accept it too, because the injunction to prevent what is bad applies only when nothing comparably significant is at stake. Thus the principle cannot lead to the kinds of actions of which non-consequentialists strongly disapprove—serious violations of individual rights, injustice, broken promises, and so on. If a non-consequentialist regards any of these as comparable in moral significance to the bad thing that is to be prevented, he will automatically regard the principle as not applying in those cases in which the bad thing can only be prevented by violating rights, doing injustice, breaking promises, or whatever else is at stake. Most non-consequentialists hold that we ought to prevent what is bad and promote what is good. Their dispute with consequentialists lies in their insistence that this is not the sole ultimate ethical principle: that it is *an* ethical principle is not denied by any plausible ethical theory.

Nevertheless the uncontroversial appearance of the principle that we ought to prevent what is bad when we can do so without sacrificing anything of comparable moral significance is deceptive. If it were taken seriously and acted upon, our lives and our world would be fundamentally changed. For the principle applies, not just to rare situations in which one can save a child from a pond, but to the everyday situation in which we can assist those living in absolute poverty. In saying this I assume that absolute poverty, with its hunger and malnutrition, lack of shelter, illiteracy, disease, high infant mortality and low life expectancy, is a bad thing. And I assume that it is within the power of the affluent to reduce absolute poverty, without sacrificing anything of comparable moral significance. If these two assumptions and the principle we have been discussing are correct, we have an obligation to help those in absolute poverty which is no less strong than our obligation to rescue a drowning child from a pond. Not to help would be wrong, whether or not it is intrinsically equivalent to killing. Helping is not, as conventionally thought, a charitable act which it is praiseworthy to do, but not wrong to omit; it is something that everyone ought to do.

This is the argument for an obligation to assist. Set out more formally, it would look like this.

First premise: If we can prevent something bad without sacrificing anything of comparable significance, we ought to do it.

Second premise: Absolute poverty is bad.

Third premise: There is some absolute poverty we can prevent without sacrificing anything of comparable moral significance.

Conclusion: We ought to prevent some absolute poverty.

The first premise is the substantive moral premise on which the argument rests, and I have tried to show that it can be accepted by people who hold a variety of ethical positions.

The second premise is unlikely to be challenged. Absolute poverty is, as McNamara put it, 'beneath any reasonable definition of human decency' and it would be hard to find a plausible ethical view which did not regard it as a bad thing.

The third premise is more controversial, even though it is cautiously framed. It claims only that some absolute poverty can be prevented without the sacrifice of anything of comparable moral significance. It thus avoids the objection that any aid I can give is just 'drops in the ocean' for the point is not whether my personal contribution will make any noticeable impression on world poverty as a whole (of course it won't) but whether it will prevent some poverty. This is all the argument needs to sustain its conclusion, since the second premise says that any absolute poverty is bad, and not merely the total amount of absolute poverty. If without sacrificing anything of comparable moral significance we can provide just one family with the means to raise itself out of absolute poverty, the third premise is vindicated.

I have left the notion of moral significance unexamined in order to show that the argument does not depend on any specific values or ethical principles. I think the third premise is true for most people living in industrialized nations, on any defensible view of what is morally significant. Our affluence means that we have income we can dispose of without giving up the basic necessities of life, and we can use this income to reduce absolute poverty. Just how much we will think ourselves obliged to give up will depend on what we consider to be of comparable moral significance to the poverty we could prevent: colour television, stylish clothes, expensive dinners, a sophisticated stereo system, overseas holidays, a (second?) car, a larger house, private schools for our children . . . For a utilitarian, none of these is likely to be of comparable significance to the reduction of absolute poverty; and those who are not utilitarians surely must, if they subscribe to the principle of universalizability, accept that at least *some* of these things are of far less moral significance than the absolute poverty that could be prevented by the money they cost. So the third premise seems to be true on any plausible ethical view—although the precise amount of absolute poverty that can be prevented before anything of moral significance is sacrificed will vary according to the ethical view one accepts.

Objections to the Argument

Taking Care of Our Own.   Anyone who has worked to increase overseas aid will have come across the argument that we should look after those near us, our families and then the poor in our own country, before we think about poverty in distant places.

No doubt we do instinctively prefer to help those who are close to us. Few could stand by and watch a child drown; many can ignore a famine in Africa. But the question is not what we usually do, but what we ought to do, and it is difficult to see any sound moral justification for the view that distance, or community membership, makes a crucial difference to our obligations.

Consider, for instance, racial affinities. Should whites help poor whites before helping poor blacks? Most of us would reject such a suggestion out of hand: . . . people's need for food has nothing to do with their race, and if blacks need food more than whites, it would be a violation of the principle of equal consideration to give preference to whites.

The same point applies to citizenship or nationhood. Every affluent nation has some relatively poor citizens, but absolute poverty is limited largely to the poor nations. Those living on the streets of Calcutta, or in a drought-stricken region of the Sahel, are experiencing poverty unknown in the West. Under these circumstances it would be wrong to decide that only those fortunate enough to be citizens of our own community will share our abundance.

We feel obligations of kinship more strongly than those of citizenship. Which parents could give away their last bowl of rice if their own children were starving? To do so would seem unnatural, contrary to our nature as biologically evolved beings—although whether it would be wrong is another question altogether. In any case, we are not faced with that situation, but with one in which our own children are well-fed, well-clothed, well-educated, and would now like new bikes, a stereo set, or their own car. In these circumstances any special obligations we might have to our children have been fulfilled, and the needs of strangers make a stronger claim upon us.

The element of truth in the view that we should first take care of our own, lies in the advantage of a recognized system of responsibilities. When families and local communities look after their own poorer members, ties of affection and personal relationships achieve ends that would otherwise require a large, impersonal bureaucracy. Hence it would be absurd to propose that from now on we all regard ourselves as equally responsible for the welfare of everyone in the world; but the argument for an obligation to assist does not propose that. It applies only when some are in absolute poverty, and others can help without sacrificing anything of comparable moral significance. To allow one's own kin to sink into absolute poverty would be to sacrifice something of comparable significance; and before that point had been reached, the breakdown of the system of family and community responsibility would be a factor to weigh the balance in favour of a small degree of preference for family and community. This small degree of preference is, however, decisively outweighed by existing discrepancies in wealth and property.

Property Rights.   Do people have a right to private property, a right which contradicts the view that they are under an obligation to give some of their wealth away to those in absolute poverty? According to some theories of rights (for instance, Robert Nozick's) provided one has acquired one's property without the use of unjust means like force and fraud, one may be entitled to enormous wealth while others starve. This individualistic conception of rights is in contrast to other views, like the early Christian doctrine to be found in the works of Thomas Aquinas, which holds that since property exists for the satisfaction of human needs, 'whatever a man has in superabundance is owed, of natural right, to the poor for their sustenance'. A socialist would also, of course, see wealth as belonging to the community rather than the individual, while utilitarians, whether socialist or not, would be prepared to override property rights to prevent great evils.

Does the argument for an obligation to assist others therefore presuppose one of these other theories of property rights, and not an individualistic theory like Nozick's? Not necessarily. A theory of property rights can insist on our *right* to retain wealth without pronouncing on whether the rich *ought* to give to the poor. Nozick, for example, rejects the use of compulsory means like taxation to redistribute income, but suggests that we can achieve the ends we deem morally desirable by voluntary means. So Nozick would reject the claim that rich people have an 'obligation' to give to the poor, in so far as this implies that the poor have a right to our aid, but might accept that giving is something we ought to do and failing to give, though within one's rights, is wrong—for rights is not all there is to ethics.

The argument for an obligation to assist can survive, with only minor modifications, even if we accept an individualistic theory of property rights. In any case, however, I do not think we should accept such a theory. It leaves too much to chance to be an acceptable ethical view. For instance, those whose forefathers happened to inhabit some sandy wastes around the Persian Gulf are now fabulously wealthy, because oil lay under those sands; while those whose forefathers settled on better land south of the Sahara live in absolute poverty, because of drought and bad harvests. Can this distribution be acceptable from an impartial point of view? If we imagine ourselves about to begin life as a citizen of either Kuwait or Chad—but we do not know which—would we accept the principle that citizens of Kuwait are under no obligation to assist people living in Chad?

Population and the Ethics of Triage.   Perhaps the most serious objection to the argument that we have an obligation to assist is that since the major cause of absolute poverty is overpopulation, helping those now in poverty will only ensure that yet more people are born to live in poverty in the future.

In its most extreme form, this objection is taken to show that we should adopt a policy of 'triage'. The term comes from medical policies adopted in wartime. With too few doctors to cope with all the casualties, the wounded were divided into three categories: those who would probably survive without medical assistance, those who might survive if they received assistance, but otherwise probably would not, and those who even with medical assistance probably would not survive. Only those in the middle category were given medical assistance. The idea, of course, was to use limited medical resources as effectively as possible. For those in the first category, medical treatment was not strictly necessary; for those in the third category, it was likely to be useless. It has been suggested that we should apply the same policies to countries, according to their prospects of becoming self-sustaining. We would not aid countries which even without our help will soon be able to feed their populations. We would not aid countries which, even with our help, will not be able to limit their population to a level they can feed. We would aid those countries where our help might make the difference between success and failure in bringing food and population into balance.

Advocates of this theory are understandably reluctant to give a complete list of the countries they would place into the 'hopeless' category; but Bangladesh is often cited as an example. Adopting the policy of triage would, then, mean cutting off assistance to Bangladesh and allowing famine, disease and natural disasters to reduce the population of that country (now around 80 million) to the level at which it can provide adequately for all.

In support of this view Garrett Hardin has offered a metaphor: we in the rich nations are like the occupants of a crowded lifeboat adrift in a sea full of drowning people. If we try to save the drowning by bringing them aboard our boat will be overloaded and we shall all drown. Since it is better that some survive than none, we should leave the others to drown. In the world today, according to Hardin, 'lifeboat ethics' apply. The rich should leave the poor to starve, for otherwise the poor will drag the rich down with them. . . .

Anyone whose initial reaction to triage was not one of repugnance would be an unpleasant sort of person. Yet initial reactions based on strong feelings are not always reliable guides. Advocates of triage are rightly concerned with the long-term consequences of our actions. They say that helping the poor and starving now merely ensures more poor and starving in the future. When our capacity to help is finally unable to cope—as one day it must be—the suffering will be greater than it would be if we stopped helping now. If this is correct, there is nothing we can do to prevent absolute starvation and poverty, in the long run, and so we have no obligation to assist. Nor does it seem reasonable to hold that under these circumstances people have a right to our assistance. If we do accept such a right, irrespective of the consequences, we are saying that, in Hardin's metaphor, we would continue to haul the drowning into our lifeboat until the boat sank and we all drowned.

If triage is to be rejected it must be tackled on its own ground, within the framework of consequentialist ethics. Here it is vulnerable. Any consequentialist ethics must take probability of outcome into account. A course of action that will certainly produce some benefit is to be preferred to an alternative course that may lead to a slightly larger benefit, but is equally likely to result in no benefit at all. Only if the greater magnitude of the uncertain benefit outweighs its uncertainty should we choose it. Better one certain unit of benefit than a 10% chance of 5 units; but better a 50% chance of 3 units than a single certain unit. The same principle applies when we are trying to avoid evils.

The policy of triage involves a certain, very great evil: population control by famine and disease. Tens of millions would die slowly. Hundreds of millions would continue to live in absolute poverty, at the very margin of existence. Against this prospect, advocates of the policy place a possible evil which is greater still: the same process of famine and disease, taking place in, say, fifty years time, when the world's population may be three times its present level, and the number who will

die from famine, or struggle on in absolute poverty, will be that much greater. The question is: how probable is this forecast that continued assistance now will lead to greater disasters in the future?

Forecasts of population growth are notoriously fallible, and theories about the factors which affect it remain speculative. One theory, at least as plausible as any other, is that countries pass through a 'demographic transition' as their standard of living rises. When people are very poor and have no access to modern medicine their fertility is high, but population is kept in check by high death rates. The introduction of sanitation, modern medical techniques and other improvements reduces the death rate, but initially has little effect on the birth rate. Then population grows rapidly. Most poor countries are now in this phase. If standards of living continue to rise, however, couples begin to realize that to have the same number of children surviving to maturity as in the past, they do not need to give birth to as many children as their parents did. The need for children to provide economic support in old age diminishes. Improved education and the emancipation and employment of women also reduce the birthrate, and so population growth begins to level off. Most rich nations have reached this stage, and their populations are growing only very slowly.

If this theory is right, there is an alternative to the disasters accepted as inevitable by supporters of triage. We can assist poor countries to raise the living standards of the poorest members of their population. We can encourage the governments of these countries to enact land reform measures, improve education, and liberate women from a purely child-bearing role. We can also help other countries to make contraception and sterilization widely available. There is a fair chance that these measures will hasten the onset of the demographic transition and bring population growth down to a manageable level. Success cannot be guaranteed; but the evidence that improved economic security and education reduce population growth is strong enough to make triage ethically unacceptable. We cannot allow millions to die from starvation and disease when there is a reasonable probability that population can be brought under control without such horrors.

Population growth is therefore not a reason against giving overseas aid, although it should make us think about the kind of aid to give. Instead of food handouts, it may be better to give aid that hastens the demographic transition. This may mean agricultural assistance for the rural poor, or assistance with education, or the provision of contraceptive services. Whatever kind of aid proves most effective in specific circumstances, the obligation to assist is not reduced.

One awkward question remains. What should we do about a poor and already overpopulated country which, for religious or nationalistic reasons, restricts the use of contraceptives and refuses to slow its population growth? Should we nevertheless offer development assistance? Or should we make our offer conditional on effective steps being taken to reduce the birthrate? To the latter course, some would object that putting conditions on aid is an attempt to impose our own ideas on independent sovereign nations. So it is—but is this imposition unjustifiable? If the argument for an obligation to assist is sound, we have an obligation to reduce absolute poverty; but we have no obligation to make sacrifices that, to the best of our knowledge, have no prospect of reducing poverty in the long run. Hence we have no obligation to assist countries whose governments have policies which will make our aid ineffective. This could be very harsh on poor citizens of these countries—for they may have no say in the government's policies—but we will help more people in the long run by using our resources where they are most effective. (The same principles may apply, incidentally, to countries that refuse to take other steps that could make assistance effective—like refusing to reform systems of land holding that impose intolerable burdens on poor tenant farmers.)

Review and Discussion Questions

1. What's the difference between absolute and relative poverty? Do we have absolute poverty in the U.S.?

2. Describe the analogy Singer uses to develop his argument for an obligation to assist. What is the key moral premise in this argument? Is Singer's principle as uncontroversial as he thinks?

3. How large a sacrifice do you think Singer's principle would require of us? What is "of comparable moral significance" to the reduction of absolute poverty?

4. How would a libertarian respond to Singer's argument? Do you think Singer is correct in maintaining that his argument can survive, even if we accept Nozick's theory?

5. Describe triage and its relevance to Singer's position. On what grounds does Singer reject the triage argument?

6. Do you see any possible objections to Singer's argument that he has overlooked or failed to answer satisfactorily? Do you think that our obligation to assist people in other lands who are in serious distress is a matter of *justice*?

Is Inheritance Justified?

D. W. Haslett

Many people support inheritance because they believe it is essential to capitalism. After reviewing some facts about wealth distribution and inheritance in the United States today, D. W. Haslett argues against this view. He contends not only that inheritance is not essential to capitalism, but that it is inconsistent with the fundamental values that underlie capitalism—in particular, with "distribution according to productivity," "equal opportunity," and "freedom." Haslett maintains, accordingly, that the practice of inheritance, as it exists today, should be abolished.

I. Background Information

Family income in the United States today is not distributed very evenly. The top fifth of American families receives 57.3 percent of all family income, while the bottom fifth receives only 7.2 percent.[1]

But, for obvious reasons, a family's financial well-being does not depend upon its income nearly

D. W. Haslett, "Is Inheritance Justified?" *Philosophy and Public Affairs* 15 (Spring 1986). Copyright © 1986 by Princeton University Press. Reprinted by permission of Princeton University Press.

as much as it does upon its wealth, just as the strength of an army does not depend upon how many people joined it during the year as much as it does upon how many people are in it altogether. So if we really want to know how unevenly economic well-being is distributed in the United States today, we must look at the distribution not of income, but of wealth.

Although—quite surprisingly—the government does not regularly collect information on the distribution of wealth, it has occasionally done so. The results are startling. One to two percent of American families own from around 20 to 30 percent of the (net) family wealth in the United States; 5 to 10 percent own from around 40 to 60 percent.[2] The top fifth owns almost 80 percent of the wealth, while the bottom fifth owns only 0.2 percent.[3] So while the top fifth has, as we saw, about eight times the income of the bottom fifth, it has about 400 times the wealth. Whether deliberately or not, by regularly gathering monumental amounts of information on the distribution of income, but not on the distribution of wealth, the government succeeds in directing attention away from how enormously unequal the distribution of wealth is, and directing it instead upon the less unequal distribution of income. But two things are clear: wealth is distributed far more unequally in the United States today than is income, and this inequality in the distribution of wealth is enormous. These are the first two things to keep in mind throughout our discussion of inheritance.

The next thing to keep in mind is that, although estate and gift taxes in the United States are supposed to redistribute wealth, and thereby lessen this inequality, they do not do so. Before 1981 estates were taxed, on an average, at a rate of only 0.2 percent—0.8 percent for estates over $500,000—hardly an amount sufficient to cause any significant redistribution of wealth.[4] And, incredibly, the Economic Recovery Act of 1981 *lowered* estate and gift taxes.

Of course the top rate at which estates and gifts are *allegedly* taxed is far greater than the 0.2 percent rate, on the average, at which they are *really* taxed. Prior to 1981, the top rate was 70 percent, which in 1981 was lowered to 50 percent. Because of this relatively high top rate, the average person is led to believe that estate and gift taxes succeed in breaking up the huge financial empires of the very rich, thereby distributing wealth more evenly. What the average person fails to realize is that what the government takes with one hand, through high nominal rates, it gives back with the other hand, through loopholes in the law. Lester Thurow writes, ". . . it is hard to understand why we go through the fiction of legislating high nominal rates and then nullifying them with generous loopholes—unless someone is to be fooled. The most obvious purpose of high nominal rates and low effective rates is to use the high nominal rates as a smokescreen to hide the transfer of wealth from generation to generation."[5] I do not know if the government deliberately intends the law on estate and gift taxation to be deceptive but, due to the complications, exceptions, and qualifications built into this law, it *is* deceptive and, more seriously still, it is ineffective as a means of distributing wealth more evenly. Indeed, as George Cooper shows, estate and gift taxes can, with the help of a good attorney, be avoided so easily they amount to little more than "voluntary" taxes.[6] As such, it is not surprising that, contrary to popular opinion, these taxes do virtually nothing to reduce the vast inequality in the distribution of wealth that exists today.

Once we know that estate and gift taxes do virtually nothing to reduce this vast inequality, what I am about to say next should come as no surprise. This vast inequality in the distribution of wealth is (according to the best estimates) due at least as much to inheritance as to any other factor. Once again, because of the surprising lack of information about these matters, the extent to which this inequality is due to inheritance is not known exactly. One estimate, based upon a series of articles appearing in *Fortune* magazine, is that 50 percent of the large fortunes in the United States were derived basically from inheritance.[7] But by far the most careful and thorough study of this matter to date is that of John A. Brittain.[8] Brittain shows that the estimate based upon the *Fortune* articles actually is too low;[9] that a more accurate estimate of the amount contributed by inheritance to the wealth of "ultra-rich" males is 67 percent.[10] In any case, it is clear that, in the United States today, inheritance plays a large role indeed in perpetuating a vastly unequal distribution of wealth. This is the final thing to keep in mind throughout the discussion which follows.

II. Inheritance and Capitalism

Capitalism (roughly speaking) is an economic system where (1) what to produce, and in what quantities, is determined essentially by supply and demand—that is, by people's "dollar votes"—rather than by central planning, and (2) capital goods are, for the most part, privately owned. In the minds of many today, capitalism goes hand in hand with the practice of inheritance; capitalism without inheritance, they would say, is absurd. But, if I am right, the exact opposite is closer to the truth. Since, as I shall try to show in this section, the practice of inheritance is incompatible with basic values or ideals that underlie capitalism, what is absurd, if anything, is capitalism *with* inheritance. . . .

I do not try to show here that the ideals underlying capitalism are worthy of support; I only try to show that inheritance is contrary to these ideals. And if it is, then from this it follows that, *if* these ideals are worthy of support (as, incidentally, I think they are), then we have prima facie reason for concluding that inheritance is unjustified. What then are these ideals? For an answer, we can do no better than turn to one of capitalism's most eloquent and uncompromising defenders: Milton Friedman.

Distribution According to Productivity

The point of any economic system is, of course, to produce goods and services. But, as Friedman tells us, society cannot very well *compel* people to be productive and, even if it could, out of respect for personal freedom, probably it should not do so. Therefore, he concludes, in order to get people to be productive, society needs instead to *entice* them to produce, and the most effective way of enticing people to produce is to distribute income and wealth according to productivity. Thus we arrive at the first ideal underlying capitalism: "To each according to what he and the instruments he owns produces."[11]

Obviously, inheritance contravenes this ideal. For certain purposes, this ideal would require further interpretation; we would need to know more about what was meant by "productivity." For our purposes, no further clarification is necessary. According to *any* reasonable interpretation of "productivity," the wealth people get through inheritance has nothing to do with their productivity. And one need not be an adherent of this ideal of distribution to be moved by the apparent injustice of one person working eight hours a day all his life at a miserable job, and accumulating nothing, while another person does little more all his life than enjoy his parents' wealth, and inherits a fortune.

Equal Opportunity

But for people to be productive it is necessary not just that they be *motivated* to be productive, but that they have the *opportunity* to be productive. This brings us to the second ideal underlying capitalism: equal opportunity—that is, equal opportunity for all to pursue, successfully, the occupation of their choice.[12] According to capitalist ethic, it is OK if, in the economic game, there are winners and losers, provided everyone has an "equal start." As Friedman puts it, the ideal of equality compatible with capitalism is not equality of outcome, which would *discourage* people from realizing their full productive potential, but equality of opportunity, which *encourages* people to do so.[13]

Naturally this ideal, like the others we are considering, neither could, nor should, be realized fully; to do so would require, among other things, no less than abolishing the family and engaging in extensive genetic engineering.[14] But the fact that this ideal cannot and should not be realized fully in no way detracts from its importance. Not only is equal opportunity itself an elementary requirement of justice but, significantly, progress in realizing this ideal could bring with it progress in at least two other crucial areas as well: those of productivity and income distribution. First, the closer we come to equal opportunity for all, the more people there will be who, as a result of increased opportunity, will come to realize their productive potential. And, of course, the more people there are who come to realize their productive potential, the greater overall productivity will be. Second, the closer we come to equal opportunity for all, the more people there will be with an excellent opportunity to become something other than an ordinary worker, to become a professional or an entrepreneur of sorts. And the more people there are with an excellent opportunity to become something other than an ordinary worker, the more people there will be who in fact become something other than an ordinary worker or, in other words, the less people there will be available for doing ordinary work. As elementary economic theory tells us, with a decrease in the supply of something comes an increase in the demand for it, and with an increase in the demand for it comes an increase in the price paid for it. An increase in the price paid for it would, in this case, mean an increase in the income of the ordinary worker vis-à-vis that of the professional and the entrepreneur, which, surely, would be a step in the direction of income being distributed more justly.

And here I mean "more justly" even according to the ideals of capitalism itself. As we have seen, the capitalist ideal of distributive justice is "to each according to his or her productivity." But, under capitalism, we can say a person's income from some occupation reflects his or her productivity only to the extent there are no unnecessary limitations upon people's opportunity to pursue, successfully, this occupation—and by "unnecessary limitations" I mean ones that either *cannot* or (because doing so would cause more harm than good) *should not* be removed. According to the law of supply and demand, the more limited the supply of people in some occupation, then (assuming a healthy demand to begin with) the higher will be the income of those pursuing the occupation. Now if the limited supply of people in some high-paying occupation is the consequence of a "natural" scarcity—a scarcity that is not the result of unnecessary limitations upon opportunity, but is the result instead of few people having the inborn capacity to pursue this occupation, or of few people freely choosing to do so—then (it is fair to say) the high pay does reflect productivity. Willingness or capacity to do what few people are willing or have the capacity to do *is* socially valuable, and those who in fact do it *are* therefore making an unusually valuable contribution; they are, in other words, being highly productive. But if, on the other hand, the limited supply of people in some high-paying occupation is the result of unnecessary limitations upon people's opportunity to pursue that occupation, then the scarcity is an "artificial" one, and the high pay can by no means be said to reflect productivity. The remedy is to remove these limitations; in other words, to increase equality of opportunity. To

what extent the relative scarcity of professionals and entrepreneurs in capitalist countries today is due to natural scarcity, and to what extent to artificial scarcity, no one really knows. I strongly suspect, however, that a dramatic increase in equality of opportunity will reveal that the scarcity is far more artificial than most professionals and entrepreneurs today care to think—*far* more artificial.

If my suspicions are correct, a dramatic increase in equality of opportunity not only would be desirable for its own sake (since equal opportunity is itself an elementary requirement of justice) but would also be desirable for the sake of greater productivity, a more equal distribution of income, *and* fuller realization of the ideal of distribution according to productivity. Indeed, a dramatic increase in equality of opportunity would, I suspect, do more to meet the objections that many throughout the world today have against American capitalism than could anything else.[15]

That inheritance violates the (crucial) second ideal of capitalism, equal opportunity, is, once again, obvious. Wealth *is* opportunity, and inheritance distributes it very unevenly indeed. Wealth is opportunity for realizing one's potential, for a career, for success, for income. There are few, if any, desirable occupations that great wealth does not, in one way or another, increase—sometimes dramatically—one's chances of being able to pursue, and to pursue successfully. And to the extent that one's success is to be measured in terms of one's income, nothing else, neither intelligence, nor education, nor skills, provides a more secure opportunity for "success" than does wealth. Say one inherits a million dollars. All one then need do is purchase long-term bonds yielding a guaranteed interest of ten percent and (presto!) one has a yearly income of $100,000, an income far greater than anyone who toils eight hours a day in a factory will probably ever have. If working in the factory pays, relatively, so little, then why, it might be asked, do not all these workers become big-time investors themselves? The answer is that they are, their entire lives, barred from doing so by a lack of initial capital which others, through inheritance, are simply handed. With inheritance, the old adage is only too true: "The rich get richer, and the poor get poorer." Without inheritance, the vast fortunes in America today, these enormous concentrations of economic power, would be broken up, allowing wealth, and therefore opportunity, to become distributed far more evenly.[16]

Freedom

But so far I have not mentioned what many, including no doubt Friedman himself, consider to be the most important ideal underlying capitalism: that of liberty or, in other words, freedom. This ideal, however, takes different forms. One form it takes for Friedman is that of being able to engage in economic transactions free from governmental or other types of human coercion. The rationale for this conception of freedom—let us call it freedom in the "narrow" sense—is clear. As Friedman explains it, assuming only that people are informed about what is good for them, this form of freedom guarantees that ". . . no exchange will take place unless both parties benefit from it."[17] If at least the parties themselves benefit from the transaction, and it does not harm anyone, then, it is fair to say, the transaction has been socially valuable. So people with freedom of exchange will, in doing what is in their own best interests, generally be doing what is socially valuable as well. In other words, with this form of freedom, the fabled "invisible hand" actually works.

All of this is a great oversimplification. For one thing, a transaction that benefits both parties may have side effects, such as pollution, which harm others and, therefore, the transaction may not be socially valuable after all. So freedom, in the narrow sense, should certainly not be absolute. But the fact that freedom, in this sense, should not be absolute does not prevent it from serving as a useful ideal. . . .

There are others whose conception of freedom is that of not being subject to any governmental coercion (or other forms of human coercion) for any purposes whatsoever—a conception sometimes referred to as "negative" freedom. It is true that governmental (or other) coercion for purposes of enforcing the abolition of inheritance violates this ideal, but then, of course, so does any such coercion for purposes of *maintaining* inheritance. So this "anticoercion" ideal . . . neither supports nor opposes the practice of inheritance, and therefore this conception of freedom need not concern us further here either.

A very popular variation of the anticoercion conception of freedom is one where freedom is, once again, the absence of all governmental (or other human) coercion, *except for any coercion necessary for enforcing our fundamental rights*. Prominent among our fundamental rights, most of those who espouse such a conception of freedom will tell us, is our right to property. So whether this conception of freedom supports the practice of inheritance depends entirely upon whether our "right to property" should be viewed as incorporating the practice of inheritance. But whether our right to property should be viewed as incorporating the practice of inheritance is just another way of stating the very point at issue in this investigation. . . . Consequently, this popular conception of freedom cannot be used here in support of the practice of inheritance without begging the question.

But there is still another conception of freedom espoused by many: that which we might call freedom in the "broad" sense. According to this conception of freedom, to be free means to have the ability, or the opportunity, to do what one wants. For example, according to this conception of freedom, rich people are, other things being equal, freer than poor people, since their wealth provides them with opportunities to do things that the poor can only dream about.

I think it is clear that when Friedman, and most other *conservative* defenders of capitalism, speak about the importance of freedom, they have something like what I have labelled the "narrow" sense in mind, along with perhaps one of the senses of freedom we have dismissed as irrelevant to our investigation. Those who, on the other hand, espouse freedom in the broad sense are often opponents of capitalism, and they use the broad sense of freedom to try to show how capitalism, with the vast inequalities of wealth to which it gives rise, is actually inconsistent with freedom. But those who espouse the broad sense of freedom need not be opponents of capitalism since, arguably, capitalism, or some modified version of it, provides even the less well off with more wealth and opportunities than does any other system and, accordingly, may be quite compatible with freedom in the broad sense after all. Indeed, it is, I think, freedom in the broad sense that is espoused by most *liberal* defenders of capitalism, those who, although they believe in the free market, are more sympathetic to governmental aid for the poor than are conservatives. Therefore, I include freedom in the broad sense among the ideals that underlie capitalism even though this ideal is not supported by all defenders of capitalism, and is, in fact, supported by many of its foes.

Let us now see whether inheritance and freedom are inconsistent. Consider, first, freedom in the narrow sense. Although inheritance may not be inconsistent with this ideal, neither is the *abolishment* of inheritance. This ideal forbids governmental interference with free exchanges between people; it does not necessarily forbid governmental interference with *gifts* or *bequests* (which, of course, are not *exchanges*). Remember, Friedman's rationale for this ideal is, as we saw, that free exchange promotes the "invisible hand"; that is, it promotes the healthy functioning of supply and demand, which is at the very heart of capitalism. Supply and demand hardly require gifts, as opposed to exchanges, in order to function well.

If anything, gifts and bequests, and the enormous concentrations of economic power resulting from them, hinder the healthy functioning of supply and demand. First of all, gifts and bequests, and the enormous concentrations of economic power resulting from them, create such great differences in people's "dollar votes" that the economy's demand curves do not accurately reflect the needs of the population as a whole, but are distorted in favor of the "votes" of the rich. And inheritance hinders the healthy functioning of supply and demand even more, perhaps, by interfering with supply. As we have seen, inheritance (which, as I am using the term, encompasses large gifts) is responsible for some starting out in life with a vast advantage over others; it is, in other words, a major source of unequal opportunity. As we have also seen, the further we are from equal opportunity, the less people there will be who come to realize their productive potential. And, of course, the less people there are who come to realize their productive potential, the less overall productivity there will be or, in other words, the less healthy will be the economy's *supply* curves. So, while inheritance may not be *literally* inconsistent with freedom in the narrow sense, it does, by hindering indirectly both supply and demand, appear to be inconsistent with the "spirit" of this ideal. . . .

So we may conclude that, at best, inheritance

receives no support from freedom in the narrow sense. But it remains for us to consider whether inheritance receives any support from the other relevant ideal of freedom, an ideal many, including myself, would consider to be the more fundamental of the two: freedom in the broad sense—being able to do, or having the opportunity to do, what one wants. So we must now ask whether, everything considered, there is more overall opportunity throughout the country for people to do what they want with inheritance, or without it.

On the one hand, without inheritance people are no longer free to leave their fortunes to whomever they want and, of course, those who otherwise would have received these fortunes are, without them, less free to do what they want also.

But to offset these losses in freedom are at least the following gains in freedom. First, as is well known, wealth has, generally speaking, a diminishing marginal utility. What this means is that, generally speaking, the more wealth one already has, the less urgent are the needs which any given increment of wealth will go to satisfy and, therefore, the less utility the additional wealth will have for one. This, in turn, means that the more evenly wealth is distributed, the more overall utility it will have.[18] And since we may assume that, generally speaking, the more utility some amount of wealth has for someone, the more freedom in the broad sense it allows that person to enjoy, we may conclude that the more evenly wealth is distributed, the more overall freedom to which it will give rise. Now assuming that abolishing inheritance would not lessen *overall* wealth . . . and that it would indeed distribute wealth more evenly, it follows that, by abolishing inheritance, there would be some gain in freedom in the broad sense attributable to the diminishing marginal utility of wealth. Next, abolishing inheritance would also increase freedom by increasing equality of opportunity. Certainly those who do not start life having inherited significant funds (through either gift or bequest) start life, relative to those who do, with what amounts to a significant handicap. Abolishing inheritance, and thereby starting everyone at a more equal level, would obviously leave those who otherwise would have suffered this handicap (which would be the great majority of people) more free in the broad sense.

I, for one, believe these gains in freedom—

that is, those attributable to the diminishing marginal utility of wealth and more equality of opportunity—would *more* than offset the loss in freedom resulting from the inability to give one's fortune to whom one wants. Abolishing inheritance is, I suggest, analogous to abolishing discrimination against blacks in restaurants and other commercial establishments. By abolishing discrimination, the owners of these establishments lose the freedom to choose the skin color of the people they do business with, but the gain in freedom for blacks is obviously greater and more significant than this loss. Likewise, by abolishing inheritance the gain in freedom for the poor is greater and more significant than the loss in freedom for the rich. So to the list of ideals that inheritance is inconsistent with, we can, if I am right, add freedom in the broad sense.

To recapitulate: three ideals that underlie capitalism are "distribution according to productivity," "equal opportunity," and "freedom," the latter being, for our purposes, subject to either a narrow or a broad interpretation. I do not claim these are the *only* ideals that may be said to underlie capitalism; I do claim, however, that they are among the most important. Inheritance is inconsistent with both "distribution according to productivity," and "equal opportunity." Perhaps it is not, strictly speaking, inconsistent with the ideal of freedom in the narrow sense, but neither is the abolishment of inheritance. On the other hand, it probably *is* inconsistent with what many would take to be the more fundamental of the two relevant ideals of freedom: freedom in the broad sense. Since these are among the most important ideals that underlie capitalism, I conclude that inheritance not only is not essential to capitalism, but is probably inconsistent with it.[19] . . .

[III. A Proposal for Abolishing Inheritance]

First, my proposal for abolishing inheritance includes the abolishment of all large gifts as well—gifts of the sort, that is, which might serve as alternatives to bequests. Obviously, if such gifts were not abolished as well, any law abolishing inheritance could be avoided all too easily.

Of course we would not want to abolish along with these large gifts such harmless gifts as ordinary birthday and Christmas presents. This, however, raises the problem of where to draw the line. I do not know the best solution to this problem. The amount that current law allows a person to give each year tax free ($10,000) is too large a figure at which to draw the line for purposes of a law abolishing inheritance. We might experiment with drawing the line, in part at least, by means of the distinction between, on the one hand, consumer goods that can be expected to be, within ten years, either consumed or worth less than half their current value and, on the other hand, all other goods. We can be more lenient in allowing gifts of goods falling within the former category since, as they are consumed or quickly lose their value, they cannot, themselves, become part of a large, unearned fortune. The same can be said about gifts of services. But we need not pursue these technicalities further here. The general point is simply that, so as to avoid an obvious loophole, gifts (other than ordinary birthday presents, etc.) are to be abolished along with bequests.

Next, according to my proposal, a person's estate would pass to the government, to be used for the general welfare. If, however, the government were to take over people's property upon their death then, obviously, after just a few generations the government would own virtually everything—which would certainly not be very compatible with capitalism. Since this proposal for abolishing inheritance *is* supposed to be compatible with capitalism, it must therefore include a requirement that the government sell on the open market, to the highest bidder, any real property, including any shares in a corporation, that it receives from anyone's estate, and that it do so within a certain period of time, within, say, one year from the decedent's death. This requirement is, however, to be subject to one qualification: any person specified by the decedent in his will shall be given a chance to *buy* any property specified by the decedent in his will before it is put on the market (a qualification designed to alleviate slightly the family heirloom/business/farm problem discussed below). The price to be paid by this person shall be whatever the property is worth (as determined by governmental appraisers, subject to appeal) and any credit terms shall be rather lenient (perhaps 10 percent down, with the balance, plus interest, due over the next 30 years).

Finally, the abolishment of inheritance proposed here is to be subject to three important exceptions. First, there shall be no limitations at all upon the amount a person can leave to his or her spouse. A marriage, it seems to me, should be viewed as a joint venture in which both members, whether or not one stays home tending to children while the other earns money, have an *equally* important role to play; and neither, therefore, should be deprived of enjoying fully any of the material rewards of this venture by having them taken away at the spouse's death. And unlimited inheritance between spouses eliminates one serious objection to abolishing inheritance: namely, that it is not right for a person suddenly to be deprived, not only of his or her spouse, but also of most of the wealth upon which he or she has come to depend—especially in those cases where the spouse has, for the sake of the marriage, given up, once and for all, any realistic prospects of a career.

The second exception to be built into this proposal is one for children who are orphaned, and any other people who have been genuinely dependent upon the decedent, such as any who are mentally incompetent, or too elderly to have any significant earning power of their own. A person shall be able to leave funds (perhaps in the form of a trust) sufficient to take care of such dependents. These funds should be used only for the dependent's living expenses, which would include any educational or institutional expenses no matter how much. They should not, of course, be used to provide children with a "nest egg" of the sort others are prohibited from leaving their children. And at a certain age, say twenty-one (if the child's formal education has been completed), or upon removal of whatever disability has caused dependency, the funds should cease. This exception eliminates another objection to abolishing inheritance—the objection that it would leave orphaned children, and other dependents, without the support they needed.[20]

The third and final exception to be built into this proposal is one for charitable organizations—ones created not for purposes of making a profit, but for charitable, religious, scientific, or educational purposes. And, in order to prevent these organizations from eventually controlling the economy, they must, generally, be under the same constraint as is the government with respect to any real property they are given, such as an operating factory: they must, generally, sell it on the open market within a year.

Notes

1. Lester C. Thurow, "Tax Wealth, Not Income," *New York Times Magazine*, 11 April 1976, p. 33. These figures do not represent "income," as defined by the census bureau, but "income" as defined more broadly so as to include also any income received from wealth. Somewhat more recent figures are, of course, readily available. I am, however, using the figures set out by Thurow for two reasons. First, figures representing the distribution of income (as opposed to the amount of income) have varied little over the past twenty-five years. Second, these figures are compared by Thurow directly to figures representing the distribution of *wealth* in the United States, figures which are set out below.

2. The latest governmental study of the distribution of wealth, carried out in 1983, estimates the amount of net wealth held by the top 2 percent to be 28 percent, and that held by the top 10 percent to be 57 percent. R. Avery, G. Elliehausen, G. Canner, and T. Gustafson, "Survey of Consumer Finances, 1983: Second Report," *Federal Reserve Bulletin* 70 (December 1984): 865. These estimates "account for all financial assets, and equity in homes and other real property as well as consumer credit and other debts. [They] exclude the value of consumer durables such as automobiles and home furnishings, the cash value of life insurance, equity in small businesses and farms, and the present value of expected future benefits from pensions or social security" (p. 861). . . .

3. Thurow, "Tax Wealth, Not Income," p. 33.

4. Lester C. Thurow, *The Impact of Taxes on the American Economy* (New York: Praeger Publishers, 1971), p. 127.

5. Thurow, "Tax Wealth, Not Income," pp. 100–101.

6. George A. Cooper, *A Voluntary Tax? New Perspectives on Sophisticated Estate Tax Avoidance* (Washington, D.C.: Brookings Institution, 1979).

7. Richard A. Smith, "The Fifty-Million Dollar Man," *Fortune* (November 1957); Arthur M. Louis, "America's Centimillionaires," *Fortune* (May 1968); and Arthur M. Louis, "The New Rich of the Seventies," *Fortune* (September 1973).

8. John A. Brittain, *Inheritance and the Inequality of National Wealth* (Washington, D.C.: Brookings Institution, 1978).

9. Ibid., pp. 14–16.

10. Ibid., p. 99.

11. Milton Friedman, *Capitalism & Freedom* (Chicago: University of Chicago Press, 1962), pp. 161–162.

12. For a useful analysis of the concept of "equal opportunity," see Douglas Rae, *Equalities* (Cambridge, MA: Harvard University Press, 1981), ch. 4. Using Rae's terminology, the ideal of equal opportunity being discussed here is "means-regarding," rather than "prospect-regarding."

    In spite of the usefulness of Rae's analysis, it is, I think, mistaken in one crucial respect. According to Rae, means-regarding equal opportunity receives whatever ideological, or moral, credibility it has only by being confused with prospect-regarding equal opportunity (pp. 67, 73). If what I say below about the value of (means-regarding) equal opportunity is correct, this is a serious mistake.

13. Milton & Rose Friedman, *Freedom to Choose* (New York: Harcourt Brace Jovanovich, 1979), pp. 131–40. Friedman also talks favorably of another ideal of equality, which he calls "equality before God." But equality before God turns out to be a restatement of the ideal of liberty, which is discussed below.

14. See, for example, Bernard Williams, "The Idea of Equality," *Philosophy, Politics and Society*, ser. 2, ed. Peter Laslett and W. G. Runciman (Oxford: Basil Blackwell, 1962).

15. I say this fully aware of the criticism of equal opportunity, and meritocracy in general, made by Michael Young in *The Rise of Meritocracy* (Harmondsworth, England: Penguin Books, 1961). The problem with these criticisms is that they are based upon taking equal opportunity (along with productivity) to be, not merely a prima facie value as it should be, but absolute. Any legitimate prima facie value can easily be reduced to absurdity if it is wrongly viewed as being absolute.

16. Although abolishing inheritance would, I should think, do more to increase equal opportunity than any single other (feasible) reform, it is by no means the only reform that is needed for this purpose. If we are serious about achieving significantly more equality of opportunity within a capitalistic framework—and I think we certainly should be—we should combine inheritance reform with, among other things, the following two additional reforms: a program that guarantees access to higher education for all who are qualified, and a program to bring about equal access to medical care for all. This latter reform would remove the financial obstacle preventing children of the very poor from receiving prompt and reliable medical care; prompt and reliable medical care is, in turn, necessary for preventing their medical needs from progressing to the point where they have suffered irreversible damage that could handicap them for the rest of their lives. One way of achieving equal access to medical care for all is through a program of "socialized" medicine, but this is not the only way.

17. Friedman, *Capitalism & Freedom*, p. 13.

18. The more evenly wealth is distributed, the more overall utility it will have since any wealth that "goes" from the rich to the poor, thereby making the distribution more even, will (given the diminishing marginal utility of wealth) have more utility for these poor than it would have had for the rich, thus increasing overall utility.

19. Inheritance is, no doubt, equally inconsistent with the ideals that underlie socialism, but we need not pursue this matter here.

20. Society must not, of course, forget about orphans, and other dependents, of the relatively poor either; they should be adequately provided for somehow by the state. Yet it might be prohibitively expensive for the state to care for orphans of the poor at the level of luxury at which this exception to the abolishment of inheritance would allow orphans of the rich to be cared for, thus raising a question of fairness. But if we accept the proposition that (since we do not want to abolish the family) it is justified for the children of the rich to live in more luxury than those of the poor while their parents are alive, then it is reasonable for us to allow this higher standard to continue even if these parents happen to die. It is usually traumatic enough for a child to have to adapt to the death of both parents without, at the same time, having to adapt to an altogether different standard of living as well.

Review and Discussion Questions

1. Has Haslett correctly identified the fundamental ideals underlying capitalism? Would you agree that inheritance is contrary to capitalism's fundamental values?

2. Distinguish freedom in the narrow sense from freedom in the broad sense. Which is the more useful concept? What are the implications of freedom (in both senses) for inheritance?

3. How would a utilitarian, a libertarian, and a Rawlsian evaluate inheritance?

4. How feasible do you find Haslett's proposal for abolishing inheritance? Would it be just?

For Further Reading

John Arthur and **William H. Shaw**, eds., *Justice and Economic Distribution* (Englewood Cliffs, N.J.: Prentice-Hall, 1978) contains substantial extracts from Rawls's *A Theory of Justice* and Nozick's *Anarchy, State, and Utopia*, two contemporary presentations of the utilitarian approach, and various recent essays discussing the topic of economic justice.

Joel Feinberg, *Social Philosophy* (Englewood Cliffs, N.J.: Prentice-Hall, 1973), Chapter 7, discusses the different types of justice and injustice.

Philip Pettit, *Judging Justice* (London: Routledge & Kegan Paul, 1980) presents a useful account of the major rival theories of justice.

Robert M. Stewart, ed., *Readings in Social and Political Philosophy* (New York: Oxford University Press, 1986), Part III, provides a number of important essays on justice and equality, including contributions from Rawls and Nozick.

PART II

AMERICAN BUSINESS AND ITS BASIS □——————

CHAPTER 4

THE NATURE OF CAPITALISM □————————————————

The floor of the New York Stock Exchange, the heart of American capitalism, is a noisy and often chaotic place. Now, suddenly, it was becoming eerily quiet, as if someone had turned down the volume on a television set. The hustle and bustle of traders, brokers, and clerks scurrying across the massive floor practically ceased. All eyes were glued to the computer screens hanging above the floor's seventeen trading kiosks, some of which were suddenly and inexplicably going blank. It was Monday morning, October 19, 1987, and those on the stock market floor were witnessing the beginning of what was to be called the "Panic of '87," the "Market Meltdown," or simply "Black Monday."[1]

From 10:30 A.M. until 12:30 P.M., the Dow Jones industrial average fell as fast as anyone ever thought it could. Down 50 points in fifteen minutes. Down 100 in forty-five minutes. Down 167 in an hour. Down 200 in an hour and a half. A few traders left, unable to watch. "Holy sh——," someone said softly, "I just lost a million." "There was absolute terror," reported one broker, "things were collapsing all around you." Others simply described it as a "bloodbath." It was like "looking into the abyss," said Michael Starkman, a stockbroker for thirty years, as he recalled watching the plunging figures flicker across the Quotron machine in his Beverly Hills office.

By the end of the day stocks had lost almost a quarter of their value, twice as much as in the famous crash of October 1929, which had helped pave the way for the Great Depression. The loss of market value of U.S. securities was staggering. An incredible $500 billion blown in a single day. How did it happen? What does it mean? Is it the long-predicted end of capitalism, as some of its critics almost gleefully suggested? Or was it simply the expected "market readjustment" after a five-year bull market? In the aftermath, experts debated the causes of the crash and its likely economic repercussions. Lots of opinions were aired, but nobody seemed to agree on anything. One thing was clear, though. Wall Street's bust was reverberating around the globe. Stocks quickly tumbled in markets as far away as London, Tokyo, Australia, and Hong Kong.

That is not surprising. Capitalism is a worldwide system. Multinational firms operate without regard for traditional political boundaries, and the economies of the various capitalist nations are intricately interconnected. But what exactly is the nature of the economic system called *capitalism*? What is its underlying economic philosophy? What has it accomplished and what are its prospects for the future? In this chapter we will look at these and related questions.

Looking back in history, one must definitely credit capitalism with having helped to break the constraints of medieval feudalism that had severely limited individual possibilities for improvement. In place of a stifling economic system, capitalism offered opportunities limited only by one's imagination, ability to plan, willingness to work, and courage to seize the opportunity. In short, capitalism increased the possibilities for individualism and, many would argue, continues to.

Capitalism must also be credited with having enhanced the numbers and diversity of goods beyond Adam Smith's wildest dreams. It has increased our ownership of material goods and our standard of living and has converted our cities from bazaars into treasure troves of dazzling merchandise.

In the light of such accomplishments and the acculturation process that tends to glorify them, it is possible to overlook capitalism's theoretical and operational problems, which have serious moral import. This chapter will attempt to identify some of these problems and their moral implications. It will provide some basic historical and conceptual categories for understanding the socioeconomic framework within which business transactions occur and moral issues arise. In particular, this chapter will address the following topics:

1. The definition of capitalism and its major historical stages.

2. Four of the key features of capitalism: companies, profit motive, competition, and private property.

3. Two classical moral justifications of capitalism—first, in terms of the right to property and, second, by means of the "invisible hand" of Adam Smith.

4. Fundamental criticisms of capitalism—in particular, its implicit view of human nature, the rise of economic oligarchies, the decline of price competition, and the employee's experience of alienation and exploitation on the job.

5. The problem of stagnating productivity and lack of competitiveness that American capitalism faces today—in particular (a) the fixation on short-term performance, (b) the declining interest in the actual manufacturing of goods, and (c) our changing attitudes toward work.

CAPITALISM

Capitalism can be defined ideally as *an economic system in which the major portion of production and distribution is in private hands, operating under what is termed a profit or market system.* The U.S. economy is the world's leading capitalistic economy. This means all manufacturing firms are privately owned, including those that produce military hardware for the government. The same applies to banks, insurance companies, and most transportation companies. All businesses—small, medium, and large—are also privately owned, as are power companies. With the exception of government expenditures for such things as health, education, welfare, highways, and military equipment, no central governing body dictates to these private owners what or how much of anything will be produced. For example, officials at Ford, Chrysler, and General Motors set production goals according to anticipated consumer demand.

The private ownership and market aspects of capitalism contrast with its polar opposite, socialism. Ideally, *socialism* is an economic system characterized by public ownership of property and a planned economy. Under socialism a society's equipment is not owned by individuals (capitalists) but by public bodies. Socialism depends primarily on centralized planning rather than on the market system for both its overall allocation of resources and its distribution of income. This means that crucial economic decisions are made not by individuals but by government. In the Soviet Union, for example, government agencies decide the number of automobiles—including models, styles, and colors—to be produced each year. Top levels of government formulate production and cost objectives, which are then converted to specific production quotas and budgets that individual plant managers must follow.

A hybrid economic system, advocated by some socialists and approximated by Yugoslavia, is that of *worker control socialism*.[2] Under this system there is a market to which individual firms respond in acquiring the necessary factors of production and in deciding what to produce. The work force of each enterprise controls the enterprise (though it may elect or hire managers to oversee day-to-day operations), and the profits accrue to the workers as a group to divide in whatever manner they agree upon. But although the workers manage their factories, the capital assets of each enterprise are owned by society as a whole, and not by private individuals.

Historical Background of Capitalism

What we call capitalism did not fully emerge until the Renaissance, the rich outpouring of art, science, and philosophy in Europe during the fifteenth and sixteenth centuries. Prior to the Renaissance, business exchanges in medieval Europe were organized through guilds, which were associations of persons of the same trade, pursuit, or interests. People joined guilds pretty much for the same reasons that they have always joined clubs, groups, and organizations: for self-protection, mutual aid, maintenance of standards, furtherance of common goals.

Today if you want a pair of shoes, you head for a shoe store. There you find an array of shoes awaiting your perusal. If nothing strikes your fancy, you set out for another

shop, and perhaps another, until at last you find what you want. Or, still disappointed, you might tell the store clerk to order you a pair from "the factory." You certainly wouldn't tell the clerk to have someone make you a pair of shoes. And yet that's precisely how the medieval guild economy worked.

Under the guild organization, shoemakers, who were also shoe sellers, only made shoes to fill orders. If they had no orders, they made no shoes. The shoemaker's sole economic function was to make shoes for people when they wanted them. His labor allowed him to maintain himself, not advance his station in life. When the shoemaker died, his business went with him—unless he had a son to inherit and carry on the enterprise. As for shoe quality and cost, the medieval shopper could generally count on getting a good pair of shoes at a fair price, since the shoemakers' guild strictly controlled quality and price.

Like shoemaking, weaving was another big medieval trade. In fact, in the fourteenth century, it was the leading industry in the German town of Augsburg. Little wonder, then, that an enterprising young man named Anton Fugger became a weaver when he settled there in 1380. But young Anton had ambitions that stretched far beyond the limits of the weaving trade and the handicraft guild system. And they were grandly realized, for within three short generations a family of simple weavers was transformed into the great German bankers of the fifteenth century.[3]

Discontent with being a weaver, Anton Fugger began collecting and selling the products of other weavers. Soon he was employing lots of weavers, paying them for their labor, and selling their products as his own. His son, Jacob Fugger I, continued the business, which was expanded by Jacob Fugger II, the foremost capitalist of the Renaissance. Under his direction, the family's interests expanded into metals and textiles. Jacob Fugger II also lent large sums of money to the Hapsburg emperors to finance their wars, among other things. In return, he obtained monopoly rights on silver and copper ores, which he then traded. When Fugger bought the mines themselves, he had acquired all the props necessary to erect an extraordinary financial dynasty.

Like latter-day American titans of industry, Fugger employed thousands of workers and paid them wages, controlled all his products from raw material to market, set his own quality standards, and charged whatever the traffic would bear. It was thus that in one brief century, what was once a handicraft inseparable from the craftsperson had become a company that existed outside any family members. What had once motivated Anton Fugger—maintenance of his station in life—had given way to gain for gain's sake, the so-called "profit motive." Under Jacob Fugger II, the company amassed "profits," a novel concept, that well exceeded the needs of the Fuggers. And the profits were measured, not in goods or in land, but in money.

The story of the Fugger family can help us discover some of the key features of capitalism. Before identifying those, however, it is important to realize that capitalism, like any other economic system, has undergone changes and passed through stages.[4] For example, the kind of capitalism that emerged in the Fuggers' time is often termed *mercantile capitalism*, which was based on mutual dependence between state and commercial interests. Implicit in mercantile capitalism are the beliefs that national good and merchant profit are complementary, that money is wealth, that political unification requires strong government, and that the role of government is to provide laws and economic policies designed to promote national supremacy.

In America, in the period after the Civil War, *industrial capitalism* emerged, which, as the name implies, is associated with the development of large-scale industry. The confluence of many post-war factors produced industrial expansion in America, including a sound financial base, the technology for mass production, expanding markets for cheaply manufactured goods, and a large and willing labor force. Exploiting these fortuitous conditions was a group of hard-driving, visionary entrepreneurs called "Robber Barons" by their critics and "Captains of Industry" by their supporters: Cornelius Vanderbilt, Cyrus McCormick, Andrew Carnegie, John D. Rockefeller, John Gates, and others.

As industrialization increased, so did the size and power of business. The private fortunes of a few individuals could no longer underwrite the accelerated growth of business activity. The large sums of capital necessary could be raised only through a corporate form of business in which risk and potential profit were distributed among numerous investors.

As competition intensified, an industry's survival depended on its financial strength to reduce prices and either eliminate or absorb competition. To shore up their assets, industries engaged in *financial capitalism*, characterized by pools, trusts, and holding companies, and in general by an interpenetration of banking, insurance, and industrial interests. Hand in hand with this, the trend continued toward larger and larger corporations, controlling more and more of the country's economic capacity.

The economic and political challenges of the Great Depression of the 1930s helped to usher in still another phase of capitalism, often called *state welfare capitalism*, in which government plays an active role in regulating economic activities in an effort to smooth out the boom-and-bust pattern of the business cycle. In addition, governmental programs like social security and unemployment insurance seek to enhance the welfare of the work force, and legislation legitimizes the existence of trade unions. Today state welfare capitalism prevails, and while conservative politicians sometimes advocate less government control of business, in reality the governments of all capitalist countries are deeply involved in the management of their economies.

While the study of capitalism's evolution is best left to the history of economics, it is important to keep in mind capitalism's dynamic nature. So doing reminds us that there is nothing fixed and immutable about this or any other economic system, that it is as susceptible to the social forces of change as any other institution. This notwithstanding, capitalism does have some prominent features that were evident in the earliest capitalistic businesses.

KEY FEATURES OF CAPITALISM

Complete coverage of capitalism's features would and has filled many a book. Here we will isolate and briefly discuss just four of significance for our study: the existence of companies, profit motive, competition, and private property.

Companies

In Chapter 2 we mentioned the Firestone case in which a media misrepresentation was left uncorrected. When asked why Firestone officials had not corrected the error, a Firestone spokesperson said that *Firestone's policy* was to ask for corrections only when it was *beneficial to the company* to do so. Expressions like "Firestone's policy" and "beneficial to the company" reflect one key feature of capitalism: the existence of companies separate from the human beings who work for and within them.

"It's not in the company's interests," "The company thinks that," "From the company's viewpoint," "As far as the company is concerned"—all of us have heard, perhaps even used, these expressions that treat the business organization like a person or at least like a separate and distinct entity. Such personifications are not mere lapses into the figurative but bespeak a basic characteristic of capitalism: Capitalism permits the creation of companies or business organizations that exist separately from the people associated with them.

Today the big companies we're familiar with—Exxon, IT&T, Ford, IBM—are, in fact, incorporated businesses or corporations. In the next chapter, we will inspect the nature of the modern corporation, including its responsibilities and the positions of those who work inside them. Let it suffice here merely to observe that in the nineteenth century, Chief Justice John Marshall defined a corporation as "an artificial being, invisible, intangible, and existing only in the contemplation of law." This definition essentially means that, although a corporation is not something that can be seen or touched, it does have prescribed rights and legal obligations within the community. Like you or me, a corporation may enter into contracts and may sue or be sued in courts of law. It may even do things that the corporation's (or company's) members disapprove of. The corporations that loom large on our economic landscape harken back to a feature of capitalism evident as early as the Fugger dynasty: the existence of the company.

Profit Motive

A second characteristic of capitalism lies in the motive of the company: to make profit. As dollar directed and gain motivated as our society is, most of us blithely assume that the human being is by nature an acquisitive creature who, left to his or her own devices, will pursue profit with all the instinctual vigor of a cat chasing a mouse. In fact, as economist Robert Heilbroner points out, the "profit motive, as we understand it, is a very recent phenomenon. It was foreign to the lower and middle classes of Egyptian, Greek, Roman, and medieval cultures, only scattered throughout the Renaissance times, and largely absent in most Eastern civilizations." The medieval Church taught that no Christian ought to be a merchant. "Even to our Pilgrim forefathers," Heilbroner writes, "the idea that gain ought to be a tolerable—even a useful—goal in life would have appeared as nothing short of a doctrine of the devil." Heilbroner concludes: "As a ubiquitous characteristic of society, the profit motive is as modern an invention as printing."[5]

Modern or not, profit, taken as the acquisition of money, is the life blood of the capitalistic system. Companies and capitalists alike are motivated by an insatiable appetite for more and more money profit. Indeed, profit motive implies and reflects an economic arrangement based on two critical assumptions about human nature: (1) that human beings act out of self-interest and personal advantage and (2) that they are basically economic creatures who recognize and are motivated by their own economic self-interests.

Competition

If self-interest and an appetite for money profit drive individuals and companies, then what stops them short of holding society up for exorbitant ransom? What stops capitalists from bleeding society dry?

Adam Smith, in his monumental treatise on commercial capitalism, *An Inquiry Into the Nature and Causes of the Wealth of Nations* (1776), provided an answer. Free competition, said Smith, is the regulator that keeps a community activated only by self-interest from degenerating into a mob of ruthless profiteers. When all restraints of every sort are removed from the sale of goods and from wages, when all individuals have equal access to raw materials and markets (the doctrine of *laissez faire*, from the French meaning "leave alone"), all of us are free to pursue our own interests. In pursuing our own interests, however, we come smack up against others similarly motivated. If any of us allows blind self-interest to dictate our actions—for example, by price gouging or employee exploitation—we will quickly find ourselves beaten out by a competitor who, let's say, charges less and pays a better wage. Competition thus regulates individual economic activity.

To sample the flavor of Smith's argument, let's imagine a young woman who, presumably like all of us, is acquisitive: She wants to pile up as much wealth as possible. She looks about her and sees that people need and want a strong, twilled cotton pair of trousers. So she takes her investment capital and sets up a jeans factory. She charges forty-five dollars for a pair and soon realizes handsome profits. The woman's success is not lost on other business minds, especially manufacturers of formal slacks and dresses, who observe a sharp decline in those markets. Wanting a piece of the jeans action, numerous enterprises start up jeans factories. Many of these start selling jeans for forty dollars a pair. No longer alone in the market, our hypothetical businesswoman must either check her appetite for profit by lowering her price or risk folding. As the number of jeans on the market increases, their supply eventually overtakes demand, and the price of jeans declines further and further. Inefficient manufacturers start dropping like flies. As the competition thins out, the demand for jeans slowly catches up with the supply, and the price regulates itself. Ultimately a balance is reached between supply and demand and the price of jeans is stabilized, yielding a fair profit to the efficient producer.

With his "impetus of self-interest and his regulator of competition,"[6] Smith thus tried to explain several things: first, how prices are kept from escalating; second, how society can induce producers to provide it with what it wants (formal slacks and dress manufacturers were enticed into jeans production); and, third, why high prices are self-correcting—they increase supply.

Private Property

While examining the libertarian theory of justice in the previous chapter, we emphasized that "property" should not be simply identified with physical objects like houses, cars, or video recorders. Nor should "ownership" be thought of as a simple relationship between the owner and the thing owned. First, one can have property rights over things that are not simple physical objects, as when one owns stock in a company. Second, property ownership involves a generally complex bundle of rights and rules, governing how, under what circumstances, and in what ways both the "owner" and others can use, possess, dispose of, or have access to the thing in question.

Private property is central to capitalism. Or, to put it another way, capitalism as a socioeconomic system is a specific form of private property. What matters for capitalism is not private property simply in the sense of personal possessions, because a socialist society can certainly permit people to own houses, television sets, and jogging shoes. Rather capitalism requires, as our earlier definition indicated, private ownership of the major means of production and distribution. The means of production and distribution include factories, warehouses, offices, machines, computer networks, trucking fleets, agricultural land, and whatever else makes up the economic resources of a nation. Under capitalism private hands control these basic economic assets and productive resources. Thus, the major economic decisions are made by individuals or groups acting on their own in pursuit of profit. These decisions are not directly coordinated with those of other producers, nor are they the result of some overall plan. Any profits (or losses) that result from these decisions about production are those of the owners.

Capital, as an economic concept, is closely related to private property. Putting it simply, capital is money that is invested for the purpose of making more money. Individuals or corporations purchase various means of production or other related assets and use them

to produce goods or provide services, which are then sold. They do this not for the purpose of being nice or of helping people out, but rather in order to make money—more money, hopefully, than they spent to make the good or provide the service in the first place. Using money to make money is at the heart of the definition of capitalism.

MORAL JUSTIFICATIONS OF CAPITALISM

Whether or not capitalism is morally justified will depend, at least in part, on which general theory of justice turns out to be the soundest. In Chapter 3 we explored in detail the utilitarian approach, the libertarian alternative, and the theory of John Rawls. Now, against that background, we will look at two basic ways in which defenders of capitalism have sought to justify their system: first, the argument that the moral right to property guarantees the legitimacy of capitalism and, second, the utilitarian-based economic argument of Adam Smith.

The Natural Right to Property

Both the readers and writers of this book live in a socioeconomic system that guarantees them certain property rights. Although we are no longer permitted to own other people, we are certainly free to own a variety of other things, from livestock to stock certificates, from our own homes to whole blocks of apartment buildings. A common defense of capitalism is the argument that people have a fundamental moral right to property and that our capitalistic system is simply the outcome of this natural right. Let's examine this defense.

In Chapter 3, we saw how Locke attempted to base the right to property in human labor. When individuals mix their labor with the natural world, they are entitled to the results. And this seems plausible in many cases. For example, if Carl diligently harvests coconuts on the island he shares with Adam, while Adam himself idles away his days, then Carl, most of us would agree, has an entitlement to those coconuts that Adam lacks. But we also saw that property ownership as it actually exists, not in some supposedly natural state, but in the real world today, is a very complex, socially shaped phenomenon. This is especially true when we speak of various sophisticated forms of corporate and financial property—for example, bonds or stock options.

One could, of course, reject the whole idea of a natural right to property as a fiction, as, for example, utilitarians do. In their view, while there are various property systems, there is no *natural* right that things be owned privately, collectively, or in any particular way whatsoever. The moral task is to find that property system, that way of organizing production and distribution, that has the greatest utility. Yet even if one believes that there is a natural right to property, at least under some circumstances, one need not believe that this right is a right to have a system of property rules and regulations just like the one we now happen to have in the U.S. That is, even if Carl has a natural right to his coconuts, there may still be moral limits on how many coconuts he can rightfully amass and what he can use them for. When he takes his coconuts to the coconut bank and receives further coconuts as interest, his newly acquired coconuts are not the result of any new labor on his part. When we look at capitalistic property, that is, at socioeconomic environments in which people profit from ownership alone, then we have left Locke's world far behind.

A defender of capitalism may reply, "Certainly, there's nothing unfair about Carl's accruing these extra coconuts through his investment; after all, he could have eaten his original coconuts instead." And, indeed, within our system this reasoning seems perfectly correct. It is the way things work in our society. But this fact doesn't prove that Carl

has some natural right to use his coconuts to make more coconuts—that is, that it would be unfair or unjust to set up a different economic system (for example, one in which he had a right to consume his coconuts but no right to use them to earn more coconuts). The argument here is simply that the issue is not an all-or-nothing one. There may be certain fundamental moral rights to property, without those rights being unlimited and without them guaranteeing capitalism as we know it.

The Invisible Hand of Adam Smith

The idea of a natural right to property is not the only, and probably not the best, way in which capitalism can be defended. Another, very important argument defends capitalism in terms of the many economic benefits that the system brings, claiming that a free and unrestrained market system, which exists under capitalism, is more efficient and more productive than any other possible system, and is thus to be preferred on moral grounds. Essentially, this is a utilitarian argument, but one doesn't have to be a utilitarian to take it seriously. As we mentioned in Chapter 2, almost every normative theory puts some moral weight on the consequences of actions. Thus, if capitalism does indeed work better than other ways of organizing economic life, then this will be a very relevant moral fact—one that will be important, for instance, for Rawlsians.

In this section we sketch Adam Smith's economic case for capitalism, as presented in *The Wealth of Nations*. Smith argues that when people are left to pursue their own interests, they will, without intending it, produce the greatest good for all. Each person's individual and private pursuit of wealth results—as if, in Smith's famous phrase, "an invisible hand" were at work—in the most beneficial overall organization and distribution of economic resources. Although the academic study of economics has developed greatly since Smith's times, his classic arguments have been, and remain, extraordinarily influential. Let us see what assumptions led Smith to his famous justification of capitalism.

We have already mentioned the first of Smith's assumptions: human beings are acquisitive creatures. Self-interest and personal advantage, specifically in an economic sense, may not be all that motivate people, but they do seem to motivate most people much of the time. At any rate, they are powerful enough forces that any successful economic system must strive to harness them. People are, Smith thought, strongly inclined to act so as to acquire more and more wealth.

A second assumption concerns Smith's labor theory of value. Labor, said Smith, creates value and is the source of all wealth within a nation. Value does not emerge from nature or the world around us. Rather than emanating from agriculture, for example, value comes out of human labor making something out of the natural environment. In brief, nothing but labor has any real value. Everything else is for human manipulation.

Third, humans have a natural propensity for trading. Unlike other species, humans have almost constant need for the assistance of others. Being creatures of self-interest, it is folly for us to expect others to act benevolently toward us. We can only secure what we need from others by offering, in turn, something they need from us.

> Whoever offers to another a bargain of any kind proposes to do this. Give me that which I want, and you shall have this which you want, is the meaning of every such offer; and it is in this manner that we obtain from one another the far greater part of those good offices which we stand in need of. It is not from the benevolence of the butcher, the brewer, or the baker that we expect our dinner, but from their regard to their own interest. We address ourselves not to their humanity, but to their self love, and never talk to them of our own necessities, but of their advantages.[7]

This disposition to barter, said Smith, gives occasion to the division of labor—dividing the labor and production process into areas of specialization, which in theory increases capital and strengthens economic productivity.

Smith's fourth assumption is that individuals have natural endowments that should determine the kind of work they will do. The disposition to trade will lead them to work that harmonizes with their talents. This collection of talents provides a common stock from which each of us can purchase whatever part of another's talents we need or desire.

The preceding assumptions led Smith to claim that the greatest utility will result from unfettered pursuit of self-interest. Individuals should be allowed unrestricted access to raw materials, markets, and labor. Government interference in private enterprise should be eliminated, free competition encouraged, and enlightened self-interest made the rule of the day. Because human beings are acquisitive creatures with natural talents, we will, if left free, engage in labor and exchange goods in a way that results in the greatest benefit to society. In our efforts to advance our own economic interests, we inevitably act so as to promote the economic well-being of society generally.

> Every individual is continually exerting himself to find the most advantageous employment for whatever capital he can command. It is his own advantage, indeed, and not that of the society, which he has in view. . . . [But] by directing that industry in such a manner as its produce may be of the greatest value, he [is] . . . led by an invisible hand to promote an end that was no part of his intention. By pursuing his own interest

he frequently promotes that of society more effectually than when he really intends to promote it.[8]

To explain why pursuit of self-interest necessarily leads to the greatest social benefit, Smith invoked the law of supply and demand, which we alluded to in discussing competition. The law of supply and demand will temper the pursuit of self-interest exactly as competition keeps the enterprising capitalist from becoming a ruthless profiteer. The law of supply and demand similarly will solve the problems of adequate goods and fair price.

The law of supply and demand will even, some think, solve the problem of fair wages, for labor is another commodity that is up for sale, just as are shoes or jeans. Just as the price of a new product, such as the jeans in our hypothetical example, at first is high, so too will the wages of labor in a new field. But as labor becomes more plentiful, wages will decline. Eventually labor in this field will so increase that the wages will fall to a subsistence level. At this point, inefficient laborers will be eliminated and forced to seek other work, just as the inefficient manufacturers of jeans were forced out of that business and into others. And, again like the price of jeans, the price of labor will then stabilize at a fair level. As for the inefficient laborers, they will find work and a living wage elsewhere. In seeking new fields of labor, they will help maximize the majority's opportunities to enjoy the necessities, conveniences, and trifles of human life.

Some modern capitalists still claim that capitalism operates as Smith envisioned and can be justified on the same utilitarian grounds. But others disagree.

CRITICAL QUESTIONS FOR CAPITALISM

Criticisms of capitalism generally fall into two categories, which are not mutually exclusive: theoretical and operational. Theoretical criticisms challenge capitalism's basic assumptions; operational criticisms question whether capitalism has delivered on its promises. The following four inquiries are a mix of these two critical thrusts.

Are Humans Basically Economic Creatures?

Classical capitalism views human beings—whether producers, workers, or consumers—as essentially economic creatures, individuals who recognize and are motivated by their own economic self-interests. To sample some implications of this assumption, consider human beings as consumers.

Capitalism assumes that consumers have full knowledge of the diverse choices available to them in the marketplace. They know the different price structures of different producers of similar products, are aware of differences in product quality, and can make the "best choice" regarding price and quality. But the key choices facing today's consumer are rarely simple. From foods to drugs, automobiles to appliances, fertilizers to water conditioners, the modern marketplace is a cornucopia of products whose nature, composition, and nuances require a high level of consumer literacy. Even with agencies and interest groups to represent them, today's consumers rarely are an equal match for powerful industries that can influence prices and create and shape markets. By some estimates, business spends about $100 billion a year on advertising. "Wherever we turn," writes Theodore Levitt, "advertising is forcibly thrust on us in an intrusive orgy of abrasive sound and sight, all to induce us to do something we might not ordinarily do, or to induce us to do it differently. This massive and persistent effort crams increasingly more commercial noise into the same, few, strained 24 hours of the day."[9] What's more, the capitalistic view of human nature assumes that consumers who need a good or service will have the resources to buy it. The economic facts of life belie this.

But, according to some critics of capitalism, the chief moral significance of capitalism's view of the economic creature is that it presents little in the way of an ideal to which either individuals or societies may properly aspire. It presents no high sense of human mission or purpose on either the personal or the collective level, as other views of human nature have.

Christianity, for example, has long aspired to the ideal of a truly religious community united in *agape*, selfless love. And socialism, because it views human nature as malleable, hopes to see people transformed from the "competitive, acquisitive beings that they are (and that they are *encouraged* to be) under all property-dominated, market-oriented systems." In the more "benign environment of a propertyless, non-market social system," socialists believe that more cooperative and less selfish human beings will emerge.[10] Such positive ideals and aspirations as those displayed by Christian or socialist belief systems are lacking in capitalism—or so its critics charge.

Does Capitalism Breed Oligopolies?

As early as the middle of the nineteenth century, the German philosopher and political economist Karl Marx (1818–1883) argued that capitalism leads to a concentration of property and thus a concentration of resources and power in relatively few hands. Exorbitant costs, complex machinery, increasing demands, and intense competition all work against the survival of small firms, said Marx. Many see proof of Marx's observation in today's economy.

Whereas the earlier economy of the Industrial Revolution was characterized by comparatively free and open competition, today's is made up largely of a handful of enormous companies that can, to a distressing extent, conspire to fix prices, eliminate competition, and monopolize an industry. The food industry is a perfect example, as Texas Commissioner of Agriculture Jim Hightower points out in "Food Monopoly: Who's Who in the Thanksgiving Business?"[11] According to Hightower, the merger activity of giant firms has produced a series of shared monopolies in the food industry, with four or fewer firms controlling a majority of sales of a given product. Here are the levels of market control by just the top three brands in various categories:

Product	Share of Market Held by Top Three Brands
Table salt	91.7%
Flour	80.4%
Catsup	86.1%
Mustard	76.2%
Peanut Butter	78.6%
Salad & cooking oil	85.5%
Vinegar	84.1%
Gelatin desserts	98.4%
Whipped toppings	85.6%
Canned evaporated milk	82.3%
Marshmallows	98.2%
Instant puddings	96.0%
Shortenings	81.0%
Jams & jellies	75.2%
Nuts	80.7%
Honey	82.2%
Frozen potato products	82.2%
Frostings	97.7%
Spaghetti sauce	85.9%
Pickle relish	79.2%
Instant tea	86.0%
Frozen dinners	92.8%
Corn & tortilla chips	86.7%
Canned spaghetti & noodles	96.0%
Ready-to-serve dips	81.5%
Nondairy cream substitutes	86.1%
Pretzels	85.6%
Dry milk	80.1%
Add-meat dinner mixes	90.7%
Canned stews	83.6%
Instant potatoes	83.9%
Pizza mix	86.6%
Instant breakfast products	90.8%

Why is this kind of market control significant? Since there is little competition, the "natural" regulator of prices is lost, and the consumer pays the price. "Once a few firms gain a monopoly position in a product category," says Hightower, "the market for the category is considered to be 'mature,' . . . and the companies are able to 'harvest' it, meaning that they can push up prices. Taking one product at a time, such artificial inflation doesn't make a dramatic impression on shoppers—a few cents more on shortening, a little extra for the pizza mix. But when the whole market basket is pushed to the cash register, consumers have been nickle-and-dimed to death."

It is true that antitrust actions have tried to foster competition and break up monopolies, as in the cases of such corporate behemoths as Standard Oil and AT&T. But on the whole, such actions have proved largely ineffectual in halting the concentration of economic power in large, oligopolistic firms. In some cases, corporate giants have spawned even larger offspring: firms called multinationals that do business in several countries. And it is no secret that the cumulative power of business resulting from greater and greater profits has placed it in the position of a kind of industrial corporate state, an economic colossus that can negotiate independently with governments, solicit favorable franchises and tariffs, and influence self-serving legislation.

Heilbroner, for one, suggests that the rise of such giant enterprises is changing the face of capitalism. Unable to function in the highly irrational system of ruthless competition, guided by some metaphysical "invisible hand," the big corporations attempt to alter the market setting through a system of public and private planning. The planning takes the form of efforts to create an atmosphere orderly and stable enough to allow the pursuit of profitable growth. Heilbroner says the planning assumes many guises, from union contracts that eliminate uncertainties in the labor market to

sophisticated advertising calculated to create dependable product markets to cozy relationships with government in order to create programs that will ensure continuing high levels of aggregate demands. "At its worst," he writes, "we find it in the military-industrial complex—the very epitome of the new symbiotic business-government relations."[12]

Has Capitalism Promoted Competition?

As previously noted, free competition is, theoretically, the lifeblood of capitalism. Unfettered competition supposedly serves the collective interest, while offering the richest opportunities for the individual. And yet, some of the same true believers who rabidly preach the doctrine of competition at home often balk at applying it to international trade. There they want protection, not competition. Indeed, Robert Reich, for one, claims that America's basic industries lost the "habit of competing" over 20 years ago.[13]

Reich says that by the mid-1960s the industries forming the U.S. industrial base (e.g., steel and auto) had become "stable oligopolies of three or four major firms, led by the largest and most entrenched." Woefully unprepared to compete in technology and price, American producers were quick to seek government protection from the 1960s influx of low-priced Japanese steel, autos, and televisions. The next twenty years witnessed a variety of protective measures. One of the most publicized were the restrictions that the U.S. forced Japan to impose on its auto exports. Among the lesser known, though not trivial, protections:

> Duties on $3.8 billion worth of imports from Southeast Asia and Latin America, which had the effect of protecting domestic manufacturers of car parts, electrical goods, fertilizers, and chemicals.

Special duties on 132 products, ranging from South Korean bicycles to Italian shoes, and including the lowly clothespin.

Special tax credits and tax depreciation allowances for specific industries threatened by foreign competition (total cost: $62.4 billion, or about 3% of the GNP).

Federal loan guarantees for specific industries totaling $221.6 billion.[14]

A Congressional Budget Office study estimates that business collects more than $60 billion annually through subsidy and credit programs.[15] And at least one writer contends that corporate America receives more in direct and indirect subsidization than it pays in taxes.[16]

Perhaps "free competition" is nice in theory but ultimately unworkable: Governmental intervention is necessary to protect vital economic interests (as with protective tariffs). Or maybe latter-day capitalists have not kept the faith: They have abandoned or perverted the doctrine of free competition because it has become inconvenient or unprofitable to maintain it. Whatever the explanation, myriad indicators point to the fact that, insofar as competition is concerned, capitalism functions differently from how it was conceived to work. Professor of business Robert B. Carson makes the point as follows:

> In surveying the American business system it is obvious that competition still exists; however, it is not a perfect competition. Often it is not price competition at all. With the possible exception of some farm markets where there are still large numbers of producers of similar and undifferentiated products (wheat, for instance), virtually every producer of goods and services has some control over price. The degree of control varies from industry to industry and between firms within an industry. Nevertheless,

it does exist and it amounts to an important modification in our model of a free-enterprise economy.[17]

Does Capitalism Exploit and Alienate?

Marx argued that as the means of production becomes concentrated in the hands of the few, the balance of power between capitalists (bourgeoisie) and laborers (proletariat) tips in favor of the bourgeoisie. Because workers have nothing to sell but their labor, said Marx, the bourgeoisie is able to exploit them by paying them less than the true value created by their labor. In fact, Marx thought, it is only through such an exploitative arrangement that capitalists make a profit and increase their capital. And the more capital they accumulate, the more they can exploit workers. Marx predicted that eventually workers would revolt. Unwilling to be exploited further, they would rise and overthrow their oppressors and set up an economic system that would truly benefit all.

The development of capitalistic systems since Marx's time belies his forecast. Legal, political, and other institutions have tempered many of the greedy, exploitative dispositions of capitalism. The twentieth century has witnessed legislation curbing egregious worker abuse, guaranteeing a minimum wage, and ensuring a safer and more healthful work environment. The emergence of labor unions and their subsequent victories have significantly enlarged the worker's share of the economic pie. Indeed, many of the specific measures proposed by Marx and his collaborator Friedrich Engels in the *Communist Manifesto* (1848) have been implemented in capitalistic countries: a program of graduated income tax, free education for all children in public schools, investiture of significant economic control in the state, and so on.

Still, many would say that, although democratic institutions may have curbed some of the excesses of capitalism, they can do nothing to prevent the alienation of workers that results from having to do unfulfilling work. Again, because of the unequal positions of capitalist and worker, laborers must work for someone else—they must do work imposed on them as a means of satisfying the needs of others. As a result, they must eventually feel exploited and debased.

But what about workers who are paid handsomely for their efforts? They too, said Marx, remain alienated, for as the fruits of their labor are enjoyed by someone else, their work ultimately proves meaningless to them. In the following selection from his "Economic and Philosophic Manuscripts" (1844), Marx summarizes his notion of alienation as the separation of individuals from the objects they create, which in turn results in one's separation from other people, from oneself, and ultimately from one's human nature.

> The worker is related to the *product of his labor* as to an *alien* object. For it is clear on this presupposition that the more the worker expends himself in work the more powerful becomes the world of objects which he creates in face of himself, the poorer he becomes in his inner life, and the less he belongs to himself. . . . The worker puts his life into the object, and his life then belongs no longer to himself but to the object. The greater his activity, therefore, the less he possesses. What is embodied in the product of his labor is no longer his own. The greater this product is, therefore, the more he is diminished. The *alienation* of the worker in his product means not only that his labor becomes an object, assumes an *external* existence, but that it exists independently, *outside himself*, and alien to him, and that it stands opposed to him as an autonomous power. The life which he has given to the object sets itself against him as an alien and hostile force. . . .

What constitutes the alienation of labor? First, that the work is *external* to the worker, that it is not part of his nature; and that, consequently, he does not fulfill himself in his work but denies himself, has a feeling of misery rather than well-being, does not develop freely his mental and physical energies but is physically exhausted and mentally debased. The worker, therefore, feels himself at home only during his leisure time, whereas at work he feels homeless. His work is not voluntary but imposed, *forced labor*. It is not the satisfaction of a need, but only a *means* for satisfying other needs. Its alien character is clearly shown by the fact that as soon as there is no physical or other compulsion it is avoided like the plague. External labor, labor in which man alienates himself, is a labor of self-sacrifice, of mortification. Finally, the external character of work for the worker is shown by the fact that it is not his own work but work for someone else, that in work he does not belong to himself but to another person. . . .

We arrive at the result that man (the worker) feels himself to be freely active only in his animal functions—eating, drinking and procreating, or at most also in his dwelling and in personal adornment—while in his human functions he is reduced to an animal. The animal becomes human and the human becomes animal.

Eating, drinking and procreating are of course also genuine human functions. But abstractly considered, apart from the environment of human activities, and turned into final and sole ends, they are animal functions.

We have now considered the act of alienation of practical human activity, labor, from two aspects: (1) the relationship of the worker to the *product of labor* as an alien object which dominates him. This relationship is at the same time the relationship to the sensuous external world, to natural objects, as an alien and hostile world; (2) the relationship of labor to the *act of production* within *labor*. This is the relationship of the worker to his own activity as something alien and not belonging to him. . . . This is *self-alienation* as against the above-mentioned alienation of the *thing*.[18]

In Marx's view, when workers are alienated they cannot be free. They may have the political and social freedoms of speech, religion, and governance. But even with these freedoms that guarantee noninterference, individuals still are not free, because freedom from government interference and persecution are not necessarily guarantees of freedom from economic exploitation. And it is for this kind of freedom, freedom from alienation, that Marx and Engels felt such passion.

Some would say that one need not wade through Marxist philosophy to get a feel for what he and others mean by worker alienation. Just talk to workers themselves, as writer Studs Terkel has done. In different ways the hundreds of workers Terkel has interviewed from diverse occupations speak of the same thing: dehumanization.

> Mike Fitzgerald . . . is a laborer in a steel mill. "I feel like the guys who built the pyramids. Somebody built 'em. Somebody built the Empire State Building, too. There's hard work behind it. I would like to see a building, say the Empire State, with a foot-wide strip from top to bottom and the name of every bricklayer on it, the name of every electrician. So when a guy walked by, he could take his son and say, 'See, that's me over there on the 45th floor. I put that steel beam in.' . . . Everybody should have something to point to."
>
> Sharon Atkins is 24 years old. She's been to college and acidly observes, "The first myth that blew up in my face is that a college education will get you a worthwhile job." For the last two years she's been a receptionist at an advertising agency. "I didn't look at myself as 'just a dumb broad' at the front desk, who took phone calls and messages. I thought I was something else. The office taught me differently."
>
> . . . Harry Stallings, 27, is a spot welder on the assembly line at an auto plant. "They'll give better care to that machine than they will to you. If it breaks down, there's somebody out there to fix it right away. If I break down, I'm just pushed over to the other side till another man takes my place. The only thing the company has in mind is to keep that machine running. A man would be more eager to do a better job if he were given proper respect and the time to do it." . . .
>
> The words of Ken Brown, owner of a repair shop: "You get enemies in the business, especially if you're successful. Ones that have grown up and started with you. You want to be liked and you want to help people. I've found out that you can't. It's not appreciated. They never thank you. If you're successful in business, you're around phonies all the time. There's always some guy slappin' you on the back, tryin' to get you to buy something from him or lend him money.
>
> "You remember old friends and good times. This relationship is gone. The fun you used to have. They're envious of what you have. They wonder why they didn't do it. When I opened a repair shop in Old Town I was paying my partner $250 a week. I gave him a car and helped with his tuition in college. Someone offered him double what I paid. I said, 'If you go, there's no comin' back.' So he left. We grew up together, went to grammar school. I lived with him. There's no loyalty when it comes to money."[19]

TODAY'S ECONOMIC CHALLENGES

Capitalism, as we have just seen, gives rise to a number of important critical questions, both theoretical and operational. But in looking at possible moral justifications for capitalism as well as at criticisms of it, we have so far discussed general issues, relevant to any capitalist society. Now we will look more specifically at some of the socioeconomic challenges facing the United States as we enter the last decade of the century.

At the beginning of Chapter 3 we discussed the trend toward a more inequitable distribution of national income. To many experts, it seems that the problem begins with a decreasing rate of growth in the country's gross national product, which has essentially halved in the past two decades, from 3.8 percent per year in the 1960s to 2 percent per year or less in the 1980s. This slowdown reflects a declining rate of growth in productivity, from 2.7 percent per year between 1960 and 1970 to .9 percent in the 1980s. Economists do not agree about the ultimate causes of this slowdown, but it is clear that it is not an international phenomenon. The growth of productivity in such countries as West Germany and Japan is three to five times the U.S. rate. Declining productivity and increased foreign competition have pushed many workers down the earnings ladder.[20]

If slow growth is not reversed, one way or another, Americans will become poorer and their standard of living will sink. By some measures this is already happening. Nonsupervisory workers—some four-fifths of the work force—have seen their wages (adjusted for inflation) steadily decline since their peak in 1972.[21] Increasing productivity is the key to enhanced international competitiveness and, thus, to an American economic recovery. But this requires bucking a discouraging long-term trend, because in the last quarter century the U.S. has been steadily losing its share of both foreign and domestic markets. The nation's huge balance of trade deficit is only the most visible sign of this. It was over $160 billion in 1988 and is not expected to sink dramatically in the foreseeable future.

The many complex causes of feeble productivity growth and declining competitiveness go beyond the scope of this book. But recent commentators have drawn attention to three that deserve discussion here because they suggest new areas of business responsibility. They are (1) a fixation with short-term performance over long-term strategies, (2) an abandonment of the traditional capitalist orientation toward the manufacturing of goods, and (3) changes in attitude toward work, which may foreshadow a whole new era of employer-employee relations.

Short-Term Performance

Long before his well-publicized trial, John DeLorean used to run General Motors Pontiac Division and then Chevrolet. He quit GM in 1973 and subsequently started manufacturing his own stainless steel cars. Shortly after leaving GM, DeLorean wrote *On A Clear Day You Can See General Motors*, an inside look at the prototypical well-run American business. At one point in the book DeLorean writes:

> Never once while I was in GM's management did I hear substantial concern raised about the impact of our business on America, its consumers, or the economy. When we should have been planning switches to smaller, more fuel-efficient, lighter cars in the late 1960s, in response to a growing demand in the market place, GM refused because "we make more money on big cars." It mattered not that customers wanted the smaller cars, or that a national balance-of-payments deficit was being built in large part because of the burgeoning sales of foreign cars in the American market.
>
> Refusal to enter the small car market when the profits were better on bigger cars, despite the needs of the public and the national economy, was not an isolated case of corporate insensitivity. It was typical. And what disturbed me is that it was indicative of fundamental problems with the system.[22]

One of the "fundamental problems" explicit in DeLorean's observation is American industry's preoccupation with short-term planning. The auto industry, as DeLorean suggests, is a perfect example. In part as a result of such planning, by 1980 imported cars had captured 28.4 percent of the U.S. market, up from about 15 percent in 1970. This erosion contributed to Chrysler Corporation's struggle for survival and to GM's, Ford's, and American Motors's scramble to contain their crumbling shares of the market.

But preoccupation with short-term performance at the expense of long-term strategies is hardly confined to the automotive industry. The same mentality characterizes most corporate executives and managers of industries that grew up together with the rising U.S. population and affluence in the 1950s and 1960s. For these business people, planning consisted largely of increasing productive capacity at the right times in the right places and using short-term profit as the exclusive measure of success. Today's population and economic realities are far different. For one thing, the U.S. population has stabilized. For another, wealth in the world has been so distributed that new competition has arisen between domestic companies and between U.S. and foreign companies. As a result, many planning strategists say that U.S. companies must become more visionary, that they must define long-term goals and be willing to stick to them even at the expense of short-term profit. The problem, of course, is how to get business people to do this when they have been trained to think and do otherwise.[23]

A focus on short-term results often goes hand in hand with an effort to avoid genuine economic competition. This was recently illustrated by Donald Petersen, chairman of the Ford Motor Company.[24] At the end of 1987, Ford was the world's most profitable auto company, with $9 billion in spare cash. Its cars were once again popular, and its plants were operating at near full capacity. Against this backdrop one might suppose that Ford would be ready to drop the "temporary" quotas on Japanese imports in effect since 1980. Wrong. Petersen instead proposed sharp, new limits on Japanese imports (the first cutback would be 600,000 cars).

The problem from Petersen's point of view is that the auto industry's total sales are declining. In part, however, this is due to high prices. In 1987 the average car buyer paid $13,520 for a new car, an increase of nearly 80 percent over the 1980 price tag of $7,574, only a small part of which reflects consumers buying bigger cars or selecting more options. Normally in this situation, supply and demand pressure would push prices down. Ford could still sell all its cars, but at a lower profit margin. But Petersen and Ford are not interested in this. They would rather avoid competition, restrict supply, keep prices and profits high—and let the consumer pick up the tab.

This attitude contrasts sharply with the competitive mentality at Toyota. In 1987 the value of the dollar against the yen was 50 percent of what it had been two years earlier. Normally, this would greatly increase the price of foreign imports like Japanese cars and make American products more competitive. (This is why the Reagan administration was pleased with the dollar's fall: a 50 percent fall in the dollar is like a 50 percent tariff on Japanese products.) Toyota's response, however, was to sacrifice profit and increase productivity in order to hold price increases to a minimum. In this way, Toyota was successfully pursuing a long-term strategy of keeping its sales and market share high, even at the cost of lower short-term profit margins.[25]

Lack of Interest in Production

Traditionally, capitalists have made money by producing goods. Manufacturing was the backbone of the American economy and the basis of our prosperity. Yet today, in industry after industry, American manufacturers are closing up shop or curtailing their operations and becoming marketing organizations for other producers, usually foreign. The result is the evolution of a new kind of company: manufacturers that do little or no manufacturing. They may perform a host of profit-making functions—from design to distribution—but they lack their own production base. Companies long identified with making goods of all sorts now often produce only the package and the label. In contrast to traditional manufacturers, they have become "hollow corporations."[26]

U.S. manufacturers are pursuing a strategy of "outsourcing," that is, buying parts or whole products from other producers, both at home and abroad. This breaks down the manufacturer's traditional vertical structure, in which it makes virtually all critical parts, and replaces it with a network of small suppliers. Proponents of the new system describe it as flexible and efficient—a logical outcome of the drive to lower the costs of doing business. But critics doubt that the U.S. can prosper without a strong manufacturing base. As Tsutomu Ohshima, a senior managing director of Toyota Motor Corp., puts it: "You can't survive with just a service industry." In terms of wages, productivity, and innovation, the service-sector fails to compare with basic industry. Nor can the service economy thrive, if the latter is allowed to wither.

Closely related to the "hollowing" of corporations is the enormous recent wave of corporate mergers and acquisitions. These days the most exciting action in town and the best opportunity for making quick, enormous profits lie in taking over—or threatening to take over—existing corporations. The players include the nation's large *Fortune* 500 corporations, the big Wall Street investment banks, corporate raiders like Carl Icahn and Sir James Goldsmith, and risk arbitrageurs like the fallen Ivan Boesky. With them has come a whole

new vocabulary: mergers, hostile takeovers, greenmail, stock buybacks, poison pills, divestitures, leveraged buyouts, and junk bonds. And when the corporate raiders are successful, the result usually means retrenching, selling subsidiaries, and eliminating jobs (both middle management and factory workers), as the raiders ruthlessly cut costs to drive up the value of their new stock.[27]

Takeovers, and the vast "corporate restructuring" that has resulted, are one of the most visible economic trends of the 1980s. Between 1983 and 1987, for example, no fewer than 12,200 companies and corporate divisions were bought and sold in deals worth $490 billion. The value of mergers and acquisitions jumped from below $40 billion in 1980 to nearly $170 billion in 1986. To take the oil industry as an example, in 1984 Chevron bought Gulf for $13.4 billion, Texaco bought Getty Oil for $10.2 billion, and Mobil shelled out $5.7 billion for Superior Oil.[28] Yet all this activity is directed toward making money through the manipulation of existing assets, rather than toward the actual production of new or better goods. Many American entrepreneurs and capitalists seem to have found better and easier ways to make profit than the time-honored technique of competing in the manufacture and production of goods.

In their defense, corporate raiders claim that takeovers oust incompetent managers, eliminate useless bureaucracy, and liquidate unproductive assets. Corporate managers, however, claim the opposite. Takeovers force them to waste time trying to keep their stock price high, to cut back on research and development, and to close plants to pay for stock repurchases. Chrysler chairman Lee Iacocca asserts:

> I see billions of dollars tied up in new corporate debt to keep the raiders at bay while research and development go begging. I see billions going for greenmail that ought to be building new high-tech factories. I also see a huge share of

America's best management talent wasted on takeover games when it should be devoted to strengthening the industrial base of the country.[29]

Changes in Attitudes Toward Work

The decline in U.S. productivity growth is rooted in more than a short-term performance mentality, outsourcing, and takeovers. It is also rooted in attitudes toward government, social institutions, business, and especially work.

As American productivity growth, once the high performance engine of national wealth, has sputtered to an embarrassingly uncompetitive low, management is apt to lament: "Nobody wants to work any more." What management probably means is that the work ethic is dead. Is it?

The so-called work ethic stresses the value of work for its own sake as something necessary for every person. It also emphasizes the belief that hard work pays off in the end. "If you work hard enough," the expression goes, "you'll make it."

As Paul Bernstein points out in "The Work Ethic That Never Was," the idea of work as an abstraction arrived rather late in the history of toil.[30] The vast majority of humankind has always tried to avoid work and has viewed it at best as a necessary evil. What is termed the "Protestant Work Ethic" took root in the Protestant Reformation of the sixteenth century and is identified with Martin Luther and John Calvin, who saw work as a collaborative act with God to do the work of the universe. Looked at this way, human labor was linked to God's will.

Although the idea of work's inherent virtue may have seemed a pious platitude to generations of immigrants who toiled in the mines and mills and factories of nineteenth-century industrial America, the idea of work as a means of improving the lot of self and family was passionately held. For countless millions of American workers building the industrial might of a young and vigorous nation, work would get them to the proverbial pot of gold at the end of the rainbow. In short, the immigrant work ethic, grounded in secular pragmatism, eventually merged with the Protestant work ethic, based in theological purpose. The upshot? A view of the value of work in terms of motive. To work for mere survival was desperate, dehumanizing, and ignoble. But to labor for a better life for self and posterity gave work a fierce dignity. It is that dignity, that indefatigable energy and undaunted hope in a better tomorrow, that many find lacking today in the American worker.

The work ethic, though not dead, is certainly much damaged today, because the attitudes toward work are different. As painful memories of the Great Depression have waned, so has the disciplined and docile approach to work that it produced. As financial support systems have been welded into society (e.g., unemployment insurance, union benefits, welfare payments, food stamps, and the like), job loss, though still traumatic, is not the catastrophe it once was. As young people have become increasingly more educated, they have rearranged their ideas about what they want out of life. For these and other reasons, the long-held and widely cherished work ethic has indeed changed.

The evidence of this change can be seen in the workplace itself. For example, it is not uncommon for operative workers to balk at doing the monotonous tasks their ancestors once accepted, albeit grudgingly. Loyalty to employers seems on the decline, and loyalty to fellow workers seems on the rise. Turnover rates in many industries are enough to make discontinuity an expensive problem. Organizational plans, schedules, and demands no longer carry the authoritative clout they once did; workers today will often subordinate them to personal needs, which results in rampant absenteeism. Moreover, employee sabotage and violence, once unheard of, happen frequently enough today to worry management. Adding to industry's woes, drug use at the office is increasingly the cause of employee theft, absenteeism, and low productivity. According to Ira Lipman, president of Guardsmark Inc., a security services company in Memphis, "If you could get rid of drugs, we'd be far ahead of other countries in productivity."[31]

Although it is impossible to pin down precisely today's workers' attitudes toward work, basically they seem willing to work hard on a job they find interesting and rewarding so long as they have the freedom to influence the nature of their jobs and pursue their own life-styles. They have a growing expectation that work will provide self-respect, nonmaterial rewards, and substantial opportunities for personal growth. And they have a growing willingness to demand individual rights, justice, and equality on the job.[32]

Jerome M. Rosow of the Work in America Institute sums up some of his own observations on our changing life-styles and attitudes to work this way:

> The permissive society has fostered a change in authority roles. The young workers have higher expectations and place intelligent limits upon the exercise of authority over their lives.
>
> The general mistrust toward big business is no longer limited to the public at large. Now it also appears to an increasing degree in employees at all levels who are puzzled at or critical of the behavior of their own employer. . . .
>
> Changing attitudes toward work reflect the values of a postreligious society which no longer views work as punishment with a reward in the afterlife.
>
> Youth reflects much less commitment to the work ethic and greater cynicism in many areas. Even managers and executives have been searching for a better balance between work goals and life goals. Work is increasingly challenged by the leisure society.

> Older workers do not look retrospectively upon their careers with a real sense of achievement. Instead of seeking to change the system, they have chosen to seek the escape route of early retirement. . . .
>
> The era of rising entitlements has created a feeling that jobs, income, and a rising standard of life are no longer privileges, but instead are a secured right.[33]

If industry is to improve productive capacity and be more competitive, it must confront seriously these changing social attitudes. As Paul Bernstein argues, it is counterproductive to compare the contemporary worker with an idealized worker of yesteryear. Rather, we must acknowledge that we have a new "work ethic," which, in Bernstein's words,

> is unrelated to religious demands of ministers and manufacturer's representatives, but is part and parcel of the individual desire for meaningful and challenging labor in which some autonomy is an integral feature. An increasingly professionalized work force will not accept a golden embrace unless it is accompanied by fulfilling jobs that have been designed for a labor force that sees work in relation to family, friends, leisure and self-development. Work, for most of us, continues as an important part of our lives, but only in relation to our total experience.[34]

SUMMARY

1. Capitalism is an economic system in which the major portion of production and distribution is in private hands, operating under a profit or market system. Socialism is an economic system characterized by public ownership of property and a planned economy.

2. Capitalism has gone through several stages: mercantile, industrial, financial, and state welfare.

3. Four key features of capitalism are: the existence of companies, profit motive, competition, and private property.

4. One basic defense of capitalism rests upon a supposed natural moral right to property. Utilitarians deny the existence of such rights. Other critics doubt that this right entitles one to have a system of property rules and regulations identical to the one we now have in the U.S.

5. Another basic defense of capitalism is utilitarian and is associated with the classical economic arguments of Adam Smith. Smith insisted that when people are left free to pursue their own economic interests, they will, without intending it, produce the greatest good for all. Smith based his claim on these assumptions: (1) only labor creates value, (2) human beings are acquisitive, (3) they have a natural propensity for trading, and (4) they have natural endowments, which should determine the kind of work they do.

6. Critics question the basic assumptions of capitalism (theoretical challenges) and whether it has delivered on its promises (operational challenges). Specifically, they ask: (1) Are humans basically economic creatures? (2) Does capitalism breed oligopolies? (3) Has capitalism promoted competition? (4) Does capitalism exploit and alienate?

7. As we enter the last decade of the century, our capitalist socioeconomic system faces a number of challenges. Among the problems that must be overcome are (1) a fixation on short-term performance at the expense of long-term strategies and (2) a lack of interest in the actual manufacturing of goods. In addition, we must come to grips with (3) our society's changing attitudes toward work.

CASE 4.1
Frayed Blue Collars

On January 31, 1980, the press release hit the mayor's desk and the mayor hit the ceiling. "This is devastating!" he shouted. "It's a clear case of corporate bad faith!"

Some months earlier, General Motors chairman Thomas A. Murphy had come to St. Louis and announced plans to invest $100 million in expanding and renovating the 175-acre St. Louis plant. But that was before the gasoline lines abruptly changed the car-buying habits of Americans, leaving GM with little choice but to switch from manufacturing big cars to smaller ones. The city hadn't anticipated the gas crunch either. City officials were so pleased with Murphy's news that they jumped at a GM request for more land to assist in the expansion. In fact, before the January 31 announcement that GM was moving, the city committed $2 million in public funds to acquire a 44-acre site adjacent to the plant.

"Not only were we misled," fumed the mayor, "we're left holding the bag for $2 million."

What happened in St. Louis is happening with alarming frequency in the industrial heartland of America. Old industrial cities, their economies intertwined with the economic health of aging and obsolete manufacturing plants, are ailing as those plants are being forced to close, cut back, or relocate in more modern but sometimes remote locales. Such dislocations devastate the lives of individuals and the well-being of communities.

These plant closings and relocations especially dominate the headlines throughout the industrial crescent of the North and Midwest. Among the areas hardest hit has been Akron, Ohio, once an industrial center for the production of rubber products. Today most of Akron's factories that once employed nearly 100,000 workers are maintained by skeleton crews. Mismanagement, foreign competition, the recession, and labor demands all have conspired to cripple the once vibrant industry. For the thousands of displaced workers in Akron, and the tens of thousands nationwide, the "American dream" has turned into a nightmare. What once appeared to be a never-ending ascent to higher and higher levels of the "good life" has suddenly turned into a downward spiral in income and self-esteem. In the resulting struggle for survival, some make it, some don't—but nobody succeeds as easily as before.

When Frank Burton was in high school in 1960, he had a part-time job at an Akron convenience store, stocking shelves and ringing the register.[35] Like so many local youngsters his age, Burton eagerly awaited the day he'd graduate and "hire on" at the nearby Firestone tire factory. Burton did just that, and for the next twenty years he worked in the plant from dawn until dusk, just as his father and grandfather had before him. But all that ended in 1981 when the plant shut down.

After he was laid off, Burton tried to get other jobs. He studied 980 hours of computer science. But no one in Akron needed his new skills. He finally landed a job at the old convenience store, doing what he did when he was in high school.

"I got my heart torn out," he says. "At forty-two I should be reaching my top income potential." In fact, he makes $7,000 at the convenience store, a fraction of the $30,000 he earned at the plant. To pay off debts, he has been forced to sell his pension rights.

Professor of industrial relations Dennis Ahlburg has a cold, hard message for people like Frank Burton: ". . . they're lucky they did

so well for so long. . . . For a lot of these people it really is over."[36]

An urban historian who agrees scolds organized labor for holding out false hope of a return to the glory days of the 60s and 70s. "Spokesmen for the working class have tried to build a sense of self-pride in the dignity of labor," he says. "But to keep mouthing old phrases—to attempt to breathe new life into words no longer relevant to our present social vocabulary—will produce bitterness, frustration, and possible rising social disorder."[37]

There's some basis for the grim outlook and stoic advice. In 1980 Japan produced eleven million vehicles, exceeding U.S. production by about 40 percent. That made Japan the world's premiere automaker, a claim it still holds. Many believe the U.S. will never regain its top spot and thus never be able to reemploy the thousands of Frank Burtons in their old jobs.

Social forecaster John Naisbitt, writing in his best-selling *Megatrends*, even doubts that Japan or any single nation can maintain the top position long because the world auto industry is undergoing "globalization." Naisbitt explains what he means:

> Half the American population owns a car already, and in Europe, where public transportation is superior to that of the United States, the demand is satisfied with one-third of the people owning cars. The replacement market in automobiles that's left will fall far short of the dynamic growth market that we've known for the past thirty years.
>
> Furthermore, if we think we are going to supply automobiles to satisfy the Third World's growing demand, we had better think again.
>
> There are eighty-six countries in the world that have automobile assembly lines. Mexico, for example, is fast becoming a major auto producer. Volkswagen, Nissan, Ford, GM, and others operate plants in Mexico, which produced nearly

300,000 autos in 1979. Countries with their own auto plants will be in the best position to meet the local demand for automobiles as the developing world becomes rich enough to purchase them. Furthermore, many developing countries have clearly indicated they will act to protect their own growing auto industries from any invasion by big auto makers.

Incredible though it seems, it's in this environment that the United States government bailed out Chrysler. If we continue in that direction, this country will turn its automobile industry into an employment program. . . .[38]

Indeed, the government not only bailed out Chrysler but propped up the entire auto industry by pressuring Japan to impose "voluntary" quotas on the number of autos it sent to the U.S. Detroit argued that the quotas were needed to buy time to regain its competitiveness. Labor organizations agreed, adding that the quotas were the only way to protect American jobs and offer people like Frank Burton any hope of reemployment in the industry. Both automakers and workers insisted that Japan must be forced to "play on a level playing field." By this they meant that Japan's remarkable success could be explained largely in terms of the advantages enjoyed by its automakers (for example, tax breaks) but denied its U.S. counterparts. Overlooked in the emotion-charged atmosphere were studies that showed an effective corporate tax rate of about 50 percent for Japanese companies, compared with about 27 percent for U.S. manufacturers. Also disregarded were studies that attributed the Japanese advantage to superior management and production-line techniques. And while automakers and labor leaders lobbied government for protectionist legislation, car buyers who would be denied the Japanese auto alternative were effectively ignored.

In 1980, the auto industry received its quota protection. For the next four years Japan did limit the number of cars it exported to the U.S. But by the end of 1984, only months before the quota agreement was to expire, the industry admitted that it still wasn't ready to compete with Japan—apparently the playing field was not yet quite level.

Lee Iacocca of Chrysler Corporation and labor officials began lobbying for an extension of the "voluntary" quotas, due to expire in March 1985. They focused their efforts on U.S. Trade Representative William E. Brock who, believing that the quotas could no longer be justified, expressed no interest in extending them. While Brock's anti-quotas position shook up Detroit, it came as good news to many consumers and free-market advocates. Brock's mail began running 6-to-1 in support of his stand.

Faced with such staunch resistance, Iacocca was reported as ready to make a deal on Japanese auto quotas.[39] If Brock would extend the quotas, Iacocca would freeze the prices of his U.S.-built small cars. He would also limit buying auto parts from abroad.

Labor's reaction to the Iacocca plan was mixed. It liked the idea of capping the purchase of imported parts, because that would mean more jobs for Americans, possibly even the rehiring of people like Frank Burton. Moreover, quotas probably would increase the purchases of U.S.-made cars, thereby providing job security. But frozen prices would also mean frozen wages, a revolting prospect to labor organizations that were still bristling over the $7 million plus that Ford chairman Philip Caldwell earned in 1983 and the $180 million GM paid in executive bonuses in the same year. Furthermore, as some consumer groups were quick to point out, frozen prices didn't necessarily mean savings for car buyers; for the prices were already bloated as a result of limited competition from abroad. Why, they asked, should car buyers be made to carry the burden of propping up an ailing industry?

Those opposing quotas on auto imports point out that despite such protection in the recent past, the auto industry continues to deteriorate—Chrysler's resurrection notwithstanding. High wages, antiquated plants and equipment, inappropriate management techniques, corporate short-sightedness, superior imports—none of these causes of the industry's malaise, they argue, will be remedied by "voluntary" quotas. Moreover, some claim that the quotas are unfair to consumers by pushing up the prices of cars and auto-related products. Although quotas may immediately save some jobs, over the long haul they may increase unemployment by reducing the purchasing power of other countries that spend their money in the U.S.

These same people do admit, however, that avoiding the protectionist reflex will not come cheaply. The costs in terms of human suffering and social upheaval will be high, perhaps higher than some can pay. Thousands like Frank Burton already are feeling the psychological toll exacted by a forced move to a low-status, poor-paying job.

"We define ourselves in terms of our jobs," says Walter Nord, a professor of organizational psychology, "and that identity permeates our families, especially in towns where one industry is prominent. . . . When you're suddenly working at a hamburger joint instead of Bethlehem Steel, that's a blow to your self-esteem. And the loss of health and other benefits has to have family-life consequences."[40]

Sometimes the consequences can be unbearable, as in the case of an Akron rubber worker who lost his job and then stood by, seemingly powerless to stop his life from shriveling. When his wife divorced him and took their children, he snapped. The day the divorce was final, he drove to her place of business, and waited for her to come outside.

When she did, he drew alongside her and fatally shot himself with a deer rifle.[41]

Experts fear that as more and more blue-collar workers are laid off and find themselves on a downward spiral, the personal and social problems associated with a diminishing blue-collar work force will worsen. Although the problem already is grave, not much is being done about it.

"We stand last among the major industrial and post-industrial nations in public expenditures on job training and retraining," says urban historian Stanley Schultz. "Because of trends in the economy, we must make a genuine national commitment to education and job retraining for many of our working-class citizens."[42]

As politicians, economists, and academics debate the need for a new industrial policy, General Motors has begun formulating one of its own. Seizing the new technologies of robots, lasers, and computers, GM is innovating in the work its employees do and how they do it.[43] Take, for example, GM's computer-programmed automated guided vehicle (AGV), which, by tracking wires in a plant floor, tirelessly and correctly delivers parts to various points of the assembly line where cars are being assembled. The AGV is only one of many pieces of computer-guided equipment GM uses, including over 100 welding robots and a score of painting robots, bar-coded gates and computer-equipped gatekeepers, and data banks that make information instantly available to workers on the plant floor.

What's more, GM intends to sell many of its high-tech innovations to industries around the world. In other words, the automotive giant is getting into the business of computer software, which it fully expects will run the next generation of factory automated systems. Speaking of his company's new ventures, GM chairman Roger B. Smith says, "We're going to . . . grow a whole new era of diversification for the corporation."[44]

Diversification hardly has been the hallmark of the U.S. auto industry. Indeed, Naisbitt says, "It was part of the conceit of the U.S. automobile companies that they never diversified. They thought they would go on forever, and then even Henry Ford III, whose grandfather gave the world the car, got out while the getting was good."[45] And yet, diversification is quite clearly what GM has in mind—not to mention building better cars more efficiently through high technology.

While admitting it's inevitable, organized labor has mixed feelings about the introduction of high technology into the workplace. For if high-tech means better products that ultimately make jobs more secure, it also means fewer workers and only ones who are trainable. At full production, an auto plant utilizing merely current technology requires one-third fewer workers to produce the same number of cars as a conventional plant. And workers lacking basic computational and language skills have about as much chance of getting a job in a computerized plant as a tone-deaf horn blower has of playing with the Boston Pops.

For those still employed, high-tech represents their last, best chance to keep their jobs. "We don't look at automation as job elimination," says the head of a United Auto Workers local. "We look at it as a way of making cars of much higher quality. If you don't get the quality at the right price, you don't get the sales. You don't get the sales, you don't get any jobs."[46] The local this man heads represents 14,500 workers, 3,000 on indefinite layoffs, at two GM plants in Lansing, Michigan. At an adjacent plant, which together with the other two constitutes the largest GM assembly complex in the U.S., 1,400 of its 42,000 workers are on indefinite layoff. As increasingly sophisticated instruments intrude into the automotive work place, the odds dwindle that many of these 4,200 laid-off workers will ever return to their jobs. And those still working fear that

while high-tech may salvage the automotive companies and other U.S. manufacturers, it may do so at their expense. They're scared for their jobs and are demanding to be protected— not merely by protectionist legislation but by the companies that they and their predecessors helped make big and rich and powerful.

Under the terms of a ground-breaking agreement between GM and the UAW in October 1984, GM agreed to invest $100 million in new business ventures designed to employ laid-off UAW members and to allow GM workers an equal voice in how the money should be invested. Moreover, the company agreed at a cost of $1 billion to protect 100 percent of the workers' pay and fringe benefits for six years, if jobs are eliminated, work is transferred to other companies here or abroad, operations are consolidated, or new technology eliminates positions. And displaced workers would continue to get their regular pay and could be assigned to other jobs at GM, be trained for a new job with GM or someone else, or get work in one of the new ventures that the union and company plan to start with the $100 million fund.

Both management and labor have praised the innovative provisions as potential models for other industries. They consider it a fair and just response to economically stressful conditions. They hope that it will ease the transitions that thousands of workers like Frank Burton will have to make over the next ten years.

Discussion Questions

1. How do you assess the future of American manufacturing? Will it be able to increase productivity and meet the challenge of foreign competition?

2. Do you find anything in the current plight of America's blue-collar workers that confirms the Marxist view of capitalism?

3. Do you think that the government bailout

of Chrysler and such protectionist legislation as "voluntary" quotas on auto imports are fair? Do they make economic sense? What would Adam Smith say?

4. Do corporations like GM have a responsibility to retain workers laid off as a result of foreign competition or new technologies?

5. How do you assess the GM-UAW pact? Should it be a model for other companies? Explain.

6. The costs incurred by GM's 1984 agreement with the UAW are reflected in the price of its products and thus borne by consumers. Do you think this is right?

CASE 4.2
Hucksters in the Classroom

Increased student loads, myriad professional obligations, and shrinking school budgets have sent many public school teachers scurrying for teaching materials to facilitate their teaching.

They don't have to look far. Into the breach has stepped business, which is ready, willing, and able to provide current print and audiovisual materials for classroom use.[47] These activities and industry-supplied teaching aids are advertised in educational journals, distributed to school boards, and showcased at educational conventions. The Dr. Pepper Company, for example, displays at such conventions a recipe booklet entitled *Cooking with Dr. Pepper*. Each recipe includes sugar-filled Dr. Pepper.

One collective tack taken by the business community has been the ABC Education Program of American Industry, whose annual publication, *Resourcebook*, consists of product-specific "sponsored pages" or ads with accompanying teacher guide sheets. Food and toiletry products are featured, such as the following:

A is for AGREE: the Creme Rinse and Conditioner that helps the greasies.

C is for COCONUT: a tantalizing tropical treat from Peter Paul candies.

E is for EFFECTIVE double deodorant system in Irish Spring (soap).[48]

Advertising space in *Resourcebook* doesn't come cheap: A single ad can run as much as $30,000. But ABC official Art Sylvie thinks it's worth it. After all, he asks, where else are manufacturers going to get such widespread and in-depth product exposure? He has a point: About 2,700,000 or 35 percent of all junior high school students in the United States participate in the ABC program, not to mention their 95,000 teachers.

An integral part of the ABC program is an annual essay-writing contest. Essays must deal with some aspect of the product in *Resourcebook*—the history or importance of an industry to a community or nation, the production and marketing of a particular product, and the like. To be eligible, entries must be signed by a teacher and include a product label or reasonable facsimile. Student writers can earn up to $50 for entering.

The people at ABC say they want to reflect the positive aspects of the world outside the classroom. And they're convinced that the way to do it is through depicting the wonders and genius of industry. "Thus," says researcher Sheila Harty, "history is taught in terms of 'innovative industrial genius,' as students write their essays on the value of soft drinks (C is for Canada Dry) or the production of tires (G is for Goodyear)."[49]

Evidently teachers go for corporate freebies with all the gusto of a softball player at a company picnic. In a survey of its members, the National Education Association found that about half of its members were using industry materials and the ten resource guides published annually by Educators Progress Services (EPS). A cursory look at the guides suggests that the offerings are comprehensive and impartial. A closer look reveals that most are privately, not publicly, sponsored. A near majority come from corporations, trade groups, and U.S. military agencies.

The introduction to EPS's "Educators Guide to Free Social Studies Materials" boasts: "Factual errors, visual misconceptions, and perceptual stereotypes are minimal because of the quality of the productions."[50] Yet, of the 466 listings in the "History" section, 382 or 82 percent are from U.S. military branches—films such as "Drawing of the Battle Lines" and "Another Day of War." One from McDonnell Douglas Corporation entitled "Counterpunch" deals with marine combat.

Some people think that corporate-sponsored teaching materials do more than fill curriculum needs. They are also public relations gambits. Thus, in his book *Corporate Response to Urban Crisis*, professor of sociology Ken Neubeck writes:

> Corporations must continually respond to problems which they had a hand in creating in the first place. From this perspective, corporate social responsibility becomes a defensive strategy to be employed whenever the social and political climate become hostile to the active pursuit of corporate economic goals. It is a strategy of 'enlightened self-interest.'"[51]

Two years before the publication of Neubeck's book, General Motors published a booklet entitled "Professor Clean Asks . . . What Is Air Pollution?" Apparently GM officials wanted to counteract the negative attitudes toward auto companies that pollsters found among children. Throughout the booklet Disneyesque characters such as "Professor

Clean," "Charlie Carbon Monoxide," and "Harry Hydrocarbon" valiantly strive to allay any anxieties about the hazards of air pollution. With the advent of antipollution devices, the good Professor assures young minds, air pollution will no longer be a problem. Presumably readers would have to learn about the auto industry's dogged resistance to government emission controls elsewhere.

Discussion Questions

1. Is industry's thrust into education consistent with the features of capitalism?

2. Are any moral issues involved in the industrial/educational affiliation?

3. Do you think that students have a "moral right" to be free from the commercial indoctrination described?

4. Some might say that teachers participating in the ABC program are little more than industry shills—unwitting, perhaps, but shills nonetheless. Would you agree?

5. The materials that industry provides teachers for classroom use fall predominantly into four subject areas: nutrition, energy, the environment, and economics. Rarely is the subject of English addressed. How do you account for this bias, and what do you think the implications are?

6. Do you think that industry is intentionally using teachers and students as a means to profit ends?

7. If you were a member of a school board contemplating the use of the materials described, what would you recommend and why?

NOTES

1. See *Newsweek* (international edition), November 2, 1987, from which the details that follow are taken.

2. See David Schweickart, *Capitalism or Worker Control?* (New York: Praeger, 1980).

3. For their succinct treatment of the rise of the Fugger dynasty, we are especially indebted to: Ned M. Cross, Robert C. Lamm, and Rudy H. Turk, *The Search for Personal Freedom* (Dubuque, Iowa: Wm. C. Brown Company, 1972), 12.

4. Ibid., 13. See also Robert B. Carson, *Business Issues Today: Alternative Perspectives* (New York: St. Martin's Press, 1982), 3–30.

5. Robert Heilbroner, *The Worldly Philosophers*, 5th ed. (New York: Simon & Schuster, Touchstone edition, 1980), 22–23.

6. Ibid., 55.

7. Adam Smith, *The Wealth of Nations* (New York: Modern Library, 1937), 419.

8. Ibid., 421–423.

9. "The Morality (?) of Advertising," *Harvard Business Review*, 48. July/August 1970.

10. Robert Heilbroner, *The Economic Problem* (Englewood Cliffs, N.J.: Prentice-Hall, 1972), 725.

11. *The Texas Observer*, November 17, 1978.

12. Heilbroner, *Worldly Philosophers*, 302.

13. Robert Reich, *The Next American Frontier* (New York: Penguin Books, 1983), 174.

14. Ibid., 178.

15. Doug Brandon, "Corporate America: Uncle Sam's Favorite Welfare Client," *Business and Society Review* 55 (Fall 1985): 48.

16. Martin Carnoy, *The State and Political Theory* (Princeton University Press, 1984), 246.

17. Robert B. Carson, *Business Issues Today: Alternative Perspectives* (New York: St. Martin's Press, 1982), 29.

18. This entire extract is from *Karl Marx: Early Writings*, translated by T. B. Bottomore, 1963. Used with permission of McGraw-Hill Book Company.

19. Studs Terkel, "Here I Am a Worker," in Leonard Silk, ed., *Capitalism: The Moving Target* (New York: Quadrangle, 1974), 68–69.

20. Lester C. Thurow, "A Surge in Inequality," *Scientific American*, May 1987. See also "Slower Pace for Productivity Gains," *The New York Times*, February 5, 1988.

21. "Can America Compete?" *Business Week*, April 20, 1987. See also "U.S. Standard of Living Under Pressure," *International Herald Tribune*, Feb. 20-21, 1988.

22. John DeLorean and J. Patrick Wright, *On A Clear Day You Can See General Motors—John Z. DeLorean's Look Inside the Automobile Giant* (New York: Wright Enterprises, 1979), 132.

23. See Richard T. Wise and Stephan W. McDaniel, "American Competitiveness and the CEO—Who's Minding Shop?" *Sloan Management Review* 29 (Winter 1988); and "Managers Need Milestones," *The Economist*, January 23, 1988.

24. This paragraph and the next are based on Robert J. Samuelson, "Clobbering Car Buyers," *Newsweek* (international edition), December 14, 1987, 43.

25. John Burgess and Fred Hiatt, "How Toyota Clung to Its U.S. Sales," *International Herald Tribune*, February 17, 1988, 1.

26. "The Hollow Corporation," *Business Week*, March 3, 1986, on which this and the following paragraph draw.

27. "The Raiding Game," *Dollars and Sense*, March 1987. See also the film *Wall Street* for a dramatic portrayal of the world of corporate raiders.

28. *Business and Society Review*, 53 (Spring 1985), 76.

29. "The Raiding Game," 14.

30. Paul Bernstein, "The Work Ethic That Never Was," *The Wharton Magazine* 4 (1980).

31. Stanley Penn, "Losses Grow from Drug Use at the Office," *The Wall Street Journal*, July 29, 1981, 27.

32. Thomas A. Kochan, Harry C. Katz, and Robert B. McKersie, *The Transformation of American Industrial Relations* (New York: Basic Books, 1986), 209.

33. "Changing Attitudes to Work and Life Styles," *Journal of Contemporary Business* 8 (1980): 18. Reprinted by permission of the publisher.

34. Bernstein, "The Work Ethic That Never Was."

35. See Richard Manning and John McCormick, "The Blue-Collar Blues," *Newsweek*, June 4, 1984, 52, 53, 55.

36. Ibid., 53.

37. Ibid.

38. John Naisbitt, *Megatrends* (New York: Warner Books, Inc., 1982), 64.

39. See Hobart Rowen, "Iacocca's Rinky-Dink Idea," *The Washington Post Weekly Edition*, June 4, 1984, 5.

40. Manning and McCormick, "Blue Collar Blues," 55.

41. Ibid.

42. Ibid.

43. See Warren Brown and Michael Schrage, "An Industrial Policy, Built by G.M.," *The Washington Post National Weekly Edition*, August 20, 1984, 6–8.

44. Ibid., 6.

45. Naisbitt, *Megatrends*, 64.

46. Brown and Schrage, "Industrial Policy," 7.

47. This case is based on research conducted by Sheila Harty and reported in Sheila Harty, *Hucksters in the Classroom: A Review of Industry Propaganda in Schools* (Washington, D.C.: Center for Study of Responsive Law, 1979).

48. Harty, *Hucksters in the Classroom*, 5.

49. Ibid., 11.

50. Ibid., 6.

51. Ken Neubeck, *Corporate Response to Urban Crisis* (New York: D. C. Heath, 1974), 117. Quoted in Harty, *Hucksters in the Classroom*, 11–12.

Buddhist Economics

E. F. Schumacher

When thinking about economic matters, people in our society make a number of assumptions. These assumptions have important theoretical and practical consequences, but we simply take their truth for granted. Author and economist E. F. Schumacher exposes several of these implicit dogmas simply by showing how the thinking of a Buddhist economist would differ from that of a modern Western economist on some basic issues: the nature of work, the benefits of mechanization, the relation between material wealth and human well-being, and the use of natural resources.

'Right Livelihood' is one of the requirements of the Buddha's Noble Eightfold Path. It is clear, therefore, that there must be such a thing as Buddhist economics.

Buddhist countries have often stated that they wish to remain faithful to their heritage. So Burma: "The New Burma sees no conflict between religious values and economic progress. Spiritual health and material wellbeing are not enemies: they are natural allies." Or: "We can blend successfully the religious and spiritual values of our heritage with the benefits of modern technology." Or: "We Burmans have a sacred duty to conform both our dreams and our acts to our faith. This we shall ever do."

All the same, such countries invariably assume that they can model their economic development plans in accordance with modern economics, and they call upon modern economists from socalled advanced countries to advise them, to formulate the policies to be pursued, and to construct the grand design for development, the Five-Year Plan or whatever it may be called. No one seems to think that a Buddhist way of life would call for Buddhist economics, just as the modern materialist way of life has brought forth modern economics.

Economists themselves, like most specialists, normally suffer from a kind of metaphysical blindness, assuming that theirs is a science of absolute and invariable truths, without any presuppositions. Some go as far as to claim that economic laws are as free from 'metaphysics' or 'values' as the law of gravitation. We need not, however, get involved in arguments of methodology. Instead, let us take some fundamentals and see what they look like when viewed by a modern economist and a Buddhist economist.

There is universal agreement that a fundamental source of wealth is human labour. Now, the modern economist has been brought up to consider 'labour' or work as little more than a necessary evil. From the point of view of the employer, it is in any case simply an item of cost, to be reduced to a minimum if it cannot be eliminated altogether, say, by automation. From the point of view of the workman, it is a 'disutility'; to work is to make a sacrifice of one's leisure and comfort, and wages are a kind of compensation for the sacrifice. Hence the ideal from the point of view of the employer is to have output without employees, and the ideal from the point of view of the employee is to have income without employment.

The consequences of these attitudes both in theory and in practice are, of course, extremely far-reaching. If the ideal with regard to work is to get rid of it, every method that 'reduces the work load' is a good thing. The most potent method, short of automation, is the so-called 'division of labour' and the classical example is the pin factory eulogised in Adam Smith's *Wealth of Nations*. Here it is not a matter of ordinary specialisation, which mankind has practised from time immemorial, but of dividing up every complete process of production into minute parts, so that the final product can be produced at great speed without anyone having had to contribute more than a totally insignificant and, in most cases, unskilled movement of his limbs.

The Buddhist point of view takes the function of work to be at least threefold: to give a man a chance to utilise and develop his faculties; to enable him to overcome his ego-centredness by joining with other people in a common task; and to bring forth the goods and services needed for a becoming existence. Again, the consequences that flow from this view are endless. To organise work in such a manner that it becomes meaningless, boring, stultifying, or nerve-racking for the worker would be little short of criminal; it would indicate a greater concern with goods than with people, an evil lack of compassion and a soul-destroying degree of attachment to the most primitive side of this worldly existence. Equally, to strive for leisure as an alternative to work would be considered a complete misunderstanding of one of the basic truths of human existence, namely that work and leisure are complementary parts of the same living process and cannot be separated without destroying the joy of work and the bliss of leisure.

From the Buddhist point of view, there are therefore two types of mechanisation which must be clearly distinguished: one that enhances a man's skill and power and one that turns the work of man over to a mechanical slave, leaving man in a position of having to serve the slave. How to tell the one from the other? "The craftsman himself," says Ananda Coomaraswamy, a man equally competent to talk about the modern west as the ancient east, "can always, if allowed to, draw the delicate distinction between the machine and the tool. The carpet loom is a tool, a contrivance for holding warp threads at a stretch for the pile to be woven round them by the craftsmen's fingers; but the power loom is a machine, and its significance as a destroyer of culture lies in the fact that it does the essentially human part of the work." It is clear, therefore, that Buddhist economics must be very different from the economics of modern material-

ism, since the Buddhist sees the essence of civilisation not in a multiplication of wants but in the purification of human character. Character, at the same time, is formed primarily by a man's work. And work, properly conducted in conditions of human dignity and freedom, blesses those who do it and equally their products. The Indian philosopher and economist J. C. Kumarappa sums the matter up as follows:

"If the nature of the work is properly appreciated and applied, it will stand in the same relation to the higher faculties as food is to the physical body. It nourishes and enlivens the higher man and urges him to produce the best he is capable of. It directs his free will along the proper course and disciplines the animal in him into progressive channels. It furnishes an excellent background for man to display his scale of values and develop his personality."

If a man has no chance of obtaining work he is in a desperate position, not simply because he lacks an income but because he lacks this nourishing and enlivening factor of disciplined work which nothing can replace. A modern economist may engage in highly sophisticated calculations on whether full employment 'pays' or whether it might be more 'economic' to run an economy at less than full employment so as to ensure a greater mobility of labour, a better stability of wages, and so forth. His fundamental criterion of success is simply the total quantity of goods produced during a given period of time. "If the marginal urgency of goods is low," says Professor Galbraith in *The Affluent Society*, "then so is the urgency of employing the last man or the last million men in the labour force." And again: "If . . . we can afford some unemployment in the interest of stability—a proposition, incidentally, of impeccably conservative antecedents—then we can afford to give those who are unemployed the goods that enable them to sustain their accustomed standard of living."

From a Buddhist point of view, this is standing the truth on its head by considering goods as more important than people and consumption as more important than creative activity. It means shifting the emphasis from the worker to the product of work, that is, from the human to the subhuman, a surrender to the forces of evil. The very start of Buddhist economic planning would be a planning for full employment, and the primary purpose of this would in fact be employment for everyone who needs an 'outside' job: it would not be the maximisation of employment nor the maximisation of production. Women, on the whole, do not need an 'outside' job, and the large-scale employment of women in offices or factories would be considered a sign of serious economic failure. In particular, to let mothers of young children work in factories while the children run wild would be as uneconomic in the eyes of a Buddhist economist as the employment of a skilled worker as a soldier in the eyes of a modern economist.

While the materialist is mainly interested in goods, the Buddhist is mainly interested in liberation. But Buddhism is 'The Middle Way' and therefore in no way antagonistic to physical well-being. It is not wealth that stands in the way of liberation but the attachment to wealth; not the enjoyment of pleasurable things but the craving for them. The keynote of Buddhist economics, therefore, is simplicity and non-violence. From an economist's point of view, the marvel of the Buddhist way of life is the utter rationality of its pattern—amazingly small means leading to extraordinarily satisfactory results.

For the modern economist this is very difficult to understand. He is used to measuring the 'standard of living' by the amount of annual consumption, assuming all the time that a man who consumes more is 'better off' than a man who consumes less. A Buddhist economist would consider this approach excessively irrational: since consumption is merely a means to human well-being, the aim should be to obtain the maximum of well-being with the minimum of consumption. Thus, if the purpose of clothing is a certain amount of temperature comfort and an attractive appearance, the task is to attain this purpose with the smallest possible effort, that is, with the smallest annual destruction of cloth and with the help of designs that involve the smallest possible input of toil. The less toil there is, the more time and strength is left for artistic creativity. It would be highly uneconomic, for instance, to go in for complicated tailoring, like the modern west, when a much more beautiful effect can be achieved by the skilful draping of uncut material. It would be the height of folly to make material so that it should wear out quickly and the height of barbarity to make anything ugly, shabby or mean. What has just been said about clothing applies equally to all other human requirements. The ownership and the consumption of goods is a means to an end, and Buddhist economics is the systematic study of how to attain given ends with the minimum means.

Modern economics, on the other hand, considers consumption to be the sole end and purpose of all economic activity, taking the factors of production—land, labour, and capital—as the means. The former, in short, tries to maximise human satisfactions by the optimal pattern of consumption, while the latter tries to maximise consumption by the optimal pattern of productive effort. It is easy to see that the effort needed to sustain a way of life which seeks to attain the optimal pattern of consumption is likely to be much smaller than the effort needed to sustain a drive for maximum consumption. We need not be surprised, therefore, that the pressure and strain of living is very much less in, say, Burma than it is in the United States, in spite of the fact that the amount of labour-saving machinery used in the former country is only a minute fraction of the amount used in the latter.

Simplicity and non-violence are obviously closely related. The optimal pattern of consumption, producing a high degree of human satisfaction by means of a relatively low rate of consumption, allows people to live without great pressure and strain and to fulfil the primary injunction of Buddhist teaching: 'Cease to do evil; try to do good.' As physical resources are everywhere limited, people satisfying their needs by means of a modest use of resources are obviously less likely to be at each other's throats than people depending upon a high rate of use. Equally, people who live in highly self-sufficient local communities are less likely to get involved in large-scale violence than people whose existence depends on world-wide systems of trade.

From the point of view of Buddhist economics, therefore, production from local resources for local needs is the most rational way of economic life, while dependence on imports from afar and the consequent need to produce for export to unknown and distant peoples is highly uneconomic and justifiable only in exceptional cases and on a small scale. Just as the modern economist would admit that a high rate of consumption of transport services between a man's home and his place of work signifies a misfortune and not a high standard of life, so the Buddhist economist would hold that to satisfy human wants from faraway sources rather than from sources nearby signifies failure rather than success. The former tends to take statistics showing an increase in the number of ton/miles per head of the population carried by a country's transport system as proof of economic progress, while to the latter—the Buddhist economist—the same statistics would indicate a highly undesirable deterioration in the *pattern* of consumption.

Another striking difference between modern economics and Buddhist economics arises over the use of natural resources. Bertrand de Jouvenel, the eminent French political philosopher, has characterised 'western man' in words which may be taken as a fair description of the modern economist:

"He tends to count nothing as an expenditure, other than human effort; he does not seem to mind how much mineral matter he wastes and, far worse, how much living matter he destroys. He does not seem to realise at all that human life is a dependent part of an ecosystem of many different forms of life. As the world is ruled from towns where men are cut off from any form of life other than human, the feeling of belonging to an ecosystem is not revived. This results in a harsh and improvident treatment of things upon which we ultimately depend, such as water and trees."

The teaching of the Buddha, on the other hand, enjoins a reverent and non-violent attitude not only to all sentient beings but also, with great emphasis, to trees. Every follower of the Buddha ought to plant a tree every few years and look after it until it is safely established, and the Buddhist economist can demonstrate without difficulty that the universal observation of this rule would result in a high rate of genuine economic development independent of any foreign aid. Much of the economic decay of south-east Asia (as of many other parts of the world) is undoubtedly due to a heedless and shameful neglect of trees.

Modern economics does not distinguish between renewable and non-renewable materials, as its very method is to equalise and quantify everything by means of a money price. Thus, taking various alternative fuels, like coal, oil, wood, or water-power: the only difference between them recognised by modern economics is relative cost per equivalent unit. The cheapest is automatically the one to be preferred, as to do otherwise would be irrational and 'uneconomic'. From a Buddhist point of view, of course, this will not do; the essential difference between non-renewable fuels like coal and oil on the one hand and renewable fuels like wood and water-power on the other cannot be simply overlooked. Non-renewable goods must be used only if they are indispensable, and then only with the greatest care and the most meticulous concern for conservation. To use them heedlessly or extravagantly is an act of violence, and while complete non-violence may not be attainable on this earth, there is nonetheless an ineluctable duty on man to aim at the ideal of non-violence in all he does.

Just as a modern European economist would not consider it a great economic achievement if all European art treasures were sold to America at attractive prices, so the Buddhist economist would insist that a population basing its economic life on non-renewable fuels is living parasitically, on capital instead of income. Such a way of life could have no permanence and could therefore be justified only as a purely temporary expedient. As the world's resources of non-renewable fuels—coal, oil and natural gas—are exceedingly unevenly distributed over the globe and undoubtedly limited in quantity, it is clear that their exploitation at an ever-increasing rate is an act of violence against nature which must almost inevitably lead to violence between men.

This fact alone might give food for thought even to those people in Buddhist countries who care nothing for the religious and spiritual values of their heritage and ardently desire to embrace the materialism of modern economics at the fastest possible speed. Before they dismiss Buddhist economics as nothing better than a nostalgic dream, they might wish to consider whether the path of economic development outlined by modern economics is likely to lead them to places where they really want to be. Towards the end of his courageous book *The Challenge of Man's Future*, Professor Harrison Brown of the California Institute of Technology gives the following appraisal:

"Thus we see that, just as industrial society is fundamentally unstable and subject to reversion to agrarian existence, so within it the conditions which offer individual freedom are unstable in their ability to avoid the conditions which impose rigid organisation and totalitarian control. Indeed, when we examine all of the foreseeable difficulties which threaten the survival of industrial civilisation, it is difficult to see how the achievement of stability and the maintenance of individual liberty can be made compatible."

Even if this were dismissed as a long-term view there is the immediate question of whether 'modernisation,' as currently practised without regard to religious and spiritual values, is actually producing agreeable results. As far as the masses are concerned, the results appear to be disastrous—a collapse of the rural economy, a rising tide of unemployment in town and country, and the growth of a city proletariat without nourishment for either body or soul.

It is in the light of both immediate experience and long-term prospects that the study of Buddhist economics could be recommended even to those who believe that economic growth is more important than any spiritual or religious values. For it is not a question of choosing between 'modern growth' and 'traditional stagnation.' It is a question of finding the right path of development, the

Middle Way between materialist heedlessness and traditionalist immobility, in short, of finding 'Right Livelihood.'

Review and Discussion Questions

1. From the Buddhist point of view, what is the function of work? What do you see as the main social and economic implications of the Buddhist perspective?

2. Schumacher sees simplicity as a keynote of Buddhist economics. Why does it value simplicity? Does capitalism promote needless complexity?

3. What distinguishes Buddhist economics from modern economics in its approach to material wealth? To natural resources? With which approach are you more sympathetic and why?

4. Is a capitalist economic system compatible with a Buddhist perspective? Is any other economic system?

5. Would you agree that Buddhism has something to teach us about economics?

Kratylus Automates His Urnworks

Tolly Kizilos

The great Greek philosopher Socrates (469–399 B.C.) was convinced that the way to attain knowledge was through a practice of developed conversation, a method he called dialectic. The goal of this dialogue or conversation was the clarification of key philosophic terms and ideas.

We are told that Socrates, accordingly, would haunt the streets of ancient Athens, buttonholing powerful men and asking them probing questions about their opinions. To those who pretended to knowledge about justice, he would ask: What is justice? When you say something or somebody is just, what do you mean? Similarly, he would investigate their ideas about virtue or knowledge or morality. By careful questioning, Socrates would plumb their belief systems, exposing cherished certainties to critical scrutiny. Socrates's persistent demand for clarity of thought and exactness often aggravated his fellow citizens, some of whom began to consider him a threat to social stability. In the end they were successful in suppressing Socrates, but not in stilling his method of dia-

lectic, which continues to resonate in the philosophical enterprise.

In this chapter we have seen that a declining rate of productivity growth lies behind the economic challenges facing us today. But on reflection it is not obvious what productivity is or why we should value it. In the following selection, Tolly Kizilos uses the dialectic to air difficult questions about the meaning of productivity, about measuring an individual's contribution to a goal, and about the desirability of furthering human productiveness. Implicitly at stake as well are hard questions about the purposes of human production, the nature of capitalism, and the treatment of workers in an era of rapid technological advance.

These issues arise when Nikias and seven others are fired after Kratylus automates his workshop in Athens. In addition to Nikias, those participating in the dialogue are Ipponikos, a rich landowner, Kallias, a politician and member of the Assembly, and, of course, Socrates.

Kallias: Here comes Nikias, troubled as usual about some social injustice or other.

Socrates: Good morning, Nikias. Isn't it a bit early in the day to be looking so troubled?

Nikias: Good morning, my friends, if you can call good a morning on which you lose your job. . . . I showed up for work at Kratylus's urnworks this morning, as I've done for three years, and he told me and seven others that we were no longer needed. He's installed some new foot-operated potter's wheels with pulleys, so he doesn't need as many people to do the work. Just like that, I'm unemployed.

Kallias: It wasn't all that sudden, though, was it, Nikias? I heard Kratylus almost a month ago talking openly at the agora about the new wheels he was buying from Corinth. It was no secret that he was going to install them to raise productivity. He had to do it, he told me, or he'd go out of business. I realize that you and a few others will suffer for a while, but he has to increase the productivity of his business or everyone working for him could end up without a job. And if he and others don't become more productive, Athens itself will take a backseat to Corinth and other cities, and all its citizens will suffer the consequences.

Nikias: We knew about it, all right, but we were hoping there would be other jobs we could do. Is it more productive to have people out of work, doing nothing, than to have them gainfully employed? How can the city's productivity grow if a lot of people are out of work? As far as I'm concerned, that kind of narrow-minded productivity increase helps no one but Kratylus; it just feeds his greed.

Kallias: Come now, Nikias; you can't possibly mean that! Productivity gains, no matter where, benefit everyone in the long run. You'll find another job soon, or Kratylus's business will expand and he'll need more workers to operate the faster wheels.

Socrates: Is productivity then both good and evil? Is it both the requirement for the workers' prosperity and the cause of their misfortunes? . . . Perhaps productivity is such an elusive concept that we can reach only a partial understanding of it, which, however, is acceptable to all of us. Let us be hopeful. . . .

Kallias: I'll tell you what productivity is, Socrates, or at least what it means to me—take it as you like. It's not such a difficult concept. It's simply the ratio of useful work output for a given valuable input. The higher the output for the same input, the higher the productivity is.

Take, for example, Kratylus's urnworks. I know something about his business because occasionally he asks for my opinion. Kratylus produces about 200 urns a day and used to employ about 20 workers. If he can produce the same number of urns with half the work force, then he doubles his shop's productivity. It's as simple as that.

Ipponikos: It's so simple, it's idiotic. Whose productivity has he increased? Nikias isn't productive anymore. He worked hard and still got laid off. Kratylus's productivity gain is Nikias's productivity loss.

Nikias: More productivity for Kratylus means more satisfaction of his greed. . . .

Kallias: I know it's hard to be objective right now, but the facts are irrefutable. When you were working for Kratylus—I'm sure very hard—you weren't very productive because you were using a slow wheel to shape the urns. You were paid wages to produce something that cost so much it couldn't be sold easily. Activity isn't productivity, Nikias.

What's needed is more output for a given input; what's needed is more drachmas from the sale of urns per drachma of wages. Now you produce nothing, but your wages are also nothing; so, it makes no sense to talk about your productivity. Only when you get paid to produce something of value, that is, when there's an input and an output, can we talk meaningfully about productivity.

Ipponikos: This input-output stuff may be useful when talking about machines or oxen, but it makes no sense when we're discussing human beings. Productivity means productive activity. Human beings can be very productive even when they're supported by handouts. Why, only two weeks ago I heard that the geometer Diomedes, a pauper, mind you, if there ever was one, invented an instrument for measuring angles he calls a theodolite. I heard Telemachus say it will save thousands of workdays for his surveying crew when they're setting the boundaries of farmers' fields all around Attica. Diomedes received no wages—no input, as you would say, Kallias—but does that mean we can't talk about his productivity? He *is* productive, very productive.

Kallias: Of course he is, my dear Ipponikos. Your example of Diomedes is precisely what I've been looking for to make my point. Maximum output with minimum possible input yields the highest productivity.

Nikias: So, productivity according to you is using up people. Humanity subordinated to the goddess of productivity. Perhaps you'd like to add another goddess to the 12 Olympians? It wouldn't surprise me.

Kallias: I said minimum *possible* input, not minimum input. Possible is the essential. . . .

Ipponikos: I don't understand why you keep using inputs and outputs when you talk about human beings, Kallias. We could never define such things for humans, capable of an infinite variety and an infinite number of possible inputs and outputs, none of them exactly predictable. No man can be bound by defining him in terms of input and output. "Man is the measure of all things," as Protagoras said—he cannot himself be measured.

Nikias: But to Kratylus and others who own shops, Ipponikos, there's little difference among men, beasts, or machines. A person at work is told exactly what input he'll have (that is, what wages he'll be paid), exactly what he has to do, and what he's expected to produce. That's what happens when you work for someone else; you're dehumanized.

Kallias: You're too angry to contribute to this discussion, Nikias.

Ipponikos: Since when has anger been proven to be an obstacle in the search for truth?

Socrates: Nikias agrees with you, Ipponikos, that man is fundamentally different from the machine, and one of the reasons is that only machines have finite and measurable inputs and outputs by design.

Ipponikos: It's even more fundamental than that: Kallias talks about wages as inputs, but that's so narrow-minded it's absurd. People can get more than wages for doing their jobs; they can get satisfaction, learning, enjoyment; they can be frightened or encouraged by what happens around them; they can be made to feel stronger or weaker by the actions of others. Their productive activity is often the result of all these impressions, shaped by thinking, feeling, and judgment. And as for their output, sometimes it's so unpredictable as to instill awe, admiration, and delight. . . .

Kallias: . . . According to you, a workshop owner should hire workers and pay them wages, but demand nothing specific of them. Some of them may want to loaf; others may decide to take up playwriting or singing instead of making urns; and some of them may even choose to work and produce urns once in a while. Now and then, perhaps, a worker will invent a new tool that improves the quality of urns or the productivity of the shop, but there will be no guarantees. And the wages have to keep coming steadily, guaranteed.

Is this a responsible way to run a business? Could the workshop owner entrust his future to the whims of his workers? The workers have no stake in the business and, if the shop went broke, they could leave at a moment's notice to take jobs elsewhere. And what about those who really work hard to produce urns and urns alone? Wouldn't this irresponsible approach be unfair to them?

Ipponikos: You talk as if the workers want to loaf and behave irresponsibly toward the owner and their fellow workers. You don't trust them.

Kallias: Not everyone is responsible and trustworthy.

Ipponikos: Perhaps not. But if the owner trusts his people and rewards them fairly, I believe that the workers would strive to do their best for the business. Some will be less productive than others, but the productivity of the whole place will be higher when people feel free to use all their talents and skills. As for fairness, the workers themselves will set standards and require that everyone pull his weight.

Socrates: I hear a lot of views being expressed, but no conclusions. If this were a workshop, its productivity would be very low, and some of us, I fear, would have to be replaced by more productive philosophers, probably from Sparta. Can't we first agree on what productivity means? . . .

Kallias: Sooner or later, I suppose, we'll have to talk about effectiveness and efficiency. I believe that productivity is high only when both efficiency and effectiveness are high.

Socrates: All right, let's see what you mean. Suppose you hire me for a drachma a day to pick olives fallen from your olive trees in Eleusis. While I'm working, I notice that the fence protecting your property from the wild pigs is down. Pigs can get into your fields and devour the ripe olives that have fallen on the ground. Because I think this is more urgent and because I'm much better at repairing fences than gathering olives, I decide to fix your fence instead.

I work hard all day long and by sunset I'm done and I'm sitting on a rock admiring the good work I did. You return from your day's debates at the Assembly and find me in this contemplative pose. You see that I have picked no olives but have fixed your fence. The question is, will you pay me as we agreed or not?

Kallias: Of course not. You changed our contract arbitrarily. I could suffer losses because of that. You shouldn't have changed the output.

Nikias: He means he didn't want you to think; do only what you were told. Be a machine or a mindless ox.

Socrates: But a contract is a contract, Nikias. What if he was counting on me to pick the olives so he could deliver them to someone who had a contract with him to buy them that same evening? I was productive, all right, but not productive doing what we agreed on. In that, my productivity was zero. So isn't it true that productivity has meaning only when there's an agreement on the inputs or wages, and the outputs or the goals?

Kallias: Of course it is.

Ipponikos: And if someone produces something very valuable without any agreement?

Socrates: It appears that it doesn't make sense to talk about productivity when there's no agreement, explicit or implicit.

Kallias: Exactly. Productivity pertains to work toward a goal. There must be expectation of output and fulfillment of that expectation.

Socrates: I'm glad you agree with what I said. But I have some difficulty with it, and you may be able to help me. It has to do with something that happened when they were building the mound commemorating the glorious dead who fell at the battle of Marathon. . . . After Pericles gave his marvelous funeral oration on that hallowed ground, he left behind General Meno from Orchomenos in charge of 100 slaves and ordered him to build the mound in 30 days. Meno was determined to obey the order even though he estimated that the project would take twice that time. It is said that General Meno became a tyrant with the slaves, driving them ruthlessly to work.

One day, during an inspection of the project, he discovered a slave who sat on the nearby edge of the marsh in blissful repose. Furious, he ordered his lieutenants to flog him until he was hardly alive. General Meno wanted to make this laggard an example for the other slaves, demonstrating to them that because the slave didn't produce, he made everyone else work harder. "He is a weight upon the earth!" he shouted for all to hear, using Homer's words.

Kallias: I still don't see. . . .

Socrates: Then one of the most productive slaves stepped forward and asked to speak. General Meno could hardly hold back his anger, but because he valued this slave greatly he allowed him to say his piece. "This man, sir," the slave said, pointing to his doomed comrade, "is one of the most productive slaves you have. It is true that he neither sweats nor strains his back digging and shoveling earth, but he contributes to the building of the mound more than anyone else."

"And how does he do this? Gazing at his belly button while you and the others break your backs?" the general demanded.

"You see, General," the slave said with conviction, "he is a storyteller, not a digger. If he was shoveling dirt with all his might, he couldn't do in a day more than I do in an hour. But after work, when we all return to camp, dog-tired, miserable, and hopeless—for what can we expect from the future but more bondage and more misery?—when we are gathered around the campfire at night, this man spins tales of hope for us and makes our lot bearable. We listen to him and dream of a better life after we end this project. He makes our burdens lighter, and we can fall asleep with dreams of freedom in our heads. Next day we are ready for work, believing that if our work pleases you and the Athenians, we may some day gain our freedom."

Kallias: I think I'm beginning . . .

Socrates: Please let me finish. "So," the slave went on, "this man does his part. If you beat him senseless, or cripple him, or—worst of fates!—kill him, who will keep us hoping, dreaming, and working? If hope vanishes, punishment and death hold no fear, General. We may not be able to build your mound. Think of that, sir, and allow this man to go on producing what he is best able to produce: tales of hope. You need him as much as, if not more than, we do.''

So spoke the valued slave, and General Meno listened. He ordered his lieutenants to release the man, who went on to tell tales until the project was finished—exactly on time. The question, dear Kallias, is this: Was the storytelling slave productive or not?

Kallias: Of course he was productive, probably the most productive of all. He contributed to the achievement of the goal, didn't he? Whether he knew it or not, he worked toward the same goal as all the other slaves.

Socrates: So, you say, productivity is work toward a goal. You wouldn't pay me for fixing your fence because you had set the goal as gathering fallen olives. What about here? Here, the goal was to build a mound, just as Kratylus's goal is to produce urns, and ours is to come up with the truth. But this slave wasn't building the mound, I wasn't gathering olives, and some workers at Kratylus's urnworks may not be producing as many urns as their fellows.

Yet you just told us that this slave was probably the most productive slave working on the mound. Could I have been more productive to you by fixing your fence? Could Nikias, who wasn't producing as much with his old wheel, and I, bumbling now on my way to the truth, be more productive than others who achieve stated goals? Could it be, Kallias, that Nikias, now that he is searching for the truth with us, is more productive to our city (and of course to Kratylus) than when he was making urns? . . .

Kallias: . . . It seems to me, Socrates, that you are mixing two kinds of productivity. Yes, Nikias is more productive to our city when he's searching for the truth with us than he would be if he were doing nothing. To the extent that Kratylus is a citizen of Athens, he benefits from Nikias's philosophizing as does every other citizen. But Nikias is not productive to Kratylus because he simply isn't making urns any more.

Socrates: But if our city is more productive, doesn't Kratylus have a better chance to sell his wares? And if that is so, isn't it fair to say that Kratylus, as the owner of the workshop, is benefiting from Nikias's philosophizing?

Kallias: Productivity loses all meaning if you put it that way. Humanity benefits from anything productive anyone does. But I still say that productivity is a useful concept only when it's limited to specific goals achieved by specific persons.

Ipponikos: Come on, Kallias, use your imagination! Think of all the ways the workers, even at Kratylus's workshop, can contribute to the production and sale of urns even when they're not actually making or selling urns. No one can say whether a person is productive by just looking at him or by measuring only specific inputs and outputs.

Kallias: Use your reason, Ipponikos.

Socrates: But Kallias, how can you tell when a person is doing something or nothing? And how can you say that a person can be productive to the city but not to Kratylus's workshop, which is, after all, a part of the city? And how can you tell if a person is productive when the goals set for that person are different from the goals toward which a person works? One can still contribute to the goals if one interprets goals more broadly.

Kallias: All I know is that somehow or other using a new wheel makes Kratylus's workshop more productive because he can lay off Nikias and some other workers and still produce the same number of urns. Then Nikias, as Kratylus had thought, finds something else to do—philosophize, in this case—and he becomes productive again to the city and to Kratylus, because he is also a citizen.

Socrates: That's well put, Kallias. But if Nikias is now productive to the city, he must be paid for his productivity. Yet I haven't heard of anyone willing to put philosophers on the public payroll. Would you propose that the Assembly pass a law to do that? It certainly would help us all, Nikias and me in particular, since we are not influential politicians like you or wealthy landowners like Ipponikos.

Ipponikos: It's not only philosophers who are productive and should be compensated but also geometers, poets, musicians, and all kinds of other people who work with their minds.

Kallias: Everyone would become a freeloader.

Nikias: Are you saying that all thinkers are freeloaders?

Kallias: Don't be absurd, Nikias. I'm saying that people with no talent for geometry or music or bent for philosophical search would claim to be geometers, musicians, and philosophers in order to collect money from the city and avoid sweating in workshops and fields. Since there is no way to measure their output, no one could tell whether Socrates was more productive than the man who sweeps the steps leading up to the Parthenon. The sweeper could claim, for example, that gazing at the blue sky was helpful in proving the Pythagorean theorem in a new way.

Socrates: And so we have arrived at a point where we must make distinctions: there is productivity and there is productivity, and unless we sort these out we will never come to any conclusions. There is productivity of persons who perform manual work with a physical output; productivity of persons whose output is thoughts, poems, songs, inventions, proofs, and so on; and productivity of groups, such as ours, organizations or institutions, such as Kratylus's workshop or our beloved city of Athens. There are the entities to which we have attached potential for productivity.

Nikias: I'll start by defining the productivity of manual workers.

Kallias: Their productivity depends simply on their output, be it urns made, olives picked, marble slabs quarried, or what have you, divided by the cost of production, which is mostly wages.

Nikias: You may think it's that simple, but I don't. Even a manual worker has a mind that he can use when he does his work. His productivity can be defined your way only if you rob him of his mind. If one does that by rigidly defining the input and the output, that is, if one dehumanizes him, then one can define his productivity accurately—so many urns per drachma of wages, so much earth moved to build a mound per loaf of bread, so many olives gathered per day's wage.

One can go even further and define the productivity of those workers who work with their intellect that way—so many plays written, or songs composed, or theorems proved, or philosophical conclusions reached per drachma. But remember, the only way this can be done is if you set rigid, unalterable inputs and outputs. If a philosopher wrote a poem and an urnmaker proved a theorem of geometry, their productivity would be nothing.

Ipponikos: In other words, Kallias, you have to choose between having a precise definition of productivity and missing a lot of good work, or having at best a sloppy definition and allowing other, unanticipated but valuable work to be encouraged.

Kallias: I can't believe this! You argue with the same cunning as some unscrupulous colleagues of mine in the Assembly. I will give you a precise definition that at the same time encourages all valuable work to proceed: set outputs that are to be met unless more valuable outputs are produced. General Meno set goals, but when a slave produced stories that helped the goal indirectly, the general recognized that his output was more valuable than his manual output would have been in furthering the goal directly.

This way the worker whose output is supposed to be the production of urns will be rewarded when he produces urns or something else, a new potter's wheel or a great poem perhaps, which the person who set the goals and must pay for their accomplishment finds equally valuable or even more valuable than the production of urns. This is my position, and I challenge you to find fault with it!

Socrates: It is indeed an excellent position, Kallias. You have said that productivity for an individual worker is his valuable output per given input. It is a good definition, but you haven't told us how the value of the output is determined or whether the person who evaluated it is competent to do so. . . .

Kallias: I don't believe that shop owners are any less competent to evaluate the relative worth of urns and plays than anyone else. Judgment, after all, is one of the most important attributes one must have to succeed in business.

Socrates: Wouldn't it perhaps be better if the employer and the wage earner could discuss the value of the work or the productivity of the wage earner and agree on it? After all, the person who produces something may be the only one who can explain the purpose for which he produced that thing and judge its value from his perspective.

Kallias: That process might work in Socrates' ideal state, but I don't think it has a chance in Athens. The wage earner can discuss all you like him to discuss, but when the time comes to decide how productive he is, when it comes to making a decision on how much he should be paid, the one who has the power, who pays the wages, will have the final word. . . .

Socrates: Even if we assume that power is what one needs to set standards, what I said still stands. The wage earner also has power because the employer needs him to be as productive as possible, not be a mere machine executing set goals. If the employer doesn't evaluate him correctly, the wage earner will cease coming up with new products, new methods, or new ideas, and the productivity of the organization will suffer. Since the employer cannot *make* the wage earner be creative or take the initiative, or modify goals to suit changed situations, he must ensure that the wage earner stays motivated. And the best way for the employer to achieve that is not to be arbitrary or authoritarian but to share his power of evaluation with him.

I see you're shaking your head, Kallias. When you reflect on these thoughts you may become less skeptical. In any case, it is an alternative way of settling the issue we were discussing. Productivity increases come not only from getting faster wheels in the workshops but also from workers such as Nikias who feel in a way like owners of the workshop. Isn't it then correct to say that productivity is defined by whatever reasonable input and output both wage earner and employer agree on?

Kallias: Though I don't believe that this process will work, I agree that it is worth an experiment to find out. But I don't think we have really defined productivity. . . .

Socrates: Definitions can get us only so far. It's the dialogue between well-meaning people that gains our ends. This is the process, it seems to me, that will also determine the productivity of organizations such as Kratylus's workshop or our beloved city of Athens. Plato may not agree entirely with me on this, but I believe that the productivity of Athens is great because we all partake in making the decisions that govern our lives. Democracy is a form of participation, and it's surprising that it hasn't been applied to our workshops in some appropriate form. . . .

Nikias: Before you go any further . . . , Socrates, I would like to know if anyone here intends to inform Kratylus of my contributions to our discourse and ask him whether he would reconsider his decision to lay me off. If this isn't anyone's intention, I'd like to move on and look for another job before my family has to beg for food.

Kallias: I can certainly talk to him about it. But would you be willing to moderate your demands on wages? At least until his workshop begins to make profits again?

Nikias: I'll do anything reasonable to keep my job, of course. But if the job could be a little more satisfying than what I used to do, or if I have some say on what I do and how I am evaluated, then I'll bear the load more comfortably and I may even turn out more urns than ever before.

Socrates: I'm sure, Nikias, that you're speaking the truth.

Review and Discussion Questions

1. What view of productivity does Kallias present at the beginning of the dialogue? Is capitalism committed to looking at productivity this way? Why do Nikias and Ipponikos object to it?

2. Should we value productivity in Kallias's sense? Is it always desirable to further human productiveness? What would a Buddhist economist say?

3. What point is Socrates trying to make with the example of the story-telling slave? Can we objectively measure an individual's contribution to a group project? To an economic goal? To society in general?

4. Kallias insists that productivity only makes sense when it is limited to specific goals and when there are inputs and outputs that can be measured. Do you see any problems with this position?

5. Explain the position that Socrates defends at the end of the dialogue. Is it compatible with

capitalism? What are its implications for relations between workers and owners and, even
more broadly, for our understanding of the
nature and purpose of human production?

6. Do you think the concept of human productivity is an important one, and, if so, what do
you see as central to it? What is the relevance
of productivity as you see it to economic
justice?

For Further Reading

R. C. Edwards, M. Reich, and T. E. Weisskopf,
eds., *The Capitalist System*, 3rd ed. (Englewood
Cliffs, N.J.: Prentice-Hall, 1986) contains critical
essays on capitalism, with an emphasis on economic issues.

Tibor R. Machan, ed., *The Main Debate: Commu-
nism versus Capitalism* (New York: Random
House, 1986) is a collection of accessible essays
that debate the relative merits of capitalism and
socialism.

David Schweickart, *Capitalism or Worker Control?*
(New York: Praeger, 1980) is an argument for
worker-control socialism.

Lester C. Thurow, *The Zero-Sum Society* (New
York: Penguin, 1980) presents a respected economist's analysis of our current economic
difficulties.

CHAPTER 5

CORPORATIONS

Thirty-five years ago the vice president of Ford Motor Company described the corporation as the dominant institution of American society. Today that dominance has reached a logical crescendo: Not only do corporations produce most of the goods and services we buy, but they and their ethos permeate everything from politics and communications to athletics and religion.

While as an aggregate corporations wield awesome economic clout, some are so vast that individually they exercise influence over the whole of American society. Hundreds of corporate organizations employ thousands of people, and the largest have hundreds of thousands in their employment ranks. Exxon Corporation, for example, employs about 170,000, a figure that pales beside General Motors's approximately 764,000 and General Electric's 405,000. Moreover, such companies receive parts and materials from thousands of suppliers and sell or service their finished products to even more small companies.

By any measurement, the biggest corporations are colossi that dominate the earth. Exxon's annual revenue of more than $100 billion exceeds the gross national product (the total market value of all the goods and services produced by a nation during a specified period) of some countries. In recent years, Exxon's net income from its revenue has exceeded $4 billion annually, more than the combined profits of DuPont, Procter & Gamble, Eastman Kodak, RCA, and Sears, Roebuck, which are themselves corporate giants.

Like the hundred or so corporations that have assets of at least $1 billion and hold about one-half of all of America's combined

industrial profits and earnings, Exxon does not really sell the products that produce its mind-boggling revenues. Its oil, chemicals, electronic typewriters, and motors are actually sold by an array of companies that Exxon owns. Business analyst Anthony J. Parisi thus describes Exxon as "a fabulously wealthy investment club with a limited portfolio."[1] It invests in thirteen affiliate companies, whose heads, says Parisi, "oversee their territories like provincial governors, sovereigns in their own lands but with an authority stemming from the power center in New York. The management committee exacts its tribute (the affiliate's profits from current operations) and issues doles (the money needed to sustain and expand those operations)." Most remarkable about Exxon's empire, however, is its scope. It operates in nearly 100 countries. "Its 195 oceangoing tankers, owned and chartered, constitute a private navy as big as Britain's."[2]

Like all modern corporations Exxon consists of a three-part organization made up of stockholders, who provide the capital, own the corporation, and enjoy liability limited to the amount of their investments; managers, who run the business operations; and employees who produce the goods and services. In the best-run organizations the management system is highly structured and impersonal. It provides the corporation's overall framework, the formal chain of command, that ensures the company's profit objectives.

The emergence of corporate giants like Exxon is one of the more intriguing chapters in the evolution of capitalism. Certainly the political theory of John Locke and the economic theory of Adam Smith admitted no such conglomerates of capital as those which originated in the nineteenth century and to-day dominate America's, even the world's, economic, political, and social life. This book isn't the place to analyze why a people committed to an individualistic social philosophy and a free-competition market economy allowed vast oligopolistic organizations to develop. Rather our concern is with the problem of applying moral standards to corporate organizations and with understanding their social responsibilities. Specifically, in this chapter we will look at the following topics:

1. The meaning of "responsibility" and the debate over whether corporations can be meaningfully said to have moral responsibility.

2. The controversy between the "narrow" and the "broad" views of corporate social responsibility.

3. Four key arguments in this debate—the "invisible hand" argument, the "hand of government" argument, the "inept custodian" argument, and the "materialization of society" argument.

4. The importance of institutionalizing ethics within corporations and how this may be done.

5. The role and history of unions in our corporation-dominated economic system, their ideals and achievements, and the moral issues they raise.

CORPORATE MORAL AGENCY

In 1976 the citizens of Massachusetts were asked in a referendum whether they wanted to amend the state constitution to allow the legislature to enact a graduated personal income tax. Predictably enough, they said no.

What made an otherwise unremarkable exercise of the initiative process noteworthy was that the First National Bank of Boston and four other businesses in the state wanted to spend money to express opposition to the referendum. The Massachusetts Supreme Judicial Court said they could not, that banks and business corporations are prohibited by law from spending corporate funds to publicize political views that do not materially affect their property, business, or assets. In 1978, however, the U.S. Supreme Court in a 5–4 decision (*First National Bank of Boston v. Bellotti*) struck down the Massachusetts court's decision and thereby defined the free-speech rights of corporations for the first time.

Writing for the majority, Justice Lewis Powell said: "If the speakers here were not corporations, no one would suggest that the state could silence their proposed speech. It is the type of speech indispensable to decision making in a democracy, and this is no less true because the speech comes from a corporation rather than from an individual." In a dissenting opinion, Justice Byron R. White said that states should be permitted to distinguish between individuals and corporations. "Ideas which were not a product of individual choice," said White, "are entitled to less First Amendment protection."

Immediately some viewed the decision as a major blow to consumers and citizens, although the Court seems to have moderated its position since then.[3] Whatever its precise legal ramifications, *First National Bank of Boston v. Bellotti* did have the effect of blurring the distinction between corporations and individuals. For in deciding that corporations enjoy protection under the First Amendment, the Court laid a basis for claiming that corporations should be treated as individuals in every way. Thus, since individuals can be held morally responsible for particular actions, so can corporations.

The problem, of course, is that corporations are not individuals but artificial persons, fictions created by society. They are collections of individuals who set goals and policies and perform specific actions. Since corporations are not actual persons, in what sense can they be held morally responsible for their actions?

To begin, it helps to understand what is meant by calling an individual "morally responsible." At least three senses of "moral responsibility" can be distinguished, which we'll designate as Sense 1, Sense 2, and Sense 3.

Meanings of "Moral Responsibility"

In Sense 1, "responsibility" refers to holding people morally accountable for their past actions. If you leap into a river and save a drowning child, you are morally responsible or praiseworthy for the action. If I lie to you or break a promise I made to you, I am ordinarily morally responsible or blameworthy. Responsibility in this sense of accountability for actions, therefore, refers to assigning blame or praise for past actions. Assigning such responsibility requires an assessment of various causal and moral factors that need not concern us here.

In Sense 2, "moral responsibility" refers to accountability not for past actions but for the care or welfare of others as derived from specific social roles we happen to play. Thus, parents are "responsible" for their children, teachers are "responsible" for what occurs in their classrooms, doctors are "responsible" for their patients, and so on. The specific role responsibilities we have typically are set by societal or organizational conventions.

Sense 3 of "moral responsibility" refers to one's being capable of making moral or rational decisions on one's own. When parents hire a babysitter for their young children, they implicitly recognize that their children lack the mental and emotional maturity to make informed decisions. Likewise when the law grants parents almost complete legal control over their young children, it implicitly asserts that children cannot be trusted to make important decisions regarding their own welfare. On the other hand, the babysitter and the parents presumably are "responsible"— that is, reliable and trustworthy and mature enough to allow their judgment to be informed by appropriate factors.

The three senses of "moral responsibility" can be further illustrated as follows. If in the statement "Fred Smith is morally responsible," "morally responsible" carries Sense 1, then Smith is praiseworthy or blameworthy for some action. If "morally responsible" carries Sense 2, then Smith is ethically accountable for the care or welfare of another. If "morally responsible" carries Sense 3, then Smith can be trusted to make rational or moral decisions on his own.

If a person is not morally responsible in Sense 3, he or she cannot be considered morally responsible in either of the other two senses. If Smith cannot make rational or moral decisions on his own, he cannot be held accountable for his actions or for the welfare of anyone else. On the other hand, if he can make such decisions, then in theory he can be held accountable for his actions and the welfare of others. The relation between Sense 3 of "morally responsible" and the other two, then, is that Sense 3 is a necessary, though not a sufficient, condition for Senses 1 and 2.

The importance of recognizing the logical priority of Sense 3 is that once it is established, then there is a theoretical basis for holding individuals "responsible" in Senses 1 and 2. This, in turn, simplifies the task of talking about corporate moral agency. If corporations, like individuals, can make rational and moral decisions on their own, then in theory they can be held blameworthy or praiseworthy for their actions and for the welfare of others.

While simplified, the task of determining whether corporations can make such decisions is anything but simple. Immediately, we must ponder whether it makes sense to say that any entity other than individual persons can make decisions in the first place, moral or otherwise.

Can Corporations Make Moral Decisions?

Corporations have so-called internal decision (CID) structures, which amount to established procedures for accomplishing specific goals. For example, consider Exxon's system, as depicted by Anthony J. Parisi:

> All through the Exxon system, checks and balances are built in. Each fall, the presidents of the 13 affiliates take their plan for the coming year and beyond to New York for review at a meeting with the management committee and the staff vice presidents. *The goal is to get a perfect corporate fit.* Some imaginary examples: The *committee might decide* that Exxon is becoming too concentrated in Australia and *recommend* that Esso Eastern move more slowly on that continent. Or *it might conclude* that if the *affiliates were to build* all the refineries *they are proposing, they would create* more capacity than the *company could profitably use. One of the affiliates would be asked to hold off, even though, from its particular point of view,* a new refinery was needed to serve its market.[1] (all italics added)

The italicized portions of this depiction reflect the commonplace personhood status granted corporations in and outside the corporate organization. More important here, though, is the implication that any decisions coming out of Exxon's annual sessions are formed and shaped to effect corporate goals, "to get a perfect corporate fit." Metaphorically, all data pass through the filter of corporate procedures and objectives. The remaining distillation constitutes "the decision." Certainly the participants actively engage in the decision making. But in addition to individual persons, the other major component of corporate decision making consists of the framework in which policies and activities are determined.

The CID structure lays out lines of authority and stipulates under what conditions personal actions become official corporate actions. And, just like individual persons, it collects data about the impact of its actions. It monitors work conditions, employee efficiency and productivity, environmental impacts. In short, it seemingly can show the same kind of rationality and respect for persons that individual human beings can. This has led Goodpaster and Matthews to argue by analogy that it makes just as much sense to speak of corporate moral responsibility, as it does to speak of individual moral responsibility.[5]

Philosopher Peter French arrives at the same conclusion in a slightly different way.[6] The CID structure, says French, in effect absorbs the intentions and acts of individual persons into a "corporate decision." Perhaps no corporate official intended the course or objective charted by the CID structure. But, says French, the corporation did. And he believes that these corporate intentions are enough to make corporate acts "intentional" and thus make corporations "morally responsible."

Professor of philosophy Manuel Velasquez demurs. "Even if its CID structure shows that a corporation per se can have intentions," he writes, "it does not establish intentionality."[7] An act is intentional, says Velasquez, only if the entity that formed the intention brings about the act through its bodily movements. "The intentions French attributes to corporations, then, do not mark out corporate acts as intentional because the intentions are attributed to one entity (the corporation) whereas the acts are carried out by another entity (the corporate members)." In Velasquez's view, then, the corporation's members, and not the corporation, bring about the acts of the corporation. This leads Velasquez to conclude that only corporate members, not the corporation itself, can be held morally responsible.

Vanishing Individual Responsibility

Some might argue that whether or not corporations as artificial entities can properly be held morally responsible, the nature and structure of modern corporate organizations allow virtually everyone to share moral accountability for an action—Sense 1 of "morally responsible." But in practice this can mean that no one person is held morally responsible. The masking of moral accountability, while worrisome, isn't so unusual: In and outside corporations, assigning praise and blame can be problematic. But what the masking phenomenon may reflect is of significant concern. Perhaps the impersonality of the corporate entity so envelops its members that they in effect lose their moral agency. It may be that, for all practical purposes, members of corporate organizations cannot be considered capable of making moral decisions (Sense 3 of "morally responsible") in a corporate context. A case in point: National Semiconductor Corporation.

In 1984, National Semiconductor, California's largest maker of microelectronic circuits, pleaded guilty to a forty-count indictment and was fined $1.75 million for selling parts between 1978 and 1981 that were not subjected to the tests prescribed by the contracting party, the Defense Department. In June 1984, the Pentagon proposed to suspend National Semiconductor from military sales, a ban that it subsequently lifted after the company promised to conduct such tests in the future. What really rankled the defense agency was that Semiconductor refused to identify the company employees responsible for the incomplete testing. Why the refusal? National Semiconductor president Charles Sporch said that no individuals should be singled out for punishment because the incomplete testing was "an industry pattern beyond any one individual's responsibility."[8]

This incident points to the inherent difficulties of assigning personal responsibility to members of corporations. For argument's sake, let us assume that Sporch is correct: It's virtually impossible to assign moral responsibility to any single individual for the incomplete testing. But why couldn't we rightly expect the appropriate parties to have

acted otherwise than they did? Sporch suggests an explanation: An industry-wide pattern placed the acts of noncompliance outside the realm of personal responsibility. If he's right, then CIDs not only gave rise to the industry pattern but effectively paralyzed, if not usurped, the moral agency of corporate members with respect to the pattern. From here it is an easy step to the conclusion that while it may not make any sense to speak of corporate moral agency, it can be equally vacuous to speak of individual moral agency in the contexts of particular organizational activities. This, in turn, raises the spectre of actions without actors in any moral sense—of flouted contracts, as in the case of National Semiconductor, without any morally responsible parties.

There are at least two ways to escape the intellectual discomfort posed by morally actorless actions. One would be to attribute moral agency to corporations, to follow the lead of the Supreme Court's decision in *First National Bank of Boston v. Bellotti* and assign responsibilities to corporations just as we do to individual persons. The other choice, not necessarily incompatible with the first, is to determine whether explanations like Sporch's are nothing but lame excuses to protect the blameworthy. It may well be that cases like National Semiconductor really dramatize how easy and automatic it has become to conveniently submerge personal responsibility in the protoplasmic CID structures of modern corporate organizations and that until CID structures are reconstituted to deal with noneconomic matters we can expect more of the same evasion of personal responsibility.

While the issue of corporate moral agency undoubtedly will continue to exercise scholars, the inescapable fact is that increasingly corporations are being accorded the status of biological persons, with all the rights *and* responsibilities implied therein. Indeed, recent criminal prosecutions such as the case of Ford's Pinto gas tanks suggest that society accepts in principle the notion of corporate moral responsibility. And corporate officials themselves are gradually moving to this position. Continental Oil Company's in-house booklet on moral standards expresses the public perception and its implications as follows:

> No one can deny that in the public's mind a corporation can break the law and be guilty of unethical and amoral conduct. Events of the early 1970s, such as corporate violation of federal laws and failure of full disclosure, confirmed that both our government and our citizenry expect *corporations* to act lawfully, ethically, and responsibly.
>
> Perhaps it is then appropriate in today's context to think of Conoco as a *living corporation*; a sentient being whose conduct and personality are the collective effort and responsibility of its employees, officers, directors, and shareholders.[9]

If, then, it makes sense to talk about the social and moral responsibilities of corporations, as most of us think, either in a literal sense or as a shorthand way of referring to the obligations of the individuals that make up the corporation, what are these responsibilities? Here we encounter a fundamental debate.

CORPORATE RESPONSIBILITY

In 1963 Tennessee Iron & Steel, a subsidiary of United States Steel, was by far the largest employer, purchaser, and taxpayer in Birmingham, Alabama. In the same city at the same time, racial tensions exploded in the bombing of a black church, killing four black children. The ugly incident led some to blame U.S. Steel for not doing more to improve race relations. But Roger Blough, chairman of U.S. Steel, defended his company:

> I do not either believe that it would be a wise thing for United States Steel to be

other than a good citizen in a community, or to attempt to have its ideas of what is right for the community enforced upon the community by some sort of economic means. . . .

> When we as individuals are citizens in a community we can exercise what small influence we may have as citizens, but for a corporation to attempt to exert any kind of economic compulsion to achieve a particular end in the racial area seems to me quite beyond what a corporation can do.[10]

Not long afterward, Sol M. Linowitz, chairman of the board of Xerox Corporation, declared in an address to the National Industrial Conference Board: "To realize its full promise in the world of tomorrow, American business and industry—or, at least, the vast portion of it—will have to make social goals as central to its decisions as economic goals; and leadership in our corporations will increasingly recognize this responsibility and accept it."[11] Thus the issue of business's corporate responsibility was joined. Just what responsibilities does a corporation have? Is its responsibility to be construed narrowly as merely profit making? Or more broadly to include refraining from harming society and even contributing actively and directly to the public good?

Narrow View: Profit Maximization

As it happened, the year preceding the Birmingham incident had seen the publication of *Capitalism and Freedom*, in which author Milton Friedman forcefully argued that business has no social responsibilities other than to maximize profits.

> The view has been gaining widespread acceptance that corporate officials and labor leaders have a social responsibility that goes beyond serving the interest of their stockholders or their members.

This view shows a fundamental misconception of the character and nature of a free economy. In such an economy, there is one and only one social responsibility of business—to use its resources and engage in activities designed to increase its profits so long as it stays within the rules of the game, which is to say, engages in open and free competition, without deception or fraud. . . . Few trends could so thoroughly undermine the very foundations of our free society as the acceptance by corporate officials of a social responsibility other than to make as much money for their stockholders as possible.[12]

Although from Friedman's perspective, the only responsibility of business is to make money for its owners, this obviously does not mean that a business may do literally anything whatsoever to increase its profits. Gangsters pursue profit maximization when they ruthlessly rub out their rivals, but such activity falls outside what Friedman refers to as "the rules of the game." Harvard professor Theodore Levitt echoes this point when he writes, "In the end business has only two responsibilities—to obey the elementary canons of face-to-face civility (honesty, good faith, and so on) and to seek material gain."[13]

What, then, are the rules of the game? Obviously, elementary morality rules out deception, force, and fraud, and the rules of the game are intended to promote open and free competition. The system of rules in which business is, in Friedman's view, to pursue profit is one that is conducive to the laissez-faire operation of Adam Smith's invisible hand (which was discussed in the previous chapter). Friedman is a conservative economist who believes that by allowing the market to operate with only the minimal restrictions necessary to prevent fraud and force, society will maximize its overall economic well-being. Pursuit of profit is what makes our system go. Anything that dampens this incentive or inhibits its operation will weaken the ability of Smith's invisible hand to deliver the economic goods.

Because the function of a corporate organization is to make money, the owners of corporations employ executives to accomplish this goal, thereby obligating these managers always to act in the interests of the owners. According to Friedman, to say that executives have social responsibilities means that at least sometimes they must subordinate owner interests to some social objective, such as controlling pollution or fighting inflation. This, in turn, means that they must spend stockholder money for general social interests—in effect, taxing the owners and spending these taxes on social causes. But taxation is a function of government, not private enterprise; and executives are not public employees but employees of private enterprise. The doctrine of social responsibility thus transposes executives into civil servants and business corporations into government agencies, thereby diverting business from its proper function in the social system.

Friedman is critical of those who would impose on business any duty other than that of making money, and he is particularly harsh with those business leaders who themselves take a broader view of their social responsibilities; that is, who

believe that they are defending free enterprise when they declaim that business is not concerned "merely" with profit but also with promoting desirable "social" ends; that business has a "social conscience" and takes seriously its responsibilities for providing employment, eliminating discrimination, avoiding pollution and whatever else may be the catchwords of the contemporary crop of reformers. . . . Businessmen who talk this way are unwitting puppets of the intellectual forces that have been undermining the basis of a free society these past decades. . . .

[This] short-sightedness is also exemplified in speeches by businessmen on social responsibility. This may gain them kudos in the short run. But it helps to strengthen the already too prevalent view that the pursuit of profits is wicked and immoral and must be curbed and controlled by external forces.[14]

Friedman believes that by conceding the necessity for a broader view of corporate social responsibility, businesspersons are helping to propagate ideas that are damaging to capitalism. He acknowledges, however, that often corporate activities are described as an exercise of "social responsibility" when, in fact, they are intended simply to advance a corporation's self-interest.

To illustrate, it may well be in the long-run interest of a corporation that is a major employer in a small community to devote resources to providing amenities to that community or to improving its government. That may make it easier to attract desirable employees, it may reduce the wage bill or lessen losses from pilferage and sabotage or have other worthwhile effects. . . .

In each of these—and many similar—cases, there is a strong temptation to rationalize these actions as an exercise of "social responsibility." In the present climate of opinion, with its widespread aversion to "capitalism," "profits," the "soulless corporation" and so on, this is one way for a corporation to generate goodwill as a by-product of expenditures that are entirely justified in its own self-interest.[15]

Friedman has no problem with a company pursuing its self-interest by these means, although he rues the fact that "the attitudes of the public make it in [corporations'] self-interest to cloak their actions in this way." Friedman's bottom line is that the bottom line is all that counts. And he rejects any notion of corporate social responsibility that would hinder a corporation's profit maximization.

The Broader View of Corporate Social Responsibility

The rival position to that of Friedman and Levitt is simply that business has other obligations in addition to pursuing profit. The phrase "in addition to" is important. Critics of the narrow view do not as a rule believe there is anything wrong with corporate profit. They maintain, rather, that corporations have other responsibilities as well—to consumers, to their employees, and to society at large. If the adherents of the broader view share one belief, it is that corporations have responsibilities that go beyond simply enhancing their profits because, as a matter of fact, they have such great social and economic power in our society. With that power must come social responsibility. As professor of business administration Keith Davis puts it:

One basic proposition is that *social responsibility arises from social power*. Modern business has immense social power in such areas as minority employment and environmental pollution. If business has the power, then a just relationship demands that business also bear responsibility for its actions in these areas. Social responsibility arises from concern about the consequences of business's acts as they affect the interests of others. Business decisions do have social consequences. Businessmen cannot make decisions that are solely economic decisions, because they are interrelated with the whole social system. This situation requires that businessmen's thinking be broadened beyond the company gate to the whole social system. Systems thinking is required.

Social responsibility implies that a business decision maker in the process of serving his own business interests is obliged to take actions that also protect and enhance society's interests. The net effect is to improve the quality of life in the broadest possible way, however quality of life is defined by society. In this manner, harmony is achieved between business's actions and the larger social system. The businessman becomes concerned with social as well as economic outputs and with the total effect of his institutional actions on society.[16]

Adherents of the broader view, like Davis, stress that modern business is intimately integrated with the rest of society. Business is not some self-enclosed world, like a private poker party. Rather, business activities have profound ramifications throughout society. As a result, although society expects business to pursue its economic interests, business has other responsibilities as well.

Melvin Anshen has cast the case for the broader view in a historical perspective.[17] He maintains that there is always a kind of "social contract" between business and society. This contract is, of course, only implicit, but it represents a tacit understanding within society about the proper goals and responsibilities of business. In effect, in Anshen's view, society always structures the guidelines within which business is permitted to operate in order to derive certain benefits from business activity. In the nineteenth century, society's prime interest was rapid economic growth, which was viewed as the source of all progress, and the engine of economic growth was identified as the drive for profits by unfettered, competitive, private enterprise. This attitude was reflected in the then existing social contract.

Today, however, society has concerns and interests other than rapid economic growth—in particular, a concern for the quality of life and for the preservation of the environment. Accordingly, the social contract is in the process of being modified. In particular, Anshen writes, "it will no longer be acceptable for corporations to manage their affairs solely in terms of the traditional internal costs of doing business, while thrusting external costs on the public."

In recent years we have grown more aware of the possible deleterious side effects of business activity, or what economists call *externalities*. Externalities are the unintended negative (or, in some cases, positive) consequences that an economic transaction between two parties can have on some third party. Industrial pollution provides the clearest illustration. Suppose, for example, that a factory makes widgets and sells them to your firm, which uses them in manufacturing some other product. A by-product of this economic transaction is the waste that the rains wash from the factory yard into the local river, waste that damages recreational or commercial fishing interests downstream. This damage to third parties is an unintended side effect of the economic transaction between the seller and buyer of widgets.

Defenders of the new social contract, like Anshen, maintain that externalities should no longer be overlooked. In the jargon of economists, externalities must be "internalized." That is, the factory should be made to absorb the cost, either by disposing of its waste in an environmentally safe (and presumably more expensive) way or by paying for the damage the waste does downstream. On the one hand, basic fairness requires that the factory's waste no longer be dumped onto third parties. On the other hand, from the economic point of view, requiring the factory to internalize the externalities makes sense, for only when it does so will the price of the widgets it sells reflect their true social cost. The real production cost of the widgets includes not just labor, raw materials, machinery, and so on, but also the damage done to the fisheries downstream. Unless the price of widgets is raised sufficiently to reimburse the fisheries for their losses or to dispose of the waste in some other way, then the buyer of widgets is paying less than their true cost. Part of the cost is being paid by the fishing interests downstream.

Some advocates of the broader view, like Keith Davis, go beyond requiring business to internalize its externalities in a narrow economic sense. Davis maintains that, in addition to considering potential profitability, a business must weigh the long-range social costs of its activities as well. Only if the overall benefit to society is positive should business act.

> For example, a firm that builds row upon row of look-alike houses may be saving $500 on each house and passing along $400 of the saving to each buyer, thus serving consumer interests. In the long run, however, this kind of construction may encourage the rapid development of a city slum. In this instance, the lack of long-range outlook may result in serious social costs. . . .

> In sum, the expectation of the social responsibility model is that a detailed cost/benefit analysis will be made prior to determining whether to proceed with an activity and that social costs will be given significant weight in the decision-making process. Almost any business action will entail some social costs. The basic question is whether the benefits outweigh the costs so that there is a net social benefit. Many questions of judgment arise, and there are no precise mathematical measures in the social field, but rational and wise judgments can be made if the issues are first thoroughly explored.[18]

Corporations, Stockholders, and the Promissory Relationship

Advocates of the narrow view argue that Davis and others do not understand the proper relationship between management and the owners (or stockholders) of a corporation. This relationship is a *promissory* relationship, and it imposes an obligation on management that is inconsistent with any social responsibility other than profit maximization. In effect, management agrees to maximize stockholder wealth in return for specific compensation. It's as if you turned $10,000 over to an investment adviser and told her:

"Make me as much money with this as you can. In return, I'll give you 10 percent of the earnings." If the consultant agrees to the terms, then you would properly consider any whimsical investment of your capital immoral and probably illegal. Of course, the adviser could refuse your offer, thus precluding any such obligation.

Law professor Christopher D. Stone uses a similar example to demonstrate that the relationship between corporate management and its shareholders is not the same as between you and the investment adviser.[19] For one thing, rarely if ever is an investment in a corporation couched in such explicitly promissory terms. Would-be investors ordinarily have brokers buy shares for them in specific companies or, not trusting their own judgment, simply tell their brokers to purchase what "looks good." The brokers then purchase shares from current shareholders, who in turn have acquired the shares the same way. Very few investors really put their money directly into the corporation but buy shares that were issued years ago through some underwriting syndicate. The impersonality of these transactions, says Stone, points up several differences between them and the case of your investment adviser: (1) Most shareholders aren't even aware who the managers of "their" corporations are; (2) most shareholders never have direct contact with management; (3) the complexity of management systems in most modern corporations makes it impossible to pinpoint a single manager or group of managers directly responsible for "keeping the promise"; (4) the managers were never given a choice, as your adviser was, of refusing to maximize your profits as a shareholder.

But even if a promissory agreement exists between shareholder and management obligating management to make the most possible money for shareholders, must such a promise always be kept? Stone notes that most people would agree that promises create moral presumptions. But, he says, few would claim that the existence of a promise automatically settles all the moral issues. For example, if I promise to meet you on the corner of Main and State at noon, I have an obligation to keep that promise. But few would regard my promise as exceptionless. For example, we wouldn't regard it as justification for refusing to give a heart attack victim cardiopulmonary resuscitation. Better to break the promise and save a life than keep the promise and lose a life. The point is that even if a promise to maximize profits runs from management to shareholders, it's doubtful that the typical shareholder interprets this as a mandate for management to maximize profits at all social costs.

Even if it is so construed, we can still ask: Is such an agreement moral? After all, a contract to do evil—for example, to kill someone—is invalid. By the same token, a promise that obligates management to subordinate all moral considerations—for example, a healthful environment or safe products—to the end of stockholder profits would be immoral. Management, therefore, would not be obliged to honor it and, in fact, should break it.

But then precisely what is the nature of and the basis for the shareholder/corporate executive relationship? Just whom are managers working for and responsible to: shareholders, society, both? Friedman raises this point when he writes:

> The whole justification for permitting the corporate executive to be selected by the shareholders is that the executive is an agent serving the interest of his principal. This justification disappears when the corporate executive imposes taxes and spends the proceeds for "social" purposes. He becomes in effect a public employee, a civil servant, even though he remains in name an employee of a private enterprise.[20]

But is it true that stockholders actually select corporate executives? Corporate watch-dogs like Ralph Nader and Mark Green make the point that, in modern corporate governance, management, in fact, selects board members by controlling proxy votes. And the board typically rubber-stamps the policies and executive-officer recommendations of management. Furthermore, corporate boards often are ignorant of the activities of chief executive officers, as the case of the multi-million-dollar bribery by Gulf Oil executives illustrates. For well over a year *after* disclosure of the bribes, the Gulf Board of Directors claimed it didn't know that the company's chief executive officer and chairman of the board had been personally involved. In big corporations, as a 1978 Senate Committee on Government Affairs observed, the tightly interlocked nature of corporate boards has the effect of concentrating their power in the hands of a small elite.[21]

But even if stockholders do select corporate executives, it doesn't follow that the executives are therefore solely bound to act in the interest of stockholder profits. Some stockholders, for example, might expect executives to act in an environmentally responsible manner, even if that means less profit. And why shouldn't stockholders who want to expand the notion of corporate responsibility fight for just that? Friedman dismisses such cases as "some stockholders trying to get other stockholders . . . to contribute against their will to 'social' causes. . . ." But why couldn't it be a case of the activists trying to open debate about the nature of their corporation's social responsibility? Besides, if activist stockholders wish to make their corporations more socially responsible, why, as owners, don't they have a right to do that?

Friedman further believes that if executives "impose taxes on stockholders and spend the proceeds for 'social' purposes, they then become 'civil servants,' and thus should be selected through a political process." He considers such a proposition absurd, or at best socialistic. And yet others, such as Nader and

Green, see a need to counterbalance the increasing power of modern corporate management and have suggested some ways to do this: a new stockholder electoral system, the prohibition of interlocking directorates, the creation of the position of professional director who would do nothing but supervise the corporation's activities.

Even if Friedman's critics are correct and broadening the notion of corporate responsibility does not violate a promissory relationship between stockholders and management, we can still ask: Should it be broadened?

THE ADVISABILITY OF BROADENING CORPORATE RESPONSIBILITY

Four powerful arguments against broadening corporate responsibility, which we will now sketch and critique, can be conveniently termed: (1) the "invisible hand" argument; (2) the "hand of government" argument; (3) the "inept custodian" argument; and (4) the "materialization of society" argument.[22] Advocates of broadened corporate responsibility base their case in part on a rejection of these arguments.

The "Invisible Hand" Argument

Adam Smith claimed that when each of us acts to promote our own best interest we are led by an "invisible hand" to promote the general good. Like-minded contemporary thinkers like Friedman agree. They point out that corporations, in fact, were chartered by states precisely with utility in mind. If businesses are permitted to seek self-interest, their activities will inevitably yield the greatest good for the greatest number. To invite corporations to base their policies and activities on anything other than profit making is, in effect, to sully the contract between society and corporations, to politicize business's

unique economic function. Accordingly, corporations should not be invited to fight racial injustice, poverty, or pollution, to broaden competition, or to help reduce prices or increase accessibility to products, except insofar as these activities are a natural outgrowth of improved corporate efficiency.

This does not mean that corporations should not be held accountable for their actions. To the degree that they fulfill or fail to fulfill their economic role, they can be praised or blamed. But corporations should not be held morally responsible for noneconomic matters. To do so would distort the economic mission of business in society and undermine the foundations of the free enterprise system.

Perhaps within a very restricted area of economic exchange, where parties to the exchange are roughly equal, each pursuing self-interest can result in the greatest good for the greatest number. But when economic exchanges involve giant corporations, the concept of an "invisible hand" orchestrating the common good stretches credulity.

Modern corporations bear about as much resemblance to Smith's self-sufficient farmers and craftpersons as today's military complex bears to the Continental Militia. Today's modern corporation, notes Professor Virginia Held, is "an almost feudal institution in its hierarchical structure and lack of democratic organization."[23] Moreover, they are no more "private" in their ability to control our lives than are state governments. If an "invisible hand" has been operating, its movements have been decidedly clumsy. The United States is not becoming more egalitarian. The percentages of rich and poor have not materially changed over the years, although the disparity between them has widened. And whereas large corporations generally can escape the ravages of economic downturns, the unskilled, members of minority groups, women, the aged, and the infirm often cannot find work or even lose the jobs they had.

The "Hand of Government" Argument

Others, like economist and social critic John Kenneth Galbraith, agree that business's social role is purely economic and that corporations should not be considered moral agents.[24] But they reject the assumption that Smith's "invisible hand" will have the effect of "moralizing corporate activities." Left to their own self-serving devices, they warn, modern corporations will enrich themselves while impoverishing society. They will pollute, allow racial and sexual inequalities to fester, deceive consumers, strive to eliminate competition, and keep prices high through oligopolistic practices. And they will use their abundant resources to pressure legislators into enacting legislation that is favorable to them but not necessarily to the rest of us. They will do these things, the argument continues, because being economic institutions they are quite properly profit motivated. But what is profitable is not necessarily socially useful or desirable; and what is socially useful and desirable is not always profitable.

Then how is the corporation's natural and insatiable appetite for profit to be controlled? Through government regulation. The strong hand of government, through a system of laws and incentives, can and should bring corporations to heel.

As Professors Kenneth E. Goodpaster (philosophy) and John B. Matthews (business administration) point out, these two views obviously differ in identifying the locus of moral force: For one it is the invisible hand of the market; for the other it is the visible hand of government. Both, however, agree that corporate social responsibility should not be expanded.[25]

Critics respond that the "hand of government" view is dangerously naive. It's a blueprint, they say, for big, intrusive government. Besides, they wonder if government can control any but the most egregious corporate immorality. Necessarily overlooked, they fear, will be many questionable activities that can be safely hidden within the labyrinth of corporate structure. Moreover, lacking the intimate knowledge of the goals and subgoals of specific corporations, as well as of their daily operations, government simply can't anticipate a specific corporation's moral challenges. Rather, it can prescribe behavior only for broad, cross-sectional issues, such as bribery, price fixing, unfair competition, and the like.

Finally, is government a credible custodian of morality? If recent experience has taught anything, it is that government officials are not always paragons of virtue. Looked at as another organization, government manifests many of the same structural characteristics that test moral behavior inside the corporation. Furthermore, given the awesome clout of political action committees (PACs), one wonders whether in serving as moral policemen government officials will do anything more than impose the value systems of their most generous financiers. And since business and corporate interests number among the most influential of PACs, can we seriously expect government to bite the hand that feeds it?

The "Inept Custodian" Argument

Some who argue against broadening corporate responsibility say that corporate executives lack the moral and social expertise to make other than economic decisions. To charge them with noneconomic responsibilities would be to put the social welfare in the hands of inept custodians. Thus, business analyst Walter Goodman writes: "I don't know of any investment adviser whom I would care to act in my behalf in any matter except turning a profit. . . . The value of these specialists . . . lies in their limitations; they ought not allow themselves to see so much of the world that they become distracted."[26]

It may be true, as Goodman suggests, that corporate members lack the moral or social expertise that a broader view of corporate responsibility would seem to require of them. But more or less the same can be said of most people in organizations: They are not trained moral philosophers or social scientists. And yet we don't ordinarily restrict the activities of these parties, individually or collectively, to carefully circumscribed organizational goals. Physicians, for example, are to provide health care. Is it therefore objectionable for them as physicians to protest nuclear war and campaign for an end to the nuclear arms race—indeed, to conceive of their social responsibility in such terms? Is it beyond the role of pediatricians to publicly support legislation requiring seat belts and other restraining devices in automobiles? Again, every year the Committee on Public Doublespeak of the National Council of Teachers of English gives a "Doublespeak Award," usually to a business or political leader, for flagrant use of language that pretends to communicate but really does not. Should the committee's members, all of whom are teachers of English, confine their language instruction to the classroom, and avoid trying to attract public attention to what is good, clear, solid language usage?

Of course, the analogy between the physicians and English teachers, on the one hand, and corporate executives on the other, is imperfect. For one thing, English teachers know of what they speak—proper language usage. And physicians are qualified to address the health aspect of nuclear war and the health hazards of driving without restraining devices. Furthermore, the social activism of these professionals does not diminish the earnings of their employers. Nevertheless, such comparisons do make the larger point that "responsibility" is not always defined within the strict limits of a profession's or organization's role in society. If we consider

physician and teacher activities like the aforementioned defensible, then it seems fair to ask: What, if anything, makes the social role of the corporation unique, so that its responsibility and that of those it employs should be confined solely to profit making?

The "Materialization of Society" Argument

Related to the "inept custodian" argument is one that expresses fear that, permitted to stray outside strictly economic matters, corporate officials will impose their materialistic values on all of society. Thus, rather than "moralizing" corporate activity, broadening corporate responsibility will "materialize" society.

Over thirty years ago Harvard professor Theodore Levitt expressed this concern when he wrote:

> The danger is that all these things resulting from having business pursue social goals other than profit making will turn the corporation into a twentieth century equivalent of the medieval church. . . . For while the corporation also transforms itself in the process, at bottom its outlook will always remain materialistic. What we have then is the frightening spectacle of a powerful economic functional group whose future and perception are shaped in a tight materialistic context of money and things but which imposes its narrow ideas about a broad spectrum of unrelated noneconomic subjects on the mass of man and society. Even if its outlook were the purest kind of good will, that would not recommend the corporation as an arbiter of our lives.[27]

This argument seems to assume that corporations do not already exercise enormous discretionary power over us. But as Keith Davis points out, business already has immense social power. "Society has . . . entrusted to business large amounts of society's resources," says Davis, "and business is expected to manage these resources as a wise trustee for society. In addition to the traditional role of economic entrepreneurship, business now has a new social role of trusteeship. As trustee for society's resources, it serves the interests of all claimants on the organization, rather than only those of owners, or consumers, or labor."[28]

In a similar vein Paul Camenisch ("Business Ethics: On Getting to the Heart of the Matter," p. 224) claims that business currently is propagating, consciously or unconsciously, a view of humanity and the good life. Implicit in the barrage of advertisements to which we are subjected daily are assumptions about happiness, success, and human fulfillment. Sometimes corporations speak out in unvarnished terms about social issues, as United Technologies did in the following blurb, entitled "The Decline of Standards," which occupied a full page in *The Wall Street Journal*:

> A big city school system requires a student in seventh grade to be able to read as well as a fifth grader, who, by the way, must be able to read as well as a fourth grader, who, in turn, must be able to read as well as a third grader. What's wrong with demanding that a seventh grader be required to read like a *seventh* grader? How would you like to be operated on by a brain surgeon who graduated from a school that allowed its students to be a year and a half behind in their skills?[29]

For several years, Mobil Corporation has run advertisements in the form of essays on industry-related social issues. One appeared right after William Ruckelshaus, the new administrator of the Environmental Protection Agency (EPA), called on scientists to help EPA formulate a public policy free from politics. Mobil seized on the opportunity to divide the population into two categories: scientists, who best know what constitutes pollution and hazardous waste, and the rest of us well-intentioned but dangerously benighted souls. Here's an excerpt from the essay:

> Too often, U.S. environmental policy has been based on political considerations or has been influenced by one-sided TV reportage. Time after time, the American people have watched as so-called experts paraded across their television screens warning of doomsday disasters from nuclear power plants and waste disposal sites. Never mind that "expert" A was a geology professor but was holding forth on nuclear power, and that "expert" B was a lawyer spouting off about hazardous waste. . . .
>
> One result is that despite the fact that industry has marshalled thousands of scientists and billions of dollars to clean up the environment and keep it clean, and that the results to date have been impressive, the public perception often is that nothing is being done.

In praising Ruckelshaus's emphasis on the central position of scientists in setting standards, Mobil in effect was making industry scientists custodians of the environment.

INSTITUTIONALIZING ETHICS WITHIN CORPORATIONS

The criticisms of the four arguments we have just presented have led many people inside and outside business to adopt the broader view of corporate responsibility—that there is no firm basis for saying that the sole obligation of the modern corporation is simply to make money. Society grants corporations the right to exist, gives them legal status as separate entities, and permits them to use natural resources. It does this not to indulge the profit appetites of owners and managers but, as Camenisch says, because it needs "the available raw materials transformed into needed goods and services, and because business in its contemporary form has been conspicuously successful in doing just that." In return for its sufferance of corporations, society has the right to expect that, at the very least, corporation activities will not cause harm.

Some argue further that the list of corporate responsibilities goes beyond such negative injunctions as "Don't pollute," "Don't misrepresent products," "Don't bribe." Included also are affirmative duties: "Hire the hardcore unemployed," "Give special consideration to members of historically disadvantaged groups," "Contribute to the arts and education," "Locate plants in economically depressed areas." This class of affirmative responsibilities would include activities that are not intrinsically related to the operations of the corporation—responsibilities that each of us, whether individuals or institutions, has equally, simply by virtue of our being members of society.[30] Precisely how far each of us must go to meet these responsibilities depends largely on our capacity to fulfill them, which, of course, varies from person to person, institution to institution. But given their considerable power and resources, corporations seem better able to promote the common good than individuals or small businesses.

Although precisely how corporations are to promote the common good cannot be answered very specifically, proponents of broadening corporate responsibility probably would agree that the first step is to create an ethical atmosphere within the corporation. This means making ethical behavior a high priority. How to do this? At least four actions seem called for:

1. Corporations should acknowledge the importance, even necessity, of conducting business morally. Their commitment to ethical behavior should be unequivocal and highly visible.

2. Corporations should make a real effort to encourage members to take moral responsibilities seriously. This action would mean ending all forms of retaliation against those who "buck the system."

3. Corporations should terminate their defensiveness in the face of criticism. They should stop responding with righteous indignation to charges of irresponsibility and give up the belief that anything done in the name of commerce is automatically exempt from considerations of decency and humanity. They should also refrain from wrapping themselves in the red-white-and-blue of free enterprise, thereby reducing legitimate inquiry to some sort of political subversion. Instead, corporations should actively solicit other views, especially those expressed by their primary claimants: stockholders, managers, employees, customers, and society as a whole. This means corporations should invite outside opinions instead of waiting until dissenters are storming the citadel.

4. Corporations must recognize the pluralistic nature of the social system of which they are a part. Society consists of diverse, interlocked groups all vying to maintain their autonomy and advance their interests. These groups are so related that the actions of one inevitably affect the standing of another on a variety of levels: economic, political, educational, cultural. As part of society, corporations affect many groups and these groups affect corporations. Failing to realize this or act on it, corporations lose sight of the social framework that governs their relationship with the external environment.

Undoubtedly other general directives could be added to this list. Still, if corporate responsibility should be expanded, then something like the preceding approach seems basic.

Limits to What the Law Can Do

In discussing the "hand of government" argument earlier in this chapter, we saw that critics questioned Galbraith's view that society should not expect business to behave morally, but rather should simply use government to direct business's pursuit of profit in socially acceptable directions. This issue is worth returning to in the present context. All defenders of the broad view of corporate social responsibility believe that more than laissez-faire is necessary to insure that business behavior is socially and morally acceptable. But there is a tendency to believe that law is a fully adequate vehicle for this purpose.

Law professor Christopher Stone has argued, however, that there are limtis on what the law can be expected to achieve.[31] Three of his points are particularly important. First, many laws, like controls on the disposal of toxic waste, are inevitably passed only after there is general awareness of the problem; in the meantime, damage has already been done. The proverbial barn door has been shut only after the horse has left.

Second, formulating appropriate laws and designing effective regulations are difficult. It is hard to achieve consensus on the relevant facts, to determine what remedies will work, and to decide how to weigh conflicting values. In addition, in our political system corporations and their lobbyists have significant input into the writing of laws. Not only that, but the specific working regulations and the day-to-day interpretation of the law require the continual input of industry experts. This is not a conspiracy, but a fact of life. Government bureaus generally have limited time, person-power, and expertise, so that they must rely on the cooperation and assistance of those they regulate.

Third, enforcing the law is often cumbersome. Legal actions against corporations are expensive and can drag on for years. Often the judicial process is too blunt an instrument to use as a way of managing complex social and business issues. In fact, recourse to the courts can be counterproductive, and Stone argues that sometimes the benefits of doing so may not be worth the costs. Legal action may simply make corporations more furtive, breeding distrust, destruction of documents,

and an attitude that "I won't do anything more than I am absolutely required to do."

What conclusion should we draw? Stone's argument is not intended to show that regulation of business is hopeless. Rather, what he wants to stress is that the law cannot do it alone. We do not want a system in which business people believe that their only obligation is to obey the law and that it is morally permissible for them to do anything which is not (yet) illegal. With that attitude on the part of business, disaster is just around the corner. More socially responsible business behavior requires, instead, that business not just respond to the requirements of the law, but that corporations and the people who make them up have high moral standards—and that they themselves monitor their own behavior.

Ethical Codes and Economic Efficiency

It is, therefore, important that corporations examine their own implicit and explicit codes of conduct and the moral standards that are being propagated to their employees. Yet, when there is talk of ethical behavior in the business world, the assumption is often that this must be at the expense of economic efficiency. Defenders of the broader view like Anshen as well as defenders of the narrow view like Friedman seem to make this assumption. Anshen believes that other values should take priority over economic efficiency, while Friedman contends business should only concern itself with profit and, in this way, maximize economic well-being. In his essay "Social Responsibility and Economic Efficiency" (reprinted on page 213), Nobel Prize-winning economist Kenneth Arrow has challenged this assumption.

First, any kind of settled economic life requires a certain degree of ethical behavior, some element of trust and confidence. Much business, for instance, is done on the basis of verbal assurance. In addition, says Arrow, "there are two types of situation in which the simple rule of maximizing profits is socially inefficient: the case in which costs are not paid for, as in pollution, and the case in which the seller has considerably more knowledge about his product than the buyer. . . ."

We have already discussed the first type of situation and the demand that corporations "internalize" their "externalities." In the second situation, where the buyer lacks the expertise and knowledge of the seller, an effective moral code, requiring either full disclosure or setting minimal standards of performance (for example, the braking ability of a new automobile), enhances, rather than diminishes, economic efficiency. Without such a code, buyers may purchase products or services they don't need. Or, because they don't trust the seller, refrain from purchasing products and services they do need. Either way, from the economist's point of view, the situation is inefficient.

An effective professional or business moral code—as well as the public's awareness of this code—is good for business. Most of us, for example, have little medical knowledge and are thus at the mercy of doctors. Over hundreds of years, however, a firm code of ethical conduct has developed in the medical profession. As a result people generally presume that their physician will perform with their welfare in mind. They rarely worry that their doctor might be taking advantage of them or exploiting them with unnecessary treatment. By contrast, used-car companies have historically suffered from a lack of public trust.

For a code to be effective it must be realistic, Arrow argues, in the sense of connecting with the collective self-interest of business. And it must become part of the corporate culture, "accepted by the significant operating institutions and transmitted from one generation of executives to the next through standard operating procedures [and] through education in business schools."

For both Arrow and Stone, then, the development of feasible and effective business and professional codes of ethics must be a central focus of any effort to enhance or expand corporate responsibility. Thus, we need to pursue further the question of how a corporate atmosphere conducive to moral decision making can be created.

Corporate Moral Codes

What can be done to so improve the organizational climate that individual members can reasonably be expected to act ethically? If those inside the corporation are to behave ethically, they need clearly stated and communicated ethical standards that are equitable and enforced. This seems possible only if the standards of expected behavior are institutionalized—that is, become a fixture in the corporate organization. To institutionalize ethics within corporations, Professors Milton Snoeyenbos and Donald Jewell suggest that corporations (1) adopt a corporate ethical code, (2) set up a high-ranking ethics committee, and (3) include ethics training in their management development programs.

The code should not be window dressing or so general as to be useless. It should set *reasonable* goals and subgoals, with an eye on blunting unethical pressures on subordinates. In formulating the code, the top-level ethics committee should solicit the views of corporate members at *all* levels regarding goals and sub-goals, so that the final code articulates "a fine-grained ethical code that addresses ethical issues likely to arise at the level of subgoals."[32] Moreover, the committee should have full authority and responsibility to (1) communicate the code and decisions based on it to all corporate members, (2) clarify and interpret the code when the need arises, (3) facilitate the code's use, (4) investigate grievances and violations of the code, (5) discipline violators and reward compliance, and (6) review, update, and upgrade the code.

The institutionalization of ethics within the corporation can be further aided by the corporation's devoting part of all employee-training programs to ethics. This could include, but need not be limited to, the study of the code, orientation to the ethics committee, and discussion of employer and employee responsibilities. Snoeyenbos and Jewell believe that institutionalizing ethics within the corporation will, in the context of developing an industry-wide code of ethics that addresses issues beyond a particular firm, go far toward establishing a corporate climate conducive to individual moral decision making.

UNIONS

We cannot conclude our discussion of corporations here, for it is not possible to understand fully contemporary corporations and the factors influencing their behavior without also discussing their relationship to organized labor. In the next chapter we look at a number of moral issues that arise in the context of employer-employee relations, but here we must examine one of the basic institutions through which corporations relate to their employees—namely, unions. We turn briefly, then, to the history and economic role of unions, to the ideals that motivate them, and to some of the moral dilemmas they raise.

History of the Union Movement

Many economists and students of the union movement give it primary credit for raising the standard of living and increasing the security of working people in this country. They argue that almost all the benefits enjoyed by employees today, whether they happen to be in unions or not, can be traced back to union victories or to union-backed legisla-

tion. At the same time, the higher wages, benefits, and increased security that unions have brought have, in turn, contributed to social stability in the country and, through enhanced effective demand, to economic growth itself. Yet, as the history of the labor movement reveals, unionization and union demands have, with few exceptions, been opposed at every step of the way by employers—and often with violence. Let's take a brief look at that history.

Just as the roots of capitalism can be traced to the handicraft guilds, so the earliest efforts of American unionism can be found in the craft unions of the eighteenth century.[33] At that time, groups of skilled artisans—carpenters, shoemakers, tailors, and the like—formed secret societies for two basic reasons: (1) to attempt to equalize their relationship with their employers and (2) to attempt to "professionalize" their crafts. They agreed on acceptable wages and working hours and pledged not to work for any employer who didn't provide them, and they set minimal admission standards for their crafts. They also agreed to keep their allegiance secret—and for good reason. If found out they would be fired, and if discovered trying to cause a strike they could be jailed.

Labor historians generally consider the Knights of Labor (K of L) established in 1869 as the first truly national trade union. What distinguished the K of L from previous craft unions was that it assembled in one labor organization both skilled and unskilled workers from an industry. Although this arrangement gave the organization the strength of numbers, it also created resentment among the skilled workers who viewed the unskilled as inferior and therefore unworthy of their association. Friction and destructive rivalries also broke out among the organization's more radical national leadership and its more conservative local directors. Outside the organization, public sentiment, although never wildly supportive, turned sharply against unions in the wake of the Chicago Haymarket Riot of 1886, in which a bomb was lobbed into a group of policemen trying to halt a labor rally. Compounding the fledgling union's problems was a sour national economy that left workers fearing for their jobs and, thus, avoiding any entanglements that might land them among the growing ranks of the unemployed. In any event, between 1885 and 1890, K of L membership plummeted from 700,000 to 100,000.

But while the K of L was tottering, a new union was being born. In 1886, the American Federation of Labor (AFL) was founded. Within seven years, under the astute and temperate leadership of Samuel Gompers, it built a membership of 500,000, which increased to about 2 million by 1917. Curiously, the survival and prosperity of the AFL must be attributed in no small measure to business itself which, fearing the radical and revolutionary tendencies of the Industrial Workers of the World (the "Wobblies"), embraced Gompers's union as the lesser of the evils.

The cause of unionism was significantly advanced in 1935 with the passage of the National Labor Relations Act (also called the Wagner Act). This legislation prohibited employers from interfering with employees trying to organize unions, attempting to gain control over labor unions, treating union workers differently than nonunion workers, and refusing to bargain with union representatives. The act helped increase union membership to almost 12 million by the end of World War II in 1945. Most of these members belonged to the Congress of Industrial Organizations (CIO), an offshoot of the AFL that brought together various workers—auto, sheet metal, steel, and so on—into industry-wide unions. The distinct advantage of the CIO over the AFL was that it could call upon all its members to strike, rather than just a few skilled workers within a firm.

But increasing union strength also brought public suspicions and fears of union power.

Many business people and political critics encouraged these worries and were quick to point to the large wave of strikes after World War II as evidence of union abuse of power. In 1947 a newly elected Republican Congress passed the Taft-Hartley Act, which amended the National Labor Relations Act. The new act outlawed the closed shop (where a person must be a member of the union before being hired), and Section 14(b) permits individual states to outlaw union shops (where a person must join the union within a specified time after being hired). Today some twenty-one states, mostly in the South and West, are so-called "right-to-work" states, with "open shop" laws on their books. These laws prohibit union contracts requiring all employees on a job site to pay union dues or their equivalent, once hired. The Taft-Hartley Act also prohibits various labor practices designated as "unfair," such as sympathy strikes or secondary boycotts (see below).

Since the merging of the AFL and CIO in 1955, unions have attempted to increase membership by recruiting outside basic industry—for example, in education, government, white-collar professions, and service jobs. But they have been only moderately successful. Between 1968 and 1978, for instance, union membership increased by two million while the workforce itself swelled by twenty million. Union membership as a percentage of the workforce has, in fact, declined: from 34 percent in 1947 to less than 20 percent today. This makes it lower than unionization rates in most Western nations—for instance, Australia, Belgium, France, Japan, the Netherlands, West Germany, and the United Kingdom.

In recent years unions have been more and more on the defensive, as the industries in which they have been traditionally based have declined. Strike incidence in 1982, for instance, reached its lowest level since World War II, and many unions have been forced to go along with decreases in wages and benefits. Nor has the general political climate been favorable to labor, as two recent, unsuccessful strikes showed. In 1981 President Reagan fired the striking air controllers and broke their union (PATCO). And the 1987 strike of NFL players (for, among other things, free agency, a right already won by baseball players and enjoyed by all other employees) collapsed after the television networks went along with the owners and broadcast the games of replacement players, despite lower than usual ratings.[34] Both unions had been considered powerful, but they were soundly defeated.

Richard Edwards and Michael Podgursky sum up labor's current situation this way:

> Bargaining structures built up over many years are crumbling and collapsing. . . . Rising product market competition, deregulation, and technological changes; adverse labor force dynamics; worsening public policy; and the legacy of the long stagnation have thrust the labor movement into a qualitatively new stage. This new period is characterized . . . by: (a) greater corporate mobility, power, and militancy; (b) ineffective labor law and a growing indifference, and in some cases, outright opposition of the government towards organized labor and collective bargaining; and (c) a waning belief in unions as the agents of working class interests. In these hostile circumstances, American unions face a difficult and troubling future.[35]

Union Ideals

From the beginning unions have been driven by an attempt to protect workers from abuses of power at the hands of employers. This effort is based on the indisputable premise that employers have tremendous power over individual workers. They can hire and fire, relocate and reassign, set work hours and wages, create rules and work conditions. Acting individually, a worker rarely, if ever, is an employer's equal in negotiating any of these items. The position of most workers acting independently is further weakened by their lack of capital, occupational limitations, and personal and family needs. Add to this that while employers obviously need workers, they rarely need any particular worker. They can select whomever they want, for whatever reasons they choose. In the raw, then, the employer-employee relationship is no more equal than the master-slave.

In an attempt to effect a balance of power in their dealings with employers, workers band together. In acting as a single body, a union, workers in effect make employers dependent on them in a way that no individual worker can. The result is parity based on mutual dependence. And this rough equality serves as a basis for collective bargaining—negotiations between the representatives of organized workers and their employers over things such as wages, hours, rules, work conditions, and, increasingly, participation in decisions affecting the work place.

Certainly no one can object to unionism's initial and overriding impulse: to protect workers from abuse and give them a voice in matters that affect their lives. Indeed, these two purposes are specifications of two lofty moral ideals: noninjury and autonomy. Curiously, it is out of respect for these ideals that some individuals criticize modern unions.

The critics argue that union shops infringe the autonomy and right of association of individual workers. Even if workers are not required to join the union, but only to pay some equivalent to union dues, the critics contend that this still infringes their freedom. In addition, evidence suggests that companies in alliance with unions sometimes treat nonunion personnel less favorably than union members. Some workers have gone to court to argue that favoritism to union members is discriminatory and unlawful (see Case 5.3 on page 210). Whether or not it is, it certainly raises a moral question about the right to determine for oneself organizational membership and participation.

Taking the union's viewpoint reveals competing ideals and other consequences that must be considered. First, there is organized labor's ideal of solidarity, which is vital to collective bargaining and to winning worker equality. Union proponents point to the fact that per capita personal income is higher in free collective bargaining states than in "right-to-work" states. In 1985, for example, of the twenty then existing right-to-work states, only Nevada and Virginia had personal incomes above the national average.

Second, there is a question of fairness. Is it fair for a nonunion member to enjoy the benefits often won at great personal and organizational expense by the union? This question arises most forcefully where unions are attempting to establish an "agency shop," which is a pattern in which all employees must pay union dues but are not required to join the union. The agency shop is designed to eliminate "free riders," while at the same time respecting the worker's freedom of choice. Opponents claim that an agency shop does not so much eliminate free riders as create "forced passengers."

Enforcement Tactics

The tactics unions employ to enforce their demands on management also raise moral issues.

Direct Strikes.   The legal right to strike is labor's most potent tool in labor-management negotiations. A strike occurs when an organized body of workers withholds its labor to force its employer to comply with its demands. Since strikes can cause financial injuries to both employer and employee, inconvenience and perhaps worse to consumers, and economic dislocations in society, they always raise serious moral questions. On the other hand, there may be times when workers cannot obtain justice and fair play in the work place in any other way than by striking. Aus-

tin Fagothey and Milton A. Gonsalves suggest the following conditions of a justified strike:[36]

1. *Just cause.* "Just cause" refers to job-related matters. Certainly, inadequate pay, excessive hours, dangerous and unhealthful working conditions are legitimate worker grievances and provide just cause for a strike. Revenge, personal ambition, petty jealousies, and the like do not constitute just cause and thus cannot justify a strike.

2. *Proper authorization.* For a strike to be justified it must spring from proper authorization. This means, first, that workers themselves must freely reach the decision without coercion and intimidation. Second, if the workers are organized, then the proposed strike must receive union backing (although this condition of Fagothey and Gonsalves becomes difficult to apply when the local union chapter and the national organization don't see eye-to-eye).

3. *Last resort.* To be justified a strike must come as a last resort. This condition acknowledges the serious potential harm of strikes. A basic moral principle is that we should always use the least injurious means available to accomplish the good we desire. Since there is an array of collective-bargaining tactics that can and usually do achieve worker objectives, all these should be exhausted before a strike is called.

Simply because a strike is justified, however, does not mean that any manner of implementing it is morally justified. Peaceful picketing and an attempt by striking workers to publicize their cause and peacefully persuade others not to cross the picket line typically are considered moral means of striking. Physical violence, threats, intimidation, and sabotage are not. More controversially, Fagothey and Gonsalves argue that if workers have the right to withhold their labor and strike, then employers have a right to fill their jobs with other workers but not professional strikebreakers whose presence incites violence and whose function extends beyond doing work to denying strikers justice and the right to organize.

The preceding observations deal with what sometimes are termed direct strikes—that is, cessation of work by employees with the same industrial grievance. There is, however, another kind of strike, far more controversial than the direct strike—the sympathetic strike.

Sympathetic Strikes. A sympathetic strike occurs when workers who have no particular grievance of their own and who may or may not have the same employer decide to strike in support of others. The bigger unions become and the more diverse workers they count among their members, the more likely are sympathetic strikes aimed at different employers. Indeed, the sympathetic strike can take on global proportions, as when American dockside workers refused to unload Russian freighters in order to show support of the Solidarity movement in Poland.

Sometimes the sympathetic strike involves several groups of workers belonging to different unions but employed by the same individuals or company. Acting on a grievance, one group strikes. But because it is so small, it enlists the aid of the other groups—it asks them to engage in a sympathetic strike. Cases like these do not seem to differ in any morally significant way from direct strikes. Indeed, it could be argued that the affiliated groups have obligations of loyalty and beneficence to join the strike. It is true, of course, that the sympathetic strikers do not have personal grievances, but they do have the same unjust employer, and they are in a unique position to help remedy that injustice by withholding their labor.[37]

Sympathetic strikes involving groups of employees working for different employers differ in several morally significant ways from the direct strike or the sympathetic strike against the same employer. Many of the employers being struck out of sympathy may be perfectly innocent victims whose treatment of workers is beyond reproach. They have lived up to their end of the work contract, only to have their workers repudiate theirs.

On the other hand, such sympathetic strikes can be very effective. J. P. Stevens & Co., the second largest company in the U.S. textile industry, fought unionization for two decades. They engaged in a variety of flagrantly unfair labor practices and refused to recognize or bargain collectively with the union, despite various court orders to do so.[38] During the boycott of J. P. Stevens products, UAW members at a GM plant in Canada refused to install Stevens carpeting in the cars, thus shutting down the assembly line. In less than half a day Stevens carpeting was gone from the plant. Had U.S. workers done something similar, both they and the textile workers union would have been subject to legal action, but J. P. Stevens would not have been able to refuse to bargain as long as it did.

Boycotts and "Corporate Campaigns." Besides strikes, unions also employ two kinds of boycotts to enforce their demands. A primary boycott occurs when union members and their supporters refuse to buy products from a company being struck. A secondary boycott occurs when people refuse to patronize companies that handle products of struck companies. Although the Taft Hartley Act prohibits secondary boycotts, they still occur, as when members of the United Farm Workers Union organized a secondary boycott in the 1970s. The union urged shoppers nationwide not to buy grapes from stores that had purchased them from farms being struck. A secondary boycott was also used against the Adolph Coors brewery in the early 1980s.

The express purpose of any boycott is the same as a strike: to hurt the employer or company financially and thus enforce union demands. And, in general, a boycott is justifiable when it meets the same conditions as a strike. In the case of the secondary boycott, which is like a sympathetic strike, the damage is extended to those whose only offense is that they happen to be handling the products of the allegedly unjust employer—and perhaps they are handling them out of financial necessity. In such cases, Fagothey and Gonsalves reject secondary boycotts. But this assessment seems too automatic and doesn't allow us to weigh the likely harms and benefits in particular cases.[39]

A relatively new pressure tactic is the so-called "corporate campaign," in which unions enlist the cooperation of a company's creditors to pressure the company to unionize or comply with union demands. The tactic first gained national recognition in 1974 after it was successfully used to help Amalgamated Clothing & Textile Workers' Union win contracts with Farah Manufacturing Company, a Texas-based men's garment maker. Union representatives persuaded retailers in Birmingham, Alabama, to stop selling the slacks by threatening them with a consumer boycott and then persuaded Farah's major creditors to "help mediate" the dispute.

A corporate campaign was also used with effect against J. P. Stevens. Stevens ultimately abandoned its battle against unionization when the union pressured banks and insurance companies to intervene. Among other pressures, union officials told banks and insurance companies that if they didn't intervene on the union's behalf, the union would withdraw deposits and cancel insurance policies.

In September 1984, officials of United Steel Workers of America threatened a corporate campaign against Phelps Dodge Corporation, the nation's second largest copper producer. Union spokespersons said they intended to consult with high-level officials of all major creditors of Phelps Dodge in order to persuade them to pressure the copper company to comply with union demands. If the creditors rejected the union's plans, union officials said they would consider withdrawing

more than $250 million in bank deposits and get other major unions to follow suit.[40]

At the heart of the corporate campaign tactic is the issue of corporate governance, for in pressuring financial institutions with mass withdrawals and cancellations of policies, unions and administrators of public-employee pension funds are trying to exert an influence over institutional policy. And when the financial institutions accede to union demands, they, in turn, effectively dictate to the recalcitrant company its policy with respect to unions. The harshest critics of the corporate campaign call it corporate blackmail. Its most enthusiastic champions view it as an effective way to get financial institutions and companies to become good corporate citizens. Such tactics, they say, are necessary at a time when legal sentiment seems to be running against unions, as illustrated in the Bildisco decision of 1984.

In that case, involving a small New Jersey firm, the Bildisco Manufacturing Co., the Supreme Court ruled 5–4 that once a company has voluntarily filed bankruptcy it can void its labor contracts—even before the bankruptcy court has acted. The decision in effect means that a financially faltering company can void its labor contract even if labor costs aren't a major reason for its financial trouble. It can now do with the Supreme Court's blessing what Continental Airlines did in October 1983 when it filed for bankruptcy, reneged on its labor contracts, and thus cut its pay scales in half—and then kept on flying.

SUMMARY

1. The question of corporate moral agency is whether corporations are the kind of entity that can have moral responsibilities. There are at least three senses of "morally responsible." If corporations can make rational and moral decisions, then they can be held blameworthy or praiseworthy for

their actions. Philosophers disagree about whether the corporate internal decision (CID) structure makes it reasonable to assign moral responsibility to corporations.

2. This problem is compounded by the difficulty of assigning moral responsibility to individuals inside corporations.

3. Despite these controversies, the courts and the general public find the notion of corporate responsibility useful and intelligible—either in a literal sense or as shorthand for the obligations of individuals in the corporation.

4. The debate over corporate responsibility concerns whether it should be construed narrowly as solely profit maximization or more broadly to include refraining from socially undesirable behavior and contributing actively and directly to the public good.

5. Proponents of the narrow view like Milton Friedman contend that diverting corporations from the pursuit of profit makes our economic system less efficient. Business's only social responsibility is to make money within the "rules of the game." Private enterprise should not be forced to undertake public responsibilities that properly belong to government.

6. Defenders of the broader view maintain that corporations have additional responsibilities because of their great social and economic power. Business is governed by an implicit "social contract," which requires it to operate in ways that benefit society. In particular, corporations must take responsibility for the unintended side effects of their business transactions (externalities) and weigh the full social costs of their activities.

7. Advocates of the narrow view stress that management has a promissory relation with the owners (stockholders) of a corporation, which obligates it to focus on profit maximization alone. Critics challenge this argument.

8. Should corporate responsibility be broadened? Four arguments against doing so are the "invisible hand" argument, the "hand of government" argument, the "inept custodian" argument, and the "materialization of society" argument. Finding flaws with each of these arguments, critics claim that there is no solid basis for restricting corporate responsibility to profit making.

9. Those proposing broader corporate responsibilities see the creation of an ethical atmosphere within the corporation as an important first step. Essential to this atmosphere would be (1) corporate acknowledgement of the critical importance of ethics, (2) corporate encouragement of moral conduct by its members, (3) an end to corporate defensiveness in the face of criticism, and (4) corporate recognition of the pluralistic nature of our social system.

10. Corporations and the people who make them up must have high moral standards and monitor their own behavior because there are limits to what the law can do to ensure that business behavior is socially and morally acceptable.

11. All settled economic life requires trust and confidence. The adoption of realistic and workable codes of ethics in the business world can actually enhance business efficiency. This is particularly true when there is an imbalance of knowledge between the buyer and the seller.

12. To improve the organizational climate such that individuals can reasonably be expected to act ethically, some writers recommend that, in addition to adopting a corporate ethical code, corporations set up a high-ranking ethics committee and include ethics training in their management development programs.

13. Unions attempt to protect workers from abuse and give them a voice in matters that affect their lives. Critics charge that forcing workers to join unions infringes autonomy and the right of association. They allege the existence of discriminatory and unlawful favoritism to union workers.

14. A direct strike is justified, argue some moral theorists, when there is just cause and proper authorization and when it is called as a last resort.

15. Sympathetic strikes involve the cessation of work by workers in support of other workers with a grievance. When the companies involved are different, questions arise concerning possible injury and injustice to innocent employers, consumers, other workers, and the public.

16. Primary boycotts—refusing to patronize companies being struck—seem morally comparable to direct strikes. Secondary boycotts—refusing to patronize companies handling products of struck companies—are morally analogous to sympathetic strikes. In "corporate campaigns," unions enlist the cooperation of a company's creditors to pressure the company to permit unionization or to comply with union demands.

CASE 5.1
Selling Infant Formula Abroad

In 1860 Henry Nestlé developed infant formula to save the life of an infant who couldn't be breastfed. According to officials at Nestlé, a $12 billion Swiss-based corporation, the Frenchman's concoction has been saving lives ever since, especially in developing countries. They point to relief organizations like the International Red Cross, which has used the formula to feed thousands of starving infants in refugee camps, for example. Without its infant formula, the Nestlé people say, Third World mothers considering use of a breast-milk substitute would use less nutritious local alternatives. Maybe so. But a hundred years after it was first developed, Henry Nestlé's sweet idea turned sour, and Nestlé Corporation's dominant share of the $12 billion international market for infant formula was threatened.

The infant formula controversy began to heat up in November 1970 at a United Nations–sponsored meeting on infant feeding in Bogota, Colombia. Meeting to discuss different aspects of world hunger, the Protein Advisory Group (PAG)—made up of nutritionists, pediatricians, and food industry representatives— hammered out a broad framework for cooperation among business, health care, and government. But some PAG members bristled up at what they thought was PAG's failure to engage a critical issue: the implications of marketing infant formula in Third World countries.

Straightaway the media began reporting some of the common marketing practices of formula companies.

Item—Dressed as health care professionals, representatives of formula companies visited villages to promote the use of infant formula.

Item—While interned in clinics and hospitals, new mothers were given free infant formula samples.

Item—Free or low-cost supplies of infant formula were given to health institutions, thus routinizing bottle feeding within the hospitals and discouraging breast feeding.

Item—Product labels failed to warn of potential dangers from incorrect use of infant formula.

Most damaging from the industry's viewpoint was infant formula's alleged complicity in the death of Third World infants. Dr. Derrick B. Jelliffe, then director of the Caribbean Food and Nutrition Institute, claimed that millions of infants suffered and died due to bottle feeding. A major reason was that Third World mothers could not take sterilization and storage precautions commonplace in homes with modern kitchens.

Outraged by these allegations, the Infant Formula Action Coalition (INFACT) was formed in 1977 and focused its indignation on Nestlé, the largest producer of infant formula worldwide. Chaired by Douglas A. Johnson and joined by a hundred other religious and health organizations, INFACT instituted an international boycott against the Nestlé Company, charging it with aggressive marketing tactics designed to pressure mothers in underdeveloped countries to switch from breast feeding to bottle feeding, thus contributing to high infant mortality rates.

In May 1981, the World Health Organization (WHO) adopted a "Code of Marketing of Breastmilk Substitutes," which called on governments to prohibit advertising of infant formula that discourages breast feeding. The code would prohibit, for example, sending women dressed as nurses to rural villages or paying local health workers to push infant formula. Of the 119 WHO members who voted, 118 voted for adoption. The sole opposition vote was cast by the United States, which invoked the principles of free trade and free speech. At the White House, President Reagan's Deputy Press Secretary James Speakes said, in effect, that the WHO had no business telling private business how to sell its products, that the United States didn't want to make the WHO an international Federal Trade Commission. American officials of the WHO resigned in protest of U.S. opposition to the code.

Condemnation of the U.S. vote roared through the international community like a prairie fire. The U.S., said its harshest critics, preferred profits to babies. Dr. Stephen Joseph, a senior executive of the Agency for International Development (AID), charged that the Reagan administration had been swayed by the self-serving arguments of the infant formula lobby and threatened to resign. AID administrator M. Peter McPherson chided Joseph for public "spleen venting" and said he would accept Joseph's resignation effective immediately.

Speaking in his capacity as president of the International Council of Infant Food Industries, E. W. Saunders, a Nestlé vice president, branded the code unacceptably ambiguous. Nevertheless, Nestlé officials announced that Nestlé would support the code and wait for individual countries to implement it through their own codes. But few such codes appeared. By the end of 1983, only 25 of 157 member nations of the WHO had established national codes.

INFACT and others yelled noncompliance. They identified four areas that they said Nestlé had to review: educational materials dealing with infant formula, hazard warnings and labels, gifts to health professionals, and free supplies to hospitals. Until Nestlé complied, INFACT threatened to pursue its campaign against the company. Nestlé said it already was complying, that the charges of noncompliance were based on subjective interpretations of the code. To safeguard its reputation, as well as its infant formula market, Nestlé dipped into its war chest—to the tune, some say, of $40 million—to fight the boycott.

While on one front Nestlé was waging a battle to preserve its reputation, on another it was moving toward a constructive resolution to the problem.

Since WHO had no enforcement authority, there thus was no neutral party to monitor compliance with its "Code of Marketing of Breastmilk Substitutes." So, Nestlé formed the Nestlé Infant Formula Audit Commission (NIFAC). NIFAC, which was chaired by former Senator Edmund S. Muskie, was asked to review Nestlé's company instructions to field personnel to see if they could be improved to better implement the code. This novel approach to the seemingly intractable situation was like hiring a private judge to arbitrate a personal dispute. At the same time, Nestlé continued to meet with officials at WHO and the United Nations International Children's Emergency Fund (UNICEF) to obtain the most accurate interpretation of the code.

NIFAC labored for eighteen months, issuing quarterly reports to the public and requesting from WHO/UNICEF several clarifications of the code. Its efforts eventually bore fruit.

On January 26, 1984, the international boycott against Nestlé was suspended when Nestlé developed procedures for dealing with the four specific points of the code in dispute.

Regarding Point 1, educational material, Nestlé agreed to include in all materials dealing with the feeding of infants information on: (1) the benefits and superiority of breastfeeding, (2) maternal nutrition and the preparation for maintenance of breastfeeding, (3) the negative effect on breastfeeding of introducing partial bottle feeding, (4) the difficulty of reversing the decision not to breastfeed, (5) possible health hazards of inappropriate food or feeding methods, and (6) the social and financial consequences of the decision to use infant formula.

Regarding Point 2, hazard warning labels, Nestlé agreed to test different statements in Third World countries, with the help of specialized consultants recommended by WHO and UNICEF, to ensure correct product use. It specifically promised to ensure that product users fully understood the consequences of inappropriate or incorrect use arising from unclean water, dirty utensils, improper dilution, and storage of prepared foods without refrigeration.

Regarding Point 3, gifts to health professionals, Nestlé agreed not to give gifts such as chocolate, key-rings, and pens to health professionals. It also agreed to avoid product-brand advertising in the distribution of technical and scientific publications.

Regarding Point 4, low-cost supplies of infant formula to health institutions, Nestlé recognized that this might inadvertently discourage breastfeeding. So, it agreed to restrict the distribution of supplies to situations where infants had to be fed on breastmilk substitutes and to help specify the conditions that would warrant such substitutes.

In announcing that a truce had been reached, Nestlé officials and protestors literally broke candy together—Nestlé chocolate, naturally—to celebrate the end of the six-and-a-half-year conflict. Douglas Johnson praised Nestlé for moving forward to become a model for the entire industry. The WHO Code, said Johnson, has changed from "an urgent moral mandate to the accepted business practice of the largest and singly most important factor in the world."[41] Nestlé officials viewed the settlement as "proof that its efforts" to comply with the WHO Code "have finally been recognized."[42] They boasted that Nestlé was the first company to "unilaterally apply the Code in developing countries" and to "submit its activities in this area to examination by an independent commission. . . . The time has now come for all interested parties to concentrate their effort on solutions to the fundamental cause of infant mortality and malnutrition in the Third World."

Discussion Questions

1. Identify the views of corporate social responsibility held by the different actors and organizations in this case.

2. Do you think the United States was justified in voting against the WHO Code? Was the United States, as critics charged, preferring profits to babies? If you had been a U.S. official at WHO, would you have resigned in protest of the U.S. vote?

3. Do you think that the facts of this case

belie the capitalistic assumption that consumers have full knowledge of the diverse choices available to them in the marketplace?

4. Would you as an individual have any moral obligation to participate in the boycott against Nestlé?

5. Some think that the boycott resolution shows that protest can be effective; it demonstrates that there is a natural and effective countervailing force to the capitalist's tendency toward profiteering. Do you agree?

6. In your opinion, does the infant formula controversy involve any moral issues? If so, what are they? What moral rights, if any, are involved in this controversy?

7. Do you find anything objectionable about the alleged marketing techniques used to sell infant formula?

8. Throughout the six-year dispute, Nestlé insisted that the WHO Code was ambiguous and that its critics were holding Nestlé accountable to their own subjective interpretation of the Code. Does Nestlé's

charge point up an inherent problem with codes? Was Nestlé wrong in apparently interpreting the Code to its own benefit?

9. Utilitarianism would not consider any of the alleged marketing tacks intrinsically wrong. The only morally relevant consideration is whether Nestlé gave each affected party equal consideration and gave the pleasure and preferences of each equal weighting in determining these techniques. Do you think Nestlé did? Do you think its final statement does?

10. In your view, did Nestlé treat consumers and health professionals as ends in themselves? Do you think Nestlé officials would be willing to be subjected to similar advertising techniques were they the consumers and health professionals?

11. Identify the ideals, obligations, and effects Nestlé should have considered in devising its marketing strategy. What weight would you give to those considerations? Does Nestlé's final statement, crafted in consultation with WHO/UNICEF, reflect attention to these elements?

CASE 5.2
Living and Dying with Asbestos

Asbestos is a fibrous mineral used for fireproofing, electrical insulation, building materials, brake linings, and chemical filters. If you are exposed long enough to asbestos particles—usually ten or more years—you can develop a chronic lung inflammation called asbestosis, which makes breathing difficult and infection easy. Also linked to asbestos exposure is mesethelioma, a cancer of the chest lining that sometimes doesn't develop until 40 years after the first exposure. Although the first major scientific conference on the dangers of asbestos was not held until

1964, the asbestos industry knew of its dangers 50 years ago.

As early as 1932, the British documented the occupational hazards of asbestos dust inhalation.[43] Indeed, on September 25, 1935, the editors of the trade journal *Asbestos* wrote Sumner Simpson, President of Raybestos-Manhattan, a leading asbestos company, asking permission to publish an article on the dangers of asbestos. Simpson refused and later praised the magazine for not printing the article. In a letter to Vandivar Brown, Secretary of Johns-Manville, another asbestos manufacturer, Simpson observed: "The less said about asbestos the better off we are." Brown agreed, adding that any article on asbestosis should reflect American, not English, data.

In fact, American data were available, and Brown, as one of the editors of the journal, knew it. Working on behalf of Raybestos-Manhattan and Johns-Manville and their insurance carrier, Metropolitan Life Insurance Company, Anthony Lanza had conducted research between 1929 and 1931 on 126 workers with three or more years of asbestos exposure. But Brown and others were not pleased with the paper Lanza submitted to them for editorial review. Lanza, said Brown, had failed to portray asbestos as milder than silicosis, a lung disease caused by long-term inhalation of silica dust and resulting in a chronic shortness of breath. Under the then pending Workmen's Compensation law, silicosis was categorized as a compensible disease. If asbestosis was worse than silicosis or indistinguishable from it, then it, too, would have to be covered. Apparently, Brown didn't want this, and thus requested that Lanza depict asbestosis as less serious than silicosis. Lanza complied and also omitted from his published report that more than half of the workers examined—67 of 126—were suffering from asbestosis.

Meanwhile Sumner Simpson was writing F. H. Schulter, President of Thermoid Rubber Company, suggesting that several manufacturers sponsor further asbestos experiments at Saranac Laboratories. The sponsors, said Simpson, could exercise oversight prerogatives: They "could determine from time to time after the findings are made whether we wish any publication or not." Added Simpson: "It would be a good idea to distribute the information to the medical fraternity, providing it is of the right type and would not injure our companies." Lest there should be any question about the arbiter of publication, Brown wrote to Saranac officials:

It is our further understanding that the results obtained will be considered the property of those who are advancing the required funds, who will determine whether, to what extent and in what manner they shall be made public. In the event it is deemed desirable that the results be made public, the manuscript of your study will be submitted to us for approval prior to publication.

Industry officials were concerned with more than controlling information flow. They also sought to deny workers early evidence of their asbestosis. Dr. Kenneth Smith, medical director of a Johns-Manville Canadian plant, explained why seven workers he found to have asbestosis should not be informed of their disease:

It must be remembered that although these men have the X-ray evidence of asbestosis, they are working today and definitely are not disabled from asbestosis. They have not been told of this diagnosis, for it is felt that as long as the man feels well, is happy at home and at work, and his physical condition remains good, nothing should be said. When he becomes disabled and sick, then the diagnosis should be made and the claim submitted *by the Company*. The fibrosis of this disease is irreversible and permanent so that eventually compensation will be paid to each of these men. But as long as the man is not disabled, it is felt that he should not be told of his condition so that he can live and work in peace and the Company can benefit by his many years of experience. Should the man be told of his condition today there is a very definite possibility that he would become mentally and physically ill, simply through the knowledge that he has asbestosis.

When lawsuits filed by asbestos workers who had developed cancer reached the industry in the 1950s, Smith suggested that the

Asbestos Textile Institute retain the Industrial Health Foundation to conduct a cancer study that would, in effect, squelch the asbestos-cancer connection. The Institute refused, claiming that such a study would only bring further unfavorable publicity to the industry and that there wasn't enough evidence linking asbestos and cancer industry-wide to warrant it.

Shortly before his death in 1977, Kenneth Smith was asked whether he had ever recommended to Johns-Manville officials that warning labels be placed on insulation products containing asbestos. Smith provided the following testimony:

> The reasons why the caution labels were not implemented immediately, it was a business decision as far as I could understand. Here was a recommendation, the corporation is in business to make, to provide jobs for people and make money for stockholders and they had to take into consideration the effects of everything they did, and if the application of a caution label identifying a product as hazardous would cut out sales, there would be serious financial implications. And the powers that be had to make some effort to judge the necessity of the label vs. the consequences of placing the label on the product.

Smith's testimony and related documents have figured prominently in hundreds of asbestos-related lawsuits, totaling more than $1 billion. In March 1981, a settlement was reached in nine separate lawsuits brought by 680 New Jersey asbestos workers at a Raybestos-Manhattan plant. Several asbestos manufacturers as well as Metropolitan Life Insurance were named as defendants. Under the terms of the settlement, the workers affected will share in a $9.4 million court-administered compensation fund. Each worker will be paid compensation according to the length of exposure to asbestos and the severity of the disease contracted. Still pending are an estimated 10,000 to 15,000 cases involving asbestos exposure. New ones are being filed at the rate of 1,000 a year.

Effects of asbestos exposure outside the workplace also have become of increasing concern to health authorities around the country. During the 1950s and 1960s, asbestos ducts were used widely in buildings with forced-air heating systems, including schools. In fact children are at special risk owing to their higher breathing rate and frequent through-mouth inhalation. Since they stand closer to the floors than adults, they are near the asbestos particles that may have settled there and get stirred up by activity.

Although in 1978 the Environmental Protection Agency banned the use of spray-on asbestos as an insulation and fireproofing material, it has not mandated its removal. The only existing requirements, which have been in effect since 1980, are that school buildings must be inspected and employees and parents informed of the presence and specific location of asbestos.

Discussion Questions

1. Should the asbestos companies be held morally responsible in the sense of being capable of making a moral decision about the ill effects of asbestos exposure? Or does it make sense only to consider the principal people involved morally responsible—for example, Simpson and Brown?

2. We can presume that Simpson and Brown acted in what they thought were the best profit interests of their companies. Nothing that they did was illegal. Would you conclude, therefore, that they acted responsibly?

3. Suppose that Simpson and Brown reasoned this way: "While it may be in our firms' short-term interests to suppress data about the ill effects of asbestos exposure, in the long run it may ruin our companies. We could be sued for millions and

the reputation of the entire industry could be destroyed. So, we should come clean about what asbestos-exposure research indicates and let the chips fall where they may." Would this kind of reasoning reflect a broad or narrow view of corporate responsibility? Explain.

4. If you were a stockholder in Raybestos-Manhattan or Thermoid Rubber, would you approve of Simpson's and Brown's conduct? If not, why not?

5. "Hand of government" proponents would say that it's the responsibility of government, not the asbestos industry, to ensure health and safety with respect to asbestos. In the absence of appropriate government regulations, asbestos manufacturers have no responsibility other than to operate efficiently. Do you agree?

6. Does Dr. Smith's explanation for concealing from workers the nature of their health problems illustrate how adherence to industry and corporate goals can militate against individual moral behavior? Or do you think that Smith did all that he was morally obliged to do as an employee of an asbestos firm? What about Lanza's suppression of data in his report?

7. Do you think that a corporate ethical code, together with an industry-wide code, a corporate ethics committee, and train-ing in ethics for management personnel would have encouraged more ethical behavior?

8. It's been shown that spouses of asbestos workers can develop lung damage and cancer simply by breathing the fibers carried home on work clothes and that people living near asbestos plants experience higher rates of cancer than does the general population. Would it be possible to assign responsibility for these effects to individual members of asbestos companies? Should the companies themselves be held responsible?

9. The New Jersey case, and a similar one in Texas in 1978, involved a group settlement, thus precluding any individual worker from suing the company as a private party and, in effect, placing the affected workers in competition with all other members of the group for a share of the funds. The same sort of settlement was worked out in the infamous Agent Orange case involving Vietnam veterans who were seriously harmed as a result of contact with toxic defoliants used during the war. Do you think a group settlement is fair?

10. In your opinion, should there be laws requiring the removal of asbestos from schools?

CASE 5.3
Union Discrimination?

The National Right to Work Legal Defense Foundation is one of several antiunion organizations that have been active in recent years. The "right to work," in this context, means the alleged right of an individual to work without being obliged to join a union. To put it the other way around, it means *forbidding companies to sign contracts with unions agreeing to hire only workers who are willing to join the union.*

What follows is one of the Foundation's advertisements,[44] titled "Job Discrimination . . . It Still Exists":

Reprinted by permission of the National Right to Work Legal Defense Foundation, 8001 Braddock Road, Suite 600, Springfield, VA 22160.

Paul Robertson is not a member of a persecuted minority. But he has experienced blatant discrimination all the same because he has chosen not to join a union.

Paul Robertson is a working man, a skilled licensed electrician with more than 20 years experience. He found out the hard way how a big company and a big union can discriminate on the job.

Paul was hired by the Bechtel Power Corporation to work on their Jim Bridger Power Plant project in the Rock Springs, Wyoming area. Only three months later, he was fired, supposedly because of a reduction in force.

But during the week preceding his discharge, Bechtel hired at least 19 union electricians referred by the local union and retained at least 65 unlicensed electricians.

A determined Paul Robertson filed unfair labor practice charges against the company and the union.

An administrative law judge ruled and was upheld by the full National Labor Relations Board that the union and the employer had indeed discriminated. The judge ordered that Robertson and seven other electricians be given the back pay they would have earned if they had been treated fairly.

The NLRB later reversed part of its decision, but Paul Robertson did not give up. With the help of the National Right to Work Legal Defense Foundation, he appealed the Board's decision to the U.S. Court of Appeals, arguing that hiring hall favoritism is discriminatory and unlawful.

Paul Robertson was fortunate. He found experienced legal help—all important because the case dragged on for nearly four years in the courts and the union still refuses to obey the NLRB's backpay order.

The National Right to Work Legal Defense Foundation is helping everyone it can—currently in more than 75 cases involving academic and political freedom, protection from union violence, and other fundamental rights. But it would like to do even more.

If you'd like to help workers like Paul Robertson write: The National Right to Work Legal Defense Foundation. . . .

Discussion Questions

1. Assuming the Foundation's description of the case as accurate, was Paul Robertson treated unfairly? Was this a case of discrimination?

2. Does it make a difference to your assessment of the case whether or not someone like Robertson knows, when he accepts a job, that he must join the union or that nonunion employees will be the first to be laid off?

3. Presumably Paul Robertson could have joined the union, but he chose not to. What principle, if any, do you think he was fighting for?

4. What do you see as the likely motivations of Bechtel Power and the union? How would they justify their conduct?

5. Why did the Foundation run this ad? Do you think it is sincerely interested in the rights of individual workers?

6. Assess the idea of union and agency shops from the moral point of view. What conflicting rights, interests, and ideals are at stake? What are the positive and negative consequences of permitting union shops?

NOTES

1. Anthony J. Parisi, "How Exxon Rules Its Great Empire," *San Francisco Chronicle*, August 5, 1980, 27.

2. Ibid.

3. In 1986, for example, the Court upheld the government of Puerto Rico's ban on casino-gambling advertising, even though casino gambling is legal there.

4. Parisi, "How Exxon Rules," 38.

5. See Kenneth Goodpaster and John B. Matthews, Jr., "Can a Corporation Have a Conscience?" *Harvard Business Review* 60 (January–February, 1982): 132–141.

6. See Peter French, "The Corporation as a Moral Person," *American Philosophical Quarterly* 16 (July 1979): 207–215.

7. Manuel G. Velasquez, "Why Corporations Are Not Morally Responsible for Anything They Do," *Business and Professional Ethics Journal* 2 (Spring 1983): 8.

8. Paul Richter, "Pentagon Lifts Threat to Ban National Semi," *Los Angeles Times*, August 8, 1984, part IV, p. 1.

9. "The Conoco Conscience," Continental Oil Company, 1976, quoted in Goodpaster and Matthews, "Can a Corporation Have a Conscience?" 141.

10. Quoted in Clarence C. Walton, *Corporate Social Responsibilities* (Belmont, Calif.: Wadsworth, 1967), 169–170.

11. Quoted in Bernard D. Nossiter, *The Mythmakers: An Essay on Power and Wealth* (Boston: Houghton Mifflin, 1964), 100.

12. Milton Friedman, *Capitalism and Freedom* (Chicago: The University of Chicago Press, 1962), 133.

13. "The Dangers of Social Responsibility," *Harvard Business Review* 36 (September–October 1958).

14. Milton Friedman, "The Social Responsibility of Business Is to Increase Its Profits," *New York Times Magazine*, September 13, 1970. Copyright © 1970 by The New York Times Company. Reprinted by permission.

15. Ibid.

16. Keith Davis, "Five Propositions for Social Responsibility," *Business Horizons* 18, (June 1975). Copyright © 1975 by the Foundation for the School of Business at Indiana University. Reprinted by permission.

17. Melvin Anshen, "Changing the Social Contract: A Role for Business," *The Columbia Journal of World Business* 5 (November–December 1970).

18. Davis, "Five Propositions for Social Responsibility."

19. See Christopher D. Stone, *Where the Law Ends* (New York: Harper & Row, 1975), 80–87.

20. Friedman, "The Social Responsibility of Business."

21. See Michael Hoffman and Jennifer Mills Moore, *Business Ethics* (New York: McGraw-Hill, 1984), 113.

22. See Goodpaster and Matthews, Jr., "Can a Corporation Have a Conscience?" 136.

23. Virginia Held, *Property, Profits, and Economic Justice* (Belmont, Calif.: Wadsworth, 1980), 11.

24. Goodpaster and Matthews, "Can a Corporation Have a Conscience?" 137.

25. Ibid.

26. Walter Goodman, "Stocks Without Sin," *Harper's*, August 1971, 66.

27. Theodore Levitt, "The Dangers of Social Responsibility," *Harvard Business Review* 36 (September–October 1958): 44.

28. Davis, "Five Propositions for Social Responsibility."

29. "The Decline of Standards," *The Wall Street Journal*, February 18, 1982, 24.

30. See Robert C. Solomon and Kristine R. Hanson, *Above the Bottom Line: An Introduction to Business Ethics* (New York: Harcourt Brace Jovanovich, 1983), 238.

31. See Stone, *Where the Law Ends*, chapter 11.

32. Milton Snoeyenbos and Donald Jewell, "Morals, Management and Codes" in Milton Snoeyenbos, Robert Almeder, James Humber, eds., *Business Ethics* (Buffalo, N.Y.: Prometheus Books, 1983), 107.

33. The historical development of unions that is sketched here is based on the clear and succinct presentation in Robert B. Carson, *Business Issues Today: Alternative Perspectives* (New York: St. Martin's Press, 1984), 139–142.

34. Not surprisingly, many people are unsympathetic with strikes by well-paid athletes. But the average football player's professional career lasts only three seasons, and he is rarely trained for anything else.

35. "Labor Unions: Context and Crisis" in R. C. Edwards, M. Reich, and T. E. Weisskopf, eds., *The Capitalist System*, 3rd ed. (Englewood Cliffs: Prentice-Hall, 1986), 165.

36. Austin Fagothey and Milton A. Gonsalves, *Right and Reason: Ethics in Theory and Practice* (St. Louis: Mosby, 1981), 428–429.

37. Ibid., 429.

38. See chapter 4 of Mary Gibson, *Workers' Rights* (Totowa, N.J.: Rowman and Allanheld, 1983). The film *Norma Rae* portrays the dogged resistance of a company like J. P. Stevens to unionization.

39. Fagothey and Gonsalves, *Right and Reason*, 428–429.

40. See "Unions Pressure Phelps Dodge's Creditors Over 15-Month Copper Strike," *Los Angeles Times*, September 17, 1984, part IV, p. 1.

41. Statement of Douglas A. Johnson, National Chairperson, Infant Formula Action Coalition (INFACT), Washington, D.C., January 26, 1984.

42. "Boycott Against Nestlé Over Infant Formula to End Next Month," *The Wall Street Journal*, January 27, 1984, 1.

43. See Samuel S. Epstein, "The Asbestos 'Pentagon Papers,'" in Mark Green and Robert Massie, Jr., eds., *The Big Business Reader: Essays on Corporate America* (New York: The Pilgrim Press, 1980),

154–165. This article is the primary source of the facts reported here and is the source of the quotations reported in this case.

44. Reprinted by permission of the National Right to Work Legal Defense Foundation, Inc., 8001 Braddock Road, Suite 600, Springfield, VA 22160.

Social Responsibility and Economic Efficiency

Kenneth J. Arrow

As an economist, Arrow examines and rejects the argument that firms ought only to pursue profit maximization, an argument that ignores the fact of imperfect competition, the unequal distribution of income resulting from unrestrained profit maximization, and the decline in altruism that profit-maximizing, self-centered economic behavior encourages. In addition, profit maximization is socially inefficient in two important cases: where costs are not paid for (externalities) and where there is an imbalance of knowledge between the seller and the buyer. Arrow concludes by discussing ways of institutionalizing the social responsibility of firms through the establishment of stable ethical codes.

Let us first consider the case against social responsibility: the assumption that the firms should aim simply to maximize their profits. One strand of that argument is empirical rather than ethical or normative. It simply states that firms *will* maximize their profits. The impulse to gain, it is argued, is very strong and the incentives for selfish behavior are so great that any kind of control is likely to be utterly ineffectual. This argument has some force but is by no means conclusive. Any mechanism for enforcing or urging social responsibility upon firms must of course reckon with a profit motive, with a desire to evade whatever response of controls are imposed. But it does not mean that we cannot expect any degree of responsibility at all.

One finds a rather different argument, frequently stated by some economists. It will probably strike the noneconomist as rather strange, at least at first hearing. The assertion is that firms *ought* to maximize profits; not merely do they like to do so but there is practically a social obligation to do so. Let me briefly sketch the argument:

Firms buy the goods and services they need for production. What they buy they pay for and therefore they are paying for whatever costs they impose upon others. What they receive in payment by selling their goods, they receive because the purchaser considers it worthwhile. This is a world of voluntary contracts; nobody *has* to buy the goods. If he chooses to buy it, it must be that he is getting a benefit measured by the price he pays. Hence, it is argued, profit really represents the net contribution that the firm makes to the social good, and the profits should therefore be made as large as possible. When firms compete with each other, in selling their goods or in buying labor or other services, they may have to lower their selling prices in order to get more of the market for themselves or raise their wages; in either case the benefits which the firm is deriving are in some respects shared with the population at large. The forces of competition prevent the firms from engrossing too large a share of the social benefit. For example, if a firm tries to reduce the quality of its goods, it will sooner or later have to lower the price which it charges because the purchaser will no longer find it worthwhile to pay the high price. Hence, the consumers will gain from price reduction at the same time as they are losing through quality deterioration. On detailed analysis it appears the firm will find it privately profitable to reduce quality under these circumstances only if, in fact, quality reduction is a net social benefit, that is, if the saving in cost is worth more to the consumer than the quality reduction. Now, as far as it goes this argument is sound. The problem is that it may not go far enough.

Kenneth J. Arrow, "Social Responsibility and Economic Efficiency," *Public Policy* 21 (Summer 1973). Reprinted by permission.

Under the proper assumptions profit maximization is indeed efficient in the sense that it can achieve as high a level of satisfaction as possible for any one consumer without reducing the levels of satisfaction of other consumers or using more resources than society is endowed with. But the limits of the argument must be stressed. I want to mention two well-known points in passing without making them the principal focus of discussion. First of all, the argument assumes that the forces of competition are sufficiently vigorous. But there is no social justification for profit maximization by monopolies. This is an important and well-known qualification. Second, the distribution of income that results from unrestrained profit maximization is very unequal. The competitive maximizing economy is indeed efficient—this shows up in high average incomes—but the high average is accompanied by widespread poverty on the one hand and vast riches, at least for a few, on the other. To many of us this is a very undesirable consequence.

Profit maximization has yet another effect on society. It tends to point away from the expression of altruistic motives. Altruistic motives are motives whose gratification is just as legitimate as selfish motives, and the expression of those motives is something we probably wish to encourage. A profit-maximizing, self-centered form of economic behavior does not provide any room for the expression of such motives.

If the three problems above were set aside, many of the ways by which firms affect others should not be tampered with. Making profits by competition is, if anything, to be encouraged rather than discouraged. Wage and price bargains between the firm and uncoerced workers and customers represent mutually beneficial exchanges. There is, therefore, no reason within the framework of the discussion to interfere with them. But these examples far from exhaust the list of interactions with which we started. The social desirability of profit maximization does not extend to all the interactions on the list. There are two categories of effects where the arguments for profit maximization break down: The first is illustrated by pollution or congestion. Here it is no longer true (and this is the key to these issues) that the firm in fact does pay for the harm it imposes on others. When it takes a person's time and uses it at work, the firm is

paying for this, and therefore the transaction can be regarded as a beneficial exchange from the point of view of both parties. We have no similar mechanism by which the pollution which a firm imposes upon its neighborhood is paid for. Therefore the firm will have a tendency to pollute more than is desirable. That is, the benefit to it or to its customers from the expanded activity is really not as great, or may not be as great, as the cost it is imposing upon the neighborhood. But since it does not pay that cost, there is no profit incentive to refrain.

The same argument applies to traffic congestion when no change is made for the addition of cars or trucks on the highway. It makes everybody less comfortable. It delays others and increases the probability of accidents; in short, it imposes a cost upon a large number of members of the society, a cost which is not paid for by the imposer of the cost, at least not in full. The person congesting is also congested, but the costs he is imposing on others are much greater than those he suffers himself. Therefore there will be a tendency to overutilize those goods for which no price is charged, particularly scarce highway space.

There are many other examples of this kind, but these two will serve to illustrate the point in question: some effort must be made to alter the profit-maximizing behavior of firms in those cases where it is imposing costs on others which are not easily compensated through an appropriate set of prices.

The second category of effects where profit maximization is not socially desirable is that in which there are quality effects about which the firm knows more than the buyer. In my examples I will cite primarily the case of quality in the product sold, but actually very much the same considerations apply to the quality of working conditions. The firm is frequently in a better position to know the consequences (the health hazards, for example) involved in working conditions than the worker is, and the considerations I am about to discuss in the case of sale of goods have a direct parallel in the analysis of working conditions in the relation of a firm to its workers. Let me illustrate by considering the sale of a used car. (Similar considerations apply to the sale of new cars.) A used car has potential defects and typically the seller knows more about the defects than the buyer. The buyer is not in a position to distinguish among used cars, and therefore he will be willing to pay the same amount for two used cars of differing quality because he cannot tell the difference between them. As a result, there is an inefficiency in the sale of used cars. If somehow or other the cars were distinguished as to their quality, there would be some buyers who would prefer a cheaper car with more defects because they intend to use it very little or they only want it for a short period, while others will want a better car at a higher price. In fact, however, the two kinds of car are sold indiscriminately to the two groups of buyers at the same price, so that we can argue that there is a distinct loss of consumer satisfaction imposed by the failure to convey information that is available to the seller. The buyers are not necessarily being cheated. They may be, but the problem of inefficiency would remain if they weren't. One can imagine a situation where, from past experience, buyers of used cars are aware that cars that look alike may turn out to be quite different. Without knowing whether a particular car is good or bad, they do know that there are good and bad cars, and of course their willingness to pay for the cars is influenced accordingly. The main loser from a monetary viewpoint may not be the customer, but rather the seller of the good car. The buyer will pay a price which is only appropriate to a lottery that gives him a good car or a bad car with varying probabilities, and therefore the seller of the good car gets less than the value of the car. The seller of the bad car is, of course, the beneficiary. Clearly then, if one could arrange to transmit the truth from the sellers to the buyers, the efficiency of the market would be greatly improved. The used-car illustration is an example of a very general phenomenon. . . .

Defenders of unrestricted profit maximization usually assume that the consumer is well informed or at least that he becomes so by his own experience, in repeated purchases, or by information about what has happened to other people like him. This argument is empirically shaky; even the ability of individuals to analyze the effects of their own past purchases may be limited, particularly with respect to complicated mechanisms. But there are two further defects. The risks, including death, may be so great that even one misleading experi-

ence is bad enough, and the opportunity to learn from repeated trials is not of much use. Also, in a world where the products are continually changing, the possibility of learning from experience is greatly reduced. Automobile companies are continually introducing new models which at least purport to differ from what they were in the past, though doubtless the change is more external than internal. New drugs are being introduced all the time; the fact that one has had bad experiences with one drug may provide very little information about the next one.

Thus there are two types of situation in which the simple rule of maximizing profits is socially inefficient: the case in which costs are not paid for, as in pollution, and the case in which the seller has considerably more knowledge about his product than the buyer, particularly with regard to safety. In these situations it is clearly desirable to have some idea of social responsibility, that is, to experience an obligation, whether ethical, moral, or legal. Now we cannot expect such an obligation to be created out of thin air. To be meaningful, any obligation of this kind, any feeling or rule of behavior has to be embodied in some definite social institution. I use that term broadly: a legal code is a social institution in a sense. Exhortation to do good must be made specific in some external form, a steady reminder and perhaps enforcer of desirable values. Part of the need is simply for factual information as a guide to individual behavior. A firm may need to be told what is right and what is wrong when in fact it is polluting, or which safety requirements are reasonable and which are too extreme or too costly to be worth consideration. Institutionalization of the social responsibility of firms also serves another very important function. It provides some assurance to any one firm that the firms with which it is in competition will also accept the same responsibility. If a firm has some code imposed from the outside, there is some expectation that other firms will obey it too and therefore there is some assurance that it need not fear any excessive cost to its good behavior.

Let me then turn to some alternative kinds of institutions that can be considered as embodying the possible social responsibilities of firms. First, we have legal regulation, as in the case of pollution where laws are passed about the kind of burning that may take place, and about setting maximum standards for emissions. A second category is that of taxes. Economists, with good reason, like to preach taxation as opposed to regulation. The movement to tax polluting emissions is getting under way and there is a fairly widely backed proposal in Congress to tax sulfur dioxide emissions from industrial smokestacks. That is an example of the second kind of institutionalization of social responsibility. The responsibility is made very clear: the violator pays for violations.

A third very old remedy or institution is that of legal liability—the liability of the civil law. One can be sued for damages. Such cases apparently go back to the Middle Ages. Regulation also extends back very far. There was an ordinance in London about the year 1300 prohibiting the burning of coal, because of the smoke nuisance.

The fourth class of institutions is represented by ethical codes. Restraint is achieved not by appealing to each individual's conscience but rather by having some generally understood definition of appropriate behavior. . . .

Let me turn to the fourth possibility, ethical codes. This may seem to be a strange possibility for an economist to raise. But when there is a wide difference in knowledge between the two sides of the market, recognized ethical codes can be, as has already been suggested, a great contribution to economic efficiency. Actually we do have examples of this in our everyday lives, but in very limited areas. The case of medical ethics is the most striking. By its very nature there is a very large difference in knowledge between the buyer and the seller. One is, in fact, buying precisely the service of someone with much more knowledge than you have. To make this relationship a viable one, ethical codes have grown up over the centuries, both to avoid the possibility of exploitation by the physician and to assure the buyer of medical services that he is not being exploited. I am not suggesting that these are universally obeyed, but there is a strong presumption that the doctor is going to perform to a large extent with your welfare in mind. Unnecessary medical expenses or other abuses are perceived as violations of ethics. There is a powerful ethical background against which we make this judgment. Behavior that we would regard as highly reprehensible in a physician is judged less

harshly when found among businessmen. The medical profession is typical of professions in general. All professions involve a situation in which knowledge is unequal on two sides of the market by the very definition of the profession, and therefore there have grown up ethical principles that afford some protection to the client. Notice there is a mutual benefit in this. The fact is that if you had sufficient distrust of a doctor's services, you wouldn't buy them. Therefore the physician wants an ethical code to act as assurance to the buyer, and he certainly wants his competitors to obey this same code, partly because any violation may put him at a disadvantage but more especially because the violation will reflect on him, since the buyer of the medical services may not be able to distinguish one doctor from another. A close look reveals that a great deal of economic life depends for its viability on a certain limited degree of ethical commitment. Purely selfish behavior of individuals is really incompatible with any kind of settled economic life. There is almost invariably some element of trust and confidence. Much business is done on the basis of verbal assurance. It would be too elaborate to try to get written commitments on every possible point. Every contract depends for its observance on a mass of unspecified conditions which suggest that the performance will be carried out in good faith without insistence on sticking literally to its wording. To put the matter in its simplest form, in almost every economic transaction, in any exchange of goods for money, somebody gives up his valuable asset before he gets the other's; either the goods are given before the money or the money is given before the goods. Moreover there is a general confidence that there won't be any violation of the implicit agreement. Another example in daily life of this kind of ethics is the observance of queue discipline. People line up; there are people who try to break in ahead of you, but there is an ethic which holds that this is bad. It is clearly an ethic which is in everybody's interest to preserve; one waits at the end of the line this time, and one is protected against somebody's coming in ahead of him.

In the context of product safety, efficiency would be greatly enhanced by accepted ethical rules. Sometimes it may be enough to have an ethical compulsion to reveal all the information available and let the buyer choose. This is not necessarily always the best. It can be argued that under some circumstances setting minimum safety standards and simply not putting out products that do not meet them would be desirable and should be felt by the businessman to be an obligation.

Now I've said that ethical codes are desirable. It doesn't follow from that that they will come about. An ethical code is useful only if it is widely accepted. Its implications for specific behavior must be moderately clear, and above all it must be clearly perceived that the acceptance of these ethical obligations by everybody does involve mutual gain. Ethical codes that lack the latter property are unlikely to be viable. How do such codes develop? They may develop as a consensus out of lengthy public discussion of obligations, discussion which will take place in legislatures, lecture halls, business journals, and other public forums. The codes are communicated by the very process of coming to an agreement. A more formal alternative would be to have some highly prestigious group discuss ethical codes for safety standards. In either case to become and to remain a part of the economic environment, the codes have to be accepted by the significant operating institutions and transmitted from one generation of executives to the next through standard operating procedures, through education in business schools, and through indoctrination of one kind or another. If we seriously expect such codes to develop and to be maintained, we might ask how the agreements develop and above all, how the codes remain stable. After all, an ethical code, however much it may be in the interest of all, is, as we remarked earlier, not in the interest of any one firm. The code may be of value to the running of the system as a whole, it may be of value to all firms if all firms maintain it, and yet it will be to the advantage of any one firm to cheat—in fact the more so, the more other firms are sticking to it. But there are some reasons for thinking that ethical codes can develop and be stable. These codes will not develop completely without institutional support. That is to say, there will be need for focal organizations, such as government agencies, trade associations, and consumer defense groups, or all combined to make the codes explicit, to iterate their doctrine and to make their presence felt. Given that help, I think the emergence of ethical codes on matters such as safety at least, is possible.

One positive factor here is something that is a negative factor in other contexts, namely that our economic organization is to such a large extent composed of large firms. The corporation is no longer a single individual; it is a social organization with internal social ties and internal pressures for acceptability and esteem. The individual members of the corporation are not only parts of the corporation but also members of a larger society whose esteem is desired. Power in a large corporation is necessarily diffused; not many individuals in such organizations feel so thoroughly identified with the corporation that other kinds of social pressures become irrelevant. Furthermore, in a large, complex firm where many people have to participate in any decision, there are likely to be some who are motivated to call attention to violations of the code. This kind of check has been conspicuous in government in recent years. The Pentagon Papers are an outstanding illustration of the fact that within the organization there are those who recognize moral guilt and take occasion to blow the whistle. I expect the same sort of behavior to occur in any large organization when there are well-defined ethical rules whose violation can be observed.

One can still ask if the codes are likely to be stable. Since it may well be possible and profitable for a minority to cheat, will it not be true that the whole system may break down? In fact, however, some of the pressures work in the other direction. It is clearly in the interest of those who are obeying the codes to enforce them, to call attention to violations, to use the ethical and social pressures of the society at large against their less scrupulous rivals. At the same time the value of maintaining the system may well be apparent to all, and no doubt ways will be found to use the assurance of quality generated by the system as a positive asset in attracting consumers and workers.

One must not expect miraculous transformations in human behavior. Ethical codes, if they are to be viable, should be limited in their scope. They are not a universal substitute for the weapons mentioned earlier, the institutions, taxes, regulations, and legal remedies. Further, we should expect the codes to apply only in situations where the firm has superior knowledge of the situation. I would not want the firm to act in accordance with some ethical principles in regard to matters of which it has little knowledge. For example, with quality standards which consumers can observe, it may not be desirable that the firm decide for itself, at least on ethical grounds, because it is depriving the consumer of the freedom of choice between high-quality, high-cost and low-quality, low-cost products. It is in areas where someone is typically misinformed or imperfectly informed that ethical codes can contribute to economic efficiency.

Review and Discussion Questions

1. Explain how Arrow's used-car example illustrates his claim that unrestricted profit maximization can be socially inefficient.

2. What are the four ways in which social responsibility can be institutionalized?

3. What characteristics must an ethical code have to be useful? How do such codes develop? Why does Arrow think that the existence of large firms is a positive factor in this context?

4. Do you think business today sees itself as governed by an ethical code? If so, is this code something that is explicitly discussed and thought about, or is it only implicit in business behavior? In your opinion, do business courses and business schools do enough to develop and transmit a sense of social responsibility among future businesspersons?

Ethical Issues in Plant Relocation

John P. Kavanagh

When a company or plant operates in a community, a web of relationships and interdependencies develop among it, its employees, and the community in general. Its shutdown or relocation can seriously hurt the community in which it has operated and the people who have worked for it and have built their lives around it. Kavanagh argues that companies are responsible for the unintended (although foreseeable) results of their business activities. Accordingly, fairness requires that they avoid moving, if possible, and, if they must move, that they take steps to reduce the harm their relocation causes.

The location of a major new manufacturing plant in a community is often the occasion of great rejoicing. City fathers welcome the enterprise as a vital addition to the town's economy. Visions of augmented tax base to support municipal services, jobs for the unemployed and for entrants into the work force, opportunities for local entrepreneurs to expand markets for goods and services, additional sources of support for civic and charitable endeavors, new challenges for educators to provide education and training—all these contribute to the euphoria of a new plant in the community.

Contrast this picture with that of a community experiencing the shutdown or relocation of a major plant, particularly one which has operated in the community for many years. Many people are hurt.

For some it means actual hardship; others find their future expectations diminished to the point of despair. The community as a whole feels a shock to its economic vitality and perhaps to its fiscal stability as well. . . .[1]

The thesis which I would like to establish is simple, but it has relatively far-reaching implications. In its basic form it may be stated:

In deciding whether or not to relocate a manufacturing operation, a company has moral obligations to its employees and to the community in which the operation is located which require that the company

1. take into account the impact of the proposed move on employees and the community;
2. avoid the move if reasonably possible;
3. notify the affected parties as soon as possible if the decision is to make the move; and
4. take positive measures to ameliorate the effects of the move.[2]

In making a decision whether or not to move, companies often do not take into account the impact on employees and the community. The management weighs economic reasons very carefully.

Reprinted by permission of the author from Tom L. Beauchamp and Norman E. Bowie, eds., *Ethical Theory and Business* 2nd ed. (Englewood Cliffs, N.J.: Prentice-Hall, 1983).

It considers the effect on production, sales, public relations and, ultimately, profit. On the basis of reasonable assumptions, it projects the outcomes expected to result from each of the options under consideration. Too often, however, there is no place in the economic calculus for any recognition of the effect the move will have on the work force or the community. Our thesis asserts that the company is not morally free to ignore this impact, since employees and members of the community are not mere things but people, whom the company has an obligation not to harm.[3] This moral fact not only deserves consideration along with economic facts but should be the overriding consideration unless there are countervailing moral reasons.

If the company takes this obligation seriously, it ought to start with a strong presumption that the move should be avoided if at all reasonably possible. It should consider every reasonable alternative: rehabilitation of the existing facility, construction of a new plant within the same community, renegotiation of the labor contract, financial assistance from civic or governmental sources, negotiation of special tax incentives, even acceptance of less than maximum profit return. Only after ruling out other available options should the company decide in favor of the move.[4]

After giving serious consideration to other alternatives, the company may still decide it has no reasonable choice but to move. In that case, two obligations remain: the company should notify the affected parties as soon as possible, and it should do whatever is necessary to ameliorate the effects of the move.

Timely notification is important. If given before the final decision is taken, it might provide the opportunity for labor organizations, civic groups, or government agencies to offer options which would enable the company to continue operations. In any event, notification is essential to permit planning for an orderly transition and preparation of programs to accommodate the change.

Ameliorating the effects of the move is not likely to be easy. Companies often offer employees the opportunity to transfer to the new location; for some this might be acceptable, but for others it would be a real hardship. Alternatively, the company might provide effective out-placement efforts as well as income maintenance for displaced workers, at least during a transition period.

To offset adverse effects on the community, the company should make a serious attempt to find a new employer to replace the lost job opportunities. A large corporation might be able to find a replacement within its own organization. Another approach would be to seek another employer among customers, vendors, competitors, or other companies who could utilize the facilities and work force being abandoned. The departing company might donate its plant, if still usable, to the community or local development organization. In some cases the better offer might be to demolish existing facilities and make the improved site available, along with financial help to the local agency concerned with promoting the location of new industries.[5]

These steps may help to make the community whole again, but some situations may require additional effort. In close consultation and cooperation with municipal officials, the company may have to work out a plan to relieve the community of financial burdens of infrastructure improvements, for instance, which were made to serve the company's special needs.

Argument in Support of Thesis

It should be a little clearer now what the proposed thesis means. Before proceeding to argue directly in favor of this position, however, I would like first to establish the following "Externalities Lemma":

> By locating and operating a manufacturing plant (or similar job-creating operation) in a community, a company produces certain externalities, affecting both workers and the community, which are pertinent to the relocation issue.

The term "externalities" is common enough in the literature of economics. It refers to unintended side effects—good or bad—which an operation produces along with its intended product. In recent years environmentalists have emphasized externalities which affect the quality of the air or water in the vicinity of manufacturing plants. A firm really interested in producing paper, for example, also produces physical and chemical waste products which may affect the surrounding environment adversely if not properly controlled. The company has no interest in producing these products nor any direct intention of doing so, but in doing what it does intend—making paper—it also perforce produces these unwanted products.[6] . . .

The "Externalities Lemma" asserts that the operation of a plant results in certain externalities pertinent to the issue of plant relocation. Although the company's intention is simply to manufacture and distribute its product, the act of doing so produces unintended results which seriously affect its workers and the community in which the company operates.

When a person agrees to work for a company, her pay is a return for effort expended to produce the product. These wages, however, do not take into account the myriad relationships which the employee builds up as a result of accepting the job. In addition to providing labor for the company, the worker adopts a life style which contributes to the work. Many people move their place of residence, enroll children in school, join local churches, become members of clubs, take interest in civic affairs—in short, make a total commitment of their lives to the community and the company. They build up a whole network of relationships based on their association with the company.

These life style commitments are advantageous to the worker, to be sure. They enable him to live a fully rounded life. But the advantage is not one-sided. The company benefits from having an employee involved in these relationships. The situation enhances the worker's ability to do his job, encourages loyalty to the company, and facilitates the employee's continuing progress in learning to do his job effectively.

The stable relationships developed benefit the community as well, but the company's presence also affects the community in other ways. City engineers adjust traffic patterns to accommodate traffic generated by workers going to or leaving the plant as well as incoming and outgoing freight movements. The municipality may have to plan, build, and maintain water and sewerage facilities on a much larger scale to serve the company's needs. Police and fire departments may require more personnel and equipment because of the plant's presence.

Assuming an equitable tax structure, the company will pay its fair share for services provided. Other taxpayers are usually willing to contribute as well because of the indirect benefits they receive.

The whole system can work smoothly because of the symbiotic relationship between the plant, its workers, and the community. Merchants, purveyors of services, schools, and private support agencies of all kinds prosper so long as the relationship continues.

When a major plant discontinues operations, however, it becomes evident that an unintended situation has been created. Not only are employees out of work, deprived of their livelihood or dependent on others for it, but the community itself suffers. Businesses dependent on the company or its employees feel the impact. The municipality and its taxpayers are left with more employees and infrastructure than they need, with continuing cost burdens far out of proportion with revenue. Schools, churches, and private associations all find themselves overbuilt as people leave or are unable to contribute to their support.

Results of the kind described are especially obvious in a small community with a single major employer. In such circumstances it is easy to isolate the phenomenon. The same effects occur, however, in larger communities with more complex economies, only they tend to be less easily observed. In the larger setting the impact on the total community may be somewhat less, but it is no less real on those affected. What remains in any case is the whole web of relationships built up which would not exist if the company had not started the operation and particularly if it had not continued over a relatively long period. The company did not intend to create this web, but it is there nevertheless because of the plant—and the operation could not have survived without it.

In light of what we can observe, the "Externalities Lemma" seems to be inescapably true. If that is indeed the case, it is not difficult to establish our thesis. One of the accepted dicta in the law of property, clearly grounded in basic ethical principles of fairness and justice, is the maxim *sic utere tuo ut alienum non laedas*—use that which is yours in such a way that you do not injure another. A company which has established a plant in a community, particularly when it had continued the operation over a long period, would clearly be injuring others if it closed or moved that operation without taking into account—in a significant way— the impact of that move on its workers and the community. By its presence the plant has created the externalities described. It is the company's moral obligation to internalize them—to replace its divot, so to speak. It can move toward meeting this obligation by undertaking the kind of actions discussed above. . . .

Almost any moral system recognizes that every moral agent has an obligation to treat human beings as persons rather than as things. Hiring a person creates a special kind of relationship. For the employer it is not like buying a piece of material or a machine: these are things, which the buyer is free to use as a means of achieving an end, with no moral responsibility owed to the purchased objects. But the employer is not free, morally speaking, to use an employee as a thing, as simply a means to an end. Since the employee is a person, the employer has an obligation to respect her integrity as a person: her feelings, values, goals, emotional relationships, cultural attachments, self-regard. As an autonomous living entity the employee is the center of a complex web of relationships and it is this whole composite with which the employer becomes involved. Obviously, the employer is not responsible for everything which happens to or within this web; but he is responsible for whatever his actions change or otherwise affect. The relationships mentioned in discussing the "Externalities Lemma" are ones which the employer's actions affect adversely in (unmitigated) plant closure decisions. Even though the company no longer needs its workers as a means to its end of profitable production, it may not with moral impunity treat them like excess material or machines, but has an obligation to protect them from the adverse consequences brought about by the company's use of them.

A company which closes or relocates a plant without ameliorating actions is acting unfairly toward its employees and the community. The general idea of fairness is that anyone who chooses to get involved with others in a cooperative activity has to do his share and is entitled to expect others involved to do likewise.[7]

In the kind of situation we are concerned with there is a reasonably just cooperative arrangement under which a person agrees to work for a company; the primary *quid pro quo* is the employer's fair day's pay for the employee's fair day's work. But each party to the agreement has additional legitimate expectations about the other. The employer expects the worker to make a commitment to the job; one of the largest corporations has this to say:

> . . . The challenges of the workplace impose strong mutual responsibilities upon General Motors and its employees. . . .
>
> An employee's most basic responsibility is to work consistently to the best of his or her ability—not just to follow instructions, but to ask questions, think independently, and make constructive suggestions for improvement.
>
> A first-rate job requires employees to maintain their good health and mental alertness, to be prompt and present on the job, to cooperate with fellow workers, and to be loyal to the Corporation—its people and products. Because GM people *are* General Motors—in the eyes of their friends and neighbors—employees also are encouraged to take interest in the basic goals, problems, and public positions of the Corporation.
>
> . . . General Motors encourages employees as individual citizens to involve themselves in community service and politics. . . .[8]

The employee, in turn, expects the company to do somewhat more than simply pay agreed-on wages. For example, no one would question that being provided a safe and at least tolerably pleasant workplace is within the worker's legitimate expectations. Beyond that, if it is fair for the company to expect that employees will take all the actions and have all the attitudes which a company like General Motors encourages and considers requisite to "a first-rate job" it also seems reasonable for workers to expect that the employer will not suddenly shut up shop and leave them high and dry with unpaid mortgages (on houses bought so they could be "prompt and present on the job" and involved in "community service and politics"), children in school, and commitments to various people or organizations; all this is part of a lifestyle to which they committed themselves when they entered into their agreement to work for the company—the kind of agreement which the GM statement calls a "partnership which can help assure the Corporation's success in the years to come, as well as contribute to an improved quality of life for the men and women of General Motors."[9]

There is nothing extraordinary in all this. In most social relationships the parties involved in an agreement have legitimate expectations which are often not expressed in the agreement itself. Fairness requires that a company either avoid a move which would cause grave hardship to workers or at least take action which would render the action harmless, since this is a legitimate expectation of the implicit "partnership" agreement between employer and employee.

Objections to the Thesis

. . . [One] objection rests on the notion of the risks inherent in the capitalistic system. It is essential to "free enterprise" that entrepreneurs freely undertake the risk of losing the time and money they invest in a venture in return for the opportunity of gain. In the nature of things there are inherent risks in establishing a manufacturing operation and everybody knows they don't last forever. These employees didn't have to go to work for us, the company may argue. They know, or should have known, the risk involved. It was their free choice when they agreed to accept the job.

All this is true so far as it goes, but it doesn't wipe out the company's moral obligations. The workers are not free to the same extent as the employer; the way the system works, they have to accept some job just to stay alive and support their families and in most instances their choice of employment is extremely limited. The entrepreneur's reward for undertaking risk is the profit generated by the enterprise, a reward shared to some extent by higher salaried management employees but not by the ordinary worker. Wages are compensation for work performed, not for assumption of risk. They are carried on the company's books as a cost item which the company has an obligation to pay whether or not it makes a profit. What our thesis asserts is that the company has certain unacknowledged structural costs consequent on the fact that it is operating the plant, over and above the operational obligation of wage payments.

Like the workers, the community is not a partner in the company's entrepreneurial risk, nor does it expect to share in the venture's profit. The company presumably pays its fair share of operational expenses through taxes (and perhaps to some extent through charitable contributions to civic causes). When the plant moves or shuts down, the community is left with significant structural changes brought about by company operations; it is the problem brought about by these changes which the company has a moral obligation to help solve.

One additional objection to the proposed thesis is that a company accepting it would be unable to compete with others which do not. The expense to the company, this argument holds, would make its costs higher than others producing the same product; others could then establish lower prices and gain a clear market advantage.

This is a powerful objection and gets to the heart of the question. Against it, one could urge that there are certain countervailing advantages in terms of worker morale, community cooperation and public relations; but in the end I would have to concede the economic soundness of the argument. What I would not concede is that the objection is a persuasive refutation of our thesis. To act in accordance with a moral obligation not infrequently entails acceptance of personal disadvantage in terms of nonmoral goods. Personal and economic advantage or disadvantage doesn't count as an argument against the existence of a moral obligation.

The thesis asserts the existence of an obligation, on the part of a company, to give appropriate moral weight to the adverse consequences of its action in moving or discontinuing an operation and to take appropriate action to avoid those consequences even in the face of an economic disadvantage. If all companies similarly situated were to recognize this obligation, of course, the competitive disadvantage would disappear. Assuming the costs were internalized—anticipated and treated like other expense items—they would be reflected in the pricing mechanism and only market factors would determine the effect on profits.

But isn't this an unlikely outcome? Is it not more probable that those companies which recognize their moral obligations will suffer for it and lose the competitive edge to those which do not? If corporate management attempts to act morally in this regard and ends up with lower profits, will not stockholders replace them with less conscientious management or invest their money elsewhere? Will not consumers refuse to pay a price for a product which is higher simply because it reflects true costs previously borne by workers and the community?

An affirmative answer to those questions might well be appropriate in a purely descriptive account of the existing economic system. In considering the proposed thesis, however, we are concerned with normative rather than descriptive issues. The question is what should be done, not how does in fact the present system work. This thesis asserts a moral obligation to be concerned about certain human consequences of a company's action: it does not assert that other consequences should be disregarded. Certainly company management should consider what effect its decision will have on profits. Certainly stockholders will consider whether managers are acting in their best interest and whether their money could be invested more profitably elsewhere. Certainly consumers will express their preference in the market and decide whether the price asked for a product is a fair one which they are willing to pay. But the proposed thesis insists that there are moral questions which must be asked, along with economic questions; important as the economic issues may be, they should be considered relevant only within a context of morally permissible actions: the moral issues are overriding.

Notes

1. The author gratefully acknowledges support from the Rockefeller Foundation and the Center for the Study of Values, University of Delaware. These initial observations, as well as several others throughout the paper, are based on the author's direct involvement in plant relocation situations in the course of more than twenty-five years of work as a senior official in Michigan state government agencies concerned with economic development programs. . . .

2. For brevity's sake I will generally speak of "relocation," although I mean also to include discontinuation of operations in the community without removal to another location.

3. The question of whether a company, a corporation or any collective can be the subject of moral acts is much controverted, but it is not the point at issue here. For those who reject the collective responsibility position, substitute the phrase "those persons morally responsible for the actions of the company" for the "company." In support of collective responsibility, see Peter A. French, "The Corporation as a Moral Person," *American Philosophical Quarterly*, 16 (1979), p. 207.

4. See John M. Clark, *Economic Institutions and Human

Welfare (New York: Alfred A. Knopf, 1957), pp. 195–197, for an interesting discussion from an economist's viewpoint of social obligations of a company in a relocation situation.

5. One plan which has received considerable attention calls for the company to transfer ownership to former workers or the community or a joint community-employee corporation. This has worked well in particularly favorable circumstances but has failed in other cases. See Robert N. Stern, K. Haydn Wood, and Tove Helland Hammer, *Employee Ownership in Plant Shutdowns* (Kalamazoo, Michigan: The W. E. Upjohn Institute for Employment Research, 1979). A current (November, 1981) instance is a planned purchase of the New Departure-Hyatt Bearing Division of General Motors Corp. at Clark, N.J. by former employees after GM announced its intention to close the plant.

6. Externalities can be beneficial. A paper operation may require management of forest resources to assure an adequate supply of timber. This may open previously inaccessible land for recreational use. Although the company may only intend to improve its timber holdings, it may also enhance the wildlife capabilities of the forest. The paper plant itself may become a tourist attraction, providing an unintended benefit to the community.

7. See John Rawls, *A Theory of Justice* (Cambridge, Mass.: Harvard University Press, 1971), p. 343.

8. *1980 General Motors Public Interest Report*, p. 83.

9. Citing of General Motors' statement should not be interpreted as critical of that company; the Corporation has a policy of replacing obsolete plants with new facilities in the same area "whenever it is economically feasible" and also, under its union contracts and salaried worker policies, pays substantial compensation to laid-off employees. GM has currently committed $10 billion to the rehabilitation and replacement of production facilities in Michigan alone.

Review and Discussion Questions

1. How is the concept of "externalities" relevant to Kavanagh's argument?

2. What moral principle or principles underlie his argument? Practically speaking, how far do companies have to go to live up to the obliga-

tion that Kavanagh imposes upon them? Assess Kavanagh's argument from the different ethical perspectives discussed in Chapter 2 and Chapter 3.

3. What would Milton Friedman say in response to Kavanagh's position?

4. What is Kavanagh's reply to the argument that companies that accept his thesis will be at a competitive disadvantage?

5. Someone might point out that we all know that nothing lasts forever and that anyone who accepts a job knows, or should know, that there is a chance the firm might decide to relocate or close the plant down. Does this point pose a problem for Kavanagh's argument?

Business Ethics: On Getting to the Heart of the Matter

Paul F. Camenisch

It's common in discussions of business ethics to make one of two assumptions. Assumption One holds that business ethics is essentially the prevailing moral code of the society applied to business. Assumption Two is that business ethics is essentially applying to the corporate member of society some standards of social responsibility. DePaul University professor of religious studies Paul F. Camenisch argues in the following essay that neither approach gets to the heart of business ethics. To do this, we must inquire about the fundamental nature of business—what it is, what it claims to do, and what distinctive functions it performs.

Camenisch keys on two definitive elements in business: profit and the provision of goods and services. We might call these elements dual ideals of business. By Milton Friedman's account, the profit ideal takes precedence over the other: if business makes a profit, it meets its responsibility to society. Camenisch demurs; whereas profit may be an adequate criterion for assessing a business undertaking, he says it is an inadequate ethical ideal. Camenisch goes on to argue that the business activity itself must be scrutinized according to how it affects "human flourishing directly through the kind of products or services it provides, and through the responsible or irresponsible use of limited and often non-renewable resources."

Many current discussions of business ethics seem in the end to locate the ethical concern some distance from the central and essential activity of business. One way this is done is to assume that the content of business ethics is no more and no less than the prevailing moral code of the society as applied to business activities. Business persons and institutions, like all other citizens, are expected to refrain from murder, from fraud, and from polluting the environment. But we cannot limit business ethics to such matters. In fact, perhaps we ought not even call this *business* ethics for the same reasons that we do not say that parental ethics prohibits my brutalizing my children. That is not parental ethics but just ethics plain and simple. This constraint arises from what it means to be a decent human being, not from what it means to be a parent. Similarly, the prohibition upon murdering to eliminate a business competitor is not part of a *business* ethic, for it does not arise from what it means to be engaged in business, nor does it apply to one simply because one is engaged in business. It too arises from what it means to be a decent, moral human being.

The second way of moving ethical issues to the edge of business's activities usually occurs under the rubric of "business's social responsibilities." The most remote of the issues raised here involve the question of whether corporations should devote any of their profits to philanthropic, educational and other sorts of humanitarian undertakings. This is a controversial issue which will not be easily resolved, but even if we concluded that this was a social responsibility of business, it would again fail to be business ethics in any specific and distinctive sense. It would simply be the application to this corporate member of a general societal expectation that members of a society existing in extensive interdependence with and benefitting from that society ought, if able, to contribute some portion of their wealth to such worthy causes. It should in

Paul Camenisch, "Business Ethics: On Getting to the Heart of the Matter," *Business & Professional Ethics Journal* 1 (Fall 1981): 59–69. Reprinted by permission of the author.

passing be noted that there are persuasive grounds for rejecting this form of social responsibility for business.

Another class of social responsibilities urged upon business is somewhat closer to business activity as such since they can be fulfilled in the course of business's central activity of producing and marketing goods and services. These are the negative duties of neither creating nor aggravating social ills which might arise from business activity such as discriminatory employment, advancement and remuneration along racial, sexual, or other irrelevant lines, dangerous working conditions, and avoidable unemployment or worker dislocation.

Still we have not yet reached the heart of business ethics because we have said nothing of the ethics which come to bear on business *as business*, on business at its very heart and essence. But what is this "heart" of the business enterprise, and how and why are business ethics to be grounded in it?

Imagine a corporation which observes all the moral claims already noted—it does not commit fraud or murder, it freely contributes from its profits to various community "charities," its employment practices are above reproach, and it sells quality products at a fair and competitive price while securing for its investors a reasonable return on their investment. So far so good. Its moral record is impeccable. But imagine that the only conceivable use of its products is for human torture. Can we say that here there are no moral or ethical judgments to be made? That the kind of service or product which is at the heart of the enterprise is entirely inconsequential in any and all moral assessments of that enterprise? I do not see how morally sensitive persons or societies can set aside their moral perceptions at this point.

Of course one good reason for resisting this suggestion is the great difficulty in making such assessments of goods and services. *Whose* assessments will prevail? We might get general agreement on instruments of human torture—although even here I would not expect unanimity. But what of other goods such as napalm, Saturday-night specials, pornographic materials, junk foods, tobacco, liquors, etc., and services such as prostitution, the training of military mercenaries, or even the provision of such, or the training of the armed forces of repressive regimes, offensive-oriented "survival" courses, the construction of the usually

redundant fast-food outlets along suburban slurp strips? In addition to these items in which virtually everyone should be able to see some detrimental elements, there is an additional class of items which some would list here because of their use of limited, even nonrenewable, resources for no purpose beyond momentarily satisfying the whimsey of the indiscriminate wealthy, the bored, the vain, or of increasing corporate profits. . . .

But how do we carry business ethics to the very heart of the business enterprise? I would argue that we can begin by asking the question of what the business sector is and claims to do, what its distinctive function is in the larger society of which it is a part. The norms, both moral and otherwise, for the conduct of an agent, whether individual or corporate,[1] can be determined only after we have established what that agent's relations are to other agents in the moral community, what role the agent plays in relation to them, what the agent's activities in the context of that community aim at. . . .

In looking for the essential or definitive element in business I would suggest that it is necessary and helpful to see business as one form of that activity by which humans have from the beginning sought to secure and/or produce the material means of sustaining and then of enhancing life. It is plausible to assume that in earlier times individuals and small groups did this for themselves in immediate and direct ways such as gathering, hunting and fishing, farming, producing simple tools and weapons, etc. With the passage of time developments such as co-operative efforts, barter and monetary exchange modified this simple and idyllic situation. Business, I would suggest, enters this picture as that form of such activities in which the exchanges engaged in are no longer motivated entirely by the intention of all participants to secure goods or services immediately needed to sustain and/or enhance their own lives, but by the design of at least some of the participants to make a profit, i.e., to obtain some value in excess of what they had before the exchange which is sufficiently flexible that it can be put to uses other than the immediate satisfaction of the recipient's own needs and desires. It should be noted that this last point is as much or more a matter of defining business, as it is of charting its historical emergence.

In the above statement I am suggesting that

there are two essential elements in any adequate definition of business, the *provision of goods and services*, and the fact that this is done with the intention of making a *profit*. The first of these shows business's continuity with the various other human activities just noted by which life has been sustained and enhanced throughout the ages and enables us to understand business in relation to the larger society. The second is a more specific characteristic and sets business off from these other activities by revealing its distinctive internal dynamic. But this element does *not* sever business's connection with those predecessors. The crucial moral points to be made here are that moral/ethical issues arise around both of these elements and that the most important ones concern the "goods and services" element, i.e., the connection between business and the larger society of which it is a part.

This appears to put me in definite tension with Milton Friedman who attempts to ground business ethics, or at least that portion of it which he calls the social responsibility of business, in the profit element only: "In . . . [a free] economy, there is one and only one social responsibility of business—to use its resources and engage in activities designed to increase its profits so long as it stays within the rules of the game, which is to say, engages in open and free competition, without deception or fraud."[2]

Of course it is unfair to Friedman to say that for him the maximization of profit is business's only moral duty since he may assume that playing by the rules of the game and that even conducting oneself so as to make a profit in such a "game" would bring additional restraints to bear on business, restraints which many of us would consider to be *moral* restraints. Nevertheless, Friedman's statement does seem to put undue emphasis on business's profit-making function in answering the question of its social and/or moral responsibility.

But however one interprets Friedman's statement, we do here encounter a question fundamental to our present point. This is the question of whether, in defining business and understanding it as a moral reality, we should focus primarily on its goal of producing goods and services or of generating a profit. One can attempt to resolve this question in several ways. There is the rather common sense way of looking at the way most persons generally apply the label "business." A producer of goods and services intending to make a profit but

failing to do so is still, by most accounts, engaged in business. Of course some might respond that the concept of profit is still crucial to this activity's being considered business even though here it is present in intention only. But consider the other side. What if profit is present but the provision of goods and services is entirely absent as in a bank robbery? Most, I take it, would deny that here we have just another instance of business, or even an instance of business of a rather unusual sort. Most would simply want to deny that the bank robber was engaged in business at all. Of course one might salvage the position that business is defined by profit-making and yet avoid having to consider the bank robber a businessman by arguing that profit is not just any kind of gain at all, but is a particular sort of gain or is gain realized only under certain circumstances. But even this move would tend to support my position that a single simple concept of profit is not by itself sufficient to define what we mean by business. Whether these additional defining characteristics are written into a more complex definition of profit or are seen as additional to profit is a matter of indifference in terms of the present argument.

Secondly, one could take a more reflective, analytical approach and ask what the relation between these two elements—providing goods and services and profit-making—is, to see if that relation grants a kind of priority to either of them. I would argue, consistent with the above scenario of the emergence of business, that business's primary function, like that of the activities it supplants, is the producing of goods and services to sustain and enhance human existence. Profit then, given the way business functions in the marketplace, becomes one of the necessary means by which business enables itself to continue supplying such goods and services. This would mean that the goods and services element must be given priority in our understanding of business as a social reality and in our moral/ethical response to it. For in the absence of goods and services which are really *goods* and *services*, the making of a profit is at best morally irrelevant. In the absence of the end sought, the means for achieving it are otiose. . . .

Finally, in trying to settle the question of the relation between profits on the one hand and goods and services on the other, one might look at business in terms of its social function and ask why societies have generated and now support and sustain business. Surely it is not for business's own sake, nor for the sake of the few who own and manage businesses so that they can make a profit. Society has no need for profit-making as such. But rather, societies generate, encourage and sustain business because societies need the available raw materials transformed into needed goods and services, and because business in its contemporary form has been conspicuously successful in doing just that. In fact, in the current setting it may be that only business has the resources and the know-how to do that job on the needed scale.

All three of these ways of addressing the relation between these two elements would seem to confirm my position that the provision of goods and services can, perhaps must, be given priority over the profit element in our understanding of business. The major implication of this position for the resulting business ethics would be that the assessment of business as such and of specific business enterprises would begin with the question of whether the goods and services produced thereby serve to enhance or detract from the human condition, whether they contribute to or obstruct human flourishing. Implicit here is the suggestion that businesses engaged in producing goods and services which do not contribute to human flourishing are engaged in a morally questionable enterprise, and those engaged in producing goods and services inimical to human flourishing are engaged in immoral activity. . . .

Of course this suggestion concerning the heart of business ethics is rife with problems. Chief among them is the question of how we define the human flourishing which business is to serve. While we cannot resolve this question here, raising it at least serves to demonstrate that business ethics, like any serious ethics, will need to develop a philosophical or theological anthropology, a view of humanity and what its proper pursuit, its appropriate fulfillment is.

Some, of course, will argue that the only proper answers to such questions are the ones given by consumers in the marketplace as they use their purchasing power to vote for or against the various answers business implicitly offers in the form of diverse goods and services. While this may be an acceptable answer when one focuses exclusively on the relation between the individual consumer and the marketplace, it is clearly inadequate when we focus on the marketplace in relation to the total society, its present condition and needs and its future prospects. And clearly it is unrealistic, even irresponsible, to attempt to view an enterprise as large and as extensively intertwined with the total fabric of the society as is business only in its relation to individual consumers and their choices. Furthermore, the "marketplace as voting booth" answer to these questions is a costly trial and error method. And given advertising and other forms of demand formation, the significance of consumer "votes" is very unclear. Yet to have such judgments made by any agency outside the marketplace has serious implications for citizen-consumer freedom and rights in a free society.

In light of these difficult problems it might be tempting to give up the search for criteria by which to assess the performance of business at the level of its central function. And yet there are at least three important reasons for attempting this assessment in spite of the obvious problems. As we become increasingly aware of the limits of the earth and its resources within which all of humanity both present and future must live, and of the fact that in our present setting only business has the means and the know-how to transform those resources on any significant scale into the needed goods and services, it becomes increasingly clear that the total society has a crucial stake in, and should therefore have a say about what business does with this our common legacy. As Keith Davis has suggested, ". . . business now has a new social role of . . . trustee for society's resources . . ."[3] The knowing use of non-renewable resources to make products of little or no human value and/or with short useful life solely for the sake of an immediate profit thus becomes a serious dis-service to the larger society. An ethic of the sort here proposed provides a framework within which we could raise the question of how this trusteeship can best be exercised.

Secondly, this enterprise of assessing business in terms of its contribution to human flourishing is called for and legitimated by the fact that business in its various activities is already propagating, whether consciously or not, a view of humanity and of what human flourishing consequently means, views which of course assign a major role to the consumption of the goods and services business produces.[4] Even if this view of humanity is only implicit or perhaps especially if it is implicit, its content and potential impact call for assessment by parties outside the business sector.

Finally, the difficult task of responding to business on these central issues is worth undertaking because of the role business plays in contemporary America and similar societies. In observing the role of business and related economic matters in contemporary America one might almost suggest that we have moved from a sacralized society dominated by religious concerns, through a secularized one in which various major sectors attained considerable autonomy in their own spheres, to a commercialized or an economized culture in which the common denominators which unify and dominate all areas of activity are business related or business grounded considerations such as dollar-value, profitability, marketability, efficiency, contribution to the gross national product, etc. And as Thomas Donaldson and Patricia Werhane have written:

> There may be nothing inherently evil about the goals of economic growth, technological advance, and a higher material standard of living; but critics such as Galbraith have argued that when these become the primary goals of a nation there is a significant lowering in the quality of human life. Economic goals are able to distract attention from crucial human issues, and freedom, individuality, and creativity are lost in a society dominated by large corporations and economic goals.[5]

If the above is a plausible interpretation of the role of business, broadly understood, in contemporary America, and of some of its implications for human flourishing, then it should be obvious that we have need for an ethic which responds to the central activity of business, since the crucial human implications of such cultural domination by business arise from this central function and not from the less central concerns often raised in business ethics. . . .

But why should business submit to the scrutiny and recommendations of an ethic such as is proposed here? One answer would be because such an ethic is predicated on what business *is*—one important part of society's efforts to enable its members to flourish, specifically that part which deals with the provision of the material means for sustaining and enhancing life.

"Of course," the critic might respond, "this answer works *if* we agree on what you say business is. But if we maintain that business must be defined and understood in terms of its own internal dynamics and goals, e.g., profit-making, rather than in terms of society's needs and goals, then the answer falls apart." True enough. But given business's extensive interdependence with society—its reliance on society's educational system to provide educated workers, on society's maintenance of transportation systems, of a stable social and political setting in which to do business, of a legal system by which business can adjudicate its disputes with competitors and customers, of what E. F. Schumacher has called the "infrastructure"[6]—it is naive to suggest that business is a self-sufficient and self-contained entity which can define its own goals and functions entirely independently of the society's goals and needs. As Robert A. Dahl has written:

> Today it is absurd to regard the corporation simply as an enterprise established for the sole purpose of allowing profit making. We the citizens give them special rights, powers, and privileges, protection, and benefits on the understanding that their activities will fulfill purposes. Corporations exist only as they continue to benefit us . . . Every corporation should be thought of as a social enterprise whose existence and decisions can be justified only insofar as they serve public or social purposes.[7]

Furthermore, anyone who argues that business should be permitted to define its own goals and purposes and thus its own ethics independently of societal interests will have to explain why business should be granted latitude at this point that is denied to other major sectors of societal activity such as politics, education, or the traditional professions such as law and medicine. (This last of course is of special interest and relevance in light of the fact already noted that increasing numbers of business persons wish to be considered professionals.) And the questions raised here cannot be put to rest by facile references to the public vs. the private sector. First of all, much of education and certainly most of the legal and medical professions are not in the public sector. So that would not explain or justify different treatment for business at this point. But more fundamentally, such a response would miss the basic question being raised here, the question of whether in a society as complex and interdependent as ours there actually is a "private sector" in the simple, straightforward sense suggested by that response.

There are numerous varied matters which are legitimately included in any adequate definition of business ethics. In fact, in a nascent field such as this it is as yet impossible to say with any certainty what is within and what is without its borders. But it does seem clear that any business ethic that does not respond first and foremost to business's contribution to or detraction from human flourishing through its essential and definitive activity of generating life sustaining and enhancing goods and services will have failed to lay a foundation from which to address all other questions for it will not yet have gotten to the heart of the matter.

Notes

1. I am not prepared to enter here into the current debate concerning the existence and/or nature of corporate moral agency. For my present point it is sufficient to note that the moral stances, decisions and actions of various persons engaged in business and working together as, or through a corporation, do have impacts on the life of society and of its members of the sort I here have in mind. Whether these impacts are to be credited to those individual persons or to the corporation seems to make little difference in the present analysis.

2. Milton Friedman, *Capitalism and Freedom* (Chicago: University of Chicago Press, 1962), 133.

3. Keith Davis, "Five Propositions for Social Responsibility," in Tom L. Beauchamp and Norman E. Bowie, eds., *Ethical Theory and Business* (Englewood Cliffs, N.J.: Prentice-Hall, 1979), 170.

4. For one interpretation of the understanding of human flourishing assumed and propagated by much of business in a consumer society, see Edward Stevens, *Business Ethics* (New York: Paulist Press, 1979), 205–211.

5. Thomas Donaldson and Patricia H. Werhane, eds., *Ethical Issues in Business* (Englewood Cliffs, N.J.: Prentice-Hall, 1979), 330.

6. E. F. Schumacher, *Small Is Beautiful* (New York: Harper and Row, 1975), 273–274.

7. Robert A. Dahl, "A Prelude to Corporate Reform," in Robert L. Heilbroner and Paul London, eds., *Corporate Social Policy* (Reading, MA: Addison-Wesley Publishing Company, 1975), 18–19, as cited

in Norman E. Bowie, "Changing the Rules," in Tom L. Beauchamp and Norman E. Bowie, eds., *Ethical Theory and Business* (Englewood Cliffs, N.J.: Prentice-Hall, 1979), 148.

Review and Discussion Questions

1. Could a company that makes products for human torture be a "socially responsible" company? Explain your answer.

2. What are Camenisch's three reasons for maintaining that the business goal of providing goods and services takes priority over making a profit? Do you agree with them?

3. Camenisch argues that business should promote "human flourishing." What does that mean to you? Do you think that there is any means other than the marketplace itself to decide what goods and services promote human flourishing?

4. Why does Camenisch believe that it is justified and important to develop criteria for assessing business in terms of human flourishing?

5. Would you agree that Camenisch has taken us to the "heart" of business ethics? What practical implications does his approach have?

For Further Reading

On Corporations

Thomas Donaldson, *Corporations and Morality* (Englewood Cliffs, N.J.: Prentice-Hall, 1982) discusses the moral status of corporations, arguments for and against corporate social responsibility, and the idea of a social contract for business, among other issues.

Elizabeth Gatewood and **Archie B. Carroll**, "The Anatomy of Corporate Social Response: The Rely, Firestone 500, and Pinto Cases," *Business Horizons* 24 (September–October 1981) analyzes different corporate responses in these three cases.

Saul W. Gellerman, "Why 'Good' Managers Make Bad Ethical Choices," *Harvard Business Review* 64 (July–August 1986) examines the rationalizations that lead to corporate misconduct.

Christopher McMahon, "Morality and the Invisible Hand," *Philosophy and Public Affairs* 10 (Summer 1981) is an insightful but advanced analysis of the relation between common morality and the implicit morality of business.

On Unions

Richard O. Boyer and **Herbert M. Morais,** *Labor's Untold Story,* 3rd ed. (New York: United Electrical, Radio, and Machine Workers of America, 1975) is a moving prolabor account of the history of the union movement in America.

Barbara Reisman and **Lance Compa,** "The Case for Adversarial Unions," *Harvard Business Review* 63 (May–June 1985) and **Jack Barbash,** "Do We Really Want Labor on the Ropes?" *Harvard Business Review* 63 (July–August 1985) are two interesting discussions of labor-management relations today.

PART III

THE ORGANIZATION AND THE PEOPLE IN IT

CHAPTER 6

THE WORKPLACE: BASIC ISSUES AND NEW CHALLENGES

Scientists first described Acquired Immune Deficiency Syndrome, commonly known as AIDS, in 1981. Apparently the result of a new infection of human beings, AIDS probably stems originally from central Africa, possibly emerging as recently as the 1950s. Within three years scientists in the United States and France had isolated "human T-lymphotropic virus III," or HTLV-III, as the cause. HTLV-III is the parent virus of AIDS and a couple of related diseases. To be infected with the virus[1] is not automatically to have AIDS, but recent evidence suggests that most of those infected will go on to develop AIDS symptoms. After identifying the virus, scientists quickly developed blood tests for its presence. As of this writing, the scientific race to develop a vaccine is on. And the stakes are high. Two million people in the United States alone are estimated to be infected. Spread primarily by intimate contact, the virus has the potential to infect virtually all human beings.[2]

No one today can doubt the seriousness of AIDS. Media attention has ensured that the public is taking this deadly disease and its threat of epidemic seriously, and this is a good thing. But when fear of some danger com-

bines with ignorance about its nature and causes, panic is often the result. And this has sadly been the case with AIDS—not least in the workplace.

Take what is, unfortunately, a typical case. John L—— is a white-collar employee, working in the downtown branch of a firm operating in a middle-sized West Coast city. In recent months, he had been feeling generally run-down and complained of various small ailments to his physician. When a routine checkup didn't reveal anything specific, John's doctor encouraged him to undergo a blood test for AIDS. He tested positive, which means that the antibodies for HTLV-III are present in his body. Their presence means that he is infected by the virus and that it is probable, given his symptoms, that he has AIDS.

A few of John's friends in the office know of his recent ill health, and gradually word of his test results circulates. And now problems begin—not just for John, but for his co-workers and for management. John's colleagues feel uneasy being around him; they're not sure what to do or to say, and some of them are very worried about possible contagion. A few coworkers feel strongly that John should not be permitted to go on working there. The boss is naturally concerned not just with the prospect of a declining work performance from John, but with the effects of his presence on office morale. She may herself also have doubts about the wisdom or even the safety of allowing John to continue to interact with the public, which is part of his job description.

The myriad problems, doubts, tensions, possibly even mild hysteria that the mere presence of John L—— can create in an organizational context are easy to imagine, but sorting out the morally relevant factors and deciding how the situation ought to be dealt with is less easy. What are John's rights and interests? How are these to be weighed against the interests and rights of both his coworkers and the organization itself? What responsibilities does an organization have to one of its members who may be facing a terminal illness? Given the size and organizational structure of John's workplace and the type of work in question, how—morally speaking— ought management to respond?

Traditionally, the obligations between a business organization and its employees could be boiled down to the following adage: "A fair wage for an honest day's work." Thus, business's primary, if not sole, obligation to its employees was to pay a decent wage. In return, employees were expected to work efficiently and to be loyal and obedient to their employer. This model of employer/employee relations is obviously too simple and fails to come to terms seriously not just with the dilemmas facing John's office, but also with many other major moral issues that arise in today's workplace. In this chapter we will look at some of these issues. In particular, we will discuss:

1. The state of civil liberties in the workplace.

2. The efforts of some successful companies to respect the rights and moral dignity of their employees.

3. Moral issues that arise with respect to personnel matters: namely, hiring, promotions, discipline and discharge, and wages.

4. The nature of privacy and the problems of organizational influence over private decisions.

5. Moral issues raised by the use of polygraphs and personality tests, the monitoring of employees, and drug testing in the workplace.

6. Working conditions—in particular, health and safety, styles of management, and provision of day-care facilities and maternity leave.

7. Job satisfaction and dissatisfaction and the prospects for enhancing the quality of work life.

CIVIL LIBERTIES IN THE WORKPLACE

Employees have all sorts of job-related concerns. Generally speaking, they want to do well at their assignments, to get on with their colleagues, and to have their contributions to the organization recognized. Their job tasks, working conditions, wages, and the possibility of promotion are among the many things that occupy their day-to-day thoughts. Aside from the actual work that they are expected to perform, employees, being human, are naturally concerned about the way their organizations treat them. Frequently, they find that treatment to be morally deficient and complain that the organizations for which they work violate their moral rights and civil liberties.

Consider the case of Louis V. MacIntire, who worked for the DuPont Company in Orange, Texas, from 1956 until 1972. As a chemical engineer he was well paid, and during the course of his career at DuPont he received several promotions. MacIntire also had literary ambitions and wrote a novel, *Scientists and Engineers: The Professionals Who are Not*, which was published by him in 1971. Several characters in the novel inveigh against various management abuses at the novel's fictional Logan Chemical Company and argue for a union for technical employees. Logan Chemical at least superficially resembles MacIntire's real-life employer, DuPont, and some of MacIntire's supervisors were unhappy with his thinly veiled criticisms. He was fired. MacIntire sued DuPont, claiming that his constitutional right of free speech had been violated. A Texas district judge threw that charge out of court.[3]

MacIntire's case illuminates what many see as the widespread absence of civil liberties in the workplace. David W. Ewing is one of those writers. He sees the corporate invasion of employees' civil liberties as rampant, and attacks it in scathing terms:

> In most . . . [corporate] organizations, during working hours, civil liberties are a will-o'-the-wisp. The Constitutional rights that employees have grown accustomed to in family, school, and church life generally must be left outdoors, like cars in the parking lot. As in totalitarian countries, from time to time a benevolent chief executive or department head may encourage speech, conscience, and privacy, but these scarcely can be called rights, for management can take them away at will. . . . It is fair to say that an enormous corporate archipelago has grown which, in terms of civil liberties, is as different from the rest of America as day is from night. In this archipelago . . . the system comes first, the individual second.[4]

Two historical factors, in Ewing's view, lie behind this loss of civil liberties and the prevalence of authoritarianism in the workplace. One of these factors was the rise of profes-

sional management and personnel engineering at the turn of the century, following the emergence of large corporations. This shaped the attitudes of companies to their employees in a way which is hardly conducive to respecting their rights. As Frederick Winslow Taylor, generally identified as the founder of "scientific management," bluntly put it, "In the past, the man has been first. In the future, the system must be first."[5]

The second historical factor is that the law has traditionally given the employer a free hand in hiring and firing employees. A century ago a Tennessee court expressed this doctrine in memorable form. Employers, the court held, "may dismiss their employees at will . . . for good cause, for no cause, or even for cause morally wrong, without thereby being guilty of legal wrong." Similarly, a California court upheld this traditional rule shortly before World War I, observing that the "arbitrary right of the employer to employ or discharge labor, with or without regard to actuating motives" is a proposition "settled beyond peradventure." And in 1975 a U.S. district court in Missouri upheld the traditional position in ruling against a whistleblowing engineer at General Motors.[6]

In addition, common law requires that an employee be loyal to an employer, acting solely for the employer's benefit in matters connected to work. The employee is also duty bound "not to act or speak disloyally," except in pursuit of his own interests outside work. It's no wonder, then, that traditional employer-employee law has hardly been supportive of the idea of freedom of speech and expression for employees. Against that background, DuPont's treatment of MacIntire and the court's refusal to see a First Amendment issue in his case are not surprising.

According to common law, then, unless there is an explicit contractual provision to the contrary, every employment is employment "at will," and either side is free to terminate it at any time without advanced notice or reason. The common law, however, has been modified in important ways by congressional and state statutory provisions. The Wagner Act of 1935 was, in this respect, a watershed. It prohibited firing workers because of union membership or union activities. The Civil Rights Act of 1964 and subsequent legislation make discrimination on the basis of race, creed, nationality, sex, or age illegal. Federal and state laws also protect war veterans and public employees in civil service. And many workers are protected by their union contracts from unjust dismissals.

Thus, today, working people have protection against some forms of unjust termination, and many of them enjoy the assurance that they can expect due process and that at least some of their civil liberties and other moral rights will be respected on the job. "But," writes Clyde Summers in the *Harvard Business Review*, "random individuals who are unjustly terminated are isolated and without organizational or political voice. For them the harsh common law rule remains."[7]

Companies That Look Beyond the Bottom Line

The law is not static, however, and some courts have been willing in specific cases to break with tradition and to protect the rights of speech, privacy, and conscience of employees.[8] But while the law seems to be gradually changing, leaving the common-law heritage of employer-employee doctrine behind, these recent legal developments are complicated and hard for the layperson to assess. The results depend not only on the details of each case, but can vary from jurisdiction to jurisdiction and from court to court. As argued in Chapter 1, though, our moral obligations extend beyond merely keeping within the law. Thus, from the authors' point of view, it is particularly significant that more and more corporations are themselves coming to acknowledge, and to design institu-

tional procedures that respect, the rights of their employees. Moreover, the firms that are taking the lead in this regard are often among the most successful companies in the country.

This fact cuts against the old argument that corporate efficiency requires that employees sacrifice their civil liberties and other rights between 9 and 5. Without strict discipline and the firm maintenance of management prerogatives, it is claimed, our economic system would come apart at the seams. An increasing body of evidence, however, suggests just the opposite. As Ewing writes:

> Civil liberties are far less of a threat to the requirements of effective management than are collective bargaining, labor-management committees, job enrichment, work participation, and a number of other schemes that industry takes for granted. Moreover, the companies that lead in encouraging rights—organizations such as Polaroid, IBM, Donnelly Mirrors, and Delta Airlines—have healthier-looking bottom lines than the average corporation does.[9]

Although under no legal compulsion to do so, a small but growing number of companies encourage employee speech—questions and criticisms about company policies affecting the welfare of employees and the community. Some companies foster open communication through regular, but informal, exchanges between management and other employees. Others, like Delta Airlines, have top officials answer questions submitted anonymously by employees—in the absence of supervisors or foremen. Still others, like General Electric or New England Telephone, have a "hot line" for questions, worries, or reports of wrongdoing. Finally, some, like Dow Chemical, open the pages of company publications to employee questions and criticisms.

Union contracts frequently require companies to set up grievance procedures and otherwise attempt to see that their members are guaranteed due process on the job. Some enlightened nonunionized companies have done the same. Polaroid, for instance, has a well-institutionalized committee whose job it is to represent an employee with a grievance. The committee members are elected from the ranks, and reportedly a fair number of management decisions are overruled in the hearings. If the decision goes against the aggrieved employee, he or she is entitled by company rules to submit the case to an outside arbitrator.

Some companies, like Johnson Wax, Procter & Gamble, and Aetna Life and Casualty, go beyond ensuring due process and respecting the right to free expression and other civil liberties of their employees. As Tad Tuleja has shown, these companies have long followed no-layoff policies.[10] IBM is another example. Motivated by the personal philosophy of its founder, Thomas Watson, IBM promised in 1914 never to lay off an employee for purely economic reasons, a promise it has kept for over seventy years. Even during the Great Depression in the 1930s, IBM maintained a full payroll, despite a severely diminished market for its machines. In discussing this policy, Richard T. Liebhaber, IBM's director for business practices and development in 1984, says that IBM begins

> with an unusual premise—the idea that the individual comes first. A lot of companies begin somewhere else—with profit or productivity or growth—and try to work the individual in. We start with respect for the person and hang everything else on that concept. When you come at business from that direction, decisions take on a very different tone, because the personal dimension is already built into your options.

Hewlett-Packard is another company with a firm commitment to full employment. During the recession in the early 1970s, orders had fallen so badly that management was considering a 10 percent cut in the work force. Since laying off people was anathema, HP went a different route. It set up a working schedule of nine days out of ten for everybody in the company, from the CEO on down. The program stayed in place for six months, when orders picked up, and the full ten-day schedule returned. "The net result of this program," says William Hewlett, "was that effectively all shared the burden of the recession, good people were not turned out on a very tough job market, and, I might observe, the company benefited by having in place a highly qualified work force when business returned."

Not only, then, is it a moral duty of companies to respect the rights and dignity of their employees, in particular by acknowledging their civil liberties and guaranteeing them due process, but doing so can also work to the company's benefit by enhancing employee morale and, thus, the competitive performance of the company. Hence, there is little basis for the widespread belief that there is an incompatibility between efficient management and a workplace environment that is fair. Of course, a company that is not sincerely committed to respecting employee rights as something that is of inherent moral importance is not likely to reap the benefits of enhanced business performance. Employees can tell the difference between a company that has a genuine regard for their welfare and a company that only pretends to have moral concern.

So far we have affirmed that the workplace should provide an environment in which employees are treated fairly and their inherent dignity respected, and we have argued that doing so can be perfectly compatible with a firm's business goals. Although important, these points are generalities. They do not provide much guidance for dealing with the specific moral issues and dilemmas that arise day in and day out on the job. The remainder of this chapter takes a closer look at some of these.

PERSONNEL POLICIES AND PROCEDURES

People make up organizations, and how an organization impinges on the lives of its own members is a morally important matter. One obvious, but nonetheless very important, way in which organizational conduct affects the welfare and rights of its employees and potential employees is through its personnel policies and procedures—that is, how the organization handles the hiring, firing, paying, and promoting of the people who work for it. These procedures and policies structure an organization's basic relationship with its employees. In this section we look at some of the morally relevant concerns to which any organization must be sensitive.

Hiring

A basic function of the employer or personnel manager is hiring. Employers generally hire people who will maximize the efficiency of the firm, which is an organizational ideal. In meeting this obligation employers must be careful to treat job applicants fairly. As you might imagine, determining the fair thing to do is not always easy. One useful way to approach some of the moral aspects of hiring is to examine the principal steps involved in the process: screening, testing, and interviewing.

Screening. When firms recruit employees, they attempt to screen them—that is, to attract only those applicants who have a good chance of qualifying for the job. When done properly, screening ensures a pool of competent candidates and guarantees that everyone has been dealt with fairly. But when screening is done improperly, it undermines effective recruitment and invites injustices into the hiring process.

Screening begins with a job description and specification. A *job description* lists all pertinent details about a job, including its duties, responsibilities, working conditions, and physical requirements. A *job specification* describes the qualifications an employee needs, such as skills, educational experience, appearance, and physical attributes. Completeness is important. When either the job description or job specification is inadequate or unspecific, firms risk injuring candidates. Suppose, for example, candidate Rita Cox takes a day off from work and travels 200 miles at her own expense to be interviewed for a position as a computer programmer with Singleton Computer Company. During the interview Cox discovers that Singleton needs someone with IBM background, not Sperry Rand, as is hers. Mention of that detail in the job specification could have prevented Cox's loss of time and money. But even when specifications don't directly injure candidates as in this case, they can cause indirect injury by depriving candidates of information they need in order to make informed decisions about their job prospects.

Age, race, national origin, religion, and sex are obvious examples of items that generally should never appear in job specifications nor figure in hiring. Such requirements exclude candidates from consideration on non-job-related grounds.

Less obvious, but potentially objectionable, are ill-considered education requirements. Requiring more formal education than a job demands is not fair to candidates or firm. Yet, increasingly employers are arbitrarily erecting an inflated educational barrier to employment. The thinking seems to be: "If I can get someone with at least two years of college (or a college degree, or post-graduate training), then why not?" An inflated educational requirement thins out the field of applicants, thereby reducing recruitment costs. But if the education requirement exceeds job demands, then can it be called relevant? Not only are candidates without the bogus requirement denied equal consideration, but one of them may be the best person for the job. Thus the firm, as well as the "undereducated" applicant, stands to lose. Beyond this, companies may be inviting considerable frustration for themselves and the employee when the job does not challenge the worker's educational preparation.

The other side of the coin is to deny an applicant job consideration because he or she is "overqualified." Certainly, some candidates are by education or experience overqualified for jobs. To avoid the personal and organizational frustrations that often result from hiring overqualified people, companies are justified in raising the issue. But "raising the issue" is different from assuming that because on paper an applicant appears overqualified the applicant necessarily spells trouble for the company. The fact is that the employment ranks are filled with people successfully doing jobs for which they are technically overqualified. In times of rapid change like the present, when the glitter of an occupational field can tarnish within a few short years, seasoned workers inevitably will hopscotch around the employment board. Employers do such workers and themselves grave injustice in summarily dismissing them as "overqualified." Moreover, they encourage such workers to misrepresent their backgrounds on job applications for fear of being passed over.

One additional matter. As traditional sex roles change, more and more men are leaving the work world for personal reasons, such as to help raise children while their wives complete professional training. More often than not, when these men try to return to work they are thwarted. Employers assume that since the man quit work once for personal reasons, he may very well do so again. Thus, discontinuity of employment is cutting some men off from job consideration, as it traditionally has for women.

"The hurdles men face returning to the job market are about three times greater" than those faced by women, says Charles Arons, president and chief executive officer of Casco Industries, a Los Angeles–based employment and recruiting firm. "There isn't a male I know of in an executive position who would accept raising kids as a legitimate excuse for not working for three years."[11]

Thomas Schumann, director of selection and placement for Dayton-based Mead Corporation, agrees. "If other qualified candidates are available," he says, "my guess is that a personnel manager would go with somebody who doesn't raise that question."[12]

Certainly, employers in highly technical, rapidly changing fields are warranted in suspecting that an individual's hiatus may have left him (or her) "out of touch." But to automatically disqualify a candidate on the basis of deliberately chosen career interruption raises a question of fairness.

Tests. Testing is an integral part of the hiring process, especially with large firms. Tests are generally designed to measure the applicant's verbal, quantitative, and logical skills. Aptitude tests help determine job suitability; skill tests measure the applicant's proficiency in specific areas such as typing and shorthand; personality tests help determine the applicant's maturity and sociability. In addition, some firms engaged in the design and assembly of precision equipment administer dexterity tests to determine how nimbly applicants can use their hands and fingers.

To be successful, a test must be valid. *Validity* refers to the quality of measuring precisely what a test is designed to determine. Just as important, tests must be reliable. *Reliability* refers to the quality of exhibiting a reasonable consistency in results obtained. Clearly not all tests are valid or reliable. Many tests are not able to measure desired qualities, and others exhibit a woefully low level of forecast accuracy. Some companies use tests that haven't been designed for the company's particular situation.

Legitimizing tests can be an expensive and time-consuming project. But if tests are used, the companies using them are obliged to ensure their validity and reliability. Otherwise, companies risk injuring applicants, stockholders, and even the general public. At the same time, companies must be cautious about the importance they place on such tests, because a test is only one measure in an overall evaluative process. Ignoring these things, firms can easily introduce injustices into the hiring process.

Even when tests are valid and reliable they can be unfair. For example, people who have studied intelligence tests contend that they favor a white, middle-class test taker, because the questions contain points of reference that this group relates to well as a result of their cultural and educational background. For ghetto-bred blacks, however, the tests can be as mystifying as if they were composed in a foreign language, because they don't relate to black culture. As a result, such tests can measure one's mastery of cultural assumptions more than one's intellectual capacity or potential. This was precisely the issue when, in July 1963, a young black male named Leon Myart applied for a job as an analyzer and phaser at Motorola's plant in Franklin Park, Illinois.

After Myart had filled out an application form he was given General Ability Test No. 10, a test designed to measure candidates' abilities to acquire technical information by evaluating their verbal comprehension and simple reasoning skills. Myart scored four, two points below the minimum requirement. As a result, personnel gave Myart no further tests. He was briefly interviewed and dismissed, the entire process taking about 15 minutes.

Myart, who had extensive background in electronics, sued Motorola, charging discrimination in its hiring practices. He claimed that Test No. 10 was discriminatory because it did not take trainability into account and because it tested for education and skills that were not actually needed on the job or that could easily be learned or compensated for by other skills.

On March 14, 1966, the Supreme Court of Illinois found Motorola innocent of discrimination in its hiring practices. But the court never decided whether Test No. 10 was discriminatory.

In 1971, however, the United States Supreme Court took a decisive stand on testing in the case of *Griggs v. Duke Power Company*. The case involved thirteen black laborers who were denied promotions because they scored low on a company-sponsored intelligence test involving verbal and mathematical puzzles. In its decision the Court found that the Civil Rights Act prohibits employers from requiring a high-school education or the passing of a general intelligence test as a prerequisite for employment or promotion without demonstrable evidence that the associated skills relate directly to job performance. Many firms responded by eliminating such tests. A more constructive response seemingly would have been to ensure that the tests were not culturally discriminatory.

Interviews.   When moral issues arise in interviewing, they almost always relate to the manner in which the interview was conducted. The literature of personnel management rightly cautions against rudeness, coarseness, hostility, and condescension in interviewing job applicants. In guarding against these qualities, personnel managers would do well to focus on the humanity of the individuals who sit across the desk from them, mindful of the very human need that has brought those people into the office. But interviewers still risk treating applicants unfairly when they forget or ignore their own personal biases.

The human tendency in interviewing is to like and prefer persons we identify with. Thus, Greg Tremont feels especially sympathetic to applicant George Horner because Horner has recently graduated from Tremont's alma mater. As a result of this bias, Tremont treats Horner preferentially, thereby harming other applicants and the firm.

Those in hiring positions should recognize their own biases, what the English philosopher Francis Bacon (1561–1626) once termed the "idols of the mind." As Bacon put it: "The human understanding is like a false mirror, which, receiving rays irregularly, distorts and discolors the nature of things by mingling its own nature with it."[13] In short, we view things, people included, through the lens of our own preconceptions. It's true that Bacon's remarks were addressed to the nature of scientific method, but his observations seem appropriate here as well. For failing to heed Bacon's "idols," interviewers can easily sacrifice the objectivity that both the nature of their jobs and fairness require of them.

Promotions

In theory, the same essential criterion that applies to hiring also applies to promotions: job qualifications. But like all generalizations about standards for decisions in the workplace, this one needs delimiting.

It's no secret that factors besides job qualifications often determine promotions. How long you've been with a firm, how well you're liked, whom you know, even when you were last promoted—all these influence promotions in the real business world. As with hiring, the key moral ideal here is fairness. Nobody would seriously argue that promoting the unqualified is fair or justifiable. It's a serious breach of duty to owners, employees, and ultimately the general public. But many reasonable people debate whether promoting by job qualification alone is the fairest thing to do. Are other criteria admissible? If so, when, and how much weight should those criteria carry? These are tough questions with no easy answers. They require a well-honed concept of fair play, an ability to compare and contrast the courses available, and even a fertile imag-

ination for devising alternatives. To highlight the problem, let's consider seniority, inbreeding, and nepotism, three factors that sometimes serve as bases for promotions.

Seniority. *Seniority refers to longevity on a job or with a firm.* Frequently job transfers or promotions are made strictly on the basis of seniority; individuals with the most longevity automatically receive the promotions. But problems can occur with this promotion method.

To illustrate, personnel manager Manuel Rodriguez needs to fill the job of quality control supervisor. Carol Martin seems better qualified for the job than Jim Turner, except in one respect: Turner's been on the job for three years longer than Martin. Whom should Rodriguez promote to quality control supervisor?

The answer isn't easy. Those who'd argue for Carol Martin—opponents of seniority—would undoubtedly claim that the firm has an obligation to fill the job with the most qualified person. In this way the firm is served and the most qualified are rewarded. Those advancing Turner's promotion—proponents of seniority—would contend that the firm should be loyal to its senior employees, that it should reward them for faithful service. In this way, employees have an incentive to work hard and to remain with the firm.

When company policies indicate what part seniority should play in promotions and job transfers, the problem abates but does not vanish. We can still wonder about the morality of the policy itself. In cases where no clear policy exists, the problem begs for an answer.

The role seniority should play in promotions is compounded by the fact that seniority in itself does not necessarily indicate competence or loyalty. Simply because Jim Turner has been on the job three years longer than Carol Martin, he is not necessarily more competent or more loyal. Of course there are instances when seniority may be a real indicator of job qualifications. A pilot who has logged hundreds of hours of flying time with an airline is more qualified for captaincy than one who hasn't.

Then there's the question of employee expectations. If personnel expect seniority to count substantially, management can injure morale and productivity by overlooking it. True, worker morale might suffer equally should seniority solely determine promotions. Ambitious and competent workers might see little point in refining skills and developing talents when positions are doled out strictly on a longevity basis.

It seems impossible, then, to say precisely what part, if any, seniority ought to play in promotions—all the more reason, therefore, for management to consider carefully its seniority policies. Of paramount importance in any decision is that management remember its twin responsibilities of promoting on the basis of qualifications and of recognizing prolonged and constructive contributions to the firm. A policy that provides for promotions strictly on the basis of qualifications seems heartless, whereas one that promotes by seniority alone seems mindless. The challenge for management is how to merge these dual responsibilities in a way that is beneficial to the firm and fair to all concerned.

Inbreeding.   All that we've said about seniority applies with equal force to *inbreeding, the practice of promoting exclusively from within the firm.* In theory, whenever managers must fill positions they should look only to competence. The most competent, whether within or without the firm, should receive the position. In this way responsibilities to owners are best served.

In practice, however, managers must seriously consider the impact of outside recruitment on in-house morale. Years of loyal service, often at great personal expense, invariably create a unique relationship between employer and employee, and with it unique obligations of gratitude. The eighteen years

that Becky Thompson has worked for National Textiles creates a relationship between her and the firm that does not exist between the firm and an outsider it may wish to hire for the job Thompson seeks. Some would argue that management has a moral obligation to remember this loyalty when determining promotions, especially when outside recruitment departs from established policy.

Nepotism.   *Nepotism is the practice of showing favoritism to relatives and close friends.* Suppose a manager hired a relative strictly because of the relationship between them. Such an action would raise a number of moral concerns; chief among them would be disregard both of managerial responsibilities to the organization and of fairness to all other applicants.

Not all instances of nepotism raise serious moral concerns. For example, when a firm is strictly a family operation and has as its purpose providing work for family members, nepotistic practices are generally justified. Also, the fact that a person is a relative or friend of firm members should not automatically exclude him or her from job consideration. Nevertheless, even when such people are qualified for a position, responsible management must consider the impact of nepotistic hiring. Will the selection breed resentment and jealousy among other employees? Will it discourage qualified outsiders from seeking employment with the firm? Will it create problems in future placement, scheduling, or dismissal of the relation? Will it make the relation an object of distrust and hostility within the organization?

It's worth noting that nepotism is by no means confined to business organizations. It can arise anywhere employers and employees come together. A few years ago, for example, a nationally syndicated columnist alleged widespread nepotism in hiring and promoting at the Los Alamos National Laboratory, the nuclear research facility in New Mexico.

At about the same time, *U.S. News & World Report* ran an article on nepotism in the nation's labor unions. The article presented a compelling case for the claim that "some of the nation's largest and most powerful unions are run like family businesses, with relatives of high-ranking officers holding influential and often high-paying positions."[14]

Discipline and Discharge

In order for an organization to function in an orderly, efficient, and productive way, personnel departments establish guidelines for behavior based on such factors as appearance, punctuality, dependability, efficiency, and cooperation. We don't intend to debate the morality of specific rules and regulations here, but only the organization's treatment of employees when infractions occur.

At the outset, let's note that managers are obliged to discipline workers who violate behavioral standards, because it is necessary for the good of the firm, other employees, and society at large. Most moral issues in this area relate to *how* the manager imposes the discipline. For example, it's one thing to speak with a person privately about some infraction and quite another to chastise or punish the person publicly. Also, trying to correct someone's behavior on a graduated basis, from verbal warning to dismissal, is different from firing someone for a first infraction. The point is that discipline, while desirable and necessary, raises concerns about fairness, noninjury, and respect for persons in the way it's administered. In order to create an atmosphere of fairness, one in which rules and standards will be fair and equally applied, the principles of just cause and due process must operate.

Just cause refers to reasons for discipline or discharge that deal directly with job performance. In general, whatever leads directly or indirectly to employee infractions of the job description may be considered a job-related reason. Thus, Phil Bruen's boss Charlie Whyte is justified in disciplining Bruen for chronic tardiness, but not for voting Republican.

Of course, the distinction between a job-related and nonrelated issue is not always as apparent as in this simple example. How a person behaves outside work is often incompatible with the image a company wishes to project. Does the organization have a right to discipline its employees for off-the-job behavior? The answer depends largely on one's concept of company image and private lives, on precisely where the company image stops and the private life begins, and on the legitimate extent of organizational influence over individual lives. Such concerns involve complex questions of personal and group rights that we'll consider later in this chapter.

The second principle related to fair worker discipline and discharge is *due process*, which refers to *the specific and systematic means workers have of appealing discipline and discharge.* Due process deals with the step-by-step procedure by which an employee can appeal a managerial decision. Where employees are unionized, such a procedure usually exists. Where no procedure exists, serious moral questions of fairness regarding employee discipline inevitably arise because the worker has no way of appealing what may be unfair treatment.

All that has been said about discipline can also be applied to firing and discharge. In most cases, work contracts prescribe termination procedures. But strict reliance on the contract may fall short of the fairness ideal. For example, unless it is stated in the contract or employees have union representation, a company may not be legally obligated to give reasons for firing an employee, nor must it give advance notice. When employers fire someone without notice or cause, they may have been strictly faithful to contractual agreement, but have they been fair?

In answering this question, it's helpful to distinguish between two employer responsibilities. Employers bear the responsibility of terminating the employment of workers who don't discharge their contractual obligations, but they are also obliged to terminate these workers as painlessly as possible. In other words, although employers have the right to fire, this does not mean they have the right to fire however they choose. Because firing can be so materially and psychologically destructive to employees, we should consider what management can do to ease its effects.

One obvious thing employers can do to ease the trauma of firing is to provide sufficient notice. Just what constitutes sufficient notice depends primarily on the nature of the job, the skill involved, the availability of similar jobs, and the longevity of employees. Where employers have reason to suspect that employees will react to notice of their terminations in a hostile, destructive way, "sufficient notice" might merely take the form of severance pay. Ideally, the length of notice should be spelled out in a work contract. Even when it is not, management still has responsibilities in this area.

For most people who have to do it, firing a worker is painfully difficult, at times impossible. In part to help managers to perform the dirty job of terminating, enlightened organizations are enlisting the services of displacement companies. For a fee the displacement company sends in a counselor who assists the displaced employee to assess personal strengths and weaknesses, analyze the causes of the dismissal, and start planning a job search. This makes the distasteful task of firing a little more palatable than it would otherwise be. And, to be sure, in such lawsuit-loony times as ours, it protects the company from being sued by the seasoned, middle-aged executive who may feel trifled with. Self-serving interests notwithstanding, companies utilizing experts with terminations show more than imagination. They deserve recognition for their humanitarian attempt to ease the anguish of those who must fire and help

those terminated salvage both their interrupted careers and their self-respect.

Today—with the frequency of plant shutdowns and relocations, sizable layoffs, and increasing automation—moral management requires careful study of responsibilities to workers in times of termination.[15] It is crucial to remember that termination affects not only workers but their families and the larger social community as well. It is impossible here to specify further what measures can or should be taken to ease the effects of displacement. Different circumstances will suggest different approaches. In some instances, job retraining might be appropriate, together with adequate notice and sufficient severance pay. Where mergers are involved, firms probably should notify workers well in advance and provide them with alternatives. Whatever the approach, the point remains that when firms terminate workers, serious moral questions regarding fair treatment arise.

Wages

Every employer faces the problem of setting wage rates and establishing salaries. From the moral point of view it is very easy to say that firms should pay a fair and just wage, but what constitutes such a wage? There are so many variables involved that no one can say with mathematical precision what a person should be paid for a job. The contribution to the firm, the market for labor and products, the competitive position of the company, the bargaining power of the firm and unions, seasonal fluctuations, and individual needs all conspire to make a simple answer to the fair and just wage issue impossible.

The impossibility of precisely determining a fair wage, however, does not mean that employers may pay workers anything they choose. In general, because work functions to fill human needs, employers should seek to pay a wage that significantly helps individuals satisfy their basic needs. Obviously, this directive is vague. A wage of significant help in one case may be rather meager in another. Moreover, factors sometimes impinge on the employer's ability to pay an ideal wage. But the issue of a *fair wage* is not as morally insoluble as it appears to be.

We can isolate a number of factors that bear on fairness. None of these alone is enough to determine a fair wage; indeed, all of them taken together can't guarantee it. But introducing these factors minimizes the chances of setting unfair wages and salaries and provides the well-intentioned business manager with some ethical guidelines.

1. *What is the prevailing wage in the industry?* Although this factor is not foolproof, or even a moral barometer, the salaries similar positions in the industry earn can provide some direction for arriving at a fair wage.

2. *What is the community wage level?* This point recognizes that some communities have a higher cost of living than others. New York City, for example, is more expensive to live in than St. Louis. The cost of living relates to basic maintenance needs and must be considered very seriously in establishing a wage. To ignore the cost of living would be to seriously jeopardize worker welfare.

3. *What is the nature of the job itself?* Some jobs require more training, experience, and education than others. Some are physically or emotionally more demanding. Some jobs are downright dangerous; others socially undesirable. Risky or unskilled jobs often attract the least educated and the most desperate for work, thus occasioning worker exploitation. Although it is impossible to draw a precise correlation between the nature of the job and what someone should be paid, a relationship exists that must be taken into account.

4. *Is the job secure?* A job that promises little or no security offends a basic worker need. In such cases employers should seek to compensate workers for this deprivation. Compensation could take the form of higher pay, fringe benefits, or a sensible distribution of the two. On the other hand, guarantees of job security are grounds for wage compromises by labor.

5. *What are the employer's financial capabilities?* What can the organization afford to pay? A company's profit margin may be so narrow that it cannot afford to pay higher than a minimum wage. Another's may be so large that it can easily afford to pay more than it does.

6. *What is the law?* Federal law requires that businesses pay at least minimum wage. Even when a particular business is exempt from the law, this minimum can serve as a guide in setting wages. At the same time, of course, one can satisfy the minimum requirements of the law and still not act morally. Considering all factors involved, not just legislative guidelines, will help businesspeople set fair wages.

Naturally there are other factors that employers should consider in determining wages. Some of these should include supply and demand, the wage philosophy of the firm, and comparative rates of various key jobs within the organization.

Equally important in determining what the wage will be is *how* the wage is established. The fairness of a wage is largely determined by a fair work contract. Just what makes up a fair work contract, in turn, demands a consideration of how the contract was wrought. Was it arbitrarily imposed? Did management unilaterally draw up a contract and present it to workers on a take-it-or-leave-it basis? Did a union present it to management with a take-it-or-else ultimatum? Or was the contract arrived at through mutual consent of employer and employee? Answering these questions will help to determine the fairness of a contract and, by implication, the fairness of the wage.

Invariably the fairness of a work contract hinges on free and fair negotiations, which exhibit several characteristics. Fair negotiations must be representative of the interests of those persons directly concerned and sometimes of persons indirectly concerned. All parties should enjoy the freedom to express themselves openly without coercion or fear of reprisal. And they should operate in good faith, carefully avoiding the use of fraud, deceit, power, or institutional blackmail in effecting agreements.

In sum, a consideration of the factors upon which a wage is based and of the procedure that was followed in establishing the wage usually determines the fairness of the wage, which is the primary moral concern in discussions about wages. Establishing wages in this way will positively affect work environment by removing a potential cause of job dissatisfaction. Just as important, wages so established go a long way toward helping management discharge its responsibilities to employees.

ORGANIZATIONAL INFLUENCE IN PRIVATE LIVES

Today privacy is widely acknowledged to be a fundamental right, and clearly corporate behavior and policies often pose a threat to it, especially in the case of employees. We are all familiar with bosses who unhesitatingly rummage through the files of their workers, even when they are marked "Private," and we know of companies that, on various grounds, eavesdrop on their employees' phone calls. Equally important is the way in which organizations can influence behavior that ought properly be left to the discretion of their employees.

There is, however, no consensus among philosophers or lawyers with regard to how to define the right to privacy, how far this right extends, and how to balance it against other rights. All of us would agree, nonetheless, that there are certain definite areas of our lives that we have a clear right to keep private, and that we need to have our privacy respected if we are to function as complete, self-governing

entities. Particularly important is our right to make personal decisions autonomously, free from the illegitimate influence of our employer.

Even when a genuine privacy right is identified, the strength of that right will depend on circumstances—in particular, on competing rights and interests. The right to privacy is not absolute. Corporations and other organizations often have legitimate interests that may conflict with the privacy rights of employees. Determining when organizational infringement on a person's private sphere is morally justifiable is, of course, precisely the question at issue here.

Consider the case of Virginia Rulon-Miller, an IBM sales manager who was demoted for dating a sales executive with a competing company. Even though IBM's decision was based on written policy governing conflicts of interest, a California jury decided that her privacy had been invaded. It awarded her $300,000.

As a general rule, whenever an organization infringes on what can reasonably be considered the personal sphere of an individual, it bears the burden of establishing the legitimacy of that infringement. The fact that a firm thinks an action or policy is justifiable does not, of course, prove that it is. The firm must establish both that it has some legitimate interest at stake and that the steps it is taking to protect that interest are reasonable and morally permissible. But what are the areas of legitimate organizational influence over the individual?

Legitimate and Illegitimate Influence

The work contract; the firm's responsibilities to owners, consumers, and society at large; and the purpose of the firm itself all support the proposition that the firm is legitimately interested in whatever significantly influences work performance. But no precise definition of a significant influence on work performance can be given because the connection between an act or policy and the job is often fuzzy. Take, for example, the area of dress. Ace Construction seems to have a legitimate interest in the kind of shoes Doug Bell wears while framing its houses because the quality of the shoes could affect his safety and job performance as well as the firm's liability. On the other hand, whether executive Margaret Rheingold may forbid her secretary Peg Morrison to wear slacks or a pantsuit to the office is not as clear. Does wearing a pantsuit significantly affect the work that Morrison does? Maybe so. Perhaps good public relations underlies Rheingold's demands. On the other hand, maybe her demands are narrowminded, provincial, and idiosyncratic.

The same rule applies to off-the-job conduct. What occurs off the job might relate significantly to the job. For example, how would you decide the following case?

In an off-the-job fight, a plant guard drew his gun on his antagonist. Although no one was injured, when the guard's employer learned of the incident, he viewed it as grounds for dismissal. He reasoned that such an action indicated a lack of judgment on the part of the guard in his use of firearms. Do you think the employer had a right to fire the guard under these circumstances? The courts did.

By contrast, consider the employee who sold a small amount of marijuana to an undercover agent or the employee who made obscene phone calls to the teenage daughter of a client. Their employers fired them, only to have the employees reinstated by arbitrators or the courts.

Then there's the amorphous area of company image. Determining where organizational image ends and individual privacy begins isn't always easy. For example, the political activities of a firm's corporate executive could significantly affect the image a firm wishes to project. On the other hand, what an obscure worker on the firm's assembly line does politically might have a comparatively insignificant impact on the company's image.

Companies and other organizations have an interest in protecting their good names. The off-duty conduct of employees might damage an organization's reputation, but in practice this is often hard to establish. For example, two IRS agents were suspended for "mooning" a group of women after leaving a bar. Would you agree with their suspension? An arbitrator didn't and revoked it. He couldn't see that their conduct damaged the IRS's reputation.[16]

Obviously we can't spell out exactly when off-duty conduct affects the company image in some major way, any more than we can say precisely what constitutes a significant influence on job performance. But that doesn't prevent us from being able to judge that in many cases organizations clearly step beyond legitimate boundaries and interfere with what should properly be personal decisions by their employees. This interference can take many forms, but we'll discuss two: one traditional, the other modern.

Involvement in Civic Activities. Business and other organizations have traditionally encouraged or pressured employees to participate in seemingly public-spirited activities off the job—presumably, in order to enhance the image of the company. Sometimes, for instance, organizations urge employees to participate in civic activities such as running for the local school board or heading up a commission on the arts. At other times business will encourage employees to join civic service organizations such as Kiwanis, Lions, or Rotary. Still other times, firms may encourage and even compel employees to contribute to charities. Not too long ago a newspaper reported that an office worker was fired for not contributing more than $10 to the United Way. Such a "meager" contribution violated the firm's policy of requiring each employee to give the equivalent of an hour's pay each month. For this employee, a $2.30 an hour desk clerk, the donation would have amounted to $27.60. True, in this case the firm compelled workers to contribute; in many other instances organizational "urgings" or "suggestions" have the impact of orders.

In 1979, members of the Army Band won a suit claiming that the posting of soldiers' names who had not contributed to the United Way constituted coercion. The federal judge who heard the case not only addressed the soldiers' specific complaint but barred all federal departments from setting 100 percent participation goals, holding group meetings to raise money, or using supervisors as fund collectors. His ruling also prohibited making noncontributors return their payroll-deduction cards and restricted the cards of contributors to personnel use. Although this ruling may someday limit the scope of fund-raising practices in other organizations, so far it has not.

Attempts by companies to influence off-the-job behavior often constitute invasions of privacy, specifically the privacy of personal decisions. By explicitly or implicitly requiring employees to associate themselves with a particular activity, group, or cause, firms are telling workers what to believe, what values to hold, and what goals to seek outside work.

In recent years company interference has taken a more subtle form. Modern psychology has made us aware that most people never realize their potential for perceiving, thinking, feeling, creating, and experiencing. Attempts to enlarge the potential for personal growth have resulted in the human potential movement. The focus of this movement is on developing ways to help people lower their defenses, remove their masks, become more aware and open to experience, feel more deeply, express themselves more effectively, be more creative, and become everything they can be.[17] The human potential movement has affected virtually every aspect of contemporary life, business included, as has one

of its most important tools, intensive group experience.

Intensive Group Experience. Intensive group experience goes by various names such as sensitivity training groups, encounter groups, T-groups, awareness groups, creativity groups, and workshops. Industry frequently employs a form of intensive group experience called team-building groups in order to facilitate the attainment of production and related goals as well as to provide opportunities for improved human relations and personal growth.[18] Whatever form it takes, the intensive group experience brings together a group of people who through various exercises attempt to realize the goals of the human potential movement.

Although the potential benefits of such experiences in the workplace are exciting, especially in terms of filling higher-level needs, they nevertheless pose a threat to psychic privacy. This occurs when groups lay bare a participant's innermost feelings. Although this doesn't always occur, it can. When it does, privacy can be violated.

Obviously, as with most questions about organizational interference with individual privacy, the issue of voluntary participation arises. When employees are genuinely free to participate or not, then such group sessions are provided by management primarily as a means of job enrichment and function as legitimate vehicles to job satisfaction. But where coercion exists, infringement on personal decision making arises, and we must be morally concerned. The coercion may take an oppressive form, as when employers demand that employees participate in such group activities. At other times it can take a subtle form, for example, when participation in such groups becomes an unwritten prerequisite for job promotion. Sometimes the coercion can take an apparently munificent form, as when employers—rather than discharging workers for reprehensible behavior—order participation in an encounter group. Whatever the form, the presence of coercion raises moral concerns relative to privacy. In the next section, we look at the issue of privacy in relation to organizational efforts to obtain information about employees.

OBTAINING INFORMATION

It's no secret that firms frequently seek, store, or communicate information about employees without their consent. Thus, without consulting or informing its employees, a firm bugs employee lounges, hoping to discover who's responsible for the widespread pilfering that's been occurring. Another firm uses a managerial grapevine: Supervisors meet once a month to exchange anecdotal material about employees, some of it obtained in confidence, all of it gathered with the hope of anticipating potential troublemakers. Still another company keeps detailed files on the personal lives of its employees to ensure compatibility with organizational image and reputation. Of special interest to us here are two common practices organizations engage in: subjecting employees to various tests, and monitoring employees on the job to discover sundry information. Before beginning, however, a word is in order about the concept of "informed consent" and how it connects with these topics.

Informed Consent

Certainly no employee is ever "compelled" to take a lie-detector test in the sense that someone puts a loaded revolver to the person's head and says, "Take the test or else." But compulsion, like freedom, comes in degrees. Although an employee may not be compelled to take a test in the same way that a prisoner of war, for example, is compelled to cooperate with a captor, enough coercion may be present to significantly diminish the worker's capacity to consent freely to privacy-invading procedures. Indeed, coercing some-

one to behave against the person's will is a grave violation of personal autonomy.

The critical issue in the information-gathering techniques we will sketch is not whether workers agree or consent to participate in them. Obviously if workers sit for a lie-detector test, for example, they agree to do so. But was their agreement or consent *informed*—that is, valid or legitimate? That's the issue, and we are assuming that it is altogether reasonable to raise it because information collected on workers is often intimately personal and private and, when used carelessly, can injure them.

Informed consent implies deliberation and free choice. This means that workers must understand what they are agreeing to, including its full ramifications, and must voluntarily choose it. Deliberation requires not only the availability of facts but also a full understanding of them. Workers must be allowed to deliberate on the basis of enough *usable* information—information that they can understand. This is precisely why professor of politics Christopher Pyle insists that polygraphers be required to give subjects the following warning:

> Before you waive your rights, you should know that many decent people have come out of these interviews feeling demeaned.
> You should also know that your superior or personnel manager will receive my report and, if he is typical, will rarely risk his career by employing a person who has damaging information of any kind in his record. If you reveal embarrassing information, it may remain in somebody's file for years and you can never be sure who will see it or use it against you. And you should know that polygraphers have been known to wrongly accuse more than 10 percent of those they question.[19]

But usable information is not of itself enough to guarantee informed consent. Free choice is also important—the *consent* part is as significant as the *informed* part of informed consent.

Everyone agrees that for consent to be legitimate, it must be voluntary. Workers must willingly agree to the privacy-invasion procedure. This in turn means that workers must be in a position to act voluntarily with respect to the procedures. One big factor that affects the voluntariness of consent is the pressures, expressed and implied, exerted on employees to conform to organizational policy. These pressures often elicit employee behavior based more on the worker's perception of organizational expectation than on personal preference. The structure and dynamics of the organization can function to exact conformity among its members. When these pressures to conform are reinforced with implicit reprisals, they can effectively undercut the voluntariness of consent. Thus, employers who ignore organizational pressures on workers to comply with privacy-invading procedures can misinterpret consent to a lie-detector test, for example, as voluntary, when it is not.

Polygraph Tests

When an individual is disturbed by a question, certain detectable physiological changes occur in the person. The person's heart may begin to race, blood pressure may rise, respiration may increase. The polygraph is an instrument that simultaneously records changes in these physiological processes and, thus, is often used in lie detection.

More than 20 percent of the country's employers routinely administer polygraph tests to their employees and use the results to hire and fire. Businesses cite several reasons for their use of the polygraph to detect lying. First, the polygraph is a fast and economical way to verify the information provided by a job applicant. Lying on résumés is common, and as the nation's population becomes pro-

gressively mobile, more and more individuals are seeking employment outside the areas where they grew up. Sometimes they haven't even lived in the community where they are seeking work long enough to establish verifiable records. For small businesses the cost for running background checks on such applicants can be prohibitive. In contrast, for a mere $80 or $90, the polygraph supposedly can give employers all the answers they need about the applicant.

A second reason for the growing use of the polygraph in business concerns the staggering annual losses companies suffer through in-house theft. The polygraph, say its supporters, allows employers to identify dishonest employees, or likely ones.

Third, companies argue that in certain decentralized retail operations like small chain groceries, the use of polygraphs permits business to abolish audits and oppressive controls. They say the use of polygraphs actually increases workers' freedom.

Fourth, employers say the polygraph is a good way to screen candidates for employment. So used it can help reveal personal philosophy, behavioral patterns, or character traits incompatible with the organization's purpose, function, and image.[20]

Relevant to the morality of polygraph use in the workplace are three major assumptions made by its supporters.[21] First, it's assumed that lying triggers an involuntary distinctive response that truth telling does not. But this is not necessarily the case. What the polygraph can and does do is to record that the respondent was more disturbed by one question than by another. But it cannot determine *why* the person was disturbed. Perhaps the question made the person feel guilty or angry or frightened. But deception does not necessarily lurk behind the emotional response.

A classic case that makes the point involved Floyd Fay of Toledo, Ohio, who in 1978 was sentenced to life for murder, in part, on the basis of having failed two polygraph tests.

The tests included "control" questions like "Before the age of twenty-five, did you ever think of hurting someone for revenge?" Because Fay's heart beat harder and his palms perspired more when he was asked about the crime than when asked about the "control" question, he was regarded as "deceptive." Fay spent two years in jail before the real killers confessed.

Second, it is assumed that polygraphs are extraordinarily accurate. Lynn March, president of the American Polygraph Association, says that "when administered correctly by qualified operators, the tests are accurate more than 90 percent of the time."[22] F. Lee Bailey, the device's most celebrated enthusiast, treats the lie detector almost as an infallible truth machine. But David T. Lykken, a psychiatry professor and author of *A Tremor in the Blood: Uses and Abuses of the Lie Detector*, claims that these boasts are not borne out by three scientifically credible studies of the accuracy of polygraphs used on actual criminal suspects. The accuracies obtained by qualified operators in these experiments were 63 percent, 39 percent, and 55 percent.[23] Whether the polygraph is accurate 90 percent of the time or less than that, there is no certainty that a person is or is not telling the truth.

The third major assumption about polygraphs is that they cannot be beaten. Lykken, for one, suggests otherwise. The easiest way to beat the polygraph, the psychiatrist claims, is by "augmenting" your response to the control question by some form of covert self-stimulation, like biting your tongue. He says Fay taught some augmenting techniques to twenty-seven fellow inmates who were charged with smuggling drugs. Twenty-three of them subsequently beat the lie detector.

If there is a question about the polygraph's validity, then serious moral questions arise about its fairness. And if, by even the most generous estimates, the polygraph has 90 percent accuracy, then questions of fairness and noninjury arise concerning the inno-cents judged guilty and the guilty judged innocent.

Beyond this, polygraphs infringe on privacy. As professor of politics Christopher Pyle says, they violate "the privacy of beliefs and associations, the freedom from unreasonable searches, the privilege against self-accusation, and the presumption of innocence."[24] This does not mean that employers never have the right to abridge privacy or that employees never have an obligation to reveal themselves. In cases of excessive in-house theft, employers may be justified in using a polygraph as a last resort. But the threat to privacy remains, together with the other moral concerns that shroud polygraph use. And even if companies have moral justification for resorting to polygraphs, they must be judicious in how they administer them.

The use of polygraphs in business often creates the sinister impression among workers that they will be judged by a machine or that they are being presumed guilty until the machine proves them otherwise. Giving such impressions raises serious moral questions of justice and injury to worker morale. Moreover, casually regarding the polygraph as just another screening device or inventory-control measure may invite employers to extend the sphere of questioning and investigation to non-job-related issues, such as marriage, sex, politics, religion, and so on.

The moral concerns embedded in the use of polygraphs suggest three points to consider in evaluating the use of polygraphs in the workplace:

1. The information the organization seeks should be clearly and significantly related to the job. This harkens back to a determination of the legitimate areas of organizational influence over the individual.

2. Because the polygraph intrudes on psychic freedom, those applying it should consider whether they have compelling job-related reasons for so doing. Some persons contend that among the reasons must be the

fact that the polygraph represents the *only* way that the organization can get information about a significant job-related matter. They claim that a firm should think seriously about the morality of subjecting employees to polygraph tests without having first exhausted all other means of preventing pilferage and discovering its source.

3. We must be concerned with how the polygraph is being used, what information it's gathering, who has access to this information, and how it will be disposed of.

All of this notwithstanding, it's conceivable, as some contend, that individuals always retain the right to protect their privacy and refuse to submit to such tests.

Personality Tests

Companies often wish to determine whether prospective employees are emotionally mature and sociable and whether they would fit in with the organization; so they sometimes administer personality tests. These tests concern us because they are character probes that can reveal highly personal information, perhaps more so than polygraph tests. In brief, personality tests can invade privacy by collecting data about employees without their full consent. Consent is usually lacking because, like polygraphs, personality tests rarely are taken on a strictly voluntary basis. They generally function as part of a battery of tests that job applicants must take if they wish to be considered for a position.

Used properly, personality tests serve two purposes in the workplace. First, they help screen applicants for jobs by indicating areas of adequacy and inadequacy. Second, in theory, they simplify the complexities of business life by reducing the amount of decision making involved in determining whether a person can relate to others. For example, if a firm knows that Frank Smith is an introvert, it would hardly place him in personnel or public relations.

But one key premise underlying the use of such tests is highly questionable. That premise is that all individuals can usefully and validly be placed into a relatively small number of categories in terms of personality and character traits. In other words, people are pure personality types, such as the classic introvert or extrovert. In fact, the pure type is the exception, not the rule. Most of us are neither purely introvert nor purely extrovert. We possess a mixture of these traits in varying degrees.[25] When organizations attempt to categorize employees, they force them into oversimplified and artificial arrangements that may be fair neither to employees nor to the firms.

Personality tests also screen for organizational compatibility, which has serious moral implications. From the firm's view, it is ironic that such a function can eliminate prospective employees whose creativity may be exactly what the firm needs. Thus personality tests can actually injure the firm. More important, when used in this way personality tests elicit a pressing moral issue in the employer-employee relationship: conformity of the individual to organizational ideals.

About thirty years ago William H. Whyte, Jr., wrote *The Organization Man*,[26] still a widely read work. In this book, Whyte observed the growing tendency in business to elevate organizational conformity and loyalty to the level of moral imperatives. Organization people, argued Whyte, are ones who dedicate themselves totally to the firm; unquestioningly accept its maxims, standards, and ethos; and unflinchingly believe that ideas and creativity emanate not from the individual but from the group. In other words, Whyte shows concern not only for the organizational threat to individual autonomy but also for individuals using the organizational ethic to rationalize away a sense of personal responsibility.

In 1957, one year after Whyte's publication, Chris Argyris published *Personality and the Organization*, which gave some credence to

Whyte's organization man theory. Argyris's study dealt with psychological problems of work, specifically alienation, frustration, and suppression of self-actualization. Argyris concluded that the basic goals of individuals and organizations are at odds. This incongruence creates conflict, frustration, and failure for the participants. In other words, according to Argyris, blind conformity to organizational standards can be self-destructive, and the organization that requires it cultivates this subversion of personal meaning and self-fulfillment.

We mention Whyte's organization man theory and Argyris's psychological findings not to characterize business as a thoroughgoing vehicle of conformity. On the contrary, there are a number of indications that business today significantly fosters individualism. But organizations by nature represent a danger to individual freedom and independence. When personality tests are used to screen for conformity to organizational values, goals, and philosophy, they can catalyze this natural tendency into a full-blown assault on the human personality. For this reason the use of such tests always raises moral concerns.

Monitoring Employees on the Job

Where in-house theft, sabotage, or other behavior that threatens the firm occurs, organizations frequently install monitoring devices both to apprehend employees responsible and to curtail the problem. These devices take the forms of mirrors, cameras, or electronic devices. They can be used to monitor either suspected trouble spots or private acts. As with personality and polygraph tests monitoring can gather information about employees without their informed consent.

Organizations frequently confuse notification of such practices with employee consent, but notification does not constitute consent. When employee rest rooms, dressing rooms, locker rooms, and other private places are being bugged, an obvious and serious threat to privacy exists—posted notices notwithstanding. It's true that in some cases surveillance devices may be the only way to apprehend the guilty. Nevertheless, they can do more harm than good by violating the vast majority of innocent employees. An evaluation of the morality of using these devices must include a careful analysis of the circumstances under which they're used. Even when the circumstances are extraordinary, some persons argue that monitoring employees without their full and informed consent is not justified. Obviously even more serious moral questions arise when monitoring devices are not used exclusively for the purposes intended but for cajoling, harassing, or snooping on employees.

Drug Testing

With the NCAA's banning of college football players from 1987 postseason bowl competition as a result of steroid testing, and with President Reagan's proposal to test federal employees for cocaine and other illicit drugs and his encouraging of private industry to do the same, drug testing has generated wide controversy. In principle, though, testing employees to determine whether they are using illegal drugs raises the same questions that we have discussed concerning other tests: Is there "informed consent"? How reliable are the tests? Is testing really pertinent to the job in question? Are the interests of the firm significant enough to justify encroaching on the privacy of the individual? But rather than reiterate the above issues, all of which are important and relevant, we offer four additional observations:

1. The issue of drug testing by corporations and other organizations arises in the broader context of the problem in America today of drug abuse (which includes the abuse not just of illegal "street drugs," but of

alcohol and prescription medicines as well). To discuss this problem intelligently, one needs good information, reliable statistics, and sociological insight, yet these are notoriously hard to come by. For instance, 1988 was a bumper year for news stories on drugs, particularly cocaine and crack. *Newsweek* ran several alarming cover stories on drug abuse, and hours of the year's nightly network news were given over to sensationalistic drug related stories. Likewise, many politicians found it advantageous to portray themselves as battling courageously against a rising flood of drugs. Yet this coverage was at best superficial, at worst misleading and even hysterical. For example, the public was presented with no hard evidence that substance abuse was a greater problem in 1988 than in, say, 1978.

We do not wish to minimize the problems that drug abuse can pose for business and other organizations—some writers believe that 10 percent of the work force is addicted to alcohol or drugs[27]—but rather to observe that excessive media attention and political posturing can create a false sense of crisis, leading people perhaps to advocate unnecessarily extreme measures.

2. Drugs differ, so one must carefully consider both what drugs one is testing for and why. Steroids, for instance, are a problem for the NCAA, but not for IBM. In addition, drug testing can only be defensible when it is really pertinent to employee performance and when there is a lot at stake. Testing airline pilots for alcohol consumption is one thing; testing the luggage crews is something else. To go on a "fishing trip" in search of possible employee drug abuse, when there is no evidence of a problem or of a significant danger, seems unreasonable.

3. Drug abuse by an individual is a serious problem, calling for medical and psychological assistance, rather than punitive action. The moral assessment of any program of drug testing must rest in part on the potential consequences for those taking the test—will they face immediate dismissal and potential criminal proceedings, or therapy and a chance to retain their positions? To put the issue another way, when an organization initiates a testing program, does it approach this as a kind of police function? Or is it responsive to the needs and problems of individual employees? Some argue that voluntary, nonpunitive drug-assistance programs are far more cost effective for companies, in any case, than testing initiatives.[28]

4. Any drug-testing program, assuming it is warranted, must be careful to respect the dignity and rights of the persons to be tested. "Due process" must also be followed, including advance notification of testing as well as procedures for retesting and appealing test results. All possible steps should be taken to ensure individual privacy.

WORKING CONDITIONS

In a broad sense, the conditions under which people work include personnel policies and procedures, as well as the extent to which an organization is committed to respecting the rights and privacy of its employees. In this section, however, we will examine three other aspects of working conditions: health and safety on the job, styles of management, and the organization's maternity and day-care arrangements.

Health and Safety

By some estimates, 95 percent of the nation's 10,000 or so grain elevators have the ingredients necessary for a major explosion. The difficulty of the problem is underscored by studies that suggest that even tiny amounts of dust—possibly as little as $\frac{1}{64}$ of an inch—can be dangerous. When air and highly flammable grain dust come together in a confined space, as in a grain elevator, an explosion can all too easily occur. Ask the workers in the

Galveston elevator that exploded in 1980. A Federal grand jury in Texas subsequently handed down the first criminal indictments ever in a grain-elevator explosion, against two former supervisors at the Galveston operation.[29] The case is a dramatic example of how some workplaces can threaten the safety of employees.

Behind the glitter and glow of the burgeoning electronics industry, to take another example, lurk health hazards for workers. Corrosive hydrochloric and hydrofluoric acids, poisons such as arsine gas and cyanide, known or suspected carcinogens like vinyl chloride and trichloroethylene, and other toxic chemicals are indispensable to the fabrication of computer chips. It is not surprising, then, that industrial hygienists report that production workers in the San Francisco Bay area's Silicon Valley, a world center of the semiconductor industry, are increasingly suffering illnesses caused by chemical exposures. In an industry whose profits are as dazzling as its accomplishments, most of these workers get little more than minimum wage. Many of them speak little English and may not even be aware that they are working with suspected carcinogens and toxic substances with possible long-range health and reproductive effects. Even if they could understand English well, it probably wouldn't help, for in 1981 the electronic lobby helped defeat a California Assembly bill that would have required companies to give workers written warnings on each chemical they handle.[30]

Despite legislation the scope of occupational hazards remains awesome and generally unrecognized. A Mt. Sinai Hospital report, for example, estimates that occupational disease is the fourth-ranked cause of death in New York State, killing between 4,686 and 6,592 employees each year.[31] Of 80 million workers nationwide, there are over 7 million annual work-related diseases and injuries, of which millions are disabling and

many fatal. Estimates of losses run as high as 250 million person-working days, costing $1.5 billion in wages and an annual loss to the gross national product (GNP) of $8 billion.[32] Before presuming that things are getting better, reflect on the fact that the incidence of disabling injuries in manufacturing industries is greater now than it was thirty years ago.

Although the thrust of the 1970 Occupational Safety and Health Act is ". . . to ensure so far as possible every working man and woman in the nation safe and healthful working conditions," implementation of the act has been spotty. Consider the fact that there are fewer than 100 qualified Occupational Safety and Health Administration (OSHA) industrial hygienists and approximately 500 OSHA inspectors for about 4 million workplaces. Add to this that OSHA has established only one permanent standard—for asbestos.

Compounding things is the cozy relationship that seems to be developing between OSHA and industry. Taking issue with OSHA's sometimes aggressive tactics, the Reagan Administration has taken measures that weaken the protective organization. In a widely publicized move, the Administration announced in 1981 that OSHA would target specific industries known to be especially hazardous. While economic, the move has effectively relieved OSHA of one of its most potent weapons—the threat of an unannounced inspection. It has also left unguarded millions of workers in "untargeted" industries. Despite the emphasis on specific industries, the percentage of inspections resulting in citations has dropped compared to 1980. The number of "Serious Citations" has fallen to about half of what it used to be, and "Willful Citations" have plunged even lower. Furthermore, under current policy, regional OSHA offices are encouraged to reduce fines and the number of contested citations. Now any penalty above $10,000 must be approved in Washington. Between April 1981 and March 1982, for example, there were six such fines, compared to one hundred between October 1979 and September 1980.

Has OSHA become a paper tiger? Critics think so. Consider the case of Stephan Golab, a 59-year-old immigrant from Poland who worked for a year stirring tanks of sodium cyanide at the Film Recovery Services plant in Elk Grove, Illinois. On February 10, 1983 he became dizzy from the cyanide fumes, went into convulsions, and died. OSHA then inspected the plant and fined Film Recovery Services $4,855 for twenty safety violations. Later, OSHA cut the fine in half. Contrast this with the actions of the State Attorney General for Cook County, who filed criminal charges. Three company officials were convicted of murder and on fourteen counts of reckless conduct. The company itself was also convicted of manslaughter and reckless conduct and was fined $24,000.

Ironically, employers, who staunchly opposed the creation of OSHA in the first place, are now trying to use the organization as a shield. They argue that the existence of OSHA legally preempts state criminal prosecutions in cases like the above—that is, that it prevents states from imposing stronger civil or criminal penalties on companies for health and safety violations. This legal argument has met with success in some state courts.[33]

One aspect of work life over which OSHA exercises little direct control is the shifts people work. Yet, a team of scientists from Harvard and Stanford Universities believe that the health and productivity of twenty-five million Americans whose work hours change regularly can be measurably improved if employers schedule shift changes to conform with the body's natural and adjustable sleep cycles. They reached this conclusion after studying workers at the Great Salt Lake Chemical and Minerals Corporation plant in Ogden, Utah. Corporate officials commissioned the study after workers kept complaining to management about experiencing insomnia, fatigue, digestive disorders, and falling asleep on the job. The workers had been changing shifts every week, usually to earlier rather than later starting times. The researchers discovered that moving workers to a later shift every three weeks enables them to so adjust that they can sleep when they have to and be alert on the job.

Another aspect of work life, the health implications of which we have only recently begun to appreciate fully, is stress. Three-quarters of Americans say their jobs cause them stress, and stress now accounts for 14 percent of workers' compensation claims and costs business an estimated $150 billion annually.[34] Revamping work environments that produce stress and helping employees learn to cope with stress are among the major health challenges facing us in the 1990s.

Management Styles

How managers conduct themselves on the job can do more to enhance or diminish the work environment than any other single facet of employer-employee relations. Mightily influencing management conduct are the general assumptions managers make about human beings and the subsequent leadership styles they adopt.

For example, the late Douglas McGregor proposed two basic sets of culturally induced assumptions about human beings that he observed in managers.[35] He called these Theories X and Y. According to McGregor, managers who espouse Theory X believe that workers essentially dislike work and will do everything they can to avoid it. Such managers insist that the average person wishes to avoid responsibility, lacks ambition, and values security over everything else. He or she must be coerced and bullied into conformity to organizational objectives.

In contrast, Theory Y managers believe workers basically like work and view it as something natural and potentially enjoyable. Workers are motivated as much by pride and a desire for self-fulfillment as by money and job security. They don't eschew responsibility, but accept and seek it out.

These basic assumptions about human nature can lead to contrasting styles of management. Theory X managers are likely to provide autocratic leadership. They closely shepherd workers by giving orders and directions. They rarely solicit ideas about how tasks should be performed, but tell employees what to do and how to do it. They expect little more of employees than that they follow orders. Theory Y managers, on the other hand, are more likely to be democratic. While informing workers of the tasks to be performed, they also invite new ideas from them about how to do those tasks. They use this information to refine their own ideas about job performance. Theory Y managers can be virtually nondirective. Viewing themselves as resource persons, troubleshooters, and supporters rather than directors of the work force, they can be inclined to leave decisions on work methods to the workers. In either case, X or Y, culturally conditioned views of human nature influence management style.

There is no absolutely correct or incorrect set of assumptions about human nature, nor is there a perfectly "right way" to manage. But that's precisely the point. Moral problems inevitably arise when managers routinize their leadership style regardless of the idiosyncrasies of their employees. Some employees at whatever level respond to and need little managerial orchestration; others need and want close supervision. When managers ignore this, they overlook people's needs and run risks of creating a work atmosphere that's not only hostile to workers but also unconducive to optimum productivity. They invite injustice into the workplace as well, for injustice can arise as much from treating people identically as from treating them unequally. If these problems are to be avoided, it seems that managers must choose a style of leadership suitable to the needs, abilities, and predilections of those in their charge.

More and more critics are charging that American managerial style is too conservative, traditional, and inflexible and that many managers put their personal ambition ahead of everything else. Take the case of Texan H. Ross Perot. A self-made billionaire, Perot became General Motors's largest shareholder and a member of its corporate board when he sold his computer services company, Electronic Data Systems Corporation, to GM in 1984 for $2.5 billion. Two years later GM ousted Perot from the board, buying back his GM stock for $700 million.

Why the buy-back? Observers agree that the fiery Perot was more than GM, one of the most tradition-bound corporations in America, could handle. Perot dared to question long-standing management practices; he would talk to workers on the factory floor about new ideas; and he would shop anonymously at GM dealerships, trying to evaluate customer service. All that was too much for GM. Under the buy-back agreement, Perot isn't supposed to make negative comments about GM, but he does say the corporation is beset by power hungry executives who spend all their time trying to move up the corporate ladder and care little about their product. "Corporate infighting," "management power struggles," "maneuvering and politics and power-grabbing," and "Machiavellian intrigues" are his phrases to describe the reality of corporate life today.[36]

We must be careful about generalizing from the experiences of one person in one company, but Perot's reports tally with too many others' to write him off as a crank. Managers who devote their energies to corporate infighting and personal advancement, and corporations that are too tradition bound to handle strong criticism, even inside the boardroom itself, are real problems. Dealing with them is part of the economic challenge facing America today, as we discussed in Chapter 4. But problems of management style also affect unfavorably employees' working conditions.

Day Care and Maternity Leave

One often overlooked area in discussions of working conditions is the provision of maternity/paternity leave and child-care services for workers with children. The need for day-care services is clearly growing, yet the United States falls behind many industrialized nations in the provision of such services. The situation is even more striking with respect to maternity leave. While at least 117 other countries provide *paid* maternity leave, a California law requiring employers to provide *unpaid* leave and reinstatement of pregnant employees was fought all the way to the Supreme Court before finally being upheld in January 1987.[37] Four other states have joined California in guaranteeing pregnant workers leave and reinstatement in their previous jobs or equivalent positions.

Today females constitute about 45 percent of the paid labor force, a higher figure than at any time in history. While in 1950 only 20 percent of the married women with children under the age of eighteen were in the paid labor force, this number had grown to over 50 percent by 1980. Today two-thirds of all women with children under eighteen work, and only half of those with children under one stay home.[38] And the rise in the employment participation rates of women with small children is expected to continue.[39] Experts anticipate that two-thirds of all new workers through the year 2000 will be women.[40]

Given that women in our society continue to bear the primary responsibility for child rearing, their increasing participation in the paid work force represents a growing demand for reasonable maternity-leave policies and affordable child-care services. Nor is this demand likely to diminish. But despite their need for day care and related child services, many families are unable to make satisfactory child-care arrangements, either because the services are unavailable or for the simple reason that the parents cannot afford them.[41] An estimated five million children are thus left alone without any supervision while their parents work. The need for child-care services is particularly acute among single-parent families, 91 percent of which are headed by women. Single mothers have a higher rate of participation in the labor force than do married mothers. Despite this, many of them are poverty stricken and, hence, unable to pay for satisfactory child-care services.[42]

Very few companies do much to help with employee child care. Campbell's Soup is one of the exceptions. It offers on-site day care, spending over $200,000 annually to subsidize 50 percent of tuition costs at the child-care center for the children of its employees at its corporate headquarters. Procter & Gamble holds priority for 75 percent of the spaces in two off-site centers near its Cincinnati headquarters. It also provides a day-care resource and referral service for the entire community. IBM provides a free nationwide system referral for its 237,000 employees and has helped to develop both the quantity and quality of child-care services where they have been deficient or lacking. Polaroid Corporation provides assistance with child-care costs for permanent employees earning less than $30,000.[43] Despite these examples, the overall corporate record on child care is poor.

Employers are in a good position to provide, or assist in the provision of, child-care services, especially in light of recent cutbacks in federal funding. Few if any employers, however, currently feel under an obligation to offer child-care services, primarily because initiating and maintaining such programs costs money. Yet viewed from a broader perspective, day-care arrangements set up by companies themselves or by several companies together in the same area are socially "cost-effective." With in-house day-care arrangements parents do not have to make special trips to pick up and deposit their children. Since the parents are not far away, they can have more interaction with their children. Depending on the specific organization of work and the firm's flexibility, parents could share in the actual running of the child-care facility itself at assigned intervals during the course of their working day.

Some have argued, moreover, that offering child care as a fringe benefit may prove advantageous for most employers.[44] Such benefits can be cost effective in the narrower sense by decreasing absenteeism, boosting morale and loyalty to the firm, and enhancing productivity. This is an important consideration. Even more important are the underlying moral issues. Let's look briefly at the relevant ethical factors.

First, women have a right to compete on an equal terrain with men. Firms that do not provide at least unpaid maternity leave and reinstatement clearly fail to respect this right. It is doubtful that those who oppose requirements like that of the California law mentioned previously could sincerely universalize their position. Nor have they been able to point to any competing economic considerations strong enough to override women's right of equal opportunity. Whether firms should also provide paid maternity leave is more controversial, although one might argue that paid leave is necessary to give substance to this right. Or one might defend such a policy on the utilitarian ground that it would enhance total social welfare. In fact, many organizations find it in their self-interest to provide paid leave in order to attract better and more-talented employees.

Second, from various ethical perspectives, the development of our potential capacities is a moral ideal—perhaps even a human right. For this reason, or from the point of view of promoting human well-being, many theorists would contend that women should not be forced to choose between childbearing and the successful pursuit of their careers. Nor should they be forced to reduce the quality of their commitment either to their children or to their careers. If circumstances of work force them to do so, and if those circumstances could reasonably be changed, then we have not lived up to the ideal of treating those women as persons whose goals are worthy of respect.

Third, while the last two decades have seen many criticisms of, and attempts to move beyond, the traditional male-female division of labor within the family, there can be little doubt that the world of work tends to reproduce those patterns. For instance, as we mentioned earlier in this chapter, men who leave work to help raise children often face enormous hurdles when returning to the job market. It seems clear, though, that many fathers today feel hampered by societal work arrangements that pit meaningful career advancement against a fully developed family life. Enhanced opportunities for part-time employment and job sharing, along with generous *parental* leave arrangements and flexible, affordable, and accessible firm-sponsored child-care facilities could enable individuals, both fathers and mothers, to achieve a more personally desirable balance between paid work and family relations.

The moral value here is not to promote any single vision of the good life, but rather to permit individuals, couples, and families as much autonomy as possible, given other social goals, to define the good life for themselves, and to seek the arrangement of work and personal relations that makes that life possible. Firm-affiliated child-care services and other institutional arrangements that better accommodate parental needs can clearly play a key role in the overall redesigning of work in a way that enhances the worker's well-being. We will discuss that need in the following section.

REDESIGNING WORK

In an earlier chapter we looked at alienation under capitalism and changing attitudes toward work in America. And it remains true that many, perhaps even most, employees—at all levels—are dissatisfied with their jobs to a greater or lesser extent. Any investigation of the moral issues arising in and around the workplace and any discussion of the challenges facing business today must confront this basic problem and consider ways of improving the quality of work life.

Dissatisfaction on the Job

In the early 1970s the government conducted a study of work in America, whose basic findings are still relevant today.[45] The study identified three chief sources of worker dissatisfaction. The first concerned industry's preoccupation with quantity, not quality; the rigidity of rules and regulations; and the fracturing of work into the smallest possible tasks together with the monotonous repetition of doing these tasks. The second source of dissatisfaction concerned the lack of opportunities to be one's own boss. The third source of dissatisfaction concerned "bigness": more people work for large corporations now than ever before. Other studies since then have cited workers' feelings of powerlessness, meaninglessness, isolation, and self-estrangement or depersonalization.

The *Work in America* survey reported similar feelings in the managerial ranks. One of three middle managers at that time was willing to join a union. A similar study by the American Management Association found that about half of the middle managers surveyed favored a change in the National Labor Relations Act to allow collective bargaining between middle and top management. Moreover, just as industrial workers voiced general complaints about work, so did middle managers. Some objected to the little influence they had in their organizations, and others objected to the organization's goals, policies, and ways of operating. Still other managers complained about tension, frustration, and infighting that intraorganizational competition can breed. Beyond these, the *Work in America* survey reported that many managers felt like cogs in a machine, like parts that could and would be replaced when a better part came along.

Recent studies confirm that an increasing number of workers at all occupational levels express declining confidence and satisfaction with employer policies and practices and with the behavior of top management.[46] If industry is to improve productive capacity and be more competitive, it must seriously confront these attitudes and the sources of employee dissatisfaction. It must devise ways to make work more satisfying, thereby motivating workers to be more productive, and it must make certain work-practice reforms that will improve the quality of work life.

As early as the 1920s, researchers began to realize that workers would be more productive if management met those needs that money cannot buy. Managers at the Hawthorne factory of Western Electric Company were conducting experiments to determine the effect of the work environment on worker productivity. In the literature of work motivation, these studies have become known as the Hawthorne studies. What they discovered has been termed the "Hawthorne effect."

Researchers in the Hawthorne studies chose a few employees to work in an experimental area, apart from the thousands of employees in the rest of the factory. Every effort was made to improve working conditions, from painting walls a cheerful color to making lights brighter. Worker productivity increased with each improvement.

Then experimenters decided to reverse the process. For example, lights were made dimmer. To everyone's surprise, productivity continued to increase.

The conclusion researchers drew was that workers were producing more because they were receiving attention. Instead of feeling that they were cogs in the organizational wheel, they felt important and recognized. The attention had the effect of heightening their sense of personal identity and feeling of control over their work environment. Recognition of this represents an insight into how management can effectively discharge its responsibilities to employees in terms of worker motivation and job satisfaction and meet its obligation to increase productivity.

More recent studies tend to corroborate and deepen the application of the Hawthorne effect. In an important study conducted to shed light on the problem of poor worker motivation, Frederick Herzberg discovered that factors producing job satisfaction differed from those producing job dissatisfaction. Herzberg found that job dissatisfaction frequently arises from extrinsic problems relating to pay, worker supervision, working conditions, and leadership styles. But resolving those extrinsic problems does not necessarily produce satisfied workers. They can still express little or no job satisfaction. The reason, Herzberg contends, is that worker satisfaction is a function of work content, and work satisfaction depends on such factors as a sense of accomplishment, responsibility, recognition, self-development, and self-expression.

Other surveys lend credence to Herzberg's findings. When 1,533 workers at all occupational levels were asked to rank in order of importance to them some twenty-five aspects of work, they listed: interesting work; sufficient help, support, and information to accomplish the job; enough authority to carry out the work; good pay; opportunity to develop special skills; job security; and seeing the results of their work.[47]

To dramatize the moral import of the work design question, consider a study conducted by the Institute of Social Research. In studying a cross section of American workers, the Institute found numerous mental health problems directly attributable to lack of job satisfaction. These problems included psy-chosomatic diseases such as ulcers and hypertension, low self-esteem, anxiety, and impaired interpersonal relations.[48] Similarly, in an exhaustive study of industrial workers, A. W. Kornhauser found that about 40 percent of all auto workers exhibited some symptoms of mental health problems related to job satisfaction.[49] In general, studies indicate that greater mental health problems occur in low-status, boring, unchallenging jobs that offer little autonomy. These findings are of particular relevance to today's work force, in which many persons of relatively high educational achievement occupy comparatively low-status jobs.

One of the most intriguing studies done not only suggests a correlation between longevity and job satisfaction but also contends that job satisfaction is the strongest predictor of longevity.[50] The second major factor for longevity is happiness. Both these factors predict longevity better than either the physical health or genetic inheritance of individuals.

The moral thrust of this is that the design of work materially affects the total well-being of workers. This fact alone would make work content and job satisfaction paramount moral concerns. But, of course, there is the additional issue of increasing worker productivity. If we assume that a happier, more contented worker is generally a more productive one, then it follows that business has an obligation to devise ways, in concert with labor and perhaps even government, to improve the quality of work life (QWL).

Quality of Work Life (QWL)

This book isn't the place for determining precisely what QWL measures firms should take. For some firms it may mean providing workers with less supervision and more autonomy. For others it may mean providing work opportunities to develop and refine skills. Still other firms might try to provide workers with greater participation in the conception, design, and execution of their work—that is, with greater responsibility and a deeper sense of achievement. Perhaps all companies ought to examine the impact of technology on job satisfaction. While typically increasing efficiency of operations and eliminating the physical drudgery that plagued yesterday's workers, today's technology sometimes results in repetitive and boring tasks that, in the long run, may inhibit productivity. So serious is this problem that many recommend sweeping reforms and innovations in the workplace aimed at recapturing the spirit, sense of commitment, and enthusiasm of today's workers at all occupational levels.

One purpose of QWL programs is to thaw the antagonistic worker-boss climate that exists in many plants and inhibits production. But the key purpose is to involve workers more fully in the production process by seeking their ideas. Accordingly, QWL programs go by various names: "worker participation," "labor-management teams," "industrial democracy," and so on. In the steel industry, to name one, labor-management participation teams have been used to deal with both quality and productivity challenges and with worker job satisfaction. Bethlehem Steel, for example, now brings outside consultants into its Los Angeles works to hold consciousness-raising seminars for its steelworkers and to induce supervisors to get more teamwork from crews by reducing antagonisms. The results are encouraging: In the first three weeks after the initial seminar ended, daily output on two rolling mills increased by 30 percent.

One very promising response to the need for QWL programs is "quality control circles," which two American personnel consultants introduced to Japanese industries about twenty-five years ago. Now widely used in Japan, the circles consist of committees of workers and supervisors who meet to discuss product quality improvement. Curiously, some U.S. companies are now rediscovering the circle concept. Westinghouse, for one, has established about 150 "quality circles" at 50 locations. By Westinghouse's account, these circles have resulted in changes that have saved the company more than $1 million in two years.

But the only way management can implement such programs is with the full cooperation of workers and their representatives. Investigators believe that the success of QWL programs and other workplace reform efforts over time depends on the ability of the organization to reinforce and sustain high levels of trust. To the extent that it does so, organizational performance can improve.[51]

But if management has an obligation to improve work quality in order to improve productivity and meet worker needs, then workers have an obligation to cooperate in these efforts. Too often, however, workers have resisted these efforts as managerial ploys to reduce the work force or as diversions from "bread-and-butter" issues: wages, job security, overtime, and the like. In effect, labor has reinforced the classical management view that sufficient extrinsic rewards could motivate someone to do almost any job. If management must alter its concept, so must workers. This calls for a less jaundiced view of QWL programs on the part of workers; they should begin seeing these efforts as means of insuring their jobs. After all, the more competitive a company is, the greater the share of the market it will garner, and the more secure will be the worker's job. A classic example can be seen in the case of GM's assembly plant at Tarrytown, New York, which is widely regarded as having highly successful QWL programs.

Back in the early 1970s, Tarrytown was in serious trouble. Rampant absenteeism, poor product quality, and strained labor-management relations all threatened to halt operations. As a result, United Auto Worker (UAW) representatives and plant managers began to meet informally to solve labor problems. From these informal meetings emerged full-scale QWL programs throughout the plant. The core of the Tarrytown program is a three-day orientation seminar for all plant workers. In these meetings, company and union goals are explained, workers are shown the interrelation of various assemblyline jobs, and they are introduced to workers in other departments. At the same time, UAW local and plant management meet regularly to *anticipate* problems before they become unwieldy. Worker input is invited, dress codes are relaxed, and socializing on the job is permitted. As a result, while 135,000 other GM workers were idled by layoffs in the middle of 1980, Tarrytown's full force of 4,600 hourly employees was working nine hours every day, as well as three Saturdays every month. The UAW says it cooperates in the QWL programs because they make jobs more satisfying. For its part, management fosters the programs because they seem to improve productivity. In this case, the ideals of improved job atmosphere and worker job security have meshed with the ideal of increased productivity.

But, unfortunately, these ideals don't always mesh. Sometimes an apparent improvement in quality of work can lead to a decrease in productivity. For example, although diversifying tasks may make work more satisfying, it may hurt both productivity and quality. Japanese carmakers, to cite one case, have effectively reduced the number of rejects on their assembly line not by diversifying but by standardizing the cars produced. Again, Volkswagen has found that its productivity and quality were higher when production consisted solely of the standard Rabbit than when other models were introduced. Job enlargement programs, by definition, add to the variety of tasks the worker is assigned; and job enrichment programs add some of the planning, design, and scheduling to the operative worker's tasks. Both programs tax the abilities of workers and in some cases may slow output and bruise quality. Such instances that involve a conflict of obligations to make work more satisfying and to increase productivity likely will be at the heart of moral

decisions in this area for years to come. To resolve them will require a cooperative effort by labor and management, rooted in the recognition that trade-offs are inevitable.

SUMMARY

1. Writers like David Ewing believe that too many corporations routinely violate the civil liberties of their employees. Historically, this authoritarianism stems from (a) the rise of professional management and personnel engineering and (b) the common-law doctrine that employees can be discharged without cause.

2. Some very successful companies have taken the lead in respecting employees' rights. Corporate profits and efficient management are compatible with a fair workplace environment.

3. Fairness in personnel matters requires, at least, that policies, standards, and decisions affecting workers are directly job related and applied equally.

4. Incomplete or unspecific job descriptions can injure candidates by denying them information they need to reach informed occupational decisions.

5. Ordinarily, questions of sex, race, national origin, and religion are non–job related and thus should not enter into personnel decisions. Education may also be non–job related, as when (a) employers require more formal education than a job demands or (b) employers summarily disqualify a candidate for being "overqualified." Automatically disqualifying a candidate because of a self-selected career interruption raises a question of fairness.

6. A test is valid if it measures precisely what it is designed to determine and reliable when it provides reasonably consistent results. Tests that lack either validity or reliability are unfair. Tests may also be unfair if they are culturally biased or if the

performance they measure does not relate directly to job performance.

7. Most moral concerns in interviewing relate to how the interview is conducted. Interviewers should focus on the humanity of the candidate and avoid allowing their personal biases to color their evaluations.

8. A key issue in promotions is whether job qualification alone should determine who gets promoted. Seniority, or longevity on the job, is not necessarily a measure of either competency or loyalty. The challenge for management is to accommodate its twin responsibilities of promoting on the basis of qualifications and recognizing long-term contributions to the company.

9. Inbreeding, promoting exclusively within the organization, presents challenges similar to those presented by seniority. Nepotism, showing favoritism to relatives or close friends, is not always objectionable, but it may overlook managerial responsibilities to the organization and may result in unfair treatment to other applicants.

10. Most moral issues in disciplining and discharge concern how management carries out these unpleasant tasks. Due process and just cause must operate if treatment is to be fair. Due process refers to specific and systematic means allowed workers for appealing discipline and discharge. To ease the trauma associated with discharge, employers should provide sufficient warning, severance pay, and perhaps "displacement counseling."

11. The factors that bear on the fairness of wages include the prevailing wage in the industry, the community wage level, the nature of the job, the security of the job, the company's financial capabilities, and the law. Especially important is the manner in which the wage is established.

Fairness requires a legitimate work contract, one arrived at through free and fair negotiation.

12. Individuals have a right to privacy, in particular a right to make personal decisions autonomously, free from illegitimate influence. Whenever an organization infringes on an individual's personal sphere, it must justify the reasonableness of that infringement.

13. A firm is legitimately interested in whatever significantly influences job performance, but there is no precise definition of "significant influence." Organizations can invade privacy when they coerce employees to contribute to charities or to participate in so-called intensive group experience.

14. Information-gathering on employees can be highly personal and subject to abuse. The critical issue here is informed consent, which implies deliberation and free choice. Deliberation requires that employees are provided all significant facts concerning the information-gathering procedure and understand their consequences. Free choice means the decision to participate must be voluntary and uncoerced.

15. Polygraph tests, personality tests, drug tests, and the monitoring of employees on the job can intrude into employee privacy. The exact character of these devices, the rationale for using them to gather information in specific circumstances, and the moral costs of doing so must always be carefully evaluated.

16. Health and safety remain of foremost moral concern in the workplace. The scope of occupational hazards, including shift work and stress, and the number of employees harmed by work-related injuries and diseases are greater than many

people think. Enforcement of existing regulations is too lax.

17. Management style greatly affects the work environment. Managers who operate with rigid assumptions about human nature or who devote themselves to infighting and political maneuvering damage employees' interests.

18. Day-care services and reasonable parental-leave policies also affect working conditions. Despite the genuine need for, and the ethical importance of, both day care and parental leave, only a handful of companies makes serious efforts at providing them.

19. Studies report extensive job dissatisfaction at all levels. Various factors influence satisfaction and dissatisfaction on the job. The redesigning of the work process can enhance the quality of work life, the well-being of workers, and even productivity.

CASE 6.1
Burger Beefs

When seventeen-year-old Wendy Hamburger applied for a summer job at a Wendy's Old Fashioned Hamburgers outlet near her Barrington, Illinois, home, she hoped to earn some money for college. But after working there for only three months, she quit when a manager threatened to fire her if she refused to work an extra shift on a holiday.

Wendy wasn't too upset with losing a job that earned her forty dollars for fifteen hours work a week. "It seemed like the job cost me more than I made,"[52] she says. She does concede, though, that Wendy's International, Inc., did pay her a little attention during her brief connection with the company. It used her to get a lot of free publicity in Chicago-area newspapers, and its president and founder, R. David Thomas, mailed her an autographed photograph of himself, which presumably she didn't have to return when she quit.

Actually, there's nothing atypical about Wendy's experience. Rock-bottom pay, unpleasant working conditions, and bossy bosses—all are familiar to the millions of teenage employees in the fast-food industry. Little wonder the average teenage worker quits in disgust within four months of being hired.

Such a rapid turnover would disembowel most businesses. Not so for those that peddle billions of burgers, fries, and shakes a year. For them frequent turnover is the rank fodder for their multimillion dollar operations, at least according to critics.

"The whole system is designed to have turnover," says Robert Harbrant, secretary-treasurer for the AFL-CIO Food and Beverage Trades Department in Washington, D.C. That way the industry averts pay increases and thwarts union efforts to organize workers.

Industry executives deny such nefarious motives. They point out, correctly, that for most youngsters a fast-food job is their first work experience. Such unseasoned workers usually are undisciplined and unreliable. No sooner are they trained, say fast-food executives, than they up and leave.

Harlow F. White, president of Systems for Human Resources, Inc., thinks otherwise. He publicly wonders whether the 300 percent annual turnover of fast-food workers is the cause or effect of industry operations. He suspects that "the industry has managed to manufacture a self-fulfilling prophecy: 'We're going to have turnover. And by God, we do.'" White points out that an abrupt decline in employment turnover would turn the industry on its head. But there's little chance of that happening. A survey conducted by White finds that one-third of management employees and a whopping four-fifths of hourly employees in the fast-food industry plan to bolt at the first opportunity.

Nevertheless, while admitting that the teenage part-timer is crucial to fast-food success, industry officials insist that they do not purposely encourage turnover. "Turnover costs us money," asserts a spokesperson for Burger King, even while conceding that it doesn't take more than a day or two to train a new worker. He profiles the typical worker as a teenage student wanting temporary part-time or summer work in order to earn some spending money.

Despite industry's declared good intention, the White survey turns up widespread discontent among fast-food workers. A teenage waitress in an Atlanta Steak n' Shake complains that she is scheduled for a two-hour work day, although it takes her that much time to make a round-trip from home to work. (A company official says this is a management problem, that the policy of Steak n' Shake is to pay workers for a minimum of three hours.) A seventeen-year-old applicant in Westchester County, New York, recalls being kept waiting for weeks until Burger King informed him that he didn't get a job after all. The delay, he says, cost him a month of job hunting and $200 in foregone pay. (Burger King, says a spokesperson, deplores such delays, which it feels the installation of a new scheduling technique will prevent in the future.) A teenage part-timer at a New York McDonald's shop says management there routinely has workers appear up to an hour ahead of work time and then "wait in the back room and punch in later when they need you."[53] (A McDonald's official insists that this is an isolated case, that McDonald's does not condone such a policy.)

Some believe that company insistence that such problems lie with local management, not the home office, is buck passing. Richard Gilber, a compliance official in the U.S. Labor Department's wage and hour division, places the blame squarely on the store-manager training programs conducted by the home offices. He says, "We find in many cases that the twenty-year-old managers are sales oriented and cleanliness oriented. But they aren't taught much about employee relations. And the Wage Hour Law is just another three pages in the operating manual."

Wendy Hamburger agrees. "I went through three managers in the short time I was at Wendy's," she recalls. "They needed managers so badly they hired anyone. They got a lot of young guys in there who think they're Mr. Macho and want to exercise their power. They don't know anything."

A Burger King official conceded that much of the criticism is warranted. The industry, he says, has put people in their early twenties in charge of a million-dollar restaurant and sometimes forty employees under age eighteen and expects them to function like professionals. The results are often less than ideal. "You can train someone to fix a piece of equipment a lot easier than you can to deal with people," he says. Burger King, for one, is trying to remedy the situation by including "people skills" as part of its ten-day training courses for managers at its new $1.6 million Burger King University in Miami. Other fast-food companies are following suit.

White's survey indicates that low pay is workers' chronic complaint. Although most chains come under minimum wage and over-time-pay laws, they don't always abide by them. Thus in 1977, Kentucky Fried Chicken of Middlesboro, Kentucky, had to make up $2,086 in overtime pay to thirty-five employees. In 1978, a federal court in Miami, Florida, ordered one of Lum's and Ranch House's restaurants to pay $100,000 to 1,290 employees who weren't paid the required minimum and overtime wages. In the same year, in New Jersey, the Department of Labor charged eighteen Burger King restaurants with systematically underpaying their workers and not keeping proper wage reports. Such cases can be multiplied across the country.

While hourly employees almost universally bristle up at management policies and conduct, the manager's job is no bowl of cherries. Ask the young woman who is paid $12,000 a year to run a McDonald's outlet that grosses $750,000 annually. "They don't pay managers enough," she complains. "I'm on my feet from 6 A.M. to 6 P.M. Often I don't have time to eat all day. On days off I come in a couple of hours or call in to check on my assistant managers. And I have to take work home, like the weekly scheduling."

Discussion Questions

1. Do you think that the fast-food industry is encouraging turnover?

2. What ideals, obligations, and effects would you consider in evaluating a policy that encourages turnover? Where do you think the weight should lie?

3. Do you think companies have responsibilities for how licensees conduct their operations?

4. Some would say that so long as the fast-food operators comply with minimum wage and overtime laws, they pay a fair wage. Do you agree?

5. If you were an executive of a fast-food company like McDonald's or Burger King, what measures, if any, would you recommend to remedy the constant worker irritants that Mr. White's survey turned up?

6. Discuss the merits and liabilities of unionizing fast-food workers.

7. Do you think that conditions in the fast-food industry support or belie Adam Smith's assumption that the natural interplay between employer and employee will produce a fair wage and hospitable work conditions?

8. Rapid turnover in the fast-food industry, some would argue, just goes to show that young people today lack loyalty, industry, and perseverance—in short, that they really don't want to work. Would you agree?

CASE 6.2
Freedom to Fire

When can dancing get you fired? Apparently, when you're on a business trip, your partner is a coworker, and your clothes are too tight. Ask Elizabeth Bellissimo.

Bellissimo, a twenty-six-year-old attorney for Westinghouse Electric Corporation, happily accepted a fellow worker's invitation to dance while they were on a business trip. Her supervisor didn't approve and told her so when she returned to the office. He accused the young attorney of "unprofessional behavior" and suggested that, rather than trotting

out to the dance floor, she should have trotted out some excuse like a headache, and returned to her room. He also chided Bellissimo for her fashion choices. Her clothes, he told her, were definitely too tight and the colors too flashy.

When Bellissimo threatened to report the reprimand to a company vice-president, she was fired. Claiming sex discrimination, Bellissimo sued her supervisors and won $121,670 for lost pay and future wages.[54]

The court's ruling wasn't unusual. Federal and state laws have long prohibited companies from discriminating against workers on the basis of sex, race, national origin, and age. Many states also have laws prohibiting employers from discharging workers for filing a worker's compensation claim and from cheating them out of pensions or commissions. And several states have even passed legislation protecting whistle blowers from organizational retaliation. The courts have thus made it clear that employers may not fire workers at will—that is, for any reason whatever or for no reason. Now, state court decisions in California, Michigan, and New York threaten to further restrict the employer's freedom to fire.

In 1981, American Airlines fired an agent with eighteen years of service. The agent sued in the California courts, claiming that he had not been given a hearing prescribed in the corporation's internal regulations. While admitting its corporation regulations make such a provision, American claimed it is under no contractual obligation to provide one. About the same time, the New York Court of Appeals heard a similar case involving a man let go after working for a company for eight years.

In both instances, the courts ruled in favor of the dismissed workers and thereby elevated to contractual status expressed or implied personnel policies contained in such corporate documents as job applications, handbooks, and stock option plans. The courts said, in effect, that discharge of an employee is a breach of contract where assurances are made in company handbooks that termination can be for just cause only, after all practical steps toward rehabilitation have been made. Employment manuals and related documents thus appear to constitute still another restriction on the employer's freedom to fire.

Experts think that those who stand to benefit the most from these rulings are lower- and middle-level professionals and managers not covered by collective bargaining agreements or personal contracts given to senior executives.[55] Already companies are beginning to shudder at the prospect of being held legally accountable for statements made in personnel handbooks. They're convinced it will make firing employees increasingly difficult and expensive. In the wake of the American Airlines decision, one of its executives had this caution for California corporations: "Companies that operate in California will have to be aware that when they fire managers and other unorganized employees, they had better document the reason pretty thoroughly because they might end up in court. And they had better be prepared to spend tens of thousands of dollars in attorney's fees."

Others maintain that there is an even more fundamental issue at stake: a company's right to manage its business as it sees fit.

McGraw-Hill, Inc., for example, believes that the court rulings are tantamount to abrogating company self-governance in matters of discharge. "Treatment of personnel handbooks as creating enforceable contract rights would . . . put upon the courts the burden of making, or at least second guessing, the myriad of personnel decisions which are currently made by the managers of business enterprises in the exercise of their business judgment," company officials claim.

Perhaps the courts ultimately will side with such arguments. In the meantime, legal consultants are advising corporate clients to protect themselves. Blue Cross & Blue Shield of Michigan, which lost in a precedent-setting 1980 decision by the Michigan Supreme Court that gave personnel policy statements the status of employee contractual rights, is taking the advice to heart. Karen S. Kienbaum, the insurer's assistant general counsel, explains: "We have changed our employee handbook so that it very explicitly states that you can be terminated at any time for any reason. It also says that it is not an employment contract."

Officials at McGraw-Hill predict that if other courts rule like California's and Michigan's, "employers would withdraw their personnel handbooks or plaster them with disclaimers."

Discussion Questions

1. Do you think Ms. Bellissimo's supervisor had just cause to fire her?

2. Some would so apply the concept of property rights to a business that owners and their representatives should be allowed to terminate a worker for any reason whatever. Do you agree?

3. Do you agree with McGraw-Hill's position: that the court ruling in effect undermines the company's self-governance in matters of discharge?

4. In your opinion, should statements that appear in job descriptions and employee handbooks have the status of contractual rights?

5. What do you think of the Blue Cross & Blue Shield of Michigan's employee handbook statement that an employee "can be terminated at any time for any reason just as you [the employee] can [quit] at any time for any reason"? Evaluate the insurer's policy from the perspectives of egoism, utilitarianism, and Kant's ethics.

CASE 6.3
Testing for Honesty

"Charity begins at home." If you don't think so, ask the Salvation Army, which has a severe problem with theft among its kettlers, the street people who collect money for the Army during the Christmas season. Some of the Army's kettlers—who are usually poor, unemployed individuals, paid minimum wage—were helping themselves to the Army's loot before the organization had a chance to dole it out. To put a stop to the problem, Army officials sought the assistance of Dr. John Jones, Director of Research of London House Management Consultants, Inc.

London House is one of several recently hatched companies that market honesty tests for prospective employees. Some of these tests, like London House's Personnel Selection Inventory (PSI), also measure the applicant's tendency toward drug use and violence. All three categories—honesty, drugs, and violence—play a major part in company losses, according to the makers of these tests.

The company losses in question are astronomical. By some estimates, U.S. companies lose about $25 billion annually because of employee dishonesty, neglect, and disruption. The American Management Association estimates that as many as 20 percent of the businesses that fail do so because of employee crime. Bank losses alone, says the FBI, cost $250 million a year. Compounding things are losses due to employee drug use, which London House estimates at about $43 billion each year in absenteeism, lost initiative, inattentiveness, accidents, and diminished productivity.[56] Employee violence also costs companies millions of dollars in damages, lost productivity, and lawsuits.

Honesty-test makers say that the only way to deal with these problems is before workers are hired, not after—by subjecting them to a pre-employment psychological test that will identify the one-third of all prospective employees who will likely steal, the 15 percent who have a history of violence or emotional instability, the 25 percent who have a history of marijuana abuse, and the 10 percent who have used other illegal drugs on a regular basis.[57]

For many the honesty test is an economical alternative to the polygraph. It costs about six to fourteen dollars per test compared to fifty-five to seventy-five dollars for a polygraph.[58] Also, honesty tests don't seem to raise the legal questions associated with polygraphs, which are restricted in fourteen states. Under the Equal Employment Opportunity Commission's "Uniform Guidelines on Employee Selection Procedures" (1978), tests that measure psychological traits are permissible since they do not appear to have any adverse impact—that is, their results don't show significantly lower scores among members of minority, racial, sex, or ethnic groups. Furthermore, the tests are easily administered at the workplace by a staff member to any category of worker, are easily and quickly evaluated by the test maker, and assess the applicant's overall answers, rather than a few isolated responses.

A typical test begins with some cautionary remarks. Test takers are told to be truthful, because dishonesty can be detected; and they are warned that incomplete answers will be considered incorrect, as will any unanswered questions. Then applicants ordinarily sign a waiver permitting the results to be known to their prospective employer and authorizing the testing agency to check out their answers. Next come the questions—and the source of growing controversy.

The test taker must answer a battery of questions like the following: "How strong is your conscience?" "How often do you feel guilty?" "Do you always tell the truth?" "Do you occasionally have thoughts you wouldn't want made public?" "Does everyone steal a little?" "Do you enjoy stories of successful crimes?" "Have you ever been so intrigued by the cleverness of a thief that you hoped the person would escape detection?"

A big part of some tests consists of a behavioral history of the applicant. Applicants are asked to reveal the nature, frequency, and quantity of specific drug use, if any. They also must indicate if they have ever engaged in drunk driving, illegal gambling, selling or using pot, traffic violations, forgery, vandalism, and a host of other unseemly behaviors. They must also state their opinions about the social acceptance of drinking alcohol and using other drugs.

Once the tests are completed, they are evaluated by the test maker, who gives the applicant a "risk" rating of high, moderate, or low. The assessment is reported to the prospective employer, who can use it as part of the overall assessment of the employee.

Those who market the tests boast of their validity and reliability, as established by field studies. They insist that the tests do make a difference—they do enable employers to ferret out potential troublemakers, as in the Salvation Army case.

Dr. Jones administered London House's PSI to eighty kettler applicants, which happened to be the number that the particular theft-ridden center needed. The PSIs were not scored, and the eighty applicants were hired with no screening. Throughout the fund-raising month between Thanksgiving and Christmas 1980, the center kept a record of each kettler's daily receipts. After the Christmas season, the tests were scored and divided into "recommended" and "not recommended" for employment. After accounting for the peculiarities of each collection neighborhood, Jones discovered that those kettlers the PSI had not recommended turned in on the average seventeen dollars per day less than those the PSI had recommended. Based on this analysis, he placed the center's loss to employee theft during the fund drive at $20,000. In the future the Salvation Army plans to identify high-risk applicants, which it intends to hire but place in non–money-handling positions.

The list of these psychological-test enthusiasts is growing by leaps and bounds, as reflected in the annual sales of just two test makers, which together exceed $10 million. But the tests also have their detractors, chief among whom are applicants who complain of having to reveal some of the most intimate details of their lives and opinions. In fact, some unions and lawyers brand the tests "confessional sheets," which ask many non–job-related questions that invade privacy. In California the American Civil Liberties Union (ACLU) and the United Food and Commercial Workers Union unsuccessfully attempted to get legislation prohibiting such tests. They dismiss business's claim that no one's privacy is being invaded, since applicants can always refuse to take the test.

"Given the unequal bargaining power," says former ACLU official Kathleen Baily, "the ability to refuse to take a test is one of theory rather than choice—if one really wants a job."[59]

Discussion Questions

1. Describe how you'd feel having to take a psychological test as a precondition for employment. Under what conditions, if any, would you take such a test?

2. Do you think psychological tests invade privacy? Explain why or why not.

3. Assuming that psychological tests like those described are valid and reliable, do you think they are fair? Explain.

4. What do you think a business's reaction would be if the government required its executive officers to submit to a personality test as a precondition for the company's getting a government contract? The tests would probe questionable business practices, such as bribery, product misrepresentation, unfair competition, and so forth. If, in your opinion, the business would object, does it have any moral grounds for subjecting workers to comparable tests?

5. Utilitarians would not find anything inherently objectionable about psychological tests so long as the interests of all parties are taken into account and given equal consideration before such tests were made a pre-employment screen. Do you think this is generally the case?

6. What ideals, obligations, and effects are included in using psychological tests as pre-employment screens? In your view, which is the most important consideration?

7. Should there be a law prohibiting psychological tests as a pre-employment screen, or should the decision be left to the employer? Explain.

8. Do you think that a decision to use these tests should be made jointly by management and labor or is testing for employment an exclusive employer right?

CASE 6.4
Speak, If You Dare

Martin Davis, senior vice-president for the National Power Company, wrote an article for a widely circulated magazine. It wasn't just any article. It questioned his company's social responsibility in planning to put a nuclear power plant near a small California town.

Davis not only raised serious doubts about the safety of nuclear power plants in general but also suggested that a plant in the proposed location would seriously undermine agricultural interests in that area by diverting much needed water to the power plant. It was the kind of article that could only hurt National Power.

There were those who wholeheartedly supported Davis's position and told National that. But also responding were those who didn't support Davis and were irritated that National apparently had succumbed to political and social pressure to abort a project that would ease the country's energy burden and provide an alternative that might stabilize or even reduce the costs of soaring fuel bills. In addition, National received a large outpouring of local labor resentment. The company, according to charges, was preventing the creation of perhaps thousands of much-needed jobs in the area.

Needless to say, none of this was lost on the top management at National. They felt that as vice-president, Davis had acted irresponsibly. They thought that such a plant was not only safe but absolutely vital to the national welfare. And yet Davis had entirely overlooked these points. He had even suggested awesome legal responsibilities National might incur should some remotely possible accident occur.

National's chief operating officer, at the request of the board, instructed Davis never again to so comment publicly without first clearing his remarks with the firm. Davis was outraged. National was way off base and was "invading," as he termed it, his duties as a responsible citizen. He wouldn't have it and told the officer as much. In fact, Davis intended to honor several speaking engagements to air further what he viewed as "a matter of conscience."

The chief operating officer relayed Davis's feelings to the board, which, in turn, issued Davis an ultimatum. Either he would conform with their order or submit his resignation immediately.

The chief operating officer delivered the message. "They expect your answer by the end of the week, Marty," he told the vice-president.

Discussion Questions

1. What are the rival ideals involved in this case?

2. Do you think that National has a right to abridge Davis's freedom of expression on this issue?

3. Do you think Davis acted irresponsibly, as the board charges?

4. What do you think Davis ought to do? Defend your answer by appeal to ethical principles.

CASE 6.5

She Snoops to Conquer

Jean Fanuchi, manager of a moderately large department store, was worried. Shrinkage in the costume jewelry department had continued to rise for the third consecutive month. In fact, this time it had wiped out the department's net profit in sales. Worse, it couldn't be attributed to damage or improper handling of markdowns or even to shoplifting. The only other possibility was in-house theft.

Based on a case reported in Thomas Garrett et al., *Cases in Business Ethics* (Englewood Cliffs, N.J.: Prentice-Hall, 1968), 9–10.

Fanuchi ordered chief of security Matt Katwalski to instruct his security people to keep a special eye on the jewelry department employees as they went about their business. She also instructed that packages, purses, and other containers employees carried with them be searched when workers left the store. When these measures failed to turn up any leads, Katwalski suggested they hire a couple of plainclothes officers to observe the store's guards. Fanuchi agreed. But still nothing turned up.

"We're going to have to install a hidden camera at the checkout station in the jewelry department," Katwalski informed the manager.

"I don't know," Fanuchi replied.

"Of course," said Katwalski, "it won't be cheap. But you don't want this problem spreading to other departments, do you?" Fanuchi didn't.

"One other thing," Katwalski said, "I think we should install some microphones in the rest room, stockroom, and employee lounge."

"You mean snoop on our own employees?" Fanuchi asked, surprised.

"We could pick up something that could crack this thing wide open," Katwalski explained.

"But what if our employees found out? How would they feel, being spied on? And then there's the public to consider. Who knows how they'd react? Why, they'd probably think that if we are spying on our own workers, we were surely spying on them. No, Matt," Fanuchi decided. "Frankly, this whole approach troubles me."

"Okay, Ms. Fanuchi, but if it was my store—"

Fanuchi cut in, "No."

"You're the boss," said Katwalski.

When the shrinkage continued, Fanuchi finally gave in. She ordered Katwalski to have the camera and microphones installed. Within ten days the camera had nabbed the culprit.

The microphones contributed nothing to the apprehension of the thief. But because of them Fanuchi and Katwalski learned that at least one store employee was selling "grass" and perhaps hard drugs, that one was planning to quit without notice, that three were taking food stamps fraudulently, and that one buyer was out to discredit Fanuchi. In solving their shrinkage problem, the pair had unwittingly raised another: What should they do with the information they had gathered while catching the thief?

Discussion Questions

1. Do you think Jean Fanuchi acted immorally in ordering the installation of the viewing and listening devices?

2. Evaluate her action by appeal to ethical principles.

3. How should Fanuchi and Katwalski handle the information they've gathered about their employees? Explain by appealing to relevant ideals, obligations, and effects.

CASE 6.6
Democracy at Harman

Harman Industries, on the edge of Bolivar, Tennessee (pop. 7,000), makes most of the rearview mirrors in the U.S. Second only to the state mental hospital in the number of people it employs, Harman is a central force in Bolivar and surrounding Handeman County. Although this alone may distinguish Harman in the minds of the local population, Harman has another, more important claim to fame: It is the site of the first and perhaps most important management-union experiment in worker participation in the U.S. Launched in 1972 by the United Auto Workers (UAW), Harman management, and consultants from the Harvard Project on Technology, Work, and Character, Harman's Work Improvement Program (WIP) has involved virtually every worker in the factory.

WIP was a response to the less-than-ideal work conditions that had soured the attitudes of Harman workers. Before WIP, the 1,000 or so Harman employees were housed in three huge Quonset huts, relics of World War II. When the project was just beginning, a consultant described the work atmosphere as dirty, noisy, and chaotic.[60] Beyond this, the economics of the auto parts industry, unblinking competition, uneven demand for cars, and price squeezing by customers all intensified the dehumanizing conditions of work that served to feed worker insecurity. In brief, workers viewed themselves as standardized, replaceable parts of the manufacturing process. This perception produced anger, hostility, and depression and blunted creativity. Clearly something had to be done.

In the summer of 1973, management, the union, and a third-party team led by project director Michael Maccoby met to hammer out what would become WIP. The group decided to take a step at a time, ensuring a solid base before moving on to the next development. The first step consisted of gathering information about employee attitudes. The study, conducted with the help of the W. E. Upjohn Institute for Employment Research, was based on in-depth, four-hour interviews with 60 workers plus shorter interviews with about 300 more workers and 50 managers. The findings confirmed everyone's worst suspicions. Workers didn't trust the company, felt management was ignoring them, and were convinced that Harman cared more about profit than people. Indeed, the study discovered that workers at Harman were so hostile toward management that many admitted sabotaging plant operations by intentionally working badly, slowly, or incorrectly.

The next step in the experiment was to set up a management-union structure for the purpose of screening and approving all project developments. A top-level management-union advisory committee was formed, consisting of the company executives, members of UAW International, and QWL experts. Maccoby stressed that a key strategy of the project structure was never to bypass the conventional management-union structures but to strengthen them.

Management and union then agreed to pursue a common set of principles. Whereas many other work-participation projects in the U.S. have aimed at improving productivity or reducing absenteeism, turnover, or sabotage, the Harman-UAW WIP program set out to reorganize the way the company itself operated. The Harvard Project declared pointedly: "The purpose is *not* to increase productivity" but "to make work better and more satisfying for all employees, salaried and hourly, while maintaining the necessary productivity for job security."[61] (The Harvard Project claims that labor-management projects can succeed only if they are committed to a set of principles of human development.) Specifically, the committee agreed that all workplace changes had to fulfill these four principles:

1. Security: creating conditions that free workers from fear of losing jobs and that maximize their financial earnings.

2. Equity: guaranteeing fairness in hiring, pay, and promotions; ending sexual and racial discrimination; and sharing profits with workers when productivity increases.

3. Individuation: understanding that each worker is different, and allowing each worker to satisfy his or her individual development.

4. Democracy: fostering free speech and due process, and permitting worker participation in decisions that directly affect them.

Having agreed on these basic principles, the participants then began to address specific problems at Harman. At first they focused on issues that workers had identified in survey interviews such as temperature extremes in the plant, the irritating air pollution, traffic jams in the parking lot, and management's policy of permitting bill collectors to track down debtors inside the factory.

Then experimental groups in three different departments were set up. One was in the assembly department, where the rearview mirrors were put together. Building on the principles of individuation and democracy, a steering committee, termed the Working Committee, had workers themselves analyze problems with their jobs and propose their own solutions.

Similarly, in the polish and buff department workers were encouraged to decide their own work assignments as a team rather than merely to obey the directives of foremen. Also, individuals who finished their jobs early were urged to help out slower teammates; and the worker team was asked to keep its own records of parts, productivity, efficiency, and the number of "bonus" hours team members were accumulating as a result of achieving product quotas before quitting time on a given day. (Workers could use bonus hours to take time off in the future.) At the same time, workers in the preassembly department came up with eight goals, including helping each other achieve new production quotas, gaining free time to learn new skills or go home early, making the workplace more attractive, improving the quality of their work, reducing "downtime," and installing better tools and fixtures at their workstations.

But the heart of Harman's project was a network of thirty shop-floor committees, termed core groups, which consisted of management, local union, and employee representatives. Most suggestions for work changes originated in these core groups, whose meetings all workers were free to attend. When a core group approved an idea it was sent to the company's Working Committee for final approval or revision.

Beyond this, the Harman WIP attempted to bridge the gap between workers' work and private lives. The most unusual innovation in this regard was the in-plant school. Workers, their families, and even community residents were invited to attend a wide array of classes held before, after, or during a shift, or at lunch. Formed in 1975, the school today offers more than forty classes such as paint technology, die technology, computer language, leadership styles, hydraulics, introduction to data processing, metric measurement, square dancing, theatre group, ceramics, typing, car care for women, and even a class that earns for its students a high school diploma. Two of the most popular courses are first aid and art appreciation. Such courses are financed by the union-management project fund and by the county under its vocational education budget.

While the Harman WIP may seem an unqualified success, it has its critics. Some say that QWL changes have been few and that the program is, in fact, a management ruse to get more out of workers. Others charge that employees really have gained little power, that only company ideas get implemented. Part of the discontent seems to have resulted from the gap between worker expectations and the intent of the project. Some workers evidently expected the core groups and Working Committee to give employees sweeping decision-making powers. But, as Maccoby has stressed, the project intended nothing of the kind.

In late 1977 Sidney Harman sold the company to Beatrice Corporation, an international conglomerate. The Beatrice Corporation maintains that it supports WIP and encourages worker participation. For their part, workers say the program is in limbo: Core groups meet, classes are held, workers occasionally initiate change on the shop floor. But there have been no major new initiatives. Still, consultants say that workers have learned much about analyzing problems and proposing solutions on their own initiative. Perhaps most important, they have learned that change is possible. So has management.

Discussion Questions

1. Do you think the idea of the best possible work environment for workers should take precedent over the idea of profit and productivity?

2. Broadly speaking, could one say that the best possible workplace for employees takes root in nonconsequential considerations, whereas productivity is based on consequential concerns? Explain.

3. Workers at Harman feared the effects of giving productivity top priority in any work improvement program. What might some of these effects be?

4. Do you agree with the Harvard Project's assumption that such programs can succeed only if there is a commitment to a set of principles of human development?

5. The case indicates that some workers today feel they still lack decision-making powers. Their expectations of individual autonomy are understandable in the light of the "democracy" principle, which calls for worker participation in decisions that directly affect them. This principle seemingly is at odds with traditional prerogatives and rights of management (e.g., appointing supervisors, deciding who will run the company, and setting prices). Do you think, then, that this makes democracy an idle principle and ideal in the workplace? Or would you say that democracy remains a legitimate goal inasmuch as it can be used to carve out areas of worker participation in analysis and decision making that can grow as participants develop greater understanding

of the business? Can there be genuine democracy in the workplace if employees are not in some way owners of the enterprise?

NOTES

1. Also called HIV, for "human immunodeficiency virus."

2. Robert C. Gallo, "The AIDS Virus," *Scientific American*, January 1987.

3. See David W. Ewing, "Civil Liberties in the Corporation," in Tom L. Beauchamp and Norman E. Bowie, eds., *Ethical Theory and Business*, 2nd ed. (Englewood Cliffs, N.J.: Prentice-Hall, 1983), 141.

4. Ibid., 139–140.

5. Ibid., 139.

6. Ibid., 140–141.

7. Clyde W. Summers, "Protecting All Employees Against Unjust Dismissal," *Harvard Business Review* 58 (January–February 1980); but see also "Business for Lawyers," *The Economist*, January 23, 1988.

8. See "Business for Lawyers," 61 and Ewing, "Civil Liberties."

9. Ewing, "Civil Liberties," 148.

10. See chapter 5 of Tuleja's *Beyond the Bottom Line* (New York: Penguin, 1987), from which the following paragraphs are drawn.

11. Dean Rotbart, "Father Quit His Job for the Family's Sake; Now Hirers Shun Him," *The Wall Street Journal*, April 13, 1981, 1.

12. Ibid.

13. Francis Bacon, *The New Organon*, Fulton H. Anderson, ed. (New York: Bobbs-Merrill, 1960), 48.

14. Jeffrey L. Sheller, "Nepotism: No Stranger to American Labor Unions," *U.S. News & World Report*, September 20, 1982, 40–41.

15. In a wave of cost cutting and restructuring, the Fortune 500 companies alone slashed 2.8 million employees from their payrolls between 1977 and 1988. Millions more have surrendered jobs or taken pay cuts in the name of corporate streamlining. "Management for the 1990s," *Newsweek* (international edition), April 25, 1988, 34.

16. Terry L. Leap, "When Can You Fire for Off-duty Conduct?" *Harvard Business Review* 66 (January–February 1988): 36.

17. See James C. Coleman and Constance L. Hammen,

Contemporary Psychology and Effective Behavior (Glenview, Ill.: Scott, Foresman, 1974), 424.

18. Ibid., 425.

19. Christopher H. Pyle, "These Tests Are Meant to Scare People," *USA Today*, February 17, 1983, 10A.

20. See Keith Davis and Robert L. Blomstrom, *Business and Society* (New York: McGraw-Hill, 1975), 319.

21. See David T. Lykken, "Three Big Lies About the Polygraph," *USA Today*, February 17, 1983, 10A.

22. Lynn March, "Lie Detectors Are Accurate and Useful," *USA Today*, February 17, 1983, 10A.

23. Lykken, "Three Lies About the Polygraph," 10A.

24. Pyle, "Tests Are Meant to Scare," 10A.

25. James M. Sawrey and Charles W. Telford, *Adjustment and Personality* (Boston: Allyn & Bacon, 1975), 500–501.

26. William H. Whyte, *The Organization Man* (New York: Simon & Schuster, 1956).

27. James T. Wrich, "Beyond Testing: Coping with Drugs at Work," *Harvard Business Review* 66 (January–February 1988).

28. Ibid.

29. See Sue Shellenbarger, "Grain-Elevator Explosions Continue to Threaten Workers and Property," *The Wall Street Journal*, July 21, 1981, Sec. 2, p. 29.

30. See Sue Martinez, "Workers Suffer as Industry Booms," *The Bakersfield Californian*, March 19, 1981, C4.

31. "Workers are Dying to Make Jobsites Safe," *New York Guardian*, April 15, 1987.

32. See Rollin H. Simonds, "OSHA Compliance: Safety Is Good Business," *Personnel*, July–August 1973.

33. "Getting Away with Murder," *Harvard Law Review* 101 (December 1987), 535.

34. "Stress on the Job," *Newsweek* (international edition), April 25, 1988; see also "Stress: the Test Americans are Failing," *Business Week*, April 18, 1988.

35. Douglas McGregor, *The Human Side of Enterprise* (New York: McGraw-Hill, 1960).

36. James Risen, "For Ross Perot, GM Ouster Still Rankles," *International Herald Tribune*, November 19, 1987.

37. *California Federal Savings and Loan Association v. Guerra*, 93 L Ed 2d 613.

38. "Danger: Mother at Work," *The Economist*, April 16, 1988, p. 49; see also Janice Peterson, "The Feminization of Poverty," *Journal of Economic Issues* 21 (March 1987), 332.

39. JoAnne McCracken, "Child Care as an Employee Fringe Benefit: May an Employer Discriminate?" *Santa Clara Law Review* 26 (Summer–Fall 1986), 670.

40. *Business Week* (international edition), February 29, 1988, p. 58.

41. The average cost of day care is $3,000 per year, and licensed day-care centers have only 2.5 million places. See "Danger: Mother at Work," 49.

42. McCracken, "Child Care as an Employee Fringe Benefit," 671–672.

43. Rosalyn B. Will and Steven D. Lydenberg, "20 Corporations that Listen to Women," *Ms.*, November 1987, p. 49.

44. McCracken, "Child Care as an Employee Fringe Benefit," 668.

45. *Work in America: Report of a Special Task Force to the Secretary of Health, Education and Welfare* (Cambridge: MIT Press, 1972).

46. Thomas A. Kochan, Harry C. Katz, and Robert B. McKersie, *The Transformation of American Industrial Relations* (New York: Basic Books, 1986), 224.

47. Survey Research Center, *Survey of Working Conditions* (Ann Arbor: University of Michigan, 1970).

48. H. Sheppard and N. Herrick, *Where Have All The Robots Gone?* (New York: The Free Press, 1972).

49. A. W. Kornhauser, *Mental Health of the Industrial Worker: A Detroit Study* (Huntington, N.Y.: Re. E. Krieger, 1965).

50. E. Palmore, "Predicting Longevity: A Follow-Up Controlling for Age," *Gerontologist* 9 (1969): 247–250.

51. Kochan et al., *Transformation of American Industrial Relations*, 175–176.

52. See Jim Montgomery, "Burger Blues," *The Wall Street Journal*, March 15, 1979, p. 1. The article is the source of the facts reported here and of the quotations reported in this case.

53. This and all other quotations in this case presentation are from Montgomery, "Burger Blues," 33.

54. Cathy Trost, "Labor Letter—A Special News Report on People and Their Jobs in Offices, Fields, and Factories," *The Wall Street Journal*, May 22, 1984, p. 1.

55. See "A Fight Over the Freedom to Fire," *Business Week*, September 20, 1982, p. 116, from which the remaining quotations in this case presentation are taken.

56. "Are Your Employees Profit-Makers or Profit Takers? Know Before You Hire," *Personnel Security Digest* 1 (Summer 1981), 8.

57. Ibid.

58. Susan Tempor, "More Employers Attempt to Catch a Thief By Giving Job Applicants 'Honesty' Exams," *The Wall Street Journal*, August 3, 1981, Sec. 2, p. 1.

59. Ibid., 15.

60. Daniel Zwerdling, "Democratizing the Workplace: A Case Study," in Mark Green and Robert Massie, Jr., eds. *The Big Business Reader* (New York: The Pilgrim Press, 1980), 106.

61. Ibid., 109.

An Employees' Bill of Rights

David W. Ewing

In this selection from his book Freedom Inside the Organization, *David Ewing presents a nine-point bill of rights for employees. Any bill of rights, Ewing suggests, should take the form of succinct, practical injunctions, injunctions that are negative in form ("Thou shalt not . . . ") and that can be readily understood by ordinary people. A bill of rights should also be enforceable, not just a statement of ideals. Ewing emphasizes that his bill of rights is a "working proposal" for further discussion.*

The bill of rights that follows is one person's proposal, a "working paper" for discussion, not a platform worked out in committee. . . .

1. *No organization or manager shall discharge, demote, or in other ways discriminate against any employee who criticizes, in speech or press, the ethics, legality, or social responsibility of management actions.*

Comment: This right is intended to extend the U.S. Supreme Court's approach in the *Pickering* case* to all employees in business, government, education, and public service organizations.

What this right does not say is as important as what it does say. Protection does not extend to employees who make nuisances of themselves or who balk, argue, or contest managerial decisions on normal operating and planning matters, such as the choice of inventory accounting method, whether to diversify the product line or concentrate it, whether to rotate workers on a certain job or specialize them, and so forth. "Committing the truth," as Ernest Fitzgerald called it, is protected

*[eds.] In this important 1968 case, the Supreme Court found in favor of a public schoolteacher who had been fired for criticizing the policies of the school board in the local newspaper.

only for speaking out on issues where we consider an average citizen's judgment to be as valid as an expert's—truth in advertising, public safety standards, questions of fair disclosure, ethical practices, and so forth.

Nor does the protection extend to employees who malign the organization. We don't protect individuals who go around ruining other people's reputations, and neither should we protect those who vindictively impugn their employers.

Note, too, that this proposed right does not authorize an employee to disclose to outsiders information that is confidential.

This right puts publications of nonunionized employees on the same basis as union newspapers and journals, which are free to criticize an organization. Can a free press be justified for one group but not for the other? More to the point still, in a country that practices democratic rites, can the necessity of an "underground press" be justified in any socially important organization?

2. *No employee shall be penalized for engaging in outside activities of his or her choice after working hours, whether political, economic, civic, or cultural, nor for buying products and services of his or her choice for personal use, nor for expressing or encouraging views contrary to top management's on political, economic, and social issues.*

Comment: Many companies encourage employees to participate in outside activities, and some states have committed this right to legislation. Freedom of choice of products and services for personal use is also authorized in various state statutes as well as in arbitrators' decisions. The

Reprinted by permission from David Ewing, *Freedom Inside the Organization* (New York: Dutton, 1977).

third part of the statement extends the protection of the First Amendment to the employee whose ideas about government, economic policy, religion, and society do not conform with the boss's. It would also protect the schoolteacher who allows the student newspaper to espouse a view on sex education that is rejected by the principal, the staff psychologist who endorses a book on a subject considered taboo in the board room, and other independent spirits.

Note that this provision does not authorize an employee to come to work "beat" in the morning because he or she has been moonlighting. Participation in outside activities should enrich employees' lives, not debilitate them; if on-the-job performance suffers, the usual penalties may have to be paid.

3. *No organization or manager shall penalize an employee for refusing to carry out a directive that violates common norms of morality.*

Comment: The purpose of this right is to . . . afford job security (not just unemployment compensation) to subordinates who cannot perform an action because they consider it unethical or illegal. It is important that the conscientious objector in such a case hold to a view that has some public acceptance. Fad moralities—messages from flying saucers, mores of occult religious sects, and so on—do not justify refusal to carry out an order. Nor in any case is the employee entitled to interfere with the boss's finding another person to do the job requested.

4. *No organization shall allow audio or visual recordings of an employee's conversations or actions to be made without his or her prior knowledge and consent. Nor may an organization require an employee or applicant to take personality tests, polygraph examinations, or other tests that constitute, in his opinion, an invasion of privacy.*

Comment: This right is based on policies that some leading organizations have already put into practice. If an employee doesn't want his working life monitored, that is his privilege so long as he demonstrates (or, if an applicant, is willing to demonstrate) competence to do a job well.

5. *No employee's desk, files, or locker may be examined in his or her absence by anyone but a senior manager who has sound reason to believe that the files contain information needed for a management decision that must be made in the employee's absence.*

Comment: The intent of this right is to grant people a privacy right as employees similar to that which they enjoy as political and social citizens under the "searches and seizures" guarantee of the Bill of Rights (Fourth Amendment to the Constitution). Many leading organizations in business and government have respected the principle of this rule for some time.

6. *No employer organization may collect and keep on file information about an employee that is not relevant and necessary for efficient management. Every employee shall have the right to inspect his or her personnel file and challenge the accuracy, relevance, or necessity of data in it, except for personal evaluations and comments by other employees which could not reasonably be obtained if confidentiality were not promised. Access to an employee's file by outside individuals and organizations shall be limited to inquiries about the essential facts of employment.*

Comment: This right is important if employees are to be masters of their employment track records instead of possible victims of them. It will help to eliminate surprises, secrets, and skeletons in the clerical closet.

7. *No manager may communicate to prospective employers of an employee who is about to be or has been discharged gratuitous opinions that might hamper the individual in obtaining a new position.*

Comment: The intent of this right is to stop blacklisting. The courts have already given some support for it.

8. *An employee who is discharged, demoted, or transferred to a less desirable job is entitled to a written statement from management of its reasons for the penalty.*

Comment: The aim of this provision is to encourage a manager to give the same reasons in a hearing, arbitration, or court trial that he or she gives the employee when the cutdown happens. The written statement need not be given unless requested; often it is so clear to all parties why an action is being taken that no document is necessary.

9. *Every employee who feels that he or she has been penalized for asserting any right described in this bill shall be entitled to a fair hearing before an impartial official, board, or arbitrator. The findings and conclusions of the hearing shall be delivered in writing to the employee and management.*

Comment: This very important right is the organizational equivalent of due process of law as we know it in political and community life. Without due process in a company or agency, the rights in this bill would all have to be enforced by outside courts and tribunals, which is expensive for society as well as time-consuming for the employees who are required to appear as complainants and witnesses. The nature of a "fair hearing" is purposely left undefined here so that different approaches can be tried, expanded, and adapted to changing needs and conditions.

Note that the findings of the investigating official or group are not binding on top management. This would put an unfair burden on an ombudsperson or "expedited arbitrator," if one of them is the investigator. Yet the employee is protected. If management rejects a finding of unfair treatment and then the employee goes to court, the investigator's statement will weigh against management in the trial. As a practical matter, therefore, employers will not want to buck the investigator-referee unless they fervently disagree with the findings.

In Sweden, perhaps the world's leading practitioner of due process in organizations, a law went into effect in January 1977 that goes a little farther than the right proposed here. The new Swedish law states that except in unusual circumstances a worker who disputes a dismissal notice can keep his or her job until the dispute has been decided by a court.

Every sizable organization, whether in business, government, health, or another field, should have a bill of rights for employees. Only small organizations need not have such a statement—personal contact and oral communications meet the need for them. However, companies and agencies need not have identical bills of rights. Industry custom, culture, past history with employee unions and associations, and other considerations can be taken into account in the wording and emphasis given to different provisions.

Review and Discussion Questions

1. What are the pros and cons of each of Ewing's nine points? Examine each point for any potential problems in enacting, interpreting, and enforcing it.

2. Are there any rights that you would add to Ewing's list? Are there any that you would delete?

3. Do you see any point in proposing and discussing a possible employees' bill of rights? Do you think employees would benefit from a bill of rights? Should each company adopt its own bill of rights or should a general bill of rights be enacted by law?

4. Some might argue that, instead of a bill of rights, it is up to individual employees, or their union, to negotiate their employment terms. Would you agree?

Privacy, Polygraphs, and Work _____

George G. Brenkert

In the following essay, professor of philosophy George G. Brenkert attempts to show how polygraphs violate personal privacy when used to screen applicants. He advances three basic claims related to the reasons that polygraphs are used; namely, to verify information and corroborate responses of job applicants. The first claim is that the information polygraphing seeks to verify can violate the applicant's privacy. The second claim is that polygraphing to corroborate an applicant's responses violates privacy. Beyond this, Brenkert makes a third claim: that polygraphing cannot be justified by appeal to some ideal weightier than privacy, such as the defense of property rights. This essay attempts to clarify the ideal of privacy, to show how polygraphing violates it, and to rank-order privacy in relation to property rights.

The rights of prospective employees have been the subject of considerable dispute, both past and present. In recent years, this dispute has focused on the use of polygraphs to verify the claims which prospective employees make on employment ap-

George G. Brenkert, "Privacy, Polygraphs, and Work," *Business & Professional Ethics Journal* 1 (Fall 1981): 19–35. Reprinted by permission of the author.

plication forms. With employee theft supposedly amounting to approximately ten billion dollars a year, with numerous businesses suffering sizeable losses and even being forced into bankruptcy by employee theft, significant and increasing numbers of employers have turned to the use of polygraphs.[1] Their right to protect their property is in danger, they insist, and the use of the polygraph to detect and weed out the untrustworthy prospective employee is a painless, quick, economical, and legitimate way to defend this right. Critics, however, have questioned both the reliability and validity of polygraphs, as well as objected to the use of polygraphs as demeaning, affronts to human dignity, violations of self-incrimination prohibitions, expressions of employers' mistrust, and violations of privacy.[2] Though there has been a great deal of discussion of the reliability and validity of polygraphs, there has been precious little discussion of the central moral issues at stake. Usually terms such as "dignity," "privacy," and "property rights" are simply bandied about with the hope that some favorable response will be evoked. The present paper seeks to redress this situation by discussing one important aspect of the above dispute—the supposed violation of personal privacy. Indeed, the violation of "a right to privacy" often appears to be the central moral objection to the use of polygraphs. However, the nature and basis of this claim have not yet been clearly established.[3] If they could be, there would be a serious reason to oppose the use of polygraphs on prospective employees.

I

There are three questions which must be faced in the determination of this issue. First, is the nature of the information which polygraphing seeks to verify, information which can be said to violate, or involve the violation of, a person's privacy? Second, does the use of the polygraph itself as the means to corroborate the responses of the job applicant violate the applicant's privacy? Third, even if—for either of the two preceding reasons—the polygraph does violate a person's privacy, might this violation still be justified by the appeal to more weighty reasons, e.g., the defense of property rights? . . .

There are certain things which people (in their various roles as employers, government officials,

physicians, etc.) and institutions (governments and businesses, etc.) ought not to know about individuals, however they might come to know these facts. Indeed, since they ought not to know such facts, those individuals who are the ultimate object of this knowledge may legitimately object to a violation of their rights and demand that steps should be taken to make sure that others do not come to know this information. For example, it would be wrong, however they went about it, for government officials to make it their business to know the details of the sexual practices of each particular citizen. It would be wrong, it has been claimed, for a physician to know by what means a patient intends to pay for the health care administered.[4] Finally, the following case suggests that there is information which an employer ought not to know about an employee. A warehouse manager had an employee who had confessed to a theft on the job take a polygraph test in order to determine whether others had helped him steal some of the missing goods. The employee answered "no" to each person he was asked about—and the polygraph bore him out, except in the case of one person. Each time he was asked about this person the employee would deny that he had helped him, but each time the polygraph reported a reaction indicative of lying. At last they asked him why each time they raised this person's name there was such a great physiological response. After some hesitation, the thief "took a deep breath and explained that one day a few weeks before, he had walked into the company bathroom and found the fellow in a stall masturbating." The employer's reaction suggests that such information he considered to be information he ought not to know—however he found it out:

> I fired the thief, but I never said a word to the other guy. He was a good worker, and that's what counts. But I'll have to tell you this: Every time I saw him for months after that, I'd think about what the thief had told me, and I'd say to myself, "God, I don't have any right to know that."[5]

It is not implausible then that there are various kinds of information which people and institutions ought not to know about individuals.[6] . . .

Is it possible then to characterize the nature of privacy such that one might know what kinds of information are rightfully private? If an employer had or sought access to that information he would be said to violate the person's right to privacy. Quite often one suspects that people take the view that information about a person is private in the above sense, if that person does not want it known by others.[7] Thus, the determination of which information is protected by a right to privacy is subjectively, individually, based—it is whatever an individual does not want to be known.

There are, however, good reasons to reject this view. Though we may intelligibly talk about the privacy a person seeks and equate this with a state of affairs he wants or seeks in which he does not share himself and/or information about himself with others, we are not thereby talking about that person's right to privacy. A person might not want passers-by to know that he is bald; he may not want his doctor to know exactly which aches and pains he has; he may not want his neighbors to know about the toxic chemicals he is burying on his land. It does not follow, however, that passers-by, one's doctor, and neighbors violate a person's right to privacy in acquiring such information. It is indeed true that control of information about oneself is important in the formation of the kinds of relationships one wants to have with other people.[8] But it does not follow from this that, just because one wants—or does not want—to have a certain relationship with another person or institution, a certain piece of information which one does not want revealed to that person or institution is therefore private—that others in acquiring it would violate one's right to privacy. In this sense, privacy is not like property which is itself merely a cluster of rights. We may, on the contrary, speak intelligibly of the privacy a person seeks apart from any right to privacy to which a person may be entitled.

On the other hand, one may want some things to be public, to be exposed to the view of all, but this may also be unjustified. The person who exposes his sexual organs at mid-day on a busy downtown street or makes a practice of revealing his most intimate thoughts and feelings to unconcerned strangers may be condemned not simply for the offense he causes others but also for his refusal to treat such matters as private rather than public. . . .

Upon what basis then, if it is not simply a personal determination, do we maintain that certain information is rightfully private, that the knowledge of it by others constitutes a violation of one's right to privacy? There are two points to make here. First, there is no piece of information about a person which is by itself rightfully private. Information about one's financial concerns may be rightfully private vis-a-vis a stranger or a neighbor, but not vis-a-vis one's banker. The nature of one's sex life may be rightfully private with regard to most people, including future employers, but not to one's psychiatrist, sex therapist, or mate. Accordingly, the right to privacy involves a three place relation. To say that something is rightfully private is to say that A may withhold from or not share something, X, with Z. Thus to know whether some information, X, about a person or institution, A, is, or ought to be, treated as rightfully private, we must ask about the relationship in which A stands to Z, another person or institution. . . .

Second, then, to speak of the right to privacy is to speak of the right which individuals, groups, or institutions have that access to and information about themselves is limited in certain ways by the relationships in which they exist to others. In general, the information and access to which a person or institution is entitled with regard to another person and/or institution is that information and access which will enable the former to fulfill, perform, or execute the role the person or institution plays in the particular relationship. All other access and information about the latter is beyond the pale. Thus one cannot be a friend of another unless one knows more about another and has a special access to that person. Similarly, one cannot be a person's lawyer, physician, or barber unless one is entitled to other kinds of knowledge and access. It follows that to speak of one's right to privacy is not simply to speak of one's ability to control information and access to him, since one may be unable to control such access or information acquisition and still be said to have a right to such. Similarly, to speak of one's privacy is not to speak of a claim one makes, since one may not claim or demand that others limit their access to oneself and still have a right that they do so.[9] Such a situation might occur when one is dominated or oppressed by others such that one does not insist on—or claim—the rights one is entitled to. On the other hand, one might also, in certain situations, decide not to invoke one's right to privacy and thus allow others access to oneself which the present relationship might not otherwise permit. It is in this sense that individuals can determine for themselves which others and when others have access to them and to information about them.

II

In order to determine what information might be legitimately private to an individual who seeks employment we must consider the nature of the employer/(prospective) employee relationship. . . .

The information to which the employer qua employer is entitled about the (prospective) employee is that information which regards his possible acceptable performance of the services for which he might be hired. Without such information the employer could not fulfill the role which present society sanctions. There are two aspects of the information to which the employer is entitled given the employer/employee relationship. On the one hand, this information will relate to and vary in accordance with the services for which the person is to be hired. But in any case, it will be limited by those services and what they require. In short, one aspect of the information to which the employer is entitled is "job relevant" information. Admittedly the criterion of job relevancy is rather vague. Certainly there are few aspects of a person which might not affect his job performance—aspects including his sex life, etc. How then does the "job relevancy" criterion limit the questions asked or the information sought? It does so by limiting the information sought to that which is directly connected with the job description. . . .

However, there is a second aspect to this matter. A person must be able not simply to perform a certain activity, or provide a service, but he must also be able to do it in an acceptable manner—i.e., in a manner which is approximately as efficient as others, in an honest manner, and in a manner compatible with others who seek to provide the services for which they were hired. Thus, not simply one's abilities to do a certain job are relevant, but also aspects of one's social and moral character are pertinent. A number of qualifications are needed for the purport of this claim to be clear. First, that a person must be able to work in an acceptable manner is not intended to legitimize the consideration of the prejudices of other employees. It is not legitimate to give weight in moral delibera-

tions to the immoral and/or morally irrelevant beliefs which people hold concerning the characteristics of others. That one's present employees can work at a certain (perhaps exceptional) rate is a legitimate consideration in hiring other workers. That one's present employees have prejudices against certain religions, sexes, races, political views, etc., is not a morally legitimate consideration. Second, it is not, or should not be, the motives, beliefs, or attitudes underlying the job relevant character traits, e.g., honest, efficient, which are pertinent, but rather the fact that a person does or does not perform according to these desirable character traits. . . . The contract of the employer with the employee is for the latter to perform acceptably certain services—it is not for the employee to have certain underlying beliefs, motives, or attitudes. . . .

Consequently, a great deal of the information which has been sought in preemployment screening through the use of polygraph tests has violated the privacy of individuals. Instances in which the sex lives, for example, of applicants have been probed are not difficult to find. However, privacy violations have occurred not simply in such generally atypical instances but also in standard situations. To illustrate the range of questions asked prospective employees and the violations of privacy which have occurred we need merely consider a list of some questions which one of the more prominent polygraph firms includes in its current tests:

> Have you ever taken any of the following without the advice of a doctor? If Yes, please check:
> Barbiturates, Speed, LSD, Tranquilizers, Amphetamines, Marijuana, Others.
> In the past five years about how many times, if any, have you bet on horse races at the race track?
> Do you think that policemen are honest?
> Do you ever think about committing a robbery?
> Have you been refused credit or a loan in the past five years?
> Have you ever consulted a doctor about a mental condition?
> Do you think that it is okay to get around the law if you don't actually break it?
> Do you enjoy stories of successful crimes and swindles?[10]

Such questions, it follows from the above argument, are for any standard employment violations of one's right to privacy. An employer might ask if a person regularly takes certain narcotic drugs, if he is considering him for a job which requires handling narcotics. An employer might ask if a person has been convicted of a larceny, etc. But whether the person enjoys stories about successful larcenists, whether a person has ever taken any prescription drugs without the advice of a doctor, or whether a person bets on the horses should be considered violations of one's rightful privacy.

The upshot of the argument in the first two sections is, then, that some information can be considered rightfully private to an individual. Such information is rightfully private or not depending on the relationship in which a person stands to another person or institution. In the case of the employer/employee relationship, I have argued that that information is rightfully private which does not relate to the acceptable performance of the activities as characterized in the job description. This excludes a good many questions which are presently asked in polygraph tests, but does not, by any means, exclude all such questions. There still remain many questions which an employer might conceivably wish to have verified by the use of the polygraph. Accordingly, I turn in the next section to the question whether the verification of the answers to legitimate questions by the use of the polygraph may be considered a violation of a person's right to privacy. If it is, then the violation obviously does not stem from the questions themselves but from the procedure, the polygraph test, whereby the answers to those questions are verified.

III

A first reason to believe that use of the polygraph occasions a violation of one's right to privacy is that, even though the questions to be answered are job relevant, some of them will occasion positive, lying reactions which are not necessarily related to any past misdeeds. Rather, the lying reaction indicated by the polygraph may be triggered because of unconscious conflicts, fears and hostilities a person has. It may be occasioned by conscious anxieties over other past activities and observations. Thus, the lying reaction indicated by the polygraph need not positively identify actual lying or the commission of illegal activities. The point, however, is not to question the validity of the polygraph. Rather, the point is that the validity of the polygraph can only be maintained by seeking to clarify whether or not such reactions really indicate lying and the commission of past misdeeds. But this can be done only by the polygraphist further probing into the person's background and inner thoughts. However, inasmuch as the questions can no longer be restrained in this situation by job relevancy considerations, but must explore other areas to which an employer is not necessarily entitled knowledge, to do this will violate a person's right to privacy.

It has been suggested by some polygraphists that if a person has "Something Else" on his mind other than the direct answer to the questions asked, a "something else" which might lead the polygraph to indicate a deceptive answer, the person might, if he so feels inclined,

> tell the examiner about this "outside troubling matter" . . . but as a special precaution obtain the examiner's promise that the disclosure of this information is secret and . . . request that the matter be held in strict confidence. The examiner will comply with your wishes. The examiner does not wish to enter into your personal problems since they tend to complicate the polygraph examination.[11]

What this suggests, however, is that a person go ahead, under the threat of the polygraph indicating that one is lying, and tell the polygraphist matters that are rightfully private. This is supposedly acceptable since one "requests" that it be held in strict confidence. But it surely does not follow that a violation of one's right to privacy does not occur simply because the recipient promises not to pass the information on. If, under some threat, I tell another person something which he has no right to know about me, but I then get his promise that he will treat the information confidentially and that it will not be misused in any way, my right to privacy has still been violated.[12] Accordingly, whether the polygraphist attempts to prevent job applicants from producing misleading deceptive reactions by allowing them to reveal what else is on their minds or probes deceptive reactions once they have occurred to ascertain whether they might not be produced by job irrelevant considerations, he violates the right to privacy of the job applicant.

A second reason why the polygraph must be said to violate a job applicant's right to privacy relates to the monitoring of a person's physiological responses to the questions posed to him. By measuring these responses, the polygraph can supposedly reveal one's mental process. Now even though the questions posed are legitimate questions, surely a violation of one's right to privacy occurs. Just because I have something which you are entitled to see or know, it does not follow that you can use any means to fulfill that entitlement and not violate my privacy. . . .

But why should the monitoring by an employer or his agent of one's physiological responses to legitimate questions be an invasion of privacy—especially if one has agreed to take the test? There are several reasons.

First, the claim that one freely agrees or consents to take the test is surely, in many cases, disingenuous.[13] Certainly a job applicant who takes the polygraph test is not physically forced or coerced into taking the exam. However, it is quite apparent that if he did not take the test and cooperate during the test, his application for employment would either not be considered at all or would be considered to have a significant negative aspect to it. This is surely but a more subtle form of coercion. And if this be the case, then one cannot say that the person has willingly allowed his reactions to the questions to be monitored. He has consented to do so, but he has consented under coercion. Had he a truly free choice, he would not have done so.

Now the whole point of this polygraph test is, of course, not simply to monitor physiological reactions but to use these responses as clues, indications, or revelations of one's mental processes and acts. The polygraph seeks to make manifest to others one's thoughts and ideas. However, unless we freely consent, we are entitled to the privacy of our thoughts, that is, we have a prima facie right not to have our thoughts exposed by others, even when the information sought is legitimate. Consider such analogous cases as a husband reading his wife's diary, a person going through a friend's desk drawers, a stranger reading personal papers on one's desk, an F.B.I. agent going through one's files. In each of these cases, a person attempts to determine the nature of someone else's thoughts

by the use of clues and indications which those thoughts left behind. And, in each of these cases, though we may suppose that the person seeks to confirm answers to legitimate questions, we may also say that, if the affected person's uncoerced consent is not forthcoming, his or her right to privacy is violated. Morally, however, there is no difference between ascertaining the nature of one's thoughts by the use of a polygraph, or reading notes left in a drawer, going through one's diary, etc. Hence, unless there are overriding considerations to consent to such revelations of one's thoughts, the use of the polygraph is a violation of one's right to privacy.[14]

Second, it should be noted that even if a person voluntarily agreed to the polygraph test, it need not follow that there is not a violation of his privacy. It was argued in Section I that there are certain aspects of oneself which are obligatorily private, that is, which one ought to keep private. Accordingly, it may be wrong for one voluntarily to reveal various aspects of oneself to others, even though in so doing one would be responding to legitimate demands. For example, consider a person being interviewed by a health officer who is legitimately seeking information from the person about venereal diseases. Suppose that the person does not simply admit to having such a disease but also—instead of providing a corroborative statement from a physician—reveals the diseased organs. Further, suppose that the health officer is not shocked or offended in any way. The person has been asked legitimate questions, he has acted voluntarily, but still he has violated his own privacy. This is not the kind of access to oneself one ought to afford a bureaucrat. Now it may well be that, analogously, one ought not to allow employers access to one's physiological reactions to legitimate questions, for the reason that such access also violates one's obligatory privacy. To act in this way sets a bad precedent, it signifies that those with power and authority may disregard the privacy of an individual in order to achieve aims of their own. Thus, even if a job applicant readily agreed to reveal certain aspects of himself in a polygraph test, it would not follow without more argument that he was not violating his own privacy.

Finally, if we value privacy not simply as a barrier to the intrusion of others but also as the way by which we define ourselves as separate, autonomous persons, individuals with an integrity which lies at least in part in the ability to make decisions, to give or withhold information and access, then the polygraph strikes at this fundamental value.[15] The polygraph operates by turning part of us over which we have little or no control against the rest of us. If a person were an accomplished yogi, the polygraph would supposedly be useless—since that person's physiological reactions would be fully under his control. The polygraph works because most of us do not have that control. Thus, the polygraph is used to probe people's reactions which they would otherwise protect, not expose to others. It uses part of us to reveal the rest of us. It takes the "shadows" consciousness throws off within us and reproduces them for other people. As such, the use of the polygraph undercuts the decision-making aspect of a person. It circumvents the person. The person says such and such, but his uncontrolled reactions may say something different. He does not know—even when honest—what his reactions might say. Thus it undercuts and demeans that way by which we define ourselves as autonomous persons—in short, it violates our privacy. . . .

Thus, it follows that even if the only questions asked in a polygraph test are legitimate ones, the use of the polygraph for the screening of job applicants still violates one's privacy. In this case, the violation of privacy stems from the procedure itself, and not the questions. Accordingly, one can see the lameness of the defense of polygraphing which maintains that if a person has nothing to hide, he should not object to the polygraph tests. Such a defense is mistaken at least on two counts. First, just because someone believes something to be private does not mean that he believes that what is private is wrong, something to be ashamed about or to be hidden. Second, the polygraph test has been shown to violate a person's privacy, whether one person has really something to hide or not—whether he is dishonest or not. Consequently, if the question is simply whether polygraphing of prospective employees violates their privacy the answer must be affirmative.

IV

There remains one possible defense of the use of polygraphs for screening prospective employees. This is to admit that such tests violate the applicant's privacy but to maintain that other considerations outweigh this fact. Specifically, in light of the great amount of merchandise and money stolen, the right of the employers to defend their property outweighs the privacy of the applicant. This defense is specious, I believe, and the following arguments seek to show why.

First, surely it would be better if people who steal or are dishonest were not placed in positions of trust. And if the polygraphs were used in only these cases, one might well maintain that the use of the polygraph, though it violates one's privacy, is legitimate and justified. However, the polygraph cannot be so used, obviously, only in these cases—it must be used more broadly on both honest and dishonest applicants. Further, if a polygraph has a 90% validity then out of 1,000 interviewees, a full 100 will be misidentified.[16] Now if 10% of the interviewees are thieves, then 10 out of the 100 will steal, but 90 would not; in addition 90 out of the 900 would be thieves, and supposedly correctly identified. This means that 90 thieves would be correctly identified, 10 thieves would be missed, and 90 honest people would be said not to have cleared the test. Thus, for every thief "caught," one honest person would also be "caught"—the former would be correctly identified as one who would steal, while the latter could not be cleared of the suspicion that he too would steal. The point, then, is that this means of defending property rights is one that excludes not simply thieves but honest people as well—and potentially in equal numbers. Such a procedure certainly appears to constitute not simply a violation of privacy rights, but also, and more gravely, an injustice to those honest people stigmatized as not beyond suspicion and hobbled in their competition with others to get employment. If then using polygraph tests to defend property rights is not simply like preventing a thief from breaking into the safe, but more like keeping a thief from the safe plus binding the leg of an innocent bystander in his competition with others to gain employment, then one may legitimately doubt that this procedure to protect property rights is indeed defensible.[17]

Second, it has been claimed that just as the use of blood tests on suspected drunken drivers and the use of baggage searches at the airport are legitimate, so too is the polygraphing of prospective employees. Both of the former kinds of searches may also be said to violate a person's privacy; still they are taken to be justified whether the appeal is to the general good they produce or to the protection of the rights of other drivers or passengers and airline employees. However, neither the blood test nor the baggage search is really analogous to the use of the polygraph on job applicants. Blood tests are only administered to those drivers who have given police officers reason to believe that they (the drivers) are driving while under the influence of alcohol. The polygraph, however, is not applied only to those suspected of past thefts; it is applied to others as well. Further, the connection between driving while drunk and car accidents is quite direct; it immediately endangers both the safety and lives of others. The connection between polygraph tests of a diverse group of applicants (some honest and some dishonest) and future theft is not nearly so direct nor do the thefts endanger the lives of others. Baggage searches are a different matter. They are similar to polygraphing in that they are required of everyone. They are dissimilar in that they are made because of fears concerning the safety of other people. Further, surely there is a dissimilarity between officials searching one's baggage for lethal objects which one is presently trying to sneak on board, and employers searching one's mind for the true nature of one's past behavior which may or may not lead to future criminal intentions. Finally, there are signs at airports warning people, before they are searched, against carrying weapons on airplanes; such weapons could at that time be declared and sent, without prejudice, with the regular baggage. There is no similar aspect to polygraph tests. Thus, the analogies suggested do not hold. Indeed, they suggest that we allow for a violation of privacy only in very different circumstances than those surrounding the polygraphing of job applicants.

Third, the corporate defense of polygraphs seems one-sided in the sense that employers would not really desire the universalization of their demands. Suppose that the businesses in a certain industry are trying to get a new government contract. The government, however, has had difficulties with other corporations breaking the rules of other contracts. As a result it has lost large sums of money. In order to prevent this in the present case it says that it is going to set up devices to monitor the reactions of board members and top managers when a questionnaire is sent to them which they must answer. Any business, of course,

need not agree to this procedure but if it does then it will be noted in their file regarding this and future government contracts. The questionnaire will include questions about the corporation's past fulfillment of contracts, competency to fulfill the present contract, loopholes used in past contracts, collusion with other companies, etc. The reactions of the managers and board members, as they respond to these questions, will be monitored and a decision on the worthiness of that corporation to receive the contract will be made in part on this basis.

There can be little doubt, I think, that the management and directors of the affected corporations would object to the proposal even though the right of the government to defend itself from the violation of its contracts and serious financial losses is at stake. It would be said to be an unjustified violation of the privacy of the decision-making process in a business; an illegitimate encroachment of the government on free enterprise. But surely if this is the legitimate response for the corporate job applicant, the same kind of response would be legitimate in the case of the individual job applicant.

Finally, it is simply false that there are not other measures which could be taken which could not help resolve the problem of theft. The fact that eighty percent of industry does not use the polygraph is itself suggestive that business does not find itself absolutely forced into the use of polygraphs. It might be objected that that does not indicate that certain industries might need polygraphs more than others—e.g., banks and drug companies more than auto plants and shipyards. But even granting this point there are other measures which businesses can use to avoid the problem of theft. Stricter inventory controls, different kinds of cash registers, educational programs, hot lines, incentives, etc. could all be used. The question is whether the employer, management, can be imaginative and innovative enough to move in these directions.

In conclusion, it has been argued that the use of the polygraph to screen job applicants does indeed violate a prospective employee's privacy. First, it is plausible that the privacy of (prospective) employees may be violated by the employer acquiring certain kinds of information about them. Second, using a polygraph an employer may violate an employee's privacy even when the employer seeks the answers to legitimate questions. Third, other moral considerations employers have raised do not appear to outweigh the employee's right to privacy. Accordingly, on balance, a violation of the privacy of a job applicant occurs in the use of the polygraph. This constitutes a serious reason to oppose the use of the polygraph for such purposes.[18]

Notes

1. Cf. Harlow Unger, "Lie Detectors: Business Needs Them to Avoid Costly Employee Rip-Offs," *Canadian Business*, Vol. 51 (April 1978), p. 30. Other estimates may be found in "Outlaw Lie-Detector Tests?", *U.S. News & World Report*, Vol. 84, No. 4 (January 1978), p. 45, and Victor Lipman, "New Hiring Tool: Truth Tests," *Parade* (October 7, 1979), p. 19.

2. Both the AFL-CIO and the ACLU have raised these objections to the use of the polygraph for screening job applicants; cf. *AFL-CIO Executive Council Statements and Reports: 1956–1975* (Westport, Conn.: Greenwood Press, 1977), p. 1422. See also ACLU Policy #248.

3. See, for example, Alan F. Westin, *Privacy and Freedom* (New York: Atheneum, 1967), p. 238.

4. Cf. "A Model Patient's Bill of Rights," from George J. Annas, *The Rights of Hospital Patients* (New York: Avon Books, 1975), p. 233.

5. Frye Gaillard, "Polygraphs and Privacy," *The Progressive*, Vol. 38 (September 1974), p. 46.

6. Cf. James Rachels' comment on the importance of the privacy of medical records in "Why Privacy Is Important," *Philosophy and Public Affairs*, Vol. IV (Summer, 1975), p. 324.

7. Alan Westin's definition of privacy suggests this view; cf. Alan F. Westin, *Privacy and Freedom*, p. 7. Also, Rachels' account of privacy suggests this view at times; cf. "Why Privacy Is Important," *Philosophy and Public Affairs*, pp. 326, 329.

8. Rachels emphasizes this point in his article; cf. "Why Privacy Is Important."

9. Alan Westin characterizes privacy in terms of the "claim" which people make; cf. *Privacy and Freedom*, p. 7.

10. John E. Reid and Associates, *Reid Report* (Chicago: By the author, 1978), passim.

11. John E. Reid and Associates, *The Polygraph Examination* (Chicago: By the author, n.d.), p. 7.

12. It should be further pointed out that the polygraphist/job-applicant relation is not legally or morally a privileged relation. What one tells one's physician one can expect to be treated confidentially. There is no similar expectation that one may entertain in the present case. At most one may hope that as another human being he will keep his promise. On the other hand, the polygraphist is an agent of the employer and responsible to him. There is and can be, then, no guarantee that the promise of the polygraphist will be kept.

13. The reasons why people do not submit to the polygraph are many and various. Some might have something to hide; others may be scared of the questions, supposing that some of them will not be legitimate; some may feel that they are being treated like criminals; others may fear the jaundiced response of the employer to the applicant's honest answers to legitimate questions; finally some may even object to the polygraph on moral grounds, e.g., it violates one's right to privacy.

14. See Section IV below.

15. Cf. Jeffrey H. Reiman, "Privacy, Intimacy, and Personhood," *Philosophy and Public Affairs*, Vol. VI (Fall 1976).

16. Estimates of the validity of the polygraph range widely. Professor David Lykken has been reported as maintaining that the most prevalent polygraph test is correct only two-thirds of the time (cf. Bennett H. Beach, "Blood, Sweat and Fears," *Time*, September 8, 1980, p. 44). A similar figure of seventy percent is reported by Richard A. Sternbach et al., "Don't Trust the Lie Detector," *Harvard Business Review*, Vol. XL (Nov.–Dec. 1962), p. 130. Operators of polygraphs, however, report figures as high as 95% accuracy; cf. Sternbach, p. 129.

17. This argument is suggested by a similar argument in David T. Lykken, "Guilty-Knowledge Test: The Right Way to Use a Lie Detector," *Psychology Today* (March 1975), p. 60.

18. I wish to thank the following for their helpful comments on earlier versions of the present paper: Tom Donaldson, Norman Gillespie, Ken Goodpaster, Betsy Postow, William Tolhurst, and the editors of [*Business & Professional Ethics Journal*].

Review and Discussion Questions

1. What is problematic about saying that private information is whatever a person does not want others to know or that certain information is always private? According to Brenkert, what determines which information is rightfully private?

2. What is an employer entitled to know about an employee or about a prospective employee? Would you agree that a great deal of the information employers seek from job applicants violates their right of privacy?

3. On what grounds does Brenkert maintain that polygraph tests violate privacy even if the questions are legitimate and the person to be tested has freely consented to take the test? Do you agree?

4. An employer might maintain that even if polygraphs violate an applicant's rights, other important considerations outweigh this fact. Brenkert disagrees for several reasons. Whose position do you find the most persuasive?

5. Brenkert focuses on the use of polygraphs in the hiring process. Can his argument be extended to the testing of current employees by firms worried about, say, drug use or theft on the job?

Participation in Employment

John J. McCall

After distinguishing different types of worker participation, John McCall presents five moral reasons that argue in favor of strong worker participation in the codetermination of policy. All of these reasons derive from a need to protect centrally important human goods. McCall contends that, in practice, protection for these goods is most effective when there are strong forms of employee participation. McCall also considers some traditional arguments against participation, none of which, he concludes, are of sufficient weight for rejecting it.

Until recently, worker participation in corporate decision making was a topic largely ignored in American management training and practice. Even in recent years, the attention usually given to worker participation by management theory has been confined to small-scale experiments aimed at increasing labor productivity. Little, if any, attention has been given to the possibility that there is a moral basis for extending a right to participation to all workers.

Numerous explanations for this lack of attention are possible. One is that management sees worker participation as a threat to its power and status. Another explanation may be found in a pervasive ideology underlying our patterns of industrial organization. The ruling theory of corporate property distinguishes sharply between the decision-making rights of ownership and its management representatives on the one hand, and employee duties of loyalty and obedience on the other. The justification for that distinction lies partly in a view of the rights of property owners to

control their goods and partly in a perception that nonmanagement employees are technically unequipped to make intelligent policy decisions. The perceived threat to power and this dominant ideology of employment provide for strong resistance even to a discussion of broad worker participation in corporate decisions. But perhaps as strong a source of this resistance comes from a confusion about the possible meanings of and moral justifications for worker participation. The primary aim of this essay is to clarify those meanings and justifications. If the essay is successful, it might also suggest that the above sources of resistance to participation should be abandoned.

What people refer to when they use the term "participation" varies widely. We can get a better grasp of that variation in meaning if we recognize that it is a function of variety in both the potential issues available for participatory decisions and the potential mechanisms for that decision making. The potential issues for participation can be divided into three broad and not perfectly distinct categories. First, employees could participate in decisions involving shop-floor operations. Characteristic shop-floor issues are the schedule of employee work hours, assembly line speed, and the distribution of work assignments. Second, employees could participate in decisions that have been the traditional prerogative of middle management. Issues here are hiring or discharge decisions, grievance procedures, evaluations of workers or

Reprinted by permission from Joseph R. DesJardins and John J. McCall, eds., *Contemporary Issues in Business Ethics* (Belmont, CA: Wadsworth, 1985).

supervisors, the distribution of merit wage increases, etc. Finally, employees might participate in traditional board-level decisions about investment, product diversification, pricing or output levels, and the like. Simply put, employee participation might refer to participation in decision making over issues that arise at any or all levels of corporate policy.

The mechanisms for participation vary as widely as do the potential issues. These participatory mechanisms vary both in terms of their location within or outside the corporation and in terms of the actual power they possess. For instance, some see employees participating in the shaping of corporate policy by individual acceptance or rejection of employment offers and by collective bargaining through union membership. These mechanisms are essentially external to the particular business institution. Internal mechanisms for participation in corporate policy making include employee stock ownership plans, "quality circle" consulting groups, and bodies that extend employees partial or total effective control of the enterprise. Employee participation through stock ownership might exist either through union pension fund holdings or through individual employee profit sharing plans.

Internal participation can also exist in ways more directly related to the day-to-day functioning of the corporation. For example, quality circle participation is a recent adaptation of some Japanese approaches to the management of human resources. Employees in these quality circles are invited to participate in round-table discussions of corporate concerns such as improving productivity. It is important to note that these quality circle groups are advisory only; their function within the corporation is consultative and they have no actual authority to implement decisions.

Distinct from these advisory bodies are those mechanisms by which employees share in the actual power to make corporate policy. Among the mechanisms for such partial effective control are worker committees with authority to govern selected aspects of the work environment or worker representatives on the traditional organs of authority. An example of the former would be an employee-run grievance board; an example of the latter received significant notice in the United States when United Auto Workers' President

Douglas Fraser assumed a seat on Chrysler's Board of Directors. Either of these mechanisms provides for only partial control, since one has a highly defined area of responsibility and the other provides employees with only one voice among many.

A final form of participation provides employees with full control of the operations of the corporation. Examples of this extensive participation are rare in North America, although some midwest farm and northwest lumber cooperatives are organized in this way.

Note that these varied mechanisms combine with the potential issues for participation in numerous ways. We might see union collective bargaining influence merit wage increases or working schedules; worker committee mechanisms of participation might deal with flexible work assignments or with evaluation of supervisors. This brief survey should indicate that discussions of employee participation must be pursued with care, since arguments criticizing or supporting participation might be sufficient grounds for drawing conclusions about one form of participation but not sufficient grounds for conclusions about other forms. That caution brings us to the second major aim of this essay—the clarification of moral arguments in favor of broad extensions of worker rights to participate in corporate decisions. Five justifications, or arguments, for participation will be sketched. Comments about the issues or mechanisms required by each justification will follow each argument sketch.

Argument 1

The first . . . justification for employee participation . . . takes its cue from the fundamental objective of any morality—the impartial promotion of human welfare. That requirement of impartiality can be understood as a requirement that we try to guarantee a fair hearing for the interests of every person in decisions concerning policies that centrally affect their lives. Certainly, many decisions at work can have a great impact on the lives of employees. For instance, an employee's privacy and health, both mental and physical, can easily be threatened in his or her working life. Morality, then, requires that there be some attempt to guarantee fair treatment for workers and their interests. We might attempt to institutionalize that guarantee through government regulation of business practices. However, regulation, while helpful to some degree, is often an insufficient guarantee of fair treatment. It is insufficient for the following reasons:

1. Regulation, when it does represent the interests of workers, often does so imprecisely because it is by nature indirect and paternalistic.

2. Business can frequently circumvent the intent of regulations by accepting fines for violations or by judicious use of regulatory appeal mechanisms.

3. Perhaps most importantly, corporate interests can emasculate the content of proposed legislation or regulation through powerful lobbying efforts.

So it seems that an effective guarantee that worker interests are represented fairly requires at least some mechanisms additional to regulation.

We might avoid many of the difficulties of legislation and regulation if workers were allowed to represent their interests more directly whenever crucial corporate decisions are made. Thus, a fair hearing for workers' interests might have a more effective institutional guarantee where workers have available some mechanisms for participation in those decisions. In practice, then, morality's demand for impartiality presumptively may require worker input in the shaping of corporate policies. . . .

Clearly, if worker interests are to be guaranteed as much fair treatment as possible, the participatory mechanisms must have actual power to influence corporate decisions. For while workers might receive fair treatment even where they lack such power, possession of real power more effectively institutionalizes a *guarantee* of fairness. Thus, internal participatory mechanisms that serve in a purely advisory capacity (e.g., quality circle groups) are obviously insufficient vehicles for meeting the fairness demands of morality.

Less obvious are the weaknesses of individual contract negotiations, union membership, and stock ownership as devices for guaranteeing fairness. None of these devices, in practice, can provide enough power to protect fair treatment for workers. Individual contract decisions often find the prospective employee in a very poor bargaining

position. The amount of effective power possessed through union membership varies with the changing state of the economy and with changes in particular industrial technologies. In addition, the majority of workers are not unionized; the declining proportion of union membership in the total workforce now stands at about one-fifth. Stock ownership plans provide employees very little leverage on corporate decisions because, commonly, only small percentages of stock are held by workers. Moreover, all three of these participation mechanisms most often have little direct power over the important operating decisions which affect worker interests. Those decisions are usually made and implemented for long periods before contract negotiations, union bargaining or stockholder meetings could have any chance at altering corporate policy.

Thus, a serious moral concern for fairness, a concern central to any moral perspective, presumptively requires that mechanisms for employee participation provide workers with at least partial effective control of the enterprise. And since decisions that have important consequences for the welfare of workers are made at every level of the corporation, employees ought to participate on issues from the shop floor to the board room. Moreover, since a balanced and impartial consideration of all interests is more probable when opposing parties have roughly equal institutional power, employees deserve more than token representation in the firm's decision-making structure. Rather, they should possess an amount of authority that realistically enables them to resist policies that unfairly damage their interests. This first moral argument, then, provides strong presumptive support for the right of employees to co-determine corporate policy.

Argument 2

The second moral argument . . . derives from points that . . . are similar to those of the preceding argument. Any acceptable moral theory must recognize the inherent value and dignity of the human person. One traditional basis for that belief in the dignity of the person derives from the fact that persons are agents capable of free and rational deliberation. We move towards respect for the dignity of the person when we protect individuals from humanly alterable interferences that jeopardize important human goods and when we allow them, equally, as much freedom from other interferences as possible. Persons with this freedom from interference are able to direct the courses of their own lives without threat of external control or coercion. (Such a view of persons provides for the moral superiority of self-determining, democratic systems of government over oppressive or totalitarian regimes.)

This moral commitment to the dignity of persons as autonomous agents has significant implications for corporate organization. Most of our adult lives are spent at our places of employment. If we possess no real control over that portion of our lives because we are denied the power to participate in forming corporate policy, then at work we are not autonomous agents. Instead we are merely anonymous and replaceable elements in the production process, elements with a moral standing little different from that of the inanimate machinery we operate. This remains true of our lives *at* work even if we have the opportunity to change employers. (Many workers do not have even that opportunity, and if they did it would be of little consequence for this issue, since most workplaces are similarly organized.) The moral importance of autonomy in respecting the dignity of persons should make us critical of these traditional patterns of work and should move us in the direction of more employee participation. However, since autonomy is understood as an ability to control one's activities, the preferred mechanisms of participation should allow employees real control at work. Thus, a commitment to the autonomy and the dignity of persons, just as a commitment to fairness, appears to require that workers have the ability to co-determine any policy that directs important corporate activity.

Argument 3

These first two arguments for broad worker participation rights have ended in an explicit requirement that workers have real and actual power over corporate policy. The final three arguments focus not on actual power but on the worker's *perception* of his or her ability to influence policy. All of these last arguments concern the potential for negative consequences created when workers see

themselves as having little control over their working lives.

The third argument warns that workers who believe themselves powerless will lose the important psychological good of self-respect.[1] Moral philosophers have contended that since all persons should be treated with dignity, all persons consequently deserve the conditions that generally contribute to a sense of their own dignity or self-worth. Psychologists tell us that a person's sense of self is to a large degree conditioned by the institutional relationships she has and the responses from others that she receives in those relationships. A person will have a stronger sense of her own worth and will develop a deeper sense of self-respect when her social interactions allow her to exercise her capacities in complex and interesting activities and when they reflect her status as an autonomous human being. Of course, in contemporary America the development of the division of labor and of hierarchical authority structures leaves little room for the recognition of the worker's autonomy or for the ordinary worker to exercise capacities in complex ways. The consequence of such work organization is the well-documented worker burnout and alienation; workers disassociate themselves from a major portion of their lives, often with the psychological consequence of a sense of their own unimportance. Contemporary American patterns of work, then, often fail to provide individuals with those conditions that foster a strong sense of self-respect; instead, they more often undermine self-respect. Numerous studies have indicated that a reversal of these trends is possible where workers are provided greater opportunities for exercising judgement and for influencing workplace activities.[2]

If we take seriously a demand for the universal provision of the conditions of self-respect, we ought to increase opportunities for satisfying work by allowing workers to participate in corporate policy decisions. It would seem, however, that this argument for worker participation need not conclude that workers be given actual power. All that the argument requires is that a worker's *sense* of self-respect be strengthened, and that is at least a possible consequence of participation in an advisory capacity. In fact, worker satisfaction has been shown to increase somewhat when employees are involved in Japanese-style quality circles that offer suggestions for improving production. Nor does it appear that the self-respect argument requires that workers be able to influence all aspects of corporate activity, since an increased sense of one's own significance could be had through participation only on immediate shop-floor issues.

However, we must be careful to estimate the long-range effects on worker alienation and self-respect of these less extensive forms of participation. Some evidence indicates that, over time, workers can grow more dissatisfied and alienated than ever if they perceive the participatory program as without real power or as simply a management attempt to manipulate workers for increased productivity.[3] We should consider, then, that a concern for long-run and substantial increases in self-respect might require workers to exercise some actual authority, of a more than token amount, over the workplace.

Argument 4

The fourth argument supporting participation also takes its cue from the studies that show repetitive work without control over one's activities causes worker alienation. The specific consequence that this argument focuses on, however, is not a lessening of self-respect but a potential threat to the mental and physical health of workers. Certainly, everyone is now aware that alienated individuals suffer from more mental disturbances and more stress-related physical illnesses. Workers who are satisfied because they feel able to contribute to corporate policy are held to suffer from less alienation. Since mental and physical health are undoubtedly very central human goods, there seems strong presumptive moral reason for minimizing any negative effects on them that institutional organizations might have. Since broader powers apparently help to minimize such effects, we again have an argument for an expansion of worker rights to participate in corporate decisions.

As with the self-respect argument, however, the issues and mechanisms of participation that this requires are unclear. It could be that negative health effects are minimized in the short run through advisory bodies of participation. On the other hand, minimizing threats to mental or physical well-being in the long run might require more actual authority. Which sorts of mechanisms help

most is a question only further empirical research can answer. However, since we have already seen presumptive reasons for actual power to co-determine policy from the first two arguments and since that power can have positive effects on self-respect and health, we perhaps have reasons for preferring the stronger forms of participation if we are presented with a choice between alternatives.

Argument 5

The fifth argument for worker participation also derives from the purported negative consequences of hierarchical and authoritarian organizations of work. This argument, however, focuses on broader social consequences—the danger to our democratic political structures if workers are not allowed to participate in corporate decisions.[4]

Many political theorists are alarmed by contemporary voter apathy. They worry that with that apathy the political process will be democratic in name only, and that the actual business of government will be controlled by powerful and private economic interests. To reverse this trend that threatens democratic government demands that individual citizens become more involved in the political process. However, increased individual involvement is seen as unlikely unless citizens believe themselves to have political power. But an initial increased sense of one's own political power does not seem possible from involvement in the large macroscopic political institutions of contemporary government. Rather, involvement in smaller, more local and immediate social activities will nurture a sense of political efficacy. Since so much time and attention is devoted to one's work life, the place of employment appears a prime candidate for that training in democracy necessary for development of civic involvement. In fact, powerless and alienated workers can bring their sense of powerlessness home and offer their children lessons in the futility of involvement. Allowing those lessons to continue would only exacerbate the threat to vital democratic institutions. This fifth argument, then, sees participation at work as a necessary condition for the existence of a healthy and lasting system of democracy where citizens have the confidence to engage in self-determining political activities.

Again, since this argument focuses on the

worker's perception of his or her own power, it provides presumptive support for those mechanisms that would increase both that sense of power and the tendency for political activity. Just what mechanisms these are can be open to argument. However, as before, if workers feel that their participatory mechanisms lack power, there is the danger that they will become even more cynical about their ability to influence political decisions. And since we have already seen arguments supporting participation with actual power to co-determine policy, there should be a presumption in favor of using mechanisms with real power.

Sources of Resistance

We have, then, five significant reasons for extending to workers a broad right to co-determine corporate policy. Now, in order to determine whether the presumption in favor of worker participation can be overridden, we need only to consider some of the common reasons for resisting this employee right to participate. Common sources of resistance to worker participation are that managers perceive it as a threat to their own status or power, that owners feel entitled to the sole control of their property, and that ordinary employees are believed incompetent to make corporate decisions. We shall consider briefly each of these sources of resistance in turn. Our evaluation of these claims will show them to be unacceptable sources of resistance when measured against the above moral reasons in favor of broad participation.

First, in order for management's perception that participation threatens its power to count as an acceptable moral reason for resistance, management power must have some moral basis of its own. According to even traditional conservative theories of corporate property, management has no basic moral right of its own to control the corporation. Rather, management's authority stems from its position as an agent of the economic interests of shareholders, who are seen as the ultimate bearers of a right to use, control, or dispose of property. On the traditional theory, then, management can find a legitimate moral reason for resisting participation only if it can show that schemes of employee participation are real threats to the economic interests of shareholders. Presently, we shall refer to evidence that this case against participation cannot be supported by the available data.

(Management, of course, might still resist even without a moral reason. However, such resistance can have no claim to our support; it is merely an obstacle to be overcome if there are moral reasons to support participation.)

Does participation damage the interests of ownership in a morally unacceptable way? To answer that question, we need to consider what interests ownership has and to what benefits property ownership should entitle one. In the process of confronting these issues, we will also see reasons for suspicion about claims that workers are not capable of participating in the intelligent setting of corporate policy.

In legally incorporated businesses, shareholders commonly have a monetary return on their investment as their principal desire.[5] Moreover, corporate property owners generally have surrendered their interest in day-to-day control of the corporation.[6] The usual owner interest, then, concerns the profitability of the business. Worker participation does not pose a serious threat to this interest in monetary return. Evidence shows that worker participation schemes often improve the economic condition of the business by increasing the interest, motivation, and productivity of employees.[7] In addition, corporations seeking qualified and motivated workers in the future might, out of self-interest, have to construct mechanisms for participation to satisfy the demands of a more slowly growing but more highly educated entry-level labor force.[8] And even in those cases where experiments at worker participation have not succeeded, the failures can often be explained by shortcomings of the particular program that are not generic to all forms of participation.[9] In fact, some of those with experience in constructing participatory work schemes believe that employees can be trained to operate most efficiently with expanded responsibilities.[10] When programs are designed carefully and when time is invested in training both former managers and employees, the competence of workers has not been seen as a crucial reason behind examples of participation's lack of success. Thus, in light of both the marked economic successes of broader worker participation programs and the apparent absence of any *generic* threats to profitability (such as employee incompetence), the economic interests of owners do not appear to provide a substantial basis for a justified resistance to an employee right to participate in corporate decision making.

Some might object, however, that corporate property owners have other interests at stake. Many see a right to control one's goods as fundamental to the concept of property ownership, for example. Thus, they might claim that shareholders have, because of their property ownership, rights to retain control of the business enterprise even if they fail to exercise those rights on a day-to-day basis. This right to control one's property would effectively eliminate the possibility of an employee right to co-determine policy.

There are two reasons, however, to question whether a right to control property can provide a moral basis for denying workers a right to participate in corporate decisions. First, corporate property owners have been granted by society a limit on their legal liability for their property. If a legally incorporated business is sued, owners stand to lose only the value of their investment; an owner of an unincorporated business can lose personal property beyond the value of the business. Part of the motivation behind making this legal limit on liability available was that society would thereby encourage investment activity that would increase the welfare of its members.[11] It is not unreasonable to suggest that this justification for the special legal privilege requires that corporations concern themselves with the welfare of persons within the society in exchange for limited liability. Society, then, places limits on the extent to which owners can direct the uses of their corporate property. For example, society can require that corporations concern themselves with the environmental health effects of their waste disposal policies. Failure to require such concern is tantamount to allowing some to profit from harms to others while preventing those others from obtaining reasonable compensation for grievous harms. However, if the legal limitation on liability requires corporations to have some moral concern for the welfare of others, it can also require corporations to protect the welfare of its employees. We have already seen, though, that morally serious goods are at stake when employees are unable to participate significantly in corporate decisions. Thus, if in exchange for limited liability the control of the corporation is to be limited by a concern for others, then the shareholders' interest in controlling corporate property could be limited to allow for an employee right to participate.

A second reason for rejecting the claim that an ownership right to control prohibits employee participation looks not on the legal privileges associated with corporate property but on the very concept of property itself. This argument makes points similar to ones made in the preceding paragraph, but the points apply to property whether it is incorporated or not. It is certainly true that property ownership is meaningless without some rights to control the goods owned. It is equally true, however, that no morally acceptable system of property rights can allow unlimited rights to control the goods owned. You, for example, are not allowed to do just anything you please with your car; you cannot have a right to drive it through my front porch. We accept similar restrictions on the control of business property; we prohibit people from selling untested and potentially dangerous drugs that they produce. The point of these examples is to illustrate that control of property, corporate or not, has to be limited by weighing the constraints on owners against the significance of the human goods that would be jeopardized in the absence of the constraints. Acceptable institutions of property rights, then, must mesh with a society's moral concern for protecting the fundamental human goods of all its members.

We have seen in the first part of this essay that there are significant reasons for thinking that important moral values are linked to a worker's ability to participate in corporate decision making. If control of property, personal or corporate, is to override these moral concerns, we need to be presented with an argument showing what more central goods would be jeopardized if employees were granted strong participation rights. The burden of proof, then, is on those who want to deny an employee right to co-determine corporate policy. They must show that an owner's interest in broad control of corporate policy can stand as an interest worthy of protection as a moral right even when such protection would threaten the dignity, fair treatment, self-respect, and health of workers, as well as the continued viability of a democratic polity with an actively self-determining citizenship.

Summary

To summarize: We have seen that there are various understandings of worker participation. The difference between these various understandings is a function of the workplace issues addressed and the participatory mechanisms that address them. We have also seen sketches of five arguments that purport to show a moral presumption in favor of strong worker participation in the form of an ability to actually co-determine policy. We have seen, further, that some traditional sources of resistance to worker participation (a threat to management or owner prerogatives of control, a belief in the incompetence of workers, a fear that profits will suffer) are either not supported by the evidence or are incapable of sustaining a moral basis for rejecting participation. The provisional conclusion we should draw, then, is that our society ought to move vigorously in the direction of a broader authority for all workers in their places of employment.

Notes

1. This argument has been made by Joe Grcic in "Rawls and Socialism," *Philosophy and Social Criticism* 8:1 (1980), and in "Rawls' Difference Principle, Marx's Alienation and the Japanese Economy," a paper presented at the Ninth Plenary Session of Amintaphil, 1983. It is also suggested by John Cotter in "Ethics and Justice in the World of Work: Improving the Quality of Working Life," *Review of Social Economy* 40:3 (1982).

2. Cf. the selection in this chapter by Edward Greenberg.

3. Cf. Daniel Zwerdling, *Workplace Democracy* (New York: Harper and Row, 1980).

4. This argument is made forcefully by Carole Pateman, *Participation and Democratic Theory* (Cambridge: Cambridge University Press, 1970).

5. Of course, the matter is more complex than this simple statement indicates. Some investors might even have interests in losing money if they are attempting to avoid taxes. Others might want to guarantee that their company does not produce immoral goods (as some Dow Chemical investors claimed was the case with Dow's napalm production). Still, in most cases the primary motivation for investment is a monetary return.

6. It is, of course, not always true that shareholders surrender their interest in day-to-day control, since some corporations are headed by their principal stockholders.

7. Cf. the articles by Greenberg and Zwerdling in this section. Additional evidence is found in the experiences of the small but highly publicized Volvo experiments and of Donnelly Mirrors, Inc. Interviews with heads of both Volvo and Donnelly can be found in *Harvard Business Review*, 55:4 (1977) and 55:1 (1977), respectively. In West Germany, co-

determination is mandated by law in some major industries that have been highly competitive with their American counterparts.

8. John Cotter, *op cit.*

9. Cf. Zwerdling's analysis of the problems with the General Foods plan in the first selection of this chapter. He argues, in part, that difficulties arose because workers saw the plan as merely an experiment instituted by management in the attempt to increase productivity.

10. The Donnelly interview, *op cit.*, and Nancy Foy and Herman Gadon, "Worker Participation: Contrasts in Three Countries," *Harvard Business Review*, v. 54, no. 3 (1976).

11. Cf. W. Michael Hoffman and James Fisher, "Corporate Responsibility: Property and Liability," in *Ethical Theory and Business*, 1st ed., T. Beauchamp and N. Bowie, eds. (Englewood Cliffs, N.J.: Prentice-Hall, 1979), pp. 187–96.

Review and Discussion Questions

1. What are the different forms that employee participation can take? In your experience, how extensive is such participation today?

2. McCall argues for participation in terms of the values of fair treatment, human dignity, self-respect, physical and mental health, and the promotion of a democratic society. Explain how each of these values, according to him, supports the case for participation.

3. On what grounds does management typically resist worker participation? How sound are its reasons for doing so? Does participation violate the rights of the owners of corporate property?

4. Is worker participation compatible with the efficient functioning of a free-enterprise system?

5. Do you think that more extensive worker participation would make companies more socially responsible? Do you think that such participation is desirable?

For Further Reading

Gertrude Ezorsky, ed., *Moral Rights in the Workplace* (Albany: State University of New York Press, 1987) is a good collection of articles on the right to meaningful work, occupational health and safety, employee privacy, unions, industrial flight, and related topics.

Mary Gibson, *Workers' Rights* (Totowa, N.J.: Rowman & Allanheld, 1983), rich in factual background and actual cases, discusses the rights of employees.

David R. Hiley, "Employee Rights and the Doctrine of At Will Employment," *Business and Professional Ethics Journal* 4 (Fall 1985) argues that employers do not have an unrestricted right to terminate employees at will.

Berth Jönsson, "The Quality of Work Life—the Volvo Experience," *Journal of Business Ethics* 1 (May 1982) discusses the innovative changes in production technology and work organization made by Volvo in Sweden.

Benjamin Kleinmuntz, "Lie Detectors Fail the Truth Test," *Harvard Business Review* 63 (July–August 1985) is a recent critique of reliance on polygraph tests.

Robert Kuttner, "Sharing Power at Eastern Air Lines," *Harvard Business Review* 63 (November–December 1985) discusses Eastern's dramatic turnaround since a 1983 union contract provided for labor and management to share power and responsibility on the shop floor.

Richard M. Pfeffer, *Working for Capitalism* (New York: Columbia University Press, 1979) describes the author's experience of factory work today.

Patricia Werhane, "Individual Rights in Business," in Tom Regan, ed., *New Introductory Essays in Business Ethics* (New York: Random House, 1984) provides a useful overview of many basic moral issues in the workplace.

Daniel Zwerdling, *Workplace Democracy* (New York: Harper & Row, 1979) contains a wealth of detailed information about efforts at worker self-management.

CHAPTER 7

MORAL CHOICES FACING EMPLOYEES

George Spanton was a sixty-two-year-old federal auditor, when he blew the whistle on "irregularities" in Department of Defense contract spending at a jet-engine testing plant. That one toot launched a 1983 federal grand jury inquiry into spending by Pratt & Whitney Aircraft Group, a division of United Technologies Corporation. It also meant personal trouble for Spanton, who was due to retire at the end of 1983, after eighteen years with the agency. When in March 1983 he sought a routine ten-month extension as resident auditor at Pratt & Whitney, Charles O. Starrett, director of the Defense Contract Auditing Agency (DCAA), wrote Spanton that he had to accept a transfer or be fired.

K. William O'Connor, special counsel of the Merit System Protection Board, questioned the propriety of certain actions by DCAA.[1] He said, "I now have reasonable grounds on the basis of the investigation to date to believe that DCAA denied Spanton's request for waiver and is now rotating him out of the Atlanta region because he provided nonclassified information to the press."

For his part, Spanton promised to fight the transfer. "I will take whatever legal action is necessary to prevent them from moving me," he said. "Furthermore, I will continue to expose improper action on the part of the contractor and the agency."[2]

For someone in a situation like George Spanton's, two general issues come up. First is a question of where his or her overall moral duty lies. For a professional auditor to decide to report "irregularities" may be a more straightforward moral decision than that

faced by an employee who suspects wrongdoing in an area that is unrelated to the employee's own job. In that case, the employee may well have conflicting moral obligations, and even the auditor, having reported the irregularities to the appropriate authority, must decide whether he is morally obligated to pursue the matter further. Again, as we shall see below, other moral considerations come into play.

Second, having decided that one ought, morally, to blow the whistle, an employee must face realistically the possible negative financial and career consequences. Spanton was close to retirement, and in that respect had less to risk than many potential whistle blowers stretched by financial obligations and with their full careers in front of them. Nor is this simply a tug-of-war between moral duty and self-interest. Some moral theorists would argue that certain personal sacrifices would be so great that we cannot reasonably be seen as being morally obliged to make them.

These two themes—(1) determining one's moral responsibility amid a welter of often conflicting demands, and (2) the personal costs involved in living up to one's obligations—recur throughout this chapter as we explore the moral choices and dilemmas that employees must often face. In particular, we will look at the following topics:

1. Obligations employees have to the firm and the problem of conflicts of interest.

2. The illegitimate use of one's official position for private gain, through insider trading or access to proprietary data.

3. Domestic and foreign bribery, and the factors to consider in determining the morality of giving and receiving gifts in a business context.

4. The obligations employees have to third parties, and the considerations they should weigh in cases of conflicting moral duties or divided loyalties.

5. What whistle blowing is, and the factors that are relevant to evaluating it morally.

6. The problem of how considerations of self-interest are to be weighed by an employee facing a tough moral choice.

OBLIGATIONS TO THE FIRM AND CONFLICTS OF INTEREST

You don't have to work for an organization very long, either at a management or non-management level, before realizing that your interests often collide with those of the organization. You want to dress one way, the organization wants you to dress another way; you'd prefer to show up for work at noon, the organization expects you to be present at 8 A.M.; you'd like to receive $50,000 a year for your labor, the organization gives you a fraction of that figure. Whatever the value in question, attitudes toward it can differ. Thus the reward, autonomy, and self-fulfillment that workers seek aren't always compatible with the worker productivity that the organization desires.

Sometimes this clash of perspectives or goals can take a serious form in what is termed a conflict of interest. *In an organization a conflict of interest arises when employees, at any level, have an interest in or are parties to an interest in a transaction substantial enough that it does or reasonably might affect their independent judgment in acts for the organization.*[3] Looked at another way, the organization has the right to expect employees to use independent judgment on its behalf. Conflicts of interest arise when employees jeopardize their independence of judgment.

The primary source of the organization's right to expect independent judgment on its behalf and the concomitant employee responsibility to respect that right is the work contract. When a person is hired, he or she agrees to discharge contractual obligations in exchange for pay. Thus the employee does specific work, puts in prescribed hours, and expends energy in return for remuneration, usually in the form of money. In general, if the contents of the work agreement are legal and workers freely consent to them, then they place themselves under an obligation to fulfill the terms of the agreement.

Implicit in any work contract is that employees will not use the firm for personal advantage. This doesn't mean that individuals shouldn't seek to benefit from being employed with a firm, but that in discharging their contractual obligations employees will not subordinate the welfare of the firm to personal gain.

Conflicts of interest may be either actual or potential. An *actual conflict of interest* arises when employees allow their interest in a transaction to becloud their independent judgment on behalf of the firm. For example, Bart Williams, sales manager for Leisure Sports World, gives all his firm's promotional work to Impact Advertising because its chief officer is Bart's brother-in-law. The transaction costs Leisure World about 15 percent more in advertising costs than comparable work with another agency would. The conflict here is actual: Bart has allowed his judgment on behalf of Leisure Sports World to be influenced by his own interest in Impact. Note that Williams's interest is not a financial one. This underscores the point that an interest conflict can take various forms. The issue is always whether the transaction functions to hamper one's independent judgment on behalf of the firm.

Even if Bart Williams does not actually

compromise himself in this way, he still faces a potential conflict of interest just by being in a position where he could compromise the interest of the firm. Thus, a *potential conflict of interest* arises in cases in which an employee's ability to exercise independent judgment on behalf of the organization is likely to be in jeopardy. Williams could easily throw some business his brother-in-law's way at the expense of Leisure Sports World.

Some would point to the Bert Lance affair as one of the more celebrated recent examples of a conflict of interest. Lance was the amiable Georgian who directed the Office of Management and Budget—but not for long. In the fall of 1977, less than a year after being appointed by President Carter, Lance resigned under fire.

The several factors that led to Lance's departure can be summed up with the phrase "highly dubious banking practices." Before assuming his governmental post, Lance was president of the Calhoun First National Bank in Georgia. During that time Lance apparently drew large personal loans from banks with which his own bank had established correspondent relationships. In a "correspondent relationship," large banks perform various services for smaller banks in return for balances that the small banks keep with them. One such large bank was Georgia's Fulton National Bank.

Between 1963 and 1975 Lance and his wife LaBelle apparently received nearly twenty loans from Fulton National totaling close to $4 million. In documents related to these loans, the Fulton bank noted that "satisfactory balances are maintained by Calhoun National Bank,"[4] thus implying a direct connection between the loans and the interest-free deposits that Lance's bank had placed with Fulton to establish the correspondent relationship. In his report, Comptroller of the Currency John Heimann concluded that there was reason to believe Lance would not have received the loans had it not been for the correspondent

accounts. Heimann further indicated that Lance had established a similar pattern of personal loans with two smaller Georgia banks in which he had an interest.

Investigators also discovered that Lance might have profited from a series of sales of a Beechcraft airplane that the Calhoun bank had purchased while Lance was its president. The bank subsequently sold the plane to Lancelot Company, whose owners were Bert and LaBelle. When Lance later became president of the National Bank of Georgia, that bank purchased the Beechcraft from Lancelot.

Apparently Lance also used the Calhoun bank to help finance and promote his bid for governor in 1974. His campaign accounts at the bank, which he then headed, were at one point overdrawn by $99,529. Further investigation indicated that the bank may have paid for entertainment, supplied computers for sending out campaign literature, and provided time to help with Lance's campaign. Evidently the Calhoun bank also paid many of Lance's campaign bills but listed them as business expenses. Lance later reimbursed the bank.

Lance and his family also ran up personal overdrafts at the Calhoun bank while he was its president. Comptroller Heimann reported that Lance's account was overdrawn by about $50,000 at least twenty-five times between 1972 and 1975. Furthermore, LaBelle Lance overdrew her account by up to $110,000 in 1974. And between September 1974 and April 1975, nine Lance relatives were overdrawn by $450,000.

It's easy to become disoriented by the dizzying effect of the figures and financial razzle-dazzle in the Lance case. On top of this are the political overtones that can easily bruise objectivity. Yet most people both in and out of the banking profession would agree that, judging from the evidence, Bert Lance used his professional banking status to advance his own interests. In other words, he seems to have engaged in practices that many bankers would consider irregular and not in the best interests of one's bank—thus, a conflict of interest.

Conflict of interest can arise in all sorts of ways and take many forms. Its most common expressions, however, involve actions related to financial investments, the use of official position (especially with regard to insider trading and proprietary data), bribery, kickbacks, gifts, and entertainment. Although these phenomena do not necessarily involve conflicts of interests, they often do; and they always raise moral questions about what employees owe organizations.

Financial Investments

Conflicts of interest can be present when employees have financial investments in suppliers, customers, or distributors with whom their organizations do business. For example, Fred Walters, purchasing agent for Trans-Con Trucking, owns stock with Timberline Paper. When ordering office supplies, Fred buys exclusively through a Timberline affiliate, even though he could get the identical supplies cheaper from another supplier. This is an actual conflict of interest. But even if Fred never advantages himself in this way, he is potentially conflicted because of his interest in Timberline.

It's impossible to say how much of a financial investment compromises one's independent judgment in acts for the organization. Ordinarily it is acceptable to hold a small percentage of stock in a publicly owned supplier that is listed on a public stock exchange. Some organizations state what percentage of outstanding stock their members may own. This can vary from 1 to 10 percent. Companies may also restrict the percentage of the employee's total investment funds that are involved in an investment. Some corporations even require key officers to make a full disclosure of all outside interests or of other rela-

tionships that could cloud their judgment on behalf of the organization. Quite obviously, then, organizational policy will largely determine the morally permissible limits of outside investments and conflicts of interest. It's worth noting, however, that since such a policy can affect the financial well-being of those who fall under it, it should be subjected to the same kind of free and open negotiations that any form of compensation is.

Use of Official Position

A serious area of conflict of interest involves the use of one's official position for personal gain. Cases in this area can range from using subordinates for nonorganization-related work to using one's important position within an organization to enhance one's own financial leverage and holdings. Some persons claim that this latter form of conflict of interest was most evident in the Lance case. Lance apparently used his bank's correspondent account to float personal loans upward of $4 million. Also he seems to have used his position to overdraw his Calhoun bank account by about $100,000 while financing his gubernatorial campaign. And Lance's relatives appear to have benefited directly from Lance's position.

Insider Trading. Although not evident in the Lance case, many abuses of official position arise from "insider trading." *Insider trading refers to the use of significant facts that have not yet been made public and will likely affect stock prices.* For example, in 1983 the Justice Department was looking into the possibility that some Social Security officials, anticipating that the government was about to award Paradyne Corporation a computer contract, bought Paradyne common stock and sold short shares in one or more of the five companies that lost out to Paradyne. (In a short sale, investors sell borrowed stock, hoping to make a profit by buying back an equal number of shares at a lower price.) If the employees did do that, they engaged in insider trading.

Increasingly in the world of big business, the pervasive desire to make "a fast buck" takes the form of illegally profiting from inside information. Currently business is brisk for the Securities Exchange Commission (SEC), which is charged with policing the stock market for insider-trading violations. Not only has the SEC been filing dozens of cases annually, but it also sent a seismic tremor through Wall Street in late 1986 by arresting the financial giant Ivan Boesky for insider trading and other securities infractions. Whether Boesky's fall will halt the increase in individuals trying to trade inside information for fast and sometimes big profits remains to be seen.

Inside traders ordinarily defend their actions by claiming they didn't injure anyone. It's true that trading by insiders on the basis of nonpublic information seldom directly injures anyone. But moral concerns arise from indirect injury, as well as from direct. As one author puts it, "What causes injury or loss to outsiders is not what the insiders knew or did; rather it is what they themselves [the outsiders] did not know. It is their own lack of knowledge which exposes them to risk of loss or denies them an opportunity to make a profit."[5] Case in point: the Texas Gulf Sulphur stock case.

In 1963 test drilling by Texas Gas Company indicated a rich ore body near Timins, Ontario. In a press release of April 12, 1964, some officials at Texas Gulf attempted to play down the potential worth of the Timins property by describing it as "a prospect." But on April 16 a second press release termed the Timins property "a major discovery." In the interim, inside investors made a handsome personal profit through stock purchases. At the same time, stockholders who unloaded stock based on the first press release lost money. Others who might have bought the stock lost out on a chance to make a profit.

In 1965 the Security and Exchange Commission (SEC) charged that a group of insiders, including Texas Gulf directors, officers, and employees, violated the disclosure section of the Securities and Exchange Act of 1934 by purchasing stock in the company while withholding information about the rich ore strike the company had made. The courts upheld the charge, finding that the first press release was "misleading to the reasonable investor using due care."[6] As a result, the courts not only ordered the insiders to pay into a special court-administered account all profits they made by trading on the inside information but also ordered them to repay profits made by outsiders whom they had tipped. The courts then used this account to compensate persons who had lost money by selling their Texas Gulf Sulphur stock on the basis of the first press release. This incident illustrates how indirect injury can result from insider dealings and the legal risks that insiders run in trading on inside information.

To be sure, insider dealings raise moral questions not easily resolved. When can employees buy and sell securities in their own companies? How much information must they disclose to stockholders about the firm's plans, outlooks, and prospects? When must this information be disclosed? Also, if people in business are to operate from a cultivated sense of moral accountability, it's important for them to understand who is considered to be an insider. In general, an *insider* could be considered anyone who has access to inside information. In practice, determining precisely who this is isn't always easy. On the one hand, corporate executives, directors, officers, and other key employees surely are insiders. But what about outsiders whom a company temporarily employs, such as accountants, lawyers, and contractors?

Before 1980, the SEC's insider trading rule presumably was intended to equalize opportunity in the market place. Thus, "insider" was then taken in the broadest sense to mean anyone who gains an advantage by using inside information. But that all changed in 1980 with the case of Vincent Chiarella, a financial printer who traded on information he culled from documents passing through his shop. The Supreme Court ruled that Chiarella was not an insider and thus didn't fall under the SEC insider-trading rule.

In *SEC vs. Dirks* (1983), the Supreme Court went further in narrowing the scope of insiders. The case involved Raymond L. Dirks, a securities analyst, who is a person who recommends which stocks to buy. Just before he blew the whistle in 1973 on a huge fraud at Equity Funding Corporation of America, Dirks advised several of his clients to dump their shares in Equity. Sure enough, when the scandal broke, the company stock plunged and Dirks's clients avoided taking a bath. The SEC charged Dirks with insider trading, but the Supreme Court reversed the decision. In ruling that Dirks was not an insider, the Court established that there is nothing improper about an outsider using information, so long as the information is not obtained from an insider who seeks personal gain, such as profit or showing favor to friends.

The SEC thinks that the Court has erred in narrowing the range of "insider." Apparently the Congress agrees. In September 1983, the House passed the "Insider Trading Sanctions Act" and in the spring of 1984 the Senate Banking, Housing, and Urban Affairs subcommittee on securities began to hammer out its own version of the measure. Both bills would allow courts to levy hefty fines against traders, and the Senate bill would broaden the definition of "insiders" to encompass accountants, lawyers, consultants, and other outsiders.

John M. Fedders, the enforcement director of the SEC, welcomes the help from Capitol Hill. He likens insider trading to white-collar crime. "It is the rawest kind of misconduct without broken windows [from looting]," he says. "Simply put, it's stealing by people in white shirts and suspenders."[7]

Law professor Henry Manne disagrees. He thinks the SEC should stay totally out of the insider trading field. "The use of insider information should be governed by private contractual relationships,"[8] such as those between corporations and their personnel.

At the base of this disagreement are two opposed philosophies about what makes the market work. Fedders and like-minded analysts contend that only if the marketplace is perceived as being honest and offering equal investment opportunity can it work. Insider trading, they argue, makes that impossible. But thinkers like Manne believed that permitting insiders to trade accelerates the information flow to the rest of the shareholders and investors. As a result, information is more quickly reflected in share value, which is healthy for the market.[9]

The information that employees garner within the company is not always the kind that they can use to affect stock prices. Sometimes the information concerns highly sensitive data concerning company research, technology, product development, and so on. How employees use such secret or classified data can also raise important moral concerns.

Proprietary Data. Companies guard information that can affect their competitive standing with all the zealousness of a bulldog guarding a ham bone. Take Procter & Gamble, for example. In June 1984 it patented the baking technique of its Duncan Hines brand of homemade-style chocolate chip cookies. It then sued three rival food chains, charging them with using the patented process to make "infringing cookies." P & G further claimed that these companies had spied at a sales presentation and at cookie plants. One company allegedly even flew a spy plane over a P & G plant under construction. One of the defendants, Frito-Lay, admitted to sending a worker to photograph the outside of a Duncan Hines bakery. But it denied telling the man's college-age son to walk into the plant and ask for some unbaked cookie dough—

which the enterprising youth did, and got. Frito-Lay insisted that it destroyed both the pictures and the dough without scrutinizing either and formally apologized to P & G. It also countersued P & G for trying to eliminate competition.[10]

When information is patented or copyrighted, it is legally protected but not secret. Others may have access to the information, but they are forbidden to use it (without permission) for the life of the patent or copyright. Thus, when a company patents a process, as Kleenex did with pop-up tissues, for example, the company has a monopoly on that process. No other firm may compete in the production of pop-up facial tissues. Although on the face of it this violates the ideal of a free market and would appear to slow the spread of new processes and technology, patents and copyrights are, in fact, generally defended on the ground that without them technological innovation would be hampered. Individuals and companies would not be willing to invest in the development of a new process if other firms could then immediately exploit any new invention without having themselves invested in developing it.

Although patent law is complicated and patents are not easy to acquire, what it means for something to be patented is well-defined legally. By contrast, the concept of a "trade secret" is broad and imprecise. The standard legal definition says that a trade secret is "any formula, pattern, device, or compilation of information which is used in one's business and which gives him an opportunity to obtain an advantage over competitors who do not know or use it."[11] Virtually any information that is not generally known (or whose utility is not recognized) is eligible for classification as a trade secret, as long as such information is valuable to its possessor and is treated confidentially. On the other hand, although a growing number of states now punish theft of trade secrets, trade secrets do not enjoy the same protection as patented information. The

formula for Coca-Cola, for instance, is secret, but not patented. No competitor has yet succeeded in figuring it out by "reverse engineering," but if your company managed to do so, then it would be entitled to use the formula itself.

One of an organization's biggest challenges is to protect trade secrets and proprietary data from being misused by its own employees. This is especially troublesome in high-tech firms when employees who are privy to sensitive information leave the organization. And the problems are compounded by at least two factors: first, the individual's right to seek new employment and, second, the difficulty of separating "trade secrets" from the technical knowledge, experience, and skill that are part of the employee's own intellect and talents.

A classic case, discussed by Michael Baram in "Trade Secrets: What Price Loyalty?" (see p. 321), involved Donald Wohlgemuth, who worked in the spacesuit department of B. F. Goodrich Company in Akron, Ohio. Eventually Wohlgemuth became the general manager of the spacesuit division and learned of Goodrich's highly classified spacesuit technology for the Apollo flights. Shortly thereafter Wohlgemuth, desiring a higher salary, joined Goodrich's competitor, International Latex Corporation in Dover, Delaware. His new position was manager of engineering for the industrial area that included making spacesuits in competition with Goodrich. As you might expect, Goodrich protested by seeking an order restraining Wohlgemuth from working for Latex. In 1963 the Court of Appeals of Ohio denied Goodrich's request for an injunction, respecting Wohlgemuth's right to choose his employer. But it did provide an injunction restraining Wohlgemuth from revealing Goodrich's trade secrets.

Cases like Wohlgemuth's are fundamentally different from those involving insider trading, for they pit a firm's right to protect its secrets against an employee's right to seek employment wherever he or she chooses. This doesn't mean that moral problems don't arise in proprietary data cases or that they're easily resolved. After all, one can always ask whether Wohlgemuth was moral in what he did, the legality of his action notwithstanding. Such a question seems especially appropriate when one learns that Wohlgemuth, when asked by Goodrich management whether he thought his action was moral, replied, "Loyalty and ethics have their price and International Latex has paid this price."

Clearly, then, considerably more moral groundbreaking is needed in the areas of insider trading and use of proprietary data. But one thing seems clear: both areas raise serious ethical questions. Similar questions surround practices involving bribes and kickbacks.

Bribes and Kickbacks

A bribe is remuneration for the performance of an act that's inconsistent with the work contract or the nature of the work one has been hired to perform. The remuneration can be money, gifts, entertainment, or preferential treatment.

Bribes constitute another area where conflicts of interest arise. To illustrate, in exchange for a "sympathetic reading of the books," a company gives a state auditor a trip to Hawaii. Or a sporting goods company provides the child of one of its retailers with free summer camp in exchange for preferred display, location, and space for its products. In both instances, individuals have received payments inconsistent with the work contract or the nature of the work they contracted to perform.

Bribery sometimes takes the form of *kickbacks, a practice that involves a percentage payment to a person able to influence or control a source of income.* Thus, Alice Farnsworth, sales representative for Sisyphus Book Co., offers a book-selection committee member a percentage of the handsome commission she stands to make if a Sisyphus civics text is adopted.

The money the committee member receives for the preferred consideration is a kickback.

Because bribes are ordinarily illegal, they raise the same general moral issues as any act of lawbreaking does. This observation applies even when an organization gives gratuities without asking for or expecting favors in return, as in the case of Gulf Corporation's pleading guilty in 1977 to giving trips to an Internal Revenue Service auditor in charge of the company's tax audit. According to government sources, Gulf's plea marked one of the first times a major U.S. corporation acknowledged that gifts to public officials are illegal even when no favors are asked or expected.

Far more frequent are instances of bribes paid with the intention of getting something in return, as when U.S. companies through their foreign subsidiaries pay off foreign officials for business favors. Such acts were declared illegal in the Foreign Corrupt Practices Act of 1977, which was passed in the wake of the discovery that nearly 400 American companies had made such payments over several years amounting to about $300 million. Egregious within the sordid pattern of international bribery by some major American corporations is Lockheed Aircraft Corporation's $22 million in payoffs to foreign politicians over five years to get aircraft contracts. Lest one understate the effects of such bribery, it is worth dwelling on the fact that revelations of Lockheed bribes in Japan caused a governmental crisis there, and in Holland Prince Bernhardt was forced to resign his governmental duties after admitting that he took a $1 million payoff from Lockheed. Gulf also admitted to making secret payments of $4 million to the ruling political party in South Korea in order to firm up its investments there. Exxon Corporation said it paid $59 million to Italian politicians to promote its business objectives in that country. And only after the suicide of United Brands chairman Eli Black did an SEC investigation reveal that United Brands had paid a $1.25 million bribe to a

Honduran official to win a reduction in that country's business export tax.

The Foreign Corrupt Practices Act (FCPA) provides stiff fines and prison sentences for corporate officials engaging in bribery overseas and requires corporations to establish strict accounting and auditing controls to guard against the creation of slush funds from which bribes can be paid. The FCPA does not, however, prohibit "grease payments" to the employees of foreign governments who have primarily clerical or ministerial responsibilities. These payments are sometimes necessary to ensure that the recipients carry out their normal job duties. On the other hand, the FCPA makes no distinction between bribery and extortion. A company is extorted by a foreign official, for instance, if the official threatens to violate the company's rights, perhaps by closing down a plant on some legal pretext, unless the official is paid off.

Since passage of the FCPA, many corporations have lobbied for changes that would extract some of the teeth from the law. They claim that the law has put American corporations at a competitive disadvantage in relation to foreign competitors whose governments permit them to bribe. Some corporations further assert that the law has resulted in lost exports for the U.S. This argument has been advanced by various Reagan administration officials, among them Commerce Secretary Malcolm Baldridge and U.S. Trade Representative Bill Brock. They have consistently pushed for an easing of accounting requirements and eliminating the responsibility of U.S. companies for actions of their foreign agents.

Before accepting such arguments, one should note that competition is not always a factor in foreign bribes, as illustrated in the United Brands case. Moreover, an investigation of corporate bribery overseas conducted under the Ford administration belies the foreign-competition defense. In 1976, Elliot Richardson, then Commerce Secretary, re-ported to Congress that "in a multitude of cases—especially those involving the sale of military and commercial aircraft—payments have been made not to outcompete foreign competitors, but rather to gain a competitive edge over other U.S. manufacturers."[12] Furthermore there's no compelling evidence that U.S. companies have lost exports as a result of the Foreign Corrupt Practices Act. But even if it is true that the U.S. is losing exports and U.S. companies are being placed at a competitive disadvantage because of the 1977 law, such considerations must be carefully weighed against the ample documentary evidence of the serious harm done to individuals, companies, and governments as a result of systematic bribery overseas.

Also worth noting is that where bribes are condoned, they can have the effect of encouraging employees of organizations to take bribes and thus subordinate the interests of the organization to their own gain. But even when bribes appear to hurt no one, moral concerns still arise. In the case of the aforementioned sporting goods company that sent the child of one of its retailers to summer camp in order to obtain special treatment, let's suppose that the product is a good and fairly priced one. People buy it and are satisfied with it. Thus, the manufacturer is happy, and so are the retailer and consumer. In brief, it appears that everyone's interests are served. So what, if anything, is wrong with bribes in such cases?

Perhaps nothing. But before reaching a conclusion, remember that bribery always involves cooperation with others who are seeking to gain preferred treatment through an act that undermines the free market system. True, such a system might be inherently immoral, in which case an act that undermines it is not necessarily wrong. We need not debate this thesis again, for we have already inspected the morality of capitalism elsewhere. The point here is that bribes tend to subvert the free enterprise system, because they function to give advantage in a way that is not directly or indirectly product-related.

The multiple impacts of bribery can be succinctly drawn out in one final case, which involves Bethlehem Steel Corporation, the nation's second-largest steel company. In 1980, Bethlehem was fined $325,000 by a federal judge for bribery and other corrupt practices stretching over four years. Bethlehem admitted to paying more than $400,000 in bribes to shipowners' representatives, including officers of the Colombian Navy. The bribes were paid to ensure that ships needing repairs would be steered into Bethlehem's eight shipyards. Thus, competitive bidding for the contracts was effectively eliminated, various members of the Colombian Navy were corrupted, and the Colombian government may have ended up paying more for the repair work than they had to. Beyond this, Bethlehem generated more than $1.7 million for the payoffs by padding bills and skimming profits from legitimate shipyard repair work. Thus, unsuspecting clients of Bethlehem were made to pay the bill for Bethlehem's bribery.

Gifts and Entertainment

In determining the morality of gift giving and gift receiving in a business situation and in deciding whether a conflict of interest exists, a number of factors must be considered.

1. *What is the value of the gift?* Is the gift of nominal value, or is it substantial enough to influence a business decision? Undoubtedly definitions of *nominal* and *substantial* are open to interpretation and are often influenced by situational and cultural variables. Nevertheless, many organizations consider a gift of twenty dollars or less given infrequently—perhaps once a year—a nominal gift. Anything larger or more frequent would constitute a substantial gift. Although this standard may be arbitrary and inappropriate in some cases, it does indicate that a rather inexpensive gift might be construed as substantial.

2. *What is the purpose of the gift?* Dick Randall, a department store manager, accepts small gifts, like pocket calculators, from an electronics firm. He insists that the transactions are harmless and that he doesn't intend to give the firm any preferred treatment in terms of advertising displays in the store. So long as the gift is not intended or received as a bribe and it remains nominal, there doesn't appear to be any actual conflict of interest in such cases. But relative to the purpose of the gift, it would be important to ascertain the electronic firm's intention. Is it to influence how Randall lays out displays? Does Randall himself expect it as a palm-greasing device before he'll ensure that the firm receives equal promotional treatment? If so, extortion may be involved. Important to this question of purpose is a consideration of whether the gift is directly tied to an accepted business practice. For example, appointment books, calendars, or pens and pencils with the donor's name clearly imprinted on them serve to advertise a firm. Trips to Hawaii rarely serve this purpose.

3. *What are the circumstances under which the gift was given or received?* A gift given during the holiday season, for a store opening, or to signal other special events is circumstantially different from one unattached to any special event. Whether the gift was given openly or secretly should also be considered. A gift with the donor's name embossed on it usually constitutes an open gift, whereas one known only to the donor and recipient would not.

4. *What is the position and sensitivity to influence of the person receiving the gift?* Is the person in a position to affect materially a business decision on behalf of the gift giver? In other words, could the recipient's opinion, influence, or decision of itself result in preferential treatment for the donor? Another important point is whether the recipients have made it abundantly clear to the donors that

they don't intend to allow the gift to influence their action one way or the other.

5. *What is the accepted business practice in the area?* Is this the customary way of conducting this kind of business? Monetary gifts and tips are standard practice in numerous service industries. Their purpose is not only to reward good service but to ensure it again. But it's not customary to tip the head of the produce department in a supermarket so that the person will put aside the best of the crop for you. Where gratuities are an integral part of customary business practice they are far less likely to pose conflict of interest questions.

6. *What is the company's policy?* Many firms explicitly forbid the practice of giving and receiving gifts in order to minimize even the suspicion that a conflict may exist. Where such a policy exists, the giving or receiving of a gift would constitute a conflict of interest.

7. *What is the law?* This consideration is implicit in all facets of conflicts of interest. Some laws, for example, forbid all gift giving and receiving among employees and firms connected with government contracts. Again, where the gift transaction violates a law, a conflict of interest is always present.

Related to gift giving is the practice of entertaining. In general, entertainment should be interpreted more sympathetically than gifts because it usually occurs within the context of doing business in a social situation. Some companies distinguish entertainment from gifts as follows: If you can eat or drink it on the spot, it's entertainment.

Ordinarily the morality of entertainment may be evaluated on the same basis as gifts—that is, with respect to value, purpose, circumstances, position and sensitivity to influence of recipient, accepted business practices, company policy, and law. In each case the ultimate moral judgment hinges largely on a decision as to whether an objective party could reasonably suspect that the gift or entertainment could blur one's independent judgment. Similarly, the donor must ask whether an objective party could reasonably suspect that the gift or entertainment was aimed at blurring the recipient's independent judgment.

OBLIGATIONS TO THIRD PARTIES

A worker knows that a fellow worker occasionally snorts coke on the job. Should she inform the boss?

A chef knows that his restaurant typically reheats three- or four-day-old food and serves it as fresh. When he informs the manager, he is told to forget it. What should the chef do?

A consulting engineer discovers a defect in a structure that is about to be sold. If the owner will not disclose the defect to the potential purchaser, should the engineer do so?

An accountant learns of the illegal activities of a client, including deliberate violations of building codes. What should she do about it?

On a regular basis, a secretary is asked by her boss to lie to his wife about his whereabouts. "If my wife calls," the boss tells her, "don't forget to confirm that I'm on a business trip." In fact, as the secretary well knows, the boss is having an affair with another woman. What should the secretary do?

Such cases are not unusual, but they are different from the ones we've been considering up until now in this chapter because they involve workers caught in the cross fire of conflicting obligations. On the one hand, workers have obligations to the employer, organization, or client; on the other, they have obligations to third parties: fellow employees, customers, government, or society generally.

Conflicts between a worker's obligation to the firm and to others are at the heart of many moral decisions workers must make. A way to resolve these conflicts is needed, but that in turn requires identifying the obligations, if any, workers have to third parties.

Workers have three basic obligations to third parties as a matter of ordinary morality: truthfulness, noninjury, and fairness. In some instances the application of these obligations to outside parties is relatively straightforward. For example, in engineering codes of ethics, obligations to third parties are fundamental, and the obligation of noninjury predominates because almost all architectural and engineering projects have a potential for injuring people. Whether the design is of an automobile, airplane, building, bridge, electric power system, sewer system, or nuclear power plant, a faulty design clearly can result in injury to others.

Similarly, those commercially serving alcoholic beverages have a noninjury obligation to monitor the amount of alcohol they serve customers—this, despite the U.S. Supreme Court's 1979 ruling ending liability for overserving intoxicated customers. (People who commercially serve alcohol still can be cited for a misdemeanor if they overserve an intoxicated person, and the establishment can lose its license.)

For accountants, it is not so much the obligation of noninjury that dominates the relationship to third parties, but truthfulness and justice. This is because most of the injury accountants cause others results from deceit or unfairness. Accordingly, auditors certify that financial statements present data fairly, as determined by generally accepted accounting principles. An untruthful audit can cause others to make unwise investments. Likewise, failure to be truthful and fair in preparing an income tax statement cheats government and society generally.

Truthfulness, noninjury, and fairness are the ordinary categories of obligations that employees have to third parties, but we can still ask: How are workers to reconcile obligations to employer or organization and others? Should the employee ensure the welfare of the organization by reporting the fellow worker using drugs, or should she be loyal to the fellow worker and say nothing? Should the secretary carry out her boss's instructions, or should she tell his wife the truth? Should the accountant say nothing about the building code violations, or should she inform authorities? In each case the employee experiences divided loyalties. Resolving such conflicts is never easy, and much hangs on the specific details of the situation. How an employee resolves the moral conflict will also depend on the moral principles to which the employee subscribes and the values which are important in his or her life.

According to the procedure recommended in Chapter 2, any moral decision should take account of the relevant *obligations*, *ideals*, and *effects*. We have already mentioned the three ordinary obligations of truthfulness, noninjury, and fairness that employees have to third parties. And, as indicated, the specific responsibilities that one assumes in a given business or professional role will affect the strength of one's obligations to third parties. When an engineer or an accounting auditor, for example, suspects some "irregularity," he or she may have a stronger obligation to get to the bottom of the matter than would an ordinary employee who has a hunch that something is not in order in another department. This raises a further question. While we all have the three general obligations mentioned above, how far must we go to uncover or remedy possible violations of those obligations by others? It is unlikely that any moral theory can give a general answer to this question, applicable to all cases.

So far our talk of the obligations of employees to third parties has been a little abstract, but we must remember that these third parties are not just the "public" at large, but often our friends, coworkers, and family members—real flesh-and-blood people with whom our lives are interwoven. Our ongoing relations with them may give rise to moral obligations based on those relationships, above and beyond any moral obligations we have to third parties in general. Sometimes these obligations have to be balanced against obligations to the firm and obligations arising from the business, professional, or organizational roles we have assumed.

The impact of our action on significant moral ideals is the second consideration to be weighed. Moral decisions must take account not only of distinct ethical obligations, but also of the various ideals advanced or respected, ignored or hindered, by the alternative actions open to us. In addition, our moral choices will often be influenced strongly by the personal weight that we place on the different values that may be at stake in a specific situation. Sometimes these values can point in different directions, as when our simultaneous commitment to professional excellence, personal integrity, and loyalty to friends pulls us in three different ways.

Third, but not least, we must examine the effects of the different courses of action. Even staunch nonconsequentialists acknowledge that the likely results of our actions are relevant to their moral assessment and that we have a duty to promote human well-being. In addition, considerations of consequences can help us determine the exact strength of our different obligations in a given situation.

As discussed in Chapter 2, we must first identify the relevant obligations, ideals, and effects and then try to decide where the emphasis among them should lie. There is nothing mechanical about this, but when we as employees weigh moral decisions, two simple things can help to keep our deliberations free from the various rationalizations to which we are all prone. First, we can ask ourselves whether we would be willing to read an account of our actions in the newspaper. That is, when we have made our decisions, are the contemplated actions ones that we would be willing to defend publicly? Second, discussing a moral dilemma or ethical problem with a friend can often help us to avoid bias and to gain a better perspective. People by themselves, and especially when emotionally involved in a situation, sometimes focus unduly on one or two points, ignoring other relevant factors. Input from others can keep us from overlooking pertinent considerations, thus helping us to make a better, more objective moral judgment.

As the preceding discussion mentioned, employees frequently know about the illegal or immoral actions of a supervisor or firm. When an employee tries to correct the situation within institutional channels and is thwarted, a central moral question emerges: Should the employee go public with the information? Should a worker who is ordered to do something illegal or immoral, or who knows of the illegal or immoral behavior of a supervisor or organization, inform the public? When these questions are answered affirmatively and the public is informed, cases of whistle blowing result.

Whistle Blowing

On October 11, 1979, Morris H. Baslow, a forty-seven-year-old biologist and father of three, dropped an envelope in the mail to Thomas B. Yost, an administrative law judge with the EPA. Later that day Baslow was fired from his job with Lawler, Matusky & Skelly, an engineering consulting firm that had been hired by Consolidated Edison Co. of New York to help it blunt EPA insistence that the power company's generating plants on the Hudson River had to have cooling towers to protect fish from excessively warm water being discharged into the river from the power plants.

Baslow claims that the documents he sent showed that Con Ed and Lawler, Matusky & Skelly had knowingly submitted invalid and misleading data to the EPA that gave the false impression that the long-term effects of the utilities' effluent on fish was negligible. On the basis of his own research, Baslow believed that the fish could be significantly harmed by the warm-water discharge. He says that for two years he tried to get his employers to listen to him, but they wouldn't.

Shortly after being fired, Baslow sent seventy-one company documents supporting his allegation to the EPA, the Federal Energy Regulation Commission, and the Justice Department. In the month following these disclosures, Baslow's employers accused him of stealing the documents and sued him for defamation. Baslow countersued, citing the Clean Water Act, which protects consultants from reprisals for reporting findings prejudicial to their employers and clients.

In October 1980, Lawler, Matusky & Skelly dropped all legal action against Baslow and gave him a cash settlement of reportedly around $100,000. In return, Baslow wrote to the EPA and other governmental agencies withdrawing his complaint of wrongdoing and perjury on the part of the defendants but not recanting his own scientific conclusions. Asked why he finally accepted the cash payment, the unemployed Baslow said, "I've had to bear the brunt of this financially by myself . . . I just wish somebody had listened to me six months ago."[13]

The Baslow case and scores more like it illustrate the ethical problem and personal risks that employees face who blow the whistle on what they perceive as organizational misconduct.

Whistle blowing refers to an employee act of informing the public about the illegal or immoral behavior of an employer or organization. Professor of philosophy Norman Bowie provides the following detailed definition of a "whistle blower":

> A whistle blower is an employee or officer of any institution, profit or non-profit, private or public, who believes either that he/she has been ordered to perform some act or he/she has obtained knowledge that the institution is engaged in activities which (a) are believed to cause unnecessary harm to third parties, (b) are in violation of human rights, or (c) run counter to the defined purpose of the institution and who informs the public of this fact.[14]

This definition effectively limits the class of moral infractions that an employee should make public. Accordingly, a worker who publicizes in-house indiscretions is not a whistle blower but a gossip monger. Such persons not only exhibit character flaws but also an ignorance of their basic obligation of loyalty and confidentiality to the firm. By contrast, "whistle blowing" is reserved conceptually only for activities that are harmful to third parties, violations of human rights, or insults to the defined purpose of the firm. Also, this definition limits the scope of one's responsibility to informing the public. The responsibility does not extend to taking retaliatory action against the employer or firm, such as sabotaging operations.

Bowie correctly points out that a discussion of whistle blowing in the 80s and 90s parallels the discussion of civil disobedience in the 60s. Just as civil disobedients of that time felt their duty to obey the law was overridden by other moral obligations, so the whistle blower overrides loyalty to colleagues and to the firm or organization in order to serve the public interest. But there are dangers of whistle blowing, as Professor Sissela Bok reminds us.[15] The whistle can be blown in error or malice, privacy invaded, and trust undermined. Not least, publicly accusing others of wrongdoing can be very destructive and brings with it an obligation to be fair to the persons accused. In addition, internal prying and mutual suspicion make it hard for any organization to function.

In his essay, "In Defense of Whistle Blowing" (see page 337), professor of philosophy Gene S. James discusses the considerations that any potential whistle blower should bear in mind. For his part, Professor Bowie, in developing his analogy with civil disobedience, proposes six conditions that must be met. According to Bowie, an act of whistle blowing is morally justified if:

1. *It is done from the appropriate moral motive, namely, as provided in the definition of whistle blowing.* This criterion focuses on the crucial question of motive. For an act of whistle blowing to be justified it must be motivated by a desire to expose unnecessary harm, violation of human rights, or conduct counter to the defined purpose of the firm. Thus, desire for attention or profit, or the exercise of one's general tendency toward "wave making," is not a justificatory motive for whistle blowing.

2. *The whistle blower, except in special circumstances, has exhausted all internal channels for dissent before going public.* The duty of loyalty to the firm obligates workers to seek an internal remedy before informing the public of a misdeed.

3. *The whistle blower has compelling evidence to believe that the inappropriate actions are ordered or have occurred.* While it is impossible to say how much or what kind of evidence constitutes "compelling evidence," employees can ask themselves whether the evidence is so strong that a person in a similar situation would be convinced that the activity is illegal or immoral. Although this is not a decisive guideline, it is one that is commonly invoked in other cases, such as deceptive advertising and negligence lawsuits.

4. *The whistle blower has acted after a careful analysis of the danger. (a) How serious is the moral violation? (b) How immediate is the moral violation? (c) Is the moral violation one that can be specified?* These criteria focus on the nature of the wrongdoing. Owing loyalty to employers, employees should blow the whistle only for grave legal or moral matters. Additionally, they should consider the time factor. The greater the time before the violation is to occur, the more likely the firm's own internal

mechanisms will prevent it; and the more immediate a violation, the more justified the whistle blowing. Finally, violations must be specific. General allegations such as that a company is "not operating in the best interests of the public" or is "systematically sabotaging the competition" won't do. Concrete examples are needed that can pass the other justificatory tests.

5. *The whistle blower's action is in keeping with one's responsibility for avoiding and/or exposing moral violations.* Although the moral imperative for any worker is that he or she must do good and avoid wrong, one's work role often imposes special obligations to correct wrongdoing. In other words, sometimes one's job is described, in part, as dealing with the morality of corporate actions. For example, it is obvious that the job of corporate auditors is to check on the legitimacy of expense account statements. Similarly, quality control personnel have a special duty to ensure a safe product. But special responsibility for moral matters need not be confined to a job description. Often companies make use of consultants such as engineers or other professionals, who are always obliged to follow their professional codes of conduct, even in their roles as consultants for an outside party.

6. *The whistle blowing has some chance of success.* This criterion recognizes that the chances of remedying an immoral or illegal action are important to consider: Sometimes the chances are good; other times they're slim. Probably most cases fall somewhere between these extremes. In general, whistle blowing that stands no chance of success is less justified than that which has some chance of success. This doesn't mean that one should never blow the whistle when there is no chance of success. Sometimes merely drawing attention to an objectionable practice, though failing to improve the specific situation, encourages government and society to be more watchful of certain behavior. Still, given the potential harmful effects of whistle

moral analysis

blowing, it seems fair to say that justification for whistle blowing increases with the chances of success.

THE QUESTION OF SELF-INTEREST

Conspicuously absent so far in our discussion of obligations to third parties and the special problem of whistle blowing has been any mention of the worker's own interests. And yet for many workers, protecting themselves or safeguarding their jobs is the primary factor in deciding whether to put third-party interests above those of the firm.

Concern with self-interest in cases that pit loyalty to the firm against obligations to third parties is altogether understandable and even warranted. After all, workers who subordinate the organization's interests to an outside party's expose themselves to charges of disloyalty, disciplinary action, "freezes" in job status, forced relocations, and even dismissal. Furthermore, even when an employee successfully blows the whistle he or she can be blacklisted in an industry. Given the potential harm to self and family that employees risk in honoring third party obligations, it is perfectly legitimate to inquire about the weight self-interest considerations should be given in resolving cases of conflicting obligations. What part, if any, should self-interest considerations play in determining what a worker should do in a situation in which his or her obligation to the organization conflicts with the obligations to an outside party?

Sadly, there is no clear answer to this question. But moral theorists and society as a whole do distinguish between prudential reasons and moral reasons. Prudential (from the word "prudence") refers here to considerations of self-interest; "moral" refers here to consideration of the interests of others. In general, if prudential concerns outweigh moral ones, then employees may do what is in their own best interests. If moral reasons override prudential ones, then workers should honor their obligations to others.

Consider the case of a cashier at a truck stop who is asked by truckers to write up phony chits so the truckers can get a larger expense reimbursement from their employers than they really deserve. The cashier doesn't think this is right, so she reports it to the manager. The manager explains that the restaurant is largely dependent on trucker business and that this is a good way to ensure it. The cashier is ordered to do the truckers' bidding and is thus being told to violate the three basic moral obligations to an outside party (the trucking firms): truth, noninjury, and fairness. Given these moral considerations, the cashier ought to refuse, and perhaps she should even report the conduct to the trucking companies.

But let's suppose that the cashier happens to be a recent divorcee with no formal education. She lacks occupational skills and stands little chance of getting another job in an economy that happens to be depressed—for months she was unemployed before landing her present job. With no other means of support, the consequences of job loss for her would be serious indeed. Now, given this scenario and given that the wrongdoing in issue is relatively minor, prudential concerns would probably take legitimate precedence over moral ones. In other words, the cashier would be justified in "going along," at least on a temporary basis.

Such an analysis is particularly relevant to whistle blowing. In situations where whistle blowing threatens one's very livelihood and career, prudential concerns may properly be taken into account in deciding what one should do, all things considered. This doesn't mean that if the worker blows the whistle despite overriding prudential reasons not to, he or she is not moral. On the contrary, such an action could be highly moral. (As we saw in Chapter 2, ethicists term such actions "supererogatory," meaning that they are, so to speak, above and beyond the call of duty.) On the other hand, when the moral concerns are great (for example, when the lives of others are at stake), elementary morality and personal integrity can require people to make substantial sacrifices.

A couple of further observations are in order here. First, an evaluation of prudential reasons obviously is colored by one's temperament and perceptions of self-interest. Most of us typically have been socialized to heed authority, often to the extent of causing others great personal harm. As a result, we are disinclined to question the orders of someone "above" us, especially when the authority is an employer or supervisor who has decided power to influence our lives for the better or worse. Additionally, each of us has a tendency to magnify potential threats to our livelihood or status within a firm. It's very easy for us to assume that *any* "boat rocking" is self-destructive. We tend to exaggerate the importance of prudential reasons compared with moral ones.

It follows, then, that each of us has an obligation to perform a kind of character or personality audit. Do we follow authority blindly? Do we suffer from moral tunnel vision on the job? Do we mindlessly do what is demanded of us, oblivious to the impact of our cooperation and actions on outside parties? Have we given enough attention to our possible roles as accomplices in the immoral undoing of other individuals, businesses, and social institutions? Do we have a balanced view of our own interests versus those of others? Do we have substantial evidence for believing that our livelihoods are really threatened, or is that belief based more on an exaggeration of the facts? Have we been imaginative in trying to balance prudential and moral concerns? Have we sought to find some middle ground, or have we set up a self/other false dilemma in which our own interests and those of others are erroneously viewed as incompatible? These are just some of the ques-

tions that a personal inventory should include if we are to combat the all-too-human tendency to stack the deck in favor of prudential reasons whenever they are pitted against moral ones.

A second observation about the prudential/moral distinction concerns the welfare of society. Given that in some cases prudential reasons are *permitted* to override moral ones, how can society be protected from serious wrongdoing? Is the welfare of society to be left to those few heroic souls willing to perform superogatory actions? Perhaps the only reasonable solution is to restructure business and social institutions so that such acts no longer carry such severe penalties. Just as laws currently exist to protect whistle blowers in the public sector from reprisals, so comparable legislation is probably needed in the private sector. If this account is correct, then it seems that each of us has an obligation to advocate such legislation.

A good example of such legislation is Michigan's "Whistle Blowers Protection Act," the first law of its kind to cover corporate employees. Under this act, any employee in private industry fired or disciplined for reporting alleged violations of federal, state, or local law to public authorities can now bring an action in state court for unjust reprisal. If the employer cannot show that treatment of the employee was based on proper personnel standards or valid business reasons, the court can award back pay, reinstatement of job, costs of litigation, and attorneys' fees. Also, the employer can be fined up to $500. Every employer in Michigan must now post a notice of this new law in the workplace. Commenting on the likely impact of this legislation, professor of public law and government Alan F. Westin believes that it probably will prod large firms to draft effective fair-procedure systems to deal with alleged company violations of public protection laws. This may entail experimenting with new mechanisms: "company ombudsmen; inspector-general systems; special regulatory-compliance review committees, such as Allied Chemical recently created; or the kind of world-wide Ethical Practices Complaint Committee at corporate headquarters that Citicorp instituted in 1980."[16] The new Michigan law probably will help convince leading managements that creating the climate and procedures that encourage honest and concerned employees to blow the whistle on illegalities and actual malpractices is an important corporate priority for the 1990s.

SUMMARY

1. Conflicts of interest arise when one has a personal interest in a transaction substantial enough that it does (actual conflict) or might reasonably be expected to (potential conflict) affect one's judgment when one is acting on behalf of the organization.

2. When employees have financial investments in suppliers, customers, or distributors with whom the organization does business, conflicts of interest can arise. Company policy usually determines the permissible limits of such financial interests.

3. *Insider trading* refers to the use of significant facts that have not yet been made public and will likely affect stock prices. Insider trading seems unfair and can injure other investors. In practice, determining what counts as insider information is not easy, and the meaning of "insider" is currently under debate. Some writers defend insider trading as performing a necessary and desirable economic function.

4. *Proprietary data* refers to an organization's classified or secret information. Increasingly, problems are arising as employees in high-tech occupations with access to sensitive information and trade secrets

quit and take employment with a competitor. Proprietary-data issues pose a conflict between two legitimate rights: the right of employers to keep certain information secret and the right of individuals to work where they choose.

5. A *bribe* is payment in some form for an act that runs counter to the work contract or the nature of the work one has been hired to perform. Bribery generally involves (1) law breaking, (2) injury to individuals, competitors, or political institutions, and (3) damage to the free-market system.

6. The following considerations are relevant to determining the moral acceptability of gift giving and receiving: (1) the value of the gift, (2) its purpose, (3) the circumstances under which it is given, (4) the position and sensitivity to influence of the person receiving the gift, (5) accepted business practice, (6) company policy, and (7) what the law says.

7. Workers have three ordinary obligations to third parties based on truthfulness, noninjury, and fairness. In addition, one's professional or business role may affect the nature and strength of one's obligations to third parties.

8. Balancing these obligations against obligations to employer or organization, friends, and coworkers can create conflicts and divided loyalties. In resolving such moral conflicts, we must identify the relevant obligations, ideals, and effects and decide where the emphasis among them should lie.

9. *Whistle blowing* refers to an employee informing the public about the illegal or immoral behavior of an employer or organization.

10. An act of whistle blowing can be presumed to be morally justified if (1) it is done from the appropriate moral motive; (2) the whistle blower, except in special

circumstances, has exhausted internal channels before going public; (3) the whistle blower has compelling evidence; (4) the whistle blower has carefully analyzed the dangers; (5) the whistle blowing is in keeping with the responsibility to avoid or expose moral violations; and (6) the whistle blowing has some chance of success.

11. Prudential considerations based on self-interest can conflict with moral considerations, which take account of the interests of others. Some sacrifices of self-interest would be so great that moral considerations must give way to prudential ones. But employees must avoid the temptation to exaggerate prudential concerns, thereby rationalizing away any individual moral responsibility to third parties. Legislation can protect whistle blowing so that it involves less personal sacrifice.

CASE 7.1
Profiting on Columns Prior to Publication

In April 1984, R. Foster Winans, who wrote *The Wall Street Journal*'s highly influential stock market column, "Heard on the Street," was fired from the paper after admitting to federal investigators that he had improperly taken advantage of his position. The 36-year-old business analyst confirmed that he had leaked information about upcoming columns to associates who were able to profit from the information by buying or selling stock.

On May 17, the Securities and Exchange Commission charged Winans with violating federal law by failing to disclose to readers that he had financial interests in the securities he wrote about. Winans, whose tips about columns prior to publication helped two stockbrokers net about one-half million dollars, also was charged with personally profiting from the material.

The basis of SEC charges is an SEC rule that prohibits anyone from omitting to state a *material fact* regarding the purchase or sale of securities. But the SEC's complaint against Winans is unclear. Professor of journalism Gilbert Cranberg phrases the ambiguity this way: "Is the ownership by a reporter of stock in a company about which he writes a 'material fact' to readers sufficient to require disclosure, or must the reporter also intend to profit from the story?"[17] Ambiguous or not, the SEC's action has convinced some legal scholars that the media must disclose the financial holdings of their financial analysts.

Even before the Winans case, some publications had formulated explicit policies designed to leave no doubt in reporters' minds about the impropriety of trading on knowledge of stories. For example, the *Washington Post* requires that all its financial and business reporters submit to their editors a confidential statement outlining their stock holdings.[18] *Post* policy prohibits writers from either writing about companies in which they have an interest or buying stock in companies they have written about. *The New York Times* has a similar policy, and *Forbes* magazine and the *Chicago Tribune* require editorial employees to divulge their corporate investments. Ralph Schulz, senior vice president at McGraw-Hill, Inc.'s publication unit, says that his company has a conflict-of-interest policy based on the premise that "nobody who writes about a company ought to own stock in it."[19] And *The Wall Street Journal*'s three-and-a-half-page conflict-of-interest policy warns employees against trading in companies immediately prior to or following a *Journal* piece on that company. The policy reads in part:

> It is not enough to be incorruptible and act with honest motives. It is equally important to use good judgment and conduct one's outside activities so that no one—management, our editors, an SEC investigator with power of subpoena, or a political critic of the company—has any grounds for even raising the suspicion that an employee misused a position with the company.[20]

But such written policies remain the exception, as shown by an informal survey of the country's media conducted by *The Wall Street Journal* in 1984. Although many newspapers have formal dress codes, few have formal rules about stock trading. Moreover, few news executives show any concern about insider trading by non-editorial employees, although sensitive investigative reports generally are accessible to any employee in the newsroom.

The Wall Street Journal survey also reveals general indifference among media executives to stock trading by subjects of interviews, as in the case of G. D. Searle & Co. Early in 1984, the SEC began investigating unusual activity in options on that company's stock just prior to the mid-January "CBS Evening News" report that raised questions about NutraSweet, Searle's new low-calorie sweetener. The SEC charges that an Arizona scientist interviewed by CBS for the report bought "put" options in Searle's NutraSweet before the story aired, convinced that the stock would tumble as a result of negative comments by himself and others.

"I honestly believe I had a right to do it," says the Arizona scientist. He adds, "I don't think it's unethical. It's the American way."[21]

The scientist's lawyer and some CBS employees also were targets of the SEC investigation.

Syndicated financial columnist Dan Dorman admits that his stories may affect the price of stocks and, by implication, shrewd subjects of interviews could stand to benefit on the stories. But he doesn't think there's anything he can do about that. "It's not my job to police," Dorman says. "My job is to get information."[22]

John G. Craig, Jr., editor of the *Pittsburg Post Gazette*, agrees. In his view, preventing sources from trading on an article "is an ethical responsibility a newspaper can't assume."[23]

And yet, James Michaels, the editor of *Forbes*, recalls once holding out a story when he learned that one of the sources had sold stock short, betting the article would have a negative impact. And *The Wall Street Journal* admits to even killing stories upon learning that investors were using their knowledge of it to wheel and deal on Wall Street.

In the meantime, the government pressed its case against R. Foster Winans. In September 1984, the Justice Department brought a 61-count indictment for fraud and conspiracy against him and two alleged collaborators. Among other things, the indictment charges that in the first half of 1983, Winans and his roommate speculated on stocks about to be mentioned in forthcoming columns. They made about a $3,000 profit on a $3,000 investment.[24] Although Winans describes his role in these deals as "stupid" and "wrong," he denies he broke any law. After a long and technical legal battle, the Supreme Court in November 1987 upheld the Justice Department's contention that what he did was not just imprudent but criminal.

Professor Cranberg fears that the Winans case may ultimately make bad law. Although he thinks that the time has come for reporters and editors to report outside compensation and financial interest, he worries that the SEC and the courts may equate business news reporters with investment advisers, and, as a result, wield undue influence on the press.

Cranberg fears that such a development

not only threatens freedom of the press but would have a chilling effect on press coverage of corporate America. "Not every problem has, or should have, a legal solution," Cranberg points out. "Most problems involving the press are best handled by voluntary measures. The way for the press to show that it can keep its house in order is to do it. More actions and less self-satisfied ridicule of concern about conflicts of interest would be signs that the press can and will."[25]

Michael Missal, a lawyer for the SEC, thinks such fears are unfounded. "We don't expect every journalist to disclose all financial relationships,"[26] he said. Instead, the government wishes to prevent profiteering on foreknowledge of stories. That, Missal said, is what the Winans case is all about.

Discussion Questions

1. In your opinion, did Winans engage in insider trading?

2. Do you believe that media financial analysts should disclose to their audience any financial interests they have in the securities they write about? Do you think they should be required to make such disclosures? If so, should the requirement take the form of an institutional policy, law, or both?

3. Would you say that so long as reporters do not intend to profit from their stories, they cannot and should not be held guilty of insider trading? Or do you think that a reporter can engage in insider trading even if he or she does not intend to profit personally?

4. Do you think that McGraw-Hill's policy—that "nobody who writes about a company ought to own stock in it"—is fair and reasonable? Or do you think it is an unfair and unreasonable encroachment on the employee's right to make profit through investments?

5. Do you agree that the Arizona scientist had a "right" to trade on the information prior to the broadcast of it?

6. What ideals, obligations, and effects do you think Winans should have considered before acting as he did? Where do you think the weight should lie?

7. What do you think Kant's position on insider trading would be?

8. As a rule utilitarian, formulate a rule for insider trading. Do you think the rule is a good one?

CASE 7.2

The Tavoulareas Affair: Nepotism at Mobil?

In 1979, *The Washington Post* alleged that William Tavoulareas had used his position as Mobil Corporation's president to help his son Peter's London-based shipping firm, Atlas Maritime Co., get a $100,000-per-year contract to manage ships in which Mobil had a 30 percent interest. In November 1980, the Tavoulareases sued the *Post* for libel, and won—well, partly. A jury unanimously found that the *Post* had libeled the elder Tavoulareas but

not the younger and awarded the senior Tavoulareas $2.1 million in damages. But a year later, in 1981, Judge Oliver Gasch, who presided over the original trial, ruled that there was insufficient evidence to support the jury's finding and threw out the libel judgment. Although that may prove the end of the Tavoulareases' suit against the *Post*, it certainly hasn't ended the younger Tavoulareas's dealings with Mobil.[27]

The business relationship between Mobil and Peter Tavoulareas began in 1974 when Peter, a twenty-four-year-old MBA from Columbia University and previously a $14,000-a-year shipping clerk at Mobil, became junior partner in Atlas. (The *Post* article claimed he was set up by his father.) One of Atlas's main functions was to manage a fleet of ships owned by Saudi Maritime Co. (Samarco), in which Mobil had a 30 percent interest. The majority interest in Samarco was held by prominent Saudis, such as Prince Mohamed Bin Fahd. In 1976 Mobil and the prince set up a similar company, Arabian International Maritime Co. (Aimco), whose fleet Atlas also manages.

During the mid-70s, Atlas expanded its operations to include investing in vessels, among other things. Capitalizing on the ship market boom of 1979, Peter Tavoulareas, who had by then become the majority owner of Atlas, ordered six 39,600-ton chemical-carrying transports for launching in 1981, 1982, and 1983 and signed contracts for three more in 1981.

But the bright future for this type of ship had begun to dim by 1981. Industry analysts and trade journals warned of surplus capacity in the category of chemical-transport vessels. They suspected that the only way such vessels could remain financially afloat was for them to carry petroleum products, which Atlas's ships were capable of doing. Petroleum countries already were thinning out their fleets of large crude-oil carriers (those in excess of 160,000-ton haulage capacity) and increasingly transporting petroleum products in simpler, less expensive ships in the 25,000- to 40,000-ton category.

During the first half of 1981, shortly before the first of the nine Atlas vessels was to be delivered, Mobil officials recommended that Aimco invest in some of Atlas's chemical ships. Internal memos predicted low risk on limited cost outlays and high rates of return. As a result, in the second half of 1981, Atlas sold 50 percent interests to Aimco in three vessels, based on valuations millions of dollars above their initial construction price. In 1982 Mobil bought out Atlas's interest in a fourth and fifth of the unbuilt vessels.

Peter Tavoulareas claims that Mobil took over control "on terms which gave no financial benefit to Atlas, and I believe were generous to Mobil." Mobil officials agree. Herbert Schmertz, vice-president of Mobil, describes the transaction as simply a matter of Atlas's offering a deal to a company whose fleet it was managing, Aimco. He says that "Atlas would have and could have taken the deals elsewhere because of their attractiveness."

One of the ships was valued at $36 million, which was $20 million above construction costs, but consistent with market values in mid-1981. For its 50 percent share, then, Aimco paid $18 million, financed through relatively low-cost sources such as the shipyard mortgages. Although the costs may appear high to the untutored eye, one Aimco member described it as "realistic and attractive . . . in terms of current market prices and new building costs for similar vessels." Apparently one big factor in Aimco's decision was the belief that the ship, and others like it, would become part of a pool of chemical ships marketed by an old-time and highly reputable Norwegian firm that continued to enjoy a strong market position. As it turned out, Aimco's forecast was overly optimistic. Rather than yielding an expected $14 per deadweight ton a month, by 1983 the ships were earning between $7 and $8, enough, by some estimates, to cover their operating costs and about half of their interest costs. Industry analysts peg the current market value of the ships at between $20 and $25 million.

During the 1980 *Post* libel trial, the senior Tavoulareas was asked why he had no reservations about such a business relationship with his son. "It wasn't a question of what I could do for my son," he testified. "It was a question of would I stand in the way of my son." According to testimony, Tavoulareas informed Mobil of the situation and an internal memo was circulated emphasizing that dealings with Atlas were to be businesslike, without any regard to the family connection. Tavoulareas testified further that he had sought assurance from Mobil's outside accountants that all such dealings with Atlas were commercially sound. He said he even told his subordinates that all decisions regarding Atlas be sent not to him but to his superior, Mobil chairman and chief executive Rawleigh Warner, Jr. Tavoulareas did admit, however, that consistent with Mobil's internal procedures, he was permitted to and sometimes did participate in discussions concerning Atlas.

Vice president Schmertz asserts not only that Mobil's executive committee approved of these transactions but also that committee member William Tavoulareas didn't even vote when the approval was made. Some of Mobil's outside directors confirm that they were fully informed of the transactions. Says Samuel C. Johnson, a Mobil director: "The transactions were in the normal course of business and arm's length." Another Mobil director, Lewis M. Branscomb, praised the Mobil-Atlas relationship: "I was very impressed with the amount of care that Tav took to see that he notified the company and the board and removed himself from areas of decision making."

But some students of corporate ethics have been less impressed. Richard West, dean of business administration at Dartmouth College and director of several companies, thinks that businesses simply should not deal with relatives unless the relatives are the sole source of a product or unless there is competitive bidding. Kenneth Goodpaster of Harvard Business School believes it's naive to think it sufficient merely to tell employees to ignore the fact that they are dealing with the boss's son. It's "like telling them not to think about an elephant," he says. And shortly after the

Post story in 1979, George McGhee, who was then a Mobil director, sent a memo to the board in which he wrote: "The present arrangement is in my view a case of nepotism which is intrinsically bad policy both from the standpoint of the company and the corporate system generally." He characterized the Mobil-Atlas relationship as "setting a bad precedent within the company. It could have a negative effect on employee morale and respect for the company. It's unfair for those in the company who must deal with Atlas."

William Tavoulareas scoffs at such criticism. "If anything, when my son's involved, [Mobile employees] bend over backwards the other way around, and don't even do things for him they'd do for an outsider." As for the suggestion that company policy should prohibit dealings with relatives, Mobil's president wonders where the line should be drawn: "Friends, schoolmates, cousins, sisters-in-law? Where do we stop this?"

Discussion Questions

1. As the case is described, did William Tavoulareas have an actual or potential conflict of interest? Explain. Was this a case of nepotism?

2. Do we have an obligation to help close relatives, if possible, in business transactions? How far is an employee permitted to go in helping a relative with whom the employee's firm has business dealings?

3. Compare former Mobil director George McGhee's characterization of the Mobil-Atlas relationship with that of Mobil director Lewis M. Branscomb. With whom do you agree?

4. If you were a stockholder of Mobil, would you be satisfied with William Tavoulareas's conduct? If not, explain why not. If you think his conduct was acceptable, do you think that he should have

gone further to avoid any possible suggestion of impropriety?

5. How are the ethics of the transaction affected by the question of whether or not Mobil lost money in its dealings with Atlas?

6. Do you agree with Dean West's belief that companies should have strict policies prohibiting doing business with relatives except when relatives are the sole source of a product or unless there is competitive bidding?

CASE 7.3
Storms Makes Waves for Navy

Zeke Storms, a fifty-two-year-old retired Navy chief, began his career as a whistle blower in March 1983 when he wrote to Representative Charles Pashayan (R–Fresno, California), protesting the congressman's support of President Reagan's budget cuts.[28] Storms, who had been employed as a civilian repairing flight simulators at the Lemoore Naval Air Base station near Fresno since his retirement in 1973, suggested that instead of supporting Reagan's proposed reductions in Civil Service pay scale, Pashayan ought to take a close look at Navy procurement practices. Enclosed in the letter was a list of spare parts showing that defense contractors were charging $435 for ordinary claw hammers and $100 or more for such electric spare parts as diodes, transistors, and semiconductors, which cost less than $1 each. He also charged that the Navy purchased transistors at $100 each, which it could have obtained through the federal supply system for five cents each.

Storms's letter prompted Pashayan to query the Defense Department, which in turn kicked off an interservice investigation of military procurement practices. In May 1983, the Defense Department inspector general's office reported that the Navy had indeed failed to determine the most economical manner to acquire the spare parts Zeke Storms had listed. It also suggested that the spare-parts-overcharge problem was more widespread than at first thought. The investigative body left no doubt that the Navy was wasting more than $1 million annually and that, on first look, such waste was occurring outside the Navy as well. As a result, the inspector general's office said it planned to do an interservice audit.

In the wake of this report, Defense Secretary Caspar Weinberger ordered a tightening of procurement procedures to ensure the lowest price for spare parts. Meanwhile, Navy Secretary John Lehman ordered contractors at Lemoore to refund $160,000 in overcharges. He also gave Storms a $4,000 award.

But Storms wasn't about to lay down his muckrake. He suggested that Defense Department auditors review overpayment of jet aircraft support equipment in the base shops. The auditors did and discovered overpayment of $482,000, most of it spent on four spectrum analyzers. Had the items been bought through the Federal Supply Systems, they would have cost $47,500.

Storms then discovered that the Navy had engaged private contractors to operate its flight simulators for a new aircraft. "I got mad," he says. "They [the Navy] had spent $1 million training their own people to do the work, then they just scrapped that and turned the maintenance over to the contractor." The contractor in question apparently was demanding $785,000 to maintain the simulators, which worked out to about $100,000 per man per year. "I showed them that we [a team of

Navy and Civil Service technicians] could do it for one-fourth that cost, so the contract was dropped to $411,000," says Storms.

Four hundred eleven thousand dollars was still higher than Storms believed the Navy had to pay, especially since the Navy had been maintaining its own trainers for two decades. So he took his case directly to Lehman, arguing that the Office of Management and Budget (OMB) regulations required the Navy to do comparative cost studies to ensure the most cost-effective means. Lehman balked at Storms's proposal, saying that such studies would cost $45,000 each. That was too high a price to pay "to indulge Mr. Storms's eccentricities," the Secretary said in a letter to Congressman Pashayan. Lehman also pointed out that OMB Director David Stockman personally had rejected the need for cost studies.

Evidently deciding it was time to quiet the querulous Storms, Lehman then sent nine Navy brass to Lemoore in February 1983. In the two-hour session that ensued, Storms did most of the talking. In the end, a commodore, four captains, two commanders, and two lieutenant commanders could do nothing to divert Storms from his course.

It was shortly thereafter that the ex-Navy chief did the "unpardonable." He accused Secretary Lehman and "his admirals" of lying. He said he had turned over to OMB officials Navy documents that showed that in 1982 Navy admirals willfully ignored requirements to do cost studies for private maintenance work. One of the documents, dated March 1982, included a message from Vice Admiral Robert F. Schoultz, the commander of naval forces in the Pacific. Addressing Admiral James D. Watkins, then commander of the Pacific Fleet, Schoultz wrote: "It is our intention to contract out all major training device maintenance. . . . [However] under the [contract] program our objective is hindered with cost studies that would yield inappropriate results." Schoultz's "inappropriate results" apparently was an allusion to the Jan-

uary 1982 report by the fleet's top training officer, who estimated that the Navy's own people could do for $7 million the same work for which private contractors would charge $28 million. In mid-1984, OMB announced it was reviewing the matter but opined that the Navy was probably in compliance with regulations.

In a letter dated June 4, 1984, N. R. Lessard, officer in charge of the flight training group that Storms was working for, informed the ten-year Lemoore veteran that "your recent comments concerning senior Navy officials . . . constitutes unacceptable employee conduct."

To which Storms replied in a way most befitting a tobacco-chewing old salt: "They [the Navy] are covering up, goddammit. I've got the facts, and they know it."

Discussion Questions

1. Do you think Storms qualifies as a whistle blower? What do you think his motives were?

2. Examine Storms's actions from the perspective of Bowie's six criteria for justified whistle blowing. Are those criteria satisfied in Storms's case? Are Bowie's criteria themselves satisfactory ones?

3. What ideals, obligations, and effects do you think Storms should have considered before becoming a whistle blower? In this case, which of these considerations is the most important? Why?

4. Based on the details provided, would you consider Storms's whistle blowing morally justified? Explain.

5. If you believe Storms's whistle blowing was permissible, do you also believe that it was morally required of him? Would someone in Storms's position have been justified in subordinating moral reasons to prudential concerns and thus in remaining silent? Explain.

6. Should whistle blowers be protected by

law? How feasible would such a law be? Identify the advantages and disadvantages of such a law.

NOTES

1. "Transfer or Be Fired, Whistle Blower Told," *Bakersfield Californian*, March 18, 1983.

2. See Ronald B. Taylor, "Making Waves: Whistle-Blower Keeps Heat on Navy in Revealing Waste of Millions of Dollars," *Los Angeles Times*, June 26, 1984.

3. Keith Davis and Robert L. Blomstrom, *Business and Society* (New York: McGraw-Hill, 1975), 182.

4. "Lance: Going, Going . . ." *Newsweek*, September 19, 1977, 7. The details reported here can be found in this article.

5. John A. C. Hetherington, "Corporate Social Responsibility, Stockholders, and the Law," *Journal of Contemporary Business* (Winter 1973): 51.

6. "Texas Gulf Ruled to Lack Diligence in Minerals Case," *The Wall Street Journal* (Midwest Edition), February 9, 1970, 1.

7. A Wall Street Journal Roundup, "SEC, Professor Split on Insider Trades," *The Wall Street Journal*, March 2, 1984, 8.

8. Ibid.

9. Ibid.

10. See "Cookie Cloak and Dagger," *Time*, September 10, 1984, 44.

11. Sissela Bok, *Secrets* (New York: Random House, 1983), 136.

12. Normal C. Miller, "U.S. Business Overseas: Back to Bribery?" *The Wall Street Journal*, April 30, 1981, 22.

13. Andy Pasztor, "Speaking Up Gets Biologist into Big Fight," *The Wall Street Journal*, November 26, 1980, Sec. 2, p. 25.

14. Norman Bowie, *Business Ethics* (Englewood Cliffs, N.J.: Prentice-Hall, 1982), 142.

15. Bok, *Secrets*, chapter 14.

16. Alan F. Westin, "Michigan's Law to Protect the Whistle Blowers," *The Wall Street Journal*, April 13, 1981, 18.

17. Gilbert Cranberg, "*Wall Street Journal* Case Could Bring Overreaction," *Los Angeles Times*, June 4, 1984, Part II, p. 5.

18. See "Media Policies Vary on Preventing Employees and Others from Profiting on Knowledge of Future Business Stories," *The Wall Street Journal*, March 2, 1984, 8.

19. Ibid.

20. Ibid.

21. "Market Leaks: Illegal Insider Trading Seems to Be on Rise," *The Wall Street Journal*, March 2, 1984, 8.

22. "Media Policies . . . ," *The Wall Street Journal*, 8.

23. Ibid.

24. See William A. Henry, III, "Impropriety or Criminality?" *Time*, September 10, 1984, 45.

25. Cranberg, "Case Could Bring Overreaction," 5.

26. Henry, "Impropriety or Criminality?" 43.

27. See Paul Blustein, "Mobil President's Son Sold Tankers to Mobil in an Uncertain Market," *The Wall Street Journal*, April 6, 1983, p. 1. This article served as the primary source of the material reported in this case, and all quotations in this case presentation are from this article, pp. 1 and 26.

28. The facts and quotations in this case are drawn from Ronald B. Taylor, "Making Waves: Whistle Blower Keeps Heat on Navy in Revealing Waste of Millions of Dollars," *Los Angeles Times*, June 26, 1984.

Trade Secrets: What Price Loyalty?

Michael S. Baram

As suggested in this chapter, the problem of employees leaving firms and taking with them proprietary data raises a number of operational and moral concerns. Obviously, this problem is especially troublesome in the research and development (R&D) sector of the economy. As Michael S. Baram, attorney and executive officer of the graduate school of the Massachusetts Institute of Technology, points out in the following article, employee mobility and high personnel turnover in R&D threaten industrial reliance on trade secrets for the protection of certain forms of intellectual property. There's no question that safeguarding the right of the corporation to its trade secrets while upholding the rights of employees to depart for what they view as more favorable job opportunities poses difficult legal, practical, and ethical questions. In this reading the author examines *these seemingly irreconcilable interests and presents a five-step management approach to meet the challenge.*

In 1963, the Court of Appeals of Ohio heard an appeal of a lower court decision from the B. F. Goodrich Company. The lower court had denied Goodrich's request for an injunction, or court order, to restrain a former employee, Donald Wohlgemuth, from disclosing its trade secrets and from working in the space suit field for any other company.

This case, as it was presented in the Court of Appeals, is a fascinating display of management issues, legal concepts, and ethical dilemmas of concern to research and development organizations and their scientist and engineer employees. The case also represents an employer-employee crisis of increasing incidence in the young and vigorous R&D sector of U.S. industry. Tales of departing employees and threatened losses of trade secrets or proprietary information are now common.

Such crises are not surprising when one considers the causes of mobility. The highly educated employees of R&D organizations place primary emphasis on their own development, interests, and satisfaction. Graduates of major scientific and technological institutions readily admit that they accept their first jobs primarily for money and for the early and brief experience they feel is a prerequisite for seeking more satisfying futures with smaller companies which are often their own. Employee mobility and high personnel turnover rates are also due to the placement of new large federal contracts and the termination of others. One need only look to the Sunday newspaper employment advertisements for evidence as to the manner in which such programs are used to attract highly educated R&D personnel.

This phenomenon of the mobile employee seeking fulfillment reflects a sudden change in societal and personal values. It also threatens industrial reliance on trade secrets for the protection of certain forms of intellectual property. There are no union solutions, and the legal framework in which it occurs is an ancient structure representing values of an earlier America. The formulation of management responses—with cognizance of legal, practical, and ethical considerations—is admittedly a difficult task, but one which must be undertaken.

In this article I shall examine the basic question of industrial loyalty regarding trade secrets, using the Goodrich-Wohlgemuth case as the focal point of the challenge to the preservation of certain forms of intellectual property posed by the mobile employee, and then offer some suggestions for the development of sound management policies.

The Appeals Case

Donald Wohlgemuth joined the B. F. Goodrich Company as a chemical engineer in 1954, following his graduation from the University of Michigan, and by 1962 he had become manager of the space suit division. As the repository of Goodrich know-how and secret data in space suit technology, he was indeed a key man in a rapidly developing technology of interest to several government agencies. Nevertheless, he was dissatisfied with his salary ($10,644) and the denial of his requests for certain additional facilities for his department.

A Goodrich rival, International Latex, had recently been awarded the major space suit subcontract for the Apollo program. Following up a contact from an employment agency hired by Latex, Wohlgemuth negotiated a position with Latex, at a substantial salary increase. In his new assignment he would be manager of engineering for industrial products, which included space suits. He then notified Goodrich of his resignation, and was met with a reaction he apparently did not expect. Goodrich management raised the moral and ethical aspects of his decision, since the company executives felt his resignation would result in the transfer of Goodrich trade secrets to Latex.

After several heated exchanges, Wohlgemuth stated that "loyalty and ethics have their price and International Latex has paid the price. . . ." Even though Goodrich threatened legal action, Wohlgemuth left Goodrich for Latex. Goodrich thereupon requested a restraining order in the Ohio courts.

At the appeals court level, the Goodrich brief sought an injunction that would prevent Wohlgemuth from working in the space field for *any* other company, prevent his disclosure of *any* information or space suit technology to *anyone*, prevent his consulting or conferring with *anyone* on Goodrich trade secrets, and finally, prevent *any* future contact he might seek with Goodrich employees.

These four broad measures were rejected by the Ohio Court of Appeals. All were too wide in scope, and all would have protected much more than Goodrich's legitimate concern of safeguarding its trade secrets. In addition, the measures were speculative, since no clear danger seemed imminent. In sum, they represented a form of "overkill" that would have placed undue restraints on Wohlgemuth.

The court did provide an injunction restraining Wohlgemuth from disclosure of Goodrich trade secrets. In passing, the court noted that in the absence of any Goodrich employment contract restraining his employment with a competitor, Wohlgemuth could commence work with Latex. With ample legal precedent, the court therefore came down on both sides of the fence. Following the decision, Wohlgemuth commenced his career with Latex and is now manager of the company's Research and Engineering Department.

Common-Law Concepts

The two basic issues in crises such as the Goodrich-Wohlgemuth case appear irreconcilable: (1) the right of the corporation to its intellectual property—its proprietary data or trade secrets; and (2) the right of the individual to seek gainful employment and utilize his abilities—to be free from a master-servant relationship.

There are no federal and but a few state statutes dealing with employment restraints and trade secrets. The U.S. courts, when faced with such issues, have sought to apply the various common-law doctrines of trade secrets and unfair competition at hand to attain an equitable solution. Many of these common-law doctrines were born in preindustrial England and later adopted by English and U.S. courts to meet employment crises of this nature through ensuing centuries of changing industrial and social patterns. In fact, some of the early cases of blacksmiths and barbers seeking to restrain departing apprentices are still cited today.

To the courts, the common legal solution, as in *Goodrich v. Wohlgemuth*, is pleasing because it theoretically preserves the rights of both parties. However, it is sadly lacking in practicality, since neither secrets nor individual liberty are truly preserved.

The trade secrets which companies seek to protect have usually become an integral portion of the departing employee's total capabilities. He cannot divest himself of his intellectual capacity, which is a compound of information acquired from his employer, his co-workers, and his own self-generated experiential information. Nevertheless, all such information, if kept secret by the company from its competition, may legitimately be claimed as corporate property. This is because the employer-employee relationship embodied in the normal employment contract or other terms of employment provides for corporate ownership of all employee-generated data, including inventions. As a result, a departing employee's intellectual capacity may be, in large measure, corporate property.

Once the new position with a competitor has been taken, the trade secrets embodied in the departing employee may manifest themselves quite clearly and consciously. This is what court injunctions seek to prohibit. But, far more likely, the trade secrets will manifest themselves subconsciously and in various forms—for example, as in the daily decisions by the employee at his new post, or in the many small contributions he makes to a large team effort—often in the form of an intuitive sense of what or what not to do, as he seeks to utilize his overall intellectual capacity. Theoretically, a legal injunction also serves to prohibit such "leakage." However, the former employer faces the practical problem of securing evidence of such leakage, for little will be apparent from the public activities and goods of the new employer. And if the new employer's public activities or goods appear suspicious, there is also the further problem of distinguishing one's trade secrets from what may be legitimately asserted as the self-generated technological skills or state of the art of the new employer and competitor which were utilized.

This is a major stumbling block in the attempt to protect one's trade secrets, since the possessor has no recourse against others who independently generate the same information. It is therefore unlikely that an injunction against disclosure of trade secrets to future employers prevents any "unintentional" transfer (or even intentional transfer) of information, except for the passage of documents and other physical embodiments of the secrets. In fact, only a lobotomy, as yet not requested nor likely to be sanctioned by the courts, would afford security against the transfer of most trade secrets.

Conversely, the departing employee bears the terrible burden of sensitivity. At his new post, subconscious disclosure and mental and physical utilization of what he feels to be no more than his own intellectual capacity may result in heated exchanges between companies, adverse publicity, and litigation. He is marked, insecure, and unlikely to contribute effectively in his new position. In fact, new co-workers may consider him to be a man with a price, and thus without integrity. Frequently, caution on the part of his new employer will result in transfer to a nonsensitive post where he is unlikely to contribute his full skills, unless he has overall capability and adaptability.

The fact that neither secrets nor individual liberty will be truly preserved rarely influences the course of litigation. Similarly, these practical considerations are usually negligible factors in the out-of-court settlements which frequently terminate such litigation, because the settlements primarily reflect the relative bargaining strengths of disputing parties.

Finally, there is the full cost of litigation to be considered. In addition to the obvious court costs and attorney's fees, there is the potentially great cost to the company's image. Although the drama enacted in court reflects legitimate corporate concerns, the public may easily fail to see more than an unequal struggle between the powerful corporate machine and a lonely individual harassed beyond his employment tenure. Prospective employees, particularly new and recent graduates whose early positions are stepping stones, may be reluctant to accept employment with what appears to be a vindictive and authoritarian organization.

Practical and Legal Aspects

Trade secrets are, of course, a common form of intellectual property. Secrecy is the most natural and the earliest known method of protecting the fruits of one's intellectual labors. Rulers of antiquity frequently had architects and engineers murdered, after completion of their work, to maintain secrecy and security. The medieval guilds and later the craftsmen of pre-industrial Europe and America imposed severe restraints on apprentices and their future activities.

Recognition and acceptance of the practice of protecting intellectual property by secrecy is found throughout Anglo-American common or judge-made law, but statutory protection has not been legislated. Perhaps the failure to do so is because of the recognition by the elected officials of industrial societies that secrecy is not in the public interest and that the widest dissemination of new works

and advances in technology and culture is necessary for optimal public welfare. . . .

To summarize this common law briefly, virtually all information—ranging from full descriptions of inventions to plant layouts, shop know-how, methods of quality control, customer and source lists, and marketing data—is eligible for protection as trade secrets. No standards of invention or originality are required. If such information is not known to the public or to the trade (or it is known but its utility is not recognized), and if such information is of value to its possessor, it is eligible for protection by the courts.

Further, and of greatest importance in terms of favorably impressing the courts, there must be evidence that the possessor recognized the value of his information and treated it accordingly. In the context of confidential relationships, "treatment" normally means that the possessor provided for limited or no disclosure of trade secrets. This means many things: for example, total prohibition of disclosure except to key company people on a need-to-know basis; provision of the information to licensees, joint ventures, or employees having contractual restraints against their unauthorized disclosure or use; division of employee responsibilities so that no employee is aware of more than a small segment of a particular process; and use in labs of unmarked chemicals and materials.

There must also be evidence that particular efforts were expended for the purpose of preserving secrecy for the specific data claimed as trade secrets. General company policies indiscriminately applied to data and employees or licensees will not suffice in the legal sense to convince the courts of the presence of trade secrets.

When the possessor and his information do fulfill such criteria, court recognition and the award of compensation to damaged parties, or injunctive restraints to protect parties in danger of imminent or further damage, will follow. If there is evidence of (a) breach of confidential relationships (contracts or licenses) which were established to preserve the secrecy of company information, (b) unauthorized copying and sale of secrets, or (c) conspiracy to damage the possessor, the courts will act with greater certitude. But in many cases, such as in the Goodrich-Wohlgemuth litigation, no such evidence is present.

Finally, the courts will not move to protect

trade secrets when an action is brought by one party against another who independently generated similar information, or who "reverse-engineered" the publicly sold products of the party petitioning the court, unless there is some contractual, fiduciary, or other relationship based on trust connecting the parties in court.

Other Considerations

In addition to the foregoing practical and legal aspects, basic questions of industrial ethics and the equitable allocation of rights and risks should be examined to provide management with intelligent and humane responses to employer-employee crises that involved intellectual property. The patent and copyright systems for the stimulation and protection of such property are premised on dissemination of information and subsequent public welfare. These systems reflect public concern with the proper use of intellectual property, which the common law of trade secrets lacks.

Will the courts continue to utilize common-law concepts for the protection of trade secrets, when such concepts are based solely on the rights of the possessors of secret information, and when the application of such concepts has a detrimental effect on both the rights of employees and the public welfare? Since current court practice places the burden of industrial loyalty solely on the employee, the skilled individual has to pay the price. In other words, the law restricts the fullest utilization of his abilities. And the detrimental effect on public welfare can be inferred from recent federal studies of technology transfer, which indicate that employee mobility and the promotion of entrepreneurial activities are primary factors in the transfer of technology and the growth of new industries.

The continuation of trade secret concepts for the preservation of property rights in secret information at the expense of certain basic individual freedoms is unlikely. The law eventually reflects changing societal values, and the mobile R&D employee who seeks career fulfillment through a succession of jobs, frequently in sensitive trade secret areas, is now a reality—one not likely to disappear. Thus it is probable that the courts will eventually adopt the position that those who rely on trade secrets assume the realities or risks in the present context of public concern with technological progress and its relationship to the public good, and

with the rights of the individual. Resulting unintentional leakage of secret information through the memory of a departing employee is now generally accepted as a reasonable price to pay for the preservation of these societal values. However, the courts will never condone the theft or other physical appropriation of secret information, nor are the courts likely to condone fraud, conspiracy, and other inequitable practices resulting in some form of unfair competition.

The failings of the statutory systems serve not as justification for the inequitable application of medieval trade secret concepts, but as the basis for legislative reform. Injunctive restraints against the unintentional leakage of secrets and the harassment of departing employees through litigation should not be part of our legal system. This is especially true when there is a growing body of evidence that management can respond, and has intelligently done so, to such crises without detriment to the individual employee, the public good, or the company itself.

Management Response

How then shall managers of research and development organizations respond to the reality of the mobile employee and his potential for damage to corporate trade secrets?

Contractual Restraints

Initial response is invariably consideration of the use of relevant contractual prohibitions on employees with such potential. For a minority of companies, this means the institution of employment contracts or other agreements concerning terms of employment. For most, a review of existing company contracts, which at a minimum provide for employee disclosure of inventions and company ownership of subsequent patents, will be called for to determine the need for relevant restraints.

Contractual prohibitions vary somewhat, but they are clearly of two general types: (1) restraints against unauthorized disclosure and use of company trade secrets or proprietary information by employees during their employment tenure or at any time thereafter; (2) restraints against certain future activities of employees following their employment tenure.

A restraint against unauthorized disclosure or use is normally upheld in the courts, provided it is limited to a legitimate company concern—trade secrets. But it is usually ineffective, due to the unintentional leakage and subconscious utilization of trade secrets, and the difficulties of "policing" and proving violation, as discussed earlier. In fact, several authorities feel that this type of restraint is ineffective unless coupled with a valid restraint against future employment with competitors. . . .

Courts have been naturally reluctant to extend protection to trade secrets when the freedom of an individual to use his overall capability is at stake. In addition, the former employer faces the practical difficulty of convincing almost any court that a prohibition of future employment is necessary, since the court will look for clear and convincing evidence that the ex-employee has, or inevitably will, exercise more than the ordinary skill a man of his competence possesses. A few states—such as California by statute and others by consistent court action—now prohibit future employment restraints.

It therefore appears that a contractual prohibition of future employment in a broad area, which prevents an ex-employee from using his overall capability, is invalid in most states. And a request for an injunction to prohibit such employment, without a prior contractual provision, stands an even poorer chance of success, as Goodrich learned when it sought to prevent Wohlgemuth from working in the space suit field for any other company. . . .

Internal Policies

Another response of R&D management to the mobile employee and his potential for damage to corporate trade secrets is the formulation of internal company policies for the handling of intellectual property of trade secret potential. Such policies may call for the prior review of publications and addresses of key employees, prohibition of consulting and other "moonlighting," dissemination of trade secrets on a strict "need to know" basis to designated employees, and prohibitions on the copying of trade secret data. More "physical" policies may restrict research and other operational areas to access for designated or "badge" employees only and divide up operations to prevent the accumulation of extensive knowledge by any individual—including safety and other general plant personnel. Several companies I know of distribute unmarked materials—particularly chemicals—to employees.

Although internal policies do not necessarily prevent future employment with competitors, they can serve to prevent undue disclosures and lessen the criticality of the departure of key personnel. All must be exercised with a sophisticated regard for employee motivation, however, because the cumulative effect may result in a police state atmosphere that inhibits creativity and repels prospective employees.

Several farsighted R&D organizations are currently experimenting with plans which essentially delegate the responsibility for nondisclosure and nonuse of their trade secrets to the key employees themselves. These plans include pension and consulting programs operative for a specified post-employment period. In one company, for example, the pension plan provides that the corporate monies which are contributed to the employee pension fund in direct ratio to the employee's own contributions will remain in his pension package following his term of employment, provided he does not work for a competing firm for a specified number of years. In another company, the consulting plan provides that certain departing employees are eligible to receive an annual consulting fee for a given number of years following employment if they do not work for a competitor. The consulting fee is a preestablished percentage of the employee's annual salary at the time of his departure.

Obviously, such corporate plans are subject to employee abuse, but if limited to truly key employees, they may succeed without abuse in most cases. They not only have the merit of providing the employee with a choice, an equitable feature likely to incur employee loyalty, but they also have no apparent legal defects.

Another valid internal practice is the debriefing of departing employees. The debriefing session, carried out in a low-key atmosphere, affords management an excellent opportunity to retrieve company materials and information in physical form, to impart to the employee a sense of responsibility regarding trade secrets and sensitive areas, and to discuss mutual anxieties in full.

External Procedures

Several management responses relating to external company policies are worth noting, as they also serve to protect trade secrets in cases involving employee departures. Among several industries, such as in the chemical field, it is common to find gentlemen's agreements which provide mutuality in the nonhiring of competitors' key employees, following notice. Employees who have encountered this practice have not found the experience a pleasant one. This same practice is also found in other areas, such as the industrial machinery industry, that are in need of innovation; and it appears that the presence of such agreements helps to depict these industries in an unappealing fashion to the types of employees they need.

Another external response for management consideration is company reliance on trademarks. Given a good mark and subsequent public identification of the product with the mark, a company may be able to maintain market despite the fact that its intellectual property is no longer a trade secret. Competitors may be hesitant about utilizing the former trade secrets of any company whose products are strongly identified with trademarks and with the company itself.

Some trade secrets are patentable, and management faced with the potential loss of such secrets should consider filing for patent protection. The application is treated confidentially by the U.S. Patent Office and some foreign patent offices up to the time of award. Moreover, if the application is rejected, the secrecy of the information is not legally diminished. In any case, the subject matter of the application remains secret throughout the two- to three-year period of time normally involved in U.S. Patent Office review.

Conclusion

A major concern of our society is progress through the promotion and utilization of new technology. To sustain and enhance this form of progress, it is necessary to optimize the flow of information and innovation all the way from conception to public use. This effort is now a tripartite affair involving federal agencies, industry, and universities. A unique feature of this tripartite relationship is the mobility of R&D managers, scientists, and engineers who follow contract funding and projects in accordance with their special competence. Neither the federal agencies nor the universities rely on trade secret concepts for the protection of their intellectual property. However, industry still does, despite the fact that trade secret concepts bear the potential ancillary effect of interfering with employee mobility.

It is becoming increasingly clear that new soci-

etal values associated with the tripartite approach to new technology are now evolving, and that the common law dispensed by the courts has begun to reflect these values. A victim of sorts is trade secret law, which has not only never been clearly defined, but which has indeed been sustained by court concepts of unfair competition, equity, and confidence derived from other fields of law. The day when courts restrict employee mobility to preserve industrial trade secrets appears to have passed, except—as we noted earlier—in cases involving highly charged factors such as conspiracy, fraud, or theft.

In short, it is now unwise for management to rely on trade secret law and derivative employee contractual restraints to preserve trade secrets. Companies must now carefully weigh the nature and value of their intellectual property, present and potential employees, competition, and applicable laws in order to formulate sound management policies.

Programmed Approach

Regarding the challenge to the preservation of trade secrets posed by the mobile employee, sophisticated management will place its primary reliance on the inculcation of company loyalty in key employees, and on the continual satisfaction of such key employees. For example, management might consider adopting the following five-step basis for developing an overall approach to the challenge:

1. Devise a program for recognition of employee achievement in the trade secret area. At present, this form of recognition is even more neglected than is adequate recognition of employee inventions.

2. Make an appraisal of trade secret activities. This should result in a limitation of (a) personnel with access to trade secrets, (b) the extent of trade secrets available to such personnel, and (c) information which truly deserves the label of trade secret.

3. Review in-house procedures and the use of physical safeguards, such as restrictions on access to certain specified areas and on employee writings for outside publication. Restrictions may tend to stifle creativity by inhibiting communication and interaction conducive to innovation. Striking the balance be-

tween too few and too many safeguards is a delicate process and depends on employee awareness of what is being sought and how it will benefit them.

4. Appraise the legal systems available for the protection of intellectual property. Utility and design patents may be advisable in some cases. The copyright system now offers some protection to certain types of industrial designs and computer software. Trademarks may be adroitly used to maintain markets.

5. Recognize that all efforts may fail to persuade a key employee from leaving. To cope with this contingency, the "gentle persuasion" of a pension or consulting plan in the post-employment period has proved effective and legally sound. A thorough debriefing is a further safeguard. Other cases wherein employee mobility is accompanied by fraud, unfair competition, or theft will be adequately dealt with by the courts.

The problem of the departing employee and the threatened loss of trade secrets is not solved by exhortations that scientists and engineers need courses in professional ethics. Management itself should display the standards of conduct expected of its employees and of other companies.

Finally, let me stress again that success probably lies in the inculcation of company loyalty in key employees, not in the enforcement of company desires or in misplaced reliance on the law to subsidize cursory management. Better employee relations—in fact, a total sensitivity to the needs and aspirations of highly educated employees—requires constant management concern. In the long run, total sensitivity will prove less costly and more effective than litigation and the use of questionable contractual restraints.

Review and Discussion Questions

1. What was at stake in the *Wohlgemuth* case? Do you think that Wohlgemuth behaved unethically? Should he have been more loyal to Goodrich? Did Goodrich overreact?

2. Explain why Baram is critical of the court's decision.

3. If an employee invents a new process for a company, who owns that knowledge? Does it make a difference to your assessment whether or not the skills that made the invention possible were acquired by the employee on the job?

4. What makes something a "trade secret"? Give examples both of information that would constitute a trade secret and of information that would not. In your opinion, how important are trade secrets in business today?

5. What problems face a company trying to protect its intellectual property? What steps would you recommend that it take? Why does Baram think that it is unwise for a company to rely on the trade-secrets law or on contractual restraints?

6. Baram emphasizes the importance of inculcating company loyalty in key employees. What does "company loyalty" mean to you? What, specifically, do employees owe the company in terms of loyalty?

A Business Traveler's Guide to Gifts and Bribes

Jeffrey A. Fadiman

Americans who travel on business to other lands frequently find themselves trying to do business against a backdrop of cultural patterns and expectations which they do not fully understand. This naturally causes uncertainty, especially when the situation involves what appears to be begging, bribery, or blackmail. How should businesspeople comply with customs that conflict with both their sense of ethics and our nation's laws? In discussing this, professor of international marketing Jeffrey A. Fadiman analyzes three important non-Western traditions which American businesspeople need to understand and goes on to provide specific suggestions on how they can respond to approaches for payoffs in foreign countries.

"What do I say if he asks for a bribe?" I asked myself while enduring the all-night flight to Asia. Uncertain, I shared my concern with the man sitting beside me, a CEO en route to Singapore. Intrigued, he passed it on to his partners next to him. No one seemed sure.

Among American executives doing business overseas, this uncertainty is widespread. Consider, for example, each of the following situations:

- You are invited to the home of your foreign colleague. You learn he lives in a palatial villa. What gift might both please your host and ease business relations? What if he considers it to be a bribe? What if he *expects* it to be a bribe? Why do you feel uneasy?

- Your company's product lies on the dock of a foreign port. To avoid spoilage, you must swiftly transport it inland. What "gift," if any, would both please authorities and facilitate your business? What if they ask for "gifts" of $50? $50,000? $500,000? When does a gift become a bribe? When do you stop feeling comfortable?

- Negotiations are complete. The agreement is signed. One week later, a minister asks your company for $1 million—"for a hospital"—simultaneously suggesting that "other valuable considerations" might come your way as the result of future favors on both sides. What response, if any, would please him, satisfy you, and help execute the signed agreement?

- You have been asked to testify before the Securities and Exchange Commission regarding alleged violations of the Foreign Corrupt Practices Act. How would you explain the way you handled the examples above? Would your explanations both satisfy those in authority and ensure the continued overseas operation of your company?

Much of the discomfort Americans feel when faced with problems of this nature is due to U.S. law. Since 1977, congressional passage of the Foreign Corrupt Practices Act has transformed hypothetical problems into practical dilemmas and has created considerable anxiety among Americans who deal with foreign governments and companies. The problem is particularly difficult for those conducting business in the developing nations, where the rules that govern payoffs may differ sharply from our own. In such instances, U.S. executives may face not only legal but also ethical and cultural dilemmas: How do businesspeople comply with customs that conflict with both their sense of ethics and this nation's law?

One way to approach the problem is to devise appropriate corporate responses to payoff requests. The suggestions that follow apply to those developing Asian, African, and Middle Eastern nations, still in transition toward industrial societies, that have retained aspects of their communal traditions. These approaches do not assume that those who adhere to these ideals exist in selfless bliss, requesting private payments only for communal ends, with little thought of self-enrichment. Nor do these suggestions apply to situations of overt extortion, where U.S. companies are forced to provide funds. Instead they explore a middle way in which non-Western colleagues may have several motives when requesting a payoff, thereby providing U.S. managers with several options.

Decisions & Dilemmas

My own first experience with Third World bribery may illustrate the inner conflict Americans can feel when asked to break the rules. It occurred in East Africa and began with this request: "Oh, and Bwana, I would like 1,000 shillings as Zawadi, my gift. And, as we are now friends, for Chai, my tea, an eight-band radio, to bring to my home when you visit."

Both *Chai* and *Zawadi* can be Swahili terms for "bribe." He delivered these requests in respectful tones. They came almost as an afterthought, at the conclusion of negotiations in which we had settled the details of a projected business venture. I had looked forward to buying my counterpart a final drink to complete the deal symbolically in the American fashion. Instead, after we had settled every contractual aspect, he expected money.

The amount he suggested, although insignificant by modern standards, seemed large at the time. Nonetheless, it was the radio that got to me. Somehow it added insult to injury. Outwardly, I kept smiling. Inside, my stomach boiled. My own world view equates bribery with sin. I expect monetary issues to be settled before contracts are signed. Instead, although the negotiations were complete, he expected me to pay out once more. Once? How often? Where would it stop? My reaction took only moments to formulate. "I'm American," I declared. "I don't pay bribes." Then I walked away. That walk was not the longest in my life. It was, however, one of the least commercially productive.

As it turned out, I had misunderstood him—in more ways than one. By misinterpreting both his language and his culture, I lost an opportunity for a business deal and a personal relationship that would have paid enormous dividends without violating either the law or my own sense of ethics.

Go back through the episode—but view it this time with an East African perspective. First, my colleague's language should have given me an important clue as to how he saw our transaction. Although his limited command of English caused him to frame his request as a command—a phrasing I instinctively found offensive—his tone was courteous. Moreover, if I had listened more carefully, I would have noted that he had addressed me as a superior: he used the honorific *Bwana*, meaning "sir," rather than *Rafiki* (or friend), used between equals. From his perspective, the language was appropriate; it reflected the differences in our personal wealth and in the power of the institutions we each represented.

Having assigned me the role of the superior figure in the economic transaction, he then suggested how I should use my position in accord with his culture's traditions—logically assuming that I would benefit by his prompting. In this case, he suggested that money and a radio would be appropriate gifts. What he did not tell me was that his culture's traditions required him to use the money to provide a feast—in my honor—to which he would invite everyone in his social and commercial circle whom he felt I should meet. The radio would simply create a festive atmosphere at the party. This was to mark the beginning of an ongoing relationship with reciprocal benefits.

He told me none of this. Since I was willing to do business in local fashion, I was supposed to know. In fact, I had not merely been invited to a dwelling but through a gateway into the maze of gifts and formal visiting that linked him to his kin. He hoped that I would respond in local fashion. Instead, I responded according to my cultural norms and walked out both on the chance to do business and on the opportunity to make friends.

The Legal Side

Perhaps from a strictly legal perspective my American reaction was warranted. In the late 1970s, as part of the national reaction to Watergate, the SEC sued several large U.S. companies for alleged instances of bribery overseas. One company reportedly authorized $59 million in contributions to political parties in Italy, including the Communist party. A second allegedly paid $4 million to a political party in South Korea. A third reportedly provided $450,000 in "gifts" to Saudi generals. A fourth may have diverted $377,000 to fly planeloads of voters to the Cook Islands to rig elections there.

The sheer size of the payments and the ways they had been used staggered the public. A U.S. senate committee reported "corrupt" foreign payments involving hundreds of millions of dollars by more than 400 U.S. corporations, including 117 of the *Fortune* "500." The SEC described the problem as a national crisis.

In response, Congress passed the Foreign Corrupt Practices Act in 1977. The law prohibits U.S. corporations from providing or even offering payments to foreign political parties, candidates, or officials with discretionary authority under circumstances that might induce recipients to misuse their positions to assist the company to obtain, maintain, or retain business.

The FCPA does not forbid payments to lesser figures, however. On the contrary, it explicitly allows facilitating payments ("grease") to persuade foreign officials to perform their normal duties, at both the clerical and ministerial levels. The law establishes no monetary guidelines but requires companies to keep reasonably detailed records that accurately and fairly reflect the transactions.

The act also prohibits indirect forms of payment. Companies cannot make payments of this nature while "knowing or having reason to know" that any portion of the funds will be transferred to a forbidden recipient to be used for corrupt purposes as previously defined. Corporations face fines of up to $1 million. Individuals can be fined $10,000—which the corporation is forbidden to indemnify—and sentenced to a maximum of five years in prison. In short, private payments by Americans abroad can mean violation of U.S. law, a consideration that deeply influences U.S. corporate thinking.

The Ethical Side

For most U.S. executives, however, the problem goes beyond the law. Most Americans share an aversion to payoffs. In parts of Asia, Africa, and the Middle East, however, certain types of bribery form an accepted element of their commercial traditions. Of course, nepotism, shakedown, and similar practices do occur in U.S. business; these practices, however, are both forbidden by law and universally disapproved.

Americans abroad reflect these sentiments. Most see themselves as personally honest and professionally ethical. More important, they see themselves as preferring to conduct business accordingly to the law, both American and foreign. They also know that virtually all foreign governments—including those notorious for corruption—have rigorously enforced statutes against most forms of private payoff. In general, there is popular support for these anticorruption measures. In Malaysia, bribery is publicly frowned on and punishable by long imprisonment. In the Soviet Union, Soviet officials who solicit bribes can be executed.

Reflecting this awareness, most U.S. businesspeople prefer to play by local rules, competing in the open market according to the quality, price, and services provided by their product. Few, if any, want to make illegal payments of any kind to anybody. Most prefer to obey both local laws and their own ethical convictions while remaining able to do business.

The Cultural Side

Yet, as my African experience suggests, indigenous traditions often override the law. In some developing nations, payoffs have become a norm. The problem is compounded when local payoff practices are rooted in a "communal heritage," ideals inherited from a preindustrial past where a community leader's wealth—however acquired—was shared throughout the community. Those who hoarded were scorned as antisocial. Those who shared won status and authority. Contact with Western commerce has blurred the ideal, but even the most individualistic businesspeople remember their communal obligations.

Contemporary business practices in those regions often reflect these earlier ideals. Certain forms of private payoff have endured for centuries. The Nigerian practice of *dash* (private payments for private services), for example, goes back to fifteenth century contacts with the Portuguese, in which Africans solicited "gifts" (trade goods) in exchange for labor. Such solicitation can pose a cultural dilemma to Americans who may be unfamiliar with the communal nuances of non-Western commercial conduct. To cope, they may denigrate these traditions, perceiving colleagues who solicit payments as unethical and their culture as corrupt. . . .

My experience suggests that most non-Westerners are neither excessively corrupt nor completely communal. Rather, they are simultaneously drawn to both indigenous and Western ideals. Many have internalized the Western norms of personal enrichment along with those of modern commerce, while simultaneously adhering to indigenous traditions by fulfilling communal obligations. Requests for payoffs may spring from both these ideals. Corporate responses must therefore be designed to satisfy them both.

Background for Payoffs

Throughout non-Western cultures, three traditions form the background for discussing payoffs: the inner circle, future favors, and the gift exchange. Though centuries old, each has evolved into a modern business concept. Americans who work in the Third World need to learn about them so they can work within them.

The Inner Circle

Most individuals in developing nations classify others into some form of "ins" and "outs." Members of more communal societies, influenced by the need to strive for group prosperity, divide humanity into those with whom they have relationships and those with whom they have none. Many Africans, for instance, view people as either "brothers" or "strangers." Relationships with brothers may be real—kin, however distant—or fictional, extending to comrades or "mates." Comrades, however, may both speak and act like kin, address one another as family, and assume obligations of protection and assistance that Americans reserve for nuclear families.

Together, kin and comrades form an inner circle, a fictional "family," devoted to mutual protection and prosperity. Like the "old boy networks" that operate in the United States, no single rule defines membership in the inner circle. . . . Beyond this magic circle live the "outs": strangers, aliens, individuals with no relationship to those within. . . .

Not every U.S. manager is aware of this division. Those who investigate often assume that their nationality, ethnic background, and alien culture automatically classify them as "outs." Non-Western colleagues, however, may regard specific Westerners as useful contacts, particularly if they seem willing to do business in local fashion. They may, therefore, consider bringing certain individuals into their inner circles in such a manner as to benefit both sides.

Overseas executives, if asked to work within such circles, should find their business prospects much enhanced. These understandings often lead to implicit quid pro quos. For example, one side might agree to hire workers from only one clan; in return the other side would guarantee devoted labor. As social and commercial trust grows, the Westerners may be regarded less and less as aliens or predators and more and more as comrades or kin. Obviously, this is a desirable transition, and executives assigned to work within this type of culture may wish to consider whether these inner circles exist, and if so, whether working within them will enhance business prospects.

The Future Favor

A second non-Western concept that relates to payoffs is a system of future favors. Relationships within the inner circles of non-Western nations function through such favors. . . . All systems of this type assume that any individual under obligation to another has entered a relationship in which the first favor must be repaid in the future, when convenient to all sides.

Neither side defines the manner of repayment. Rather, both understand that some form of gift or service will repay the earlier debt with interest. This repayment places the originator under obligation. The process then begins again, creating

a lifelong cycle. The relationship that springs from meeting lifelong obligations builds the trust that forms a basis for conducting business.

My own introduction to the future favors system may illustrate the process. While conducting business on Mt. Kenya in the 1970s, I visited a notable local dignitary. On completing our agenda, he stopped my rush to leave by presenting me a live and angry hen. Surprised, I stammered shaky "thank-yous," then walked down the mountain with my kicking, struggling bird. Having discharged my obligation—at least in Western terms—by thanking him, I cooked the hen, completed my business, eventually left Kenya, and forgot the incident.

Years later, I returned on different business. It was a revelation. People up and down the mountain called out to one another that I had come back to "return the dignitary's hen." To them, the relationship that had sprung up between us had remained unchanged throughout the years. Having received a favor, I had now come back to renew the relationship by returning it.

I had, of course, no such intention. Having forgotten the hen incident, I was also unaware of its importance to others. Embarrassed, I slipped into a market and bought a larger hen, then climbed to his homestead to present it. Again I erred, deciding to apologize in Western fashion for delaying my return. "How can a hen be late?" he replied. "Due to the bird, we have *uthoni* [obligations, thus a relationship]. That is what sweetens life. What else was the hen for but to bring you here again?"

These sentiments can also operate within non-Western commercial circles, where business favors can replace hens, but *uthoni* are what sweetens corporate life. Western interest lies in doing business; non-Western, in forming bonds so that business can begin. Westerners seek to discharge obligations; non-Westerners, to create them. Our focus is on producing short-term profit; theirs, on generating future favors. The success of an overseas venture may depend on an executive's awareness of these differences.

The Gift Exchange

One final non-Western concept that can relate to payoffs is a continuous exchange of gifts. In some developing nations, gifts form the catalysts that trigger future favors. U.S. executives often wish to present gifts appropriate to cultures where they are assigned, to the point where at least one corporation has commissioned a special study of the subject. They may be less aware, however, of the long-range implications of gift giving within these cultures. Two of these may be particularly relevant to CEOs concerned with payoffs.

In many non-Western commercial circles, the tradition of gift giving has evolved into a modern business tool intended to create obligation as well as affection. Recipients may be gratified by what they receive, but they also incur an obligation that they must some day repay. Gift giving in these cultures may therefore operate in two dimensions: one meant to provide short-term pleasure; the other, long-range bonds.

This strategy is common in Moslem areas of Africa and Asia. Within these cultures, I have watched export merchants change Western clientele from browsers to buyers by inviting them to tea. Seated, the customers sip at leisure, while merchandise is brought before them piece by piece. The seller thus achieves three goals. His clients have been honored, immobilized, and placed under obligation.

In consequence, the customers often feel the need to repay in kind. Lacking suitable material gifts, they frequently respond as the merchant intends: with decisions to buy—not because they need the merchandise but to return the seller's gift of hospitality. The buyers, considering their obligation discharged, leave the premises believing relations have ended. The sellers, however, hope they have just begun. Their intent is to create relationships that will cause clients to return. A second visit would mean presentation of another gift, perhaps of greater value. That, in turn, might mean a second purchase, leading to further visits, continued gifts, and a gradual deepening of personal and commercial relations intended to enrich both sides.

The point of the process, obviously, is not the exchanges themselves but the relationships they engender. The gifts are simply catalysts. Under ideal circumstances the process should be unending, with visits, gifts, gestures, and services flowing back and forth among participants throughout their lives. The universally understood purpose is to create reciprocal good feelings and commercial prosperity among all concerned.

Gift giving has also evolved as a commercial "signal." In America, gifts exchanged by business colleagues may signal gratitude, camaraderie, or perhaps the discharge of minor obligations. Among non-Westerners, gifts may signal the desire to begin both social and commercial relationships with members of an inner circle. That signal may also apply to gifts exchanged with Westerners. If frequently repeated, such exchanges may be signals of intent. For Americans, the signal may suggest a willingness to work within a circle of local business colleagues, to assume appropriate obligations, and to conduct business in local ways. For non-Western colleagues, gifts may imply a wish to invite selected individuals into their commercial interactions.

Approaches to Payoffs

While U.S. corporations may benefit from adapting to local business concepts, many indigenous business traditions, especially in developing regions, are alien to the American experience and therefore difficult to implement by U.S. field personnel—as every executive who has tried to sit cross-legged for several hours with Third World counterparts will attest.

Conversely, many non-Western administrators are particularly well informed about U.S. business practices, thus permitting U.S. field representatives to function on familiar ground. Nonetheless, those willing to adapt indigenous commercial concepts to U.S. corporate needs may find that their companies can benefit in several ways. Through working with a circle of non-Western business colleagues, and participating fully in the traditional exchange of gifts and favors, U.S. executives may find that their companies increase the chance of preferential treatment; use local methods and local contacts to gain market share; develop trust to reinforce contractual obligations; and minimize current risk, while maximizing future opportunities by developing local expertise.

Corporations that adapt to local business concepts may also develop methods to cope with local forms of payoff. Current approaches vary from culture to culture, yet patterns do appear. Three frequently recur in dealings between Americans and non-Westerners: gifts, bribes, and other considerations.

Gifts: The Direct Request

This form of payoff may occur when key foreign businesspeople approach their U.S. colleagues to solicit "gifts." Solicitations of this type have no place in U.S. business circles where they could be construed as exploitation. Obviously, the same may hold true overseas, particularly in areas where shakedown, bribery, and extortion may be prevalent. There is, however, an alternative to consider. To non-Western colleagues, such requests may simply be a normal business strategy, designed to build long-term relationships.

To U.S. businesspeople, every venture is based on the bottom line. To non-Western colleagues, a venture is based on the human relationships that form around it. Yet, when dealing with us they often grow uncertain as to how to form these relationships. How can social ties be created with Americans who speak only of business, even when at leisure? How can traditions of gift giving be initiated with people unaware of the traditions? Without the exchange of gifts, how can obligations be created? Without obligations, how can there be trust?

Faced with such questions, non-Western business colleagues may understandably decide to initiate gift-giving relationships on their own. If powerful, prominent, or wealthy, they may simply begin by taking on the role of giver. If less powerful or affluent, some may begin by suggesting they become recipients. There need be no dishonor in such action, since petitioners know they will repay with future favors whatever inner debt they incur.

The hosts may also realize that, as strangers, Americans may be unaware of local forms of gift giving as well as their relationship to business norms. Or they may be cognizant of such relationships but may have no idea of how to enter into them. In such instances, simple courtesy may cause the hosts to indicate—perhaps obliquely—how proper entry into the local system should be made. Such was the unfortunate case with my East African colleague's request for the eight-band radio.

Cultural barriers can be difficult to cross. Most Americans give generously, but rarely on request. When solicited, we feel exploited. Solicitations may seem more relevant, however, if examined from the perspective of the non-Western peoples with whom we are concerned.

Often, in societies marked by enormous gaps between the rich and the poor, acts of generosity display high status. To withhold gifts is to deny the affluence one has achieved. Non-Western counterparts often use lavish hospitality both to reflect and to display their wealth and status within local society. When Americans within these regions both represent great wealth through association with their corporations and seek high status as a tool to conduct business, it may prove more profitable for the corporation to give than to receive.

In short, when asked for "gifts" by foreign personnel, managers may consider two options. The first option is to regard each query as extortion and every petitioner as a potential thief. The second is to consider the request within its local context. In nations where gifts generate a sense of obligation, it may prove best to give them, thereby creating inner debts among key foreign colleagues in the belief that they will repay them over time. If such requests indeed reflect a local way of doing business, they may be gateways into the workings of its commercial world. One U.S. option, therefore, is to consider the effect of providing "gifts"—even on direct request—in terms of the relationships required to implement the corporation's long-range plans.

Bribes: The Indirect Request

A second approach to payoffs, recurrent in non-Western business circles, is the indirect request. Most Third World people prefer the carrot to the stick. To avoid unpleasant confrontation, they designate third parties to suggest that "gifts" of specified amounts be made to those in local power circles. In explanation they cite the probability of future favors in return. No line exists, of course, dividing gifts from bribes. It seems that direct solicitation involves smaller amounts, while larger ones require go-betweens. On occasion, however, the sums requested can be staggering: in 1976, for example, U.S. executives in Qatar were asked for a $1.5 million "gift" for that nation's minister of oil.

U.S. responses to such queries must preserve both corporate funds and executive relationships with those in power. While smaller gifts may signal a desire to work with the local business circles, a company that supplies larger sums could violate both local antipayoff statutes and the FCPA. Conversely, outright rejection of such requests may cause both the go-betweens and those they represent to lose prestige and thus possibly prompt retaliation.

In such instances, the FCPA may actually provide beleaguered corporate executives with a highly convenient excuse. Since direct compliance with requests for private funds exposes every U.S. company to threats of negative publicity, blackmail, legal action, financial loss, and damage to corporate image, it may prove easy for Americans to say no—while at the same time offering nonmonetary benefits to satisfy both sides.

U.S. competitors may, in fact, be in a better situation than those companies from Europe and Japan that play by different rules. Since the principle of payoffs is either accepted or encouraged by many of their governments, the companies must find it difficult to refuse payment of whatever sums are asked.

Nor should the "right to bribe" be automatically considered an advantage. Ignoring every other factor, this argument assumes contracts are awarded solely on the basis of the largest private payoff. At the most obvious level, it ignores the possibility that products also compete on the basis of quality, price, promotion, and service—factors often crucial to American success abroad. U.S. field representatives are often first to recognize that payoffs may be only one of many factors in awarding contracts. In analyzing U.S. competition in the Middle East, for instance, one executive of an American aircraft company noted: "The French have savoir faire in giving bribes discreetly and well, but they're still not . . . backing up their sales with technical expertise." The overseas executive should consider to what degree the right to bribe may be offset by turning the attention of the payoff seekers to other valuable considerations.

Other Considerations: The Suggested Service

A third approach, often used by members of a non-Western elite, is to request that U.S. companies contribute cash to public service projects, often administered by the petitioners themselves. Most proposals of this type require money. Yet if American executives focus too sharply on the financial aspects, they may neglect the chance to work other nonmonetary considerations into their response. In many developing nations, nonmonetary considerations may weigh heavily on foreign colleagues.

Many elite non-Westerners, for example, are intensely nationalistic. They love their country keenly, deplore its relative poverty, and yearn to help it rise. They may, therefore, phrase their requests for payoffs in terms of a suggested service to the nation. In Kenya, for example, ministerial requests to U.S. companies during the 1970s suggested a contribution toward the construction of a hospital. In Indonesia, in the mid-1970s, a top executive of Pertamina, that nation's government-sponsored oil company, requested contributions to an Indonesian restaurant in New York City as a service to the homeland. In his solicitation letter, the executive wrote that the restaurant was in fact intended to "enhance the Indonesian image in the U.S.A., . . . promote tourism, . . . and attract the interest of the U.S. businessmen to investments in Indonesia."

Westerners may regard such claims with cynicism. Non-Westerners may not. They recognize that, even if the notables involved become wealthy, some portion of the wealth, which only they can attract from abroad, will still be shared by other members of their homeland.

That belief is worth consideration, for many elite non-Westerners share a second concern: the desire to meet communal obligations by sharing wealth with members of their inner circle. Modern business leaders in communal cultures rarely simply hoard their wealth. To do so would invite social condemnation. Rather, they provide gifts, funds, and favors to those in their communal settings, receiving deference, authority, and prestige in return.

This does not mean that funds transferred by Western corporations to a single foreign colleague will be parceled out among a circle of cronies. Rather, money passes through one pair of hands, over time, flowing slowly in the form of gifts and favors to friends and kin. The funds may even flow beyond this inner circle to their children, most often to ensure their continued education. Such generosity, of course, places both adult recipients and children under a long-term obligation, thereby providing donors both with current status and with assurance of obtaining future favors.

In short, non-Western colleagues who seek payoffs may have concerns beyond their personal enrichment. If motivated by both national and communal idealism, they may feel that these requests are not only for themselves but also a means to aid much larger groups and ultimately their nation.

A Donation Strategy

Requests for payoffs give executives little choice. Rejection generates resentment, while agreement may lead to prosecution. Perhaps appeals to both communal and national idealism can open up a third alternative. Consider, for example, the possibility of deflecting such requests by transforming private payoffs into public services. One approach would be to respond to requests for private payment with well-publicized, carefully tailored "donations"—an approach that offers both idealistic and practical appeal.

This type of donation could take several forms. The most obvious, monetary contribution, could be roughly identical to the amount requested in private funds. Donating it publicly, however, would pay off important foreign colleagues in nonmonetary ways.

At the national level, for instance, the most appropriate and satisfying corporate response to ministerial requests for "contributions" toward the construction of a hospital, such as occurred in Kenya, might be actually to provide one, down to the final door and stethoscope, while simultaneously insisting that monetary payments of any kind are proscribed by U.S. law. . . .

Yet donations alone seem insufficient. To serve as an alternative to payoffs, the concept should have practical appeal. Consider, for example, the story of a Western company in Zaire. During the 1970s, Zaire's economy decayed so badly that even ranking civil servants went unpaid. As a result, key Zairian district officials approached officers of the Western company, requesting private funds for future favors. Instead, the company responded with expressions of deference and "donations" of surplus supplies, including goods that could be sold on the black market. The resulting cash flow enabled the officials to continue in their posts. This in turn allowed them to render reciprocal services, both to their district and to the company. By tailoring their contribution to local conditions, the company avoided draining its funds, while providing benefits to both sides.

There are many ways to tailor donations. At the most obvious level, funds can support social

projects in the home areas of important local colleagues. Funds or even whole facilities can be given in their names. Production centers can be staffed by members of their ethnic group. Educational, medical, and other social services can be made available to key segments of a target population based on the advice of influential foreign counterparts. Given the opportunity, many non-Westerners would direct the contributions toward members of their inner circles profiting from local forms of recognition and prestige. These practices, often used in one form or another in the United States, can provide non-Western counterparts with local recognition and authority and supply a legal, ethical, and culturally acceptable alternative to a payoff.

Donating Services

U.S. companies may also deflect payoff proposals by donating services, gratifying important foreign colleagues in nonmonetary fashion, and thus facilitating the flow of future business. In 1983, for example, a British military unit, part of the Royal Electrical and Mechanical Engineers, planned an African overland vehicle expedition across the Sahara to Tanzania. On arrival, they were "expected" to make a sizable cash donation to that nation to be used in support of its wildlife.

Usually this meant meeting a minister, handing over a check, and taking a picture of the transfer. Instead, the British assembled thousands of dollars worth of tools and vehicle parts, all needed in Tanzanian wildlife areas for trucks on antipoaching patrols. Tanzania's weakened economy no longer permitted the import of enough good tools or parts, which left the wildlife authorities with few working vehicles. As a result, wild-game management had nearly halted. By transporting the vital parts across half of Africa, then working alongside local mechanics until every vehicle was on the road, the British reaped far more goodwill than private payments or even cash donations would have gained. More important, they paved the way for future transactions by providing services meant to benefit both sides.

Donating Jobs

A third alternative to private payoffs may be to donate jobs, particularly on projects meant to build goodwill among a host nation's elite. In the 1970s, for example, Coca-Cola was the object of a Middle

Eastern boycott by members of the Arab League. Conceivably, Coca-Cola could have sought to win favor with important individuals through gifts or bribes. Instead, the company hired hundreds of Egyptians to plant thousands of acres of orange trees. Eventually the company carpeted a considerable stretch of desert and thereby created both employment and goodwill.

More recently, Mexico refused to let IBM become the first wholly owned foreign company to make personal computers within its borders. Like Coca-Cola in Egypt, IBM employed a strategy of national development: it offered a revised proposal, creating both direct and indirect employment for Mexican nationals, in numbers high enough to satisfy that nation's elite. Such projects do more than generate goodwill. Those able to involve key foreign colleagues in ways that lend prestige on local terms may find they serve as viable alternatives to bribery.

Good Ethics, Good Business

Three strategies do not exhaust the list. U.S. executives in foreign countries should be able to devise their own variants based on local conditions. . . .

Non-Western business practices may be difficult to comprehend, especially when they involve violations of U.S. legal, commercial, or social norms. Nonetheless, U.S. business options are limited only by our business attitudes. If these can be expanded through selective research into those local concepts that relate to payoffs, responses may emerge to satisfy both congressional and indige-

nous demands. What may initially appear as begging, bribery, or blackmail may be revealed as local tradition, cross-cultural courtesy, or attempts to make friends. More important, when examined from a non-American perspective, mention of "gifts," "bribes," and "other valuable considerations" may signal a wish to do business.

Review and Discussion Questions

1. In Fadiman's first encounter with Third World bribery, what did he fail to understand about the situation? How would you have acted in his place?

2. Explain the three non-Western cultural traditions that Fadiman identifies as forming the context of payoffs.

3. Critics of the FCPA claim that the act ties the hands of American corporations by forbidding them to bribe foreign officials. Fadiman appears skeptical of this argument. Why? Do you think the FCPA is a good law?

4. Americans view bribery as immoral. But if bribery is an accepted practice in a foreign country, is it still immoral? Explain your answer. Why do we consider bribery wrong in the first place?

5. Describe the donation strategy that Fadiman recommends. Does it solve the problem of respecting local customs while remaining true to our own legal and ethical standards? Do you see any problems with the strategy?

In Defense of Whistle Blowing

Gene G. James

Professor of philosophy Gene G. James begins his examination of whistle blowing with some pertinent definitions and an overview of the current legal status of the phenomenon. He then challenges Professor DeGeorge's analysis of whistle blowing. Among other things, James believes, counter to DeGeorge's condition five, that workers have an obligation to warn the public of dangers, even if they believe that the public will ignore the warnings. He also rejects DeGeorge's claim that engineers are not obligated to blow the whistle when, by so doing, they will likely lose their jobs. In James's view that

kind of risk-running is part and parcel of the engineer's professional obligations.

James also questions DeGeorge's insistence that one must exhaust all internal channels before blowing the whistle, condition three. It all depends, says James, on the nature of the wrongdoing, the kind of organization involved, and the likelihood of retaliation.

James then sketches the factors that whistle blowers should consider "if they are to act prudently and morally."

He concludes with a brief discussion of the need for pro-

tective legislation for whistle blowers and changes within organizations to prevent the need for whistle blowing.

Whistle blowing may be defined as the attempt by an employee or former employee of an organization to disclose what he or she believes to be wrongdoing in or by the organization. Like blowing a whistle to call attention to a thief, whistle blowing is an effort to make others aware of practices one considers illegal, unjust, or harmful. Whenever someone goes over the head of immediate supervisors to inform higher management of wrongdoing, the whistle blowing is *internal* to the organization. Whenever someone discloses wrongdoing to outside individuals or groups such as reporters, public interest groups, or regulatory agencies, the whistle blowing is *external*.

Most whistle blowing is done by people presently employed by the organization. However, people who have left the organization may also blow the whistle. The former may be referred to as *current* whistle blowers; the latter as *alumni* whistle blowers. If the whistle blower discloses his or her identity, the whistle blowing may be said to be *open*; if the person's identity is not disclosed, the whistle blowing is *anonymous*.

Whistle blowers differ from muckrakers because the latter do not have any ties to the organizations whose wrongdoing they seek to disclose. They differ from informers and stool pigeons because the latter usually have self-interested reasons for their disclosures, such as obtaining prosecutorial immunity. The term *whistle blower*, on the other hand, usually refers to people who disclose wrongdoing for moral reasons. However, unless whistle blowing is *defined* as disclosing wrongdoing for moral reasons, the distinction between whistle blowing and informing cannot be a sharp one. Thus, although most whistle blowers do it for moral reasons, one cannot take for granted that their motives are praiseworthy.

Whistle blowers almost always experience retaliation. If they work for private industry, they are likely to be fired. They also receive damaging letters of recommendation and may be blacklisted so they cannot find work in their profession. If they are not fired, or work for government agencies, they are still likely to be transferred, demoted, given less interesting work, and denied salary increases and promotions. Their professional compe-

tence is usually attacked. They are said to be unqualified to judge, misinformed, and so forth. Since their actions seem to threaten both the organization and their fellow employees, attacks on their personal lives are also frequent. They are called traitors, rat finks, and other names. They are also said to be disgruntled, known troublemakers, people who make an issue out of nothing, self-serving, and publicity-seekers. Their life-styles, sex lives, and mental stability may be questioned. Physical assaults, abuse of their families, and even murder are not unknown as retaliation to whistle blowing.

Whistle Blowing and the Law[1]

The law does not at present offer whistle blowers very much protection. Agency law, the area of common law which governs relations between employees and employers, imposes a duty on employees to keep confidential any information learned through their employment which might be detrimental to their employers. However, this duty does not hold if the employee has knowledge that the employer either has committed or is about to commit a felony. In this case the employee has a positive obligation to report the offense. Failure to do so is known as misprision and makes one subject to criminal penalties.

The problem with agency law is that it is based on the assumption that unless there are statutes or agreements to the contrary, contracts between employees and employers can be terminated at will by either party. It therefore grants employers the right to discharge employees at any time for any reason or even for no reason at all. The result is that most employees who blow the whistle on their employers, even those who report felonies, are fired or suffer other retaliation. One employee of thirty years was even fired the day before his pension became effective for testifying under subpoena against his employer, without the courts doing anything to aid him.

This situation has begun to change somewhat in recent years. In *Pickering v. Board of Education* in 1968 the Supreme Court ruled that government employees have the right to speak out on policy issues affecting their agencies provided doing so does not seriously disrupt the agency. A number of similar decisions have followed and the right of government employees to speak out on policy issues now seems firmly established. But employees in private industry do not have the right to speak out on company policies without being fired. In one case involving both a union and a company doing a substantial portion of its business with the federal government, federal courts did award back pay to an employee fired for criticizing the union and the company, but did not reinstate him or award him punitive damages.

A few state courts have begun to modify the right of employers to dismiss employees at will. Courts in Oregon and Pennsylvania have awarded damages to employees fired for serving on juries. A New Hampshire court granted damages to a woman fired for refusing to date her foreman. A West Virginia court reinstated a bank employee who reported illegal interest rates. The Illinois Supreme Court upheld the right of an employee to sue when fired for reporting and testifying about criminal activities of a fellow employee. However, a majority of states still uphold the right of employers to fire employees at will unless there are statutes or agreements to the contrary. Only one state, Michigan, has passed a law prohibiting employers from retaliating against employees who report violations of local, state, or federal laws.

A number of federal statutes contain provisions intended to protect whistle blowers. The National Labor Relations Act, Fair Labor Standards Act, Title VII of the 1964 Civil Rights Act, Age Discrimination Act, and Occupational Safety and Health Act all have sections prohibiting employers from taking retaliatory actions against employees who report or testify about violations of the acts.

Although these laws seem to encourage and protect whistle blowers, to be effective they must be enforced. A 1976 study[2] of the Occupational Safety and Health Act showed that only about 20 percent of the 2300 complaints filed in fiscal years 1975 and 1976 were judged valid by OSHA investigators. About half of these were settled out of court. Of the sixty cases taken to court at the time of the study in November 1976, one had been won, eight were lost, and the others were still pending. A more recent study[3] showed that of the 3100 violations reported in 1979, only 270 were settled out of court and only sixteen litigated.

Since the National Labor Relations Act guarantees the right of workers to organize and bargain collectively and most collective bargaining agreements contain a clause requiring employers to have just cause for discharging employees, these agreements would seem to offer some protection for whistle blowers. In fact, however, arbitrators have tended to agree with employers that whistle blowing is an act of disloyalty which disrupts business and injures the employer's reputation. Their attitude seems to be summed up in a 1972 case in which the arbitrator stated that one should not "bite the hand that feeds you and insist on staying for future banquets."[4] One reason for this, pointed out by David Ewing, is that unions are frequently as corrupt as the organizations on which the whistle is being blown. Such unions, he says, "are not likely to feed a hawk that comes to prey in their own barnyard."[5] The record of professional societies is not any better. They generally have failed to come to the defense of members who have attempted to live up to their professional codes of ethics by blowing the whistle on corrupt practices.

The Moral Justification of Whistle Blowing

Under what conditions, if any, is whistle blowing morally justified? Some people have argued that it is always justified because it is an exercise of free speech. But the right to free speech, like most other rights, is not absolute. Thus, even if whistle blowing is a form of free speech, that does not mean it is justified in every case. Others have argued that whistle blowing is never justified because employees have obligations of absolute loyalty and confidentiality to the organization for which they work. However, because the actions of organizations often harm or violate the rights of others, and one has an obligation to prevent harmful actions if one can, a universal prohibition against whistle blowing is not justifiable.

Assuming that we reject such extreme views, what conditions must be satisfied for whistle blowing to be moraly justified? Richard DeGeorge believes that whistle blowing is morally permissible if it meets the following three conditions:

1. The company must be engaged in a practice or about to release a product which does *serious* harm to individuals or to society in general.

The more serious the harm, the more serious the obligation.

2. The employee should report his concern or complaint to his immediate superior.

3. If no appropriate action is taken the employee should take the matter up the managerial line. Before he or she is obliged to go public, the resources for remedy within the company should be exhausted.[6]

For whistle blowing to be morally obligatory DeGeorge thinks two other conditions must be satisfied:

4. The employee should have documentation of the practice or defect. . . . Without adequate evidence his chances of being successful . . . are slim.

5. The employee must have good reason to believe that by going public he will be able to bring about the necessary changes.[7]

DeGeorge believes that because of the almost certain retaliation whistle blowers experience, whistle blowing is frequently morally permissible but not morally obligatory. He holds that this is true even when the person involved is a professional whose code of ethics requires him or her to put the public good ahead of personal good. He argues, for example:

> The myth that ethics has no place in engineering has . . . at least in some corners of the engineering profession . . . been put to rest. Another myth, however, is emerging to take its place—the myth of the engineer as moral hero. . . . The zeal . . . however, has gone too far, piling moral responsibility upon moral responsibility on the shoulders of the engineer. This emphasis . . . is misplaced. Though engineers are members of a profession that holds public safety paramount, we cannot reasonably expect engineers to be willing to sacrifice their jobs each day for principle and to have a whistle ever at their sides. . . ."[8]

He contends that engineers only have an obligation to do their jobs as best they can. This includes reporting observations about safety to management. But engineers do not have an "obligation to insist that their perceptions or their standards be accepted. They are not paid to do that, they are not expected to do that, and they have no moral or ethical obligation to do that."[9]

There are a number of problems with this analysis of whistle blowing.

The first condition is far too strong because it requires de facto wrongdoing instead of extremely probable evidence of wrongdoing before whistle blowing is morally justified. All that should be required of whistle blowers in this regard is that they be diligent in gathering evidence and act on the basis of the best evidence available to them. They should not be held to a more rigid standard than is usually applied to moral actions.

What constitutes serious and considerable harm? Must the harm be physical? Since DeGeorge was writing on business ethics, it is understandable that he only discussed whistle blowing involving corporations. But businesses, like governments, can be guilty of wrongs other than physically harming people. Should one, for example, never blow the whistle on such things as invasions of privacy?

If the harm is physical, how many people's health or safety must be endangered before the harm can be said to be considerable? And do professionals not have an obligation to inform the public of dangerous products and practices even if they will lose their jobs? Even though some Ford engineers had serious misgivings about the safety of Pinto gas tanks and several people were killed when tanks exploded after rear-end crashes, DeGeorge says that Ford engineers did not have an obligation to make their misgivings public. He maintains that although engineers are better qualified than other people to calculate cost versus safety, decisions about acceptable risk are not primarily engineering but managerial decisions. He believes that under ideal conditions the public itself would make this kind of decision. "A panel of informed people, not necesssarily engineers, should decide . . . acceptable risk and minimum standards."[10] This information should then be relayed to car buyers who, he believes, are entitled to it.

One of the reasons it is difficult to decide when employees have an obligation to blow the whistle is that this is part of the larger problem of the extent to which people are responsible for actions by organizations of which they are members. The problem arises because it is extremely difficult to determine when a given individual in an organization is responsible for a particular decision or policy. Decisions are often the product of committees rather than single individuals. Since committee members usually serve temporary terms, none of the members who helped make a particular decision may be on the committee when it is implemented. Implementation is also likely to be the responsibility of others. Since committee membership is temporary, decisions are often made that contradict previous decisions. Even when decisions are made by individuals, these individuals seldom have control over the outcome of the decisions.

The result is that no one feels responsible for the consequences of organizational decisions. Top management does not because it only formulates policy; it does not implement it. Those in the middle and at the bottom of the chain of authority do not, because they simply carry out policy. If challenged to assume moral responsibility for their actions, they reply "I'm not responsible, I was simply carrying out orders" or "I was just doing my job." But, as DeGeorge points out, absence of a feeling of obligation does not mean absence of obligation.

Whenever one acts in such a way as to harm or violate the rights of others, one is justly held accountable for those actions. This is true regardless of one's occupation or role in society. Acting as a member of an institution or corporation does not relieve a person of moral obligations. To the contrary. Because most of the actions we undertake in such settings have more far-reaching consequences than those we undertake in our personal lives, our moral obligation is *increased*. The amount of responsibility one bears for organizational actions is dependent on the extent to which (a) one could foresee the consequences of the organizational action, and (b) one's own acts or failures to act are a cause of those consequences. It is important to include failures to act here because frequently it is easier to determine what will happen if we don't act than if we do and because we are morally responsible for not preventing evil as well as for causing it.

Although the foregoing discussion is brief and the ideas not fully worked out, if the criteria which are presented are applied to the engineers in the Pinto case, I think one must conclude that they had an obligation to blow the whistle. They knew the gas tanks were likely to explode, injuring or killing people, if Pintos were struck from behind by cars traveling thirty miles per hour. They knew that if

they did not blow the whistle, Ford would market the cars. They were also members of a profession that, because of its special knowledge and skills, has a particular obligation to be concerned about public safety.

DeGeorge thinks that the Ford engineers would have had an obligation to blow the whistle only if they had also known that doing so would have been likely to prevent the deaths. But we have an obligation to warn others of danger even if we believe they will ignore our warnings. This is especially true if the danger will come about partly because we did not speak out. DeGeorge admits that the public has a right to know about dangerous products. If that is true, it would seem that those who have knowledge about such products have an obligation to inform the public. This is not usurping the public's right to decide acceptable risk; it is supplying it with the information necessary to exercise the right.

DeGeorge also believes we are not justified in asking engineers to blow the whistle if it would threaten their jobs. It is true that we would not be justified in demanding that they blow the whistle if that would place their or their families' lives in danger. But this is not true if only their jobs are at stake. Engineers are recognized as professionals and accorded respect and high salaries, not only because of their specialized knowledge and skills, but also because of the special responsibilities we entrust to them. All people have a prima facie obligation to blow the whistle on practices that are illegal, unjust, or harmful to others. But engineers who have special knowledge about, and are partially responsible for, dangerous practices or products have an especially strong obligation to blow the whistle if they are unsuccessful in getting the practices or products modified. Indeed, if they do not have an obligation to blow the whistle in such situations, no one ever has such an obligation.

A number of people have argued that for external whistle blowing to be justified the whistle blower must first make his or her concern known within the organization. "Surely," says Arthur S. Miller, "an employee owes his employer enough loyalty to try to work, first of all, within the organization to attempt to effect change."[11] DeGeorge even states that for whistle blowing to be morally justified one must first have informed one's immediate supervisor and exhausted all possible avenues of change within the organization. The problems with this kind of advice are: (1) It may be one's immediate supervisor who is responsible for the wrongdoing. (2) Organizations differ considerably in both their mechanisms for reporting and how they respond to wrongdoing. (3) Not all wrongdoing is of the same type. If the wrongdoing is one which threatens people's health or safety, exhausting all channels of protest within the organization could result in unjustified delay in correcting the problem. Exhausting internal channels of protest can also give people time to destroy evidence needed to substantiate one's allegations. Finally, it may expose the employee to possible retaliation that he or she would have some protection against if the wrongdoing were reported to an external agency.

It has also been argued that anonymous whistle blowing is never justified. It is said, for example, that anonymous whistle blowing violates the right of people to face their accusers. The fact that the whistle blower's identity is unknown also raises questions about his or her motives. But, as Frederick Elliston points out, anonymous whistle blowing can both protect whistle blowers from unjust retaliation and prevent those on whom the whistle is blown from engaging in an ad hominem attack to draw attention away from their wrongdoing. As he also points out, people should be protected from false accusations, but it is not necessary for the identity of whistle blowers to be known to accomplish this. "It is only necessary that accusations be properly investigated, proven true or false, and the results widely disseminated."[12] Discovering the whistle blower's motive is also irrelevant as far as immediate public policy is concerned. All that matters is whether wrongdoing has taken place and, if so, what should be done about it.

It has also been argued that anonymous whistle blowing should be avoided because it is ineffective. In fact, if anonymous whistle blowing is ineffective, it is more likely to be a function of lack of documentation and follow-up testimony than of its anonymity. Moreover, anonymity is a matter of degree. For whistle blowing to be anonymous, the whistle blower's identity does not have to be unknown to everyone, only to those on whom the whistle is blown and the general public. A few key investigators may know his or her identity. It should also not be forgotten that one of the most

dramatic and important whistle-blowing incidents in recent years, Deep Throat's disclosure of Richard Nixon's betrayal of the American people, was an instance of anonymous whistle blowing.

Factors to Consider in Whistle Blowing

I have argued that because we have a duty to prevent harm and injustice to others, which holds even though we are members of organizations, we have a prima facie obligation to disclose organizational wrongdoing we are unable to prevent. The degree of the obligation depends on the extent to which we are capable of foreseeing the consequences of organizational actions and our own acts or failures to act are causes of those consequences. It also depends on the kind and extent of the wrongdoing. Even a part-time or temporary employee has an obligation to report serious or extensive wrongdoing. But, in general, professionals who occupy positions of trust and special responsibilities have a stronger obligation to blow the whistle than ordinary workers.

Although we have an obligation to document wrongdoing as thoroughly as possible, we can only act on the basis of probability, so it is possible for the whistle blower to be in error about the wrongdoing and the whistle blowing still be justified. Whether we have an obligation to express our concern within the organization before going outside depends on the nature of the wrongdoing, the kind of organization involved, and the likelihood of retaliation. Whether we have an obligation to blow the whistle openly rather than anonymously depends on the extent to which it helps us avoid unfair retaliation and is effective in exposing the wrongdoing. The same is true of alumni as opposed to current whistle blowing.

Since whistle blowing usually involves conflicting obligations and a wide range of variables and has far-reaching consequences for all people involved, decisions to blow the whistle are not easily made. Like all complicated moral actions, whistle blowing cannot be reduced to a how-to-do list. However, some of the factors whistle blowers should take into consideration, if they are to act prudently and morally, can be stated. The following is an attempt to do this.

- *Make sure the situation is one that warrants whistle blowing.* Make sure the situation involves illegal actions, harm to others, or violation of people's rights, and is not one in which you would be disclosing personal matters, trade secrets, customer lists, or similar material. If disclosure of the wrongdoing would involve the latter, make sure that the harm to be avoided is great enough to offset the harm from the latter.

- *Examine your motives.* Although it is not necessary for the whistle blower's motive to be praiseworthy for the action to be justified in terms of the public interest, examination of your motives will help in deciding whether the situation warrants whistle blowing.

- *Verify and document your information.* If at all possible, try to obtain evidence that would stand up in court or regulatory hearings. If the danger to others is so great that you believe you are justified in obtaining evidence by surreptitious methods such as eavesdropping or recording telephone calls, examine your motives thoroughly, weigh carefully the risks you are taking, and try to find alternative and independent sources for any evidence you uncover. In general, it is advisable to avoid surreptitious methods.

- *Determine the type of wrongdoing you are reporting and to whom it should be reported.* Determining the exact nature of the wrongdoing can help you decide both what kind of evidence to obtain and to whom it should be reported. For example, if the wrongdoing consists of illegal actions such as the submission of false test reports to government agencies, bribery of public officials, racial or sexual discrimination, or violation of safety, health, or pollution laws, then determining the nature of the laws being violated will also indicate which agencies have authority to enforce those laws. If, on the other hand, the wrongdoing consists of actions which are legal but contrary to the public interest, determining this will help you decide whether you have an obligation to publicize the actions and, if so, in what way. The best place to report this type of wrongdoing is usually a public interest group. Such an organization is more likely than the press to: (1) be concerned about and advise the whistle blower regarding retaliation, (2) maintain confidentiality, (3) investigate the whistle blower's allegations to try to substantiate them rather than sensationalize them by turning the issue into a "personality dispute." If releasing information to the press is the best way to remedy the situation, the public interest group can help with or do this.

- *State your allegations in an appropriate way.* Be as specific as possible without being unintelligible. If you are reporting violation of a law to a government agency and it is possible for you to do so, include information and technical data necessary for experts to verify the wrongdoing. If you are disclosing wrongdoing which does not require technical information to substantiate it, still be as specific as possible in stating the type of illegal or immoral action involved, who is being injured, and in what ways.

- *Stick to the facts.* Avoid name calling, slander, and being drawn into a mud-slinging contest. As Peter Raven-Hansen wisely points out: "One of the most important points . . . is to focus on the disclosure. . . . This rule applies even when the whistle blower believes that certain individuals are responsible. . . . The disclosure itself usually leaves a trail for others to follow to the miscreants."[13] Sticking to the facts also helps the whistle blower minimize retaliation.

- *Decide whether the whistle blowing should be internal or external.* Familiarize yourself with all available internal channels for reporting wrongdoing and obtain as many data as you can both on how people who have used these channels were treated by the organization and on what was done about the problems they reported. If you are considering blowing the whistle on an immediate supervisor, find out what has happened in the past in this kind of situation. If people who report wrongdoing have been treated fairly and problems corrected, use internal channels to report the wrongdoing. If not, decide to what external agencies you should report the wrongdoing.

- *Decide whether the whistle blowing should be open or anonymous.* If you intend to remain anonymous, decide whether partial or total anonymity is required. Also, make sure your documentation is as thorough as possible. Finally, since anonymity may be difficult to preserve, anticipate what you will do if your identity becomes known.

- *Decide whether current or alumni whistle blowing is required.* Sometimes it is advisable to resign your present position and obtain another before blowing the whistle. This protects you from being fired, receiving damaging letters of recommendation, or even being blacklisted from your profession. Alumni whistle blowing may also be advisable if you are anticipating writing a book about the wrongdoing. Since this can be profitable, anyone planning to take this step has a particularly strong obligation to examine his or her motives to make sure they are morally praiseworthy.

- *Find out how much protection is available for whistle blowers in your industry, state, or federal agency.* Follow any guidelines that have been established and make sure you meet all qualifications, deadlines, and so on for filing reports.

- *Anticipate and document retaliation.* Although it is not as certain as Newton's law of motion that for every action there is an equal reaction, whistle blowers whose identities are known can expect retaliation. Thus whether you decide to work within the organization or go outside, document every step with letters, records, tape recordings of meetings, and so forth. Unless you do this, you may find that regulatory agencies and the courts are of no help.

- *Consult a lawyer.* Lawyers are advisable at almost every stage of whistle blowing. They can help you determine if the wrongdoing violates the law, aid you in documenting information about it, inform you of any laws you might be breaking in documenting it, assist you in deciding to whom to report it, make sure reports are filed on time, and help you protect yourself against retaliation. However, since lawyers tend to view problems within a narrow legal framework and decisions to blow the whistle are moral decisions, in the final analysis you must rely on your conscience.

Beyond Whistle Blowing

What can be done to eliminate the wrongdoing which gives rise to whistle blowing? One solution would be to give whistle blowers greater legal protection. Another would be to try to change the nature of organizations so as to diminish the need for whistle blowing. These solutions of course are not mutually exclusive.

Many people are opposed to legislation protecting whistle blowers because they think it is unwarranted interference with the right to freedom of contract. However, if the right to freedom of contract is to be consistent with the public interest, it cannot serve as a shield for wrongdoing. It does this when threat of dismissal prevents people from blowing the whistle. The right of employers to dismiss at will has been restricted previously by labor laws which prevent employers from dismissing employees for union activities. It is ironic that we have restricted the right of employers to fire employees who are pursuing their economic self-interest, but allowed employers to fire employees acting in behalf of the public interest. The right of employers to dismiss employees in the interest of efficiency should be balanced against the right of the public to know about illegal, dangerous, and unjust practices of organizations. The most effective way to achieve the latter goal would be to pass a federal law protecting whistle blowers.

Laws protecting whistle blowers have also been opposed on the grounds that (1) employees would use them as an excuse to mask poor performance, (2) they would create an "informer ethos" within organizations, and (3) they would take away the autonomy of business, strangling it in red tape.

The first objection is illegitimate because only those employees who could show that an act of whistle blowing preceded their being dismissed or penalized and that their employment records were adequate up to the time of the whistle blowing could seek relief under the law.

The second objection is more formidable. A society that encourages snooping, suspicion, and mistrust is not most people's idea of the good society. Laws which encourage whistle blowing for self-interested reasons, such as the federal tax law, which pays informers part of any money that is collected, could help bring about such a society. However, laws protecting whistle blowers from being penalized or dismissed are quite different. They do not reward the whistle blower; they merely protect him or her from unjust retaliation. It is unlikely that federal or state laws of this sort would promote an informer society.

The third objection is also unfounded. Laws protecting whistle blowers would not require any positive duties on the part of organizations—only the negative duty of not retaliating against employees who speak out in the public interest. However, not every act of apparent whistle blowing should be protected. Only people who can show they had probable reasons for believing wrongdoing existed should be protected. Furthermore, the burden of proof should be on the individual. People who cannot show they had good cause to suspect wrongdoing may justly be penalized or dismissed. If the damage to the organization is serious, it should also be allowed to sue. Since these conditions would impose some risks on potential whistle blowers, they would reduce the possibility of frivolous action.

If, on the other hand, someone who has probable reasons for believing wrongdoing exists blows the whistle and is fired, the burden of proof should be on the organization to show that he or she was not fired for blowing the whistle. If the whistle blowing is found to be the reason for the dismissal, the whistle blower should be reinstated and awarded damages. If there is further retaliation after reinstatement, additional damages should be awarded.

What changes could be made in organizations to prevent the need for whistle blowing? Some of the suggestions which have been made are that organizations develop effective internal channels for reporting wrongdoing, reward people with salary increases and promotions for using these channels, and appoint senior executives, board members, ombudspersons, and so on whose primary obligations would be to investigate and eliminate organizational wrongdoing. These changes could be undertaken by organizations on their own or mandated by law. Other changes which might be mandated are requiring that certain kinds of records be kept, assessing larger fines for illegal actions, and making executives and other professionals personally liable for filing false reports, knowingly marketing dangerous products, failing to monitor how policies are being implemented,

and so forth. Although these reforms could do much to reduce the need for whistle blowing, given human nature it is highly unlikely that this need can ever be totally eliminated. Therefore, it is important to have laws which protect whistle blowers and for us to state as clearly as we can both the practical problems and moral issues pertaining to whistle blowing.

Notes

1. For discussion of the legal aspects of whistle blowing see Lawrence E. Blades, "Employment at Will vs. Individual Freedom: On Limiting the Abusive Exercise of Employer Power," *Columbia Law Review,* vol. 67 (1967); Philip Blumberg, "Corporate Responsibility and the Employee's Duty of Loyalty and Obedience: A Preliminary Inquiry," *Oklahoma Law Review,* vol. 24 (1971); Clyde W. Summers, "Individual Protection Against Unjust Dismissal: Time for a Statute," *Virginia Law Review,* vol. 62 (1976); Arthur S. Miller, "Whistle Blowing and the Law," in Ralph Nader, Peter J. Petkas, and Kate Blackwell, *Whistle Blowing,* New York: Grossman Publishers, 1972; Alan F. Westin, *Whistle Blowing!,* New York: McGraw-Hill, 1981; Martin H. Marlin, "Current Status of Legal Protection for Whistleblowers," paper delivered at the Second Annual Conference on Ethics in Engineering, Illinois Institute of Technology, 1982. See also Gene G. James, "Whistle Blowing: Its Nature and Justification," *Philosophy in Context,* vol. 10 (1980).

2. For a discussion of this study which was by Morton Corn see Frank von Hipple, "Professional Freedom and Responsibility: The Role of the Professional Society," *Newsletter on Science, Technology and Human Values,* vol. 22, January 1978.

3. See Westin, op. cit.

4. See Marlin, op. cit.

5. David W. Ewing, *Freedom Inside the Organization,* New York: E. P. Dutton, 1977, pp. 165–166.

6. Richard T. DeGeorge, *Business Ethics,* New York: Macmillan, 1982, p. 161. See also DeGeorge, "Ethical Responsibilities of Engineers in Large Organizations," *Business and Professional Ethics Journal,* vol. 1, no. 1, Fall 1981, pp. 1–14. He formulates the first criterion in a slightly different way in the last work, saying that the harm must be both serious and considerable before whistle blowing is justified.

7. Ibid.

8. DeGeorge, "Ethical Responsibilities of Engineers in Large Organizations," op. cit., p. 1.

9. Ibid., p. 5.
10. Ibid., p. 7.
11. Miller, op. cit., p. 30.
12. Frederick A. Elliston, "Anonymous Whistleblowing," *Business and Professional Ethics Journal*, vol. 1, no. 2, Winter 1982.
13. Peter Raven-Hansen, "Dos and Don'ts for Whistleblowers: Planning for Trouble," *Technology Review*, May 1980, p. 30. My discussion in the present section is heavily indebted to this article.

Review and Discussion Questions

1. James and DeGeorge differ over what the engineers at Ford were morally required to do. With whom do you side and why?

2. Writers like DeGeorge and Bowie maintain that potential whistle blowers should first exhaust internal channels. Other authors maintain that whistle blowing should not be anonymous. James rejects both claims. Do you agree?

3. How important are the motives of a whistle blower? How important is the likelihood that blowing the whistle will bring results?

4. Do you think that laws protecting whistle blowers are a good idea? Do such laws reward disloyalty? Can internal organizational changes prevent the need for whistle blowing?

5. Compare the approaches of Bowie, DeGeorge, and James to whistle blowing. Whose analysis is the most persuasive?

For Further Reading

Sissela Bok, in *Secrets* (New York: Vintage, 1983), writes insightfully on trade secrets and patents in chapter 10 and on whistle blowing in chapter 14.

Richard T. George, in "Ethical Responsibilities of Engineers in Large Organizations," *Business and Professional Ethics Journal* 1 (Fall 1981), discusses whistle blowing in the context of the Ford Pinto case.

Martin Snoeyenbos, Robert Almeder, and **James Humber**, eds., *Business Ethics* (Buffalo: Prometheus, 1983), Part 3, provides essays and cases on conflict of interest, gifts and payoffs, patents, and trade secrets.

Mark Pastin and **Michael Hooker** criticize the FCPA in "Ethics and the Foreign Corrupt Practices Act," *Business Horizons* 23 (December 1980).

CHAPTER 8

JOB DISCRIMINATION

"Sick humor and racist clichés" abound at the White House. So says Terrell H. Bell, President Reagan's first Secretary of Education.[1] When the Reagan administration was vigorously fighting passage of the bill to establish Martin Luther King, Jr.'s birthday as a national holiday, "midlevel" staffers referred to Dr. King as "Martin Lucifer Coon." Over at the Attorney General's office, the section of the Civil Rights Act that safeguards women against discrimination was nicknamed "the lesbian's bill of rights." Staffers at the State Department, when discussing the Middle East, quipped that Arabs are just "sand niggers." And women will have a hard time forgetting Chief of Staff Don Regan's widely published denigrations. After the first Reagan-Gorbachev summit meeting, he stated that women are more interested in fashion than arms control. On another occasion he claimed they cared more about their diamonds (many of which come from South Africa) than they did about apartheid.

If the attitudes these remarks display are prevalent in the highest reaches of government, it is hard to believe that they are not also to be found in the boardrooms and executive suites of many American corporations. Many people would of course reject such racist and sexist jokes as at best crude and unseemly, at worst immoral. But explicit prejudice is just part of the problem. Even openminded men may operate on implicit assumptions that work to the disadvantage of women, and often whites who believe themselves to be unprejudiced may harbor unconscious racist attitudes.

Stanford Law Professor Charles R. Law-

rence III, for instance, recalls his college days as a token black presence in a white world. Companions would say to him, "I don't think of you as a Negro." Their conscious intent was benign and complimentary. The speaker was saying, "I think of you as a normal human being, just like me."

> But he was not conscious of the underlying implications of his words. What did this mean about most Negroes? Were they not normal human beings? . . . To say that one does not think of a Negro as a Negro is to say that one thinks of him as something else. The statement is made in the context of the real world, and implicit in it is a comparison to some norm. In this case the norm is whiteness. The white liberal's unconscious thought . . . is, "I think of you as different from other Negroes, as more like white people."[2]

In other cases, unconscious racist stereotypes, which are normally repressed, slip out, as when sportscaster Howard Cosell, carried away by the excitement of the game, referred to a black football player as a "little monkey," or when Nancy Reagan told a public gathering that she wished her husband could be there to "see all these beautiful white people."[3]

Slavery in our country resulted in a long legacy of legally institutionalized racism and of the socioeconomic subordination of blacks and other minorities. That history, and centuries of discrimination against women, lie behind the conscious and unconscious racially and sexually prejudiced attitudes so prevalent in the United States. We must bear that his-

347

tory and those attitudes in mind as we explore the area of job discrimination. In particular, this chapter examines the following topics:

1. The meaning of job discrimination and its different forms.

2. The statistical and attitudinal evidence of discrimination.

3. The history and legal context of affirmative action.

4. The moral arguments for and against affirmative action.

5. The doctrine of comparable worth and the controversy over it.

6. The problem of sexual harassment in employment—what it is, what forms it takes, what the law says about it, and why it's wrong.

THE MEANING OF JOB DISCRIMINATION

According to Professor Manuel G. Velasquez to discriminate in employment is to make an adverse decision against employees based on their membership in a certain class.[4] Included in this definition of discrimination in employment are three basic elements: (1) The decision is against employees solely because of their membership in a certain group. (2) The decision is based on the assumption that the group is in some way inferior to some other group and thus deserving of unequal treatment. (3) The decision in some way harms those it's aimed at. Since, traditionally, most of the discrimination in the American workplace has been aimed at women and minorities such as blacks and Hispanics, the following discussion will focus on these groups.

Job discrimination can take different forms. Individuals can intentionally discriminate out of personal prejudice or on the basis of stereotypes. For example, a member of a company's personnel department might rou-tinely downgrade applications from women who want to work in the company's production plant because he believes, and knowingly acts on the belief, that "ladies don't understand machines."

On the other hand, individuals may discriminate because they unthinkingly or unconsciously adopt traditional practices and stereotypes. For example, if the male in the preceding case acted without being aware of the bias underlying his decisions, his action would fall into this category.

Institutions can also discriminate. Sometimes this can be explicit and intentional as, for example, when it is company policy to pass over women for supervisory positions because "the boys in the company don't like to take orders from females." Or the routine operating procedures of a company may reflect sexually or racially prejudiced stereotypes, assumptions, and practices of which it is not fully aware.

In addition, institutional practices that appear neutral and nondiscriminatory, according to the definition proposed above, may nonetheless be discriminatory, in a broader sense, in their effects. When membership in an all-white craft union, for instance, requires nomination by those who are already members, this is likely to result in maintaining racial exclusion even if the motivation of those who do the nominating is purely nepotistic in character and results from no ill-will toward, or stereotyping of, members of another race. Institutional procedures like this may not involve job discrimination in the narrow sense, but they clearly work to the disadvantage of women and minority groups, denying them full equality of opportunity.

From a variety of moral perspectives there are compelling moral arguments against job discrimination on racial or sexual grounds. Since discrimination as defined above involves false assumptions about the inferiority of a certain group and harms individual members of that group, utilitarians would reject it because of its ill effects on total human welfare. Kantians would clearly repudiate it as failing to respect people as ends in themselves. Universalizing the maxim underlying discriminatory practices is virtually impossible. No people who now discriminate would be willing to accept such treatment themselves. Sexual and racial discrimination also violate people's basic moral rights and mock the ideal of human moral equality. Furthermore, such discrimination is unjust. To use Rawls's theory as an illustration, parties in the original position would clearly choose for themselves the principle of equal opportunity.

On the other hand, there are no respectable arguments in favor of racial and sexual discrimination. Whatever racist or sexist attitudes people might actually have, no one today is prepared to defend job discrimination publicly, any more than they would publicly defend slavery or repealing the Nineteenth Amendment (which gave women the right to vote). This attitude toward job discrimination is reflected in legal and political efforts to develop programs to root out job discrimination and ameliorate the results of past discrimination. Before looking at the relevant legal history and the controversies surrounding various antidiscrimination measures, we need to examine the relative positions of whites and minorities and of males and females in the American workplace to see if they say anything about ongoing discrimination.

EVIDENCE OF DISCRIMINATION

Determining the presence of discrimination isn't easy, because many factors could possibly account for the relative positions of various groups in the work world. But generally speaking, there are reasonable grounds for thinking that an institution is practicing discrimination (intentional or unintentional) when (1) statistics indicate that members of a group are being treated unequally in comparison with other groups, and (2) endemic attitudes and formal and informal practices and policies are biased in ways that seem to account for the skewed statistics.

Statistical Evidence

As we noted in a previous chapter, racial minorities bear the brunt of poverty in our nation. Blacks are about three times more likely to be poor than whites. While one out of every nine white Americans is poor, one out of every three blacks and Native Americans is poor and more than one out of every four Hispanics is poor. Today, a black child has nearly one chance in two of being born into poverty.[5]

Overall black family income is only 55 percent of white family income. This is down from 62 percent in 1975, and many fear that the gap will further widen. William F. Buckley notes that if we put the income of the average American at 100, then Native Americans are at 60, blacks at 62, Puerto Ricans at 63, and Mexican-Americans at 76.[6] In the 1980s the salary gap between whites and blacks also increased.[7]

Unemployment hits racial minorities hard, since they are often last hired and first fired. Unemployment among blacks is in general twice as high as that of whites. Of every three minority workers, one is employed irregularly or has given up looking for work, and one in three is engaged primarily in a job that pays less than a living wage. Official unemployment figures for inner-city black youths exceed 40 percent, while the actual figures are thought to be much higher.

Black and other minority workers are overwhelmingly clustered in low-paying, low-prestige, dead-end work. U.S. government statistics reveal clearly the extent to which the most desirable occupations (in management and administration, professional and technical jobs, sales and crafts) are dominated by whites, while blacks, Hispanics, and other ethnic minorities are relegated to less desirable jobs like manual labor, service, and farm work.[8] As Gertrude Ezorsky remarks, today every other person involved by occupation with dirt or garbage is black.[9] Of roughly two million engineers in America, about 2 percent are blacks and 2 percent Hispanics. Of approximately 225,000 physical scientists, 3 percent are blacks and less than 2 percent Hispanics.[10] The *National Law Journal* reports that blacks make up about 1.5 percent of the lawyers in the nation's one hundred largest law firms. The percentage of Hispanic lawyers in these firms is even smaller: .65 percent.[11] Education does not account for this disparity in pay and position. In 1977, a white head of household with one to three years of *high school* earned more than a black head of household with one to three years of *college*.[12]

Women, too, are clustered in poorer paying jobs. They work as librarians, nurses, elementary school teachers, sales clerks, secretaries, bank tellers, and waitresses, while the top paying occupations have been, and to a large extent continue to be, almost exclusively male preserves. (For example, 99 percent of dental hygienists, but only 6.2 percent of dentists, are women.) Nor is it simply that men monopolize the very top positions. Figures from the Bureau of Labor Statistics show that traditionally "female occupations" like those listed above pay less than traditionally "male occupations" like pharmacist, mail carrier, and shipping clerk. Sixty percent of all women work in only ten occupations, and most new jobs for women are in areas with low pay and limited chances of advancement.[13] A Cornell study found that one-quarter of the 1,315 working women it polled earned a poverty-level income (which varies according to the number of children in the household). The situation is even worse for black women. Nearly 20 percent of full-time-employed black women in the survey were poor.[14]

Here, too, education does not explain the differences in position and pay. The typical male full-time worker with no more than a *grammar school education* earned nearly as much in 1977 as a female full-time worker with a *college degree*.[15] At almost all occupational levels, women make less money than men—even for the same work—despite legislation forbidding discrimination on the basis of sex and requiring equal pay for equal jobs. According to a Rand Corporation study released in October 1984, however, the wage gap between men and women is supposed to be closing.[16] The study concluded that the average hourly wage for working women will rise from 64 percent to 75 percent of the average for working men by the year 2000. In fact, the male-female wage differential has increased slightly since 1984, but even if the study's long-term prediction is correct, a 25 percent average wage difference is far from parity. Moreover, the 64 percent figure, while up from 1979 when women's earnings were 58.9 percent of men, is no more than it was in 1955. The fact is that, although recent years have seen women enter the work force in greater numbers and in more diverse fields than ever before, men remain ahead in pay. Consider, for example, a comparison of men's and women's earnings in the following ten professions, as reported by the Bureau of Labor Statistics.[17]

Occupation	Average Weekly Earnings	
	Men	Women
Lawyer	$653	$492
Engineer	$592	$479
Social Scientist	$580	$420
Physician	$564	$412
College Teacher	$528	$412
Computer Programmer	$478	$382
Accountant	$468	$325
Real Estate Agent	$435	$292
Wholesale, Retail Buyer	$412	$271
Elementary Teacher	$411	$339

It's important to realize that the differences between men's and women's earnings do not appear merely after a period of time on the job but often begin as soon as men and women leave school.

Women and minorities have made inroads into white-collar and professional ranks, but few have made it to the top of their professions. For example, only 5 percent of law partnerships are held by women. About 40 percent of working blacks hold white-collar jobs, up from 11 percent in 1960, although still 14 percent behind whites. Yet two surveys of *Fortune* 1000 companies reveal that there is little penetration of the top rungs of America's largest corporations. The 1979 survey of 1,708 senior executives discovered only 3 blacks, 2 Asians, 2 Hispanics, and 8 women. The 1985 survey of 1,362 senior executives found little improvement: 4 blacks, 6 Asians, 3 Hispanics, and 29 women.[18] And *Business Week*'s 1987 directory of the CEOs of the top 1,000 publicly held companies lists 2 women and no blacks, while in 1988 *Fortune* magazine found 1 black CEO among its 1,000 corporations and 1 black among its top 500 industrials.[19]

Attitudinal Evidence

In 1972 Elizabeth Hishon went to work for King & Spaulding, a big Atlanta law firm closely associated with the Jimmy Carter administration. Customarily, associates like Hishon are given a period of time to make partner or seek another job. So, when Hishon had not attained partner status by 1979, she was terminated. Immediately she filed a suit seeking monetary damages under Title VII of the Civil Rights Act of 1964, which prohibits sexual and racial discrimination at work. Hishon claimed that her failure to become a partner was due to systematic sexism practiced by the law firm, as evidenced in the fact that no woman had ever made partner in the 100-lawyer firm. (Since then, two women have been made partners.)

A district court held that rights guaranteed by Title VII did not apply to the selection of partners in a law firm. But on May 27, 1984, the Supreme Court in a unanimous decision overturned that ruling and held that women could bring sex-discrimination suits against law firms that unfairly deny them promotions to partner.

The Hishon decision is having a significant impact on the one million nationwide partnership concerns. Promotional practices are being reevaluated not only in law firms but also in accounting firms, advertising agencies, securities firms, architectural concerns, and engineering firms. Beyond this the case is noteworthy because the defendants expressed no specific complaints about Hishon's work. They denied her a partnership apparently on a general feeling that "she just didn't fit in."[20] In the words of another woman who had been an associate at King & Spaulding, "If you can't discuss the Virginia-North Carolina basketball game, you're an outcast."[21] Her pithy comment speaks volumes about how deep-seated attitudes operate against women and minorities in the workplace.

Although some would disagree, the statistics alone don't conclusively establish discrimination, for one can always argue that other things account for these disparities. But there are indications of widespread attitudes and formal and informal institutional practices and policies which, taken collectively, point to discrimination as the cause of these statistical disparities.

For example, in a questionnaire submitted to 5,000 of its subscribers, the *Harvard Business Review* found a double standard with regard to managerial expectations of men and women. In sum, managers expect male employees to put job before family when conflicting obligations arise, but they expect females to sacrifice their career to family responsibilities. Also, when personal conduct threatens an employee's job, managers go to greater lengths to retain a valuable male employee than an equally qualified female. The survey also turned up antifemale bias: In employee selection and promotion and in career-development decisions, managers clearly favor males.[22] And over the years, various reports indicate that myths, stereotypes, and false preconceptions victimize women and minorities. For example, studies of MBA students in recent years show male students remaining consistently negative in their attitudes toward women as executives.[23]

When women and minorities enter male-dominated areas, they frequently are assumed incompetent until they prove otherwise. A good example is scientific fields, where women and minorities often confront implicit assumptions by white male scientists about who is competent in science. "Employers make certain assumptions about what the best look like," says Shirley Malcolm, head of the office of opportunities in science of the American Association for the Advancement of Science.[24] Betty Vettr, executive director of the Scientific Manpower Commission in Washington, elaborates: "When men come in as new engineers into a job, they are assumed to be competent until proved otherwise. . . . When women come in, they are assumed to be incompetent until they have proved over and over and over again that indeed they are not."[25]

Moreover, a woman entering "male turf" can find herself uncomfortably measured according to the predominant male value system. Here's how Florence Blair, a twenty-five-year-old black civil engineer describes working as a civil engineer at Corning Glass Works:

> As a minority woman, you are just so different from everyone else you encounter. . . . I went through a long period of isolation. . . . When I came here, I didn't have a lot in common with the white males I was working with. I didn't play golf, I didn't drink beer, I didn't hunt. All these things I had no frame of reference to.
>
> You need to do your job on a certain technical level, but a lot of things you do on the job come down to socializing and

how well you mesh with people. Sometimes I look at my role as making people feel comfortable with me.

> Sometimes it's disheartening. You think why do I have to spend all of my time and my energy making them feel comfortable with me when they're not reciprocating?[26]

Blair also says she experienced a double standard. Soon after she started work, with an engineering degree from Purdue, she was told by her supervisor that her drafting skills were not up to par and that she should take a remedial drafting course at a local community college. In contrast, when young white males showed less than adequate drafting skills, Blair says, they were told by supervisors, "We know that your skills are rusty, but we'll work with you a little bit, and through practice you will improve."[27] While this worker's experience may not be typical, it does point up how ill-considered assumptions and stereotypes, which admittedly can sometimes victimize all of us, are a special problem that women and minorities face in the workplace.

A recent survey of Ivy League graduates, class of 1957, illustrates the prevalence of racial stereotypes and assumptions. For these men, "dumb" came to mind when they thought of blacks. Only 36 percent of the Princeton class, 47 percent at Yale, and 55 percent at Harvard agreed with the statement, "Blacks are as intelligent as whites." These are graduates of three leading universities who are now in their fifties, the age of promotion into senior corporate positions. In discussing this survey, Edward W. Jones, Jr. writes:

> All people possess stereotypes, which act like shorthand to avoid mental overload. . . . Most of the time stereotypes are mere shadow images rooted in one's history and deep in the subconscious. But they are very powerful. For example, in controlled experiments the mere insertion of the word black into a sentence

has resulted in people changing their responses to a statement.

One reason for the power of stereotypes is their circularity. People seek to confirm their expectations and resist contradictory evidence, so we cling to beliefs and stereotypes that become self-fulfilling. If, for example, a white administrator makes a mistake, his boss is likely to tell him, "That's OK. Everybody's entitled to one goof." If, however, a black counterpart commits the same error, the boss thinks, "I knew he couldn't do it. The guy is incompetent." The stereotype reinforces itself.[28]

Taken together, the statistics and the personal and institutional attitudes, assumptions, and practices provide powerful evidence of intractable discrimination against women and minorities in the American workplace. Recognizing the existence of such discrimination and believing that, for a variety of reasons, it is wrong, we have as a nation passed laws intended to provide equality of opportunity to women and minorities. They expressly forbid discrimination in recruitment, screening, promotion, compensation, and firing. But antidiscrimination laws do not address the present-day effects of past discrimination. In order to remedy the defects of past discrimination and to counteract visceral racism and sexism, some companies and institutions have adopted stronger and more controversial affirmative action measures. After discussing their legal context, we will turn to the moral evaluation of these measures.

AFFIRMATIVE ACTION: THE LEGAL CONTEXT

In 1954 the Supreme Court decided in the case of *Brown v. Board of Education* that racially segregated schooling was unconstitutional. In doing so, they conclusively rejected the older doctrine that "separate but equal" facilities were legally permissible. Not only were segregated facilities in fact unequal, the court found, but the very ideal of separation of the races, based as it was on a belief in black racial inferiority, inherently led to unequal treatment. That famous decision helped to launch the civil rights movement in this country. One fruit of that movement was a series of federal laws and orders that attempt to implement the right of each person to equal treatment with respect to employment.

It began in 1961, when President John F. Kennedy signed Executive Order 10925, which decreed that federal contractors should "take affirmative action to ensure that applicants are employed without regard to their race, creed, color, or national origin." In 1963 the Equal Pay Act was passed by Congress. Aimed especially at wage discrimination against women, it guaranteed the right to equal pay for equal work. That was followed by the Civil Rights Act of 1964 (which was later amended by the Equal Employment Opportunity Act of 1972). It prohibits all forms of discrimination based on race, color, sex, religion, or national origin. Title VII, the most important section of the act, prohibits discrimination in employment. It says:

It shall be an unlawful employment practice for an employer (1) to fail or refuse to hire or to discharge any individual, or otherwise discriminate against any individual with respect to his compensation, terms, conditions, or privileges of employment, because of such individual's race, color, religion, sex, or national origin; or (2) to limit, segregate, or classify his employees or applicants for employment in any way that would deprive or tend to deprive any individual of employment opportunities or otherwise adversely affect his status as an employee, because of such individual's race, color, religion, sex, or national origin.

The Civil Rights Act of 1964 applies to all employers, both public and private, with fifteen or more employees. In 1967 the Age Discrimination in Employment Act was passed (amended in 1978). In addition, there have been several acts and Executive Orders that regulate government contractors and subcontractors, and that require equal opportunities for the handicapped and for veterans. All of these acts are enforced through the Equal Employment Opportunity Commission (EEOC).[29]

By the late 1960s and early 1970s companies contracting with the federal government, first in construction and then generally, were required to develop *affirmative-action programs*, designed to correct imbalances in employment that exist directly as a result of past discrimination. These programs corresponded with the courts' recognition that job discrimination can exist even in the absence of conscious intent to discriminate.[30] Affirmative action riders were added, with varying degrees of specificity, into a large number of federal programs. Many state and local bodies adopted comparable requirements.[31]

What do affirmative action programs involve? The EEOC lists general guidelines as steps to affirmative action. Under these steps, firms must issue a written equal-employment policy and an affirmative-action commitment. They must appoint a top official with responsibility and authority to direct and implement their program and to publicize their policy and affirmative action commitment. In addition, firms must survey current female and minority employment by department and job classification. Where underrepresentation of these groups is evident, firms must develop goals and timetables to improve in each area of underrepresentation. They then must develop specific programs to achieve these goals, establish an internal audit system to monitor them, and evaluate progress in each aspect of the program. Finally, companies must develop supportive in-house and community programs to combat discrimination.

Critics of affirmative action charge that it means, in practice, illegal quotas, preferential treatment of blacks and women, and even "reverse discrimination" against white men. In the 1960s and early 1970s, however, federal courts dismissed legal challenges to affirmative action, and in 1972 Congress gave it increased legislative validity by passing the Equal Employment Opportunity Act. Eventually, though, the Supreme Court had to address the question. Although its decisions determine the law of the land with regard to affirmative action, the Court's rulings have not always been as simple and straightforward as one might wish. Let's look at the Court's most important decisions.

The Supreme Court's Position

The Supreme Court's first major ruling on affirmative action was in 1978, in the case of *Bakke v. Regents of the University of California*. Allan Bakke is a white male who applied for admission to the Medical School at the University of California at Davis. Only a tiny percentage of doctors are not white. In order to help remedy this situation, Davis had an affirmative action program that set aside sixteen out of its hundred entrance places for minority students. If qualified minority students could not be found, those places were not to be filled. In addition to the special admissions process, minority students were free to compete through the regular admissions process for one of the unrestricted eighty-four positions. Bakke was refused admission, but he sued the University of California, contending that he had been discriminated against in violation of both the 1964 Civil Rights Act and the Constitution. He argued that he would have won admission if those sixteen places had not been withdrawn from open competition and reserved for minority students. Bakke's grades, MCAT scores, and so on were higher than several minority students who were admitted. The University did not deny this, but defended its program as legally permissible, and socially necessary, affirmative action.

Bakke won his case, although it was a close five to four decision. Four justices sided with the University of California at Davis, four found that Davis's program was illegal in light of the 1964 Civil Rights Act, and one justice (Powell) held that while the program did not violate that act, it was invalid on constitutional grounds. In announcing the judgment of the court, Powell's opinion rejected explicit racial criteria that set rigid quotas and that exclude nonpreferred groups from competition. At the same time he held that the selection process can take race and ethnic origin into account as one factor and pointed to Harvard's admission program as a model. In such a program "race or ethnic background may be deemed a 'plus' in a particular applicant's file, yet it does not insulate the individual from comparison with all other candidates for the available seats." Powell also granted that numerical goals may be permissible when the institution in question has illegally discriminated in the past.

A year later, in *United Steelworkers of America v. Weber*, the Supreme Court took up the issue again—but in a different situation and with a different verdict. Brian Weber worked at Kaiser Aluminum's Gramercy, Louisiana, plant. The steelworkers' union had been pressing Kaiser to institute programs to train its own workers for its better-paying skilled craft positions instead of hiring craft workers from outside the company. Kaiser was also under pressure from various federal agencies to employ more black workers in skilled positions. At the Gramercy plant, for example, only 5 out of 273 skilled craft workers were black, although the local area work force was 39 percent black. Kaiser therefore entered into a collective bargaining agreement with the United Steelworkers that contained a plan "to eliminate conspicuous racial imbalances" in

Kaiser's skilled craft work positions. Kaiser agreed to set up a training program to qualify its own workers for craft positions and to choose trainees from the existing work force on the basis of seniority, except that 50 percent of the positions would be reserved for blacks until the percentage of blacks in these jobs approximated the percentage of blacks in the local work force.

Weber, a young, white, semiskilled worker, was one of several whites who had failed to gain admission to the training program for skilled craft work positions despite having more seniority than the most senior black trainee. Weber sued, arguing that he had been discriminated against on the basis of his race. This time the Supreme Court upheld the affirmative action program, in a 5–2 decision. In delivering the court's opinion, Justice Brennan makes clear that legal prohibition of racial discrimination does not prevent "private, voluntary, race-conscious affirmative action plans." He continues:

> We need not today define in detail the line of demarcation between permissible and impermissible affirmative action plans. It suffices to hold that the challenged Kaiser-USWA affirmative action plan falls on the permissible side of the line. The purposes of the plan mirror those of the [Civil Rights] statute. Both were designed to break down old patterns of racial segregation and hierarchy. Both were structured to "open employment opportunities for Negroes in occupations which have been traditionally closed to them" . . .
>
> At the same time, the plan does not unnecessarily trammel the interest of the white employees. . . . Moreover, the plan is a temporary measure . . . simply to eliminate a manifest racial imbalance.

In 1984, however, the Supreme Court upheld seniority over affirmative action in *Memphis Firefighters v. Stotts*. The city of Memphis,

Tennessee, hired its first black firefighter in 1955 and its second in 1964. Between 1950 and 1976, the firefighting department hired 1,683 whites but only 94 blacks. A class action suit was filed in 1977, charging the city with racial discrimination in hiring and promoting firefighters, and in 1980 the city signed a consent decree with the Justice Department. While not admitting it had engaged in racial discrimination, the city agreed to attempt to give 50 percent of new jobs and 20 percent of promotions to blacks. Under the plan the percentage of black firefighters rose from 4 to 11.5 percent.

When financial difficulties forced the city to lay off firefighters, it followed the seniority rules negotiated with the union. Last hired were to be let go first. Fearing that the progress black firefighters had made would be quickly lost, Carl Stotts, who had brought the original suit, asked a federal district court to protect blacks from layoffs. It did, and seventy-two whites, but only eight blacks, were laid off or demoted. The city of Memphis and the union appealed the ruling and, after losing before a federal appeals court, took their cause to the Supreme Court. In the meantime, additional funds had been found to rehire the laid-off workers, but the Supreme Court agreed to hear the case anyway.

The Supreme Court reversed the district court's ruling, holding that seniority systems are racially neutral and that the city may not lay off white workers to save the jobs of black workers with less seniority. Speaking for the majority, Justice White wrote, "It is inappropriate to deny an innocent employee the benefits of his seniority . . . to provide a remedy in a [case] such as this." The court can award competitive seniority to an individual black only when he or she has been the actual victim of illegal discrimination. He continued:

> Mere membership in the disadvantaged class is insufficient to warrant a seniority award. . . . Even when an individual shows that the discriminatory

practice has had an impact on him, he is not automatically entitled to have a nonminority employee laid off to make room for him. He may have to wait until a vacancy occurs.

These three cases illustrate well the Supreme Court's cautious approach to alleged abuses of affirmative action. Instead of trying to establish at one blow a hard and fast "line of demarcation between permissible and impermissible affirmative action plans," the Court is developing its position gradually, based on the relatively specific details of the individual cases it examines. Despite variations in the three cases just described, and despite dissenting opinions, a solid majority of the Supreme Court continues to uphold the general principle of affirmative action.

Affirmative action was upheld again in 1987, this time in a case concerning women. In *Johnson v. Transportation Agency*, the Supreme Court affirmed that considerations of sex were permissible as one factor in promoting Diane Joyce, a female county employee, to the position of road dispatcher over an equally qualified male employee, Paul Johnson. In summing up the Court's position, Justice Brennan states that the promotion of Joyce "was made pursuant to an affirmative action plan that represents a moderate, flexible, case-by-case approach to effecting a gradual improvement in the representation of minorities and women in the Agency's work force."

AFFIRMATIVE ACTION: THE MORAL ISSUES

The Supreme Court's gradually emerging position on affirmative action is important because it lets employers know what they are and are not legally permitted to do. But legal decisions by themselves do not exhaust the relevant moral issues. Employers, as well as women, minorities, and white men, want to know whether affirmative action programs are morally right.

Before we look at arguments for and against affirmative action, we have to make clear what is being debated. We shall take "affirmative action" to mean programs that take the race or sex of employees or job candidates into account as part of an effort to correct imbalances in employment that exist as a result of past discrimination, either in the company itself or in the larger society. In Professor Thomas Nagel's terminology (see "A Defense of Affirmative Action," beginning on page 373), this is "strong" rather than "weak" affirmative action. To keep the discussion relevant, we limit it to affirmative action programs that might reasonably be expected to be upheld by the Supreme Court. Excluded are programs that establish rigid, permanent quotas or hire and promote unqualified persons. Included are programs that hire or promote a woman or black who would not otherwise, according to established but fair criteria, be the best qualified candidate.

A word about terminology: Critics of affirmative action often label it as "reverse discrimination," but this is misleading. Our original definition of job discrimination involves the assumption that a certain group is inferior and deserves unequal treatment. No such assumption is at work in the affirmative action cases we have discussed. Those who designed the programs that worked to the disadvantage of Allan Bakke, Brian Weber, and Paul Johnson did not do so because they believed that white men are inferior and deserving of less respect than other human beings. Those who designed the programs in question were themselves white men.

Arguments for Affirmative Action

1. *Compensatory justice demands affirmative action programs.*

POINT: "As groups, women and minorities have historically been discriminated against, often viciously. As individuals and as a nation, we can't ignore the sins of our fathers and mothers. In fact, we have an obligation to do something to help repair the wrongs of the past. Affirmative action in employment is one sound way to do this."

COUNTERPOINT: "People today can't be expected to atone for the sins of the past. We're not responsible for them, and in any case, we wouldn't be compensating those who rightly deserve it. Young blacks and women coming for their first job have never suffered employment discrimination. Their parents and grandparents may deserve compensation, but why should today's candidates receive any special consideration? No one should discriminate against them, of course, but they should have to compete openly and on their merits, just like everybody else."

2. *Affirmative action is necessary to permit fairer competition.*

POINT: "Even if young blacks and women today have not themselves suffered job discrimination, they have suffered all the disadvantages of growing up in families that have been disadvantaged by discrimination. In our racist society, they have suffered from inferior schools and poor environment. In addition, as victims of society's prejudiced attitudes, they have been hampered by a lack of self-confidence and self-respect. Taking race and sex into account makes job competition fairer by keeping white males from having a competitive edge that they don't really deserve."

COUNTERPOINT: "Your point is better when applied to blacks than to women, it seems to me, but I'm still not persuaded. You overlook the fact that there are a lot of disadvantaged whites out there, too. Is an employer going to have to investigate everyone's life history to see who had to overcome the most obstacles? I think an employer has a right to seek the best qualified candidate, without trying to make life fair for everybody. And isn't the best qualified person entitled to get the job or the promotion?"

3. *Affirmative action is necessary to break the cycle that keeps minorities and women locked into poor, low-prestige jobs.*

POINT: "You advocate color-blind, nondiscriminatory employment practices, as if we could just ignore our whole history of racial and sexual discrimination. Statistics show that blacks in particular have been trapped in a socioeconomically subordinate position. If we want to end that and eventually heal the racial rifts in our country, we've got to break that pattern with vigorous affirmative action that pushes more blacks into middle-class jobs. Even assuming racism were dead in our society, with mere nondiscrimination alone it would take a hundred years or more for blacks to equalize their position."

COUNTERPOINT: "You ignore the fact that affirmative action has its costs, too. You talk about healing the racial rifts in our country, but affirmative action programs make everybody more racially conscious. They also cause resentment and frustration among white males. Many blacks and women resent, too, being advanced on grounds other than merit. Finally, if you hire and promote people faster and further than they merit, you're only asking for problems."

Arguments Against Affirmative Action

1. *Affirmative action injures white males and violates their rights.*

POINT: "Even moderate affirmative action programs injure the white males who are made to bear their brunt. Other people design the programs, but it is Allan Bakke, Brian Weber, Paul Johnson, and others like them who find their career opportunities hampered. Moreover, such programs violate white males' right to be treated as individuals and to have racial or sexual considerations not affect employment decisions."

COUNTERPOINT: "I'm not sure Bakke, Weber, and Johnson have the rights you are talking about. Racial and sexual considerations are often relevant to employment decisions. Jobs and medical school places are scarce resources, and society may distribute these in a way that furthers its legitimate ends—like breaking the cycle of poverty for minorities. I admit that with affirmative action programs white men do not have it as good as they did before, and I'm against extreme programs that disregard their interests altogether. But their interests have to be balanced against society's interest in promoting these programs."

2. *Affirmative action itself violates the principle of equality.*

POINT: "Affirmative action programs are intended to enhance racial and sexual equality, but you can't do that by treating people unequally. If equality is the goal, it must be the means, too. With affirmative action programs, you use racial and sexual considerations—but that is the very thing that has caused so much harm in the past and that affirmative action itself is hoping to get rid of."

COUNTERPOINT: "I admit that it is distasteful to have to take racial and sexual considerations into account when dealing with individuals in employment situations. I wish we didn't have to. But the unfortunate reality is that in the real world racial and sexual factors go a long way toward determining what life prospects an individual has. We can't wish that reality away by pretending the world is color-blind, when it is not. Formal, color-blind equality has to be infringed now, if we are ever to achieve real, meaningful racial and sexual equality later."

3. Nondiscrimination will achieve our social goals; stronger affirmative action is unnecessary.

POINT: "The 1964 Civil Rights Act unequivocally outlaws job discrimination, and numerous employees and job candidates have won discrimination cases before the EEOC or in court. We need to insist on rigorous enforcement of the law. Also, employers should continue to recruit in a way that attracts minority applicants and make sure that their screening and review practices do not involve any implicit racist or sexist assumptions, and they should monitor their internal procedures and the behavior of their white male employees to root out any discriminatory behavior. Stronger affirmative action measures, in particular the taking of racial or sexual considerations into account in employment matters, are unnecessary. They only bring undesirable results."

COUNTERPOINT: "Without affirmative action, progress often stops. The percentage of minorities and women employed by employers subject to federal affirmative action requirements has risen much higher than it has with other employers. Or take the example of Alabama. In the late 1960s, a federal court found that only 27 out of 3,000 clerical and managerial state employees were black. Federal Judge Frank Johnson ordered extensive recruiting of blacks, as well as the hiring of the few specifically identified individual blacks who could prove they were victims of discrimination. Nothing happened. Another suit was filed, this time just against the state police, and this time a 50 percent hiring quota was imposed, until blacks reached 25 percent of the force. Today Alabama has the most thoroughly integrated state police force in the country."[32]

The debate over affirmative action is not the only controversy connected with job discrimination. Two other issues, both primarily concerning women, have been at the center of recent moral, legal, and political debate: the issue of comparable worth and the problem of sexual harassment on the job. We will look at these in turn.

COMPARABLE WORTH

In 1983 Louise Peterson was a licensed practical nurse at Western State Hospital in Tacoma, Washington. That year she received $1,462 a month for supervising the daily care of 60 males convicted of sex crimes, which was $192 a month less than the hospital's groundskeepers earned and $700 a month less than males doing similar work to hers at Washington state prisons. Convinced of the inequity in the state's pay scale, Peterson filed a suit claiming that she and other women were being discriminated against because men of similar skills and training and having similar responsibilities were being paid significantly more. A federal judge found Washington guilty of sex discrimination and ordered the state to reimburse its female employees a whopping $838 million in back pay.

The judge's ruling sent tremors of apprehension through state capitols and city governments—Connecticut, Wisconsin, Hawaii, Los Angeles, Philadelphia among them—and through the private sector as well. It also raised to national prominence the doctrine of comparable worth, and signaled a dramatic escalation in women's fight for equal employment rights.

In essence, *the doctrine of comparable worth holds that women and men should be paid on the same scale, not just for doing equal jobs, but for doing different jobs of equal skill, effort, and responsibility.* One legal-affairs correspondent rightly says, "The issue pits against each other two cherished American values: the ethic of nondiscrimination versus the free enterprise system."[33]

Advocates of comparable worth say that

substantial statistical evidence shows that women not only are in more low-paying jobs than men but also that they have been *forced* into them. They point to the nearly 50 percent of the entire female work force that is occupied as clerical workers, teachers, and nurses. Such workers and millions of females like them are being victimized by patently discriminatory pay scales that compensate women significantly less than males who have similar skills and do jobs of similar value. In short, justice demands that women receive equal pay for work of comparable worth. Many comparable-worth advocates go further to argue that in cases where women have not received comparable pay for jobs of comparable worth, justice requires that employers pay them reparation damages in the form of monies they have lost.

Comparable-worth adherents, then, endorse the first of the following two positions and possibly the second as well: (1) Women should start receiving equal pay for doing jobs of equal value, and (2) reparation damages should be paid to women who have not received equal pay for doing jobs of equal value. While the costs of implementing both demands would be decidedly higher than implementing just the first, under any comparable-worth program pay schedules would have to be readjusted so that all jobs of similar value would pay the same salary. And that would be expensive.

Opponents of comparable worth insist that women, desiring flexible schedules and less taxing jobs, have freely chosen lower-paying occupations, and thus are not entitled to any readjustment in pay scales to accord with the doctrine of comparable worth. Phyllis Schlafly, head of the Eagle Forum and an outspoken critic of the Equal Rights Amendment and nonrestrictive-abortion legislation, calls comparable worth "basically a conspiracy theory of jobs. . . . It asserts that, first, a massive societal male conspiracy has segregated or ghetto-ized women into particular occupations by excluding them from others; and then, second, devalued the women's job by paying them lower wages than other occupations held primarily by men."[34] She adds: "Not a shred of evidence has been produced to prove these assumptions. For two decades at least women have been free to go into any occupation. . . . But most women continue to choose traditional, rather than nontraditional jobs. This is their own free choice. Nobody makes them do it."[35]

Others who are sympathetic to the concept of comparable worth worry about its implementation. How are different jobs to be evaluated and compared, they wonder. "How do you determine the intrinsic value of one job and then compare it to another?" asks Linda Chavez, staff director of the Commission on Civil Rights. She points out that "for 200 years, this has been done by the free marketplace. It's as good an alternative as those being suggested by comparable-worth advocates. I'm not sure the legislative bodies or courts can do any better."[36] Even if judgments of comparability are possible, opponents worry about the cost issue: A revision of federal workers' salaries alone could run as high as $1.8 billion in annual pay increases and extra pension costs.

Advocates of comparable worth respond to these criticisms by pointing not only to the statistical evidence that they say demonstrates the inequity of pay scales, but also to massive research documenting the reality of visceral discrimination in the workplace and to the hundreds of cases and settlements that have involved workplace discrimination. They argue that it is not by accident or free choice that women find themselves in jobs that pay them less than males doing similar work. They have been victimized by a combination of institutional discrimination and a socialization process that has directed them to "female jobs." Moreover, they reject the argument that implementing comparable worth would be prohibitively expensive. They point to Minnesota, for example, which is phasing in a comparable-worth program over several years so that the state incurs an expense of about 1 percent a year. But the core of their arguments remains an appeal to fairness and equity, which, they insist, cannot be sacrificed on the altar of economy.

Embedded in the comparable-worth debate is the interplay of two federal laws, both intended to eliminate discrimination. Under the Equal Pay Act of 1963, employers are required to pay men and women equal pay for equal jobs. Title VII of the 1964 Civil Rights Act prohibits racial and sexual discrimination in employment. Opponents of comparable worth invoke the Equal Pay Act, claiming that employers are only obliged to pay equal pay for equal jobs, not for different jobs. Advocates of comparable worth, on the other hand, claim that Title VII covers all sex-based discrimination in wages. They insist that Congress did not intend to license pay inequities not covered under the narrow prohibitions of the Equal Pay Act.[37]

The comparable-worth issue continues to engender legal controversy. The federal courts have not explicitly accepted the doctrine of "comparable worth," even when they've rendered legal decisions that seem to most legal scholars to support it. One form of job discrimination against women that the courts agree about, however, is sexual harassment.

SEXUAL HARASSMENT

When many men hear the term "sexual harassment," they find it amusing and have a hard time taking it seriously. "It wouldn't bother me," they feel certain. "In fact," they chuckle, "I wouldn't mind being harassed a little more often." Others shrug it off, saying, "What's the big deal? You know what the world is like. Men and women, love and sex, they make it go 'round. Only uptight women are going to complain about sexual advances."

But for millions of working women, the reality of sexual harassment is not something to be shrugged off. For them it is no laughing matter.

The courts agree. Sexual harassment claims have emerged in the past decade as a potent force in the effort to come to terms with, and eliminate, sex discrimination. These claims fall primarily under Title VII of the Civil Rights Act, which in certain circumstances imposes liability on employers for the discriminatory acts of their employees—including sexual harassment. While the Supreme Court has not yet addressed the issue, a variety of federal district and appeals courts have held that sexual harassment is an objectionable act based on the sex of the individual and therefore violates the Civil Rights Act.[38] In short, sexual harassment is illegal.

Men can be victims of sexual harassment as well. We shall focus mainly on women, though, since they are the ones who suffer the most from it. The U.S. Merit Systems Protection Board found that 42 percent of all female employees of the federal government reported being harassed, while only 15 percent of the male employees did. And nine-tenths of the 9,000 women who responded to a questionnaire in *Redbook* magazine reported sexual harassment experiences.[39] We are all familiar with the stereotype of construction workers who whistle at, and make lewd comments about, women who walk by. But the truth is that all types of men in all sorts of occupations have been reported as harassers. Survey after survey of women in different universities, for example, reveals that high percentages of female professors, both tenured and untenured, and female students, graduate and undergraduate, have encountered some form of sexual harassment from a person in authority at least once while they were in the university.

Critics may contend that it is odd that sexual harassment is viewed by the courts as a kind of sex discrimination. If an infatuated supervisor harasses only the particular female employee who is the object of his desires, is his misconduct really best understood as discrimination against women? He does not bother women in general, just this particular individual. In viewing sexual harassment as a violation of the 1964 Civil Rights Act, the courts, however, are rightly acknowledging that such behavior, and the larger social patterns that reinforce it, rest on male attitudes and assumptions that work against women enjoying equality of opportunity on the job.

Accepting this viewpoint still leaves us with puzzles, though. Assume the infatuated supervisor is a woman and the employee a man. How are we to interpret this as sex discrimination, since it does not take place against a backdrop of social attitudes and practices which exploit and discriminate against men? Or imagine a bisexual employer who sexually harasses both male and female employees. Since he discriminates against neither sex, is there no sexual harassment?

These conceptual puzzles have to do with the law's interpretation of sexual harassment as a kind of sex discrimination. Practically speaking, this interpretation has benefited women and brought them better and fairer treatment on the job, but it clearly has its limits. While, legally speaking, the most important aspect of sexual harassment may be that it represents discrimination, it is doubtful that discrimination is *morally* the worst aspect of sexual harassment. Morally, as we shall see, there is much more to be said about the wrongness of sexual harassment.[40]

But what exactly is sexual harassment? The Equal Employment Opportunity Commission says that it is "unwelcome sexual advances, requests for sexual favors, and other verbal or physical conduct of a sexual nature . . ." Catherine A. MacKinnon, author of *Sexual Harassment of Working Women*, describes sexual harassment as "sexual attention imposed on someone who is not in a position to refuse it." And Alan K. Campbell, Director of

the Federal Office of Personnel Management, defines it as "deliberate or repeated unsolicited verbal comments, gestures, or physical contact of a sexual nature which are unwelcome." One useful legal definition of sexual harassment, which reflects the way most courts understand it, puts it this way:

> Unwelcome sexual advances, requests for sexual favors, and other verbal or physical conduct of a sexual nature constitute sexual harassment when (1) submission to such conduct is made either explicitly or implicitly a term or condition of an individual's employment, (2) submission to or rejection of such conduct by an individual is used as the basis for employment decisions affecting such individual, or (3) such conduct has the purpose or effect of substantially interfering with an individual's work performance or creating an intimidating, hostile, or offensive working environment.[41]

This definition helps us to distinguish three different types of sexual harassment.

Sexual threats are the first type. In its crudest form: "You better agree to sleep with me if you want to keep your job." The immorality of such threats seems clear. In threatening harm, they are coercive and violate the rights of the person threatened, certainly depriving him or her of equal treatment on the job. That such threats can be seriously psychologically damaging, and hence wrong, is also obvious.

Sexual offers are the second type: "If you sleep with me, I'm sure I can help you to advance more quickly in the firm." Often such offers may harbor implied threats, and unlike genuine offers, the employee may risk something by turning them down. Larry May and John Hughes argue in their essay "Sexual Harassment" (see page 382) that such offers by a male employer to a female employee put her in a worse position than she was before and, hence, are coercive. Even sexual offers without hint of retaliation, they suggest, change the female employee's working environment in an undesirable way. In the case of both threats and offers, the employer is attempting to exploit the power imbalance between him and the employee.

The third category is the broadest, but in some ways it is the most important because it is so pervasive. Sexual harassment includes behavior of a sexual nature that is distressing to women and interferes with their ability to perform on the job, even when the behavior is not an attempt to pressure the woman for sexual favors. Sexual innuendos, leering or ogling at a woman, sexist remarks about women's bodies, clothing, or sexual activities, and unnecessary touching, patting, or other physical conduct can all constitute sexual harassment. Such behavior is humiliating and degrading to its victim. It interferes with her peace of mind and undermines her work performance.

Neither the wrongness nor the illegality of sexual harassment requires that the harassing conduct be by the employee's supervisor. This is particularly relevant in the third category, where the harassment a woman endures may come from coworkers. Firms, however, are responsible for providing a work environment in which an employee can be free from harassment, and they can be sued for damages if they fail to do so. Although different courts have reached different decisions on the question of whether supervisory personnel must be notified or aware of sexual harassment by its employees before the firm will be found legally liable,[42] one can safely say that, morally speaking, a company needs to be alert to, and to take reasonable steps to guard against, the possibility of sexual harassment by its employees.

An isolated or occasional sexist remark or innuendo, while it might be morally objectionable, does not constitute harassment. Harassment of the third type requires that the objectionable behavior be persistent. The

same holds for racial slurs and epithets. An ethnic joke by itself does not constitute discriminatory harassment, but a concerned pattern of "excessive and opprobrious" racially derogatory remarks and related abuse does violate the law.[43]

Human beings are sexual creatures, and wherever men and women work together, there are bound to be sexual undertones to their interactions. Women as well as men can appreciate, with the right persons and at the appropriate times, sexual references, sex-related humor, and physical contact with members of the opposite sex. Flirting, too, is often appreciated by both parties. The authors believe neither that a serious and professional work environment must be free from sexuality nor that this is a possible goal.

When, then, is behavior objectionable or offensive enough to constitute harassment? What one person views as innocent fun or a friendly overture may be seen as objectionable and degrading by another. Comments that one women appreciates or enjoys may be distressing to another. Who can decide what is right? In the case of sexual harassment, who determines what is objectionable or offensive?

The answer is very simple: Harassment lies in the eyes of the receiver. There is no need for a theory of what is objectively insulting or inappropriate. Even if such a theory were possible, it would be irrelevant. The moral point is to respect a person's choices and wishes. Even if it were true that the other women in the office like it when the boss gives them a little hug, it would still be wrong to hug the one woman who is made uncomfortable by it. If the behavior is unwanted—that is, if the woman doesn't like it—then persisting in it is wrong. The fact that objectionable behavior must be persistent and repeated to be sexual harassment allows for the possibility that people can honestly misread coworkers' signals or misjudge their likely response to a sexual innuendo, a joke, or a friendly pat. That may be excusable; what is not excusable is persisting in the behavior once you know it is unwelcome.

Practically speaking, what should a female employee do if she encounters sexually harassing behavior? First, she must make it clear that the behavior is unwanted. This may be harder to do than it sounds, because most of us like to please others and do not want to be thought to be prudes or to lack a sense of humor. The employee may wish to be tactful and even pleasant in rejecting behavior she finds inappropriate, especially if she thinks the offending party is well intentioned, but in any case, she has to make her feelings known clearly and unequivocally. Second, if the behavior persists, she should try to document it by keeping a record of what has occurred, who was involved, and when it happened. If others have witnessed some of the incidents, then that will help her to document her case.

The third thing the female employee must do when faced with sexual harassment is to complain to the appropriate supervisor, sticking to the facts and presenting her allegations as objectively as possible. She should do this immediately in the case of sexual threats or offers by supervisors; in the case of inappropriate behavior by coworkers, she should generally wait to see if it persists despite her having told the offending party that she objects to the behavior in question. If complaining to her supervisor does not bring quick action, then she must try whatever other channel is available to her in the organization—the grievance committee, for example, or the chief executive's office itself.

Fourth, if complaining to a supervisor does not bring results, then the employee should seriously consider seeing a lawyer and learning in detail what legal options are available to her. Many women try to ignore sexual harassment, but the evidence suggests that in most cases it continues or grows worse. When sexual threats or offers are involved, a significant number of victims are subject to unwarranted reprimands, increased work loads, or other reprisals. The employee must remember, too, that she has both a moral and a legal right to work in an environment free from sexual harassment.

SUMMARY

1. Discrimination in employment involves adverse decisions against employees based on their membership in a group that is viewed as inferior or deserving of unequal treatment. Discrimination can be intentional or unintentional, institutional or individual.

2. Statistics, together with evidence of deep-seated attitudes and institutional practices and policies, point to racial and sexual discrimination in the workplace.

3. The Civil Rights Act of 1964 forbids discrimination in employment on the basis of race, color, sex, religion, and national origin. In the late 1960s and early 1970s many companies developed affirmative action programs to correct racial imbalances existing as a result of past discrimination. Critics charge that in practice affirmative action has often meant preferential treatment of women and minorities and even "reverse discrimination" against white men.

4. In a series of decisions, the Supreme Court has adopted a moderate, case-by-case approach to affirmative action. A majority of the Court upholds the general principle of affirmative action, as long as such programs are moderate and flexible. Race can legitimately be taken into account in employment-related decisions, but only as one among several factors. Affirmative action programs that rely on rigid and unreasonable quotas or that impose excessive hardship on present employees are illegal.

5. The moral issues surrounding affirmative action are controversial. Its defenders ar-

gue that: (1) compensatory justice demands affirmative action programs; (2) affirmative action is necessary to permit fairer competition; and (3) affirmative action is necessary to break the cycle that keeps minorities and women locked into poor, low-prestige jobs.

6. Critics of affirmative action argue that: (1) affirmative action injures white males and violates their rights; (2) affirmative action itself violates the principle of equality; and (3) nondiscrimination (without affirmative action) will suffice to achieve our social goals.

7. The doctrine of comparable worth holds that women and men should be paid on the same scale for doing different jobs of equal skill, effort, and responsibility.

8. Advocates of comparable worth say that women have been forced into lower-paying jobs than men and that justice requires that women receive equal pay for doing jobs of equal worth. Some contend further that monetary reparations are due to women who in the past have not received equal pay for doing jobs of equal value.

9. Opponents of comparable worth claim that women have freely chosen their occupations and are not entitled to compensation. They contend that only the market can and should determine the value of different jobs. Revising pay scales would also be prohibitively expensive.

10. Sexual harassment is widespread. It includes unwelcome sexual advances and other conduct of a sexual nature where (1) submission to such conduct is a basis for employment decisions or (2) such conduct substantially interferes with an individual's work performance. Sexual harassment is a kind of discrimination and is illegal.

11. Employees encountering sexually harassing behavior from coworkers should make it clear that the behavior is unwanted. If it persists, harassed employees should document the behavior and report it to the appropriate person or office in the organization. In the case of sexual threats or offers from supervisors, they should do this immediately. If internal channels are ineffective, employees should seek legal advice.

CASE 8.1

Warning: Pregnancy May Be Dangerous to Job Security

As recently as the early sixties, a working woman who found herself pregnant could expect to find herself jobless. Very few employers offered disability benefits for childbirth, and many did not grant pregnancy leaves. In the 70s, as more and more women began to enter the work force, it became increasingly difficult for employers to discharge pregnant women or deny them disability benefits. Still, employers insisted that the uniqueness of pregnancy and childbirth placed it outside the realm of illness benefits. And they received support from the Supreme Court, which in 1976 ruled that despite Title VII's prohibition against sex discrimination, it was legal for General Electric to grant its workers disability benefits for every non-job-related disability except pregnancy.[44] In other words, General Electric—or any company for that matter—could compensate men recovering from male medical problems—for example, prostate operations—and still deny benefits to a woman recovering from childbirth.

Outcries of "specious" greeted the Court's

General Electric decision. Some feminist organizations viewed it not only as a misreading of Title VII, but sexist inspired. Labor leaders saw the ruling as an assault on the disability rights of a growing segment of the work force.

Reacting to widespread criticism of the court's decision, Congress initiated what became a rather long and at times acrimonious debate of the issue. The upshot was that in 1978 it passed legislation requiring employers to treat pregnancy and childbirth like any other non-occupational illness or injury. The Pregnancy Discrimination Act did not require that pregnant women receive disability leave or benefits—only that whatever the employer's disability program, it should apply equally to pregnancy and childbirth. What at the time was celebrated in many quarters, especially among feminists and others battling for female equality in the workplace, soon turned into a rat's nest of legal confusion. Ask Lillian Garland.[45]

About the same time the Supreme Court was ruling in the General Electric case, Garland was being hired by California Federal Savings and Loan Association (Cal Fed) as a receptionist in the bank's commercial loans department. She immediately took a liking to her job and over the next five years competently did her work, which included answering telephones and attending to customers. What promised to be a long and fruitful association with Cal Fed ended abruptly with Garland's pregnancy in 1981.

Garland trained a woman to do her job during her absence with every expectation of returning to the position after the birth of her child. But when she returned to the bank on April 20, 1982, two months after a Cesarean section, she was informed that there was no receptionist or similar position open at the time. It was only then that she realized that having a baby had cost her job.

"I mean, I felt cold all over," Garland recalls. "I stood there and said, 'What do you mean, you don't have a position available for me? What about my job?' They said, 'Well, we have hired somebody in your place.' And I said, 'Who?' And it was the person I trained. And I said, 'What do I do now?' And they said, 'We'll call you, as soon as a position becomes available.'"

In November Cal Fed offered Garland a position as a receptionist in accounting, and she took it. In the seven-month interim, Cal Fed had also offered her several typing jobs, which she felt unqualified to accept, and jobs at other branches, which she refused because she had no car. She had also sought but failed to get jobs as a barmaid, waitress, and salesperson.

Although Garland was relieved to have a job again with Cal Fed, she filed a complaint with the California Department of Fair Employment and Housing. The basis of her action was a California state law that requires employers not only to allow pregnant workers a disability leave but to return them to their jobs or comparable jobs, regardless of what they offer other employees. In other words, under California law no matter what a company's disability policies are it owes every pregnant woman a job-secure leave of up to four months for the time she is incapacitated by pregnancy and childbirth.

Cal Fed contended that its action was perfectly consistent with the federal law that requires employers to treat pregnancy and childbirth exactly as it does any other disability. Since under the bank's disability policy no employee is guaranteed a job immediately upon returning to work, Cal Fed claimed that Garland should not have expected nor have received special treatment.

U.S. District Judge Manuel L. Real agreed with the bank's position. Acting on a motion from Cal Fed and two major state employers' organizations, the judge ruled that the California law constituted "preferential treatment of females disabled by pregnancy, childbirth, or related medical conditions." In the judge's opinion, then, the California law is discriminatory because it violates the prohibition against sex discrimination in Title VII of the 1964 Civil Rights Act.

Eventually, the case made it to the Supreme Court. Ironically, the National Organization of Women (NOW) sided with Cal Fed, arguing that special treatment of pregnant employees reinforces gender-based stereotypes traditionally used to exclude women. The Court's 1987 decision, however, backed Garland.[46] Writing for the majority, Justice Marshall ruled that the California statute does not unlawfully discriminate against men by providing women with some benefit not provided to other disabled workers. Rather, the statute is within the meaning and the intention of the Civil Rights Act, as amended by the Pregnancy Discrimination Act. It fairly and legally promotes equality of employment for women.

Marshall added another, subtle argument, reasoning that, even if one falsely assumes that federal law makes it illegal for employers to provide pregnant women with benefits which are not already provided to other disabled employees, the California statute would still be acceptable. In requiring leave for pregnant workers, the statute does not compel employers to treat them better than other employees. Employers are still free to guarantee their other disabled workers leave and reinstatement! That was definitely a conclusion Cal Fed didn't like hearing.

Discussion Questions

1. The California law provides certain protections just for pregnant employees. Is there anything wrong about the state treating pregnant workers differently from other disabled employees or from other employees in general? What do you think of NOW's argument?

2. The courts continually discuss pregnancy as a medical disability, analogous with medical disabilities men might suffer. Is this a good analogy? Is pregnancy best understood as a "disability"?

3. Only women can become pregnant. Does that mean that the California statute is giving special privileges to women?

4. Does the statute discriminate against men? Is there anything morally objectionable about the California law?

5. Does *not* providing women with unpaid maternity leave and reinstatement constitute discrimination against women?

6. Suggest possible arguments for and against *paid* maternity leave.

CASE 8.2
Raising the Ante

Having spearheaded the women's cause on behalf of equal pay for jobs of equal value, Phyllis Warren was elated when the board decided to readjust salaries in the light of that principle. Its decision was clearly important in the sense that Phyllis and other women employed by the crafts firm would receive pay equivalent to males doing comparable jobs. But in a larger sense it constituted an admis-

sion of guilt on the part of the board, acknowledgment of a history blemished with sexual discrimination.

In the euphoria that followed the board's decision, neither Phyllis nor any of the other campaign activists thought much about the implications of such an implied admission of female exploitation. But some weeks later, Herm Leggett, a sales dispatcher, half jokingly suggested to Phyllis over lunch that she shouldn't stop with equal pay *now*. Phyllis asked Herm what he meant.

"Back pay," Herm said without hesitation. "If they're readjusting salaries for women," he explained, "they obviously know that salaries are out of line, and have been for some time." Then he asked her pointedly, "How long you been here, Phyl?" Eleven years, she told him. "If those statistics you folks were passing around last month are accurate," Herm said, "then I'd say you've been losing about $500 a year or $5,500 over eleven." Then he added with a laugh, "Not counting interest, of course."

"Why not?" Phyllis thought. Why shouldn't she and other women who'd suffered past inequities be reimbursed?

That night Phyllis called a few of the other women and suggested that they press the board for back pay. Some said they were satisfied and didn't think they should force the issue. Others thought the firm had been fair in readjusting the salary schedule, and they were willing to let bygones be bygones. Still others thought that any further efforts might, in fact, roll back the board's favorable decision. Yet, there was a nucleus that agreed with Phyllis that workers who had been unfairly treated in the past ought to receive compensation. They decided, however, that since their ranks were divided, they shouldn't wage as intense an in-house campaign as previously but take the issue directly to the board while it might still be inhaling deeply the fresh air of social responsibility.

The following Wednesday, Phyllis and four other women presented their case to the board, intentionally giving the impression that they enjoyed as much support from other workers as they had the last time they appeared before it. Although this wasn't true, Phyllis suggested it as an effective strategic ploy.

Phyllis's presentation had hardly ended when board members began making their feelings known about her proposal. One called it "industrial blackmail." "No sooner do we try to right an injustice," he said testily, "than you take our good faith and threaten to beat us over the head with it unless we comply with your request."

Another member just as vigorously argued that the current board couldn't be held accountable for the actions, policies, and decisions of previous boards. "Sure," he said, "we're empowered to alter policies as we see fit, as new conditions chart new directions. And we've done that. But to expect us to bear the full financial liability of decisions we never made is totally unrealistic—and unfair."

Still another member wondered where it would all end. "If we agree," he asked, "will you then suggest that we should track down all those women who ever worked for us, and provide them compensation?" Phyllis said no, but that the board should readjust retirement benefits for those affected.

At this point the board asked Phyllis if she had any idea what all of what she was proposing would cost the firm.

"Whatever it is, it's a small price to pay for righting wrong," she said firmly.

"But is it a small price to pay for severely damaging our profit picture?" one of the members asked. Then he added, "I needn't remind you that our profit outlook directly affects what we can offer our current employees in terms of salary and fringes. It directly affects our ability to revise our salary schedule." Finally, he asked Phyllis whether she'd be willing for the board to reduce everyone's current compensation in order for it to meet what Phyllis termed the board's "obligations to the past."

Despite its decided opposition to Phyllis's proposal, the board agreed to consider it and render a decision at its next meeting. As a final broadside, Phyllis hinted that if the board didn't comply with the committee's request, the committee was prepared to submit its demand to litigation.

Discussion Questions

1. If you were a board member, how would you vote? Why?

2. What moral values are involved in the case?

3. Do you think Phyllis Warren was unfair in turning the board's implied admission of salary discrimination on the basis of sex against it? Why?

4. Do you think Phyllis was wrong in giving the board the impression that her proposal enjoyed broad support? Why?

5. If the board rejects the committee's request, do you think the committee ought to sue? Give reasons.

CASE 8.3
Mandatory Retirement

Congress acted in 1978 to include age among the categories, discrimination on the grounds of which is contrary to the Civil Rights Act. In the year before, the Congressional Select Committee on Aging heard arguments for and against mandatory retirement from various sources—from large and small corporations, from interest groups, from labor unions, from scholars, from legal experts, and from economists. The Committee summed up their arguments this way:[47]

A. For Mandatory Retirement

1. Older persons as a group may be less well-suited for some jobs than younger workers because:
   a. Declining physical and mental capacity are found in greater proportion among older persons.
   b. Generally older persons do not learn new skills as easily as younger persons.
   c. Older workers have more inflexibility with regard to work due to work rules, seniority systems and pay scales.
   d. Older workers typically have less education than younger workers.

2. Medical science is not capable of making accurate individual assessments of physical and psychological competencies of employees which would presumably be required if there was no standard mandatory retirement age; or substantial time and money may be required to make such individual determinations of fitness. Also, it is difficult to administer any such individual test of fitness fairly.

3. Mandatory retirement saves face for the older workers no longer capable of performing his or her job adequately, who would otherwise be singled out for forced retirement.

4. Mandatory retirement provides a predictable situation allowing both management and employees to plan ahead.

5. It is sometimes more costly for employers to have an older work force in terms of maintaining various pension, health and life insurance plans.

6. By forcing retirement at an earlier age than a person might otherwise choose, there are more opportunities for younger workers. This may aid in recruiting additions and replacements to the work force and allow infusion of new ideas.

7. Older workers can often retire to social security or other retirement income, making jobs available to younger unemployed workers who do not have other income potential.

B. Against Mandatory Retirement

1. Mandatory retirement based on age alone is discriminatory against workers. It is contrary to equal employment opportunity. Mandatory retirement laws have been challenged as unconstitutional because of denying individuals equal protection of the law.

2. Chronological age alone is a poor indicator of ability to perform a job. Mandatory retirement at a certain age does not take into consideration actual, differing abilities and capacities. Studies demonstrate that many workers can continue to work effectively beyond age 65, and may be better employees than younger workers because of experience and job commitment.

3. Mandatory retirement can cause hardships for older persons. For example:

   a. Mandatory retirement often results in loss of role and income for individuals.

   b. Mandatory retirement at a certain age may very well result in a lower retirement benefit under social security if the last years the employee would have worked would have brought higher earnings than earlier years.

   c. Mandatory retirement is especially disadvantageous to some women who do not start work until after the children are grown or after being widowed or divorced. Forced retirement limits the work life of these women and reduces their ability to build up significant benefits.

   d. Mandatory retirement can cause great economic hardship on a growing number of older workers who have many financial obligations usually considered the province of younger persons, e.g., home mortgages, installment payments on cars, etc. In addition, a rapidly increasing number of older persons ages 60–65 are experiencing the financial responsibility for aged parents or other relatives.

   e. Mandatory retirement on the basis of age may well impair the health of many individuals whose job represents a major source of status, creative satisfaction, social relationships, or self-respect.

4. Mandatory retirement causes loss of skills and experience from the work force, resulting in reduced national output (GNP).

5. Forced retirement causes an increased expense to government income maintenance programs such as social security and supplemental security income, as well as to social service programs.

6. The declining birth rate will mean a proportionately smaller labor force supporting a larger retiree population early in the next century. The economics of this situation could be eased by later retirement or elimination of mandatory retirement at any set age.

Discussion Questions

1. Is mandatory retirement a form of job discrimination? Explain. What other considerations of justice and rights are involved in the debate over mandatory retirement?

2. Evaluate both the pro and the con arguments carefully from the utilitarian perspective.

3. In your view is mandatory retirement (a) morally required; (b) wise and morally permissible (but not required); (c) morally permissible, but misguided; (d) morally

suspect or questionable; or (e) flatly immoral?

4. Should corporate retirement policies be regulated by law? If so, how? If not, why not?

5. If you were hired as a company consultant on this issue, what would you recommend as a good, nondiscriminatory retirement policy?

CASE 8.4
Consenting to Sexual Harassment

In the recent case of *Vinson v. Taylor*, heard before the federal District Court for the District of Columbia, Vinson alleged that Taylor, her supervisor at Capital City Savings and Loan, sexually harassed her, but the facts of the case are contested.[48] In court, Vinson testified that about a year after she began working at the bank Taylor asked her to have sexual relations with him. She claimed that Taylor said that she "owed" him because he had obtained the job for her.

Although she turned down Taylor at first, she eventually became involved with him. She and Taylor engaged in sexual relations, both during and after business hours, during the remaining three years that she worked at the bank. The encounters included intercourse in a bank vault and in a storage area in the bank basement. Vinson also testified that Taylor often actually "assaulted or raped" her. She contended that she was forced to submit to Taylor or jeopardize her employment.

Taylor, for his part, denied the allegations. He testified that he had never had sex with Vinson. On the contrary, he alleged that Vinson had made advances toward him and that he declined them. He contended that Vinson had brought the charges against him in order to "get even" with him because of a work-related dispute.

In its ruling on the case, the court held that if Vinson and Taylor engaged in a sexual relationship, that relationship was voluntary on the part of Vinson and was not employment related. The court also held that Capital City Federal Savings and Loan did not have "notice" of the alleged harassment and was, therefore, not liable. Although Taylor was Vinson's supervisor, the court reasoned that notice to him was not notice to the bank.

Vinson appealed the case, and the court of appeals held that the district court had erred in three ways. First, the district court had overlooked the fact that there are two possible kinds of sexual harassment. Writing for the majority, Chief Judge Robinson distinguished cases where the victim's continued employment or promotion is conditioned on giving into sexual demands and those cases in which the victim must tolerate a "substantially discriminatory work environment." The lower court had failed to consider Vinson's case as possible harassment of the second kind.

Second, the higher court also overruled the district court's finding that because Vinson voluntarily engaged in a sexual relationship with Taylor, she was not a victim of sexual harassment. Voluntariness on Vinson's part had "no bearing," the judge wrote, on "whether Taylor made Vinson's toleration of sexual harassment a condition of her employment." Third, the court of appeals held that *any* discriminatory activity by a supervisor is attributable to the employer, regardless of whether the employer had specific notice.

In his dissent to the court of appeals's decision, Judge Bork rejected the majority's claim that "voluntariness" did not automatically rule out harassment. He argued that this would have the result of depriving the accused person of any defense since he could no longer establish that the supposed victim was really "a willing participant." Judge Bork contended further that an employer should not be held vicariously liable for a supervisor's acts that it didn't know about.

Discussion Questions

1. According to her own testimony Vinson acquiesced in the sexual demands of Taylor. In this sense her behavior was "voluntary." Does the voluntariness of her behavior mean that she had "consented" to Taylor's advances? Does it mean that they were "welcome"? Do you agree that Vinson's acquiescence shows there was no sexual harassment? Who was right about this, the district court or the court of appeals? Defend your position.

2. In your opinion, under what circumstances would acquiescence be a defense to charges of sexual harassment? When would it not be a defense? Can you formulate a general rule for deciding such cases?

3. Assuming the truth of Vinson's version of the case, should her employer, Capital City Savings and Loan, be held liable for sexual harassment it was not aware of? Should the Savings and Loan have been aware of it? Does it make a difference that Taylor was at a supervisory level? In general, when should an employer be liable for harassment?

4. What steps do you think Vinson should have taken when Taylor first pressed her for sex? Should she be blamed for having given in to him? Assuming that there was sexual harassment despite her acquiescence, does her going along with Taylor make her partly responsible or mitigate Taylor's wrongdoing?

5. In court Vinson's allegations were coun-

tered by Taylor's version of the facts. Will there always be a "your word against mine" problem in sexual harassment cases? What could Vinson have done to strengthen her case?

NOTES

1. "So Who's Laughing?" *Guardian* (New York), November 4, 1987.

2. Charles R. Lawrence III, "The Id, the Ego, and Equal Protection: Reckoning with Unconscious Racism," *Stanford Law Review* 39 (January 1987): 318, 340.

3. Ibid., 339–340.

4. Manuel G. Velasquez, *Business Ethics: Concepts and Cases* (Englewood Cliffs, N.J.: Prentice-Hall, 1982), 266–267.

5. See Michael Parenti, *Democracy for the Few*, 4th ed. (New York: St. Martin's, 1983), 29, 33; and the National Conference of Catholic Bishops, *Economic Justice for All* (Washington: U.S. Catholic Conference, 1986), 89–90.

6. On his television show "Firing Line," a transcript of which appears in John Arthur, ed., *Morality and Moral Controversies*, 2nd ed. (Englewood Cliffs, N.J.: Prentice-Hall, 1986). Buckley goes on to argue, implausibly in the eyes of the authors, that differences in median age account for this income disparity among ethnic groups.

7. *Newsweek* (international edition), March 8, 1988, 36.

8. Velasquez, *Business Ethics*, 272–273.

9. "Individual Candidate Remedies: Why They Won't Work," in Gertrude Ezorsky, ed., *Moral Rights in the Workplace* (Albany: State University of New York Press, 1987), 260.

10. Lee Lembart, "Science: Still Few Chances for Women," *Los Angeles Times*, March 7, 1984.

11. Reported in "Women Lawyers Gain, Blacks Lose, Survey Finds," *USA Today*, May 17, 1984.

12. U.S. Bureau of the Census, *Statistical Abstract of the U.S. 1978* (Washington: U.S. Government Printing Office, 1978), 457.

13. *Economic Justice for All*, 88; and Doug Grider and Mike Shurden, "The Gathering Storm of Comparable Worth," *Business Horizons* 30 (July–August 1987): 61.

14. See "Women Finding Jobs, Less Money," *Santa Barbara News Press*, October 3, 1984.

15. U.S. Bureau of the Census, *Statistical Abstract*, 457.

16. Allan Parachini, "Male-Female Wage Gap Closing," *Los Angeles Times*, October 31, 1984, Part I, p. 3.

17. Reported in *USA Today*, May 29, 1984, p. 4D.

18. Edward W. Jones, Jr., "Black Managers: the Dream Deferred," *Harvard Business Review* 64 (May–June 1986): 84; and Colin Leinster, "Black Executives: How They're Doing," *Fortune*, January 18, 1988, 110.

19. *Business Week*, October 23, 1987; *Fortune*, January 18, 1988, 109.

20. Ellen Goodman, "Women Gain a Better Shot at Top Rungs," *Los Angeles Times*, May 29, 1984, Part II, p. 45.

21. Ibid.

22. Benson Rosen and Thomas H. Jerdee, "Sex Stereotyping in the Executive Suite," *Harvard Business Review* 52 (May–June 1974): 45–58.

23. Peter Dubno, "Is Corporate Sexism Passé?" *Business and Society Review* 53 (Spring 1985).

24. Lee Dembart, "Science: Still Few Chances For Women," *Los Angeles Times*, March 7, 1984, 1.

25. Ibid.

26. Ibid., 3, 19.

27. Ibid., 3.

28. Jones, "Black Managers," 88.

29. Richard T. DeGeorge, *Business Ethics*, 2nd ed. (New York: Macmillan, 1986), 247–248.

30. See *Griggs v. Duke Power Co.*, 401 U.S. 424 (1971).

31. James E. Jones, "'Reverse Discrimination' in Employment," in Joseph R. DesJardins and John J. McCall, eds., *Contemporary Issues in Business Ethics* (Belmont, Calif.: Wadsworth, 1985), 431–432.

32. Herman Schwartz, "Affirmative Action," in Gertrude Ezorsky, ed., *Moral Rights in the Workplace* (Albany: State University of New York Press, 1987), 276.

33. Nina Totenberg, "Why Women Earn Less," *Parade Magazine*, June 10, 1984, 5.

34. Caroline E. Mayer, "The Comparable Pay Debate," *The Washington Post National Weekly Edition*, August 6, 1984, 9.

35. Ibid.

36. Ibid.

37. See Stephen Wermiel, "High Court Looks at Women's Pay in Dispute on 'Comparable Worth.'" *The Wall Street Journal*, May 14, 1981, Sec. 2, p. 25.

38. Mary Jo Shaney, "Perceptions of Harm: The Consent Defense in Sexual Harassment Cases," *Iowa Law Review* 71 (May 1986): 1109.

39. Ibid., 1112n.

40. By analogy, compare the fact that often the only grounds on which the federal government can put a murderer on trial is on the charge of having violated the civil rights of his or her victim. The charge of violating the victim's civil rights doesn't get to the heart of the murderer's wrongdoing, even if it is the only legally relevant issue.

41. Shaney, "Perceptions of Harm," 1109.

42. Ibid., 1110n.

43. Terry L. Leap and Larry R. Smeltzer, "Racial Remarks in the Workplace: Humor or Harassment?" *Harvard Business Review* 62 (November–December 1984).

44. *General Electric Co. v. Gilbert*, 429 U.S. 125 (1976).

45. See Cynthia Gorney, "The Law's the Same for a Man: Have a Baby, Lose Your Job," *The Washington Post National Weekly Edition*, April 23, 1984, 6. The quotations reported here are from this source.

46. *California Federal Savings and Loan Assoc. v. Guerra*, 93 L Ed 2d 613 (1987).

47. From the Report by the Select Committee on Aging, *The Social and Human Cost of Enforced Idleness* (U.S. Government Printing Office, 1977); reprinted in David Braybrooke, *Ethics in the World of Business* (Totowa, N.J.: Rowman and Allanheld, 1983).

48. See Mary Jo Shaney, "Perceptions of Harm: The Consent Defense in Sexual Harassment Cases," *Iowa Law Review* 71 (May 1986) for the relevant legal citations and a presentation of the facts on which this case study relies.

A Defense of Affirmative Action

Thomas Nagel

After distinguishing between strong and weak senses of "affirmative action," Professor Nagel examines three objections to strong affirmative action: that it is inefficient, that it is unfair, and that it damages self-esteem. Although Nagel grants that the objections have weight, he argues that they are outweighed by the need to remove the stubborn residues of our racial caste system. With regard to women, however, strong affirmative action is probably not warranted.

The term "affirmative action" has changed in meaning since it was first introduced. Originally it

Testimony before the Subcommittee on the Constitution of the Senate Judiciary Committee, June 18, 1981. Reprinted by permission of Professor Nagel.

referred only to special efforts to ensure equal opportunity for members of groups that had been subject to discrimination. These efforts included public advertisement of positions to be filled, active recruitment of qualified applicants from the formerly excluded groups, and special training programs to help them meet the standards for admission or appointment. There was also close attention to procedures of appointment, and sometimes to the results, with a view to detecting continued discrimination, conscious or unconscious.

More recently the term has come to refer also to some degree of definite preference for members of these groups in determining access to positions from which they were formerly excluded. Such preference might be allowed to influence decisions only between candidates who are otherwise equally qualified, but usually it involves the selection of women or minority members over other candidates who are better qualified for the position.

Let me call the first sort of policy "weak affirmative action" and the second "strong affirmative action." It is important to distinguish them, because the distinction is sometimes blurred in practice. It is strong affirmative action—the policy of preference—that arouses controversy. Most people would agree that weak or precautionary affirmative action is a good thing, and worth its cost in time and energy. But this does not imply that strong affirmative action is also justified.

I shall claim that in the present state of things it is justified, most clearly with respect to blacks. But I also believe that a defender of the practice must acknowledge that there are serious arguments against it, and that it is defensible only because the arguments for it have great weight. Moral opinion in this country is sharply divided over the issue because significant values are involved on both sides. My own view is that while strong affirmative action is intrinsically undesirable, it is a legitimate and perhaps indispensable method of pursuing a goal so important to the national welfare that it can be justified as a temporary, though not short-term, policy for both public and private institutions. In this respect it is like other policies that impose burdens on some for the public good.

Three Objections

I shall begin with the argument against. There are three objections to strong affirmative action:

that it is inefficient; that it is unfair; and that it damages self-esteem.

The degree of inefficiency depends on how strong a role racial or sexual preference plays in the process of selection. Among candidates meeting the basic qualifications for a position, those better qualified will on the average perform better, whether they are doctors, policemen, teachers, or electricians. There may be some cases, as in preferential college admissions, where the immediate usefulness of making educational resources available to an individual is thought to be greater because of the use to which the education will be put or because of the internal effects on the institution itself. But by and large, policies of strong affirmative action must reckon with the costs of some lowering in performance level: the stronger the preference, the larger the cost to be justified. Since both the costs and the value of the results will vary from case to case, this suggests that no one policy of affirmative action is likely to be correct in all cases, and that the cost in performance level should be taken into account in the design of a legitimate policy.

The charge of unfairness arouses the deepest disagreements. To be passed over because of membership in a group one was born into, where this has nothing to do with one's individual qualifications for a position, can arouse strong feelings of resentment. It is a departure from the ideal—one of the values finally recognized in our society—that people should be judged so far as possible on the basis of individual characteristics rather than involuntary group membership.

This does not mean that strong affirmative action is morally repugnant in the manner of racial or sexual discrimination. It is nothing like those practices, for though like them it employs race and sex as criteria of selection, it does so for entirely different reasons. Racial and sexual discrimination are based on contempt or even loathing for the excluded group, a feeling that certain contacts with them are degrading to members of the dominant group, that they are fit only for subordinate positions or menial work. Strong affirmative action involves none of this: it is simply a means of increasing the social and economic strength of formerly victimized groups, and does not stigmatize others.

There is an element of individual unfairness here, but it is more like the unfairness of conscription in wartime, or of property condemnation under the right of eminent domain. Those who benefit or lose out because of their race or sex cannot be said to deserve their good or bad fortune.

It might be said on the other side that the beneficiaries of affirmative action deserve it as compensation for past discrimination, and that compensation is rightly exacted from the group that has benefited from discrimination in the past. But this is a bad argument, because as the practice usually works, no effort is made to give preference to those who have suffered most from discrimination, or to prefer them especially to those who have benefited most from it, or been guilty of it. Only candidates who in other qualifications fall on one or other side of the margin of decision will directly benefit or lose from the policy, and these are not necessarily, or even probably, the ones who especially deserve it. Women or blacks who don't have the qualifications even to be considered are likely to have been handicapped more by the effects of discrimination than those who receive preference. And the marginal white male candidate who is turned down can evoke our sympathy if he asks, "Why me?" (A policy of explicitly *compensatory* preference, which took into account each individual's background of poverty and discrimination, would escape some of these objections, and it has its defenders, but it is not the policy I want to defend. Whatever its merits, it will not serve the same purpose as direct affirmative action.)

The third objection concerns self-esteem, and is particularly serious. While strong affirmative action is in effect, and generally known to be so, no one in an affirmative action category who gets a desirable job or is admitted to a selective university can be sure that he or she has not benefited from the policy. Even those who would have made it anyway fall under suspicion, from themselves and from others: it comes to be widely felt that success does not mean the same thing for women and minorities. This painful damage to esteem cannot be avoided. It should make any defender of strong affirmative action want the practice to end as soon as it has achieved its basic purpose.

Justifying Affirmative Action

I have examined these three objections and tried to assess their weight, in order to decide how strong a countervailing reason is needed to justify such a policy. In my view, taken together they imply that strong affirmative action involving significant preference should be undertaken only if it will substantially further a social goal of the first importance. While this condition is not met by all programs of affirmative action now in effect, it is met by those which address the most deep-seated, stubborn, and radically unhealthy divisions in the society, divisions whose removal is a condition of basic justice and social cohesion.

The situation of black people in our country is unique in this respect. For almost a century after the abolition of slavery we had a rigid racial caste system of the ugliest kind, and it only began to break up twenty-five years ago. In the South it was enforced by law, and in the North, in a somewhat less severe form, by social convention. Whites were thought to be defiled by social or residential proximity to blacks, intermarriage was taboo, blacks were denied the same level of public goods—education and legal protection—as whites, were restricted to the most menial occupations, and were barred from any positions of authority over whites. The visceral feelings of black inferiority and untouchability that this system expressed were deeply ingrained in the members of both races, and they continue, not surprisingly, to have their effect. Blacks still form, to a considerable extent, a hereditary social and economic community characterized by widespread poverty, unemployment, and social alienation.

When this society finally got around to moving against the caste system, it might have done no more than to enforce straight equality of opportunity, perhaps with the help of weak affirmative action, and then wait a few hundred years while things gradually got better. Fortunately it decided instead to accelerate the process by both public and private institutional action, because there was wide recognition of the intractable character of the problem posed by this insular minority and its place in the nation's history and collective consciousness. This has not been going on very long, but the results are already impressive, especially in speeding the advancement of blacks into the middle class. Affirmative action has not done much to improve the position of poor and unskilled blacks. That is the most serious part of the problem, and it requires a more direct economic attack. But increased access to higher education and upper-level jobs is an essential part of what must be achieved to break the structure of drastic separation that was left largely undisturbed by the legal abolition of the caste system.

Changes of this kind require a generation or two. My guess is that strong affirmative action for blacks will continue to be justified into the early decades of the next century, but that by then it will have accomplished what it can and will no longer be worth the costs. One point deserves special emphasis. The goal to be pursued is the reduction of a great social injustice, not proportional representation of the races in all institutions and professions. Proportional racial representation is of no value in itself. It is not a legitimate social goal, and it should certainly not be the aim of strong affirmative action, whose drawbacks make it worth adopting only against a serious and intractable social evil.

This implies that the justification for strong affirmative action is much weaker in the case of other racial and ethnic groups, and in the case of women. At least, the practice will be justified in a narrower range of circumstances and for a shorter span of time than it is for blacks. No other group has been treated quite like this, and no other group is in a comparable status. Hispanic-Americans occupy an intermediate position, but it seems to me frankly absurd to include persons of oriental descent as beneficiaries of affirmative action, strong or weak. They are not a severely deprived and excluded minority, and their eligibility serves only to swell the numbers that can be included on affirmative action reports. It also suggests that there is a drift in the policy toward adopting the goal of racial proportional representation for its own sake. This is a foolish mistake, and should be resisted. The only legitimate goal of the policy is to reduce egregious racial stratification.

With respect to women, I believe that except over the short term, and in professions or institutions from which their absence is particularly marked, strong affirmative action is not warranted and weak affirmative action is enough. This is based simply on the expectation that the social and economic situation of women will improve quite rapidly under conditions of full equality of opportunity. Recent progress provides some evidence for this. Women do not form a separate hereditary community, characteristically poor and uneducated, and their position is not likely to be self-perpetuating in the same way as that of an outcast race. The process requires less artificial accelera-

tion, and any need for strong affirmative action for women can be expected to end sooner than it ends for blacks.

I said at the outset that there was a tendency to blur the distinction between weak and strong affirmative action. This occurs especially in the use of numerical quotas, a topic on which I want to comment briefly.

A quota may be a method of either weak or strong affirmative action, depending on the circumstances. It amounts to weak affirmative action—a safeguard against discrimination—if, and only if, there is independent evidence that average qualifications for the positions being filled are no lower in the group to which a minimum quota is being assigned than in the applicant group as a whole. This can be presumed true of unskilled jobs that most people can do, but it becomes less likely, and harder to establish, the greater the skill and education required for the position. At these levels, a quota proportional to population, or even to representation of the group in the applicant pool, is almost certain to amount to strong affirmative action. Moreover it is strong affirmative action of a particularly crude and indiscriminate kind, because it permits no variation in the degree of preference on the basis of costs in efficiency, depending on the qualification gap. For this reason I should defend quotas only where they serve the purpose of weak affirmative action. On the whole, strong affirmative action is better implemented by including group preference as one factor in appointment or admission decisions, and letting the results depend on its interaction with other factors.

I have tried to show that the arguments against strong affirmative action are clearly outweighed at present by the need for exceptional measures to remove the stubborn residues of racial caste. But advocates of the policy should acknowledge the reasons against it, which will ensure its termination when it is no longer necessary. Affirmative action is not an end in itself, but a means of dealing with a social situation that should be intolerable to us all.

Review and Discussion Questions

1. What is Nagel's reason for supporting "strong affirmative action" with respect to blacks?

2. How strong are the three objections to affirmative action that Nagel discusses? Has he overlooked any other important objections to affirmative action?

3. Assess Nagel's contention that strong affirmative action is not, in general, warranted with respect to women.

Debate Over Comparable Worth: Facts and Rhetoric

Judith Olans Brown, Phyllis Tropper Baumann, and Elaine Millar Melnick

Recent court decisions concerning job discrimination against women have given support to the principle of "equal pay for work of comparable value." After defining "comparable worth," the authors contend that the necessity for job comparison and evaluation poses no real problem. They then examine and rebut three common arguments against comparable worth: first, that the male-female wage gap is not due to discrimination; second, that it is an attempt to compare "apples and oranges"; and third, that comparable worth schemes would cripple the free market.

A. Definitions: The Heart of the Debate

"Comparable worth" means that workers, regardless of their sex, should earn equal pay for work of comparable value to their common employer. Imprecise use of the phrase hinders meaningful discussion. Comparable worth is equated indiscriminately with comparable work, work of equal worth, work of equal value, or pay equity; however, these terms are not synonymous. Comparable worth theory addresses wage inequities that are associated with job segregation. The basic premise of comparable worth theory is that women should be able to substantiate a claim for equal wages by showing that their jobs and those of male workers are of equal value to their common employer. The doctrine allows comparison of jobs which are different but which require comparable skills, effort and responsibility.[1] In other words, this doctrine permits comparison of jobs which do not come within the ambit of the Equal Pay Act requirement of equal pay for jobs which are "substantially equal."

Opponents of comparable worth, however, focus on jobs that are not demonstrably equivalent and where a comparable worth claim is thus not present. Their rhetoric too often sacrifices accuracy

to ideology.[2] In a popular but mistaken example, comparable worth opponents ask why such unrelated workers as nurses (not generally unionized) and truck drivers (highly unionized) should receive the same wages.[3] Opponents also ask why nurses and teamsters, who do not even work for the same employer, should receive the same pay. The response must emphasize that comparable worth cases always involve the same employer. The cases also always involve occupations which, according to a rational standard, are of comparable value to that employer.

The nurse/truck driver example implies that comparable worth requires equal pay for randomly selected job categories simply because the jobs being compared are ordinarily performed by members of one sex. What is really at issue, however, is equal pay for demonstrably equivalent jobs, as measured by either job content or a standard of experience, skill, or responsibility. An appropriate index against which to measure nurses' salaries might be the salaries of hospital sanitarians. Similarly, the appropriate comparable job for a truck driver is one which, although perhaps different in job content, is rated as equivalent in a job evaluation study, or which is capable of being so rated.[4]

Comparable worth doctrine differs from the Equal Pay Act formula in that it permits comparison of jobs which are not substantially similar in content. The Equal Pay Act of 1963 requires equal pay for work of equal skill, effort and responsibility performed under similar working conditions. But the statute requires pay equality only for jobs which are *substantially equal*. If the jobs are relatively equivalent yet not sufficiently similar to meet that standard, no Equal Pay Act violation exists.

[In 1981 the Supreme Court] eliminated the

requirement that Title VII plaintiffs prove the substantial equality of the jobs being compared.[5] . . . All Title VII plaintiffs alleging gender-based discrimination are comparing jobs which may have dissimilar functions but are of comparable value to the common employer.

The question for Title VII plaintiffs invoking comparable worth theory then becomes how to demonstrate that their jobs and those of male workers are of equal value to their common employer. [After the Court's 1981 decision] plaintiffs need not demonstrate job equivalency. Nor does a successful comparable worth claim require proof of undervaluation due to historical discrimination.[6] Instead, comparable worth requires proof that the employer's male and female workers perform work of comparable value and that the female workers are paid less. Such a demonstration necessarily depends upon the evaluation of jobs which are different in content.

B. Job Evaluation: The Red Herring of the Comparable Worth Debate

Job evaluation techniques provide a method for comparing jobs which are dissimilar in content. Job evaluation is a formal procedure which classifies a set of jobs on the basis of their relative value to the employer. Although the courts are uncomfortable with the concept of comparable worth, the technique of job evaluation has been familiar to American industry for decades.[7] Contrary to the claims of comparable worth critics, job evaluation does not require governmental participation. Evaluation merely eliminates resort to guesswork or unsubstantiated assertions of comparability. It provides a way of identifying situations in which wages remain artificially low because of sex, but where men and women are not performing identical or nearly identical operations.

Formal job evaluation originated in the late nineteenth century as part of a generalized expansion of organizational techniques and a restructuring of workplace control systems. Indeed, job evaluation was such a familiar method for comparing jobs that it provided the theoretical underpinning for the Equal Pay Act of 1963.[8] The various evaluation techniques all use similar methods to inject objectivity and equity into pay structures. The first stage requires a formal description of the duties, requirements and working conditions of each job within the unit being evaluated. Next, jobs are evaluated in terms of "worth" to the organization. The outcome of these two processes is a ranking of all jobs in the evaluation unit. The third stage involves setting wage rates for each job in accordance with the evaluation—the higher the ranking, the higher the wages. The job itself, not the worker performing it, is the subject of evaluation.

Any attempt to raise wages on the basis of comparable worth turns on effective use of wage rate, job classification, promotion policy and contractual data. Job evaluations assemble the relevant information in a form useful to employers, employees, and courts. Firmly grounded in existing industrial relations practice, job evaluation itself is hardly controversial. What is new is the use of this practice to address sex discrimination in wages.

Women in diverse occupations have begun to use job evaluation to demonstrate the discriminatory nature of their employers' male/female pay discrepancies.[9] The public rhetoric that characterizes job evaluation as an impossible task of comparing "apples and oranges" merely ignores the factual basis of the technique. The employer has already fashioned a wholly rational hierarchy of "apples and oranges" on the basis of relative worth to the employer. Unfortunately, the mistaken but popular notion of job evaluation has nonetheless prejudiced the courts against evaluation techniques that are essential to plaintiffs' cases.

C. Arguments Against Comparable Worth: The Crux of the Rhetoric

Intense hostility has surrounded the idea of comparable worth. In order to understand this hostility, it is necessary to examine the arguments used by opponents of comparable worth. These arguments involve three related contentions: the male/female earnings gap results, at least in large part, from factors unrelated to discrimination by particular employers; comparable worth analysis is logistically impossible since there is no objective basis for establishing comparisons between different jobs; and, third, pay equity based on comparable worth would cripple the so-called free market.

1. The Non-Discriminatory Nature of the Wage Gap

The argument that the wage gap between men and women results from non-discriminatory factors is clearly expressed in a report by the U.S. Civil Rights Commission. In its findings, the Civil Rights Commission states that:

> The wage gap between female and male earnings in America results, at least in significant part from a variety of things having nothing to do with discrimination by employers, including job expectations resulting from socialization beginning in the home; educational choices of women who anticipate performing child-bearing and child-rearing functions in the family and who wish to prepare for participation in the labor force in a manner which accommodates the performance of those functions, like the desire of women to work in the kinds of jobs which accommodate their family roles and the intermittency of women's labor force participation.

Essentially, one can reduce the Commission's argument to three basic propositions: women choose low-paying jobs because of their sociological predisposition; women make educational choices which lead to low-paying jobs; and the interrupted participation of women in the labor force leads to lower pay.

The first contention is misguided; comparable worth does not raise job *access* issues. Instead, it addresses situations where women who are already employed are paid less for jobs demonstrably similar to those of male co-workers. In comparable worth cases, women are not socialized to hold "easier" jobs: they are paid less for work of equivalent value. While the effect of socialization on job expectations is relevant to a woman's choice to become a nurse rather than a doctor, it does not address why female nurses are paid less than male orderlies or sanitarians at the same hospital. Comparable worth theory addresses inequities subsequent to access. The Commission simply misses the point in arguing that disadvantage results from the victim's choice, based on her own lower expectations.

The second and third contentions reflect the analytical framework used by human capital theorists to account for employment discrimination.[10] The touchstone of human capital theory as an explanation of wage differentials is productivity. Wages are viewed as a return on investments in human capital. The argument proceeds from the premise that individuals make investments in their productive capacity through education and training. These investments have costs, but they also produce returns in the form of higher wages. The male/female wage differential, therefore, merely reflects the different investments that men and women make.

Mincer and Polachek provide the classic formulation of the theory that women's lower wages merely reflect lower investments in human capital.[11] Productivity of men and women arguably differs . . . [due to] differences in education, training, or length of experience. [However] comparable worth theory does not rely on generalized statistical assertions; it requires a demonstration that in a particular case no other factor appears capable of explaining a proven disparity.

2. Comparing "Apples and Oranges"

The second major argument espoused by opponents of comparable worth is that no objective technique exists for comparing jobs that are not identical in content. The Civil Rights Commission contends that in comparable worth litigation job evaluations are inherently subjective and cannot establish jobs' intrinsic worth. Instead, the Commission claims that such studies function only "to establish rational pay-setting policies within an organization, satisfactory to the organization's employees and management."

This objection, though partially valid, goes too far. Although job evaluation is not absolutely objective, it is a well-established technique in American industry for determining relative wage levels. Representatives of business interests successfully sought to incorporate the concepts of job evaluation into the definition of equality in the Equal Pay Act of 1963. They argued that such a course was necessary because the use of job evaluation techniques was so widespread in industry. For example, E. G. Hester, the director of industrial relations research for Corning Glass, told the Senate Committee on Labor and Public Welfare of his company's concern over the proposed equality criteria. According to Mr. Hester, the proposed criteria would require equal pay "for equal work on jobs the performance of which requires equal skills." He asserted that this approach:

... could give a great deal of difficulty to that large part of American industry and business which has relied upon systematic methods of job evaluation for establishment of equitable rate relationships. Such job evaluation plans depend for their reliability upon other factors than skill alone.

Mr. Hester's statement to the Committee included evidence of the extent to which job evaluation was used. He argued that:

With this general acceptance of job evaluation throughout industry on the part of both management and labor, we feel it most desirable that legislation related to the equal-pay principle incorporate in its language, recognition of job evaluation (or job classification) principles that have been developed, accepted, and are in general use.

In arguing for the incorporation of job evaluation principles, Mr. Hester conceded that job evaluation was "not a precise science governed by natural laws" but still lauded it as "a systematic approach to establish relative job order . . ." He pointed out that industries using job evaluation principles had customarily constructed the hierarchy on the basis of "effort, skill, responsibility, and working conditions." The Equal Pay Act incorporates these same four factors.

Even a cursory examination of industrial relations practices demonstrates that business and industry have long used specific techniques to determine the relative wage rates of jobs which are dissimilar in content. While evaluation techniques are not absolutely objective, they are a logical starting point in any meaningful wage determination process. Comparable worth cases do not require an abstract showing of intrinsic value. Instead, plaintiffs' cases turn on proof that the employer's job worth determinations are gender-based. Since comparable worth cases always address alleged discrimination of a particular employer, they compare "pay-setting policies within an organization." The Commission itself admits that this use of job evaluation is "rational."

3. Laissez-Faire Economics and Antidiscrimination Law

The third argument commonly raised against comparable worth is that it requires an unwar-

ranted intrusion into the market. Again, the Civil Rights Commission report provides an example. The Commission notes that: "The setting of wages is not and cannot be divorced from the forces of labor supply and demand. These factors heavily influence the setting of pay in many jobs and play an important role in setting wages for virtually all other jobs." The Commission then argues that there is nothing in the language or legislative history of Title VII to indicate that Congress intended to prevent employers from relying on the operation of the market in setting wages.

Courts have also made this assertion. However, any statute governing the employment relationship must by its very nature interfere with an employer's absolute freedom to determine wages by reference to the market. The enactment of Title VII indicates congressional intent to intervene in the market to further significant policy interests.

Those who argue that comparable worth is an unwarranted interference insist that supply and demand curves create the wage disparity at issue. Thus, comparable worth theory is not a legitimate response to discrimination but rather a specious definition of discrimination. If there is no impermissible discrimination, they argue, there is no social justification for judicial interference with market forces. A recent article called equal pay for work of comparable worth "a fallacious notion that apples are equal to oranges and that prices for both should be the same, even if that means overriding the law of supply and demand."[12] Market forces are the only relevant measure of value.

The argument's proponents would cloak impermissible sex-based discrimination in the putative legality of "market operation." Yet the argument sidesteps the contention of comparable worth proponents that, despite a pay differential, the jobs are equivalent according to a rational standard. Extolling the overriding authority of supply and demand is to ignore the possibility that that "law" conflicts with Title VII, which like other regulatory legislation necessarily interferes with a laissez-faire economy. The market-based argument against comparable worth is nonetheless instructive since it links criticisms of the allegedly spurious nature of comparable worth with antipathy to the remedy—interference with the market—that comparable worth purportedly implies. It is this connection which is critical to an understanding of judicial opinions in the comparable worth area, since judges often defer to the operation of the market.

Notes

1. See, e.g., Newman and Wilson, "Comparable Worth: A Job Inequity By Any Other Name," in *Manual On Pay Equity: Raising Wages for Women's Work* 54 (J. Grune ed. undated) (on file with Harv. C.R.-C.L. L. Rev.).

2. President Reagan even dismissed comparable worth as a "cockamamie idea." Connant & Paine, "A Loss for Comparable Worth," *Newsweek*, Sept. 16, 1985, 36.

3. See, e.g., Krucoff, "Money: The Question of Men, Women, and 'Comparable Worth,'" *Wash. Post*, Nov. 13, 1979, B5, col. 1.

4. The point is not to assert that equal pay *must* be based on similarity of job content, although it may be so based. Jobs which are quite different in content may properly be the basis for an equal pay claim if it can be demonstrated that they are of equal worth. A case brought under the British Equal Pay Act of 1970 provides an illustration. In *Hayward v. Cammell Laird Shipbuilders Ltd.*, IRLR 463 (1984), ICR 71 (1985), a female cook employed in the works cafeteria at the employer's shipyard sought equal pay with men employed as painters, thermal insulation engineers and joiners. An independent expert appointed by the industrial tribunal hearing the claim assessed the various jobs under five factors: physical demands, environmental demands, planning and decisionmaking, skill and knowledge required, and responsibility involved. On the basis of this evaluation he found the jobs to be of equal value.

5. "Respondent's claims of discriminatory undercompensation are not barred by § 703(h) of Title VII merely because respondents do not perform work equal to that of male jail guards." *Gunther*, 452 U.S. at 181.

6. For a discussion of the historic undervaluation of women's jobs, see Blumrosen, "Wage Discrimination, Job Segregation, and Title VII of the Civil Rights Act of 1964," 12 *U. Mich. J.L. Ref.* 397 (1979).

7. See, e.g., *Laffey v. Northwest Airlines*, 567 F.2d 429 (D.C. Cir. 1976), vacating and remanding in part, aff'g in pertinent part, 366 F. Supp. 763 (D.D.C. 1973), cert. denied, 434 U.S. 1080 (1978) (Court of Appeals agreeing with District Court judge who found, after testimony from expert witnesses on job evaluation presented by both plaintiff and defendant, that "pursers" and "stewardesses" performed substantially equal work even though jobs had different titles, descriptions and responsibilities).

8. The "effort, skill, responsibility and working conditions" criteria which the Equal Pay Act uses to determine whether jobs are equal were derived from then-current job evaluation systems.

9. See American Federation of State, County, and Municipal Employees, AFL-CIO (AFSCME), *Guide to Comparable Worth, in Pay Equity: A Union Issue for the 1980's* 11–12 (1980). Unions representing women workers have begun to use evaluation techniques to demonstrate the extent to which women's work is undervalued and underpaid. AFSCME bargained for job evaluation studies in San Jose, California, Lane County, Oregon, and statewide in Minnesota, Wisconsin, and Michigan. *Manual on Pay Equity: Raising Wages for Women's Work* 152–53 (J. Grune ed. undated) (on file with Harv. C.R.-C.L. L. Rev.). The trend has been especially pronounced in the public sector where 100 municipalities are now re-evaluating their job classification systems. See Noble, "Comparable Worth: How It's Figured," *New York Times*, Feb. 27, 1985, p. C7, col. 1.

10. See Amsden, "Introduction," in *The Economics of Women and Work* 13–18 (A. Amsden ed. 1980).

11. See Mincer & Polachek, "Family Investments in Human Capital: Earnings of Women," 82 *J. Pol. Econ.* 76 (1974) (supp.).

12. Smith, "The EEOC's Bold Foray into Job Evaluation," *Fortune*, Sept. 11, 1978, 58. The author goes on to talk of the "enormous inflationary effect" of comparable worth, which "at the extreme [would] raise the aggregate pay of the county's 27.3 million full-time working women high enough . . . [to] add a staggering $150 billion a year to civilian payrolls." *Id*. at 59. The statement is typical of the hyperbole on which comparable worth arguments often are based. The author fails to acknowledge that no comparable worth advocate has suggested that all American working women will benefit from the implementation of the doctrine—only those doing work of demonstrably comparable value to that of a male worker of the same employer.

Review and Discussion Questions

1. How does comparable worth doctrine differ from what is required by the Equal Pay Act?

2. Can job evaluation techniques provide a satisfactory method for comparing jobs that are dissimilar in content? Are such methods better than the market?

3. Assess Brown, Baumann, and Melnick's critique of the three common arguments against comparable worth. Do you find them convincing?

4. Are there other arguments against comparable worth that Brown, Baumann, and Melnick have overlooked?

5. In your view, how strong is the overall case for comparable worth?

Sexual Harassment

Larry May and John C. Hughes

May and Hughes argue that sexual harassment on the job is not a private matter between two individuals, but a social problem. Sexual threats are immoral because of their coercive nature; they also contribute to a pattern of discrimination against women. When an employee is promised some benefit in exchange for sexual favors but is not threatened, the harm involved is more difficult to identify. The authors argue, though, that sexual offers made by male employers to female employees are closer to threats than to ordinary offers and are implicitly coercive.

A number of recent lawsuits filed under Title VII of the 1964 Civil Rights Act have brought the problem of sexual harassment into the footlights of contemporary political and moral discussion.[1] Is sexual harassment a purely private matter between two individuals, or is it a social problem? If sexual harassment is to be treated as something more than a purely personal dispute, how do we distinguish the social problem from benevolent forms of social interaction between members of a work hierarchy? We will argue here that sexual harassment of women workers is a public issue because it is inherently coercive, regardless of whether it takes the form of a threat for noncompliance, or of a reward for compliance. We will further argue that the harm of harassment is felt beyond the individuals immediately involved because it contributes to a pervasive pattern of discrimination and exploitation based on sex.

The term *sexual harassment* refers to the intimidation of persons in subordinate positions by those holding power and authority over them in order to exact sexual favors that would ordinarily not have been granted. Sexual harassment of male subordinates by female superiors is conceivable, and probably occurs, albeit infrequently. Positions of authority are more likely to be occupied by males, while women are predominantly relegated to positions of subservience and dependency. Furthermore, strong cultural patterns induce female sexual passivity and acquiescence to male initiative.[2] These factors combine to produce a dominant pattern of male harassment of females. However, it might bear reflecting that the poisoning of the work environment that may result from sexual intimidation may affect members of both sexes, so that sexual harassment should be viewed as more than merely a women's issue.

Truly systematic empirical studies of the incidence of sexual harassment are yet to be done. Most of the studies by social scientists to date suffer from severe methodological flaws. Nevertheless, they reveal a pattern of sexual harassment of working women that is too strong to ignore. Perhaps the most telling study is that conducted by Peggy Crull.[3] Working with a self-selected sample, Crull sought to discern the nature, extent, and effects of sexual harassment on women, as well as the predominant relationship between harasser and victim. Her data show the victims of harassment to be likely to occupy low-status and low-paying positions of economic vulnerability. Fifty-three percent of the victims on her survey were clerical workers (including secretaries, typists, and general office help), with another 15 percent occupying service positions (waitresses, hospital aids, and the like).

The most frequent pattern involved verbal harassment, but over half of Crull's respondents also reported incidents of physical harassment that persisted over time despite their protestations, with 39 percent reporting fondling. Twelve percent claimed to have been physically restrained during incidents of sexual harassment.

What is perhaps most significant in Crull's finding is that 79 percent of the men involved held power to fire or promote the victim, while only 16 percent threatened an explicit employment sanction. Seventy-nine percent of the victims complained about the incident to the harasser or to someone in authority (often though not always the same person), but in only 9 percent of the cases did the behavior stop. Forty-nine percent of the women who complained felt their claims were not taken seriously, while 26 percent experienced retaliation for their complaints. Crull also discovered that whether the victim complained or not, her experience of harassment placed her job in jeopardy. A full 24 percent of Crull's respondents were soon fired, while another 42 percent were pressured into resigning by the intolerable working conditions that resulted from the behavior of their supervisors. If this figure is not striking enough, 83 percent claimed the harassment interfered in some way with their job performance. Indeed, 96 percent reported symptoms of emotional stress, with 63 percent reporting symptoms of physical stress. Twelve percent sought some form of therapeutic help in dealing with these symptoms. Faced with such results, it seems fair to say that sexual harassment is a problem that must be taken seriously.

I

Like most interpersonal transactions, sexual advances may take many forms. There is of course the sincere proposal, motivated by genuine feeling for another, made in a context of mutual respect for the other's autonomy and dignity. Such offers are possible between members of a work hierarchy, but are of no concern here. Rather, we are interested in advances that take the following forms: (1) Sexual threat: "If you don't provide a sexual benefit, I will punish you by withholding a promotion or a raise that would otherwise be due, or ultimately fire you." (2) Sexual offer: "If you provide a sexual benefit, I will reward you with a promotion

or a raise that would otherwise not be due." There are also sexual harassment situations that are merely annoying, but without demonstrable sanction or reward. It is worth noting at the outset that all three forms of sexual harassment have been proscribed under recently promulgated Equal Employment Opportunity Commission guidelines implementing Title VII.[4]

Sexual harassment in the form of threats is coercive behavior that forces the employee to accept a course of conduct she wouldn't otherwise accept. What is wrong with this? Why can't she simply resist the threats and remain as before? Viewed in the abstract, one can seemingly resist threats, for unlike physical restraint, threatening does not completely deny individual choice over her alternatives. A person who is physically restrained is literally no longer in control of her own life. The victim is no longer reaching decisions of her own and autonomously carrying them out. Threats do not have this dramatic effect on a person's autonomy. Rather, the effect of the threat is that the recipient of a threat is much less inclined to act as she would have absent the threat—generally out of fear. Fear is the calculation of expected harm and the decision to avoid it. Reasonably prudent individuals will not, without a sufficiently expected possibility of gain, risk harm. The first thing wrong with sexual threats then is that, for the reasonable person, it now takes a very good reason to resist the threat, whereas no such strength of reasoning was required before to resist a sexual advance.

Sexual threats are coercive because they worsen the objective situation the employee finds herself in. To examine this claim, consider her situation before and after the threat has been made (preproposition stage and postproposition stage).[5] In the preproposition stage, a secretary, for example, is judged by standards of efficiency to determine whether she should be allowed to retain her job. She would naturally view her employer as having power over her, but only in the rather limited domain concerning the job-related functions she performs. Her personal life would be her own. She could choose her own social relationships, without fear that these decisions might adversely affect her job. In the postproposition stage, she can no longer remain employed under the same conditions while not choosing to have relations with her employer. Further, the efficient performance of job-related functions is no longer sufficient for the retention of her job. She can no longer look to her supervisor as one who exercises power merely over the performance of her office duties. He now wields power over a part of her personal life. This may help to explain Crull's finding that many women leave their jobs after such a proposition has been tendered. They cannot simply go on as before, for their new situation is correctly perceived as worse than the old situation.

It is the worsening of the woman's situation after the threat has been made that contributes to the likelihood of her acquiescence to the threat. The perception of job insecurity created by the threat can only be alleviated by her acceptance of the sexual proposition. But what of the woman who prefers to have a sexual relationship with her employer than not to do so? Has this woman also been made objectively worse off than she was before the threat occurred? We contend that she has, for before the threat was made she could pursue her preference without feeling forced to do so. If the liaison developed and then turned sour, she could quit the relationship and not so clearly risk a worsening of her employment situation. Now, however, her continued job success might be held ransom to the continued sexual demands of her employer. This also may adversely affect other women in the business organization. What the employer has done is to establish a precedent for employment decisions based upon the stereotype that values women for their sexuality rather than for their job skills. This has a discriminatory impact on women individually and as a group. Focusing on this effect will shed some light on the harm of both sexual threats and sexual offers.

II

Consider the following case.[6] Barnes was hired as an administrative assistant by the director of a federal agency. In a preemployment interview, the director, a male, promised to promote Barnes, a female, within ninety days. Shortly after beginning her job, (1) the director repeatedly asked her for a date after work hours, even though she consistently refused; (2) made repeated remarks to her that were sexual in nature; and (3) repeatedly told her that if she did not cooperate with him by engaging in sexual relations, her employment status would be affected. After consistently rebuffing him, she finally told him she wished for their relationship to remain a strictly professional one. Thereafter the director, sometimes in concert with others, began a campaign to belittle and demean her within the office. Subsequently she was stripped of most of her job duties, culminating in the eventual abolition of her job. Barnes filed suit, claiming that these actions would not have occurred but for the fact that she was a woman.

Under Title VII, it is now widely accepted that the kind of sexual threat illustrated by this case is an instance of sex discrimination in employment.[7] Such threats treat women differently than men in employment contexts even though gender is not a relevantly applicable category for making employment-related decisions. The underlying principle here is that like persons should be treated alike. Unless there are relevant differences among persons, it is harmful to disadvantage one particular class of persons. In the normal course of events, male employees are not threatened sexually by employers or supervisors. The threats disadvantage a woman in that an additional requirement is placed in her path for successful job retention, one not placed in the path of male employees. When persons who are otherwise similarly situated are distinguished on the basis of their sex, and rewards or burdens are apportioned according to these gender-based classifications, illegal sex discrimination has occurred. Applying this theory of discrimination to Barnes' complaint, the federal appellate court ruled:

> So it was, by her version, that retention of her job was conditioned upon submission to sexual relations—an exaction which the supervisor would not have made of any male. It is much too late in the day to contend that Title VII does not outlaw terms of employment for women which differ appreciably from those set for men and which are not genuinely and reasonably related to the performance on the job. . . . Put another way, she became the target of her superior's sexual desires because she was a woman and was asked to bow to demands as the price for holding her job.[8]

There is a second way in which this behavior might be viewed as discriminatory. Sexual threats also contribute to a pervasive pattern of disadvantaged treatment of women as a group. Under this approach, the harm is not viewed as resulting from the arbitrary and unfair use of gender as a criterion for employment decisions. Rather, emphasis is on the effect the classification has of continuing the subordination of women as a group. The harm results regardless of whether the specific incident could be given an employment rationale or not. Sexual harassment perpetuates sex discrimination, and illustrates the harm that occurs for members of a group that have historically been disadvantaged. This theory was applied to sexual harassment in another federal lawsuit, *Tomkins v. Public Service Gas and Electric Co.*[9] The plaintiff's lawyers argued that employer tolerance of sexual harassment and its pattern of reprisals had a disparate impact upon women as an already disadvantaged group and was inherently degrading to all women.

Sexual threats are harmful to the individual woman because she is coerced and treated unfairly by her employer, disadvantaging her for no good reason. Beyond this, such practices further contribute to a pervasive pattern of disadvantaged status for her and all women in society. The sexual stereotyping makes it less likely, and sometimes impossible, that women will be treated on the basis of job efficiency, intelligence, or administrative skill. These women must now compete on a very different level, and in the case where sexual threats are common or at least accepted, this level is clearly inferior to that occupied by men. The few male employees who are harassed in the workplace suffer the first harm but not the second. We shall next show that there are also two harms of sexual offers in employment, only one of which can also be said to befall men.

III

The harm of sexual offers is much more difficult to identity and analyze. Indeed, some may even see sexual offers as contributing to a differentiation based on sex that advantages rather than disadvantages women, individually and as a group. After all, males cannot normally gain promotions by engaging in sexual relations with their employers. We shall argue, on the contrary, that a sexual offer disadvantages the woman employee by changing the work environment so that she is viewed by others, and may come to view herself, less in terms of her work productivity and more in terms of her sexual allure. This change, like the threat, makes it unlikely that she can return to the preproposition stage even though she might prefer to do so. Furthermore, to offset her diminished status and to protect against later retaliation, a prudent woman would feel that she must accept the offer. Here, sexual offers resemble the coercive threat. The specific harm to women becomes clearer when one looks at the group impact of sexual offers in employment. Women are already more economically vulnerable and socially passive than men. When sexual offers are tendered, exploitation of a woman employee is accomplished by taking advantage of a preexisting vulnerability males generally do not share.

Seduction accomplished through sexual offers and coercive threats blend together most clearly in the mixed case of the sexual offer of a promotion with the lurking threat of retaliation if the offer is turned down. Both combine together to compel the woman to engage in sexual relations with her employer. Gifts are so rare in economic matters that it is best to be suspicious of all offers and to look for their hidden costs. As Crull's study showed, only 16 percent of those harassed were explicitly threatened. Yet 24 percent were fired, and another 42 percent reported that they were forced to resign. This evidence leads us to surmise that sexual offers often contain veiled threats and are for that reason coercive.

Why are the clearly mixed cases, where there is both an offer and a (sometimes only implied) threat, coercive rather than noncoercive? To return to our initial discussion, why is it that one is made worse off by the existence of these proposals? In one sense they enable women to do things they couldn't otherwise do, namely, get a promotion that they did not deserve, thus seeming to be noncoercive. On the other hand, if the woman prefers not having sexual relations with her employer (while retaining her job) to having sexual relations with him (with ensuing promotion), then it is predominantly a threat and more clearly coercive. The best reason for not preferring the postproposition stage is that she is then made worse off if she rejects the proposition, and if she accepts, she nonetheless risks future harm or retaliation. This latter condition is also true for more straightforward offers, as we shall now show.

A number of contemporary philosophers have argued that offers place people in truly advantageous positions, for they can always be turned down with the ensuing return to the preoffer stage.[10] In the case of sexual offers, however, the mere proposal of a promotion in exchange for sexual relations changes the work environment. Once sexual relations are seriously proposed as a sufficient condition for employment success, the woman realizes that this male employer sees her (and will probably continue to see her) as a sex object as well as an employee. A prudent woman will henceforth worry that she is not being regarded as an employee who simply happens to be a woman, but rather as a woman made more vulnerable by the fact that she happens to be an employee. If she accepts the offer, she lends credence to the stereotype, and because of this, it is more likely that she may experience future offers or even threats. She would thus worry about her ability to achieve on the basis of her work-related merits. If she rejects the offer, she would still worry about her employer's attitude toward her status as a worker. Furthermore, because of the volatility of sexual feelings, these offers cannot be turned down without the risk of offending or alienating one's employer, something any employee would wish to avoid. She may reasonably conclude from these two considerations that neither postoffer alternative is desirable. This is one of the hidden costs of sexual offers in the workplace.

It may be claimed that such environmental changes are no different for men who can also be the objects of sexual offers in the workplace. One needs to show that the changed environment is worse for those who are women. Sexual employment offers take advantage of unequal power relations that exist between employer and employee so as to force a particular outcome further benefitting those who are already in advantageous positions. But beyond this, sexual offers are doubly exploitative for female employees, because women already enter the employment arena from a position of vulnerability. As we have indicated, this is true because of the history of their economic powerlessness and because of their culturally ingrained passivity and acquiescence in the face of male initiatives. Women enter the employment arena much more ripe for coercion than their male colleagues. Thus, women are more likely to be harmed by these offers.

This may partially explain Crull's finding that women frequently experience extreme stress and sometimes even require professional therapy when harassed in this way. Men are not similarly harmed by sexual offers because they do not have the same history of sexual exploitation. Men are likely to regard such seductive offers either humorously or as insults to be aggressively combatted, while women have been socialized to be passive rather than combative in such situations. The woman to whom the offer is made becomes less sure of her real abilities by virtue of the proposal itself. This self-denigrating response to an unwelcomed proposal is a vestige of women's history of subordination. Even without the veiled threat, sexual offers can cause women to act in ways they would not choose to act otherwise. To this extent, these sexual offers are coercive.

Most offers are not coercive because one would prefer to have the offer made. This is because one of the postoffer alternatives (rejecting the offer) is equivalent to the preoffer alternative (having no offer at all). Sexual offers made by male employers to female employees are different, however, because they more closely resemble threats than ordinary offers.[11] As we have shown, the preoffer alternative—being employed, unpromoted, yet able to obtain promotion according to one's merits—is different from, and preferable to, either of the postoffer alternatives—accepting the promotion, and having sexual relations with her employer, with all of its negative consequences, or rejecting the offer of promotion, but with the risk that the promotion may now prove unobtainable on the basis of merit. By blocking a return to the more preferable preoffer alternative, the male employer has acted similarly to the employer who uses sexual threats. The woman is forced to choose between two undesirable alternatives because she cannot have what she would have chosen before the proposal was made. Stressing these hidden costs, which are much greater for women than for men, exposes the coercive element inherent in sexual offers as well as in sexual threats. We are thus led to conclude that both of these employment practices are harmful to women and recently were properly proscribed by the U.S. Equal Employment Opportunity Commission.

Notes

1. For a careful analysis of these cases we recommend Catherine MacKinnon's book, *Sexual Harassment of Working Women* (New Haven, Conn.: Yale University Press, 1979).

2. For the historical evidence, see William Chaffe, *Women and Equality* (New York: Oxford University Press, 1977). For the sociological evidence, see J. R. Feagin and C. B. Feagin, *Discrimination American Style* (Englewood Cliffs, N.J.: Prentice-Hall, 1978).

3. Peggy Crull, "The Impact of Sexual Harassment on the Job: A Profile of the Experiences of 92 Women," *Sexuality in Organizations*, ed. D. A. Neugarten and J. M. Shafritz (Oak Park, Ill.: Moore Publishing Co., 1980), 67–72.

4. 45 Fed. Reg. 74, 677 (1980); 29 C.F.R. 1604.11 (a).

5. We proceed from the general analysis developed by Robert Nozick, "Coercion," *Philosophy, Science and Method*, ed. Morgenbesser, Suppes, and White (New York: St. Martin's Press, 1969). A very large literature has grown out of this analysis. We recommend the essays by Bernard Gert, Michael Bayles, and especially Virginia Held, collected in *NOMOS XIV: Coercion* (New York: Lieber Atherton, 1973).

6. Summary of the Facts for *Barnes v. Costel*, 561 F.2d 984 (D.C. Cir. 1977).

7. For more elaboration, see Section II of our essay, "Sexual Harassment," *Social Theory and Practice* (1980), 256–68.

8. 561 F.2d 989, 990, 992 n. 68 (D.C. Cir. 1977).

9. 568 F.2d 1044 (3rd Cir. 1977).

10. See Michael Bayles, "Coercive Offers and Public Benefits," *The Personalist*, vol. 55 (1974); Donald Vandeveer, "Coercion, Seduction and Rights," *The Personalist*, vol. 58 (1977); and Nozick, "Coercion," among others.

11. Some other employment offers have been seen as coercive also. See David Zimmerman, "Coercive Wage Offers," *Philosophy and Public Affairs*, vol. 10 (1981).

Review and Discussion Questions

1. Why do May and Hughes maintain that sexual harassment is a form of discrimination?

2. Are sexual offers by an employer to an employee (where no threat is involved) wrong? Do you think such sexual offers are really a form of sexual harassment?

3. Assess May and Hughes's contention that women are more likely than men to be harmed by sexual offers. Does their position lead to a "double standard"?

4. May and Hughes's definition of sexual harassment seems to be narrower than that presented in the text. How do you think sexual harassment is best defined?

For Further Reading

There is an extensive literature on affirmative action. The following three volumes, which provide a selection of philosophical essays both for and against it, are a good place to start: **Marshall Cohen, Thomas Nagel**, and **Thomas Scanlon**, eds., *Equality and Preferential Treatment* (Princeton, N.J.: Princeton University Press, 1976); **Joseph R. DesJardins** and **John J. McCall**, eds., *Contemporary Issues in Business Ethics* (Belmont, Calif.: Wadsworth, 1985); and **Richard Wasserstrom**, ed., *Today's Moral Problems*, 3rd ed. (New York: Macmillan, 1985).

For an introduction to some of the issues surrounding comparable worth, see **Laurie Shrage**, "Some Implications of Comparable Worth," *Social Theory and Practice* 13 (Spring 1987).

Daniel R. Fischel and **Edward R. Lazear**'s challenging essay, "Comparable Worth and Discrimination in Labor Markets," *The University of Chicago Law Review* 53 (Spring 1986), is followed by a reply by **Mary E. Becker** and a rejoinder to Becker by Fischel and Lazear. It is a thorough and intelligent debate.

PART IV

BUSINESS AND SOCIETY

CHAPTER 9

CONSUMERS

The "Marlboro man" has long mesmerized people around the world, and few can deny the glamor of the ruggedly good-looking Marlboro cowboy, with boots, hat, chaps— and, of course, a cigarette in his mouth. Product of one of the most successful advertising campaigns in history, the "Marlboro man" revolutionized the image of Marlboro cigarettes, making it a top-selling brand year in, year out. Few people remember, though, that the actor who originally portrayed the Marlboro man died of lung cancer as a result of smoking.

Everybody, of course, knows that smoking is hazardous to one's health. Although the percentage of Americans that smoke is dropping, the absolute number of smokers—and smoking's death toll—remains as high as ever. According to figures released in 1987 by the federal Center for Disease Control, smoking remains the leading cause of preventable deaths and is responsible for 16 percent of deaths overall.[1] Hardly any consumer good compares to cigarettes in terms of individual injury and social costs.

In May 1986 the American Medical Association proposed that the federal government ban all promotion and advertising of cigarettes. Meanwhile, waves of lawsuits continue to crash against the tobacco industry. Cigarette smokers are going to court and suing tobacco companies for injuries allegedly caused by their deadly habit. Despite the warning labels that have been required since 1966, many smokers—or their estates—contend that they were addicted and couldn't stop. They have also produced evidence that the tobacco companies suppressed research showing that cigarette smoke contains carcinogens. If the smokers win, cigarette manufacturers may be held accountable for an estimated $80 billion a year in losses related to smoking. And cigarette prices may jump to three dollars a pack—thus reducing the numbers of smokers and saving millions from premature death.[2]

Cigarettes are an especially dangerous product, and their manufacture, marketing, advertising, and sale raise in an acute form a number of questions that are relevant to the consumer issues of this chapter. For instance, what responsibility to consumers do companies have that sell potentially or (in the case of cigarettes) inherently dangerous products? To what extent do manufacturers abuse advertising? How should we decide what is or is not deceptive advertising? Can advertisements create or at least stimulate desires for products that consumers would not otherwise want or would not otherwise want as much? How, if at all, should advertising be restricted?

What about possibly deceptive labeling and packaging? Are consumers sufficiently well informed about the products they buy? How far should we go in monitoring the claims of advertisers, in regulating the packaging and labeling of products, and in upholding set standards of reliability and safety? In a market-oriented economic system, how do we balance the interests of business with the rights of consumers? How do we promote social well-being while still respecting the choices of individuals?

These are among the issues probed in this chapter. In particular we look at the following:

1. Product safety—the legal and moral responsibilities of manufacturers, and the pros and cons of government regulations designed to protect us.

2. The responsibilities of business to consumers in the areas of product quality, prices, labeling, and packaging.

3. Deceptive and morally questionable techniques used in advertising.

4. The choice between the ''reasonable'' consumer and ''ignorant'' consumer standards as the basis for identifying deceptive advertisements.

5. Advertising and children.

6. The debate over the social desirability of advertising in general—is it a positive feature of our economic system? Does it manipulate, or merely respond to, the needs of the consumer?

PRODUCT SAFETY

Business's responsibility for understanding and providing for consumer needs derives from the fact that citizen-consumers are completely dependent on business to satisfy their needs. This dependence is particularly true in our highly technological society, characterized as it is by a complex economy, intense specialization, and urban concentration. Contrast these conditions with those prevailing in the United States when the country was primarily agrarian, composed of people who could satisfy most of their own needs. In those times one had little difficulty practicing the virtues of self-reliance, independence, and rugged individualism in providing for oneself and one's family.

Today, however, we find ourselves parts of an economic and social network of interdependency. More and more we rely on others to provide the wherewithal for our survival and prosperity. We no longer make our own clothing, produce our own food, provide our own transportation, manufacture our own tools, or construct our own homes.

The increasing complexity of today's economy and the growing dependence of consumers on business for their survival and enrichment have heightened business's responsibilities to consumers. This is particularly true in the area of product safety. From toys to tools, consumers use products believing that they won't be harmed or injured by them. Since consumers are not in a position of technical expertise to judge the sophisticated products that are necessary for contemporary life, they must rely primarily on the conscionable efforts of business to ensure consumer safety. This extreme dependency underscores business's obligations in the area of consumer safety.

Unfortunately, statistics indicate that the faith consumers must place in the manufacturers of products to ensure consumer safety is often misplaced. Over 20 million Americans per year require medical treatment from product-related accidents. Of these persons, 110,000 are permanently disabled and 30,000 die; in addition, roughly $5.5 billion is lost to the economy.[3]

The Legal Liability of Manufacturers

If you are injured by a defective product, then you can sue the manufacturer of that product. We take this legal fact for granted, but it wasn't always so. Before the famous case of *MacPherson v. Buick Motor Car* in 1916, injured consumers could only recover damages from the retailer of the defective product—that is, from the party with whom they had actually done business. That made sense in an older day of small-scale, local capitalism. If the shoes you bought from the local shoemaker were defective, then your complaint was against him. By contrast, when a wheel fell off MacPherson's Buick, the firm he had bought the Buick from hadn't actually made it.

Legal policy before *MacPherson* reflected a view of manufacturer's liability which based that liability on the contractual relationship between the producer and the consumer. Their contractual relationship is simply the sale, that is, the exchange of money for a commodity of a certain description. That contractual relationship, though, is an important source of moral and legal responsibilities for the producer. The contractual relationship obligates business firms to provide consumers with a product that lives up to the claims that the firm makes about the product. Those claims form the basis of the customers' expectations about what they are buying and lead them to enter into the contract in the first place. The question in *MacPherson*, though, was whether a manufacturer's liability for defective products was limited to those with whom it had a direct contractual relationship.

The New York Court of Appeals' *MacPherson* decision recognized the twentieth-century economic reality of large manufacturing concerns and national systems of product distribution. Among other things, local retailers are not as likely as large manufaturers to be able to bear financial responsibility for defective products that injure others. One can also see the court in *MacPherson* moving to a "due care" theory of the manufacturer's duties to consumers. "Due care" is the idea that consumers and sellers do not meet as equals and that the consumer's interests are particularly vulnerable to being harmed by the manufac-

turer, who has a knowledge and an expertise that the consumer does not have.[4] MacPherson, for instance, was in no position to have discovered, or to have known about, the defective wheel before the Buick was purchased. According to the "due care" view, then, manufacturers have an obligation, above and beyond any contract, to exercise due care to prevent the consumer from being injured by defective products.

As an emphasis on "due care" spread, legal policy moved decisively beyond the old doctrine of *caveat emptor*, which was on its last legs by the time of *MacPherson* anyway. *Caveat emptor* means "let the buyer beware," and today we associate it with an era of patent medicines and outrageously false product claims. Although legally the doctrine of "let the buyer beware" was never upheld across the board, it still symbolized a period in which the law put a greater responsibility on consumers themselves to accept the consequences of their product choices.

Consumers were held to the ideal of being knowledgeable, shrewd, and skeptical. It was their free choice whether to buy a certain product. Accordingly, they were expected to take the claims of manufacturers and salespersons with a grain of salt, to inspect any potential purchase carefully, to rely on their own judgment, and to accept any ill results of their decision to use a given product. In the first part of the twentieth century, though, the courts repudiated this doctrine, largely on grounds of its unrealistic assumptions about consumer knowledge, competence, and behavior.

Despite *MacPherson*'s support for the "due care" theory and for a broader view of manufacturer's liability, the case still left the burden on the injured consumer to prove that the manufacturer had been negligent. Not only might such an assertion be hard to prove, but also a product might be dangerously defective despite the manufacturer having taken reasonable steps to avoid such a defect.

Two important cases changed that. In the

1960 New Jersey case *Henningsen v. Bloomfield Motors* and in the 1963 California case *Greenman v. Yuba Power Products*, injured consumers were awarded damages without their having to prove that the manufacturers of the defective products were negligent. Consumers, the courts ruled, have a right to expect that the products they purchase are reasonably safe when used in the intended way. On the basis of these cases, and hundreds of subsequent cases, the "strict liability" approach to product safety has come to dominate legal thinking.

Strict products liability is the doctrine that the seller of a product has legal responsibilities to compensate the user of that product for injuries suffered due to a defective aspect of the product, even though the seller has not been negligent in permitting that defect to occur.[5] For example, a judgment for the recovery of damages could conceivably be won even if the manufacturer adhered to strict quality-control procedures that demanded that a high sample proportion of its products undergo safety tests.[6] Strict liability, however, is not absolute liability. The manufacturer is not responsible for any injury whatsoever that might befall the consumer. The product must be defective, and the consumer always has the responsibility to exercise care.

Strict products liability is not without its critics, however. They contend that the doctrine is unfair. If a firm has exercised "due care" and taken reasonable precautions to avoid or eliminate foreseeable dangerous defects, they argue, then it should not be held liable for defects that are not its "fault," that is, for defects that happen despite its best efforts to guard against them. To hold the firm liable, anyway, seems unjust.

The argument for strict liability is basically utilitarian. Its advocates contend, first, that only such a policy leads firms to bend over backwards to guarantee product safety. Since they know that they will be held liable for injurious defects no matter what, then they will make every effort to enhance safety.

Second, proponents of strict liability contend that the manufacturer is best able to bear the cost of injuries due to defects. Naturally, firms raise the cost of their products to cover their legal costs (or pay for liability insurance). Defenders of strict liability do not disapprove of this. They see it rather as a perfectly reasonable way of spreading the cost of injuries among all the consumers of the product, rather than letting it fall on a single individual—a kind of insurance scheme.

Protecting the Public

The developments and doctrines just discussed set the general legal framework within which manufacturers must operate. In addition, a number of government agencies are involved in regulating product safety. Congress created one of the most important of these in 1972 when it passed the Consumer Products Safety Act. This act empowers the Consumer Products Safety Commission to "protect the public against unreasonable risks of injury associated with consumer products." The five member commission sets standards for products, bans products presenting undue risk of injury, and in general polices the entire consumer-product marketing process from manufacture to final sale.[7]

The commission aids consumers in evaluating product safety, develops uniform standards, gathers data, conducts research, and coordinates local, state, and federal product safety laws and enforcement. The commission's jurisdiction extends to more than 10,000 products, and it has the power to require recalls, public warnings, and refunds. Exceptionally risky products can, by court order, be seized and condemned. Rather than stressing punitive action, though, the commission's emphasis is on developing new standards and redesigning products to accommodate possible consumer misuse.[8] It is less concerned with assigning liability than with avoiding injuries in the first place.

Despite the obvious benefits to the public

of safety regulations, critics are worried about the economic costs, as new standards add millions of dollars to the cumulative price tag of goods like power lawn mowers. Recalls, too, are expensive. General Motors had to spend $3.5 million for postage alone to notify by certified mail, as required by law, the 6.5 million owners of cars with questionable engine mounts. The cost to Panasonic to recall and repair 280,000 television sets, as ordered by the commission because of harmful radiation emission, was probably equal to the company's profits in the United States for several years.[9]

Safety regulations, critics charge, prevent individuals from choosing to purchase a riskier, though less expensive, product. Take the notorious Ford Pinto with its unsafe gas tank for example. In 1978, after all the negative publicity, scores of lawsuits, and the trial of Ford Motor Company for reckless homicide, the sale of Pintos fell dramatically. Consumers preferred a safer car for comparable money. The state of Oregon took all the Pintos out of its fleet and sold them. At least one dealer involved in selling turned-in Pintos, however, reported brisk sales at their low, second-hand price.[10] These consumers were willing to accept the risks of a Pinto, if the price was right.

Economists worry that preventing individuals from balancing safety against price can be inefficient. Philosophers have the different worry that we are interfering with people's freedom of choice. Take automobile safety, again. We know that small cars are more dangerous than large cars in that people in small cars are less likely to survive accidents. Bigger, safer cars are more expensive, however, and many would prefer to spend less on their cars, despite the increased risk. If we only allowed cars to be sold that were as safe as, say, a Mercedes, then there would be fewer deaths on the highways. There would also be fewer people who could afford cars.

Here we touch on the larger controversy over *legal paternalism*, which is the doctrine that the law may justifiably be used to restrict the freedom of individuals for their own good. No one doubts that the law justifiably restricts people from harming other people, but a sizable number of moral theorists deny that it should do so simply to prevent people from running a risk that affects only themselves. Requiring your car to have brakes protects others; without brakes, you are more likely to run over a pedestrian. On the other hand, requiring you to wear a seat belt when you drive affects only you. Antipaternalists would protest that your being forced to wear a seat belt despite your wishes fails to respect your moral autonomy. Nonetheless, the twentieth century has seen a growing number of paternalistic laws.

Paternalism is a large issue, and we can't do justice to it here. Relevant to safety regulations, though, three comments are in order. First, the safety of some products or some features of products (like a car's brakes) affects not just the consumer who purchases the product, but third parties as well. Regulating these products or product features can be defended on nonpaternalistic grounds. Second, antipaternalism gains plausibility from the view that individuals know their own interests better than anyone else and that they are fully informed and able to advance those interests. But in the increasingly complex consumer world, this assumption is often doubtful. Where citizens lack knowledge and are unable to make intelligent safety judgments and comparisons, they may find it in their collective self-interest to set minimal safety standards. This is particularly true in cases where few, if any, reasonable persons would want a product that did not satisfy those standards.

Finally, the controversy over legal paternalism pits the values of individual freedom and autonomy, on the one hand, against social welfare on the other. Requiring people to wear seat belts may infringe the former, but it saves thousands of lives each year. We may simply have to acknowledge that clash of values and be willing to make trade-offs. This doesn't imply a defense of paternalism across the board. Arguably, there are paternalistic regulations that infringe autonomy more than do laws about seat belts, but yet which bring less gain in social welfare. In the end, one may have to examine paternalistic product safety legislation case by case and try to weigh the conflicting values and likely results.

How Effective Is Regulation?

There is no doubt that in some cases regulation does interfere with rather than safeguard consumer interests. Take, for example, the area of drug regulation. In the late 60s the FDA, with considerable fanfare, banned from the market the sweetener cyclamate. Several years later, when scientific bodies around the world determined that cyclamate was safe, Abbott Laboratories, makers of cyclamate, asked the FDA to rescind the ban. The FDA refused, so Abbott petitioned the court to take jurisdiction over the cyclamate proceedings, enjoin the FDA from further administrative action, and, given the evidence, override the agency and approve the sale of cyclamate. The court ruled that Abbott could proceed with what in law is called "discovery."

Emboldened with subpoena power, Abbott discovered compelling evidence of abuse of both regulatory process and scientific method as well as a massive attempt at a cover-up. In particular, Abbott put into the records affidavits that the FDA commissioner conceded at a meeting with corporate executives that cyclamate was safe but would remain banned for political reasons. Abbott also forced the agency to turn over internal memoranda and other documents that proved that throughout the extended proceedings qualified FDA staffers admitted without reservation that cyclamate was safe and that superiors merely saw no point in permitting it back on the market.

In this instance, the interests of the consuming public do not seem to have been served. But regulations often do prod business to recognize and act on their responsibilities to consumers. Sometimes even without applying the force of law, agencies can effectively safeguard consumer rights, especially in cases of health and safety. A good example concerns the connection between certain kinds of tampons and the newly identified and sometimes fatal disease called toxic shock syndrome.

Procter & Gamble, makers of Rely, which in 1980 garnered about one-quarter of the tampon market, became aware of toxic shock in May 1980 when the federal Center for Disease Control (CDC) published the first report indicating many new cases of toxic shock affecting menstruating women. In June the CDC asked Procter & Gamble and other tampon makers for market information, partly because a reporter in Los Angeles had suggested that tampons might be involved. A subsequent CDC study confirmed a correlation between toxic shock and tampon use but termed the rate of incidence too low to recommend that women stop using tampons. But studying cases of toxic shock contracted in July and August, the CDC found that of women with toxic shock more than twice as many had used Rely than a similar group of healthy women.

From the moment that the CDC's second report became public, Procter & Gamble tried to shore up its defense of Rely. Despite its many denials about its product's complicity in toxic shock, it couldn't stem the flood of bad publicity that was part of the offensive strategy of the FDA, the regulatory agency charged with acting on CDC findings. Knowing that Procter & Gamble was sensitive to bad publicity and aware of its own charge to protect the public health, the FDA deliberately used the media as a weapon to drive Rely off the market. In the words of Wayne L. Pines, associate FDA commissioner for public affairs: "Throughout the series of events, we made sure the press was notified so as to keep the story alive. We wanted to saturate the market with information on Rely. We deliberately delayed issuing press releases for a day to maximize the media impact. There was quite a concerted and deliberate effort to keep a steady flow of information before the public."[11] The upshot: On September 23, 1980, Procter & Gamble voluntarily agreed to withdraw Rely from the market.

Because Procter & Gamble remained convinced that Rely was a safe product, it's fair to surmise that it would not have withdrawn the product without agency pressure. After all, there was no laboratory evidence implicating highly absorbent tampons in the incidence of toxic shock until over a year later. Had the FDA not acted as it did and had Procter & Gamble continued to sell the product, many women undoubtedly would have suffered and even died between September 1980 and December 1981, when incontrovertible clinical evidence became available.

Do regulations, then, help business meet its responsibility to consumers? Based on these cases, the answer is: generally yes, sometimes no. Nonetheless, the prevailing view today among businesspeople favors self-regulation. Such a view certainly is in keeping with the tenets of classical capitalism and is arguably an attractive ideal. However, self-regulation can easily become the instrument of subordinating consumer interests to profit making when the two goals clash. Under the guise of self-regulation, businesses can end up ignoring or minimizing responsibility to consumers.

Consider the auto industry. For the past twenty years it has been fighting a battle against safety and pollution regulations for cars. Jolted a few years ago by the industry's staggering losses and mounting layoffs, Washington started going easier on Detroit. Sensing an opportunity to press their case, industry officials embarked on a major effort to rid themselves of many regulations they considered unnecessary and too costly. Automakers began circulating thick books in Washington detailing how dozens of sought revisions would save themselves and car

buyers vast sums of money. In particular, auto officials wanted to roll back car and truck pollution rules, completely revamp emissions enforcement, scrap a requirement for automatic crash-protection devices for passengers, and dilute existing standards for bumpers. As a result, the Reagan administration targeted some three dozen safety and pollution rules for delay, revision, or cancellation. Such steps could save the industry billions in capital outlays. Whether U.S. carmakers have been, or will be, made more competitive as a result is open to debate. But what is apparent is that some of these deregulations jeopardize the safety of drivers and add to already soaring public health costs.

To illustrate, the Reagan administration delayed requiring that future cars come equipped with air bags or automatic seat belts. A one-year delay alone saved the industry $30 million. Dropping the regulations altogether might save more than $200 million. But according to Joan Clayburn, former safety-agency chief of the U.S. Department of Transportation (DOT), passive restraints would reduce highway deaths by 9,000 a year and injuries by tens of thousands. DOT's own analysis conceded that the postponement would result in an additional 600 motor vehicle deaths and 4,300 serious injuries.[12] Using DOT's figures, the American Academy of Pediatricians estimated that although further delay would save the auto industry about $70 million in manufacturing and purchase costs, it would eventually end up costing $457,693,000 in health care costs, not to mention the tragedy of those who will be killed or injured.[13] If these observations are correct, then deregulation in this instance is not compatible with consumer safety or the economic interests of society.

The Responsibilities of Business

Simply obeying regulatory laws does not exhaust the moral responsibilities of business in the area of consumer safety. The exact nature of those responsibilities is hard to specify in general, since much will depend on the particular product or service being provided. But abiding by the following steps would do much to help business behave morally with respect to consumer safety:

1. *Business can give safety the priority warranted by the product.* This is an important factor because businesses often base safety considerations strictly on cost factors. Thus, if the margin of safety can be increased without significantly insulting budgetary considerations, fine. If not, then safety questions are shelved. Moreover, businesses frequently allow the law to determine to what extent they'll ensure safety. Although both cost and the law are factors in safety control, two other considerations seem of more moral importance. One factor is the seriousness of the injury the product can cause. The automobile, for example, can cause severe injury or death; thus it should be an item of the highest priority. Other products that can cause serious injury, such as power tools, pesticides, and chemicals, also deserve high priority. The second factor to consider is the frequency of occurrence. How often is a particular product involved in an accident? When a product scores high on both the seriousness and frequency tests, it warrants the highest priority as a potential safety hazard.

2. *Business should abandon the misconception that accidents occur exclusively as a result of product misuse and abuse.* At one time such a belief may have been valid, but in using today's highly sophisticated products, numerous people have followed product instructions explicitly and still were injured. The point is that the company shares the responsibility of product safety together with the consumer. Rather than insisting that consumers' abuse of products leads to most accidents and injuries, firms would probably accomplish more by carefully pointing out how their products can be used safely. If the product poses a potentially serious threat, a company may need to take extraordinary measures to ensure continued safe usage of it. Determining the extent to which the company must go, however, isn't an easy task. Sometimes a firm's moral responsibility for ensuring safety doesn't reach much beyond the sale of the product. Other times it may extend well beyond that. Consider, for example, the case of a company producing heavy machinery. Workers using its products could easily fall into bad and dangerous habits. Some would argue, therefore, that the company has an obligation to follow up the sale of such a product, perhaps by visiting firms using its machinery to see if they've developed dangerous shortcuts.

3. *Business must monitor the manufacturing process itself.* Frequently firms fail to control key variables during the manufacturing process, resulting in product defects. Companies should periodically review working conditions and the competence of key personnel. At the design stage of the process, they need to predict ways that the product might fail and the consequences of this failure. With respect to the materials used in production, companies ordinarily can select those that have been pretested or certified as flawless. If a company fails to do this, then we must question the priority the company gives safety. Similar questions arise when companies do not make use of research available about product safety. When none is available, a company really interested in safety can generate its own. In doing this, however, or in making use of safety research and studies, companies should rely on the findings of independent research groups. Studies by these groups ensure impartial and disinterested analysis and are usually more reliable than studies by in-house programs.

Testing should be rigorous and stimulate the toughest conditions. Tests shouldn't assume that the product will be used in just the way the manufacturer intends it to be used. Even established products should be tested.

The courts have repeatedly held that a trouble-free history does not justify the assumption that the product is free of defects.[14]

When a product moves into production, it can be changed in a variety of ways. It's important that these changes be documented and referred to some appropriate party, like the safety engineer, for analysis. This procedure means that the firm must be scrupulous about coordinating department activities to preclude one department's altering manufacturing specifications without consulting other departments to determine any potential dangers related to these changes.

4. *When a product is ready to be marketed, companies should have their product safety staff review advertising for safety-related content.* This step not only ensures accuracy and completeness but also provides consumers with vital purchase information. A corollary to this rule would be informing salespeople about the product's hazardous aspects.

5. *When a product reaches the marketplace, firms should make available to consumers in writing everything relative to the product's performance.* This information should include operating instructions, the product's safety features and under what conditions it will fail, a complete list of the ways the product can be used, and a cautionary list of the ways it should not be used. Warnings must be specific.

6. *Companies should investigate consumer complaints.* This process encourages firms to deal fairly with consumers and to utilize the most effective source of product improvement: the opinions of those who use it.

Even if firms seriously tended to each of these safety considerations, they couldn't guarantee an absolutely safe product. Some hazards invariably will attach to numerous products, heroic efforts notwithstanding. But business must acknowledge and discharge moral responsibilities in this area. Morally speaking, no one's asking for an accident- and injury-proof product—only that a manufacturer do everything reasonable to approach that ideal.

Although, unfortunately, there are many examples of companies that play fast and loose with safety—resisting product improvements and dodging responsibility for consumer injury—many companies do respond quickly to perceived or suspected hazards. Consider two examples of successful companies that place a premium on product safety.[15]

Burning Radios.   Back in the early 1960s a few of the radios sold by J. C. Penney were reported to have caught fire in customers' homes. J. C. Penney tested the radios and discovered a defective resistor in a few of them—less than 1 percent. Nonetheless, Penney informed the manufacturer, withdrew the entire line of radios, ran national ads informing the public of the danger, and offered immediate refunds. "This was before the Consumer Product Safety Commission even existed," says Penney vice-chairman Robert Gill. "I guess some people might have thought we were crazy, and said that liability insurance was specifically designed to take care of such problems. But we felt we just could not sell that kind of product."

Fluorocarbons.   In the mid-1970s environmentalists were seriously alarmed at the possibility that fluorocarbons released from aerosol cans were depleting the earth's thin and fragile ozone layer. The media rapidly picked up the story, but virtually every manufacturer of aerosol cans denounced the scientific findings and stood by their products. The exception was Johnson Wax. The company acknowledged that the scientific questions were difficult to resolve, but it took seriously consumer concern about the ozone. Years before the Federal Drug Administration ban, Johnson Wax withdrew all its fluorocarbon products worldwide. "We picked up a lot of flak from other manufacturers," recalls company chairman Samuel Johnson, "and we lost business in some areas, but I don't have any question we were right. . . . Our belief is that as long as you can make do without a potentially hazardous material, why not do without it?"

OTHER AREAS OF BUSINESS RESPONSIBILITY

Product safety is naturally a dominant concern of consumers. No one wants to be injured by the products he or she uses. But safety is far from the only interest of consumers. The last twenty-five years have seen a general increase in consumer awareness and an ever stronger consumer advocacy movement. One chief consumer issue has been advertising and its possible abuse, which we will discuss in later sections, but other areas of business responsibility and irresponsibility to consumers are equally important and are taken equally seriously by the consumer movement. We will look at three of those areas: product quality, pricing, and packaging and labeling.

Product Quality

The demand for product quality is closely related to a number of the themes mentioned in our discussion of safety. Most would agree that business bears a general responsibility to ensure that the quality of a product measures up to the claims made about it and to reasonable consumer expectations. They would undoubtedly see this responsibility as deriving primarily from the consumer's basic right to get what he or she pays for. But business's obligation for product quality also stems from its general responsibility to protect owners' interests, for just as the burden of product safety has shifted to the producer, so has product performance. This realization means a toughening of product liability law and a softening of judicial resistance to consumer

complaints. In increasing numbers consumers are going to court when products don't perform. What's more, the courts often uphold their complaints. As a result, the area of product performance incurs serious financial risks to stockholders who must increase business's responsibility in this area.

One way that business tries to meet its responsibilities is through *warranties, obligations that sellers assume to purchasers.* We generally speak of two kinds of warranties, expressed and implied. Expressed warranties are the claims that sellers explicitly state. They include assertions about the product's characteristics, assurances of product durability, and other statements on warranty cards, labels, wrappers, and packages, or in the advertising of the product. Of moral concern here is that the manufacturer ensure that a product live up to its billing. Just as important, however, is the question of reparation. When a product fails to perform as promoted, whether and how the manufacturer "makes good" the consumer loss raises moral concerns. In some cases, the manufacturer may issue a refund or a new product; in others, greater reparation may be required.

Implied warranties include the implicit claim that a particular product is fit for the ordinary use for which it is likely to be employed. Again, serious moral questions of reparation arise when injury or harm results from the failure of a product to perform as it should. Suppose, for example, that Eleanor Solano buys a new automobile. After she drives the car around for a few days under normal conditions, its steering mechanism fails and she is severely injured. In such a case, a company may bear far-reaching moral as well as legal responsibilities, even if on purchase Solano signed a disclaimer limiting the company's liability to replacement of defective parts.

Advertising can result in implied warranties, even when its claims are not very specific. For example, in one case a man named

Inglis bought a Rambler, relying on an American Motors advertising claim that a Rambler would be trouble free, economical to run, and a product of superior quality. Sadly, Inglis's expectations proved unrealistic. Not only was his Rambler's trunk out of line but it couldn't even be opened. The door handles were loose; the steering gear was improperly set; the oil pump was defective; the brakes squeaked and grated; the engine leaked oil; and loose parts inside the car occasionally fell on the floor. If not a lemon, certainly Inglis's car was of the citrus variety. Unable to get satisfaction from his dealer, Inglis went to court. The court ruled that in cases where there is a difference between advertisement claims and a product's actual performance, there is no sound reason that consumers shouldn't be permitted to recoup their losses.[16]

In sum, business has a general responsibility to ensure the quality of its product. Where there are discrepancies between explicit or implicit claims and performance, moral questions about reparation arise. At the same time it is important to note that business's responsibility for product quality and its obligation to provide clear, accurate, and adequate information to ensure product safety are tied to questions that reach beyond consumer dissatisfaction with unsafe or inferior merchandise. Obligations in this area invite serious consideration by business about its attitude toward people, about its priorities, and about whether it's cultivating a marketplace atmosphere conducive to fair treatment for all consumers, no matter what their socioeconomic standing.

Prices

Have you ever wondered why a product is priced at $9.88 rather than $9.99 or simply $10? Or why a product that retails for $3.80 on Monday is selling for $4.10 on Friday? The answers have nothing to do with inflation, production costs, overhead expenses, labor demands, or the more conventional influences on product prices.

It is true that prices do reflect the costs of material, labor, and operating expenses. But in many cases, other factors help shape the price, including a shop's location and the volume of merchandise bought and paid for at one time. And more and more, psychological factors are entering into the price-setting equation.

For example, one manufacturer eschews pricing jeans at $9.99 in favor of $9.88. Why? "When people see $9.99, they say, 'That's $10,'" explains the company's general sales manager. "But $9.88 isn't $10. It's just psychological."[17]

For a lot of consumers, higher prices mean better products. So manufacturers arbitrarily raise the price of a product to give the impression of superior quality or that the buyer is getting something special. But often as not the price is higher than the product's extra quality. For example, a few years ago Proctor-Silex's most expensive fabric iron sold for $54.95, five dollars above the company's next most expensive. Its wholesale price was $26.98 against $24.20, a difference of $2.78. The extra cost of producing the top model was less than one dollar for a light that signaled when the iron was ready.[18]

Manufacturers also trade on human psychology when they sell their own substantially identical products at different prices. In 1981, for example, Heublein, Inc., raised the price of its Popov brand vodka from about $3.80 to $4.10 a fifth without altering the vodka that went into the fifth. Why the price increase? Heublein sales representatives believed that consumers wanted a variety of vodka prices from which to choose. Apparently they were right: While Popov lost 1 percent of its market share, it increased its profits by 30 percent. Applying its theory further, Heublein offers vodka drinkers an even more expensive vodka, Smirnoff. All this, despite the insistence of analysts that there is no qualitative difference among vodkas made in the U.S.[19]

In this case the use of psychological pricing is closely related to the problem of pricing branded products higher than generic products that are otherwise indistinguishable from them. Consumers pay more, often assuming that the brand name or the higher price implies a better product. Another ethically dubious practice is that of manufacturers who print a suggested retail price on their packages that is higher than what they know the retailer will charge. When the retailer marks a new price over the "suggested price," customers receive the false impression that the item is selling below its customary price. Retailers themselves are on questionable ethical ground when they use special pricing codes, or fail to put a price on, or post it near, products, thus hindering consumers from easily comparing prices.[20]

Many practical consumers tend to think of these pricing practices more as a nuisance or as an irritant that they must live with than as something which may be morally objectionable. But these practices do raise moral questions—not least about business's view of itself and its role in the community—which businesspeople and ethical theorists are now beginning to take seriously. Much more attention has been devoted to price fixing, which despite its prevalence is widely recognized as a violation of the "rules of the game" in a market system whose ideal is open and fair price competition.

When a few companies gain control of a market, they are often in a position to force consumers to pay artificially high prices. For example, in 1960 General Electric, Westinghouse, and twenty-seven other companies producing electrical equipment were found guilty of fixing prices in that $1.75 billion industry. The companies were made to pay about $2 million in fines and many more millions to their corporate victims.[21] Given the oligopolistic nature of the electrical equipment market, consumers could not reasonably be said to have had the option to take their business elsewhere and thus drive down prices. (In fact, until it was exposed, they had no reason to believe they were being victimized by price fixing.)

Of course, controlling prices need not be done so blatantly. Firms in an oligopoly can tacitly agree to remain uncompetitive with one another, thereby avoiding losses that might result from price-cutting competition. They can then play "follow the leader": Let the lead firm in the market raise its prices and then follow suit. The result is a laundered form of price fixing.

Even without tacit price fixing, the firms that dominate a field often implicitly agree not to compete in terms of price. Nobody, they say to themselves, wants a "price war," as if price competition were a threat to a market system, rather than its lifeblood. Familiar rivals like Pepsi and Coca-Cola or McDonalds and Burger King generally choose to compete in terms of image and jingles rather than price. While deregulation and Peoples Express did much to encourage price competition among the airlines in the eighties, the carriers, judging from their advertisements, prefer to compete on the basis of meals and the uniforms of stewardesses, rather than the cost of their tickets.

From the moral point of view, prices, like wages, should be just. What is a just price? It's not enough to say that a just price exists when a merchant makes a "fair profit" after expenses, for we can still ask: What is a *fair* profit? In the end, the question, "What is a just price?" probably defies a precise answer. This does not mean that merchants can charge whatever they want or whatever the market will bear, any more than employers can pay workers whatever they (the employers) want simply because it is impossible to be precise about a "fair wage."

Jut as in the case of wages, one can approach an answer to the just price question by assessing the factors upon which the price is based and the process by which it is arrived. Certainly factors such as costs of material and production, operating and marketing expenses, and profit are relevant to price setting. In addition, consumer choice in the marketplace does, and should, affect prices. Product price, in other words, reflects in part the considered beliefs and judgments of the consuming public regarding the relative value of the article. In a capitalistic economy, these beliefs are formed and judgments made in the open market in a free interplay between sellers and buyers.

For this process to function satisfactorily, the buyers must be in a position to exercise informed consent. Informed consent, as we noted in a preceding chapter, calls for deliberation and free choice. Deliberation requires that buyers have and understand all significant facts about the goods and services they are purchasing, and then voluntarily purchase them. But clearly consumers are at least sometimes, perhaps often, denied informed consent. They do not always receive the clear, accurate, and complete information they need about products to make prudent choices with respect to quality and price.

Labeling and Packaging

Business's general responsibility to provide clear, accurate, and adequate information undoubtedly applies to product labeling and packaging. The reason is that, despite the billions of dollars spent annually on advertising, a product's label and package remain the consumer's primary source of product information. Yet labels are often hard to understand or even misleading, and what they omit to say may be more important than what they do say.

We are all familiar, too, with the ways in which package shape can exploit certain optical illusions. Tall and narrow cereal boxes look larger than short, squat ones that actually contain more cereal; shampoo bottles often have pinched waists to give the illusion of quantity; fruits are packed in large quantities of syrup; and dry foods often come in tins or cartons stuffed with cardboard.[22]

Consider a representative study made up of five randomly selected housewife-shoppers.[23] Each shopper shared the characteristics of a college education and extensive family marketing experience. The five women were taken to a supermarket, where they were each given a set amount of money and asked to purchase 14 items, the average number of purchases that shoppers make. When they finished, their selections were compared with the merchandise available in the supermarket. Of the 70 items chosen, only 36 were the "best buys"; that is, the most economical selections available of products of comparable quality. Even granting that the sample here is too small to draw firm conclusions, the results suggest that some shoppers are fooled by such things as labeling and packaging.

Language abuse partly accounts for consumer bewilderment in the marketplace. Frequently shoppers are mystified by terms such as *large*, *extra large*, and *economy size*; by the net quantities of the contents (ounces, pints, quarts, liters, grams, etc.); as well as by special products terms, such as those applied to meat, like *prime*, *choice*, *graded*, and *ungraded*. Without a pocket computer consumers find it difficult in many stores to calculate the relative prices of items. They can fall victim to terms and numbers, even though unit pricing is doing much to alleviate the problem.

What's more, although the Truth in Packaging Act (Fair Packaging and Labeling Act, 1966) empowers representative agencies to rank and list all ingredients in the order of decreasing percentage of total contents, wily marketers can sometimes circumvent this at the consumer's expense. For example, because sugar is the predominant ingredient in Shazam! breakfast cereal, it must be listed first. But breaking down sugar into its various forms—sucrose, glucose, fructose, lactose—by "precising" the sugar contents, the manufacturer of Shazam! can minimize the appearance of sugar in the product. Indeed, it can avoid the word *sugar* entirely. As a result, a consumer must not only guess at the amount of sugar in the product but must also be something of a chemist to accomplish even this.

As with product information in advertising, the moral issues that packaging and labeling raise relate primarily to truth telling and consumer exploitation. Many persons would argue that sound moral conduct in this area must rest on a strong desire to provide consumers information about the price, quality, and quantity of a product so that they can make an intelligent choice. When marketers are interested primarily in selling a product and only secondarily in providing relevant information, then morally questionable practices are bound to follow. At the same time, those responsible for labeling and packaging would be well advised to consider at least the following questions, a negative answer to any of which could signal a moral problem. Have we clearly and specifically identified the product in an appropriate part of the label? Is the net quantity prominently located? Is it readily understandable to those wishing to compare prices? If a term such as *serving* is used, as in soups or puddings, is the net quantity of the serving stipulated? Are ingredients so listed as to be readily recognized and understood? Have we indicated and represented the percentage of the contents that is filler, such as the bone in a piece of meat?

These questions represent only some that a moral person might ask. In addition, we must not forget those people whose health necessitates certain dietary restrictions. They often have great difficulty determining what products they can safely purchase. In the last analysis, moral evaluation of problems related to labeling and packaging must be based on

how well or poorly they provide clear, accurate, and adequate consumer information.

DECEPTION AND UNFAIRNESS IN ADVERTISING

We tend to take advertising for granted, yet sociologically and economically it is enormously important. Ads dominate our environment. Famous ones become part of our culture; their jingles dance in our heads, and their images haunt our dreams and shape our tastes. Advertising is also big business. Advertising agencies have an annual gross income of around $6.5 billion, and their clients pay out over $44 billion annually for space and time in the mass media. In 1983, for example, Procter & Gamble sunk $773 million into national advertising, Sears spent $732 million, Beatrice Companies $602 million, General Motors $595 million, and R. J. Reynolds $595 million.[24]

When people are asked what advertising does, their first thought is often that it provides consumers with information about goods and services. In fact, advertising conveys very little information. Nor are most ads intended to do so. Except for classified ads (by amateurs!) and newspaper ads reporting supermarket prices, very few advertisements offer any information of genuine use to the consumer. (If you want useful product information, you have to go to a magazine like *Consumer Reports*, which publishes objective and comparative studies of various products.) Instead, advertisements offer us jingles, rhymes, and attractive images of their products.

The goal of advertising, of course, is to persuade us to buy the products that are being touted. Providing objective and comparative product information may be one way to do this. But it is not the only way, and judging from ads these days—which frequently say nothing at all about the product's qualities—it is not a very common way. The similarity among many competing products may be the explanation for this. One writer identifies this as the "ethical, as well as economic, crux of the [advertising] industry," and another refers to it as the "persistent, underlying bad faith" of much American advertising.[25]

Deceptive Techniques

Since advertisers are trying to persuade people to buy their products, and since straight product information is not necessarily the best way to do this, there is a natural temptation to obfuscate, misrepresent, or even lie. In an attempt to persuade, advertisers are prone to exploit ambiguity, to conceal facts, to exaggerate, and to employ psychological appeals. Let's look at each of these aspects of advertising.

Ambiguity. When ads are ambiguous, they can be deceiving. For example, the Continental Baking Company was charged with such ambiguity by the Federal Trade Commission (FTC). In advertising its Profile Bread, Continental implied that eating the bread would lead to weight loss. The fact was that Profile had about the same number of calories per ounce as other breads but each slice contained seven fewer calories only because it was sliced thinner than most breads. Continental issued a corrective advertisement.

In all aspects of advertising, much potential moral danger lies in the interpretation. The Profile ad is a good example. A large number of people interpreted that ad to mean that eating Profile Bread would lead to a weight loss.[26] Likewise, for years consumers have inferred from its advertisements that Listerine mouthwash effectively fought bacteria and sore throats. Not so; in 1978 the FTC ordered Listerine to run a multimillion-dollar disclaimer. In such cases, advertisers and manufacturers invariably deny intending the inference that consumers draw. But some-

times the ad is so ambiguous that a reasonable person couldn't infer anything else. Thus, when a cold tablet advertises, "At the first sign of a cold or flu—Coricidin," what is the consumer likely to think? The fact is that neither Coricidin nor any other cold remedy can cure the common cold. At best it can only provide temporary symptomatic relief. But a consumer is left to draw his or her own conclusion, and it's likely to be the wrong one.

A striking example of this "open-to-interpretation" aspect of ambiguity can be seen in the battle over a seemingly harmless topic—buying a tire. Uniroyal advises consumers to buy the numbers: Use the numbers and letter molded into the sidewalls under a federally mandated tire-grading system to select the best tire value. Goodyear counters that the numbers are misleading and that the only reliable way to buy a tire is by brand name and dealer recommendations. (It is hardly any coincidence, of course, that Uniroyal has the highest tread-wear number on its first-line radials, those supplied to auto dealers; and Goodyear has the best-known brand, the biggest advertising budget, and the most stores and dealers.)

The dispute is long-standing. In the mid-1960s the government responded to concern about quality and safety by proposing a quality grading system. Producers fought tire grading for over ten years, but a 1979 court decision forced them to start using grade labels. Under the law, each manufacturer can grade its own tires, and the government randomly checks to see that the tires measure up to the ratings. Although grading began with the bias-ply tires, in 1980 tire makers also had to begin putting separate A, B, or C grade ratings on radials for traction and ability to withstand heat buildup from high-speed driving. In response, tire makers simply put on a number to indicate expected wear and left it at that.

But early in 1981 Uniroyal, which had

rated its "Steeler" at 220 (indicating 66,000 miles of useful life[27]), started advertising that its Steelers were better than Goodyear's Custom Polysteel, which had been rated at 170 (51,000 miles), and other competing brands. As a result, Goodyear, Firestone Tire and Rubber, B. F. Goodrich, and General Tire were put in the ludicrous position of having to convince tire dealers and motorists that their grade ratings were really meaningless, and that no one should take them seriously.

Each of these companies insisted that the test results on which the ratings were based are so variable that they are not reliable. Goodyear, for example, said tests on its Polysteel tires ranged from 160 to 420, with a 13-inch size ranking the lowest. Goodyear therefore assigned a grade of 160 for 13-inch tires and 170 for 14- and 15-inch sizes to assure that all tires met the grade. Fair or not, Goodyear began running ads declaring that, in comparative tests, its Custom Polysteel Tires averaged 229 and 329 ratings in 14- and 15-inch sizes, higher than the 220 and 277 averaged for Uniroyal's Steelers. For its part, Uniroyal insisted that the records of the tests they had run showed that the Goodyear tires didn't test as well as the Steelers.

What, then, does a tire grade mean? What kind of information does it provide the consumer? You be the judge.

Aiding and abetting ambiguity in ads is the use of "weasel" words, words used to evade or retreat from a direct or forthright statement or position. Consider the weasel *help*. *Help* means "aid" or "assist" and nothing else. Yet, as one author has observed, "'help' is the one single word which, in all the annals of advertising, has done the most to say something that couldn't be said."[28] Because the word *help* is used to qualify, once it's used almost anything can be said after it. Thus, we're exposed to ads for products that "help us keep young," "help prevent cavities," "help keep our houses germ-free." Consider for a moment how many times a day you hear or read phrases like these: "helps stop," "helps prevent," "helps fight," "helps overcome," "helps you feel," "helps you look." And, of course, "help" is hardly the only weasel. "Like," "virtual" or "virtually," "can be," "up to" (as in "provides relief *up to* eight hours"), "as much as" (as in "saves *as much as* one gallon of gas"), and numerous other weasels function to say what can't be said.

That ads are open to interpretation doesn't exonerate advertisers from the obligation to provide clear information. Indeed, this fact intensifies their responsibility, because the danger of misleading through ambiguity increases as the ad is subject to interpretation. At stake are not only people's money but also their health, loyalties, and expectations. The potential harm a misleading ad can cause is great, not to mention its cavalier treatment of the truth. For these reasons ambiguity in ads is of serious moral concern.

Concealed facts. When advertisers conceal facts, they suppress information that is unflattering to their products. Put another way, a fact is concealed when its availability would probably make the desire, purchase, or use of the product less likely than in its absence. Shell, for example, used to advertise that its gasoline had "platformate" but neglected to mention that all other brands did too. For years Bayer Aspirin advertised that it contained "the ingredient that doctors recommend most." What is that ingredient? Aspirin. Subway ads for the Bowery Bank in New York use former baseball star Joe DiMaggio to tout the fact that it is "federally insured," but then so is almost every bank in the country. Concealed facts concern us in ethics not only because they can exploit by misleading as much as ambiguity can but also because they wantonly undermine truth telling.

Truth rarely seems foremost in the minds of advertisers. As Samm Sinclair Baker writes in *The Permissible Lie*: "Inside the agency the basic approach is hardly conducive to truth telling. The usual thinking in forming a campaign is first what can we say, true or not, that will sell the product best? The second consideration is, how can we say it effectively and get away with it so that (1) people who buy won't feel let down by too big a promise that doesn't come true, and (2) the ads will avoid quick and certain censure by the FTC."[29] In this observation we see the businessperson's tendency to equate what's legal with what's moral, an attitude we previously alluded to. It's precisely this outlook that leads to advertising behavior of dubious morality.

One needn't look far to find examples of concealed facts in ads. Recall the old Colgate-Palmolive ad for its Rapid Shave Cream (discussed on page 417). Colgate concealed that the "sandpaper" in the ad was actually Plexiglas and that actual sandpaper had to be soaked in Rapid Shave for about eighty minutes before it came off in a stroke.

More recently Campbell vegetable soup ads showed pictures of a thick, rich brew calculated to whet even a gourmet's appetite. Supporting the soup were clear glass marbles deposited into the bowl to give the appearance of solidity.

Then there's the whole area of feminine deodorant sprays (FDS), one rife with concealed facts. Currently an industry in excess of $55 million, FDS ads not only fail to mention that such products in most cases are unnecessary but that they frequently produce unwanted side effects: itching, burning, blistering, and urinary infections. A Food and Drug Administration (FDA) "caution" now appears on these products.

If business has obligations to provide clear, accurate, and adequate information, we must wonder if it meets this charge when it hides facts relevant to the consumer's need and desire for, or purchase of, a product. Hiding facts raise serious moral concerns relative to truth telling and consumer exploitation. When consumers are deprived of comprehensive knowledge about a product, their choices are constricted and distorted.

If pushed farther, the moral demand for full information challenges almost all advertising. Even the best advertisements never point out the negative features of their products or, what is often the case, that there is no substantive difference between the product being advertised and its competitors. In this sense, they could be accused of concealing relevant information. Most advertisers would be shocked at the suggestion that honesty requires that they present objectively the pros *and cons* of their products, and in fact consumers don't expect advertisers or salespersons to be impartial. Nevertheless, it is not clear why this moral value should not be relevant to assessing advertising. And it can be noted that retail salespersons, despite a sometimes negative reputation, often do approach this level of candor—at least when they are fortunate enough to sell a genuinely good and competitive product or when they do not work on commission.

Exaggeration. Advertisers can mislead through exaggeration; that is, by making claims unsupported by evidence. For example, claims that a pain reliever provides "extra pain relief" or is "50 percent stronger than aspirin," that it "upsets the stomach less frequently" or is "superior to any other nonprescription pain killer on the market" contradict evidence that indicates that all analgesics are effective to the same degree.[30]

In recent years the FTC has been making numerous companies substantiate their claims, as in the Profile and Listerine cases. In the tire industry, the FTC has questioned Goodyear's claim that its Double-Eagle Polysteel Tires can be driven over ax blades without suffering damage. It has also asked Sears, Roebuck and Company to prove its claim that its steel-belted radial tires can give 60,000 to 101,000 miles of service. In the auto industry, the FTC has questioned Volkswagen's claim that its squareback sedan gives drivers 200 gallons of gas more a year compared with the average domestic compact. In addition, the

FTC has asked General Motors to verify its claim that its Vega's ground beams provide more side-impact collision protection than those of any other comparable compact. And it has questioned Chrysler's claim that its electronic system never needs tuning.[31]

"Antiaging" skin care products are one of the fastest growing segments of the cosmetic industry, partly because the baby boom generation is getting older. The federal Food and Drug Administration (FDA), however, is upset about cosmetic firms' claims about their antiaging skin treatments. Companies portray their products as "repairing cells" or skin layers below the surface rather than having only an external effect. The FDA says that if the companies want to keep making these claims, then they have to seek new-drug status for their treatments. And the FDA says it is prepared to take "appropriate regulatory sanctions, such as seizure or injunction," if they don't.

Part of the labeling for Avon's Bioadvance Beauty Recovery System, for example, claims that it "actually helps reverse many signs of facial aging in just six weeks . . . helps revitalize and invigorate your skin's regenerative system." Christiaan Barnard, the first heart-transplant surgeon, endorses the antiaging skin cream made by Alfin Fragrances. The product's distinctive ingredient, Glycosphingolipid—said by critics to be only a natural body fat with a fancy name—is claimed to make skin "function as if it were young again."[32]

Clearly the line between deliberate deception and what advertising mogul David Ogilvy has termed "puffery" is not always clear. By *puffery* Ogilvy means the use of "harmless" superlatives. Thus advertisers frequently boast of the merits of their products by using words such as *best, finest,* or *most,* or phrases like "King of Beers" or "Breakfast of Champions." In many instances the use of such puffery is indeed harmless, as in the claim that a soap is the "best loved in America." Other times, however, it's downright misleading, as in the Dial soap ad that claimed that Dial was "the most effective deodorant soap you can buy." When asked to substantiate that claim, Armour-Dial Company insisted that it was not claiming product superiority; all it meant was that Dial soap was *as effective as* any other soap.

Of moral importance in determining the line between puffery and deliberate deception would seem to be the advertiser's intention and the likely interpretation of the ad. Are the claims intended as no more than verbal posturing, or are they intended to sell through deceptive exaggeration? Are advertisers primarily interested in saying as much as they can without drawing legal sanction or in providing consumers with accurate information? But even when the intention is harmless, advertisers must consider how the ad is likely to be interpreted. What conclusion is the general consuming public likely to draw about the product? Is that conclusion contrary to likely performance? Without raising questions like these about their ads, advertisers and manufacturers run risks of warping truth and injuring consumers, two significant moral concerns.

Psychological appeals. A psychological appeal is one that aims to persuade exclusively by appealing to human emotions and emotional needs and not to reason. This is potentially the area of greatest moral concern in advertising. An automobile ad that presents the product in an elitist atmosphere peopled by members of the "in" set appeals to our need and desire for status. A life insurance ad that portrays a destitute family woefully struggling in the aftermath of a provider's death aims to persuade through pity and fear. Reliance on such devices, although not unethical per se, raises moral concerns because rarely do such ads fully deliver what they promise.

Ads that rely extensively on pitches to power, prestige, sex, masculinity, femininity, acceptance, approval, and the like aim to sell more than a product. They are peddling psychological satisfaction. Perhaps the best example is the increasingly explicit and pervasive use of sexual pitches in ads.

Scene:	An artist's skylit studio. A young man lies nude, the bedsheets in disarray. He awakens to find a tender note on his pillow. The phone rings and he gets up to answer it.
Woman's Voice:	'You snore.'
Artist (smiling):	'And you always steal the covers.'

More cozy patter between the two. Then a husky-voiced announcer intones: 'Paco Rabanne. A cologne for men. What is remembered is up to you.'[33]

Although sex has always been used to sell products, it has never before been used as explicitly in advertising as it is today. And the sexual pitches are by no means confined to products like cologne. The California Avocado Commission supplements its "Love Food From California" recipe ads with a campaign featuring leggy actress Angie Dickinson, who is sprawled across two pages of some eighteen national magazines to promote the avocado's nutritional value. The copy line reads: "Would this body lie to you?" Similarly, Dannon Yogurt recently ran an ad featuring a bikini-clad beauty and the message: "More nonsense is written on dieting than any other subject—except possibly sex."

Some students of marketing claim that ads like these appeal to the subconscious mind of both marketer and consumer. Purdue University psychologist and marketing consultant Jacob Jacoby contends that marketers, like everyone else, carry around sexual symbols in their subconscious that, intentionally or not, they use in ads. A case in point: the widely circulated Newport cigarette "Alive

with Pleasure" campaign. One campaign ad featured a woman riding the handlebars of a bicycle driven by a man. The main strut of the bike wheel stands vertically beneath her body. In Jacoby's view, such symbolism needs no interpretation.

Author Wilson Bryan Key, who has extensively researched the topic of subconscious marketing appeals, claims that many ads take a subliminal form. *Subliminal advertising is advertising that communicates at a level beneath our conscious awareness,* where some psychologists claim that the vast reservoir of human motivation primarily resides. Most marketing people would likely deny that such advertising occurs. Key disagrees. Indeed, he goes so far as to claim: "It is virtually impossible to pick up a newspaper or magazine, turn on a radio or television set, read a promotional pamphlet or the telephone book, or shop through a supermarket without having your subconscious purposely massaged by some monstrously clever artist, photographer, writer, or technician."[34]

Concern with the serious nature of psychological appeals is what the California Wine Institute seemed to have in mind when it adopted an advertising code of standards. The following restrictions are included:

No wine ad shall present persons engaged in activities with appeal particularly to minors. Among those excluded: amateur or professional sports figures, celebrities, or cowboys; rock stars, race car drivers.

No wine ad shall exploit the human form or "feature provocative or enticing poses or be demeaning to any individual."

No wine ad shall portray wine in a setting where food is not presented.

No wine ad shall present wine in "quantities inappropriate to the situation."

No wine ad shall portray wine as similar to another type of beverage or product such as milk, soda, or candy.

No wine ad shall associate wine with personal performance, social attainment, achievement, wealth, or the attainment of adulthood.

No wine ad shall show automobiles in a way that one could construe their conjunction.

As suggested, the code seems particularly sensitive to the subtle implications and psychological nuances of ads. In adopting such a rigorous code of advertising ethics, the California Wine Institute recognizes the inextricable connection between *what* is communicated and *how* it is communicated. In other words, as media expert Marshall McLuhan always insisted, content cannot be distinguished from form, nor form from content. Sensitivity to this proposition would go far toward raising the moral recognition level in advertising and toward alerting businesspeople to the moral overtones of psychological appeals.

The Federal Trade Commission

The Federal Trade Commission (FTC) was established over seventy-five years ago and has the legal responsibility to protect consumers against deceptive advertising. Although the FTC is not the only regulatory body which monitors advertisements, it is mainly thanks to the FTC that today we are spared the most blatant abuses of advertising.

During the Reagan administration, however, there were complaints that the FTC wasn't doing as much as it should. As a result, consumer groups and rival products with a beef have been forgetting about the FTC and going directly to court to challenge dubious advertising claims. Ironically, the laissez-faire approach of the conservative Reagan FTC can be said to have backfired, because advertisers found the courts giving them a harder and more expensive time than did the FTC in its more vigorous days. A district court, for ex-

ample, fined Jartran $20 million in punitive damages—something the FTC can't do—on top of the $20 million awarded to U-Haul to compensate it for Jartran's claim that it had newer, easier-to-drive trucks than U-Haul.[35]

One important question running through the FTC's history and relevant to all efforts to prohibit deceptive advertising is whether the FTC (or any other regulatory body) is obligated to protect only reasonable, intelligent consumers who conduct themselves sensibly in the marketplace. Or should it also protect ignorant consumers who are careless or gullible in their purchases?[36] If the FTC uses the reasonable-consumer standard, then it prohibits only advertising claims which would deceive reasonable people. People who are more gullible or less bright than average and are taken in as a result would be unprotected. On the other hand, if the FTC uses the ignorant-consumer standard and prohibits an advertisement if it misleads anyone, no matter how ill-informed and naive he or she is, then it will handle a lot more cases and restrict advertising much more. But in spending its time and resources on such cases, it is not clear that the FTC will be proceeding in response to a substantial public interest, as it is legally charged with doing.[37]

The reasonable-person standard was traditional in a variety of areas of the law long before the FTC was established. If you are sued for negligence, you can successfully defend yourself if you can establish that you behaved as a hypothetical reasonable person would have behaved under like circumstances. On the other hand, in the law of misrepresentation, when you as a deceived consumer sue a seller on grounds that you were misled, then—assuming the deception is not proved to be intentional—you must establish that you were acting reasonably in relying on the false representation. If a reasonable person would not have been misled in like circumstances, then you will not win your case. Ads which make physically impossible or obviously exaggerated claims would thus escape legal liability under the reasonable-person standard.[38]

One decisive case in the legal transition *away* from the reasonable-person standard in matters of advertising, sales, and marketing was *FTC v. Standard Education* in 1931.[39] In this case an encyclopedia company was charged by the FTC with a number of deceptive and misleading practices. Potential customers were told by the company's agents that their names had been specially selected and that the encyclopedia they were being offered was being given away free as part of an advertising plan in return for use of their name for advertising purposes and as a reference. The customer was only required to pay $69.50 for a loose-leaf extension service. Potential buyers were not told that both books and supplements regularly sold for $69.50.

In deciding the case, the Supreme Court noted the view of the appellate court, which had earlier dismissed the FTC's case. Writing for the appellate court, Judge Learned Hand had declared that the FTC was occupying itself with "trivial niceties" which only "divert attention from substantial evils." "We cannot take seriously the suggestion," he wrote, "that a man who is buying a set of books and a ten years' 'extension service,' will be fatuous enough to be misled by the mere statement that the first are given away, and that he is paying only for the second." The Supreme Court itself, however, looked at the matter in a different light and held for the FTC and against Standard Education.

First, it noted that the practice had successfully deceived numerous victims, apparently including teachers, doctors, and college professors. But instead of resting its decision on the claim that a reasonable person might have been deceived, it advocated a change of standard, to something like the ignorant-consumer standard.

The fact that a false statement may be obviously false to those who are trained and experienced does not change its character, nor take away its power to deceive others less experienced. There is no duty resting upon a citizen to suspect the honesty of those with whom he transacts business. Laws are made to protect the trusting as well as the suspicious. The best element of business has long since decided that honesty should govern competitive enterprises, and that the rule of *caveat emptor* should not be relied upon to reward fraud and deception.

The decision in *FTC v. Standard Education*, as author Ivan L. Preston notes, led the FTC to apply the ignorant-man standard liberally, even in cases where there was no intent to deceive. In the 1940s the FTC challenged ads in some cases where it is hard to believe that anyone could possibly have been deceived. For example, it issued a complaint against Bristol-Myers's Ipana Toothpaste on the grounds that its "Smile of Beauty" slogan would lead some to believe that Ipana toothpaste would straighten their teeth. Eventually, though, the FTC abandoned the ignorant consumer standard in its extreme form and ceased to attempt to protect everybody from everything that might possibly deceive them. It now follows the "modified" ignorant consumer standard and protects only those cases of foolishness that are committed by significant numbers of people.[40]

Still, deciding what is likely to be misleading to a significant number of consumers is not necessarily easy. Consider these advertising claims, which are contested by some as deceptive: that Kraft Cheez Whiz is real cheese; that Chicken McNuggets are made from "whole breasts and thighs" (when they allegedly contain processed chicken skin as well and are fried in highly saturated beef fat); that ibuprofen causes stomach irritation (as

Tylenol's ads seem to imply). Was it deceptive of Diet Coke to proclaim that it was sweetened "Now with NutraSweet" even though the product also contained saccharin? Under legal pressure, Diet Coke changed its ads to read "NutraSweet blend." Is that free of any misleading implications?[41]

Children

The FTC has always looked after one special group of consumers without regard to how reasonable they are: namely, children. Still, several consumer groups think the FTC has not done enough, and they advocate even stricter controls over advertisements that reach children. Advertising to children is big business. The text of an ad in *Broadcast* magazine directed at potential television sponsors makes that point clearly:

> If you're selling, Charlie's Mom is buying. But you've got to sell Charlie first.
> His allowance is only 50¢ a week but his buying power is an American phenomenon. He's not only tight with his Mom, but he has a way with his Dad, his Grandma, and Aunt Harriet, too.
> When Charlie sees something he likes, he usually gets it.[42]

Television and advertising play a large role in most children's lives. The person or character with the highest level of recognition among young children is not the president, not Mickey Mouse, not even Santa Claus, but—Ronald McDonald. Children, particularly young children, are, as we all know, naive and gullible and thus particularly vulnerable to advertisers' enticements. Consider, for example, General Foods Corporation's advertisements for its Honeycomb cereal in which children are shown, after eating the cereal, to have enough power to lift large playhouses.[43] No adult would be misled by that, but children lack experience and independent, critical judgment. This provides at least a *prima facie* case for protecting them.

Advertisers, however, argue that parents still have ultimate control over what gets purchased and what doesn't. But is the strategy of selling to parents by convincing the children a fair one? The president of Kellogg Foods, William La Mothe, puts the case for the advertisers this way: "Once we start deciding which group can be advertised to and which group cannot, advertising as an efficient and economic method will be on its way to oblivion."[44]

Consumer advocate Peggy Charren of Action for Children's Television challenges that. She attacks the products that are being sold to children:

> The two things sold to children most on TV are toys and food, and we've found that 98 percent of the food advertising is for products children don't have to eat, non-nutritive things. Now in fact they're designing foods that would never be on the market if it weren't for television and its ability to sell them. They actually design junk cereals like Frankenberry and Cocoa Pebbles and Cookie Crisps because they can push them to kids on television.[45]

Advertising to children obviously raises the question of children's special susceptibilities and how far we need to go to protect them from possible manipulation. It also leads to the larger question of the nature and desirability of advertising's role in today's media-dominated society, which is our next topic.

THE DEBATE OVER ADVERTISING

The controversy over advertising does not end with the issue of deceptive techniques and unfair advertising practices. Advertising, as we have seen, provides little usable information to consumers. Advertisements almost always conceal relevant, negative facts about their products, and they base themselves more and more frequently on subtle appeals to psychological needs, which the products they peddle are unlikely to satisfy. This is the basis for some critics' wholesale repudiation of advertising on moral grounds. They also desire a less commercially polluted environment, one which does not continually reinforce materialistic values.

Consumer Needs

Some defenders of advertising, though, take the above points in stride. They concede that images of glamor, sex, or adventure sell products, but they argue that this is what we, the consumers, want. We don't just want blue jeans; we want romance or sophistication or status with our blue jeans—and advertisements provide this. Harvard business professor Theodore Levitt has gone on to draw an analogy between advertising and art. Both take liberties with reality, both deal in symbolic communication, and neither is interested in literal truth or in pure functionality. Rather, both art and advertising help us to repackage the otherwise crude, drab, and generally oppressive reality that surrounds us. They create "illusions, symbols, and implications that promise more." They help us to modify, transform, embellish, enrich, and reconstruct the world around us.

This is an essential need of human beings, Levitt writes. "Without distortion, embellishment, and elaboration, life would be drab, dull, anguished, and at its existential worst." Advertising helps to satisfy this legitimate human need. Its handsome packages and imaginative promises produce that "elevation of the spirit" that we want and need. Embellishment and distortion are therefore among advertising's socially desirable purposes. To criticize advertising on these counts, Levitt argues, is to overlook the real needs and values of human beings.[46]

Critics of Levitt contend that even if advertising appeals to the same deep needs that art does, advertising promises satisfaction of those needs in the products it sells, and that promise is rarely kept. At the end of the day, blue jeans are still just blue jeans, and your love life will be unaffected by which soap you shower with. The imaginative, symbolic, and artistic content of advertising, which Levitt sees as answering to real human needs, is viewed by critics of advertising as manipulating, distorting, and even creating those needs. In his influential books *The Affluent Society* and *The New Industrial State* John Kenneth Galbraith has criticized advertising on just this point.

Galbraith argues that the process of production today, with its expensive marketing campaigns, subtle advertising techniques, and sophisticated sales strategies, creates the very wants which it then satisfies. Producers, that is, create both the goods and the consumer demand for those goods. If a new breakfast cereal or detergent were so much wanted, Galbraith reasons, why must so much money be spent trying to get the consumer to buy it? He thinks it is obvious that "wants can be synthesized by advertising, catalyzed by salesmanship, and shaped by" discreet manipulations.

Accordingly, Galbraith rejects the traditional economist's belief in "consumer sovereignty": the idea that consumers should and do control the market through their purchases. Rather than independent consumer demand shaping production, as classical economic theory says it does, nowadays it is the other way around. Galbraith dubs this the "Dependence Effect": "As a society becomes increasingly affluent, wants are increasingly created by the process by which they are satisfied."[47]

One consequence of this, Galbraith thinks, is that our system of production cannot be defended on the ground that it is satisfying urgent or important wants. We can't defend production as satisfying wants if the production process itself creates those wants in the first place. "In the absence of the massive and artful persuasion that accompanies the management of demand," Galbraith argues,

> increasing abundance might well have reduced the interest of people in acquiring more goods. They would not have felt the need for multiplying the artifacts—autos, appliances, detergents, cosmetics—by which they were surrounded.[48]

Another consequence is our general preoccupation with material consumption. In particular, our pursuit of private goods, continually reinforced by advertising, leads us, Galbraith claims, to neglect public goods and services. We need better schools, parks, artistic and recreational facilities; safer and cleaner cities and air; and more efficient, less-crowded transportation systems. There is an imbalance of public services in relation to the private production and use of goods. We are rich in the latter, Galbraith thinks, and starved in the former. Our preoccupation with private consumption leads us to overlook opportunities for enjoyment that could be provided more efficiently or cost effectively by public production.

Critics of Galbraith have concentrated their fire on a couple of points. First, Galbraith never shows that advertising has the power he attributes to it. Most new products fail, despite heavy advertising, to win a permanent place in the hearts of consumers. Advertising campaigns like that for Listerine in the 1920s, which successfully created the problem of "halitosis" in order to sell the new idea of "mouthwash," are rare.[49] While it is true that we are inundated with ads, experiments suggest that we no longer care much about them. Each of us sees an average of 1,600 advertisements a day, notices around 1,200 of them, and responds favorably or unfavorably to only about 12. We also appear to pay more attention to ads for products that we already have.[50]

Second, critics have attacked Galbraith's belief that the needs supposedly created by advertisers and producers are, as a result, "false" or "artificial" needs and, therefore, less worthy of satisfaction. Human needs, they stress, are always socially influenced and are never static. How are we to distinguish between "genuine" and "artificial" wants, and why should the latter be thought less important? Ads might produce a want that we would not otherwise have had—say, for overnight mail delivery—without that want being in any way objectionable.

Although conclusive evidence is unavailable, critics of advertising continue to worry about its power to influence our lives and shape our culture and civilization. Even if producers cannot create wants out of whole cloth, many worry that advertising can manipulate our existing desires; that is, that it can stimulate certain of our desires, both at the expense of other, nonconsumer oriented desires and out of proportion to the likely satisfaction that fulfillment of those desires will bring.

Market Economics

Defenders of advertising are largely untroubled by these worries. They see advertising as an aspect of free competition in a competitive market, which ultimately works to the benefit of all. But there are problems with this simple free-market defense of advertising. First, advertising doesn't fit too well into the economist's model of the free market. Economists can prove, if we grant them enough assumptions, that free-market buying and selling leads to optimal results.[51] One of these assumptions is that everyone has full and complete information, on the basis of which they then buy and sell. But if this were so, advertising would be pointless.

One might argue that advertising moves us closer to the ideal of full information, but we have seen already that there is good reason to doubt this. Even if we put aside the question of whether ads can create, shape, or manipulate wants, they do seem to enhance brand loyalty, which generally works to thwart price competition. A true brand-name consumer is willing to pay more for a product that is otherwise indistinguishable from its competitors. He or she buys a certain beer despite being unable to taste the difference between it and other beers.

More generally, critics of advertising stand the "invisible hand" argument on its head. The goal of advertisers is to sell you products and to make money, not to maximize your well-being. Rational demonstration of how a product will in fact enhance your well-being is not the only way advertisers can successfully persuade people to buy their products. Indeed, it is far from the most common technique. The critics charge, accordingly, that there is no reason to think that advertising even tends to maximize the well-being of consumers.

Defenders of advertising may claim that, nonetheless, advertising is necessary for economic growth which, in turn, benefits us all. The truth of this, however, is open to debate. Critics maintain that advertising is a waste of resources and only serves to raise the price of advertised goods. Like Galbraith, they may also contend that advertising in general reinforces mindless consumerism. It corrupts our civilization and misdirects our society's economic effort toward private consumption and away from the public realm. The never-ending pursuit of material goods may also divert us as a society from the possibility of a substantially reduced working day. (For a development of this argument, see G. A. Cohen's "A Distinctive Contradiction of Advanced Capitalism," reprinted beginning on page 435.)

Free Speech and the Media

Two final issues can be briefly noted. Defenders of advertising claim that, despite these criticisms, advertising enjoys protection under the First Amendment as a form of speech. Legally, this claim probably requires qualification, especially in regard to radio and television, where one requires a license to broadcast. The banning of cigarette advertisements from television, for instance, did not run contrary to the Constitution. More importantly, even if we concede advertisers the legal right to free speech, not every exercise of that legal right is morally justifiable. If advertisements in general, or of a certain type or for a certain product, were shown to have undesirable social consequences, or if certain sorts of ads relied on objectionable or nonrational persuasive techniques, then there would be a strong moral argument against such advertisements regardless of their legal status.

Advertising subsidizes the media, and that is a positive but far from conclusive consideration in its favor. This is not the place to launch a discussion of the defects of American television, but the very fact that it is free results in our consuming far more than we would otherwise and probably, as many think, far more than is good for us. Nor is the mediocrity of much American television fare accidental. The networks need large audiences. Obviously, they can't run everyone's favorite type of program because people's tastes differ, so they seek to reach a common denominator. If viewers, instead of advertisers, paid for each show they watched, things would be different.[52]

SUMMARY

1. The complexity of today's economy and the dependence of consumers on business increases business's responsibility for product safety.

2. The legal liability of manufacturers for injuries caused by defective products has evolved over the years. Today the courts have moved to the doctrine of strict liability, which holds the manufacturer of a

product responsible for any injuries suffered as a result of defects in the product, regardless of whether the manufacturer was negligent.

3. Government agencies, like the Consumer Products Safety Commission, have broad powers to regulate product safety. Critics contend that these regulations are costly and that they prevent individuals from choosing to purchase a riskier but less-expensive product. This touches on the controversy over legal paternalism, the doctrine that the law may justifiably be used to restrict the freedom of individuals for their own good.

4. Although there are exceptions, regulations generally help ensure that business meets its responsibilities to consumers. Businesspeople, however, tend to favor self-regulation and governmental deregulation.

5. To increase safety, companies need to (1) give safety the priority necessitated by the product, (2) abandon the misconception that accidents are solely the result of consumer misuse, (3) monitor closely the manufacturing process, (4) review the safety content of their advertising, (5) provide consumers with full information about product performance, and (6) investigate consumer complaints. Some successful companies already put a premium on safety.

6. Business also has other obligations to consumers: (1) Product quality must live up to express and implied warranties; (2) prices should be just, and business should refrain from manipulative pricing and the use of price fixing to avoid competition; and (3) product labeling and packaging should provide clear, accurate, and adequate information.

7. Advertising tries to persuade people to buy products. Ambiguity, the conceal-ment of relevant facts, exaggeration, and psychological appeals are among the morally dubious techniques that advertisers use.

8. The Federal Trade Commission oversees advertising and protects us from blatantly deceptive advertising. It has been debated whether the FTC should only ban advertising that is likely to deceive reasonable people or whether it should protect careless or gullible consumers as well. The FTC now seeks to prohibit advertising that misleads a significant number of consumers, regardless of whether it was reasonable for them to have been misled.

9. Advertising to children is big business, but children are particularly susceptible to the blandishments of advertising. Advertisers contend that parents still control what gets purchased and what doesn't. But critics doubt the fairness of selling to parents by appealing to children.

10. Defenders of advertising view its imaginative, symbolic, and artistic content as answering to real human needs. Critics maintain that advertising manipulates those needs or even creates artificial ones. John Kenneth Galbraith contends that today the same process that produces products also produces the demand for those products (the Dependence Effect). Galbraith argues, controversially, that advertising encourages a preoccupation with material goods and leads us to favor private consumption at the expense of public goods.

11. Defenders of advertising see it as (1) a necessary and desirable aspect of competition in a market system, (2) a protected form of free speech, and (3) usefully subsidizing the media, in particular television. Critics challenge all three claims.

CASE 9.1

Aspartame: Miracle Sweetener or Dangerous Substance?

Diet Coke stands alone as the greatest overnight success in the marketplace. But when you quaff a Diet Coke on a hot summer's day, you may be doing more than quenching your thirst. You could be inviting a headache, depression, seizure, aggressive behavior, visual impairment, or, if you're a female, menstrual disturbances. You might even be loading your tissues with a carcinogen. The reason, say some nutritionists and medical scientists, is that soft drinks like Diet Coke—and a host of other products with sugar substitutes—contain the low-calorie sweetener aspartame, which goes under the name NutraSweet.

In 1981, the Reagan administration's newly appointed FDA commissioner, Dr. Arthur Hull Hayes, Jr., approved the use of aspartame in carbonated beverages and in one stroke seemed to end the prolonged controversy over the safety of the artificial sweetener that erupted in 1974, when the FDA first approved aspartame as a food additive. No sooner has aspartame's manufacturer, G. D. Searle & Co., begun to celebrate the FDA's initial approval of its sweet-profits-promising sweetener than things turned sour. Largely as a result of the rancorous protests of lawyer James Turner, author of a book about food additives, the FDA suspended its approval. Armed with animal experiments conducted by Washington University neuropathologist and psychiatrist Dr. James Olney, Turner insisted that aspartame could damage brain chemistry, especially in infants and children. Searle pooh-poohed the charges, citing experiments of its own which, it said, established the safety of its chemical sweetener. Unconvinced, Dr. Alexander M. Schmidt, then-FDA commissioner, appointed a task force of six scientists to examine Searle's experiments.

The task force's findings did not corroborate Searle's rosy assurances of safety. In fact, it concluded that Searle had distorted the safety data to win FDA approval of aspartame, as well as five drugs and an intrauterine device it was developing. According to the task force's 1976 report, "Searle made a number of deliberate decisions which seemingly were calculated to minimize the chances of discovering toxicity and/or to allay FDA concern."[53] Schmidt not only endorsed the task force's findings but told Congress in April 1976 that he saw in Searle's experiments "a pattern of conduct which compromises the scientific integrity of the studies." He added "at the heart of the FDA's regulatory process is the ability to rely upon the integrity of the basic safety data submitted by the sponsors of regulated products. Our investigation clearly demonstrates that, in the G. D. Searle Co., we have no basis for such reliance now." Specifically addressing the tests of aspartame, the commissioner and other FDA officials reported such irregularities as test animals recorded as dead on one date and alive on another and autopsies on rats conducted a year after the rodents had died during a feeding experiment. Schmidt further branded Searle's animal studies as "poorly conceived, carelessly executed, or inaccurately analyzed or reported."

Understandably, Searle wasn't about to allow these broadsides to pass unanswered. In a May 1976 letter to Schmidt, the firm's executive vice president, James Buzard, asserted that the FDA task force investigators "totally failed to find fraud, totally failed to find concrete evidence of an intent to deceive or mislead the agency or any advisory committee, or a failure to make any required report."

Sticking to his guns, Schmidt asked the

Justice Department to investigate the possibility that Searle had deliberately misled the FDA. After looking into the matter, a grand jury brought no indictment against the company. Nevertheless, under FDA pressure Searle enlisted the services of Universities Associated for Research and Education in Pathology (UAREP), a private group of fifteen universities that work under contracts and grants for paying clients. UAREP was to scrutinize eight of the fifteen as yet unreviewed aspartame studies to check Searle's conclusions. Under the terms of its agreement with Searle, UAREP would submit its findings to the company before submitting them to the FDA. Searle said that that was necessary to ensure accuracy. But Adrian Gross, a task force member and senior FDA scientist, expressed misgivings about the arrangement to his superiors. The report that UAREP submitted, Gross argued, "may well be interpreted as nothing short of an improper white wash."

Despite Gross's concern, the UAREP body proceeded, focusing solely on the microscopic slides produced by Searle in its animal experiments. In the end, the consortium could find nothing improper in Searle's interpretation of the slides. But Turner complained that the review was unacceptably narrow and incomplete because it had failed to consider either the design or execution of Searle's experiments. He was assured in writing that these and other relevant matters would be taken up by a public board of inquiry.

That board, made up of three independent scientists, had its work cut out for it. By January 1980, when the panel convened, the FDA had amassed 140 volumes of data on aspartame. Unable to deal with the mountain of information, the board concentrated on the same studies UAREP had examined. On September 30, 1980, the panel recommended that the FDA withdraw approval of aspartame. In making its recommendation, the board said that it couldn't exclude the possibility that

aspartame causes cancer in rats. It was noted that one of the compounds that aspartame degrades into upon digestion or when left unrefrigerated in hot water is DKP (diketopiperazinel). Since experiments in which DKP was fed to rats were inconclusive, there was no basis for claiming that aspartame was noncarcinogenic.

It thus appeared that aspartame had been laid to rest. But in November the country elected a new president, and within a few short months, the chemical would be sweetening a multitude of products and making millions of dollars for its manufacturer.

The day after Ronald Reagan was inaugurated President of the United States, Searle repetitioned the FDA to approve the sale of aspartame. It based its appeal on the same data it had previously submitted. Six months later, on July 24, 1981, the new FDA commissioner, Dr. Hayes, approved the sale of aspartame as a "table-top sweetener and ingredient of dry foods."

In approving the product for sale, Hayes discounted the possible cancer connection by citing a study done in 1981 by Ajinomoto, a Japanese chemical firm. That study found that, while rats fed with aspartame did develop more brain tumors than untreated rats, the increase was not statistically significant. The commissioner took the results as breaking the tie between two similar experiments conducted earlier by Searle, which had produced differing results.

Some scientists immediately discredited the Ajinomoto experiments, claiming that they used a strain of rat different from the one used in earlier Searle studies. In reply, Searle insisted that all three rat studies demonstrated that aspartame was noncarcinogenic.

In 1983 Searle successfully petitioned the FDA to permit aspartame to be used in carbonated beverages. Hayes gave FDA approval on July 8, 1983. Worldwide sales of aspartame in 1984 were estimated at $600 million.

One month after granting Searle permission to use aspartame in soft drinks, Dr. Hayes resigned from the FDA to become dean of New York Medical College. Three months later, in November 1983, he also took a job as senior scientific consultant to Burson-Marsteller, the public relations firm that has Searle's account for aspartame.

Discussion Questions

1. Does the aspartame controversy tend to support or belie the assumption that regulatory agencies are sufficient to ensure consumer safety?

2. Do you think that the evidence supports a conclusion that Searle allowed pursuit of self-interest to bias a scientifically objective assessment of the safety of aspartame?

3. Who do you think should have the primary responsibility for ensuring product safety—manufacturer or governmental agency?

4. Do you think that requiring a label warning consumers that a diet soft drink contains carcinogenic chemicals sufficiently discharges a governmental agency's obligation to protect the public?

5. If you were a Searle shareholder, would you think that the company acted responsibly? Would you want it to have acted other than it did?

6. Do you think that on safety matters the FDA or any regulatory agency should err on the side of overprotection rather than underprotection?

7. Do you think that Dr. Hayes acted responsibly in his role as FDA commissioner?

8. Some would argue that chemical sweeteners give the weight conscious and diabetics a needed alternative to sugar. In short, the availability of products containing saccharin or aspartame enlarges consumer freedom of choice. Thus, consumers and only consumers should decide whether they want to run the health risks associated with these chemicals. Would you agree?

CASE 9.2
FTC v. Colgate-Palmolive Company

Colgate-Palmolive Company was as proud as a new papa. The baby in this case was not the cuddly cute kind found snoozing and squalling in a maternity ward, but a shaving cream, which, Palmolive boasted, outshaved them all. Rapid Shave was its name.

To inform consumers of this blessed commercial event, Colgate enlisted the service of Ted Bates & Company, Inc., an advertising agency. Bates prepared three one-minute commercials designed to show that Rapid Shave could soften even the toughness of sandpaper. Each of the commercials contained the same "sandpaper test." "To prove Rapid Shave's super-moisturizing power," the announcer proclaimed, "we put it right from the can onto this tough, dry sandpaper. It was apply . . . soak . . . off in a stroke." The accompanying visual showed Rapid Shave being applied to what looked like sandpaper and immediately thereafter a razor shaving the substance clean. To any man who ever scraped his way awake in the morning, the ad bordered on the irresistible—well, almost.

Federal Trade Commission (FTC) officials found the commercials less than compelling.

In fact, the Commission charged Colgate and Bates with false and deceptive advertising. It based the charge on evidence disclosing that sandpaper of the type depicted in the commercial could not be shaved immediately following the application of Rapid Shave. Indeed, it required about eighty minutes of soaking. What's more, the sandpaper substance of the commercials was actually a simulated prop, a plexiglas mock-up to which sand had been applied. The FTC did concede that Rapid Shave could shave sandpaper, though not in the time depicted, and that real sandpaper is not very telegenic—it photographs like plain, colored paper.

The Court of Appeals backed up the FTC's claim that it was misleading of Colgate and Bates not to inform viewers that eighty minutes were required before one could shave sandpaper with Rapid Shave. But it did not agree with the Commission that the undisclosed use of plexiglass was a second, additional misrepresentation. This aspect of the case was appealed to the Supreme Court.

The Supreme Court accepted the Commission's determination that the commercials contained three representations to the public: (1) that Rapid Shave could shave sandpaper; (2) that an experiment had been conducted which verified this claim; and (3) that TV viewers were seeing the experiment for themselves. Putting aside the question of time, the first two representations are true, but the third is false. The question, then, is: Does this constitute a "material" or significant deception?

In a 7–2 ruling, the majority of the Court answered yes. They decided that television commercials that depict an experiment with undisclosed simulated props are deceptive. Speaking for the Majority, Chief Justice Warren stated:

> Respondents . . . insist that the present case . . . is . . . like a case in which a celebrity or independent testing agency has in fact submitted a written verification of an experiment actually observed, but, because of the inability of the camera to transmit accurately an impression of the paper on which the testimonial is written, the seller reproduces it on another substance so that it can be seen by the viewing audience. This analogy ignored the finding of the Commission that in the present case the seller misrepresented to the public that it was being given objective proof of a product claim. In respondents' hypothetical the objective proof of the product claim that is offered, the word of the celebrity or agency that the experiment was actually conducted, does exist; while in the case before us the objective proof offered, the viewer's own perception of an actual experiment, does not exist . . .

> The Court of Appeals has criticized the reference in the Commission's order to "test, experiment or demonstration" as not being capable of practical interpretation. It could find no difference between the Rapid Shave commercials and a commercial which extolled the goodness of ice cream while giving viewers a picture of a scoop of mashed potatoes appearing to be ice cream. We do not understand this difficulty. In the ice cream case the mashed potato prop is not being used for traditional proof of the product claim, while the purpose of the Rapid Shave commercial is to give the reviewer objective proof of the claims made. If in the ice cream hypothetical the focus of the commercial becomes the undisclosed potato prop and the viewer is invited, explicitly or by implication, to see for himself the truth of the claims about the ice cream's rich texture and full color, and perhaps compare it to a "rival product," then the commercial has become similar to the one now before us. Clearly, however, a commercial which depicts happy actors delightedly eating ice cream that is in fact mashed potatoes . . . is not covered by the present order.

Justice Harlan wrote the dissenting opinion in favor of Colgate and Bates:

> The only question here is what techniques the advertiser may use to convey essential truth to the television viewer. If the claim is true and valid, then the technique for projecting that claim, within broad boundaries, falls purely within the advertiser's art. The warrant to the Federal Trade Commission is to police the verity of the claim itself . . .
>
> I do not see how such a commercial can be said to be "deceptive" in any legally acceptable use of that term. The Court attempts to distinguish the case where a "celebrity" has written a testimonial endorsing some product, but the original testimonial cannot be seen over television and a copy is shown over the air by the manufacturer . . . But in both cases the viewer is told to "see for himself," in the one case that the celebrity has endorsed the product; in the other, that the product can shave sandpaper; in neither case is the viewer actually seeing the proof; and in both cases the objective proof does exist, be it in the original testimonial or the sandpaper test actually conducted by the manufacturer. In neither case, however, is there a material misrepresentation, because what the viewer sees *is* an accurate image of the objective proof . . .
>
> It is commonly known that television presents certain distortions in transmission for which the broadcasting industry must compensate. Thus, a white towel will look a dingy gray over television, but a blue towel will look sparkling white. On the Court's analysis, an advertiser must achieve accuracy in the studio even though it results in an inaccurate image being projected on the home screen . . . Would it be proper for respondent Colgate, in advertising a laundry detergent, to "demonstrate" the effectiveness of a major competitor's detergent in washing white sheets; and

> then "before the viewer's eyes," to wash a white (not blue) sheet with the competitor's detergent? The studio test would accurately show the quality of the product, but the image on the screen would look as though the sheet had been washed with an ineffective detergent. All that has happened here is the converse: a demonstration has been altered in the studio to compensate for the distortions of the television medium, but in this instance in order to present an accurate picture to the television viewers.[54]

Discussion Questions

1. In what ways, if any, were television viewers misled by the Rapid Shave advertisement?

2. Do you agree with the Federal Trade Commission and with Chief Justice Warren that the Rapid Shave commercial led the public to believe that it was seeing an objective proof of Rapid Shave's claim to shave sandpaper? Do you think that viewers suffered a "material" deception by not being told about the plexiglass prop?

3. Would the hypothetical "reasonable consumer" have been deceived by this commercial? Is this the appropriate standard to use in assessing the deceptiveness of commercials? Do you think the FTC was right to have concerned itself with this case?

4. Under what circumstances is it permissible for television commercials to use props? Must viewers always be informed of this fact?

5. Do you think that the advertising agency, Ted Bates and Company, acted responsibly in designing this ad? Did Colgate-Palmolive behave in a morally justifiable way in agreeing to run it?

CASE 9.3

Warning: The Following Ad May Contain a Subliminal Embed

There's nothing like the smell of a new car, right? Well, now there is—a product called Velvet Touch, which is an aerosol fountain of youth for any moribund old clunker. With a blast or two of this vehicular elixir, you can instantly turn an auto that smells like a stockyard into a "new car scent."

Marvin Ivy, president of the National Independent Auto Dealers Association, disapproves of using such products to sell used cars. "I think you'll deceive the public," he says. "That car could have 60,000 miles on it and smell like hell."[55]

Joseph Eikenberg, owner of Aero Motors, doesn't know what hell smells like, but his nose knows the lingering fetor left in cars by dogs and smokers. And the Baltimore car dealer thinks it's okay to use the artificial odor to combat them.

Synthetic scents are by no means confined to the used car business. Have you ever been strolling through a shopping mall and been seduced by the mouth-watering aroma of a freshly baked chocolate chip cookie? If so, the source of your temptation may not have been a cookie at all, but one of the many scents made and packaged by International Flavors & Fragrances, Inc. IF&F infuses into aerosol cans the palate-pleasing scents of foods such as fresh pizza, hot apple pie, nongreasy french fries and, to be sure, the once inimitable chocolate chip cookie. Sniffing profits in the scents wafting from IF&F's olfactory factory, many merchants are time-releasing the odors into the walkways of shopping malls. They hope that shoppers will find the aromas so tempting that they will succumb to their urge to splurge.

IF&F's success comes as no surprise to Minnesota Mining and Manufacturing Co., which provides most of the music we hear in commercial buildings. "We have been told [by retailers] that it will increase impulse purchases," says Donald Conlin, project manager at 3M.[56] The specially arranged music also is supposed to reduce absenteeism, worker turnover, and customer complaints as well as increase sales volume and profit.

Hal C. Becker, president of Behavioral Engineering Corporation, claims that what people don't consciously hear can be as influential as what they do. He has developed a subliminal message machine being marketed as "Dr. Becker's Black Box." (It sells for $9,180 or leases for $4,800 a year.) The messages and recipients vary. A Louisiana supermarket beams to workers and shoppers the inaudible message, "I will not steal. If I steal I go to jail." The owner of the supermarket is thrilled with the results. Before buying the device, he claims, pilferage used to run about $4,500 over six months and cashier shortages about $125 a month. Now the pilferage is down to $1,300 and the shortages to less than $10. In a Buffalo, New York, real estate management concern, salespeople hear tapes saying, "I love my job" and "I am the greatest salesman." According to the company's president, revenue has risen 35 percent despite a drop in advertising.[57]

Many of Becker's customers don't want to be identified for fear that the American Civil Liberties Union (ACLU) will sue them. Apparently their fears have some merit.

"The potential for abuse is enormous," says Barbara Shack, executive director of the New York branch of the ACLU. "If it is a distortion of sound and camouflaged so the receiver isn't aware and can influence his behavior, it's tantamount to brainwashing and ought to be prohibited by legislation."[58] Adds Jack Novik, the ACLU's national staff counsel: "We are very skeptical and suspicious of anything that imposes outside control on behavior."[59]

Some academicians consider the "black box" no more than a money machine for Becker. Professor of business Jay Russo points to the inconclusiveness of studies in subliminal suggestions. "It's an open issue," he says. "It won't die, but every time you do research it disappears like sand through your hands."[60]

Don't tell that to Wilson Key, though. He has worked in the media and advertising for thirty years. Since *Subliminal Seduction*, his first book, in 1973, Key has been the center of the controversy over alleged widespread use of subliminals in advertising. He has at once been praised as a trenchant critic of the mass media and a "kook" and "paranoid" for suggesting that ads are glutted with subliminally suggestive graphics that, though invisible to anyone not looking for them, can manipulate the beholder. Key has compiled a massive collection of ads that he claims present shockingly erotic images disguised as something innocuous.

"The strange-but-true part is that messages might actually affect us under certain conditions," says professor of communications Phillip Bozek. "Research suggests that our minds can register and begin to process information we didn't clearly hear or see, and that subliminal techniques can suggest to us images or phrases which we may later think we conceived ourselves, and which we are therefore less likely to resist. A subliminal message could urge a consumer to go ahead and buy something after all, and he or she might never suspect the subtle prodding."[61] Bozek sees ample evidence of the commercial use of subliminals.

So does one California legislator who has sponsored a bill that would require broadcasters to warn the public of subliminally embedded communications. Assemblyman Phillip

Wyman's bill would not outlaw subliminal communications but would require consumer warnings when "sounds" and "visual images" are "conveyed to people," but which are "not immediately and consequently perceptible" to normal seeing and hearing faculties.

Discussion Questions

1. How effective do you think subliminal communication is? What examples of subliminal communication have you encountered?

2. What moral issues are raised by the use of subliminal communication? What ideals, obligations, and effects must be taken into account by a company considering using subliminal communication?

3. How would you apply the principle of utility to the issue of using subliminals in advertising?

4. Do you think the end or purpose for which a subliminal message is used affects its morality? For example, would there be a significant moral difference between the surgeon general's using subliminals on television to get people to stop smoking and cigarette manufacturers using them to get people to buy and smoke a particular cigarette?

5. Professor Bozek, for one, draws a distinction between electronic and printed subliminals according to each one's degree of perceptibility. You need special equipment to pick out the former, but you can see the latter if you know how to look for them. This distinction leads Bozek to conclude that government should regulate electronically transmitted subliminals, whereas education should inform us about print subliminals. Do you agree? Or do you think both should be regulated, or neither?

CASE 9.4

Closing the Deal

Now that she had to, Jean McGuire wasn't sure she could. Not that she didn't understand what to do. Wright Boazman, sales director for Sunrise Land Developers, had made the step clear enough when he had described a variety of other effective "deal-closing techniques."

As Wright explained it very often people actually want to buy a lot, but at the last minute they're filled with self-doubt and uncertainty. The inexperienced salesperson can misinterpret this as a lack of interest in a property. "But," as Wright pointed out, "in most cases it's just an expression of the normal reservations everyone shows when the time comes to sign our names on the dotted line."

In Wright's view, the job of a land salesperson was "to help the prospect make the decision to buy." This didn't mean that salespeople should misrepresent a piece of property or in any way mislead people about what they were purchasing. "Law prohibits this," he pointed out, "and personally I find such behavior repugnant. What I'm talking about is helping them buy a lot they genuinely want and which you're convinced will be compatible with their needs and interests." For Wright Boazman, salespeople should serve as motivators, people who could provide whatever impulse was needed for prospects to close the deal.

In Wright's experience one of the most effective closing techniques was what he termed "the other party." It went something like this.

Suppose someone like Jean McGuire had a "hot" prospect, someone who was exhibiting a real interest in a lot but who was having trouble deciding. To motivate the prospect into buying, Jean ought to tell the person that she wasn't even sure the lot was still available, since there were a number of other salespeople showing the same lot, and they could already have closed a deal on it. As Wright put it, "This first ploy generally has the effect of increasing the prospect's interest in the property, and, more important to us, in closing the deal *pronto*."

Next Jean should say something like, "Why don't we go back to the office and I'll call headquarters to find out the status of the lot?" Wright indicated that such a suggestion ordinarily "whets their appetite" even more. In addition, it turns prospects away from wondering whether they should purchase the land and toward hoping that it's still available.

When they return to the office, Jean should make a call in the presence of the prospect. The call, of course, would not be to "headquarters" but to a private office only yards from where she and the prospect sit. Wright or someone else would receive the call, and Jean should fake a conversation about the property's availability, punctuating her comments with enough contagious excitement about its desirability. When she hangs up, she should breathe a sigh of relief that the lot's still available—but barely. At any minute, Jean should explain anxiously, the lot could be "green tagged," which means that headquarters is expecting a call from another salesperson who's about to close a deal and will remove the lot from open stock. (An effective variation of this, Wright had pointed out, would have Jean abruptly excuse herself upon hanging up and dart over to another sales representative with whom she'd engage in a heated, though staged, debate about the availability of the property, loud enough, of course, for the prospect to hear. The intended effect, according to Wright, would place the prospect in the "now or never" frame of mind.)

When Jean first heard about this and

other closing techniques, she felt uneasy. Even though the property was everything it was represented to be, and the law allowed purchasers ten days to change their minds after closing a deal, she instinctively objected to the use of psychological manipulation. Nevertheless, Jean never expressed her reservations to anyone, primarily because she didn't want to endanger her job. She desperately needed it owing to the recent and unexpected death of her husband, which left her as the sole support of herself and three young children. Besides, Jean had convinced herself that she could deal with closures more respectably than Wright and other salespeople might. But the truth was that after six months of selling land for Sunrise, Jean's sales lagged far behind those of the other sales representatives. Whether she liked it or not, Jean had to admit that she was losing a considerable number of sales because she couldn't close. And she couldn't close because, in Wright Boazman's words, she lacked technique. She wasn't employing the psychological closing devices that he and others had found so successful.

Now as she drove back to the office with two "hot prospects" in hand, she wondered what to do.

Discussion Questions

1. Do you disapprove of this sales tactic, or is it a legitimate business technique? How might it be morally defended?

2. What ideals, obligations, and effects must Jean consider? What interests and rights of the customer are at stake?

3. What weight should Jean give to self-interest in her deliberations? What do you think she should do? What would you do?

4. Suppose you knew either (1) that the person would eventually decide to buy the property anyway or (2) that it would genuinely be in the person's interests to buy it. Would that affect your moral assessment of this closing technique?

5. What rule, if any, would a rule utilitarian encourage realtors in this situation to follow? What should the realtors' professional code of ethics say about closing techniques?

CASE 9.5
The Ad Too Hot to Touch

Jack Saroyan, vice-president in charge of advertising for *American Companion*, a family magazine with a multimillion circulation, had heard of Car/Puter, but he never imagined that it would pitch him into a dilemma that could cost him his job.

Saroyan knew that Car/Puter International Corporation was a firm based in Brooklyn, New York, that for ten dollars would provide any person interested in buying a specific car with a computer printout of the list prices and the dealer's cost for the car and any accessories or options available. For an-

other ten dollars it would order the car from one of 900 participating dealers at $125 above the dealer's cost, far below the usual markup.

Although Saroyan realized that millions of Americans had access to information about this unique service through newspaper and magazine articles and editorials, he also knew that rarely had Car/Puter ads appeared in the print media. Not that Car/Puter hadn't tried to place ads; dozens of periodicals had summarily rejected their ads.

To Saroyan's knowledge no periodical had ever expressed why it wouldn't sell Car/Puter some advertising space, but he realized the rationale. Car/Puter's services directly competed with automotive dealers who pay millions of dollars annually for advertising space in newspapers and magazines. If a print medium were to advertise a service that car dealers disapproved of, automobile manufacturers would be highly reluctant to continue advertising in it. The result would be a tremendous loss of advertising revenue.

Most magazines simply couldn't risk losing such a considerable source of profit. For example, Saroyan's *American Companion* attributed more than half its annual advertising revenue to ads placed by Ford, General Motors, Chrysler, and American Motors. Saroyan was no fool. To jeopardize this income by running ads for Car/Puter struck him as the height of economic folly. What's more, if he lost even a fraction of these revenues by approving Car/Puter ads, Saroyan would be held personally accountable. He didn't wish to dwell on the career implications of that.

Unfortunately, Jack Saroyan had never been one to see things entirely in economic or self-interested terms. In this instance, for example, he felt sensitive to the significant social service he would perform by running Car/Puter ads. The ads would help consumers avail themselves of information they needed to make wise and prudent decisions about a car purchase. It also offered a service calculated to help them save millions of dollars annually. Besides, Saroyan was keenly aware of the economic disadvantage that Car/Puter suffered by being denied advertising space in the print media, by being denied its general right to make its service known to the public through advertising.

Saroyan viewed his decision as a choice between rendering the public at large and Car/Puter in particular a service or doing what he thought to be in the best interests of *American Companion*. As hard as he tried, he didn't see these values as compatible.

Discussion Questions

1. What should Saroyan do? Explain by appeal to ethical principles.

2. Do you think the media ought to grant advertising space to all who desire it and can pay for it? If not, what limitations would you impose, and why?

3. If Saroyan decides to reject Car/Puter's request, does he have a moral obligation to explain to them why? (Keep in mind that anything he writes could be used in subsequent litigation that Car/Puter may wish to pursue.)

CASE 9.6
The Skateboard Scare

Colin Brewster, owner of Brewster's Bicycle Shop, had to admit that his skateboard sales had salvaged his business now that interest in the bicycle seemed to have peaked. In fact, skateboard business was so brisk that Brewster could hardly keep them in stock. But the picture was far from rosy.

Just last week a concerned consumer group visited his shop to inform Brewster that it had ample evidence to prove that skateboards presented a real and immediate hazard to consumer safety. Brewster conceded that the group surely provided enough statistical support of the shocking number of broken bones and concussions that had resulted directly and indirectly from accidents involving skateboards. But he thought the group's position was fundamentally unsound because, as he told them, "It's not the skateboards that are unsafe but how people use them."

Committee members weren't impressed with Brewster's distinction. They likened it to saying that automobile manufacturers shouldn't be conscious of consumer safety because it's not the automobiles that are unsafe but how we drive them. Brewster objected that automobiles presented an entirely different problem, because a number of things could be done to ensure their safe usage. "But what can you do about a skateboard?" he asked them. "Besides, I don't manufacture them, I just sell them."

The committee pointed out that other groups were attacking the problem on the manufacturing level. What they expected of Brewster was some responsible management of the problem at the local retail level. They pointed out that recently Brewster had run a series of local television ads portraying young but accomplished skateboarders performing fancy flips and turns. The ad implied that anyone could easily accomplish such feats. Only yesterday one parent had told the committee of her child's breaking an arm attempting such gymnastics after having purchased a Brewster skateboard. "Obviously," Brewster countered, "the woman has an irresponsible kid whose activities she should monitor, not me." He pointed out that his ad was no more intended to imply that anyone could or should do those tricks than an ad for a car that shows it traveling at high speeds while doing stunt tricks implies that you should drive that way.

The committee disagreed. They said Brewster not only should discontinue such misleading advertising but also should actively publicize the potential dangers of skateboarding. Specifically, the committee wanted him to display prominently beside his skateboard stock the statistical data testifying to its hazards. Furthermore, he should make sure that anyone buying a skateboard has read this material prior to purchase.

Brewster argued that the committee's demands were unreasonable. "Do you have any idea what effect that would have on sales?" he asked them.

Committee members readily admitted that they were less interested in his sales than in their children's safety. Brewster told them that in this matter their children's safety was their responsibility, not his. But the committee was adamant. Members told Brewster that they'd be back in a week to find out what positive steps, if any, he'd taken to correct the problem. In the event he'd done nothing, they indicated that they were prepared to picket his shop.

Discussion Questions

1. Whom do you agree with—Brewster or the committee? Why?

2. Would you criticize Brewster's advertisements? Do you think the demand that he publicize the dangers of skateboarding is reasonable?

3. What responsibilities, if any, do retailers have to ensure consumer safety? Compare the responsibilities of manufacturers, skateboarders, and parents.

4. Identify the ideals, obligations, and effects that Brewster should consider in reaching his decision. Which of the considerations do you think is the most important?

NOTES

1. "Tobacco's Toll," *Newsweek* (international edition), November 9, 1987.

2. Lawrence H. Tribe, "Federalism with Smoke and Mirrors," *The Nation*, June 7, 1986; "Taking on Big Tobacco in Dixie," *U.S. News and World Report*, Feb-

ruary 8, 1988; and "Of Mice and Men," *The Economist*, April 16, 1988.

3. Fred Luthans and Richard M. Hodgetts, *Social Issues in Business* (New York: Macmillan, 1976), 362.

4. Manuel G. Velasquez, *Business Ethics* (Englewood Cliffs, N.J.: Prentice-Hall, 1982), 235.

5. George G. Brenkert, "Strict Products Liability and Compensatory Justice," in W. Michael Hoffman and Jennifer Mills Moore, eds., *Business Ethics: Readings and Cases in Corporate Morality* (New York: McGraw-Hill, 1984).

6. Joseph R. DesJardins and John J. McCall, eds., *Contemporary Issues in Business Ethics* (Belmont, Calif.: Wadsworth, 1985), 51.

7. Murray Weidenbaum, "Consumer Product Regulation," in DesJardins and McCall, *Contemporary Issues in Business*, 79.

8. Ibid., 79–80.

9. Ibid., 83.

10. Richard T. DeGeorge, "Ethical Responsibilities of Engineers in Large Organizations," *Business and Professional Ethics Journal* 1 (Fall 1981).

11. Dean Rothbart and John A. Prestbo, "Taking Rely Off Market Cost Procter & Gamble a Week of Agonizing," *The Wall Street Journal*, November 3, 1980, 1.

12. Car crashes are currently the leading killer of Americans under 35. See Allan Parachini, "Pediatricians Raise Issue in Auto Safety Debate," *Los Angeles Times*, April 3, 1981.

13. Ibid., 7.

14. Marisa Manley, "Products Liability: You're More Exposed Than You Think," *Harvard Business Review* 65 (September–October 1987): 28–29.

15. These are taken from Tad Tuleja, *Beyond the Bottom Line* (New York: Penguin, 1987), 77–78.

16. David L. Rados, "Product Liability: Tougher Ground Rules," *Harvard Business Review* 47 (July–August 1969): 148.

17. Jeffrey H. Birnbaum, "Pricing of Product Is Still an Art, Often Having Little Link to Costs," *The Wall Street Journal*, November 25, 1981, Sec. 2, p. 29.

18. Ibid.

19. Ibid.

20. See William J. Kehoe, "Ethics, Price Fixing, and the Management of Price Strategy," in Gene R. Laczniak and Patrick E. Murphy, eds., *Marketing Ethics* (Lexington, Mass.: Lexington Books, 1985) for a discussion of ethical issues in pricing.

21. For a thorough look at this case, see M. David Er-

mann and Richard J. Lundman, *Corporate Deviance* (New York: Holt, Rinehart & Winston, 1982), chapter 5.

22. Burton Leiser, "Deceptive Practices in Advertising," in Tom L. Beauchamp and Norman E. Bowie, eds., *Ethical Theory and Business*, 2nd ed. (Englewood Cliffs, N.J.: Prentice-Hall, 1983), 337.

23. E. B. Weiss, "Marketers Fiddle While Consumers Burn," *Harvard Business Review* 46 (July–August 1968): 48.

24. Roger Draper, "The Faithless Shepherd," *New York Review of Books* (June 26, 1986): 14.

25. Ibid., 17.

26. See "Mea Culpa, Sort Of," *Newsweek*, September 27, 1971, 98.

27. A rating of 100 supposedly equals 30,000 miles of useful life.

28. Paul Stevens, "Weasel Words: God's Little Helpers," in Paul A. Eschhol, Alfred A. Rosa, Virginia P. Clark, eds., *Language Awareness* (New York: St. Martin's Press, 1974), 156.

29. Samm Sinclair Baker, *The Permissible Lie* (New York: World Publishing Co., 1968), 16.

30. The editors of *Consumer Reports*, *The Medicine Show* (Mt. Vernon, N.Y.: Consumers Union, 1972), 14.

31. Fred Luthans and Richard M. Hodgetts, *Social Issues in Business* (New York: Macmillan, 1976), 353.

32. Ann Hagedorn, "FDA Cracks Down on Cosmetic Firms' Age-Treatment Drugs," *The Wall Street Journal*, April 27, 1987.

33. Gail Bronson, "Sexual Pitches in Ads Become More Explicit and Pervasive," *The Wall Street Journal*, November 18, 1980, 1.

34. Wilson Bryan Key, *Subliminal Seduction* (New York: New American Library, 1973), 11.

35. "Deceptive Ads: The FTC's Laissez-Faire Approach Is Backfiring," *Business Week*, December 2, 1985.

36. See Ivan L. Preston, "Reasonable Consumer or Ignorant Consumer? How the FTC Decides," in Tom L. Beauchamp and Norman E. Bowie, eds., *Ethical Theory and Business*, 2nd ed. (Englewood Cliffs, N.J.: Prentice-Hall, 1983).

37. Ibid., 348.

38. Ibid.

39. 302 US 112.

40. Preston, "Reasonable Consumer," 352–355.

41. "Deceptive Ads," *Business Week*.

42. Quoted in John Culkin, "Selling to Children: Fair Play in TV Commercials," in DesJardins and McCall, 193.

43. "Deceptive Ads," *Business Week*.

44. Culkin, p. 194.

45. Ibid.

46. Theodore Levitt, "The Morality (?) of Advertising," *Harvard Business Review* 48 (July–August 1970): 84–92.

47. John Kenneth Galbraith, *The Affluent Society*, 3rd ed. (New York: Houghton Mifflin, 1976), 131.

48. John Kenneth Galbraith, *The New Industrial State* (New York: Signet, 1967), 219.

49. Since the saliva in one's mouth is completely replenished every fifteen minutes or so anyway, no mouthwash can have an effect longer than that.

50. Draper, "The Faithless Shepherd," 16.

51. Technically, it leads to a situation called *Pareto optimal*, in which no one person could be made better off without making someone else worse off.

52. For a discussion of this, see "All by the Numbers," *The Economist*, December 20, 1986.

53. Judith Randal, "Is Aspartame Really Safe? The Fight Over the Miracle Sweetener Hasn't Ended Yet," *The Washington Post National Weekly Edition*, May 28, 1984, 7–8. This article is the source of the case presented and of all the quotations that appear in the remainder of the case.

54. *Federal Trade Commission v. Colgate-Palmolive Co. et al.*, 380 U.S. 374, 85 S. Ct. 1035, 13 L Ed. 2d 904 (1965).

55. Bernard Wysocki, Jr., "Sight, Smell, Sound: They're All Arms in Retailers's Arsenal," *The Wall Street Journal*, April 17, 1979, 27.

56. Neil Maxwell, "Words Whispered to Subconscious Supposedly Deter Theft, Fainting," *The Wall Street Journal*, November 25, 1980, 26.

57. Ibid.

58. Ibid.

59. Wysocki, "Retailers's Arsenal," 1.

60. Ibid., 1, 27.

61. "Letters to Editor," *The Bakersfield Californian*, June 3, 1983, 5.

Advertising and Behavior Control

Robert L. Arrington

After defining and illustrating the meaning of "puffery" in advertising, professor of philosophy Robert L. Arrington turns to the central question of his article: "Do the advertising techniques we have discussed involve a violation of human autonomy and a manipulation and control of consumer behavior, or do they simply provide an efficient and effective means of giving the consumer information on the basis of which he or she makes a free choice?" Or more briefly: "Is advertising information, or creation of desire?"

In answering the question, Arrington examines the notions of autonomous desire, rational desire and choice, free choice, and control or manipulation. He concedes that advertising may in some individuals control behavior, produce compulsive behavior, or create irrational wants or wants not truly those of the consumer. But he does not believe that advertising does this in most cases or that there is anything about the nature of advertising that necessarily leads to violations of autonomy.

Consider the following advertisements:

1. "A woman in *Distinction Foundations* is so beautiful that all other women want to kill her."

2. Pongo Peach color from Revlon comes "from east of the sun . . . west of the moon where each tomorrow dawns." It is "succulent on your lips" and "sizzling on your finger tips (And on your toes, goodness knows)." Let it be your "adventure in paradise."

3. "Increase the value of your holdings. Old Charter Bourbon Whiskey—The Final Set Up."

4. Last Call Smirnoff Style: "They'd never really miss us, and it's kind of late already, and it's quite a long way, and I could build a fire, and you're looking very beautiful, and we could have another martini, and it's awfully nice just being home . . . you think?"

5. A Christmas Prayer. "Let us pray that the blessings of peace be ours—the peace to build and grow, to live in harmony and sympathy with others, and to plan for the future with confidence." New York Life Insurance Company.

These are instances of what is called puffery—the practice by a seller of making exaggerated, highly fanciful or suggestive claims about a product or service. Puffery, within ill-defined limits, is

Excerpted from "Advertising and Behavior Control," published in *Journal of Business Ethics* 1 (February 1982): 3–12. Copyright © 1982 by D. Reidel Publishing Company, Dordrecht, Holland.

legal. It is considered a legitimate, necessary, and very successful tool of the advertising industry. Puffery is not just bragging; it is bragging carefully designed to achieve a very definite effect. Using the techniques of so-called motivational research, advertising firms first identify our often hidden needs (for security, conformity, oral stimulation) and our desires (for power, sexual dominance and dalliance, adventure) and then they design ads which respond to these needs and desires. By associating a product, for which we may have little or no direct need or desire, with symbols reflecting the fulfillment of these other, often subterranean interests, the advertisement can quickly generate large numbers of consumers eager to purchase the product advertised. What woman in the sexual race of life could resist a foundation which would turn other women envious to the point of homicide? Who can turn down an adventure in paradise, east of the sun where tomorrow dawns? Be at the pinnacle of success—drink Old Charter. Or stay at home and dally a bit—with Smirnoff. And let us pray for a secure and predictable future, provided for by New York Life, God willing. It doesn't take very much motivational research to see the point of these sales pitches. Others are perhaps a little less obvious. The need to feel secure in one's home at night can be used to sell window air conditioners, which drown out small noises and provide a friendly, dependable companion. The fact that baking a cake is symbolic of giving birth to a baby used to prompt advertisements for cake mixes which glamorized the 'creative' housewife. And other strategies, for example involving cigar symbolism, are a bit too crude to mention, but are nevertheless very effective.

Don't such uses of puffery amount to manipulation, exploitation, or downright control? In his very popular book *The Hidden Persuaders*, Vance Packard points out that a number of people in the advertising world have frankly admitted as much:

> As early as 1941 Dr. Dichter (an influential advertising consultant) was exhorting ad agencies to recognize themselves for what they actually were—"one of the most advanced laboratories in psychology". He said the successful ad agency "manipulates human motivations and desires and develops a need for goods with which the public has at one time been unfamiliar—perhaps even unde-

sirous of purchasing". The following year *Advertising Agency* carried an ad man's statement that psychology not only holds promise for understanding people but "ultimately for controlling their behavior."[1]

Such statements lead Packard to remark: "With all this interest in manipulating the customer's subconscious, the old slogan 'let the buyer beware' began taking on a new and more profound meaning."[2]

B. F. Skinner, the high priest of behaviorism, has expressed a similar assessment of advertising and related marketing techniques. Why, he asks, do we buy a certain kind of car?

> Perhaps our favorite TV program is sponsored by the manufacturer of that car. Perhaps we have seen pictures of many beautiful or prestigeful persons driving it—in pleasant or glamorous places. Perhaps the car has been designed with respect to our motivational patterns: the device on the hood is a phallic symbol; or the horsepower has been stepped up to please our competitive spirit in enabling us to pass other cars swiftly (or, as the advertisements say, 'safely'). The concept of freedom that has emerged as part of the cultural practice of our group makes little or no provision for recognizing or dealing with these kinds of control.[3]

In purchasing a car we may think we are free, Skinner is claiming, when in fact our act is completely controlled by factors in our environment and in our history of reinforcement. Advertising is one such factor.

A look at some other advertising techniques may reinforce the suspicion that Madison Avenue controls us like so many puppets. T.V. watchers surely have noticed that some of the more repugnant ads are shown over and over again, *ad nauseum*. My favorite, or most hated, is the one about A-1 Steak Sauce which goes something like this: Now, ladies and gentlemen, what *is* hamburger? It has succeeded in destroying my taste for hamburger, but it has surely drilled the name of A-1 Sauce into my head. And that is the point of it. Its very repetitiousness has generated what ad theorists call *information*. In this case it is indirect information, information derived not from the content of what is said but from the fact that it is said so

often and so vividly that it sticks in one's mind—
i.e., the information yield has increased. And not
only do I always remember A-1 Sauce when I go to
the grocers, I tend to assume that any product
advertised so often has to be good—and so I usually buy a bottle of the stuff.

Still another technique: On a recent show of
the television program 'Hard Choices' it was demonstrated how subliminal suggestion can be used
to control customers. In a New Orleans department store, messages to the effect that shoplifting
is wrong, illegal, and subject to punishment were
blended into the Muzak background music and
masked so as not to be consciously audible. The
store reported a dramatic drop in shoplifting. The
program host conjectured whether a logical extension of this technique would be to broadcast subliminal advertising messages to the effect that the
store's $15.99 sweater special is the "bargain of a
lifetime." Actually, this application of subliminal
suggestion to advertising has already taken place.
Years ago in New Jersey a cinema was reported to
have flashed subthreshold ice cream ads onto the
screen during regular showings of the film—and,
yes, the concession stand did a landslide business.[4]

Puffery, indirect information transfer, subliminal advertising—are these techniques of manipulation and control whose success shows that many of
us have forfeited our autonomy and become a community, or herd, of packaged souls?[5] The business
world and the advertising industry certainly reject
this interpretation of their efforts. *Business Week*, for
example, dismissed the charge that the science of
behavior, as utilized by advertising, is engaged in
human engineering and manipulation. It edi-
torialized to the effect that "it is hard to find anything very sinister about a science whose principle
conclusion is that you get along with people by
giving them what they want."[6] The theme is familiar: businesses just give the consumer what he/she
wants; if they didn't they wouldn't stay in business
very long. Proof that the consumer wants the products advertised is given by the fact that he buys
them, and indeed often returns to buy them again
and again.

The techniques of advertising we are discussing have had their more intellectual defenders as
well. For example, Theodore Levitt, Professor of
Business Administration at the Harvard Business
School, has defended the practice of puffery and

the use of techniques dependent on motivational
research.[7] What would be the consequences, he
asks us, of deleting all exaggerated claims and fanciful associations from advertisements? We would
be left with literal descriptions of the empirical
characteristics of products and their functions.
Cosmetics would be presented as facial and bodily
lotions and powders which produce certain odor
and color changes; they would no longer offer hope
or adventure. In addition to the fact that these
products would not then sell as well, they would
not, according to Levitt, please us as much either.
For it is hope and adventure we want when we buy
them. We want automobiles not just for transportation, but for the feelings of power and status they
give us. Quoting T. S. Eliot to the effect that "Human kind cannot bear very much reality," Levitt
argues that advertising is an effort to "transcend
nature in the raw," to "augment what nature has so
crudely fashioned." He maintains that "everybody
everywhere wants to modify, transform, embellish, enrich and reconstruct the world around
him." Commerce takes the same liberty with reality
as the artist and the priest—in all three instances
the purpose is "to influence the audience by creating illusions, symbols, and implications that promise more than pure functionality." For example, "to
amplify the temple in men's eyes, [men of cloth]
have, very realistically, systematically sanctioned
the embellishment of the houses of the gods with
the same kind of luxurious design and expensive
decoration that Detroit puts into a Cadillac." A
poem, a temple, a Cadillac—they all elevate our
spirits, offering imaginative promises and symbolic interpretations of our mundane activities.
Seen in this light, Levitt claims, "Embellishment
and distortion are among advertising's legitimate
and socially desirable purposes." To reject these
techniques of advertising would be "to deny man's
honest needs and values."

Phillip Nelson, a Professor of Economics at
SUNY-Binghampton, has developed an interesting
defense of indirect information advertising.[8] He
argues that even when the message (the direct
information) is not credible, the fact that the brand
is advertised, and advertised frequently, is valuable indirect information for the consumer. The
reason for this is that the brands advertised most
are more likely to be better buys—losers won't be
advertised a lot, for it simply wouldn't pay to do so.

Thus even if the advertising claims made for a widely advertised product are empty, the consumer reaps the benefit of the indirect information which shows the product to be a good buy.

I don't know of any attempt to defend the use of subliminal suggestion in advertising, but I can imagine one form such an attempt might take. Advertising information, even if perceived below the level of conscious awareness, must appeal to some desire on the part of the audience if it is to trigger a purchasing response. Just as the admonition not to shoplift speaks directly to the superego, the sexual virtues of TR-7's, Pongo Peach, and Betty Crocker cake mix present themselves directly to the id, bypassing the pesky reality principle of the ego. With a little help from our advertising friends, we may remove a few of the discontents of civilization and perhaps even enter into the paradise of polymorphous perversity.[9]

The defense of advertising which suggests that advertising simply is information which allows us to purchase what we want, has in turn been challenged. Does business, largely through its advertising efforts, really make available to the consumer what he/she desires and demands? John Kenneth Galbraith has denied that the matter is as straightforward as this.[10] In his opinion the desires to which business is supposed to respond, far from being original to the consumer, are often themselves created by business. The producers make both the product and the desire for it, and the "central function" of advertising is "to create desires." Galbraith coins the term 'The Dependence Effect' to designate the way wants depend on the same process by which they are satisfied.

David Braybrooke has argued in similar and related ways.[11] Even though the consumer is, in a sense, the final authority concerning what he wants, he may come to see, according to Braybrooke, that he was mistaken in wanting what he did. The statement 'I want x,' he tells us, is not incorrigible but is "ripe for revision." If the consumer had more objective information than he is provided by product puffing, if his values had not been mixed up by motivational research strategies (e.g., the confusion of sexual and automotive values), and if he had an expanded set of choices instead of the limited set offered by profit-hungry corporations, then he might want something quite different from what he presently wants. This

shows, Braybrooke thinks, the extent to which the consumer's wants are a function of advertising and not necessarily representative of his real or true wants.

The central issue which emerges between the above critics and defenders of advertising is this: do the advertising techniques we have discussed involve a violation of human autonomy and a manipulation and control of consumer behavior, or do they simply provide an efficient and cost-effective means of giving the consumer information on the basis of which he or she makes a free choice. Is advertising information, or creation of desire?

To answer this question we need a better conceptual grasp of what is involved in the notion of autonomy. This is a complex, multifaceted concept, and we need to approach it through the more determinate notions of (a) autonomous desire, (b) rational desire and choice, (c) free choice, and (d) control or manipulation. In what follows I shall offer some tentative and very incomplete analyses of these concepts and apply the results to the case of advertising.

(a) Autonomous Desire

Imagine that I am watching T.V. and see an ad for Grecian Formula 16. The thought occurs to me that if I purchase some and apply it to my beard, I will soon look younger—in fact I might even be myself again. Suddenly I want to be myself! I want to be young again! So I rush out and buy a bottle. This is our question: was the desire to be younger manufactured by the commercial, or was it 'original to me' and truly mine? Was it autonomous or not?

F. A. von Hayek has argued plausibly that we should not equate nonautonomous desires, desires which are not original to me or truly mine, with those which are culturally induced.[12] If we did equate the two, he points out, then the desires for music, art, and knowledge could not properly be attributed to a person as original to him, for these are surely induced culturally. The only desires a person would really have as his own in this case would be the purely physical ones for food, shelter, sex, etc. But if we reject the equation of the nonautonomous and the culturally induced, as von Hayek would have us do, then the mere fact that my desire to be young again is caused by the T.V.

commercial—surely an instrument of popular culture transmission—does not in and of itself show that this is not my own, autonomous desire. Moreover, even if I never before felt the need to look young, it doesn't follow that this new desire is any less mine. I haven't always liked 1969 Aloxe Corton Burgundy or the music of Satie, but when the desires for these things first hit me, they were truly mine.

This shows that there is something wrong in setting up the issue over advertising and behavior control as a question whether our desires are truly ours *or* are created in us by advertisements. Induced and autonomous desires do not separate into two mutually exclusive classes. To obtain a better understanding of autonomous and nonautonomous desires, let us consider some cases of a desire which a person does not *acknowledge* to be his own even though he *feels* it. The kleptomaniac has a desire to steal which in many instances he repudiates, seeking by treatment to rid himself of it. And if I were suddenly overtaken by a desire to attend an REO concert, I would immediately disown this desire, claiming possession or momentary madness. These are examples of desires which one might have but with which one would not identify. They are experienced as foreign to one's character or personality. Often a person will have what Harry Frankfurt calls a second-order desire, that is to say, a desire *not* to have another desire.[13] In such cases, the first-order desire is thought of as being nonautonomous, imposed on one. When on the contrary a person has a second-order desire to maintain and fulfill a first-order desire, then the first-order desire is truly his own, autonomous, original to him. So there is in fact a distinction between desires which are the agent's own and those which are not, but this is not the same as the distinction between desires which are innate to the agent and those which are externally induced.

If we apply the autonomous/nonautonomous distinction derived from Frankfurt to the desires brought about by advertising, does this show that advertising is responsible for creating desires which are not truly the agent's own? Not necessarily, and indeed not often. There may be some desires I feel which I have picked up from advertising and which I disown—for instance, my desire for A-1 Steak Sauce. If I act on these desires it can be said that I have been led by advertising to act in a

way foreign to my nature. In these cases my autonomy has been violated. But most of the desires induced by advertising I fully accept, and hence most of these desires are autonomous. The most vivid demonstration of this is that I often return to purchase the same product over and over again, without regret or remorse. And when I don't, it is more likely that the desire has just faded than that I have repudiated it. Hence, while advertising may violate my autonomy by leading me to act on desires which are not truly mine, this seems to be the exceptional case.

Note that this conclusion applies equally well to the case of subliminal advertising. This may generate subconscious desires which lead to purchases, and the act of purchasing these goods may be inconsistent with other conscious desires I have, in which case I might repudiate my behavior and by implication the subconscious cause of it. But my subconscious desires may not be inconsistent in this way with my conscious ones; my id may be cooperative and benign rather than hostile and malign.[14] Here again, then, advertising may or may not produce desires which are 'not truly mine.'

What are we to say in response to Braybrooke's argument that insofar as we might choose differently if advertisers gave us better information and more options, it follows that the desires we have are to be attributed more to advertising than to our own real inclinations? This claim seems empty. It amounts to saying that if the world we lived in, and we ourselves, were different, then we would want different things. This is surely true, but it is equally true of our desire for shelter as of our desire for Grecian Formula 16. If we lived in a tropical paradise we would not need or desire shelter. If we were immortal, we would not desire youth. What is true of all desires can hardly be used as a basis for criticizing some desires by claiming that they are nonautonomous.

(b) Rational Desire and Choice

Braybrooke might be interpreted as claiming that the desires induced by advertising are often irrational ones in the sense that they are not expressed by an agent who is in full possession of the facts about the products advertised or about the alternative products which might be offered him. Following this line of thought, a possible criticism of advertising is that it leads us to act on irrational desires or to make irrational choices. It might be said that our autonomy has been violated by the fact that we are prevented from following our rational wills or that we have been denied the 'positive freedom' to develop our true, rational selves. It might be claimed that the desires induced in us by advertising are false desires in that they do not reflect our essential, i.e., rational, essence.

The problem faced by this line of criticism is that of determining what is to count as rational desire or rational choice. If we require that the desire or choice be the product of an awareness of *all* the facts about the product, then surely every one of us is always moved by irrational desires and makes nothing but irrational choices. How could we know all the facts about a product? If it be required only that we possess all of the *available* knowledge about the product advertised, then we still have to face the problem that not all available knowledge is *relevant* to a rational choice. If I am purchasing a car, certain engineering features will be, and others won't be, relevant, *given what I want in a car*. My prior desires determine the relevance of information. Normally a rational desire or choice is thought to be one based upon relevant information, and information is relevant if it shows how other, prior desires may be satisfied. It can plausibly be claimed that it is such prior desires that advertising agencies acknowledge, and that the agencies often provide the type of information that is relevant in light of these desires. To the extent that this is true, advertising does not inhibit our rational wills or our autonomy as rational creatures.

(c) Free Choice

It might be said that some desires are so strong or so covert that a person cannot resist them, and that when he acts on such desires he is not acting freely or voluntarily but is rather the victim of an irresistible impulse or an unconscious drive. Perhaps those who condemn advertising feel that it produces this kind of desire in us and consequently reduces our autonomy.

This raises a very difficult issue. How do we distinguish between an impulse we *do* not resist and one we *could* not resist, between freely giving in to a desire and succumbing to one? A person acts or chooses freely if he does so for a reason, that is, if

he can adduce considerations which justify in his mind the act in question. Many of our actions are in fact free because this condition frequently holds. Often, however, a person will act from habit, or whim, or impulse, and on these occasions he does not have a reason in mind. Nevertheless he often acts voluntarily in these instances, i.e., he could have acted otherwise. And this is because if there *had been* a reason for acting otherwise of which he was aware, he would in fact have done so. Thus acting from habit or impulse is not necessarily to act in an involuntary manner. If, however, a person is aware of a good reason to do *x* and still follows his impulse to do *y*, then he can be said to be impelled by irresistible impulse and hence to act involuntarily. Many kleptomaniacs can be said to act involuntarily, for in spite of their knowledge that they likely will be caught and their awareness that the goods they steal have little utilitarian value to them, they nevertheless steal. Here their 'out of character' desires have the upper hand, and we have a case of compulsive behavior.

Applying these notions of voluntary and compulsive behavior to the case of behavior prompted by advertising, can we say that consumers influenced by advertising act compulsively? The unexciting answer is: sometimes they do, sometimes no. I may have an overwhelming, T.V. induced urge to own a Mazda Rx-7 and all the while realize that I can't afford one without severely reducing my family's caloric intake to a dangerous level. If, aware of this good reason not to purchase the car, I nevertheless do so, this shows that I have been the victim of T.V. compulsion. But if I have the urge, as I assure you I do, and don't act on it, or if in some other possible world I could afford an Rx-7, then I have not been the subject of undue influence by Mazda advertising. Some Mazda Rx-7 purchasers act compulsively; others do not. The Mazda advertising effort *in general* cannot be condemned, then, for impairing its customers' autonomy in the sense of limiting free or voluntary choice. Of course the question remains what should be done about the fact that advertising may and does *occasionally* limit free choice.

(d) Control or Manipulation

Briefly let us consider the matter of control and manipulation. Under what conditions do these activities occur? In a recent paper on 'Forms and

Limits of Control' I suggested the following criteria:[15]

A person C controls the behavior of another person P iff

1. C intends P to act in a certain way A;

2. C's intention is causally effective in bringing about A; and

3. C intends to ensure that all of the necessary conditions of A are satisfied.

These criteria may be elaborated as follows. To control another person it is not enough that one's actions produce certain behavior on the part of that person; additionally one must intend that this happen. Hence control is the intentional production of behavior. Moreover, it is not enough just to have the intention; the intention must give rise to the conditions which bring about the intended effect. Finally, the controller must intend to establish by his actions any otherwise unsatisfied necessary conditions for the production of the intended effect. The controller is not just influencing the outcome, not just having input; he is as it were guaranteeing that the sufficient conditions for the intended effect are satisfied.

Let us apply these criteria of control to the case of advertising and see what happens. Conditions 1 and 3 are crucial. Does the Mazda manufacturing company or its advertising agency intend that I buy an Rx-7? Do they intend that a certain number of people buy the car? *Prima facie* it seems more appropriate to say that they *hope* a certain number of people will buy it, and hoping and intending are not the same. But the difficult term here is 'intend.' Some philosophers have argued that to intend A it is necessary only to desire that A happen and to believe that it will. If this is correct, and if marketing analysis gives the Mazda agency a reasonable belief that a certain segment of the population will buy its product, then, assuming on its part the desire that this happen, we have the conditions necessary for saying that the agency intends that a certain segment purchase the car. If I am a member of this segment of the population, would it then follow that the agency intends that I purchase an Rx-7? Or is control referentially opaque? Obviously we have some questions here which need further exploration.

Let us turn to the third condition of control,

the requirement that the controller intend to activate or bring about any otherwise unsatisfied necessary conditions for the production of the intended effect. It is in terms of this condition that we are able to distinguish brainwashing from liberal education. The brainwasher arranges all of the necessary conditions for belief. On the other hand, teachers (at least those of liberal persuasion) seek only to influence their students—to provide them with information and enlightenment which they may absorb *if they wish*. We do not normally think of teachers as controlling their students, for the students' performances depend as well on their own interests and inclinations.

Now the advertiser—does he control, or merely influence, his audience? Does he intend to ensure that all of the necessary conditions for purchasing behavior are met, or does he offer information and symbols which are intended to have an effect only *if* the potential purchaser has certain desires? Undeniably advertising induces some desires, and it does this intentionally, but more often than not it intends to induce a desire for a particular object, *given* that the purchaser already has other desires. Given a desire for youth, or power, or adventure, or ravishing beauty, we are led to desire Grecian Formula 16, Mazda Rx-7's, Pongo Peach, and Distinctive Foundations. In this light, the advertiser is influencing us by appealing to independent desires we already have. He is not creating those basic desires. Hence it seems appropriate to deny that he intends to produce all of the necessary conditions for our purchases, and appropriate to deny that he controls us.

Let me summarize my argument. The critics of advertising see it as having a pernicious effect on the autonomy of consumers, as controlling their lives and manufacturing their very souls. The defense claims that advertising only offers information and in effect allows industry to provide consumers with what they want. After developing some of the philosophical dimensions of this dispute, I have come down tentatively in favor of the advertisers. Advertising may, but certainly does not always or even frequently, control behavior, produce compulsive behavior, or create wants which are not rational or are not truly those of the consumer. Admittedly it may in individual cases do all of these things, but it is innocent of the charge of intrinsically or necessarily doing them or even, I think, of often doing so. This limited potentiality, to be sure, leads to the question whether advertising should be abolished or severely curtailed or regulated because of its potential to harm a few poor souls in the above ways. This is a very difficult question, and I do not pretend to have the answer. I only hope that the above discussion, in showing some of the kinds of harm that can be done by advertising and by indicating the likely limits of this harm, will put us in a better position to grapple with the question.

Notes

1. Vance Packard, *The Hidden Persuaders* (Pocket Books, New York, 1958), pp. 20–21.

2. Ibid., p. 21.

3. B. F. Skinner, "Some Issues Concerning the Control of Human Behavior: A Symposium," in Karlins and Andres (eds.), *Man Controlled* (The Free Press, New York, 1972).

4. For a provocative discussion of subliminal advertising, see W. B. Key, *Subliminal Seduction* (The New American Library, New York, 1973), and W. B. Key, *Media Sexploitation* (Prentice-Hall, Inc., Englewood Cliffs, N.J., 1976).

5. I would like to emphasize that in what follows I am discussing these techniques of advertising from the standpoint of the issue of control and not from that of deception. For a good and recent discussion of the many dimensions of possible deception in advertising, see Alex C. Michalos, "Advertising: Its Logic, Ethics, and Economics," in J. A. Blair and R. H. Johnson (eds.), *Informal Logic: The First International Symposium* (Edgepress, Pt. Reyes, Calif., 1980).

6. Quoted by Packard, *op. cit.*, p. 220.

7. Theodore Levitt, "The Morality (?) of Advertising," *Harvard Business Review* 48 (1970): 84–92.

8. Phillip Nelson, "Advertising and Ethics," in Richard T. DeGeorge and Joseph A. Pichler (eds.), *Ethics, Free Enterprise, and Public Policy* (Oxford University Press, New York, 1978), pp. 187–198.

9. For a discussion of polymorphous perversity, see Norman O. Brown, *Life Against Death* (Random House, New York, 1969), Chapter III.

10. John Kenneth Galbraith, *The Affluent Society*; reprinted in Tom L. Beauchamp and Norman E. Bowie (eds.), *Ethical Theory and Business* (Prentice-Hall, Englewood Cliffs, N.J., 1979), pp. 496–501.

11. David Braybrooke, "Skepticism of Wants, and Certain Subversive Effects of Corporations on American Values," in Sidney Hook (ed.), *Human Values and Economic Policy* (New York University Press, 1967); reprinted in Beauchamp and Bowie (eds.), *op. cit.*, pp. 502–508.

12. F. A. von Hayek, "The *Non Sequitur* of the 'Dependence Effect,'" *Southern Economic Journal* (1961); reprinted in Beauchamp and Bowie (eds.), *op. cit.*, pp. 508–512.

13. Harry Frankfurt, "Freedom of the Will and the Concept of a Person," *Journal of Philosophy* LXVIII (1971), 5–20.

14. For a discussion of the difference between a malign and a benign subconscious mind, see P. H. Nowell-Smith, "Psycho-analysis and Moral Language," *The Rationalist Annual* (1954); reprinted in P. Edwards and A. Pap (eds.), *A Modern Introduction to Philosophy*, Revised Edition (The Free Press, New York, 1965), pp. 86–93.

15. Robert L. Arrington, "Forms and Limits of Control," delivered at the annual meeting of the Southern Society for Philosophy and Psychology, Birmingham, Alabama, 1980.

Review and Discussion Questions

1. Give your own examples of advertisements that associate products for which we have little or no direct need or desire with symbols reflecting other, hidden needs or desires.

2. What does Arrington see as the central issue between critics and defenders of advertising?

3. Explain how Arrington defines "autonomous desire," "rational desire or choice," "free choice," and "control."

4. Explain the relevance of Arrington's analysis of each of these terms to the central issue between critics and defenders of advertising.

5. Although Arrington is skeptical of the extreme claims made by advertising's critics, he does concede that in some cases "advertising may . . . control behavior, produce compulsive behavior, or create wants which are not rational or are not truly those of the consumer." Do you think that this provides a sufficient basis for abolishing or severely regulating advertising?

A Distinctive Contradiction of Advanced Capitalism

G. A. Cohen

Capitalism has produced unprecedented technological progress. Oxford University professor G. A. Cohen argues, however, that the system is biased in favor of expanding output rather than reducing the amount of time worked and that at a certain stage of affluence this becomes irrational. Advertising encourages us to acquiesce in this systemic bias. No ads stress leisure, rather than consumption. Advertising increases our desire for consumption goods without increasing the satisfaction which that consumption brings.

Capitalist society is responsible for technological power on an unprecedented scale, progressing at an unprecedented rate. This is because the competitive position of its industrial decision-makers compels them to increase the productivity of production processes. The compulsion does not lapse when capitalism reaches its misnamed 'monopoly stage,' for competition persists in pertinent respects. Since total consumer spending power is finite, heterogeneous products of monopolized industries compete against one another for buyers. There is also competition for shareholders, for skilled labour, etc.

Improvement in productivity is a condition of persistence and success in the multidimensional competition which characterizes capitalism in *all* of its stages. 'It is therefore the economic tendency of capital which teaches humanity to husband its strength and to achieve its productive aim with the least possible expenditure of means.'[1]

Now improvements in productivity, whether labour-saving or capital-saving, are open to two uses. One way of exploiting enhanced productivity is to reduce toil and extend leisure, while maintaining output constant. Alternatively, output may be increased, while labour stays the same. It is also possible to achieve a measure of both *desiderata*.

'Leisure' is used broadly here, in rough synonymy with 'freedom from unappealing activity,' and 'toil' refers to activity in so far as it is unappealing. One is leisured to the extent that his time and energy is *not* spent in the service of goals he would prefer fulfilled without such expenditure. One toils to the extent that the motivation of his activity is remuneration or other external reward. It follows that leisure time can be filled strenuously. It also follows that amelioration of working conditions counts as expanding leisure.

The economic distinction between job time and time off coincides imperfectly with the distinction here envisaged between toil and freedom from it. Some 'gainful employment' is enjoyable, and some time off is spent toilsomely. But the distinctions are sufficiently coextensive for the purposes of our argument. What particularly matters is that, as things are, for most people most of the time earning a living is not a joy. Most people are so situated that they would benefit not only from more goods and services but also from reduced working hours and/or enhanced working conditions. It is clear that advances in productivity enable gains in either direction, typically at the expense of gains in the other direction.

Now capitalism inherently tends to promote just one of the options, output expansion, since the other, toil reduction, threatens a sacrifice of the profit associated with increased output and sales, and hence a loss of competitive strength.[2] When the efficiency of a firm's production improves, it does not simply reduce the working day of its employees and produce the same amount as before. It produces more of the goods in question, or, if that course is, because of the structure of the market, not optimal, it adopts another non-labour-reducing strategy, to be described shortly.

But first let us note that there has indeed been a titanic growth of output and a comparatively small reduction of labour expenditure since the inception of capitalism (date that where you will). That the reduction in the working day has been small by comparison with the volume of output expansion is beyond controversy. But it is arguable that it has also been fairly small in absolute terms, if sophisticated but defensible criteria of the amount of time people spend supporting themselves are used. Meriting consideration here are such activities as travelling to work, shopping in so far as it is felt to be a nuisance, and any activity in itself unattractive but performed as a means to fulfilling consumption purposes.[3] In sheer hours of work per year (admittedly, not the only relevant index), the modern American worker is not obviously better off than the European peasant of the Middle Ages, many of whose days were made idle by the weather and by observance of the Christian calendar.[4] Nor has there been stunning progress since, say, 1920, if everything pertinent, notably overtime, is taken into account. There has of course been an impressive decline in labour time since the earlier part of the nineteenth century, but the capitalist system need not be thanked for effecting it, since it was capitalism which stretched the working day in the first place. In any case, even that decline loses force in comparison with the accompanying increase in output, and the bias here attributed to capitalism is sufficiently evidenced by the relative position.

Output expansion takes different forms. If the market for the good whose production has improved is expansible, output expansion may take the immediate form of more products of the same kind. Otherwise, and especially if the market in question is more or less saturated, output expands elsewhere, as newly available funds (generated by reductions in the wages bill) flow into another line of production. This does not always occur promptly or smoothly, but eventually it occurs. Jobs are generally destroyed and created in the process.

As long as production remains subject to the capitalist principle, the output-increasing option will tend to be selected, and implemented in one way or another. Whether or not they have capitalist mentalities, it is imperative for capitalists to continue accumulating exchange-value, and thus to expand output. But it is unlikely that the principle should prevail while the mentality is wholly absent, and the mentality fortifies and augments the output-favouring effect of the purely objective constraint of competition.

Now the consequence of the increasing output which capitalism necessarily favours is increasing consumption. Hence the boundless pursuit of consumption goods is a result of a productive process oriented to exchange-values rather than consumption-values. It is the Rockefellers who ensure that the Smiths need to keep up with the Jones's. . . .

To recapitulate. The argument is that even if and when it becomes possible and desirable to reduce or transform unwanted activity, capitalism continues to promote consumption instead, and therefore functions irrationally, in the sense that the structure of the economy militates against optimal use of its productive capacity. It is undeniable that capitalist relations of production possess an output-expanding bias. So the only way of denying that they are potentially irrational in the stated respect is to assert that labour is so enjoyable (or not so unenjoyable) and resources are so plentiful and the satisfaction to be had from goods and services is so limitless that no matter how much is being consumed it remains desirable to consume more, instead of expanding freedom from labour: a rather large assertion. . . .

For a long time the benefits of this tilted decision-making perhaps outweigh the sacrifice exacted in labour. But when output is of a very high order and it remains true that most people devote most of their substance to doing what they would rather not do, then to persist in favour of further output at the expense of relief from undesired work is irrational. . . .

An Objection

Here is one way of developing the objection mentioned [earlier]: 'You have proved at most that capitalism *tends* to select output expansion. It does not follow that if it actually expands output, then this is adequately explained by the bias you identified. There are other tendencies attributable to capitalism on similar grounds—the need to accumulate capital—which are completely unfulfilled. One is the tendency of firms not to raise their workers' wages. The tendency is there, but its effect is neutralized by countervailing trade union power. Why does that same power not check the propensity towards output? Why do unions generally press for more income rather than less labour? If the system's bias harms their members' interests, why do they co-operate with it? When the contradiction looms, why does union policy not change?

If the United States has crossed the border into contradiction, why is union policy what it is?'

Note the nature of the objection. It is *not*: output expansion is favoured not by the system but only by the aims the population wants the system to accomplish. That claim cannot stand, since the system demonstrably possesses an output-expanding bias. But the presence of that tendency does not show that it explains the realization of what it is a tendency to. That lesser claim is the basis of the objection.

We shall meet the objection by exploiting quite uncontroversial premisses. It is easily met on the radical premiss that much of what is consumed gives no real satisfaction, but people cherish it because they are dupes of advertising and ideology. Later, a reduced version of that thesis will be defended, but first let us magnanimously assume that by and large the given consumer goods are desirable, that desire for them is in some relevant sense awakened, not contrived, by advertising and affiliated processes, and that the satisfaction they afford is genuine.

On the other side, the opponent must concede that plenty of labour is not desired. If God gave workers *gratis* the pay they now get, and granted them freedom to choose whether or not to work at their jobs, for as long as they pleased, without remuneration, then there would result a very substantial decline in labouring activity. Superficial observation suggests that people enjoy what they consume, but it also reveals that they do not enjoy much of what they must do to be able to consume it.

Then what advertising (etc.) may be said to do, on the most generous account, is to draw attention to and emphasize (what we have supposed are) the independently desirable qualities of the products it displays. This is balanced by no similar campaign stressing the goods of leisure. No ads say: WHEN *YOUR* UNION NEGOTIATES, MAKE IT GO FOR SHORTER HOURS, NOT MORE PAY. ELECTRIC CARVING KNIVES ARE FINE, BUT NOTHING BEATS FREEDOM. There are no 'leisure ads' because firms have no interest in financing them, nor in paying for public reminders of the unpleasant side of the labour which buys the goods.

There is, of course, promotion of so-called 'leisure products,' but rising income is required to procure them, and the advertisements do not men-

tion the sacrifice of leisure needed to sustain that income. One can imagine someone saying, in an extreme case: 'I am taking a week-end job to maintain the payments on the snowmobile I use at week-ends.'

Thus labour acquiescence in the bias is itself traceable to the bias: workers are influenced by its operation in the emphases promoted by the media.[5]

The foregoing scepticism about the process of desire formation in capitalist society does not rest on a theory disclosing the optimal desire structure for human beings: that would be difficult to supply. It would, more particularly, be hazardous to attempt a realistic general statement of the relative merits of increments of consumption and leisure at varying levels of each. Such doctrine being foresworn, what are the principles behind the critique that was given?

A distinction obtains between what a man is disposed to seek, and what would in fact afford him satisfaction. We can, on that basis, distinguish, more elaborately, between two schedules pertinently descriptive of a person's make-up and circumstances: his *pursuit* schedule and his *satisfaction* schedule. Each orders objects of his desire, but from different points of view. The pursuit schedule orders them by reference to the relative strengths of his dispositions to seek them. The satisfaction schedule orders them according to the amounts of satisfaction he would obtain from possessing them. (We ignore (a) satisfactions he would obtain from objects he does not pursue, and (b) probabilities of attaining pursued objects: suppose that whatever is pursued is attained.) These schedules are, of course, constantly changing with changes in information, taste, and external conditions, but we can say that a person's situation at a given time is likely to be unfortunate to the extent that objects are differently ordered in his two schedules. If the ordering in his satisfaction schedule differs from the ordering in his pursuit schedule, he is unlikely to be making optimal use of the resources available to him.

Now if an agency increases a man's pursuit of an object, without commensurately increasing the satisfaction he would get from possessing it, then it probably produces the unwanted misalignment of schedules, and therefore has a negative effect on his welfare, *unless* his pursuit of the object increases because the agency supplies a more accurate account than he had before of the satisfaction it would give him (in which case, an—in that respect—improved alignment results). But the agencies in capitalist society which promote a preference for output over leisure cannot be credited with a comparable tendency to increase the satisfaction to be had from output as opposed to leisure, nor may they be said to provide a more accurate account than might otherwise be available of the relative values of the two. There is therefore a case for saying that they corrupt the individual's preference structure, a claim we can make without describing the content of an uncorrupted preference structure.

We criticize capitalism not because it causes desires which might otherwise not have arisen, but because it causes desires the fulfilment of which does not afford an appropriate degree of satisfaction. The system requires the pursuit of consumption goods: it is indifferent to the quality of satisfaction which lies at the end of it, except in so far as high satisfaction might reinforce the pursuit. But it is naive to think that a particularly effective way of sustaining the commitment to consumption is to make consumption rewarding. On the contrary, there is reason to suppose—and here we approach the 'radical premiss' not used in our reply to the objection—that the pursuit of goods will, in important ranges, be stronger to the extent that their power to satisfy the pursuer is limited. The system cannot abide consumers who are content with what they already have. As Baker says:

> . . . while trying to increase sales and profits,
> a business enterprise will want to create tastes
> that are (1) cheapest to develop or stimulate
> and (2) for which palliatives can be produced
> but (3) which are never completely satisfied
> and do not cause other desires to be satiated.[6]

Business wants contented customers, but they must not be too contented. Otherwise they will buy less and work less, and business will dwindle.

Finally, a reply to those who use their leisure time arguing that if people had lots of it they would not know how to use it. No well-confirmed propositions about human beings support this arrogant pessimism. It is, moreover, predictable that a soci-

ety rigged up to maximize output will fail to develop the theory and practice of leisure.[7] And this further manifestation of the output bias adds to the explanation of general acquiescence in it. Free time looks empty when the salient available ways of filling it are inane.

Notes

1. Karl Marx, *Theories of Surplus Value*, ii, 548.
2. See *Grundrisse*, pp. 701, 707–12; *Theories of Surplus Value*, i. 223, 226–8, ii. 468. An interesting early example of the bias of capitalism was the introduction of safety lamps in mining after 1813, which initially brought 'not greater security of life to the miner, but a larger output of coal—from seams that had previously been considered too dangerous to be worked at all.' Because explosions would have damaged the mine too much? Ashton, *The Industrial Revolution*, p. 65.
3. Also needing attention, in more than just a footnote, is the complicated effect of capitalism on the amount of labour performed by women. In *some* respects their leisure can increase since the output bias leads to a proliferation of devices which reduce domestic labour. But the same devices enable women to join the remunerated labour force, so their total effect is not easy to judge.

   According to Galbraith, the net result of the increasing flow of goods into the home is to make housewives hard-pressed managers of consumption, so that 'the menial role of the woman becomes more arduous the higher the family income.' Galbraith is evidently no connoisseur of low-income family life, but there may be a grain of truth in what he says. See *Economics and the Public Purpose*, p. 32.
4. For further discussion, see Parker, *The Sociology of Leisure*, p. 24, the references he cites, and those cited by Howard and King, *The Political Economy of Marx*, p. 124, n. 7.
5. We have dealt only with the most manifest messages in favour of goods projected by capitalist society. To show how much else in its culture has the same end is more than can be done here. Advertising is no doubt a relatively secondary influence, reinforcing much deeper sources of commitment to consumption.
6. 'The Ideology of the Economic Analysis of Law,' p. 38.
7. '. . . we are now at a point at which sociologists are discussing the "problem" of leisure. And a part of

the problem is: how did it come to be a problem?'
Thompson, 'Time, Work-Discipline, and Industrial
Capitalism,' p. 67.

Review and Discussion Questions

1. Explain what Cohen sees as "a distinctive contradiction of advanced capitalism."

2. Do you agree that capitalism gives rise to this contradiction? Is Cohen correct in thinking that it is "distinctive" of capitalism?

3. What objection to his thesis does Cohen discuss, and what is his reply to it?

4. What is the relevance of the distinction between "pursuit schedule" and "satisfaction schedule" for Cohen's argument?

For Further Reading

The single best source of further readings is probably **Joseph R. DesJardins** and **John J. McCall**, eds., *Contemporary Issues in Business Ethics* (Belmont, Calif.: Wadsworth, 1985), which contains important and useful essays on products liability, consumer regulation, advertising and free speech, subliminal advertising, and advertising to children, among other issues. Also helpful is Chapter 6 of **Manuel G. Velasquez**, *Business Ethics* (Englewood Cliffs, N.J.: Prentice-Hall, 1982). **Roger Draper**, "The Faithless Shepherd," *New York Review of Books*, June 26, 1986, is a good, intelligent review of recent books on advertising.

CHAPTER 10
THE ENVIRONMENT

There is no question that in manufacturing and using products we have contaminated the environment and that contamination directly threatens the integrity of the biosphere and thus life itself. Pollution besets us.

In his book on the subject, professor of philosophy Tom Regan begins by saying: "The concerns of environmental ethics might begin with the food on our plate."[1] Food is of concern because agriculture increasingly utilizes hundreds of chemicals in crop production, including various fertilizers, herbicides, and pesticides. While chemically intensive agriculture has yielded many benefits, it also raises worries about harmful chemical residue left in food.

A public health disaster in Puerto Rico is but one dramatic and tragic example. An estimated 3,000 youngsters under ten years of age—some as young as seventeen months—are suffering from abnormal sexual development, including menstruation and fully developed breasts. Authorities suspect an environmental contaminant, probably the steroid hormone estrogen, in the food chain. One possible source of the estrogen is growth stimulant for cattle and chickens. Although estrogen is restricted, some experts believe its use is common in Puerto Rico.[2] That claim raises the spectre of government agencies that, while setting standards regarding food contaminants, are unwilling or powerless to enforce them. This conclusion approximates the one drawn by Lewis Regenstein in his book, *America the Poisoned*. Regenstein says that:

> A review of the government's policy in setting and enforcing tolerance levels of toxic pesticides leads to the inescapable conclusion that the program exists primarily to insure the public that it is being protected from harmful chemical residues. In fact, the program, as currently administered, does little to minimize or even monitor the amount of poisons in our food, and serves the interests of the users and producers of pesticides rather than those of the public.[3]

In 1972 the brand-new Environmental Protection Agency was given the job of regulating new pesticides and of reevaluating the old ones using modern standards. The old pesticides, with about 600 active ingredients, constitute the bulk of those in use, but the agency has only evaluated a handful of them. "It is almost as if the 1972 law had never been passed," the *Washington Post* has commented, calling pesticides our most serious environmental problem and the one we are doing the least about.[4]

The contaminants that infiltrate the food chain can also spread into our water. The toxic chemicals used in farming can and do run off into underground reservoirs, which are a major source of our water. "The drinking water of every American city," claims Regenstein, "contains dozens of cancer-causing chemicals and other toxins," many of which can be traced to the chemicals used in agriculture.[5]

Pollutants also contaminate the air, despoiling vegetation and crops, corroding construction materials, and threatening health and life. Automobiles and industrial smokestacks, the major sources of air pollution, disgorge a variety of pollutants producing a mix of noxious effects. If you have ever come out of a traffic jam with a headache, it could be because of the carbon monoxide you were breathing. When your eyes smart and throat stings while you're walking down a street, it's probably because the air is thick with petrochemical smog, a poisonous soup brewed up by the sun from the nitrogen oxides and hydrocarbons discharged chiefly by automobiles. If you're lucky, momentary discomfort will be all you'll suffer. If you're not, you may end up more susceptible to respiratory disease, as are people in larger cities, who are exposed to high concentrations of sulfur dioxide from oil.

Food, water, and air are only three areas of pollution that challenge us today. Millions of tons of industrial wastes—acidic chemicals, pesticides, herbicides, inorganic metals, and so on—have been deposited in thousands of sites nationwide. In many cases, the public does not know precisely where the sites are or what substances they contain and in what amounts. We do know, however, that the lion's share of what is deposited is toxic—it can seriously injure or even kill people.

So can nuclear wastes, even the small amounts released into the atmosphere during the normal operating of a nuclear power plant or in mining, processing, or transporting nuclear fuels. By government estimates, at least 1,000 people will die between the years 1975 and 2000 as a result of cancer caused by exposure to these routine emissions.[6] A nuclear plant accident, of course, could sizably increase the casualty rate in the search for a clean, efficient energy source, as the 1986 disaster at the Soviet city of Chernobyl brought vividly home to the world. And the disposal of nuclear wastes has to worry anyone who is sensitive to the legacy we leave future generations. Will the nuclear toxins we bury today in the bosom of the earth return to haunt us tomorrow?

It is little wonder, then, that considerable attention has focused on business's and industry's responsibility for preserving the integrity of our physical environment. This chapter deals with some of the moral dilemmas posed for business by our environmental relationships—not just the problem of pollution, but also the ethical issues posed by the depletion of natural resources and by our treatment of animals. The chapter's purpose is not to argue that the environmental problems facing us are serious and that industry has greatly contributed to them. Few people today doubt this. Rather, this chapter is largely concerned with the question: Given the problems of environmental degradation, of resource depletion, and of the abuse of animals for commercial purposes, what are business's responsibilities? Specifically, this chapter examines:

1. The meaning and significance of "ecology."

2. The traditional business attitudes toward the environment that have encouraged environmental degradation and resource depletion.

3. The moral problems underlying business abuse of the environment—in particular, the question of externalities, the problem of free riders, and the right to a livable environment.

4. The costs of environmental protection and the question of who should pay them.

5. Three methods—regulations, incentives, pricing mechanisms—for allocating the costs of environmental protection.

6. Some of the deeper and not fully resolved questions of environmental ethics—what obligations do we have to future generations? Does nature have value in itself? Is our commercial exploitation of animals immoral?

BUSINESS AND ECOLOGY

In order to deal intelligently with the question of business's responsibilities for the environment, one must realize that business functions within an ecological system.

Ecology refers to the science of the interrelationships among organisms and their environ-

ments. The operative term is *interrelationships*, implying that an interdependence exists among all entities in the environment. In speaking about ecological matters, ecologists frequently use the term *ecosystem*, which refers to a total ecological community, both living and nonliving. An ordinary example of an ecosystem is a pond. It consists of a complex community of animal and vegetable life. Suppose the area where the pond is located experiences a prolonged period of drought; or someone begins to fish in the pond regularly; or, during a period of excessive rainfall, plant pesticides begin to spill into it. Under any of these circumstances, changes will occur in the relationships among the pond's constituent members. Damage to a particular form of plant life may mean that fewer fish can live in the pond; a particular species might even disappear. A change in the pond's ecosystem may also affect other ecosystems. Because of water contamination, for example, a herd of deer that lived nearby may have to go elsewhere for water; their relocation may ensure an increased berry crop, which had previously been devoured by the hungry deer. The point is that in considering any ecosystem, one must remember its complex and interrelated nature and the intricate network of interdependencies that bind it to other ecosystems.

It is apparent that in some sense every living organism affects its environment. The problem to be considered as we discuss business and the environment is that human commercial activities (for example, using pesticides and establishing oil fields) have unpredicted consequences for the ecosystem. Sometimes the effects are negative; other times they appear to be positive. So, although it may be true that no organism can live without affecting its environment, at the same time the species *Homo sapiens* possesses the power to upset drastically the stability of natural ecosystems.

A good example of the consequences of ecological ignorance can be found in the indiscriminate agricultural use of pesticides. Rachel Carson spoke eloquently about this problem in her classic book *Silent Spring*. She contended that we had put biologically dangerous chemicals into the hands of persons who were ignorant of their poisonous nature. These persons were using chemicals with no understanding of their effects on soil, water, wildlife, and human beings. Carson warned that tampering with ecosystems would have serious consequences. She predicted that future generations would indict our imprudence and deplore our insensitivity to the natural world.

Subsequent research and developments have confirmed Carson's worst suspicions. We now know that some pesticides can affect the reproductive capacity of animals and can reach such high concentrations in human fatty tissues that they cause brain damage and cirrhosis of the liver. One study has revealed that a large percentage of terminal cancer patients have shown high concentrations of pesticide residues in their livers and brain tissues. Another study has observed that workers such as crop dusters who are exposed to certain pesticides exhibit dull reflexes and mental instability; they often die as a result of intolerable levels of toxicity.

Tampering with ecosystems does not always have the injurious effects evident in the use of pesticides. On the contrary, sometimes unforeseen benefits result, as was true of the expansive oil and gas drilling activity in the Gulf of Mexico. Much to everyone's surprise, the operational docks, pipes, and platforms provided a more beneficent place to which lower forms of life could attach themselves than the silt-laden sea ever did. As a result, oil drilling in the Gulf of Mexico has greatly increased the commercial fish catch in the area. But even in fortuitous instances like this, environmental intrusions affect the integrity of ecosystems. And that's the point. Because an ecosystem represents a delicate balance of interrelated entities and because ecosystems are interlocked, an intrusion into one will affect its integrity and the integrity of others.

Dr. Paul Ehrlich, one of the best-known exponents of ecological awareness, has put the matter succinctly. "There are a number of ecological rules it would be wise for people to remember," Ehrlich has written. "One of them is that there is no such thing as a free lunch. Another is that when we change something into something else, the new thing is usually more dangerous than what we had originally."[7] Clearly everyone must learn the laws of interdependence and interrelationship, including an undeniably principal polluter, business.

In its role as the major economic instrument of production in our society, business must intrude into ecosystems. This does not mean, however, that all intrusions or any kind of intrusion is thereby justifiable. In fact, precisely because of the interrelated nature of ecosystems and because intrusions generally produce serious unfavorable effects, business must be scrupulous in its actions, practices, and policies that have an impact on the physical environment. There's ample documentation to show that business traditionally has been remiss in both recognizing and adequately discharging its obligations in this area. We needn't spend time here retelling the sorry tale. But it does seem worthwhile to isolate some business attitudes that historically have supported this indifference.

Business's Traditional Attitudes Toward the Environment

Several related attitudes, prevalent in our society in general and in business in particular, have led to, or increased, our environmental problems. One of these is the tendency to view the natural world as a "free and unlimited good," that is, as something we can squander without regard to the future. Writer John Steinbeck reflects on this attitude in the following passage:

I have often wondered at the savagery and thoughtlessness with which our early settlers approached this rich continent. They came at it as though it were an enemy, which of course it was. They burned the forests and changed the rainfall; they swept the buffalo from the plains, blasted the streams, set fire to the grass, ran a reckless scythe through the virgin and noble timber. Perhaps they felt that it was limitless and could never be exhausted and that a man could move on to new wonders endlessly. Certainly there are many examples to the contrary, but to a large extent the early people pillaged the country as though they hated it, as though they held it temporarily and might be driven off at any time.

This tendency toward irresponsibility persists in very many of us today; our rivers are poisoned by reckless dumping of sewage and toxic industrial wastes, the air of our cities is filthy and dangerous to breathe from belching or uncontrolled products from combustion of coal, coke, oil, and gasoline. Our towns are girdled with wreckage and debris of our toys—our automobiles and our packaged pleasures. Through uninhibited spraying against one enemy, we have destroyed the natural balances our survival requires. All these evils can and must be overcome if America and Americans are to survive; but many of us conduct ourselves as our ancestors did, stealing from the future for our clear and present profit.[8]

Traditionally, business has considered the environment to be a free, virtually limitless good. In other words, air, water, land, and other natural resources from coal to beavers (trapped almost to extinction for their pelts in the last century) were seen as available for business to use as it saw fit. In this context, pollution and the depletion of natural resources are two aspects of the same problem:

both involve using up natural resources that are limited. Pollution uses up clean air and water, just as extraction uses up the minerals or oil in the ground. The belief that both sorts of resources are unlimited and free promotes wasteful consumption of them.

Garrett Hardin describes the consequences of this attitude in his modern parable, "The Tragedy of the Commons." Hardin asks us to imagine peasants who allow their animals to graze in the "commons," or collectively shared village pasture. It is in the interest of each to permit his or her animals to graze without limit on the public land. But the result of this is that the commons is soon overgrazed, making it of no further grazing value to anyone.[9]

This story can be generalized. When it comes to "the commons," that is to public or communal goods—like air, water, or unowned wilderness—problems arise as the result of individuals and companies following their own self-interest. Each believes that his or her own use of the commons has a negligible effect, but the cumulative result can be the gradual destruction of the public domain, which makes everyone worse off. In the "tragedy of the commons" we have the reverse of Adam Smith's "invisible hand": each person's pursuit of self-interest makes everyone worse off.

The "tragedy of the commons" also illustrates the more general point that there can be a difference between the private costs and the social costs of a business activity. We have discussed this issue in Chapter 5 when we described what economists call "externalities," but it is worth reviewing it in the present context.

Suppose a paper mill only partially treats the chemical wastes it emits into a lake that's primarily used for fishing and recreational activities. Should the amount of effluent be great enough to reduce the fishing productivity of the lake, then society, while paying a lower price for the mill's product, will pay a

higher price for fish than it otherwise would. Moreover, the pollution may make the lake unfit for such recreational activities as swimming and boating or for use as a source of fresh water. The result is that the public must pay the cost of the mill's inadequate waste treatment system. *Economists term this disparity between private industrial costs and public social costs a spillover or externality.* In viewing things strictly in terms of private industrial costs, business overlooks spillover. This is an economic problem because the price of the paper does not reflect the true cost of producing it. Paper is underpriced and overproduced, thus leading to a misallocation of resources. This is also a moral problem because the purchasers of paper are not paying its full cost. Instead, part of the cost of producing paper is being unfairly imposed on other people.

In sum, then, spillovers or externalities, pursuit of private interest at the expense of the commons, and a view of the environment as a free good that can be consumed without limit have combined with an ignorance of ecology and of the often fragile interconnections and interdependencies of the natural world to create the serious environmental problems facing us today.

THE ETHICS OF ENVIRONMENTAL PROTECTION

Much of what we do to reduce, eliminate, or avoid pollution and the depletion of scarce natural resources is in our collective self-interest. Accordingly, many measures that we take, for example, recycling our cans or putting catalytic converters on our cars, are steps that benefit all of us, collectively and individually: Our air is more breathable and our landscapes less cluttered with garbage. But even if such measures benefit each and every one of us, there will still be a temptation to shirk our individual responsibilities and be a "free rider." The individual person or company may rationalize that the little bit it adds to the total pollution problem won't make any difference. The firm benefits from the efforts of others to avoid pollution but "rides for free" by not making the same effort itself.

The unfairness here is obvious. Likewise, as we explained in the previous section, the failure of companies to "internalize" their environmental "externalities" spells unfairness. Others are forced to pick up the tab when companies do not pay all the environmental costs involved in producing their own products. As we saw in Chapter 5, those who adopt the broader view of corporate social responsibility emphasize that there exists an implicit social contract between business and the rest of society. This contract reflects what society hopes to achieve by allowing business to operate as well as the "rules of the game" governing business activity. Companies who try to be "free riders" in environmental matters or who refuse to address the spillover or external costs of their business activity violate this contract.

So far this chapter has emphasized that we need to view the environment differently if we are to improve our quality of life and even to continue to exist. And we have just stressed how the failure of an individual or business to play its part is unfair. Some moral theorists, like William T. Blackstone, have gone beyond this to argue that each of us has a human right to a livable environment. "Each person," Blackstone argues, "has this right *qua* being human and because a livable environment is essential for one to fulfill his human capacities."[10] This right has emerged, he contends, as a result of changing environmental conditions, which impact on the very possibility of human life as well as on the possibility of realizing other human rights.

Recognition of a right to a livable environment would strengthen further the ethical reasons for business to respect the integrity of the natural world. In addition, recognition of this moral right could, Blackstone suggests,

form a sound basis for establishing a *legal* right to a livable environment through legislation and even, perhaps, through a constitutional amendment or an environmental bill of rights. This in turn would enhance our ability to go after polluters and other abusers of the natural environment.

Acknowledging a human right to a livable environment, however, does not solve many of the hard problems facing us. In the effort to conserve irreplaceable resources, to protect the environment from degradation, and to restore it where it has been injured, we are still faced with difficult moral choices. And each choice has its economic and moral costs. We will focus next on pollution control, but most of our points will apply equally to other problems of environmental protection as well as to the conservation of scarce resources.

The Costs of Pollution Control

It is easy to say that we should do whatever is necessary to improve the environment. Before this answer has any operational worth, we must consider a number of things. One is the quality of environment that we want. This can vary from an environment restored to its pristine state to one minimally improved over the current state. Then there's the question of precisely what is necessary to effect the kind of environment we want. In some cases we may not at present have the technological capacity to improve the environment. But perhaps the overriding concern in any determination of what should be done to improve the environment is a calculation of what it will cost. This calculation will necessarily involve controversial judgments that will affect the moral commitment, or lack of it, that business feels toward enhancing the environment.

To draw out this point, we must consider a technique that plays a major role in determining the total costs of environmental improvement: cost-benefit analysis. This device is used to determine whether it's worthwhile to incur a particular cost; namely, the cost of employing a pollution-control and environment-improvement device. The general approach is to take a project and evaluate its direct and indirect costs and benefits, the difference being the net result for society. Consider, for example, a national project undertaken to clean up the air.

In order to determine whether it's worthwhile to initiate such a program, a multitude of cost-benefit factors must be considered. For example, the Council on Environmental Quality estimates that air-pollution-control costs will run about $106.5 billion. Included here presumably would be such items as loss in corporate profits, higher prices for consumers, unfavorable effects on employment, and adverse consequences for the nation's balance of payments. These costs must be compared with the anticipated benefits. Thus, some persons calculate a 50 percent reduction in the amount of particulates and sulfur oxide in the air over urban areas would reduce illness and premature death from bronchitis by at least 25 percent and perhaps as much as 50 percent. Also, deaths due to heart disease would decrease by 20 percent, from respiratory disease by 25 percent, and from cancer by at least 25 percent. Moreover, a reduction in air pollution would add approximately three to five years to the life expectancy of an urban dweller. These facts can be translated into 5,000 fewer deaths per year from lung cancer and 16,000 fewer from heart disease. As for the savings in medical costs and personal effects, some conservatively estimate those at $2 billion. In addition, billions more may be saved in property and crop damages.[11] It would be on the basis of such an analysis that a decision for or against air-pollution control would be made.

Even granting this strictly consequential approach to determining whether to undertake a specific program, a cost-effectiveness analysis clearly involves value judgments that will affect the nature and extent of one's moral commitment. This is so because a cost-benefit analysis does not consider costs and benefits only in terms of money. Thus, costs relative to time, effort, and discomfort can and must be introduced. Benefits can take even more numerous forms: health, convenience, comfort, enjoyment, leisure, self-fulfillment, freedom from odor, visibility, psychological conditions, and so on. Benefits are especially difficult to calculate in environmental matters because they often take the form of an aesthetic enhancement. Some environmentalists, for example, may campaign for the preservation of a remote forest visited annually by only a handful of stalwart backpackers, while developers wish to convert it into a more accessible and frequented ski resort. Should the forest be preserved or should it be converted into a ski resort? Conflicting value judgments are at stake.

Even if business seeks a social result in which benefits of all types are greater than costs of all types, this formula isn't entirely satisfactory, because, as in the case here, determination of the costs and benefits can depend foundationally on the value that one places on a pristine forest as opposed to a ski resort. The value one attaches to the forest cannot be as well quantified as the one attaching to the ski resort. It relies essentially on a qualitative judgment, which some environmentalists would argue outweighs the quantitative benefits of the ski resort. These same proponents might go further and claim that it was a strictly quantitative approach to the environment that has produced all the problems.

Clearly, then, an evaluation of costs and benefits is wed to values, assessments of worth, and an ordering of those values. Compounding this fact further is that values are constantly being affected by changes in the environment itself. Thus, the high value that some environmentalists might attach to the forest is directly related to the fact that such wilderness areas are becoming rarer, to the point of extinction. As a result, they might see the cost of obliterating it as prohibitive, whereas in former times they might not have. By the same token, others who are sensitive to the fact that recreational land is becoming scarce might consider a ski resort as a pre-mining who should pay the costs of environmental protections and restorations. Two popular answers to this question currently circulate: that those responsible for causing the pollution ought to pay, and that those who stand to benefit from protection and restoration should pick up the tab.

Who Should Pay the Costs?

One aspect of the environmental dilemma that raises questions of social justice is determining who should pay the costs of environmental protections and restorations. Two popular answers to this question currently circulate: that those responsible for causing the pollution ought to pay, and that those who stand to benefit from protection and restoration should pick up the tab.

Those Responsible.   The claim that those responsible for causing the pollution ought to pay the costs of pollution control seems eminently fair until one asks a simple question. Just who is responsible for the pollution? Who are the polluters? Proponents of this claim observe that individuals and institutions with large incomes generally produce disproportionately more pollution than those with low incomes. Thus, big business is the chief polluter, and this alone, according to the argument, is enough to justify the claim that business ought to bear the lion's share of pollution control. But there's another reason. Shifting environment-improvement costs to society or customers would only increase the economic disparity that already exists between polluters and those damaged by pollution. In effect, a policy of making polluters pick up the tab for environmental restoration would probably have the desirable social ef-

fect of shifting income from the richer to the poorer and thus providing for a more equitable distribution of wealth. In the minds of some persons, the question of who should pay the bill is connected with the fair and just distribution of wealth.

Although it's true that business probably has benefited financially more than any other group as a result of treating the environment as a free good, not all a firm's wealth or even most of it has resulted directly from its doing so. Moreover, consumers themselves have benefited to the tune of billions of dollars by not having had to pay higher costs for products.

Some would argue that consumers are primarily to blame for pollution and therefore should pay the bill for its control. Because customers create the demand for the products whose production eventually impairs the environment, then customers ought to pay for the spillover. In this way, the argument goes, social costs are not unfairly passed on to those who have not incurred them. In sum, let those who want the products pay a price for them that includes all the costs of production without degrading the environment. But questions still remain.

Consider this case, for example. The citizens of Massachusetts, wanting cleaner air, vote to pay higher prices for their electricity. It appears that they will pay the entire economic costs of the environmental improvement. But some of the costs of the cleaner air in Massachusetts may be borne by miners of high-sulfur coal in Pennsylvania who lose their jobs because this coal will no longer be used in Massachusetts. These miners neither caused the pollution nor will they benefit from controlling it. At the same time, miners of low-sulfur coal in, say, some western state stand to reap a windfall benefit along with the railroad which hauls the coal.[12] This one example is enough to illustrate that assigning pollution-control costs to customers can affect an intricate network of economic interdependence in ways that raise serious questions of social justice.

The fact is that those arguing either version of the polluter-should-pay-the-bill thesis, in attributing primary responsibility for pollution to big business or to customers, largely ignore the manifold deep-rooted causes of environmental degradation.

Causes of Pollution. One important cause is the concentration of people in urban areas. In the 60 years between 1910 and 1970 the percentage of Americans living in urban areas of 2,500 or more rose from 45.7 percent to 70 percent, the number of people increasing from 42 million to 150 million. This tremendous growth of urban population has resulted in staggering demands for goods and services. Thus, between 1960 and 1970 a 10 percent increase in the population (from 181 million to 205 million) resulted in a 14 percent rise in metropolitan population, with an accompanying 33 percent increase in vehicles, a 65 percent growth in industrial production, and a 100 percent jump in electric power generated.[13] This increase in consumer demands for goods and services has raised the levels of air, water, space, and noise pollution.

Another root cause of environmental problems is rising American affluence in this century. As people have had more money to spend, they have bought and consumed more tangible goods, discarded them more quickly, and produced more solid waste. All of this has added to environmental degradation. With the number of urban dwellers doubling and with per capita real income quadrupling about every 40 years, one wonders whether we can even meet the challenge of providing urban amenities.[14] Add to the causes our general tendency to value quantity over quality, our governmental failure to demand an accounting of the social costs of environmental pollution, and our ignorance of the interrelated nature of the global ecosystem, and a more sophisticated and accurate causal explanation of environmental decay emerges.

What's more important, we're less likely to point the finger of blame at one economic sector of society and demand that it shoulder the costs of pollution control. The enemy in the war against environmental decadence turns out to be all of us. Any solution to the question of who should pay the costs of pollution control that ignores this fact runs grave risks of committing social injustices.

Those Who Would Benefit. A second popular reply to the payment problem is that those who will benefit from environmental improvement should pay the costs.

The trouble with this argument is that every individual, rich or poor, and every institution, large or small, stand to profit from environmental improvement, albeit not to the same degree. As a result, the claim that those who will benefit should pay the costs is not satisfactory, because everyone is touched by pollution. If, on the other hand, this position means that individuals and groups should pay to the degree that they will benefit, then one must wonder how this could possibly be determined. But perhaps the most serious objection to this thesis is that it seems to leave out responsibility as a legitimate criterion.

Any equitable solution to the problem of who should pay the bill of environmental cleanup should take into account responsibility as well as benefit. The preceding analysis suggests that we all share the blame for pollution and collectively stand to benefit from environmental improvement. This doesn't mean, however, that individual entities cannot be isolated as being chronic and flagrant polluters or that certain individuals will not benefit more than others, as residents of the Los Angeles basin might benefit more from stringently enforced federal auto-emission-control standards than some Americans living in a remote corner of Wyoming. The point is that a fair and just program for assigning costs begins in a recognition that we all bear the responsibility for environmental problems and that we all stand to benefit from correcting them.

But even if we agree that it is only fair that everyone shares the cost of environmental improvement, we can still wonder about how the bill ought to be paid. What would be the fairest distribution among those who will pay the initial costs?

COST ALLOCATION

Most would probably agree that environmental pollution cannot be stopped without business and government working together. The main proposals for revitalizing the environment conceptualize government as initiating programs that will prod business into responsible action. The moral question that concerns us, then, is the fairest way of allocating costs for environmental revitalization.

Three proposals have gained the most attention: the use of regulations, incentives, and pricing mechanisms. Although similar in some respects, they carry different assumptions about the roles of government and business as well as about what's fair and just. Each approach has distinct advantages and weaknesses; each raises some questions of social justice.

Regulations

The regulatory approach makes use of direct public regulation and control in determining how the pollution bill is paid. This approach can take the form of establishing environmental standards through legislation, which are then applied by administrative agencies and courts. An effluent standard, for example, would prohibit industries from releasing more than a certain percentage of fly ash from a smokestack. Thus, an industry would be required to install a fly-ash control device in order to comply with the standard.

A clear advantage to such a regulatory approach is that standards would be legally enforceable. Firms not meeting them could be fined or even shut down. Also, from the view of morality, such standards would be fair in that they would be applied to all industries in the same way. There are, however, distinct disadvantages in this approach, which carry moral overtones.

First, there's the question of compliance. If such universal standards are applied without regard for the idiosyncratic nature of each industry, serious inequities could arise about the comparative competitive positions of firms. For example, one firm might find that its costs for complying with water-pollution standards are insignificant because it has access to high-quality water to begin with, whereas another firm might be forced to incur substantial costs because its water source is of low quality.

Then there's the problem of displacement costs resulting from industrial relocation or shutdown. For example, in the fall of 1977 Youngstown Sheet and Tube Company moved its corporate headquarters and some production lines to the Chicago area, thus eliminating 500 jobs and causing serious economic problems in nearby communities. One of the reasons for the transfer was the need to implement water-pollution controls, which stole vital capital. Consider also the marginal firms that would fail while attempting to meet the costs of such standards. When air-pollution regulations were applied to a 60-year-old cement plant in San Juan Bautista, California, the plant had to close because it was too obsolete to meet the standard economically. The shutdown seriously injured the economy of the town, which had been primarily supported by the cement plant.[15] Similarly, in one western city two paper mills announced within a period of two weeks that they were closing because they simply couldn't meet environmental standards. One mill had been in the town 80 years and had employed 750 workers with a payroll of $6 million annually. The other firm had employed over 300 workers. The closing of these plants resulted in a loss of over 1,000 jobs with attendant human suffering.[16]

Although universal environmental standards are fair in the sense that they apply to all in the same way, this very fact raises questions about their effectiveness. In attempting to legislate realistic and reliable standards for all, will government so dilute the standards that they become ineffectual? Consider the cases of areas whose physical environment is cleaner than government standards. In such cases, should an industry be allowed to pollute up to the maximum of the standard? The Supreme Court thinks not. In a case brought before it by the Sierra Club in 1973, the Court ruled that states with relatively clean air must prohibit industries from producing significant air pollution even though Environmental Protection Agency (EPA) standards are not violated. In this case a firm and ultimately the consumer are being forced to pay the costs of meeting an environmental standard that, in one sense, is sterner than the one competitors must meet elsewhere.

Clearly, then, a regulatory approach to environmental improvement, while having advantages, also raises serious questions.

Incentives

A widely supported approach to the problem of cost allocation for environmental improvement is government investment, subsidy, and general economic incentive.

The government might give a firm a tax incentive for the purchase and use of pollution equipment, or it might offer matching grants to companies that install such devices. The advantage of this approach is that it minimizes governmental interference in business operations and encourages voluntary action rather than coercing compliance, as in the case of regulation. By allowing firms to move at their own pace it avoids the evident unfairness to firms that cannot meet regulatory standards and must either relocate or fail. In addition, whereas regulated standards can encourage minimum legal compliance, an incentive approach provides an economic reason for going beyond minimal compliance. Firms have a financial inducement to do more than just meet EPA standards.

But incentives are not without disadvantages that bear moral overtones. First, as an essentially voluntary device, an incentive program is likely to be slow. Environmental problems that cry out for a solution may continue to fester. Incentive programs may allow urgently needed action to be postponed. In addition, any kind of governmental incentive program amounts to a subsidy for polluters. Polluting firms are being paid not to pollute. Although this may address the economics of pollution more effectively than any other proposal, it nonetheless raises at least theoretical questions about the justice of compensating not the victims of pollution but some of the egregious polluters. This problem grows darker when one realizes that as indirect government expenditures, incentives rarely involve governmental scrutiny. Thus a firm already guilty of pollution can rather easily bury or manipulate the total costs of antipollution equipment within a nest of other business expenditures reported in tax returns. Not only is the government thereby defrauded, but it is also left without any realistic way of determining the cost-effectiveness payoff of its incentive program.[17]

Pricing Mechanisms

A third approach to the cost-allocation problem involves programs designed to charge firms for the amount of pollution they produce. This could take the form of pricing mechanisms, or effluent charges, which spell out the cost for a specific kind of pollution in a specific area at a specific time. The prices would vary from place to place and from time to time and would be tied to the amount of damage caused. For example, during the summer months in the Los Angeles basin a firm might pay much higher charges for fly ash emitted into the environment than it would during the winter months. Whatever the set of prices, they would apply equally to every producer of a given type of pollution at the same time and place. The more a firm pollutes, the more it pays.

One advantage in this approach is that it places the cost of pollution control on the polluters. Pricing mechanisms or effluent charges would penalize, not compensate, industrial polluters. For many persons this is inherently more fair than a program that compensates polluters.

Also, because costs are internalized, firms could be encouraged to do more than meet the minimal requirements established under a strict regulatory policy. Under this approach a firm, in theory, could be charged for any amount of pollution and not just incur legal penalties whenever it exceeded an EPA standard. In effect, pollution costs become production costs.

Another plus: Pricing mechanisms and effluent charges, rather than treating firms collectively, consider them individually. They allow firms to have different levels of pollution depending on the peculiarities of their locations, the damage they are likely to cause, and the seasonal constraints they operate under.

But these programs raise noteworthy questions about the arbitrary nature of pollution costs. Who would set effluent charges? What is a fair price? Any decisions are bound to reflect debatable value judgments. What's more, companies located in areas that require strict environmental control clearly would operate at a competitive disadvantage vis-á-vis companies in a less troubled environment. As in the case of regulations, then, a question of fair treatment arises. Similarly, some companies would relocate or fail, with serious consequences not only for the firm but also for individuals and communities directly and in-

directly affected. Finally, it seems reasonable to wonder whether such a proposal, like incentives, is actually a license to pollute. After all, if a company determines that it is cheaper for it to pollute, it might feel free to do just that. Pricing mechanisms and effluent charges could in theory run counter to the objectives of a war on environmental degradation.

In sum, although each of these approaches to cost allocation has decided advantages, none is without serious weaknesses. Because there appears to be no ideal approach and because these programs or variations of them are the ones currently available for meeting this urgent problem, a combination of regulation, incentive, and effluent charge is probably called for. Any such combination must consider not only the most expeditious and effectual approach to the problem but also the fairest mix among those who will pay the bill. This will call for input from all sectors of society, a deliberate commitment on the part of all parties to work in concert, a sizable measure of good faith, and perhaps above all else a heightened and sophisticated sense of social justice. This is no mean challenge.

DEEPER INTO ENVIRONMENTAL ETHICS

So far our discussion of environmental ethics has focused on business's obligation to understand its environmental responsibilities, to acknowledge and internalize its externalities (or spillovers), and to avoid free riding. We have stressed the extent to which environmental protection is in our collective self-interest, and we have looked at the operational and moral dilemmas involved in dealing with the costs of pollution.

The subject of environmental ethics can be pushed deeper than this, and many moral theorists would advocate doing so. In particular, they would insist that we also consider our obligations to those who live outside our society. The United States has 6 percent of the world's population, but it uses 30 percent of the world's refined oil. Similar figures hold for other irreplaceable natural resources. Moreover, the United States must depend on foreign sources to supply our needs. This raises a variety of moral and political issues. Here we shall mention just two of those problems.

First is the question of how the continued availability of foreign resources is to be secured. Does, or will, our need for resources outside our territory lead us to dominate other lands, politically and economically, particularly in Asia, Africa, and Latin America? To do so is morally risky, because political and economic domination almost always involves violations of the rights and interests of the dominated population, as well as of our own moral ideals and values.

Second is the question of whether any nation has a right to consume the world's irreplaceable resources at a rate so grossly out of proportion to the size of its population. Of course, we pay to consume resources like oil that other nations own, but in the view of many the fact that other nations acquiesce in our disproportionate consumption of resources does not resolve the moral problem of our doing so. Are we respecting the needs and interests of both our present co-inhabitants on this planet and the future generations who will live on earth?

Obligations to Future Generations

Almost everybody feels intuitively that it would be wrong of us to empty the globe of resources and to contaminate the environment that we pass on to future generations. Certainly there is a strong danger that we might do both these things. But the question of what moral obligations we have to future generations is surprisingly difficult, and discussion of it among philosophers has not resolved all of the important theoretical issues.

While most of us agree that it would be

immoral to make the world uninhabitable for future people, can we talk meaningfully of those future generations having a *right* that we not do this? After all, our remote descendants are not yet alive and, thus, cannot claim a right to a livable environment. In fact, since these generations do not yet exist, they cannot at present, it seems, be said to have any interests at all. How can they then have rights?

Professor of philosophy Joel Feinberg argues, however, that whatever future human beings turn out to be like, they will have interests that we can affect, for better or worse, right now. Even though we do not know who the future people will be, we do know that they will have interests and what the general nature of those interests will be. This is enough, he contends, both to talk coherently about their having rights and to impose a duty on us not to leave ecological time bombs for them.

Feinberg concedes that it doesn't make sense to talk about future people having a right to be born. The child that you could conceive tonight, if you felt like it, cannot intelligibly be said to have a right to be born. Thus, the rights of future generations are "contingent," says Feinberg, on those future people coming into existence. But this qualification does not affect his main contention: "The interests that [future people] are sure to have when they come into being . . . cry out for protection from invasions that can take place now."[18]

Even if we are persuaded that future generations have rights, this does not tell us exactly what those rights are or how they are to be balanced against the interests and rights of present people. If we substantially injure future generations to gain some small benefit for ourselves, we are being as selfish and short-sighted as we would be by hurting other people today for some slight advantage for ourselves. Normally, though, if the benefits of some environmental policy outweigh the costs, then a strong case can be made for adopting the policy. But what if it is the present generation that receives the benefits and the future generation that pays the costs? Would it be unfair of us to adopt such a policy? Would doings so violate the rights of future people?

An additional puzzle is raised by the fact that policies we adopt will affect *who* is born in the future. Imagine that we must choose between two environmental policies, one of which would cause a slightly higher standard of living over the next century. Given the effects of those policies on the details of our lives, over time it would increasingly be true that people would marry different people under one policy than they would under the other. And even within the same marriages children would increasingly be conceived at different times.

> Some of the people who are later born would owe their existence to our choice of one of the two policies. If we had chosen the other policy, these particular people would never have existed. And the proportion of those later born who owe their existence to our choice would, like ripples in a pool, steadily grow. We can plausibly assume that, after three centuries, there would be no one living in our community who would have been born whichever policy we chose.[19]

This suggests that later generations cannot complain about an environmental policy choice that we make today that causes them to have fewer opportunities and a lower standard of living. If we had made a different choice, then those people would not have existed at all. On the other hand, it can be claimed that we act immorally in causing people to exist whose rights to equal opportunity and an equally high standard of living cannot be fulfilled. But if those future people knew the facts, would they regret that we acted as we did?[20]

Perhaps it is mistaken, though, to focus on the rights and interests of future people as individuals. Annette Baier argues that the important thing is to "recognize our obligations to consider the good of the continuing human community."[21] This suggests adopting a utilitarian perspective and seeking to maximize total human happiness through time. But this demand is also not without problems. If our concern is with total happiness, this may lead us to increase greatly the earth's population. Even if individuals on an overcrowded earth do not have much happiness, there may still be more total happiness than there would be if we followed a population-control policy that resulted in fewer, but better-off, people. This distasteful conclusion has led some utilitarians to modify their theory and maintain that with regard to population policy we should aim at the highest *average* happiness, rather than the highest *total* happiness.

John Rawls has suggested another approach to the question of our obligations to future generations, an approach that reflects his general theory of justice (which we discussed in Chapter 3). He suggests that the members of each generation put themselves in the "original position." Then, without knowing what generation they belong to, they could decide what would be a just way of distributing resources between adjacent generations. They would have to balance how much they are willing to sacrifice for their descendants against how much they wish to inherit from their predecessors. In other words, the device of the original position and veil of ignorance might be used to determine our obligations to future generations—in particular, how much each generation should save for use by those who inherit the earth from it.

The Value of Nature

A more radical approach to environmental ethics goes beyond the question of our obligations to future generations. It challenges the human-centered approach that we have so far adopted. Implicit in our discussion has been the assumption that preservation of the environment is good solely because it is good for human beings. This reflects a characteristic human attitude that nature has no intrinsic value. It only has value because, and insofar as, people value it. If human nature were different and none of us cared about the beauty of, say, the Grand Canyon, then it would be without value.

Many writers on environmental issues do not recognize their anthropocentric, or human-oriented, bias. William F. Baxter is one who does. In discussing his approach to the pollution problem, Baxter mentions the fact that the use of DDT in food production is causing damage to the penguin population. He writes:

> My criteria are oriented to people, not penguins. Damage to penguins, or sugar pines, or geological marvels is, without more, simply irrelevant. . . . Penguins are important because people enjoy seeing them walk about rocks. . . . In short, my observations about environmental problems will be people-oriented. . . . I have no interest in preserving penguins for their own sake. . . .
>
> I reject the proposition that we *ought* to respect the "balance of nature" or to "preserve the environment" unless the reason for doing so, express or implied, is the benefit of man.[22]

Contrast Baxter's position with what Holmes Rolston III calls the "naturalistic ethic." Advocates of a naturalistic ethic contend, contrary to Baxter's view, "that some natural objects, such as whooping cranes, are morally considerable in their own right, apart from human interests, or that some ecosystems, perhaps the Great Smokies, have intrinsic values, such as aesthetic beauty, from which we derive a duty to respect these landscapes."[23] Human beings may value a mountain for a variety of reasons—because they can hike it, build ski lifts on it, mine the ore deep inside it, or simple because they like

looking at it. According to a naturalistic ethic, however, the value of the mountain is not simply a function of these human interests. Nature, or at least parts of it, can have value in and of itself, apart from human beings.

Some defenders of a naturalistic ethic contend that we have a particularly strong obligation to preserve species from extinction. This attitude is shared by many and was one of the factors behind the controversial legal efforts in the 1970s to prevent construction of the Tellico Dam on the Little Tennessee River in order to save the only known population of snail darters. But do species really have value above and beyond the individuals that make them up? An estimated 5 to 10 million species now inhabit the earth (there are, for instance, over 36,000 species of beetles), and they are always coming into and going out of existence. How valuable is this diversity of species, and how far are we morally required to go in maintaining it?

Adopting a naturalistic ethic would definitely alter our way of looking at nature and our understanding of our moral obligations to preserve and respect the natural environment. Many philosophers doubt, however, that nature has intrinsic value or that we can be said to have moral duties to nature. Having interests is a precondition, they would contend, of something's having rights or of our having moral duties to that thing. Natural objects, however, have no interests. Can a rock meaningfully be said to have an interest in not being eroded or in not being smashed into smaller pieces?

Plants and trees are different from rocks and streams. They are alive, and we can talk intelligibly about what is good or bad for a tree, plant, or vegetable. They can flourish or do poorly. Nonetheless, philosophers who discuss moral rights generally hold that this is not enough for plants to be said to have rights. To have rights a thing must have genuine interests, and to have interests, most theorists contend, a thing must have beliefs and desires. Vegetative life, however, lacks any cognitive awareness. Claims to the contrary are biologically unsupportable.

Even if the plant world lacks rights, can it still have intrinsic value? Can we still have a moral obligation to respect that world and not abuse it? Or are the only morally relevant values the various interests of human beings? These are hard questions. Among philosophers there is no consensus on how to answer them.

Animals

Above a certain level of complexity, animals do have at least rudimentary cognitive awareness. No owner of a cat or dog doubts that his pet has beliefs and desires. Accordingly, a number of philosophers have recently defended the claim that animals can have rights. Because they have genuine interests, animals can have genuine moral rights—despite the fact that they cannot claim their rights, that they cannot speak, that we cannot reason with them, and that they themselves lack a moral sense. Animals, it is more and more widely contended, do not have to be equal to human beings to have certain moral rights that we must respect.

Rather than talking about animals' rights, utilitarians would stress that higher animals are sentient, that is, that they are capable of feeling pain. Accordingly, there can be no justifiable reason for excluding their pleasures and pains from the overall utilitarian calculus. As Jeremy Bentham, one of the founders of utilitarianism, put it: "The question is not, Can they *reason*? nor, Can they *talk*? but, Can they *suffer*?" Our actions have effects on animals, and these consequences cannot be ignored. When one is deciding, then, what the morally right course of action is, the pleasures and pains of animals must be taken into account, too.

Business affects the welfare of animals very substantially. One way is through experimentation and the testing of products on ani-

mals. Critics like Peter Singer contend that the vast majority of experimentation and testing cannot be justified on moral grounds. Consider the "LD 50" test, which until very recently was the standard method of testing new foodstuffs. The object of the test is to find the dosage level at which 50 percent of the test animals die. This means that nearly all of them will become very sick before finally succumbing or surviving. When the substance is harmless, huge doses must be forced down the animals until in some cases the sheer volume kills them.[24]

In principle, utilitarians are willing to permit testing and experimentation on animals, provided that the overall results justify their pain and suffering. Not only is this proviso often not satisfied, but human beings typically disregard altogether the price the animals must pay. Consider the pharmaceutical firm Merck Sharp and Dohme, which sought to import chimpanzees to test a vaccine for Hepatitis B. Chimps are an endangered species and, as we all know, highly intelligent. Capturing juvenile chimps requires shooting the mother. One analyst assessed the situation this way:

> The world has a growing population of 4 billion people and a dwindling population of some 50,000 chimpanzees. Since the vaccine seems unusually innocuous, and since the disease is only rarely fatal, it would perhaps be more just if the larger population could find some way of solving its problem that was not to the detriment of the smaller.[25]

Business's largest and most devastating impact on animals, though, is through the production of animal-related products—in particular, meat. Many of us still think of our chicken and beef as coming from something like the idyllic farms pictured in storybooks, where the animals roam around contentedly and play with the farmer's children. Meat and egg production, however, is big business, and today most of the animal products we eat are from factory farms. In 1921 the largest commercial egg farm had a flock of 2,000 hens, who ran around loose in a large pasture. Today the largest commercial flock contains 2.5 million birds, and 80 percent of the 440 million laying hens are housed in 3 percent of the known chicken farms. These birds live in small multitiered wire cages.[26]

While the individuals involved in the meat and animal-products industries are not brutal, the desire to cut business costs and to economize routinely leads to treatment of animals that can only be described as cruel. Philosopher and animal rights advocate Tom Regan describes it this way:

> In increasing numbers, animals are being brought in off the land and raised indoors, in unnatural, crowded conditions—raised "intensively," to use the jargon of the animal industry. . . . The inhabitants of these "farms" are kept in cages, or stalls, or pens . . . living out their abbreviated lives in a technologically created and sustained environment: automated feeding, automated watering, automated light cycles, automated waste removal, automated what-not. And the crowding: as many as 9 hens in cages that measure 18 by 24 inches; veal calves confined to 22 inch wide stalls; hogs similarly confined, sometimes in tiers of cages, two, three, four rows high. Could any impartial, morally sensitive person view what goes on in a factory farm with benign approval?[27]

When it comes to the protection of animals, England has stricter laws than does the United States. Consider, then, the following proposals for protecting commercially farmed animals, which were turned down by the British government as being idealistic and unrealistic: (1) Any animal should have room to turn around. (2) A dry bed should be provided for all stock. (3) Palatable roughage must be readily available to all calves after one week of age. (4) Cages for poultry should be large enough for a bird to be able to stretch one wing at a time.[28]

Moral vegetarians are people who reject the eating of meat on moral grounds. Their argument is simple and powerful: The raising of animals for meat, especially with modern factory farming, sacrifices the most important and basic interests of animals simply to satisfy human tastes. Americans eat, per capita, a phenomenal amount of meat, by some estimates twice as much as we ate in 1950. Many people eat meat three times a day. Our preference for a Big Mac over a soybean burger, however, is only a matter of taste and culture, and the extra pleasure we believe that we get from eating the former cannot justify the price the animal must pay.

Would it be wrong to eat animals who were raised humanely, like those who run around freely and happily in children's picture books of farms? Unlike the lives of animals that we do in fact eat, the lives of such humanely raised animals, before being abruptly terminated, are not painful ones. Some philosophers would contend that it is permissible to raise animals for food if their lives are on balance positive ones. Other moral theorists challenge this, contending that at least higher animals have a right to life and should not be killed.

This debate raises important philosophical issues, but it is also rather hypothetical. Given economic reality, mass production of meat at affordable prices dictates factory farming. The important moral issue, then, is the real suffering and unhappy lives that billions of creatures experience on the way to our dinner table. This is an aspect of environmental ethics that is often overlooked, but which raises profound and challenging questions for both business and consumers.

SUMMARY

1. Business functions within a global ecological system. Because of the interrelated nature of ecosystems, and because intru-

sion into ecosystems frequently creates unfavorable effects, business must be sensitive to its impact on the physical environment.

2. Traditionally, business has regarded the natural world as a free and unlimited good. Pollution and resource depletion are examples of situations in which each person's pursuit of self-interest can make everyone worse off (the "tragedy of the commons"). Business must be sensitive to possible disparities between its private economic costs and the social costs of its activities (the problem of "externalities" or spillovers).

3. Companies that attempt to be "free riders" in environmental matters or that refuse to address the external costs of their business activities behave unfairly. Some philosophers maintain, further, that each person has a human right to a livable environment.

4. Pollution control has a price, and trade-offs will have to be made. But weighing costs and benefits involves controversial value judgments. Any equitable solution to the problem of who should pay must recognize that all of us in some way contribute to the problem and will benefit from correcting it.

5. Cost allocation requires a combination of regulations, incentives, and pricing mechanisms. Such an approach must consider not only what is effective, but must also seek a fair assignment of costs.

6. A broader view of environmental ethics must also consider our obligations to those in other societies and to future generations. Some philosophers argue that we must respect now the right of future generations not to inherit a seriously damaged environment, but talk of the rights of future generations raises puzzles.

7. Philosophers disagree about whether nature has intrinsic value. Some, adopting a human-oriented point of view, contend that the environment is valuable only because, and to the extent that, human beings value it. Those adopting a naturalistic ethic believe that the value of nature is not simply a function of human interests.

8. Through experimentation, testing, and the production of animal products, business has a very substantial impact on the welfare of animals. The meat and animal-produce industries rely on factory-farming techniques, which many describe as cruel and horrible. Because of this, moral vegetarians argue that meat eating is wrong.

CASE 10.1
BKK: The Story of a Waste Site

On an otherwise uneventful Tuesday night in July, 1984, police ordered nineteen families out of their homes in West Covina, one of the many cities in the megalopolis of Los Angeles. They were told that their health was jeopardized by high levels of methane and vinylchloride gases, which had been escaping from the nearby BKK landfill into their homes.

When a plastic company makes a plastic razor or ballpoint pen, it must dispose of vinylchloride, which, when inhaled above acceptable levels, can cause cancer. Until 1980, vinylchloride was discarded at the BKK landfill—that is, in the middle of a city of more than 80,000 people. When authorities roused families out of their quarters that quiet summer evening, they did so because fumes of the deadly chemical were seeping into nearby homes at a rate ninety-nine times the acceptable standard.

Local officials quickly began urging the Environmental Protection Agency (EPA) to do something and do it fast. But amidst the urgent pleas could be heard skeptical voices that doubted the EPA would take quick and decisive action.

The skeptics had some basis for doubting the EPA's resolve. One California representative, Vic Fazio, asserted that the EPA has "omitted and ignored" 120 sites in its survey of waste dumps at federal installations and laboratories. He pointed to a study done by the General Accounting Office that indicated that some of the federal government's own facilities might be more health threatening than private-sector waste sites like BKK. Fazio charged that the EPA simply had not been aggressive enough in dealing with federal waste sites, and he wanted legislation forcing the agency to set up strict rules and schedules for waste cleanup at federal installations.[29]

Fueling the case made by Fazio and other EPA critics was a nineteen-state survey conducted in 1984 by an environmental coalition group, the National Campaign Against Toxic Hazards. The survey, said its sponsors, found that nearly 60 percent of toxic-waste dumps marked for cleanup since 1983 under the federal "superfund" program remained basically untouched. But EPA official Russell A. Dawson said the survey masked "substantial work" that would soon double at targeted "superfund" sites.[30]

Environmentalists treated Dawson's assurance as so much eyewash. They hoped that the toxic hazards report would pressure the Senate to follow the House in expanding the scope and activities of "superfund." (A month earlier the House had passed a bill that would allot $10.2 billion for toxic waste site cleanup between 1983 and 1991—six times as much as the $1.6 billion that already had been authorized for 1981 through 1985. The Senate, heeding Administration claims that the legislation was premature, too sweeping, and too expensive, had failed to move a superfund bill to the floor.)

"These sites are not like fine wine," said John O'Connor, director of the Toxic Hazards Campaign. "They get worse with age, and they get more difficult and costly to clean up."[31]

Meanwhile Representative Esteban E. Torres, whose district included the BKK landfill, was calling on the EPA to shut down the dump immediately. Federal law, Torres pointed out, allows the EPA head to close a landfill when, in the administrator's view, it "may present an imminent and substantial endangerment to health or the environment." "All he [the EPA head] has to prove is that the BKK landfill is a public nuisance," said Torres. He added, "I am sure he can prove it, but he refuses to exercise his discretion at this time."[32]

Reacting to the pressures, federal and state officials urged the BKK Corporation, operators of the landfill, to close the site. On September 26, 1984, BKK officials announced that as of November 20 it would stop receiving liquid and solid hazardous wastes. But Kenneth Kazarian, vice president of BKK Corp., wanted to make it clear that BKK was not being forced into the decision. The company, he said, was simply withdrawing its request to be granted a permanent federal permit to operate a hazardous landfill.

An official from the Health Services Department welcomed the BKK decision. "That will put them out of the hazardous waste business entirely,"[33] he said. Meanwhile state and federal officials were assuring West Covina residents that the landfill presented "no imminent danger to public health." They added that after November 30, as many as forty trucks a day carrying toxic waste to BKK would be rerouted to landfills in other California counties.

But not everyone received news of the dump shutdown with enthusiasm. One California assemblyman, whose district includes

BKK, immediately called for a hearing to determine whether the landfill is safe. ''If this is the great solution we've been hearing about . . . I'm very disappointed,''[34] he said.

And grumbles of protest reverberated within the counties earmarked for the diverted toxic wastes. One of the most emphatic cries of outrage came from Santa Barbara County, where President Reagan has his ranch. Just a few months earlier, a truck carrying toxic waste had overturned and jackknifed while passing through the city of Santa Barbara enroute to a nearby dump site. The toxins discarded in the accident caused officials to shut down the highway for several hours and evacuate people from nearby homes and businesses.

Moreover word of the BKK closure did nothing to deter Representative Torres from seeking support for a bill he was sponsoring in the House of Representatives. The bill would require hazardous-waste landfill operators to conduct health-effects studies for areas around their facilities. The legislation would make it possible for people living near a toxic waste site to make an informed judgment about possible hazards to their health.

Discussion Questions

1. Identify the values and describe the attitudes that have contributed to the problems associated with toxic waste sites.

2. What would your reaction be if you were a citizen of a county to which toxic wastes were being diverted?

3. Who do you think should pay the costs of cleaning up a site like BKK?

4. Do you think that we have any obligations to future generations regarding the disposal of our toxic wastes?

5. Do you think the EPA should have shut down BKK? Why?

6. Do you think the BKK Corporation had a moral obligation to shut down the landfill, even if it was not legally forced to? Explain by appeal to ethical principles.

CASE 10.2
The Valley of Death

It is called Brazil's ''valley of death,'' and it may be the most polluted place on the earth. It lies about an hour's drive south of São Paulo, where the land suddenly drops 2,000 feet to a coastal plane. Over 100,000 people live in the valley—along with a variety of industrial plants that produce and discharge thousands of tons of pollutants into the air every day. A reporter for *National Geographic* recalls that within an hour of his arrival in the valley, his chest began aching as the polluted air inflamed his bronchial tubes and restricted his breathing.[35]

The air in the valley is rich with toxins—among them, benzene, a known carcinogen.

Ten percent of the area's factory workers show low white-blood-cell counts, a possible precursor to leukemia. Infant mortality is 10 percent higher here than in the state as a whole. Out of 40,000 urban residents in the valley municipality of Cubatão, nearly 13,000 cases of respiratory disease were reported in a recent year.

Few of the local inhabitants complain, however. For them, the fumes smell of jobs. They also distrust bids to buy their property by local industry, which wants to expand, as well as governmental efforts to relocate them to free homesites on a landfill. One young mother says, ''yes, the children are often ill and sometimes can barely breathe. We want to live in another place, but we cannot afford to."

A university professor of public health, Dr. Oswaldo Campos views the dirty air in Cubatão simply as the result of economic priorities. "Some say it is the price of progress," Campos comments, "but is it? Look who pays the price—the poor."

Discussion Questions

1. What attitudes and values on the part of business and others lead to the creation of areas like the "valley of death"?

2. Some say "pollution is the price of progress." Is this slogan correct? What is meant by "progress"? Who does pay the price? Explain both the economic and the moral issues raised by the slogan.

3. It might be argued that if the people of the valley don't complain and don't wish to move, then they accept the risks of living there and the polluters are not violating their rights. Assess this argument.

CASE 10.3
Paying the Bill for Cleaning Up Three Mile Island

In the spring of 1986 the world's attention was riveted on the accident at the Soviet nuclear power plant at Chernobyl. Those in the West do not know all the details of what happened, nor is anyone really certain what the long-term environmental and health effects of Chernobyl will be. While American officials rushed to assure the world that a similar disaster couldn't happened here, Americans remembered only too well the events at Three Mile Island, Pennsylvania, in 1979—the costs and consequences of which we are still coming to grips with.

In his book *The Politics of Energy*, Barry Commoner identifies the key events surrounding the accident at Three Mile Island (TMI).[36] On March 28, 1979, at 3:53 A.M., a pump failed, and as a result the reactor's heat was not drawn off in the heat exchanger and in the primary loop overhead. When the pressure in the loop increased, a release valve opened, as it was designed to do on such occasions. But the valve stuck open, causing the loop system to lose the water it needed to carry off the heat generated within the reactor core. Technicians monitoring the vent misread the flash-ing lights to mean that cooling water was flooding into the hot core, when, in fact, it was draining out.

Intense heat that had built up could in theory melt the reactor's fuel rods, causing a "meltdown" that would discharge radioactive material right through the floor of the reactor. Designed for just such a catastrophic possibility, the reactor's energy cooling system was automatically activated. But when it was prematurely turned off, some of the fuel rods overheated, producing a bubble of hydrogen gas at the top of the reactor. The bubble effectively blocked the flow of cooling water, thus again presenting technicians with the threat of a meltdown. Equally alarming was the possibility that the gas contained enough oxygen to cause an explosion that would release deadly radioactive material into the surrounding countryside. But in the end the desperate efforts of the technicians to reduce the size of the gas bubble succeeded. The threat of an explosion had been averted. But the sealed-off plant was thoroughly contaminated. No one would be able to enter it for months without exposure to lethal radiation levels.

Despite their efforts, technicians were not able to contain all the radioactive material within the plant. So, upon learning that some gases had escaped, Pennsylvania Governor Richard Thornburgh urged pregnant women and children to leave the area within a radius of five miles of the plant. Other people also heeded the governor's advice—about 60,000 left within the week.

The accident at TMI proved a financial disaster for General Public Utilities Corp. (GPU), the plant's owner. The power company's earnings plummeted, its stock lost 70 percent of its value, its bond rating fell, and its stockholders no longer received dividends. Most humiliating was the $1 billion estimated cost of cleaning up the plant—humiliating because GPU said it couldn't pay the costs.

It was thus that in the fall of 1981, a fierce argument erupted over who would pay the cleanup costs at TMI. *The Wall Street Journal* phrased the question under debate as follows: "Should Americans everywhere be dunned to correct a blunder by a utility that was selling relatively cheap nuclear power to customers in Pennsylvania?"[37]

Two proposals for collecting the money quickly surfaced. The first, endorsed by the Reagan Administration, called for the government to put up $123 million in radiation clean-up money over a period of several years. But administration officials were quick to point out the federal aid would not be "open-ended." The responsibility for paying for the radiation cleanup of TMI, one of the president's key advisers emphasized, lay with those who produced and used the power from the facility.

Under the second proposal, Edison Electric Institute, which represents 200 investor-owned utilities, pledged to collect upwards of $192 million from utilities nationwide. The institute conditioned their pledge on the passage of legislation making contributions by utilities mandatory. That way the contributing utilities could convince state rate-setting commissions that their donation must be treated as operating expenses and passed on to the rate payers.

Some members of Congress balked at both legislative proposals. The first, they said, was just another government bailout, despite administration assurances to the contrary. It was also, in their view, identical to the institute's proposal in one key respect: Both would make those pay who bore no responsibility for the accident and derived no benefit from the inexpensive power generated at TMI.

Still, GPU insisted that without outside help, rate payers for TMI energy would have to shoulder an excessive burden. It reminded everyone that Metropolitan Edison Co., a GPU subsidiary that was operating TMI in 1979, already had asked the Pennsylvania Public Utilities Commission for a 22 percent rate increase to finance the cleanup. The company estimated that the increase would raise the monthly electric bill of a typical residential customer to $46.64 from $36.18.[38]

Representative Allen Ertel, whose district includes Three Mile Island, put forth a plan of his own that would require all U.S. utilities operating nuclear plants to contribute to an insurance fund to help defray the costs of cleaning up TMI and protect the industry against similar future accidents. Under Ertel's plan, electric rate payers in other states would, in effect, finance the TMI cleanup.

Governor Thornburgh voiced concern that most utilities were having to pay higher bond interest rates because of the accident. Fearing that the entire utility industry could be adversely affected, he suggested that both the industry and federal and state governments jointly cover $760 million in cleanup expenses.

While various parties haggled over who would foot the cleanup bill, the 600,000 gallons of radioactive water left by the accident continued to stand in the basement of the reactor's containment building. Cleanup experts clamored for the water's removal, lest it seep into the Susquehanna River, endangering humans and fish downstream in the Chesapeake Bay. In fact, in September, GPU had begun pumping the water out of the basement and filtering its radioactive atoms through canisters holding sand-like material. The contaminated sand would be stored on the island until the government decided its ultimate disposition. The filtered water would also be stored and used later for scrubbing down the contaminated walls of the reactor building.

The final resting place for the water concerned officials, because, despite the filtering, it still contained the radioactive material tritium. GPU officials claimed that the water could be rendered harmless by dilution with fresh water, and the resulting mix could then be safely trickled into the Susquehanna. But GPU conceded that the proposal probably would alarm people downstream.

Another alternative would be to put the water in ponds on the island and let it evaporate—a proposal hardly geared to please those who had to breathe tritium in the air. Still other alternatives called for using the water to make concrete and then shipping the concrete off to—well, somewhere. Or trucking the water to the ocean and dumping it. Or just leaving it in its two holding tanks indefinitely on the island.

Discussion Questions

1. If the TMI accident did result from error on the part of the utility company, should the company have paid all the cleanup costs?

2. Do you agree that the cleanup costs should have been borne jointly by those who produced and who used the power from the facility?

3. In your opinion, is it fair to make rate payers nationwide absorb the costs of cleaning up TMI? Should government pick up (part of) the tab?

4. Identify the ideals, obligations, and effects involved in disposing of the contaminated water.

5. Suppose that the cheapest, most efficient, and least net harmful way to dispose of the water happened to put at risk a small segment of the population. Do you think that so disposing of the water would be morally justifiable? Explain by appeal to ethical principles.

CASE 10.4
Testing Car Fumes Sparks Debate

"Emissions analyzer" is the official name of the device. But gas station owners in the New York area call it by other names, most unprintable.

An emissions analyzer is a 115-pound, computerized instrument that measures pollutants in automobile exhausts. A probe is inserted into the tail pipe, and a computer prints a tape showing the level of each pollutant. The device costs $5,850 plus $99 a month.[39]

By early 1981, about 4,000 gas station owners in the New York metropolitan area had bought or leased an emissions analyzer to comply with a state regulation that made an emissions inspection part of the existing annual safety inspection required for all New York-licensed cars and light trucks. The stringent regulation was part of a federal plan to cut pollution in the metropolitan area by 25 percent.

No one could seriously question the determination of the federal and state governments to do something about the city's filthy air. After all, next to Los Angeles, the New York metropolitan area has the most polluted air in the nation. According to the EPA, at times the levels of carbon monoxide and hydrocarbons reach twice the level of government maximum-allowed standards. To prod the state of New York into action, the EPA gave it an ultimatum in 1979: Either devise a plan to control auto emissions or lose $550 million in federal funds. The state got the message and on January 1, 1981, began requiring all cars and light trucks in the nine counties of metropolitan New York City to undergo annual emission inspections. It's doubtful, though, that state officials were fully prepared for the firestorm of protest that would follow.

All sorts of individuals and groups resented the program. Topping the list were some owners of service stations and repair shops authorized to administer safety tests. (Unlike some states that use government inspectors to administer safety tests, New York allows the tests to be conducted by authorized service stations.) Not only did the owners object to the compulsory nature of the program and to the costs of purchasing or leasing the analyzer, but they complained that the devices were troublesome. Every month, they said, the analyzers had to be calibrated by factory representatives, and on cold mornings they took up to a half hour to warm up.

To defray their costs, station owners immediately doubled the cost of an inspection, up to $12 from $6, thereby outraging some consumers. Suburbanites in eastern Long Is-

land's Suffolk County, for example, complained that, while their air was fine, they were being forced to bear the expense of helping clean up air in New York City. A consumer group in Rockland County even branded the program "the biggest consumer fraud ever to hit the state's citizens,"[40] because large trucks and buses were exempt from exhaust checks. The point was not lost on Rockland County legislators, who approved legal action to block the plan. Even the auto club worried that some motorists could be victimized by unneeded repairs.

Despite the hue and cry, the EPA stood firm. Indeed, it plans to require metropolitan areas in twenty nine states to install auto-exhaust checks.

Discussion Questions

1. Do you think the EPA emission inspection is justified? Do critics of the program have any legitimate concerns?

2. Is it fair that only cars and light trucks are required to undergo annual inspections?

3. In your opinion, is it fair that residents in an area relatively free of air pollution (such as eastern Long Island) should be made to help pay the costs of cleaning up an area with severe air pollution (like New York City)?

4. Would you support or oppose an extension of the EPA program to other metropolitan areas? Explain.

CASE 10.5
Sharing the Blame

SCENE: The office of the director of a midwestern advertising agency
CHARACTERS: Donna Ellis, assistant director of advertising
Bryan Lavelle, director

SITUATION: Donna Ellis is vehemently protesting the agency's complicity in an ad campaign commissioned by Mid-Valley Gas and Electric, a utility firm with pronounced antienvironment tendencies. Mid-Valley has consistently propagan-

dized for increased electric power use. Its latest campaign solicits public support to build more power plants to provide adequate service. Some persons doubt whether such plants are needed. Vigorously promoting less power use might accomplish what additional plants would be intended to do. Ellis is particularly incensed about a leaflet her agency has worked up to accompany the bills consumers will receive in the months ahead. The content of the leaflet is captured in the bold-print headline on the first page. It reads: "Balance Ecology With Power."

Ellis: The point is that ecology is not a thing to be balanced against anything else.

Lavelle: What do you mean?

Ellis: I mean this ad is tremendously misleading. It misses the whole concept of ecology, its essential meaning. *Ecology* refers to a science of the interrelatedness of everything. To speak of balancing it with anything else is just plain dumb. In fact, it's downright distorting. It gives the impression that somehow we must be just as concerned with energy as we are with the ecology.

Lavelle: But isn't that true?

Ellis: It's not so much a question of truth as one of emphasis and impact within an advertising gestalt.

Lavelle: Gestalt?

Ellis: That's right. Look, we both know that for years now Mid-Valley has been trying to get people to use more power. Now with the energy crunch on, they're obviously concerned with maintaining their mind-boggling profits while at the same time not appearing to be callously indifferent to environmental concerns. The result is this ad. Taken within the total framework of where Mid-Valley's coming from, it amounts to a not-so-subtle pitch calculated to marshal public sup-

port for building additional power plants, which they've already begun to lobby for in Washington and in the state capitol.

Lavelle: But you can't expect them not to. I mean, calling for power conservation and a moratorium on plant construction just isn't in their best business interests.

Ellis: Obviously. But that doesn't mean we should assist them in furthering what may be of highly questionable social value.

Lavelle: But Donna, that's totally unrealistic. You're asking us to sit in judgment of the moral worth of our clients' interests.

Ellis: I'm suggesting that on matters as serious as a firm's environmental responsibilities, we must act in a socially responsible way.

Lavelle: You realize, of course, that we already devote 20 percent of our advertising time to what we consider sound social causes? Nobody can accuse this agency of being socially indifferent.

Ellis: But that's a cop-out. Remember, only a small fraction of that time is earmarked for environmental matters. What's worse, it seems to me we're undoing what little good we may be achieving when we run ads like this. It *talks* about the research necessary to deal with environmental pollution, but we both know that Mid-Valley has done no research at all.

Lavelle: But it's not our job to sit in judgment of our clients' interests. That's the job of government.

Ellis: But certainly we should sit in judgment of our own activities, shouldn't we?

Lavelle: Okay, let's do that, let's really do it. Do you think we'd be doing the right thing if we jeopardized Mid-

Valley's three-million-dollar annual account with us by imposing our own environmental philosophy on their ads or telling them to peddle their propaganda elsewhere? What about our stockholders? Our own employees? Our other accounts? We've got obligations to them as well, you know.

Ellis: Sure we do, but that shouldn't blind us to our social obligations. Simply because we function in this society as information communicators, we're not relieved of the obligation to examine the likely impact of that information, the impressions it gives, the opinions it helps form, the attitudes it molds. That we ourselves don't operate belching smokestacks or discharge waste into rivers doesn't mean we have no business responsibilities to the environment. The fact is that on environmental questions our role is a pivotal one. We control what the most obvious vested interests can say to generate public opinion. If Mid-Valley persists in behaving in an environmentally irresponsible way, we share the blame.

Lavelle: Donna, I hear what you're saying and appreciate your concerns, but this is a decision I'm going to have to mull over. I may even have to go to the board.

Ellis: I think you should.

Discussion Questions

1. Is Donna Ellis right in speaking out? Would you, too, be critical of Mid-Valley's campaign?

2. What should Lavelle do? If he takes the matter to the board, what do you think the board should do?

3. With respect to the environment, do you think advertising agencies have any general responsibilities?

4. If the board chooses to take no action, what should Donna Ellis do?

NOTES

1. *Earthbound: New Introductory Essays in Environmental Ethics*, Tom Regan, ed. (New York: Random House, 1984), 3.

2. See Margaret Engel, "A Mystery in Puerto Rico: Why Babies Menstruate," *The Washington Post National Weekly Edition*, October 1, 1984, p. 7.

3. Lewis Regenstein, *America the Poisoned* (Washington, D.C.: Acropolis Books, 1982), 81. Quoted in Regan, *Earthbound*, 4.

4. "Tolerating Pesticides," reprinted in the *International Herald Tribune*, November 19, 1987.

5. Regenstein, 182. Quoted in Regan, *Earthbound*, 3.

6. U.S. Nuclear Regulatory Commission, "Final Generic Environmental Statement on the Use of Plutonium Recycled in Mixed Oxide Fuel in Light Water Cooled Reactors," *NUREG–0002* 1 (August 1976). Quoted in Manuel G. Velasquez, *Business Ethics: Concepts and Cases* (Englewood Cliffs, N.J.: Prentice-Hall, 1982), 183.

7. "*Playboy* Interview: Dr. Paul Ehrlich," *Playboy*, August 1970, p. 56.

8. John Steinbeck, *America and Americans* (New York: Viking Press, 1966), 127.

9. Garrett Hardin, "The Tragedy of the Commons," *Science* 162 (December 13, 1968): 1243–1248.

10. William T. Blackstone, "Ethics and Ecology," in William T. Blackstone, ed., *Philosophy and the Environmental Crisis* (Athens: University of Georgia Press, 1974).

11. George Steiner, *Business and Society* (New York: Random House, 1973), 242-243.

12. Keith Davis and Robert L. Blomstrom, *Business and Society* (New York: McGraw-Hill, 1975), 439.

13. Steiner, *Business and Society*, 235.

14. See Neal H. Jacoby, "The Environmental Crisis," *The Center Magazine* (November–December 1970): 37–48.

15. Davis and Blomstrom, *Business and Society*, 440.

16. Ibid., 454.

17. See Steiner, *Business and Society*, 247.

18. Joel Feinberg, "The Rights of Animals and Unborn Generations," in Tom L. Beauchamp and Norman E. Bowie, eds., *Ethical Theory and Business*, 2nd ed. (Englewood Cliffs, N.J.: Prentice-Hall, 1983), 435.

19. Derek Parfit, *Reasons and Persons* (New York: Oxford University Press, 1986), 361. Parfit adds: "It may help to think about this question: how many of us could truly claim, 'Even if railways and motor cars had never been invented, I would still have been born.'"

20. Ibid., 365

21. Annette Baier, "The Rights of Past and Future Persons," in Joseph R. DesJardins and John J. McCall, eds., *Contemporary Issues in Business Ethics* (Belmont, Calif,: Wadsworth, 1985), 501.

22. "People or Penguins," in Donald VanDeVeer and Christine Pierce, eds., *People, Penguins, and Plastic Trees* (Belmont, Calif.: Wadsworth, 1986), 215–216.

23. "Just Environmental Business," in Tom Regan, ed., *New Introductory Essays in Business Ethics* (New York: Random House, 1984), 325.

24. "Animal Liberation," *New York Review of Books*, April 5, 1973.

25. Quoted by Rolston, "Just Environmental Business," 340.

26. Tom L. Beauchamp, *Case Studies in Business, Society, and Ethics* (Englewood Cliffs, N.J.: Prentice-Hall, 1983), 118–119.

27. Tom Regan, "Ethical Vegetarianism and Commercial Animal Farming," in Richard A. Wasserstrom, ed., *Today's Moral Problems*, 3rd ed. (New York: Macmillan, 1985), 463–464.

28. Singer, "Animal Liberation."

29. Roberta A. Rosenblatt, "Toxic Flow From Acid Pits Creates Water Basin Peril," *Los Angeles Times*, August 7, 1984, Part II, p. 2.

30. See Michael Wines, "Waste Dumps Untouched, Survey Says," *Los Angeles Times*, September 7, 1984, Part I, p. 5.

31. Ibid.

32. Esteban E. Torres, "Solution to BKK's Hazards Starts With Closing It Now," *Los Angeles Times*, August 6, 1984, Part II, p. 5.

33. Mark Gladstone, "BKK Landfill To Cease All Hazardous Waste Dumping," *Los Angeles Times*, September 27, 1984, Part II, p. 1.

34. Ibid.

35. See Noel Grove, "Air: An Atmosphere of Uncertainty," *National Geographic* 171 (April 1987), from which this case study and the quotations below are drawn.

36. See Barry Commoner, *The Politics of Energy* (New York: Knopf, 1979), 47–48.

37. Arlen J. Large, "Fallout's Fallout: Battle Opens On Paying $1 Billion Cleanup Bill For Three Mile Island," *The Wall Street Journal*, October 21, 1981, p. 1. This article is the primary source of the facts reported in the case.

38. Ibid.

39. For the facts reported in this case, see Daniel Hertzberg, "Device To Test Car Fumes Irks Gas Stations," *The Wall Street Journal*, February 6, 1981, Section 2, p. 25.

40. Ibid., 25.

The Environmental Crisis and the Quality of Life

Nicholas Rescher

While agreeing that attempts to clean up the environment are noble, Professor Rescher believes that they are too little, too late. In Rescher's view, society simply must learn to live with scarce environmental goods and scale down its expectations for the quality of life accordingly. Our ideas about material progress, our faith in the power of technology, and our hope for a perfect future will all have to give way, Rescher argues, as a result of the environmental crisis.

Introduction

Most of us tend to think of the environmental crisis as resulting from "too much"—too much pollution, wastage, pesticide, and so forth. But from the economists' angle the problem is one of *scarcity*: too little clean air, pure water, recreationally usable land, safe fruit. The answer traditional among welfare economists to problems of scarcity is based singlemindedly on the leading idea of *production*. But alas the things which the environmental crisis leaves in too short supply—fresh air, clean rivers, unpolluted beaches, and the like are not things to which the standard, traditional concept of the production of goods and services—or anything like it—will be applicable. The project of *producing* another planet earth to live on after we have used this one up is unfortunately unfeasible.

For reasons such as this, various economists—Kenneth Boulding most prominent among them—have urged a broadening of economic horizons and redeployment of concern. Economics is to deal not just narrowly with the production and consumption of goods and services but broadly with the maintenance of a quality of life. Such a reorientation of welfare economics has profound consequences. It once again renders relevant to economics the traditional concerns of the philosopher with matters of norms and values, of ideology and the rational structure of social appraisal.

It is from this philosophical vantage point—not ignoring the concerns of the economist and sociologist and social psychologist but seeking to transcend the bounds of their disciplinary bailiwicks—that I should like to consider the impact of the environmental crisis.

Most of the discussions of the environmental crisis in which I have been a participant or witness are basically exercises in social uplift. The lesson is driven home that if only we are good and behave ourselves everything will come out just fine. To adopt more stringent legislation of control, to subject grasping enterprise to social pressure, to adopt better social values and attitudes, to espouse the program and ideology of planned parenthood or women's lib, to hand the control of affairs over to those who are younger and purer of heart . . . so runs the gamut of remedies which their respective advocates would have us adopt and which, once adopted, will—so we are told—put everything to rights. Throughout this stance there runs the fundamentally activistic optimism of the American experience: virtue will be rewarded; and by the end of the sixth reel, the good guys will be riding off into the glorious sunset.

My aim is to dash some cold water on all this. I want to propose the deeply pessimistic suggestion that, crudely speaking, the environment has had it and that we simply cannot "go home again" to "the good old days" of environmental purity. We all know of the futile laments caused by the demise of the feudal order by such thinkers as Thomas More or the ruralistic yearnings voiced by the romantics in the early days of the Industrial Revolution. Historical retrospect may well cast the present spate of hand-wringing over environmental deterioration as an essentially analogous—right-minded

but utterly futile—penchant for the easier, simpler ways of bygone days. Actually even to think of the problem as an environmental crisis is tendentious. Crises are by definition transitory phenomena: they point toward a moment of decision for life or death, not toward a stable condition of things. The very terminology indicates an unwillingness to face the prospect of a serious environmental degradation as a permanent reality, an ongoing "fact of life."

To take this view goes deep against the grain, and I have little hope of persuading many people of its correctness. I certainly do not like it myself. But perhaps it could be granted—at least for the sake of discussion—that the view might be correct. Granting this hypothesis, let us explore its implications.

First let me be clearer about the hypothesis itself. I am not saying that environmental activism is futile—that man cannot by dint of energy and effort manage to clean up this or that environmental mess. What I am saying is that we may simply be unable to solve the environmental crisis as a whole: that once this or that form of noxiousness is expelled from one door some other equally bad version comes in by another. My hypothesis in short is that the environmental crisis may well be incurable. It just may be something that we cannot solve but have to learn to live with.

This hypothesis is surely not altogether unrealistic and fanciful. Basically the environmental mess is a product of the conspiration of three forces: (1) high population densities, (2) high levels of personal consumption, and (3) a messy technology of production. Can one even realistically expect that any of these can really be eliminated? Not the population crunch surely. As the character remarked in a recent "Peanuts" cartoon: "Everybody says there are too many of us, but nobody wants to leave." So much for population. Moreover, lots of people everywhere in the world are clamoring for affluence and a place on the high-consumption bandwagon, and pitifully few are jumping off. . . .

The Escalation of Expectations

The concept of social *progress* is deeply, almost irremovably, impressed on the American consciousness. And this is so not just in the remote past but very much in our own day. Take just the most recent period since World War II. Consider the marked signs of progress:

1. The increase of life expectancy (at birth) from sixty-three years in 1940 to seventy years in 1965.

2. The rise of per capita personal income from $1,810 in 1950 to $2,542 in 1965 (in constant [1958] dollars).

3. The increase in education represented by a rise in school enrollments from 44 percent of the five-to-thirty-four-year-old group in 1950 to 60 percent in 1965.

4. The growth of social welfare expenditures from $88 per capita in 1945 to $360 per capita in 1965 (in constant [1958] dollars).

Taken together, these statistics bring into focus the steady and significant improvement in the provisions for individual comfort and social welfare that has taken place in the United States since World War II. If the progress-oriented thesis that increased physical well-being brings increased happiness were correct, one would certainly expect Americans to be substantially happier today than ever before. This expectation is not realized. In fact, the available evidence all points the reverse way.

. . . We are facing . . . an escalation of expectations, a raising of the levels of expectations with corresponding increased aspirations in the demands people make upon the circumstances and conditions of their lives. With respect to the requisites of happiness, we are in the midst of a revolution of rising expectations, a revolution that affects not only the man at the bottom, but operates throughout, to the very top of the heap.

This supposition of an escalation of expectations regarding the quality of life, and correspondingly of aspirations regarding the requisites of happiness, finds striking confirmation in the fact that despite the impressive signs that people think of themselves as less happy than their predecessors of a generation or so ago, they would be unwilling to contemplate a return to what we hear spoken of (usually cynically) as the good old days.

. . . This sort of perception of unhappiness has a surprising twist to it. It indicates a deep faith in progress—a progression of steady improvement in the circumstances of life, however little we may actually savor this improvement in terms of increased happiness.

Some Ideological Victims

Let us now return in the light of these considerations to my initial hypothesis. If in the continued unfolding an ongoing environmental crisis occurs, various conceptions integral to the American social ideology will have to go by the board: in particular the conceptions of material progress, of technological omnipotence, and of millennial orientation.

Material Progress

. . . A parting of the ways with the concept of progress will not come easy to us. It's going to take a lot of doing to accustom us to the idea that things are on balance to get worse or at any rate no better as concerns the quality of life in this nation. (And once we are persuaded of this, there may be vast social and political repercussions in terms of personal frustration and social unrest.) The conception of a deescalation of expectations, of settling for less than we've been accustomed to, is something Americans are not prepared for. We have had little preparatory background for accepting the realization that in some key aspects in the quality of life the best days may be behind us. I myself very much doubt that we are going to take kindly to the idea. The British have made a pretty good show of having to haul down the flag of empire. You will, I hope, forgive me for evincing skepticism about our ability to show equally good grace when the time comes to run down our banner emblazoned with "Standard of Living."

Technological Omnipotence

The conception of get-it-done confidence, virtually of technological omnipotence, runs deep in the American character. We incline to the idea that, as a people, we can do anything we set our mind to. In a frontier nation there was little tendency toward a serious recognition of limits of any sort. The concept of finite resources, the reality of opportunity costs, the necessity for *choice* in the allocation of effort and the inescapable prospect of unpleasant consequences of choices (negative externalities) are newcomers to American thinking.

This era of economic awareness and recognition of the realities of cost-benefit analysis is so recent it has hardly trickled down to the popular level.

The course of our historical experience has not really prepared us to face the realities of finiteness and incapacity. We expect government to "handle things"—not only the foreign wars, economic crises, and social disorders of historical experience, but now the environmental crises as well. The idea that our scientific technology and the social technology of our political institutions may be utterly inadequate to the task does not really dawn on us. If and when it finally does, you may be sure that the fur will fly.

Millennial Hankerings

Americans have manifested more millennial hankerings than perhaps any other people since the days when apocalyptic thinking was in fashion. The idea that a solution to our problems lies somehow just around the corner is deeply ingrained in our consciousness. Nobody knows the themes to which people resonate better than politicians. And from Woodrow Wilson's Fourteen Points to Franklin Roosevelt's New Deal to the quality-of-life rhetoric of Lyndon Johnson's campaign the fundamentally millennial nature of our political rhetoric is clear. "Buy our program, accept our policies, and everything in the country will be just about perfect." That is how the politicians talk, and they do so because that is what people yearn to hear. We can accept deprivation now as long as we feel assured that prosperity lies just around the corner. No political campaign is complete without substantial pandering to our millennial yearnings through assurances that if only we put the right set of men in office all our troubles will vanish and we can all live happily ever after. We as a nation have yet to learn the unpleasant lesson that such pie-in-the-sky thinking is a luxury we can no longer afford.

The ideological consequences of the demise of a faith in progress, technological omnipotence, and the millennial orientation will clearly be profound. The result cannot but be a radically altered ideology, a wholly new American outlook. What will this be? All too temptingly it may be a leap to the opposite extreme: to hopelessness, despondency, discouragement—the sense of impotence and *après nous le déluge*. I am afraid that such an era of disillusionment may well be the natural consequence of the presently popular rhetoric of the environmental crisis. And the American people do not have a particularly good record for sensible action in a time of disappointed expectations. Our basic weakness is a rather nonstandard problem of morale: a failure not of nerve but of patience.

Yet such a result—despair and disillusionment—seems to me wholly unwarranted. It is realism not hopelessness that provides the proper remedy for overconfidence. Let us by all means carry on the struggle to "save the environment" by all feasible steps. But let us not entertain misguided expectations about the prospects of success—expectations whose probable disappointment cannot but result in despondency, recrimination, and the tempting resort to the dire political measures that are natural to gravely disillusioned people.

The stance I see as necessary is not one of fatalistic resignation but of carrying on the good fight to save the environment—but doing so in fully realistic awareness that we are carrying on a limited war in which an actual victory may well lie beyond our grasp. It has taken an extraordinarily difficult struggle for us to arrive at a limited war perspective in international relations under the inexorable pressure of the political and technological facts of our times. And we have not even begun to move toward the corresponding mentality in the sphere of social problems and domestic difficulties. Yet just this—as I see it—is one of the crucial sociotechnological imperatives of our day.

Conclusion

The time has come for summing up. The conception that the quality of life—currently under threat by the environmental crisis—represents simply another one of those binds for which the welfare economists' classic prescription of "producing oneself out of it" seems to me profoundly misguided. In my discussion I have set before you the hypothesis of the environmental crisis as not really a crisis at all, but the inauguration of a permanent condition of things.

I have tried to argue that one of the main implications of this is a reversal of the ongoing escalation of expectations that is and long has been rife among Americans. In various crucial respects regarding the quality of life we just may have to settle for less. I have maintained that this development will exact from Americans a great price in terms of ideological revisionism. In particular, it will demand as victims our inclination to progressivism, our Promethean faith in man's technological omnipotence, and our penchant for millennial thinking. What is needed in the face of the environmental crisis at this point, as I see it, may well be not a magisterial confidence that things can be put right, but a large dose of cool realism tempered with stoic resignation. We had better get used to the idea that we may have to scale down our expectations and learn to settle for less in point of standard of living and quality of life.

This conclusion will very likely strike many as a repulsive instance of "gloom and doom" thinking. This would be quite wrong. The moral, as I see it, is at worst one of gloom without doom. Man is a being of enormous adaptability, resiliency, and power. He has learned to survive and make the best of it under some extremely difficult and unpleasant conditions. By all means, let us do everything we can to save the environment. But if we do

not do a very good job of it—and I for one do not think we will—it is not necessarily the end of the world. Let us not sell man short. We have been in some unpleasant circumstances before and have managed to cope.

Review and Discussion Questions

1. Why does Rescher think that the environmental "crisis" is not really a crisis at all, but a permanent condition? Do you agree?

2. Has Rescher correctly identified three main features of "American social ideology"? Would accepting his point of view require us to modify our ideology, as he maintains?

3. Is Rescher pessimistic or just "realistic"? Are Americans likely to adopt his perspective on the environmental crisis? What would be the results if they did?

The Place Of Nonhumans In Environmental Issues

Peter Singer

Professor of philosophy Peter Singer argues that the effects of our environmental actions on nonhumans should figure directly in our deliberations about what we ought to do. Because animals can feel pleasure and pain and have the capacity for subjective experience, they can therefore be said to have interests, interests we must not ignore. Singer contends that we must extend the moral principle of "equal consideration of interests" to include the interests of nonhumans, and he sketches the implications of our doing so—including the necessity of abandoning our present practice of rearing and killing other animals for food.

Not For Humans Only

When we humans change the environment in which we live, we often harm ourselves. If we discharge cadmium into a bay and eat shellfish from that bay, we become ill and may die. When our industries and automobiles pour noxious fumes into the atmosphere, we find a displeasing smell in the air, the long-term results of which may be every

bit as deadly as cadmium poisoning. The harm that humans do the environment, however, does not rebound solely, or even chiefly, on humans. It is nonhumans who bear the most direct burden of human interference with nature.

By "nonhumans" I mean to refer to all living things other than human beings, though for reasons to be given later, it is with nonhuman animals, rather than plants, that I am chiefly concerned. It is also important, in the context of environmental issues, to note that living things may be regarded either collectively or as individuals. In debates about the environment the most important way of regarding living things collectively has been to regard them as species. Thus, when environmentalists worry about the future of the blue whale, they usually are thinking of the blue whale as a species, rather than of individual blue whales. But this is not, of course, the only way in which one can think

From K. E. Goodpaster and K. M. Sayre, eds., *Ethics and Problems of the 21st Century* (Notre Dame, Ind.: University of Notre Dame Press, 1979). Reprinted by permission.

of blue whales, or other animals, and one of the topics I shall discuss is whether we should be concerned about what we are doing to the environment primarily insofar as it threatens entire species of nonhumans, or primarily insofar as it affects individual nonhuman animals.

The general question, then, is how the effects of our actions on the environment of nonhuman beings should figure in our deliberations about what we ought to do. There is an unlimited variety of contexts in which this issue could arise. To take just one: Suppose that it is considered necessary to build a new power station, and there are two sites, A and B, under consideration. In most respects the sites are equally suitable, but building the power station on site A would be more expensive because the greater depth of shifting soil at that site will require deeper foundations; on the other hand to build on site B will destroy a favored breeding ground for thousands of wildfowl. Should the presence of the wildfowl enter into the decision as to where to build? And if so, in what manner should it enter, and how heavily should it weigh?

In a case like this the effects of our actions on nonhuman animals could be taken into account in two quite different ways: directly, giving the lives and welfare of nonhuman animals an intrinsic significance which must count in any moral calculation; or indirectly, so that the effects of our actions on nonhumans are morally significant only if they have consequences for humans. . . .

The view that the effects of our actions on other animals has no direct moral significance is not as likely to be openly advocated today as it was in the past; yet it is likely to be accepted implicitly and acted upon. When planners perform cost-benefit studies on new projects, the costs and benefits are costs and benefits for human beings only. This does not mean that the impact of the power station or highway on wildlife is ignored altogether, but it is included only indirectly. That a new reservoir would drown a valley teeming with wildlife is taken into account only under some such heading as the value of the facilities for recreation that the valley affords. In calculating this value, the cost-benefit study will be neutral between forms of recreation like hunting and shooting and those like bird watching and bush walking—in fact hunting and shooting are likely to contribute more to the benefit side of the calculations because larger sums

of money are spent on them, and they therefore benefit manufacturers and retailers of firearms as well as the hunters and shooters themselves. The suffering experienced by the animals whose habitat is flooded is not reckoned into the costs of the operation; nor is the recreational value obtained by the hunters and shooters offset by the cost to the animals that their recreation involves.

Despite its venerable origins, the view that the effects of our actions on nonhuman animals have no intrinsic moral significance can be shown to be arbitrary and morally indefensible. If a being suffers, the fact that it is not a member of our own species cannot be a moral reason for failing to take its suffering into account. This becomes obvious if we consider the analogous attempt by white slave-owners to deny consideration to the interests of blacks. These white racists limited their moral concern to their own race, so the suffering of a black did not have the same moral significance as the suffering of a white. We now recognize that in doing so they were making an arbitrary distinction, and that the existence of suffering, rather than the race of the sufferer, is what is really morally significant. The point remains true if "species" is substituted for "race." The logic of racism and the logic of the position we have been discussing, which I have elsewhere referred to as "speciesism," are indistinguishable; and if we reject the former then consistency demands that we reject the latter too.[1]

It should be clearly understood that the rejection of speciesism does not imply that the different species are in fact equal in respect of such characteristics as intelligence, physical strength, ability to communicate, capacity to suffer, ability to damage the environment, or anything else. After all, the moral principle of human equality cannot be taken as implying that all humans are equal in these respects either—if it did, we would have to give up the idea of human equality. That one being is more intelligent than another does not entitle him to enslave, exploit, or disregard the interests of the less intelligent being. The moral basis of equality among humans is not equality in fact, but the principle of equal consideration of interests, and it is this principle that, in consistency, must be extended to any nonhumans who have interests.

There may be some doubt about whether any nonhuman beings have interests. This doubt may arise because of uncertainty about what it is to have an interest, or because of uncertainty about the nature of some nonhuman beings. So far as the concept of "interest" is the cause of doubt, I take the view that only a being with subjective experiences, such as the experience of pleasure or the experience of pain, can have interests in the full sense of the term; and that any being with such experiences does have at least one interest, namely, the interest in experiencing pleasure and avoiding pain. Thus consciousness, or the capacity for subjective experience, is both a necessary and a sufficient condition for having an interest. While there may be a loose sense of the term in which we can say that it is in the interests of a tree to be watered, this attenuated sense of the term is not the sense covered by the principle of equal consideration of interests. All we mean when we say that it is in the interests of a tree to be watered is that the tree needs water if it is to continue to live and grow normally; if we regard this as evidence that the tree has interests, we might almost as well say that it is in the interests of a car to be lubricated regularly because the car needs lubrication if it is to run properly. In neither case can we really mean (unless we impute consciousness to trees or cars) that the tree or car has any preference about the matter.

The remaining doubt about whether nonhuman beings have interests is, then, a doubt about whether nonhuman beings have subjective experiences like the experience of pain. I have argued elsewhere that the commonsense view that birds and mammals feel pain is well founded,[2] but more serious doubts arise as we move down the evolutionary scale. Vertebrate animals have nervous systems broadly similar to our own and behave in ways that resemble our own pain behavior when subjected to stimuli that we would find painful; so the inference that vertebrates are capable of feeling pain is a reasonable one, though not as strong as it is if limited to mammals and birds. When we go beyond vertebrates to insects, crustaceans, mollusks and so on, the existence of subjective states becomes more dubious, and with very simple organisms it is difficult to believe that they could be conscious. As for plants, though there have been sensational claims that plants are not only conscious, but even psychic, there is no hard evidence that supports even the more modest claim.[3]

The boundary of beings who may be taken as having interests is therefore not an abrupt boundary, but a broad range in which the assumption that the being has interests shifts from being so strong as to be virtually certain to being so weak as to be highly improbable. The principle of equal consideration of interests must be applied with this in mind, so that where there is a clash between a virtually certain interest and a highly doubtful one, it is the virtually certain interest that ought to prevail.

In this manner our moral concern ought to extend to all beings who have interests. Unlike race or species, this boundary does not arbitrarily exclude any being; indeed it can truly be said that it excludes nothing at all, not even "the most contemptible clod of earth" from equal consideration of interests—for full consideration of no interests still results in no weight being given to whatever was considered, just as multiplying zero by a million still results in zero.[4]

Giving equal consideration to the interests of two different beings does not mean treating them alike or holding their lives to be of equal value. We may recognize that the interests of one being are greater than those of another, and equal consideration will then lead us to sacrifice the being with lesser interests, if one or the other must be sacrificed. For instance, if for some reason a choice has to be made between saving the life of a normal human being and that of a dog, we might well decide to save the human because he, with his greater awareness of what is going to happen, will suffer more before he dies; we may also take into account the likelihood that it is the family and friends of the human who will suffer more; and finally, it would be the human who had the greater potential for future happiness. This decision would be in accordance with the principle of equal consideration of interests, for the interests of the dog get the same consideration as those of the human, and the loss to the dog is not discounted because the dog is not a member of our species. The outcome is as it is because the balance of interests favors the human. In a different situation—say, if the human were grossly mentally defective and without family or anyone else who would grieve for it—the balance of interests might favor the nonhuman.[5]

The more positive side of the principle of equal consideration is this: where interests are equal, they must be given equal weight. So where human and nonhuman animals share an interest—as in the case of the interest in avoiding physical pain—we must give as much weight to violations of the interest of the nonhumans as we do to similar violations of the human's interest. This does not mean, of course, that it is as bad to hit a horse with a stick as it is to hit a human being, for the same blow would cause less pain to the animal with the tougher skin. The principle holds between similar amounts of felt pain, and what this is will vary from case to case.

It may be objected that we cannot tell exactly how much pain another animal is suffering, and that therefore the principle is impossible to apply. While I do not deny the difficulty and even, so far as precise measurement is concerned, the impossibility of comparing the subjective experiences of members of different species, I do not think that the problem is different in kind from the problem of comparing the subjective experiences of two members of our own species. Yet this is something we do all the time, for instance when we judge that a wealthy person will suffer less by being taxed at a higher rate than a poor person will gain from the welfare benefits paid for by the tax; or when we decide to take our two children to the beach instead of to a fair, because although the older one would prefer the fair, the younger one has a stronger preference the other way. These comparisons may be very rough, but since there is nothing better, we must use them; it would be irrational to refuse to do so simply because they are rough. Moreover, rough as they are, there are many situations in which we can be reasonably sure which way the balance of interests lies. While a difference of species may make comparisons rougher still, the basic problem is the same, and the comparisons are still often good enough to use, in the absence of anything more precise. . . .

The difficulty of making the required comparison will mean that the application of this conclusion is controversial in many cases, but there will be some situations in which it is clear enough. Take, for instance, the wholesale poisoning of animals that is euphemistically known as "pest control." The authorities who conduct these campaigns give no consideration to the suffering they inflict on the "pests," and invariably use the method of slaughter they believe to be cheapest and most effective. The result is that hundreds of millions of rabbits have died agonizing deaths from the artificially introduced disease, myxomatosis, or from poisons like "ten-eighty"; coyotes and other wild dogs have died painfully from cyanide poisoning; and all manner of wild animals have endured days of thirst, hunger, and fear with a mangled limb caught in a leg-hold trap.[6] Granting, for the sake of argument, the necessity for pest control—though this has rightly been questioned—the fact remains that no serious attempts have been made to introduce alternative means of control and thereby reduce the incalculable amount of suffering caused by present methods. It would not, presumably, be beyond modern science to produce a substance which, when eaten by rabbits or coyotes, produced sterility instead of a drawn-out death. Such methods might be more expensive, but can anyone doubt that if a similar amount of human suffering were at stake, the expense would be borne?

Another clear instance in which the principle of equal consideration of interests would indicate methods different from those presently used is in the timber industry. There are two basic methods of obtaining timber from forests. One is to cut only selected mature or dead trees, leaving the forest substantially intact. The other, known as clear-cutting, involves chopping down everything that grows in a given area, and then reseeding. Obviously when a large area is clear-cut, wild animals find their whole living area destroyed in a few days, whereas selected felling makes a relatively minor disturbance. But clear-cutting is cheaper, and timber companies therefore use this method and will continue to do so unless forced to do otherwise.[7] . . .

It is not merely the act of killing that indicates what we are ready to do to other species in order to gratify our tastes. The suffering we inflict on the animals while they are alive is perhaps an even clearer indication of our speciesism than the fact that we are prepared to kill them.[8] In order to have meat on the table at a price that people can afford, our society tolerates methods of meat production that confine sentient animals in cramped, unsuitable conditions for the entire durations of their lives. Animals are treated like machines that convert fodder into flesh, and any innovation that results in a higher "conversion ratio" is liable to be adopted. As one authority on the subject has said, "cruelty is acknowledged only when profitability ceases."[9] So hens are crowded four or five to a cage with a floor area of twenty inches by eighteen inches, or around the size of a single page of the *New York Times*. The cages have wire floors, since this reduces cleaning costs, though wire is unsuitable for the hens feet; the floors slope, since this makes the eggs roll down for easy collection, although this makes it difficult for the hens to rest comfortably. In these conditions all the birds' natural instincts are thwarted: They cannot stretch their wings fully, walk freely, dust-bathe, scratch the ground, or build a nest. Although they have never known other conditions, observers have noticed that the birds vainly try to perform these actions. Frustrated at their inability to do so, they often develop what farmers call "vices," and peck each other to death. To prevent this, the beaks of young birds are often cut off.

This kind of treatment is not limited to poultry. Pigs are now also being reared in cages inside sheds. These animals are comparable to dogs in intelligence, and need a varied, stimulating environment if they are not to suffer from stress and boredom. Anyone who kept a dog in the way in which pigs are frequently kept would be liable to prosecution, in England at least, but because our interest in exploiting pigs is greater than our interest in exploiting dogs, we object to cruelty to dogs while consuming the produce of cruelty to pigs. Of the other animals, the condition of veal calves is perhaps worst of all, since these animals are so closely confined that they cannot even turn around or get up and lie down freely. In this way they do not develop unpalatable muscle. They are also made anaemic and kept short of roughage, to keep their flesh pale, since white veal fetches a higher price; as a result they develop a craving for iron and roughage, and have been observed to gnaw wood off the sides of their stalls, and lick greedily at any rusty hinge that is within reach.

Since, as I have said, none of these practices cater to anything more than our pleasures of taste, our practice of rearing and killing other animals in order to eat them is a clear instance of the sacrifice of the most important interests of other beings in order to satisfy trivial interests of our own. To avoid speciesism we must stop this practice, and each of us has a moral obligation to cease supporting the practice. Our custom is all the support that the meat industry needs. The decision to cease giving

it that support may be difficult, but it is no more difficult than it would have been for a white Southerner to go against the traditions of his society and free his slaves; if we do not change our dietary habits, how can we censure those slaveholders who would not change their own way of living?

Notes

1. For a fuller statement of this argument, see my *Animal Liberation* (New York: A New York Review Book, 1975), especially ch.1.

2. *Ibid.*

3. See, for instance, the comments by Arthur Galston in *Natural History*, 83, no. 3 (March 1974): 18, on the "evidence" cited in such books as *The Secret Life of Plants*.

4. The idea that we would logically have to consider "the most contemptible clod of earth" as having rights was suggested by Thomas Taylor, the Cambridge Neo-Platonist, in a pamphlet he published anonymously, entitled *A Vindication of the Rights of Brutes* (London, 1972) which appears to be a satirical refutation of the attribution of rights to women by Mary Wollstonecroft in her *Vindication of the Rights of Women* (London, 1972). Logically, Taylor was no doubt correct, but he neglected to specify just what interests such contemptible clods of earth have.

5. Singer, *Animal Liberation*, pp. 20-23.

6. See J. Olsen, *Slaughter the Animals, Poison the Earth* (New York: Simon and Schuster, 1971), especially pp. 153-164.

7. See R. and V. Routley, *The Fight for the Forests* (Canberra: Australian National University Press, 1974), for a thoroughly documented indictment of clear-cutting in America, see *Time*, May 17, 1976.

8. Although one might think that killing a being is obviously the ultimate wrong one can do to it, I think that the infliction of suffering is a clearer indication of speciesism because it might be argued that at least part of what is wrong with killing a human is that most humans are conscious of their existence over time, and have desires and purposes that extend into the future—see, for instance, M. Tooley, "Abortion and Infanticide," *Philosophy and Public Affairs*, vol. 2, no. 1 (1972). Of course, if one took this view one would have to hold—as Tooley does—that killing a human infant or mental defective is not in itself wrong, and is less serious than killing certain higher mammals that probably do have a sense of their own existence over time.

9. Ruth Harrison, *Animal Machines* (Stuart, London, 1964). This book provides an eye-opening account of intensive farming methods for those unfamiliar with the subject.

Review and Discussion Questions

1. Describe the human practices that most clearly demonstrate speciesism.

2. What does the principle of "equal consideration of interests" imply for our treatment of animals? What does it not imply?

3. Give examples of how adherence to the principle of equal consideration would change our conduct. What are the principle's implications for business?

4. What is Singer's argument against meat eating and how might a critic respond to it? Can meat eating be morally justified?

Should Trees Have Standing?—Toward Legal Rights For Natural Objects

Christopher D. Stone

Professor of law Christopher D. Stone argues that we should extend legal rights to forests, oceans, rivers and other natural objects. Although the proposal may sound absurd, so did earlier proposals to extend rights, for example, to blacks and women. Stone discusses what it means to be a holder of legal rights and how extending rights to natural objects would change dramatically our approach to environmental protection. Stone's proposal is in part pragmatic—a legal move to enable environmentalists to better protect the environment. But it also reflects the view that nature deserves to be protected for its own sake.

Throughout legal history, each successive extension of rights to some new entity has been, theretofore, a bit unthinkable. We are inclined to suppose the rightlessness of rightless "things" to be a decree of Nature, not a legal convention acting in support of some status quo. It is thus that we defer considering the choices involved in all their moral, social, and economic dimensions. And so the United States Supreme Court could straightfacedly tell us in *Dred Scott* that Blacks had been denied the rights of citizenship "as a subordinate and inferior class of beings, who had been subjugated by the dominant race. . . ."[1] In the nineteenth century, the highest court in California explained that Chinese had not the right to testify against white men in criminal matters because they were "a race of people whom nature has marked as inferior, and who are incapable of progress or intel-

lectual development beyond a certain point . . . between whom and ourselves nature has placed an impassable difference."[2] The popular conception of the Jew in the 13th Century contributed to a law which treated them as "men *ferae naturae*, protected by a quasi-forest law. Like the roe and the deer, they form an order apart."[3] Recall, too, that it was not so long ago that the foetus was "like the roe and the deer." In an early suit attempting to establish a wrongful death action on behalf of a negligently killed foetus (now widely accepted practice), Holmes, then on the Massachusetts Supreme Court, seems to have thought it simply inconceivable "that a man might owe a civil duty and incur a conditional prospective liability in tort to one not yet in being."[4] The first woman in Wisconsin who thought she might have a right to practice law was told that she did not, in the following terms:

> The law of nature destines and qualifies the female sex for the bearing and nurture of the children of our race and for the custody of the homes of the world. . . . [A]ll life-long callings of women, inconsistent with these radical and sacred duties of their sex, as is the profession of the law, are departures from the order of nature; and when voluntary, treason against it. . . . The peculiar qualities of womanhood, its gentle graces, its quick sensibility,

Christopher D. Stone, "Should Trees Have Standing?—Toward Legal Rights for Natural Objects," *Southern California Law Review* 45 (1972). Reprinted with the permission of the *Southern California Law Review.*

its tender susceptibility, its purity, its delicacy, its emotional impulses, its subordination of hard reason to sympathetic feeling, are surely not qualifications for forensic strife. Nature has tempered woman as little for the juridical conflicts of the court room, as for the physical conflicts of the battle field. . . . [5]

The fact is, that each time there is a movement to confer rights onto some new "entity," the proposal is bound to sound odd or frightening or laughable. This is partly because until the rightless thing receives its rights, we cannot see it as anything but a *thing* for the use of "us"—those who are holding rights at the time. In this vein, what is striking about the Wisconsin case above is that the court, for all its talk about women, so clearly was never able to see women as they are (and might become). All it could see was the popular "idealized" version of *an object it needed*. Such is the way the slave South looked upon the Black. There is something of a seamless web involved: there will be resistance to giving the thing "rights" until it can be seen and valued for itself; yet, it is hard to see it and value it for itself until we can bring ourselves to give it "rights"—which is almost inevitably going to sound inconceivable to a large group of people.

The reason for this little discourse on the unthinkable, the reader must know by now, if only from the title of the paper. I am quite seriously proposing that we give legal rights to forests, oceans, rivers and other so-called "natural objects" in the environment—indeed, to the natural environment as a whole. . . .

Toward Rights for the Environment

Now, to say that the natural environment should have rights is not to say anything as silly as that no one should be allowed to cut down a tree. We say human beings have rights, but—at least as of the time of this writing—they can be executed. Corporations have rights, but they cannot plead the fifth amendment; *In re Gault* gave 15-year-olds certain rights in juvenile proceedings, but it did not give them the right to vote. Thus, to say that the environment should have rights is not to say that it should have every right we can imagine, or even the same body of rights as human beings have. Nor

is it to say that everything in the environment should have the same rights as every other thing in the environment. . . .

For a thing to be *a holder of legal rights*, something more is needed than that some authoritative body will review the actions and processes of those who threaten it. As I shall use the term, "holder of legal rights," each of three additional criteria must be satisfied. All three, one will observe, go towards making a thing *count* jurally—to have a legally recognized worth and dignity in its own right, and not merely to serve as a means to benefit "us" (whoever the contemporary group of rights-holders may be). They are, first, that the thing can institute legal actions *at its behest*; second, that in determining the granting of legal relief, the court must take *injury to it* into account; and, third, that relief must run to the *benefit of it*. . . .

The Rightlessness of Natural Objects at Common Law

Consider, for example, the common law's posture toward the pollution of a stream. True, courts have always been able, in some circumstances, to issue orders that will stop the pollution. . . . But the stream itself is fundamentally rightless, with implications that deserve careful reconsideration.

The first sense in which the stream is not a rights-holder has to do with standing. The stream itself has none. So far as the common law is concerned, there is in general no way to challenge the polluter's actions save at the behest of a lower riparian—another human being—able to show an invasion of *his* rights. . . .

The second sense in which the common law denies "rights" to natural objects has to do with the way in which the merits are decided in those cases in which someone is competent and willing to establish standing. At its more primitive levels, the system protected the "rights" of the property owning human with minimal weighting of any values. . . . Today we have come more and more to make balances—but only such as will adjust the economic best interests of identifiable humans. . . .

Thus, we find the highest court of Pennsylvania refusing to stop a coal company from discharging polluted mine water into a tributary of the Lackawana River because a plaintiff's "grievance is for a mere personal inconvenience; and . . . mere private personal inconveniences . . . must yield to the necessities of a great public industry, which although in the hands of a private corporation, subserves a great public interest."[6] The stream itself is lost sight of in "a quantitative compromise between *two* conflicting interests."[7]

The third way in which the common law makes natural objects rightless has to do with who is regarded as the beneficiary of a favorable judgment. Here, too, it makes a considerable difference that it is not the natural object that counts in its own right. To illustrate this point let me begin by observing that it makes perfectly good sense to speak of, and ascertain, the legal damage to a natural object, if only in the sense of "making it whole" with respect to the most obvious factors. The costs of making a forest whole, for example, would include the costs of reseeding, repairing watersheds, restocking wildlife—the sorts of costs the Forest Service undergoes after a fire. Making a polluted stream whole would include the costs of restocking with fish, water-fowl, and other animal and vegetable life, dredging, washing out impurities, establishing natural and/or artificial aerating agents, and so forth. Now, what is important to note is that, under our present system, even if a plaintiff riparian wins a water pollution suit for damages, no money goes to the benefit of the stream itself to repair *its* damages. . . .

None of the natural objects, whether held in common or situated on private land, has any of the three criteria of a rights-holder. They have no standing in their own right; their unique damages do not count in determining outcome; and they are not the beneficiaries of awards. In such fashion, these objects have traditionally been regarded by the common law, and even by all but the most recent legislation, as objects for man to conquer and master and use—in such a way as the law once looked upon "man's" relationships to African Negroes. Even where special measures have been taken to conserve them, as by seasons on game and limits on timber cutting, the dominant motive has been to conserve them *for us*—for the greatest good of the greatest number of human beings. Conservationists, so far as I am aware, are generally reluctant to maintain otherwise. As the name implies, they want to conserve and guarantee *our* consumption and *our* enjoyment of these other living things. In their own right, natural objects have counted for little, in law as in popular movements.

As I mentioned at the outset, however, the rightlessness of the natural environment can and should change; it already shows some signs of doing so.

Toward Having Standing in Its Own Right

It is not inevitable, nor is it wise, that natural objects should have no rights to seek redress in their own behalf. It is no answer to say that streams and forests cannot have standing because streams and forests cannot speak. Corporations cannot speak either; nor can states, estates, infants, incompetents, municipalities or universities. Lawyers speak for them, as they customarily do for the ordinary citizen with legal problems. One ought, I think, to handle the legal problems of natural objects as one does the problems of legal incompetents—human beings who have become vegetable. If a human being shows signs of becoming senile and has affairs that he is de jure incompetent to manage, those concerned with his well being make such a showing to the court, and someone is designated by the court with the authority to manage the incompetent's affairs. . . .

On a parity of reasoning we should have a system in which, when a friend of a natural object perceives it to be endangered, he can apply to a court for the creation of a guardianship. . . .

The potential "friends" that such a statutory scheme would require will hardly be lacking. The Sierra Club, Environmental Defense Fund, Friends of the Earth, Natural Resources Defense Counsel, and the Izaak Walton League are just some of the many groups which have manifested unflagging dedication to the environment and which are becoming increasingly capable of marshalling the requisite technical experts and lawyers. If, for example, the Environmental Defense Fund should have reason to believe that some company's strip mining operations might be irreparably destroying the ecological balance of large tracts of land, it could, under this procedure, apply to the court in which the lands were situated to be appointed guardian. As guardian, it might be given rights of inspection (or visitation) to determine and bring to the court's attention a fuller finding on the land's condition. If there were indications that under the substantive law some redress might be available on the land's behalf, then the guardian would be entitled to raise the land's rights in the land's name, *i.e.*, without having to make the roundabout and often unavailing demonstration . . . that the "rights" of the club's members were being invaded. . . .

One reason for making the environment itself the beneficiary of a judgment is to prevent it from being "sold out" in a negotiation among private litigants who agree not to enforce rights that have been established among themselves. Protection from this will be advanced by making the natural object a party to an injunctive settlement. Even more importantly, we should make it a beneficiary of money awards. . . .

The idea of assessing damages as best we can and placing them in a trust fund is far more realistic than a hope that a total "freeze" can be put on the environmental status quo. Nature is a continuous theatre in which things and species (eventually man) are destined to enter and exit. In the meantime, co-existence of man and his environment means that *each* is going to have to compromise for the better of both. Some pollution of streams, for example, will probably be inevitable for some time. Instead of setting an unrealizable goal of enjoining absolutely the discharge of all such pollutants, the trust fund concept would (a) help assure that pollution would occur only in those instances where the social need for the pollutant's product (via his present method of production) was so high as to enable the polluter to cover *all* homocentric costs, plus some estimated costs to the environment *per se*, and (b) would be a corpus for preserving monies, if necessary, while the technology developed to a point where repairing the damaged portion of the environment was feasible. Such a fund might even finance the requisite research and development. . . .

A radical new conception of man's relationship to the rest of nature would not only be a step towards solving the material planetary problems; there are strong reasons for such a changed consciousness from the point of making us far better humans. If we only stop for a moment and look at the underlying human qualities that our present attitudes toward property and nature draw upon and reinforce, we have to be struck by how stultifying of our own personal growth and satisfaction they can become when they take rein of us. Hegel, in "justifying" private property, unwittingly reflects the tone and quality of some of the needs that are played upon:

A person has as his substantive end the right of putting his will into any and every thing and thereby making it his, because it has no such end in itself and derives its destiny and soul from his will. This is the absolute right of appropriation which man has over all "things."[8]

What is it within us that gives us this need not just to satisfy basic biological wants, but to extend our wills over things, to object-ify them, to make them ours, to manipulate them, to keep them at a psychic distance? Can it all be explained on "rational" bases? Should we not be suspect of such needs within us, cautious as to why we wish to gratify them? When I first read that passage of Hegel, I immediately thought not only of the emotional contrast with Spinoza, but of the passage in Carson McCullers' *A Tree, A Rock, A Cloud*, in which an old derelict has collared a twelve year old boy in a streetcar cafe. The old man asks whether the boy knows "how love should be begun?"

The old man leaned closer and whispered:

"A tree. A rock. A cloud."
"The weather was like this in Portland," he said. "At the time my science was begun. I meditated and I started very cautious. I would pick up something from the street and take it home with me. I bought a goldfish and I concentrated on the goldfish and I loved it. I graduated from one thing to another. Day by day I was getting this technique. . . .
. . . "For six years now I have gone around by myself and built up my science. And now I am a master. Son. I can love anything. No longer do I have to think about it even. I see a street full of people and a beautiful light comes in me. I watch a bird in the sky. Or I meet a traveler on the road. Everything, Son. And anybody. All stranger and all loved! Do you realize what a science like mine can mean?"[9]

To be able to get away from the view that Nature is a collection of useful senseless objects is, as McCullers' "madman" suggests, deeply involved in the development of our abilities to love—or, if that is putting it too strongly, to be able to reach a heightened awareness of our own, and others' capacities in their mutual interplay. To do so, we have to give up some psychic investment in our sense of separateness and specialness in the universe. And this, in turn, is hard giving indeed, because it involves us in a flight backwards, into earlier stages of civilization and childhood in which we had to trust (and perhaps fear) our environment, for we had not then the power to master it. Yet, in doing so, we—as persons—gradually free ourselves of needs for supportive illusions. Is not this one of the triumphs for "us" of our giving legal rights to (or acknowledging the legal rights of) the Blacks and women? . . .

The time may be on hand when these sentiments, and the early stirrings of the law can be coalesced into a radical new theory or myth—felt as well as intellectualized—of man's relationships to the rest of nature. I do not mean "myth" in a demeaning sense of the term, but in the sense in which, at different times in history, our social "facts" and relationships have been comprehended and integrated by reference to the "myths" that we are co-signers of a social contract, that the Pope is God's agent, and that all men are created equal. Pantheism, Shinto and Tao all have myths to offer. But they are all, each in its own fashion, quaint, primitive and archaic. What is needed is a myth that can fit our growing body of knowledge of geophysics, biology and the cosmos. In this vein, I do not think it too remote that we may come to regard the Earth, as some have suggested, as one organism, of which Mankind is a functional part—the mind, perhaps: different from the rest of nature, but different as a man's brain is from his lungs. . . .

Notes

1. *Dred Scott v. Sanford,* 60 U.S. (19 How.) 396, 404–05 (1856).

2. *People v. Hall,* 4 Cal. 399, 405 (1854).

3. Schechter, "The Rightlessness of Mediaeval English Jewry," 45 *Jewish Q. Rev.* 121, 135 (1954) quoting from M. Bateson, *Medieval England* 139 (1904).

4. *Dietrich v. Inhabitants of Northampton,* 138 Mass. 14, 16 (1884).

5. *In re Goddell,* 39 Wisc. 232, 245 (1875).

6. *Pennsylvania Coal Co. v. Sanderson,* 113 Pa. 126, 149, 6 A. 453, 459 (1886).

7. Hand, J. in *Smith v. Staso Milling Co.,* 18 F.2d 736, 738 (2d Cir. 1927) (emphasis added).

8. G. Hegel, *Hegel's Philosophy of Right,* 41 (T. Knox transl. 1945).

9. C. McCullers, *The Ballad of the Sad Cafe and Other Stories,* 150–51 (1958).

Review and Discussion Questions

1. What does it mean to be a "holder of legal rights"?

2. Do you think the idea of granting legal rights to natural objects is workable? What would be the practical results of doing so?

3. Singer states that "consciousness, or the capacity for subjective experiences, is both a necessary and a sufficient condition for having an interest." This suggests that he would disagree with Stone's talk of protecting the "interests" of nature. Whose point of view is more plausible? Can something without conscious awareness have rights?

4. Does our conception of our relationship to nature need to be radically changed, as Stone suggests?

For Further Reading

Tom Regan, ed., *Earthbound: New Introductory Essays in Environmental Ethics* (New York: Random House, 1984) and **Donald VanDeVeer** and **Christine Pierce,** eds., *People, Penguins, and Plastic Trees* (Belmont, Calif.: Wadsworth, 1986) are very useful collections of recent writings on various topics in environmental ethics. **Robin Attfield,** *The Ethics of Environmental Concern* (New York: Columbia University Press, 1983) is a solid introduction to the subject.

Part 4 of **Derek Parfit's** *Reasons and Persons* (Oxford: Oxford University Press, 1984) is a philosophically challenging exploration of some puzzling aspects of our obligations to future generations.

Peter Singer's *Animal Liberation* (New York: A New York Review Book [distributed by Random House], 1975) is a seminal work advocating a radical change in our treatment of animals. **Peter Singer and Tom Regan,** eds., *Animal Rights and Human Obligations* (Englewood Cliffs, N.J.: Prentice-Hall, 1976) contains good, generally pro-animal rights essays. **R. G. Frey** defends meat eating in *Rights, Animals, and Suffering* (Oxford: Basil Blackwell, 1983).

CHAPTER 11

THE PROFESSIONS

One day in January 1985 Eugene Barnes, a San Leandro, California man, suffered a serious head injury. His case might have been routine, the treatment of his wound rapid, and his name forgotten—had it not been for one thing: Barnes was uninsured. He was transferred from one hospital to another in a seven-hour search to find a neurosurgeon willing to operate on him. By the time he did receive treatment, it was too late. Eugene Barnes died.

In recent years a number of people have died as the result of "patient dumping" by hospitals and physicians who refuse to treat patients without insurance. In Contra County, California, for example, one pregnant woman was left sitting in the waiting room of a private hospital for three hours before an ambulance took her to a county hospital, which was willing to care for her. Her baby was stillborn. Such cases have led California to pass a tough, new law that imposes fines of up to $25,000 on physicians and hospitals who refuse to treat the uninsured.[1]

Only a few states have acted as vigorously and effectively as California. But regardless of what the law says about it, "patient dumping" raises important moral questions for those who practice medicine. In particular, what moral responsibilities do physicians have to treat those who need medical assistance but cannot afford it? Do they have a professional duty to use their skill and knowledge to aid whoever needs it? Or are they obligated only to those whom they have accepted as clients? Should we view physicians simply as ordinary business people, as medical entrepreneurs?

Questions like these cannot be answered without looking at what it means to be a doctor—that is, at the nature of the medical profession and at the responsibilities individuals assume by entering that profession. The fact that the California Medical Association opposed the California antidumping law, and had defeated a similar bill the year before, raises even more sharply this issue of how a profession understands its goals and its role in society. The association's opposition and the political involvement of professional organizations in general raises additional issues. What is the proper purpose of professional organizations? Are they simply special-interest groups, or do they have morally and socially important functions that extend beyond looking after the economic interests of their members?

Presumably, many members of the California Medical Association opposed the California law not because they favor patient dumping but because they believe the medical profession should be left to regulate itself. This raises further issues. To what extent should the supervision and discipline of professional and technical personnel be left to their own professional organizations? Should the professions be entirely autonomous and self-governing? What is the value of self-regulation, and how is it to be balanced against other social goals and values? What say should society have in setting the norms of professional conduct?

These topics, issues, and questions are typical problems of "professional ethics." Professional ethics includes both the moral issues that commonly face those who practice a profession as well as larger ethical and social questions about the proper role of various professions in society. Professional practice incorporates a wide range of occupations: lawyers, engineers, scientific researchers, accountants, teachers, investment consultants, nurses, and real estate agents, to name just a few.

Many of the important moral issues surrounding the professions are also issues of business and organizational ethics. Economic justice and the nature of capitalism, the treatment of people inside the workplace, the moral responsibilities of organizations, whistle blowing, advertising, testing and privacy, racial and sexual discrimination, and conflicts of interest are among the numerous topics that this book has previously discussed and that—along with Chapters 1 and 2—bear directly on professional ethics.

There are, in addition, at least three ways in which a discussion of moral issues affecting the professions connects with the problems of business and organizational ethics that have been explored by preceding chapters. First is the fact that business relies more and more on the professions. As the business world becomes more complex, the demand for specialized, professional services becomes ever greater. Engineers design the products that corporations build. Corporations spend billions of dollars annually on legal services. The intimate involvement of professionals like real estate and insurance brokers, accountants, and financial advisors in the world of business is obvious. In addition, drug firms and other companies are deeply and profitably involved in the day-to-day reality of professional medical practice.

A second and related connection is the increasingly businesslike character of the professions themselves. Professionals are more likely than ever before to be employed by large, often bureaucratic and impersonal organizations. Many work for companies that are geared toward profit and that see themselves as providing a commodity on the marketplace. Ideas about what constitutes acceptable professional practice are more in-

fluenced than ever by standard business procedures. Lawyers, for example, now advertise their services and openly engage in price competition, something that was unheard of a couple of decades ago. Hospitals launch advertising campaigns to attract patients, and with the spread of group practices and prepaid medical services, price competition is sneaking into the medical profession, too.

At the same time, and this is the third connection, more people than ever in business view themselves as professionals. The slogan of Harvard Business School, for example, commits it to "making business a profession." As Professor David Braybrooke has argued, if one defines the term *profession* broadly enough to include engineering and university teaching and research, then it is hard to deny its application to business as well. Nowadays people in business tend to share a body of specialized formal learning, often having taken an MBA or at least a bachelor's degree in business administration. Many areas of business have codes of ethics every bit as strong and effective as those of other professions.[2]

Although professional ethics fits within the general topic of business and organization ethics, there are problems that are special to it—problems concerning the nature and proper role of the professions as well as the problems that professional practitioners often confront in their daily lives. Naturally, these problems vary from profession to profession, and no single chapter can discuss all the specific moral issues facing each and every profession. The moral problems of various professions, however, have enough in common for it to be useful to look in general at ethical issues in the professions.

Questions of the proper relationship of the professional to his or her clients, of trustworthiness and confidentiality, of the balancing of the interests of client against obligations to third parties and society generally, and the nature of a professional's duties to the profession itself are problems common to most, if not all, professions. In addition are questions of the nature of the professions themselves. What is their role in society and what responsibilities does one assume by entering them? What is the relationship between one's obligations as a professional and the general demands of morality? These and related issues are also distinct enough from the questions discussed in previous chapters to deserve separate treatment here.

Specifically, this chapter examines the following topics:

1. The key features of the professions and their role in, and responsibility to, society.

2. The nature of professional norms and their relationship to other moral obligations.

3. Professional codes of ethics and how they can be improved.

4. The ideal of self-regulation and the involvement of laypersons in setting and monitoring professional standards.

5. The business side of the professions.

6. The debate over licensing.

7. The obligations of professionals to clients, the public, their colleagues, and their profession itself, and the moral dilemmas these obligations can create.

THE NATURE OF THE PROFESSIONS

Socially and economically, the professions are playing an increasingly important role, and the number of professionals is climbing. As our economy develops and technology progresses, we are more service oriented, and the services we need are of an increasingly sophisticated sort. Even within production itself the demand is more and more for a technically trained workforce. The ranks of the traditional blue-collar worker are declining in numbers, in income, and in social standing, while a majority of the new high-paying jobs are in "knowledge work." Technicians, professionals, managers, and specialists of all kinds are what our economy now requires.[3]

Business could not function without the professions, nor could we enjoy the benefits of a modern society without them. The famed sociologist Talcott Parsons claimed some years ago that the professions had already become the single most important structural component of modern societies. The truth of that claim might be disputed, but no one can deny the impressive rise of the professions. Although the roots of many modern professions like psychiatry, accounting, and some branches of engineering can be traced back centuries, there is no question that the emergence of professions and the concept of professionalism are largely twentieth-century phenomena.

In 1900 there were 1,234,000 professional and technical workers in the United States, making up 4.5 percent of the workforce. By 1970 they numbered 11,561,000 and constituted 14.5 percent of the employed population. And the figures for 1970 do not include college teachers and groups such as musicians, artists, and entertainers, which were included in 1900.[4] If we count these and other groups that have at least some of the characteristics of a profession, the number of professionals in the United States is very high indeed.

As society becomes more technologically oriented, our legal system more complex, and our economy more centralized, the importance of professionals and "knowledge workers" in general has been greatly enhanced. The professions keep modern society functioning and make its distinctive services and products possible. "Experts"—from family counselors to nuclear engineers—have more and more influence over our lives. As a result, questions of professional ethics and questions about the role of the professions in society have become more important than ever.

But what occupations count as part of the "professions," and who exactly is a "professional"? An answer to these questions is complicated by the fact that *professional* is a word with a definite positive evaluative overtone. "Professional," as contrasted with "amateur," generally indicates a higher level of skill and expertise. A professional carpenter, for example, does for pay what others do only as a hobby. If you're a "pro" at something, then you have a talent or training or devotion to your craft that others lack. In addition, having a "professional" attitude contrasts favorably with "unprofessional" behavior: The professional conducts himself or herself not only competently, but with objectivity and courtesy.

Professionals typically have greater control over their working environment than do most people. They generally enjoy wide autonomy in choosing their work tasks and are free to exercise independence of judgment in carrying them out. Professionals are not closely supervised, and they rarely punch a clock. Professionals do work that is often more challenging and more satisfying than other jobs in our society. These features of professional occupations are all desirable ones in their own right; they are also associated with higher status and better pay.

As a result, there is a natural tendency for people to stress the professional-like aspects or characteristics of their work, and more and more occupations today claim professional status. There is nothing wrong with this tendency. People sometimes smirk when, for example, janitors are designated "custodial engineers," but such changes in title reflect the desire of many occupations to obtain a more professional status. And that is nothing to smirk at. Many formerly low-skill occupations are becoming more technical in character, and the desire of people to have their work respected as meaningful and important is a reasonable one. Being viewed as a "professional" often brings this respect.

Nevertheless, inflating the concept of "profession" so much that it includes most occupations reduces its usefulness. To keep the meaning of "profession" from sprawling all over, it is necessary to focus on its key features—in particular, those features that are exemplified in the oldest and most familiar professions, like law and medicine. It will also be useful to try to keep any definitional discussion focused on the objective sociological or economic characteristics of professions. On the one hand, we want to avoid definitions that smuggle in some normative principle—for example, that being a professional means being committed to public service. On the other hand, we don't want to put down occupations that end up being described as "nonprofessional."

Key Features of the Professions

We should not expect to find an exact specification of what counts as a profession. No definition of *profession* can be given which holds for all the various professions and for only the professions. Identifying some of the main features of the professions, that is, the characteristics that are typical of them, will assist us in our discussion of professional ethics. But there will definitely be borderline occupations that share some, but not all of these features. As long as we recognize that fact, it should pose no problems.

Professor of philosophy Michael Bayles has helpfully identified three features that most writers agree on as being necessary for an occupation to be a profession. He also describes three additional characteristics that are typical of professions:[5]

First, extensive training is a prerequisite of professional practice. Lawyers and doctors must study for years, and most professionals have advanced degrees. Second, in virtue of their special training and abilities professionals provide important services in a society, which, as we have seen, is growing in complexity and which requires an ever greater application of specialized knowledge. By contrast, to use Professor Bayles's example, chess experts provide no such service, despite their years of practice and training.

Third, while one must also train for many other occupations (like barbering or bricklaying) that are socially important, the training of professionals and their distinctive skills are largely intellectual in character. Professionals are thus different from craft workers. One must practice for years to be a skilled glassblower, but this is largely a physical talent. Related to the intellectual component of professional training is the fact that many professionals are in the position of advising others about matters that the average person does not understand.

In addition to these three characteristics are three further features that are common to the professions but not necessary for professional status. First, professionals are generally licensed or certified. Lawyers, real estate brokers, and doctors—to name just three professions—must pass exams in order to be members of their profession. In addition, the professions often have a monopoly over the provision of certain services. It is illegal, for example, to practice medicine if one is not a licensed doctor, and only licensed pharmacists can dispense prescription drugs. By contrast, though, one can work as an accountant without being a certified public accountant, and there is no licensing procedure for research scientists or college teachers.

A second common feature is that the major professions have organizations that claim to represent them—organizations dedicated to advancing the goals of the profession and to defending the professional and economic interests of their members. Typically, these organizations have been subject to little public control. They have been allowed to control the criteria of membership, set the conditions of practice, and discipline their members for breaches of acceptable profes-

sional behavior. But not all professions have enjoyed as large a degree of self-regulation as medicine and law have. In addition, members of a profession sometimes do not belong to their professional organization, and sometimes there are competing organizations within a single profession.

A third common feature is autonomy. Professionals, as we mentioned earlier, are typically granted wide freedom of judgment and independence of action in their work. They have greater discretionary powers and more significant control over their work than nonprofessionals do. Naturally, they must remain within the boundaries of acceptable professional practice, although what those boundaries are will vary with the nature of the profession and with the specific work task at hand. In fact, people hire professionals because they want them to exercise their judgment within the work context and apply their skills creatively and independently to the problems they are dealing with.

MORALITY AND PROFESSIONAL RESPONSIBILITY

Some general observations about the moral responsibilities of professionals follow from our description of the key features of professions. We then turn to the relationship between professional obligations and the requirements of everyday morality.

The Social Responsibility of Professionals

All writers on the subject agree that professionals have special obligations in virtue of the role they play in society. Professionals have specialized knowledge and are charged with the provision of crucial services—from performing operations and delivering babies to building bridges and constructing nuclear reactors, from protecting our legal rights in court to designing the structures we live and work in. As a result, when one enters into a profession, one assumes special, social responsibilities.

Why is this? There are several reasons. First, society invests heavily in the training of professionals. Virtually every university, medical college, law school, and scientific research facility receives public support. This is true even of "private" institutions of higher education. Because of this investment, society expects those who receive this socially supported professional training to exercise their skills in a socially responsible way.

One must remember, too, that while every citizen has a right to primary and secondary education, in the sense that the state must provide the necessary schools and teachers, attending a professional school is a privilege. The state has no obligation, for instance, to build enough medical schools to allow everyone who would like to be a doctor to study medicine. Resources are scarce, and inevitably professional training is not available to all who might want it. Admittance to professional training is not by lottery or payment. Rather, we establish principles of selection with an eye to the qualifications that it will be socially useful to have in doctors, veterinarians, lawyers, and so on.

Society also grants the professions a wide area of self-governance. By and large the professions are left free to govern themselves, control admission to membership, choose their direction of research, enforce the quality of work, and direct the allocation of public funds within their subject area.[6] With the privilege of self-governance comes the obligation to exercise it in a socially responsible way.

In addition, when the state permits a profession to have a monopoly over the provision of certain services, it enhances its social status and ensures the economic well-being of its members. If, for example, the practice of law were not restricted to those who graduate from law school or pass a qualifying exam (or both), lawyers would have less status, and many would earn less money. When society makes an exception to free market principles and permits monopolies (utility companies are an example), it does so not to enrich those who have the monopoly but because it benefits society in some way. Again, privileges bring responsibilities.

Finally, as William Lowrance has argued, society not only invests in the professions, but also "invests *with* the professions and their institutions certain trusts, among them a trust that the professions will watch over the well-being of society." He quotes Berkeley sociologist William Kaufman's statement that "professional responsibility is based on the belief that the power conferred by expertise entails a fiduciary relationship to society." A *fiduciary* is someone who functions as a trustee—that is, someone who is entrusted to look after the interests or well-being of another party. Professional knowledge and expertise, then, bring with them responsibilities to exercise that knowledge and expertise in acceptable ways. "This 'fiduciary relationship,'" Lowrance argues, "is what gives rise to the ethical 'oughts'" that are part of the professional's role in our society.[7]

In a later section we look more specifically at the sometimes conflicting obligations facing professionals as they try to balance duties to their clients, to the public, and to the profession itself. First, though, we need to discuss the relationship between professional and moral obligations, the nature of professional ethical codes, and the ideal of professional self-regulation.

Professional Norms and Moral Obligation

We have seen that membership in a profession brings with it definite role-based social responsibilities. Such membership is of course voluntary, but if one chooses to enter a profession, then he or she assumes the responsibilities characteristic of that profession.

Professional organizations often use legalistic codes of ethics to define the duties of their members. We shall say more about these in the next section. Equally, if not more important, however, are the more informally established procedures or customary practices of the professions. Such procedures cover not only morally sensitive matters like client confidentiality or conflicts of interest, but also more mundane things like referral and billing procedures and various professional courtesies. These "rules" play a key role in guiding the day-to-day behavior of professionals and in structuring their expectations about the conduct of their peers.

Not only do professionals and their organizations have definite ideas, expectations, and rules about what constitutes appropriate professional practice, they also have certain values and ideals that they see as guiding their profession. These ideals and values may often be rather vague, and certainly there is range of individual interpretation. Sometimes, in fact, the identity or self-conception of a profession may not be settled. Engineers seem to be struggling with the question of whether business values or an ethic of service should dominate their profession, and accountants are unsure how to respond to the public's expectation that they do more to bring illegal corporate bribes, political payoffs, and other shady practices to light.[8]

For most professionals, professional practice is more than a job. They have an understanding of themselves as members of their given profession, an understanding that reflects what they see as the distinctive virtues of that profession. As we have discussed before, ideals and values influence people's moral decisions as much as the explicit moral rules they endorse, and this point is nowhere more true than with professionals.

Properly understood, one's professional obligations do not replace one's general moral obligations. Rather than being a substitute for the ordinary demands of morality, specifically professional obligations are often an addition to, or strengthening of, those demands. For example, an accountant has a stronger obligation, in virtue of his or her standing as a professional, to expose financial skulduggery than does the average employee. We all have a *prima facie* obligation to blow the whistle on practices that are illegal, unjust, or harmful to others. But, as Professor Gene James argued earlier, the professional responsibility of engineers to speak out against dangerous products or practices even when their jobs are on the line is even stronger than this.[9] Likewise, physicians have long seen themselves as having a professional duty to sacrifice family life, time, convenience, and physical comfort to render aid to those in need—a duty that goes well beyond that which is incumbent on the average person.

Professional obligations can also involve the elaboration of ordinary ethical requirements in a specifically professional context. Basic morality, for instance, requires that we respect people as ends in themselves. But this moral imperative needs to be translated into more operational directives for the handling of clients and the treatment of patients. Doing so yields specific rules and procedures for, among other things, ensuring "informed consent" on the part of clients. Such rules are not independent of ordinary morality, but rather an extension of it to the special contexts in which professionals work.

The important point here is that while the assumption of a professional role brings with it distinct obligations, these obligations are not at the expense of the universalistic demands of morality. The moral demands on professionals, and the norms to which their behavior is expected to conform, may differ from those facing nonprofessionals, but this does not imply any ethical relativism. It reflects, rather, the special training of professionals and the distinctive circumstances of professional practice. Professor Richard T. DeGeorge puts this point well:

There is no special ethics that allows people in a profession to do as professionals what it is immoral for others to do. Lawyers, for instance, have no right to lie or cheat or mislead in order to help or to defend a client. Doctors in their role as doctors may not for the good of medicine experiment on their patients without the patient's informed consent, nor may they lie to patients for the patient's own good. Those in professions do have a special relation to ethics because of the roles they fill as members of a profession. But *more* is appropriately expected of them because of their roles, not less.[10]

PROFESSIONAL CODES AND REGULATION

Professional codes of conduct, both implicit and explicit, help to determine the obligations and responsibilities of professionals. As we stressed in Chapter 1, though, such codes do not fully delineate the moral duties of a professional. First, professionals are human beings before they are members of a profession. Thus, they are always subject to the general demands of morality as well as to the specific requirements of their profession. Second, professional codes of ethics often concern themselves with conduct (like the billing of services) that is more a matter of business procedure, professional custom, or etiquette, than of morality. Third, the ethical code of a profession, even where it explicitly addresses moral issues, may stand in need of modification and revision.

The formulation of a code of ethics is one of the first steps taken by any occupation aspiring to professional status. The American Medical Association (AMA) adopted its first, very extensive code in 1847, the same year that the organization was founded. Other professions since then have followed this pattern. Some sociologists see the professional code as the institutional manifestation of the ideals of service and self-governance characteristic of professions. The code represents the profession's contract with society: In exchange for autonomy, the profession agrees to police itself. Other sociologists see professional codes more as public relations. They represent an occupational group's attempt to win status, prestige, and economic benefits.

In either case, professional codes of ethics are often justly criticized as being largely a matter of self-promotion by the professional or occupational group that promulgates it. Like their corporate counterparts, professional codes of ethics are frequently vague and general, espousing values or ideals that we all share but failing to translate them into clear and specific guidelines.

The journal *Chemical Engineering*, for instance, recently surveyed the views of chemical engineers on certain hypothetical cases in engineering ethics. In discussing the results of the survey, the journal observed that the code of ethics of the American Institute of Chemical Engineers "was almost universally ignored in determining the solutions of our survey problems. Fewer than a half-dozen [out of 4,318] respondents even mentioned a code of ethics at all."[11]

By itself this survey does not prove that existing professional codes are worthless. Experienced and mature professionals are not likely to have to study a code of conduct in order to determine how they should act. Their actions will be based on established principles, and they will not normally require long deliberation in order to decide how to act. Failure to cite a written professional code can thus reflect the fact that the members of the profession have long internalized its principles. On the other hand, the survey result does suggest that in hard cases, the chemical engineers' code was of little practical value.

Some codes, especially those governing lawyers, are very specific and detailed. They reflect the thinking of competent professionals about hard, moral issues, and members of the profession utilize the code in determining their own conduct and assessing that of their peers. Even where this is not the case, a profession's code of ethics can be the focal point for addressing, analyzing, and rethinking the moral problems that the members of that profession are likely to face. Thus, the ethical code of a profession deserves to be taken seriously, and the members of a profession should work to improve and refine their codes. A profession's code of ethics is an important basis of its claim to be self-regulating, and without a meaningful, strict, and effective code an occupational group's demand for the autonomy characteristic of professions becomes less convincing.

The 1983 National Association of Accountants Code of Ethics has been criticized on this last count. It suggests, but does not require, that accountants working within firms report false accounting, fraud, and other improper activities to the management of the firm. If management takes no action, the accountant is advised to resign; he is not required to blow the whistle. The code advises accountants, in effect, simply to do what the law requires, argues Professor DeGeorge. If the law requires public disclosure, the code requires it; if the law does not require it, the code advises silence. DeGeorge concludes: "Because the code does not require more than the law does, the code does not satisfy the conditions for a profession's autonomy, and this is partial grounds for not considering accountancy a profession."[12]

The philosophical assessment of any profession's code of ethics requires a detailed look at the nature of that profession and the moral dilemmas that are likely to confront its practitioners. Ethical analysis must be accompanied by a practical understanding of the profession's various work tasks and the specific temptations, moral pitfalls, and ethically difficult decisions that accompany them. An examination of the content of any profession's ethical code cannot be undertaken here. We can, however, offer a few comments that are relevant to the evaluation of professional codes in general.

Making Professional Codes More Effective

A professional code of ethics must be specific and detailed, describing actual situations that members of the profession are likely to encounter and laying down clear guidelines and principles for handling them. A declaration of general professional ideals and values is fine, but if the code limits itself to pious proclamations, it will be of little use. The members of the profession need to take a hard and honest look at the areas in which their conduct has been legitimately criticized. For a code to be useful it must come down to earth and deal practically and openly with those situations where its members' actions have been open to challenge.

The formulation of specific rules of conduct is important, and there will be many areas of professional life and activity that can and ought to be regulated by definite rules. Doing so eliminates ambiguity and doubt about the standards to which members of the profession are expected to conform. Obviously, though, firm and specific rules are not possible where the professional faces a situation that is not black and white. Here the code must spell out the relevant moral considerations and professional values that the conscientious professional must balance.

This last point is important, and some have argued that professional codes of ethics, particularly in engineering, should not seek to provide a set of ethical rules. Rather, they should offer "guides for ethical decision-making."[13] Professionals need ethical sensitivity to conflicting values and confusions of obligations that occur in concrete situations, in contrast to the clear-cut issues that often characterize technical problems. Instead of prepackaged codes, critical questioning and ethical reflection need to be encouraged.[14]

It is probably a mistake, however, to see this as an either-or matter. Professional codes of ethics can offer cut-and-dried rules for some situations as well as more general discussion of guidelines and considerations for handling other situations. If the goal of a professional code is to promote ethical behavior by professionals, both rules and guides for ethical decision making have a role to play.

Finally, a profession should strive to put teeth into its ethical code. In staking its claim to be recognized as an autonomous and self-regulating occupation, a profession commits itself to police its own rules. Accordingly, there should be both penalties for infringement of the code and professional institutions that can effectively enforce it. The point is not punishment for its own sake. Rather, it is to demonstrate the seriousness with which the profession views its ethical commitments and responsibilities. The point can be put this way:

> Unless a profession can demonstrate by its record that it does police its own ranks, society has little reason to believe that it is doing so. In such cases, it has no justification for allowing special privileges to the profession. Society should then, appropriately, legislate concerning the members of the profession and control their activities, as it controls those engaged in other occupations.[15]

A professional group loses credibility if it cannot ensure the compliance of its members with its own rules.

A profession's enforcement procedures should be accessible to complaints from professionals as well as clients and other nonprofessionals. Since it is possible for professionals to collude with clients, say, in defrauding an insurance company or in the utilization of substandard materials, investigation and enforcement should not depend on client complaints.[16] Lack of financing is an obvious hurdle to effective enforcement of professional norms, but unless a profession surmounts it, its commitment to ensuring the compliance of its members to its own ethical code is open to doubt.

A profession's investigative and enforcement procedures should be objective, efficient, and effective. Cases should be dealt with promptly, and the implementation of sanctions should not be needlessly deferred or delayed. Although these procedures are not legal proceedings, they do affect seriously the livelihood and professional status of those investigated. Professionals can lose some of their privileges or even their license to practice. Accordingly, while investigation and enforcement should be flexible and not unduly formalized, due process must be respected. There should also be provision for review of decisions. Procedures need to respect the privacy of those suspected of unprofessional conduct, yet the withholding of names should not be to the exclusion of the public's interest in an open process.[17]

Professional Self-Regulation

Historically, the professions have been self-regulating, and that is the ideal to which occupations seeking professional status still strive. As we have seen, the promulgating and enforcing of a code of ethics are at the heart of a profession's claim to be self-regulating and to have autonomy over its own affairs. But how successful has professional self-regulation been?

We will look at the economic aspects of that question in the next section. Critics charge that in general the professions have not succeeded in enforcing their own norms. A study of the New York City Bar found that only 2 percent of the lawyers who violated ethical norms (based on their self-reports) were officially processed, and fewer than 0.2 percent of them were subject to official censure, suspension, or disbarment. In a typical year only 937 of the 5,000 complaints received by the California Bar Association were investigated, and only 53 led to disbarment or suspension. Studies of the medical profession show that self-regulatory mechanisms are rare and that even when misconduct is observed, nothing is done about it. During a seven-and-a-half-year period in the 1970s, the American Institute of Certified Public Accountants disciplined only 121 members. The National Society of Professional Engineers has approximately 60,000 members but hears only about 150 cases of unethical conduct a year. Twenty of its fifty-two member societies have never processed a single disciplinary case.[18]

Critics of professional self-regulation argue more generally that the professions routinely sacrifice the public interest when it conflicts with professional advantage. Limiting the membership of a profession in order to protect the income of its current members is one example of this and is discussed in the next section. The claim of the critics is also supported by examples of vigorous lobbying efforts by professional groups on behalf of purely self-interested concerns. American trial lawyers have long and vocally fought attempts to introduce no-fault laws in cases of automobile accidents. Elimination or modification of adversarial proceedings in cases of automobile accidents would lower the insurance premiums of consumers significantly, but it would also deprive lawyers of a very lucrative source of income. Lawyers, too, have often fought attempts to simplify divorce, will, and bankruptcy procedures so that individuals could process simple cases themselves without hiring a lawyer.

Nor do the professions have an encouraging record when it comes to ensuring the continuing competence of their members, even though in all probability professional incompetence is a significantly greater problem for, and source of injury to, the public than is blatantly unethical behavior by professionals. With knowledge expanding, technology advancing, and laws changing, professionals must work hard to keep abreast of developments in their fields, and unfortunately it is easy to slip behind. Yet the professions do not have strong checks on their members. For example, between 3 and 5 percent of American physicians—that is, over 10,000 doctors—are estimated to be incompetent as a result of debilitating disease, addiction, or lack of training. Yet fewer than one hundred physicians are deprived of their licenses each year.[19]

Physicians are generally required to participate in some continuing education, and lawyers are beginning to follow suit. But nowhere are there periodic examinations, say, every three to five years, of continuing competence. The assumption seems to be that competence, once acquired, is permanent.[20] The principle of peer review among doctors was, in fact, set back in 1981 when Timothy A. Patrick, a surgeon in Astoria, Oregon, sued a hospital peer-review panel when it appeared likely that he would receive an unsatisfactory evaluation. Invoking federal antitrust laws, he argued that the physicians on the panel were attempting to put him out of business. When a district court awarded him $650,000 in damages, which—under antitrust law—was trebled to $1,950,000, doctors began to mute their criticisms of colleagues or to refuse to participate on peer-review panels. When the Ninth Circuit Court of Appeals finally reversed the Patrick decision in 1985, it breathed new life into the principle of peer review.

Despite these shortcomings and the flawed record of the professions when it comes to self-regulation, professional self-governance and autonomy from direct social control are widely defended on the grounds that only professionals have the necessary expertise to oversee and evaluate professional activities. The assumption is that laypersons cannot possibly judge or assess the work of professionals because they lack the requisite training. Professor Michael Bayles, however, has persuasively challenged this assumption.[21]

Laypersons can intelligently contribute to the establishing of professional norms and the general management of professional activity. Not only are they apt to be as competent as professionals in general questions of ethics, but also they are likely to be free of biases stemming from self-interest. Not all wisdom about the proper role of professions resides at the top of the professional heap; informed lay people have an important perspective to contribute.[22] Lay administrators, particularly in medicine, already judge and direct such professional matters as the types of services to be rendered, the most efficient way to provide them, and the reduction of their costs.

Much professional work is routine, and expertise is not needed to identify and judge gross mistakes—for example, failing to date a will, leaving a sponge in a patient after an operation, or designing the stairs of a house so that they go out the front door—all actual cases.[23] Likewise, great professional sophistication is not generally required to evaluate cases of ethical misconduct: the financial consultant with a conflict of interest, the lawyer who breaches client confidentiality, the physician who orders an unnecessary operation. Even when technical issues are involved, both sides can present laypersons with their interpretation of the issues and with evidence concerning the appropriate professional practices and standards. This, after all, is the basis on which trial by jury works.

This thinking leads Bayles to propose that laypersons be extensively involved in both the development of professional norms and in their enforcement.[24] There is some precedent for this. Institutional review boards for experimentation on human and animal subjects now routinely have nonprofessional members. Since 1969, two of the seven members of

the Grievance Board of the Michigan State Bar have been nonlawyers, and a few other states have begun to follow suit. In Ontario, Canada, laypersons have been involved on the governing boards of professional engineers and lawyers for years.[25] Still, the involvement of laypersons in the enforcement of professional norms is far from widespread.

The results of lay involvement, where it has occurred, have generally been perceived as beneficial and have allayed doubts about the competence of laypersons to oversee professionals. Laypersons have proved objective, unbiased, and perfectly able to respect confidentiality. Still, where only a few laypersons are added to oversight groups, their addition could be more of a public-relations effort than a serious attempt at reforming professional conduct so that it gives greater weight to the public interest. Thus, Bayles advocates that laypersons should constitute a majority of the groups charged with establishing and enforcing professional codes of ethics. No other monopolies of essential public services, he contends, are regulated solely or even primarily by representatives of the monopoly.

Extensive lay involvement in professional life weakens, by definition, the autonomy of the professions, but this is not grounds for a strong objection to lay involvement. Autonomy is not an absolute value. It has to be balanced against competing values and social concerns. Moreover, lay participation in the establishment and enforcement of professional norms need not intrude any more than peer review does on the ability of individual professionals to exercise freedom of judgment on professional matters. There is no reason to think laypersons would be inclined to interfere with technical decisions involving no significant ethical issues.

THE PROFESSIONS AS BUSINESS

Historically, the professions have attempted not only to monitor ethically the conduct of their members, but also to regulate the conditions and terms of professional practice. In doing so, they have been particularly sensitive to their own economic interests. Many practices, regulations, and customs that are defended on professional grounds appear to outside observers to have more to do with economic self-interest than with the public good.

An example is the setting of standard fees for services. This might involve set fees for certain services, but a recommended price range or minimum charge is more common. In California, for example, $300 was formerly the approximate minimum attorneys were expected to charge for handling simple, uncontested divorces. Lawyers who charged less, including lawyers in legal services offices explicitly intended to serve poor people, were the object of complaints to local bar associations. The establishing of minimum fees is normally considered price fixing or unfair restraint of trade. The absence of price competition works against the public interest and gives professional practitioners little incentive to save on costs.

The Supreme Court held in 1975 that the Sherman Anti-Trust Act prohibits minimum fee schedules in the case of lawyers doing real estate title searches. A couple buying a house had found that nineteen different attorneys quoted the county bar's recommended fee or a higher one for this service, and the Court viewed this as price fixing even though the recommended fee was not mandatory.[26] Likewise the Court has held that the National Society of Professional Engineers' prohibition on competitive bidding for contracts was an illegal suppression of competition and violated the antitrust law. Although the prohibition was defended on grounds that clients would focus on price alone and that engineers would be tempted to cut corners with materials and safety in order to bid low, the result of the prohibition clearly thwarts the ability of clients to obtain services at as low a cost as possible.[27]

Even without fee schedules, professionals are frequently reluctant to reveal their fees in advance or to compete among themselves in terms of price. Professional organizations have claimed that haggling over fees is undignified, but this position reflects, at best, a day when professions like medicine were less commercially oriented and their practitioners received only modest incomes. It fits less well an era in which physicians view themselves as profit-maximizing entrepreneurs and most doctors' offices have signs demanding immediate payment for services rendered.

Discouragement of price competition is also defended as necessary to prevent inadequate services being provided for lower costs. But this paternalistic argument seems oddly out of place in a market-oriented system. It denies people the opportunity, which they have elsewhere, to choose a lower-quality product at a lower price. Consumers must always make trade-offs, and some of us end up driving a Toyota rather than a Mercedes-Benz.

Related issues arise with regard to advertising and solicitation. Traditionally, professional organizations have viewed these practices as inappropriate and damaging to the image of the profession, probably reflecting a conception of themselves as devoted to public service rather than making money. The image of the "ambulance chasing" lawyer, who contacts persons immediately after accidents and proposes to represent them for a percentage of the court settlement, has undoubtedly embarrassed the legal profession. Approaching people like accident victims in vulnerable circumstances is ethically dubious, and the Supreme Court has upheld the validity of restrictions on solicitation that poses a threat of fraud, intimidation, or undue influence.[28]

Blanket bans on advertising, however, are different because they infringe freedom of speech, and in several cases the Supreme Court has upheld the right of lawyers and other professionals to advertise their fees. The

Court, however, has left open the possibility that restrictions by professional organizations on the quality and kind of advertising by their members would be legally permissible.

The desirability of such restrictions is an issue that leads us back to the questions discussed in Chapter 9, which we shan't reopen here. Despite the loosening of these restrictions, though, professionals still advertise relatively lightly, and when they do, it often causes comment. For example, recent efforts by therapists and counselors to snare new clients by adopting high-powered marketing methods have raised eyebrows in the media.[29]

One reason for the general lack of advertising in the professions may be that professionals simply refrain from it out of habit. Another, related reason is that advertising does not fit the self-understanding that many professionals have of themselves as professionals. A different reason may be that—unlike therapists, whose field is saturated with practitioners and running out of clients—many professionals don't need to advertise because they already have as many clients as they can handle. Why? Because restrictions on entry into these professions keeps the number of practitioners down.[30] We need to look at this issue a little more closely.

The Licensing of Professionals

One of the key objectives of professional associations has been to prevent unauthorized practice—that is, the provision of services by unqualified persons. The justification is widely accepted: If professionals are not licensed and certified as competent to practice, then the public will be victimized. Who wants to hire a "lawyer" who doesn't know the Constitution or be operated on by a "surgeon" who has never been to medical school?

University of Chicago professor of Economics Milton Friedman, whose economic views we discussed in Chapter 5, has been a long-standing critic of occupational licensure

in all fields. His reasoning is straightforward: Licensure—the requirement that one obtain a license from a recognized authority in order to engage in an occupation—restricts entry into the field. Licensure thus permits the occupational or professional group to enjoy a monopoly in the provision of services. In Friedman's view, this contravenes the principles of a free market to the disadvantage of us all.

Friedman has no objection to certification; that is, to public or private agencies certifying that an individual has certain skills. But he rejects the policy of preventing people who do not have such a certificate from practicing the occupation of their choice. Such a policy restricts freedom and keeps the price of the services in question artificially high. When one reads the long lists of occupations for which some states require a license—librarians, tree surgeons, pest controllers, well diggers, barbers, even potato growers, among many others—Friedman's case gains plausibility. But Friedman pushes his argument to include all occupations and professions.

Does this mean we should let incompetent physicians practice? Friedman's answer is yes.[31] In his view the American Medical Association (AMA) is simply a trade union, though probably the strongest one in the United States. It keeps the wages of its members high by restricting the number of those who can practice medicine.

The AMA does this not just through licensure but also, even more effectively, through controlling the number of medical schools and the numbers of students admitted to them. The medical profession limits entry into the field by turning down applicants to medical school and making standards for admission and licensure so difficult as to discourage many young people from ever trying to gain admission. (Historically, the American Bar Association has done the same thing, but with less success. The number of approved law schools has risen in recent years by 25 percent, and student enrollments have doubled. New lawyers are currently being produced at three times their mid-1960s rate.[32])

Viewed as a trade union, the AMA has been singularly effective. As recently as the 1920s, physicians were far down the list of professions in terms of income; the average doctor made less than the average accountant. Today, doctors constitute what is probably the profession with the highest status and the best pay in the country. In 1984 the average doctor made $108,000, and the average specialist considerably more. But the AMA is still worried. In July 1987 it predicted a "surplus" of doctors by the year 2000, warning that this "could lower the quality and raise the cost of physicians's services."[33]

In fact, the AMA's real worry seems to be the prospect of stabilizing or declining incomes. Its proposed remedy is the familiar one: restrict the size of medical school classes. The problem for the AMA, however, is that would-be doctors have been evading this bottleneck by going to medical school abroad. The AMA is responding to this by attempting to make it harder for the graduates of foreign medical schools to practice here—supposedly out of "concern . . . about the quality of medical training."[34]

Medical licensure restricts the freedom of people to practice medicine and prevents the public from buying the medical care it wants. Nonetheless, most people would probably defend the principle of licensure on the grounds that it raises the standards of competence and the quality of care. Friedman contests this. By reducing the amount of care available, he contends, licensure also reduces the average quality of care people receive. Furthermore, monopoly has reduced the incentive for research, development, and experimentation, both in medicine and in the organization and provision of services.

Since Friedman initially presented his argument over twenty-five years ago, some of the alternatives to traditional practice that he proposed have come to pass: prepaid services have emerged, and group and clinic-based practices are on the increase. But what about his main contention that, instead of licensure, we should allow the marketplace to sort out the competent from the incompetent providers of medical services?

Even if the licensing of professionals "involves violating a moral rule" against restricting individuals' "freedom of opportunity,"[35] one may still reply that it is immoral to allow an unqualified person to engage in potentially harmful activities without having subjected the person to adequate tests of competence.[36] Despite the appeal of Friedman's arguments on behalf of free choice, the danger still remains that people will be victimized by the incompetent.

Consider for example the quack remedies and treatments that are being peddled to AIDS patients here and abroad. Twenty-dollar bottles of processed pond scum and eighty-dollar concoctions of herbs, injections of hydrogen peroxide or of cells from the glands of unborn calves, the eating of bee pollen and garlic, $800 pills containing substances from mice inoculated with the AIDS virus, and even whacking the thymus gland of patients to stimulate the body's immune system—all these are among the treatments offered to desperate people by the unscrupulous and the eccentric.[37] Deregulation of the medical field seems most unlikely to diminish such exploitation.

Professional licensing, however, is not an all-or-nothing issue, and it is likely that restrictions on the provision of professional services have gone beyond what can be justified in terms of the public good. We want to protect people from inadequate or incompetent practitioners while allowing consumer clients to choose a lesser service at a lower cost. This suggests that services must be examined individually.[38] Could not paraprofessionals or laypersons perform less expensively but equally competently some tasks now reserved for lawyers? And wouldn't it be economically efficient to allow pharmacists, nurses, medics, and midwives to take over some medical functions now limited to doctors?

A middle road is probably the right one on the licensing issue. Michael Bayles argues that only certain core services should be restricted to specific professions. These would be services either that (1) no reasonable person would want a less than fully trained professional to provide or that (2) might burden the public if provided by inadequately trained persons.[39] The first condition holds for only a few services—like open-heart surgery and being defended on a murder charge. By contrast, a reasonable person might be willing to have his house designed by someone other than a professionally certified architect.

The second condition applies more widely. Untrained people in court could waste the court's time and run up costs. Allowing mathematically incompetent accountants to audit government accounts would cost us all a lot of money. The danger of incompetent engineers building dams and bridges is obvious, and bungled medical care could be a drain on public resources. Even so, these conditions do not justify the extent of professional-services licensing that now exists. Bayles contends, however, that restrictions that go beyond what is permitted by his two conditions unduly limit the freedom of clients to choose, and of nonprofessionals to render, services.[40]

THE OBLIGATIONS OF PROFESSIONALS

Professionals who are employed in business firms or other organizations share with their fellow employees the possibility of having to deal with the moral difficulties and ethical dilemmas that were discussed in Chapter 7. As employees they must understand their various obligations to those for whom they work. Professionals must be wary of actual or potential conflicts of interest and be careful

not to abuse their official positions. In view of their specialized professional expertise, they may be more likely than other employees to have to face the question of whistle blowing. Professionals who manage offices, on the other hand, have the same obligations as do employers in general with respect to personnel matters and working conditions. They must be sensitive to the workplace issues examined in Chapter 6.

But professionals, in particular professionals who work with clients, face a variety of moral choices that differ from those discussed in earlier chapters. In this section we will look at the distinct and sometimes conflicting obligations that professionals have with respect to clients, third parties, colleagues, and the profession itself.

Accepting Clients

The first ethically difficult decisions a professional might face are the choice of clients and the acceptance of professional projects. These are different issues. A gangster, for example, might need a lawyer for an innocuous title search or for drawing up a will. Here, even though the professional may find a potential client morally despicable, the services the client is seeking are not objectionable in themselves. On the other hand, a professional may object morally to what the client wants done. A physician, for instance, might be troubled by a patient's request that he or she perform, or refer the patient to someone who will perform, an abortion.

Professionals are generally accorded a very wide range of freedom to decide what kind of work they do, for whom they do it, and under what terms they do it. This is part of their professional autonomy, and few would want to abridge significantly their freedom of choice in these areas. In some instances, though, professional services can be of such importance that people may have a right to them. Legal representation in felony criminal cases and medical assistance in the event of serious injury or illness are examples of such instances. The medical profession has long seen itself as having a professional duty to strive to save life regardless of whose it is. No one criticizes doctors for struggling to keep even convicted murderers alive. Similarly, even the most despicable criminal defendant has a right to effective legal representation.

This establishes only that some professional must provide legal or medical assistance to the person in question; it doesn't show that any particular individual professional must agree to do so. If no other professional is available, however, or if all others have declined to handle the case, then the remaining individual practitioner would have a duty to do so. Failure to assist would violate the rights of the person in question.

Outside of dire cases, the matter would seem to be different. Refusing to assist a gangster with his or her will or with a noncriminal-related tax matter, even if you were the last lawyer in town, does not violate the gangster's rights. Likewise, a plastic surgeon could decline to perform certain cosmetic operations on ethical grounds even if the patient had nowhere else to turn. In these cases, requiring the professional to accept the case would seriously restrict his or her moral and professional autonomy.

There are hard cases in between these extremes. The matter may be of great importance to the potential client, without it being a service so fundamental that he or she has a right to it. Or the professional and the potential client may hold conflicting views about controversial ethical issues—for example, the moral permissibility of abortion. To what extent should a professional impose his or her own values and principles on the client or potential client? When does a professional do wrong in assisting immoral clients or morally objectionable projects? No general answer to such questions is possible because one needs to know the situational details, including the values motivating the professional.

As a practical matter, professionals can know what sort of cases a particular line of specialization will bring, and thus they can avoid work that they might find morally problematic. Law students who are considering becoming criminal defense lawyers, for example, soon learn that defense attorneys are not like Perry Mason. Almost all the people they represent are guilty of something. More generally, by the time their training is completed and practice is begun, young professionals should have identified the professional ideals that motivate them and have thought through the values and goals they hope to realize as they pursue their chosen careers. This self-understanding will guide them in deciding what clients and what types of projects to accept.

Because the point of the professions is to provide certain services, potential clients should be given the benefit of the doubt. Barbers and automobile mechanics are not blamed for assisting unworthy persons, nor are they at all identified with the activities of their customers. The situation is different with professionals, however, because professional services involve more personal interaction—advice, confidentiality, trust—between the professional and the client. Thus, the presumption in favor of accepting a client can be overriden.

The professional also runs a greater risk than does the barber or automobile mechanic of being judged by his or her professional associations and held at least partially responsible for activities of their clients. In this respect, a medical specialist flown into Camp David to operate on a visiting dictator is in a different position than the person who agrees to become the dictator's personal physician. The latter has no professional duty to accept the dictator as a client and, arguably, a moral duty not to. An architect might with propriety design a new post office for an evil regime, but the professional risks not just guilt by association but also his or her own moral corruption—as the history of architect Albert Speer's involvement with the Nazis shows.[41]

The Nazi-architect case also illustrates the point that professionals must not view potential work projects from a narrowly technical perspective. The designing of advanced weaponry, the setting up of an elaborate computer system, experimenting with new drugs on human subjects, or winning a suspect's release from police custody—these might all pose interesting challenges of one's professional skill. Yet, depending on the context—imagine the computer system is to facilitate the efforts of the South African police to suppress dissent or that the suspect has sworn to kill someone on the outside—the project might be grossly immoral. Professionals have a responsibility not just to assess any work task in terms of its professional or technical interest, but also to evaluate it in its actual context from the wider perspective of morality.

Dealing with Clients

From what we have said so far, it follows that a professional never relinquishes his or her independence of judgment, either on moral or professional questions. The model of relations between professionals and clients that sees the professional as simply the "hired gun" or the "mouthpiece" of the client, carrying out without question the client's wishes, overlooks this fact. The professional cannot plausibly be viewed simply as the neutral instrument of the client's purposes, because the forming of the client's plans depends on the advice, counseling, and expertise of the professional. This is true even in the case where one professional needs the services of another, as when a doctor treats a fellow physician.

In fact, given the imbalance of knowledge between the professional and the client, their relationship does not fit well the model of a standard contractual relationship between two equal parties. The contractual model does not capture the special responsibilities of professionals to their clients in view of the former's expertise and the latter's dependence. But we should not go to the opposite extreme and see the professional as the "boss" who determines what the client shall do or not do. Such a model is too paternalistic. The client is not a child in need of direction by an adult; rather, clients must be treated as persons and their choices respected.

On the other hand, it seems misguided to view the professional-client relationship as one of friendship, as Yale law professor Charles Fried has proposed.[42] The points of dissimilarity between professional involvement and personal friendship are too many and too great. For one thing, the professional is providing a service for which the client is paying.

A better model is to see the professional-client relationship as a *fiduciary* relationship,[43] a concept we mentioned earlier in discussing the social responsibility of the professions. Here, in identifying the professional's relationship to the client as fiduciary, we wish to recognize the professional's superior knowledge and hence the dependence of the client and at the same time acknowledge that the activities of the profession should ultimately be based on the consent of the client. The professional informs the client of the various options that are available and makes recommendations, with which the client can agree or disagree.

Since the client is not generally in a position to understand, without the aid of the professional, what courses of action are open and what their respective pros and cons are, the client must trust the professional to present the options in an accurate, yet understandable way. This trust is at the heart of the relationship between the professional and client and gives it its fiduciary character.

In light of this we can identify some of the professional's basic obligations to the client.[44] In addition to working diligently and competently for the client, the professional obviously has to be honest. Relatedly, the professional should also be candid with the client, striving to make sure that the consent of clients and patients is fully informed and meaningful. This can be harder than it sounds, and most of us, for example, have experienced both the problem of being told too little by our physicians as well as the problem of being told more than we could understand.

The way in which information is presented obviously influences the decisions made by clients and patients, yet there is not one right way to present that information. There are other issues as well concerning candor and full disclosure. If a physician tells some patients that he or she suspects that their ailment is psychosomatic, this might aggravate their symptoms. How candid, then, should the doctor be? Should a physician stress the financial costs when he is discussing with distraught parents whether to continue a probably futile fight to keep their defective newborn alive? The physician may believe that the fight should be abandoned as soon as possible in order to spare the parents an even greater financial burden. Yet under great emotional stress some parents might feel guilty about letting money influence their decision at all. Should the physician instead exaggerate the hopelessness of the situation in order to get the parents to consent to what the physician believes is best?

In addition to honesty and candor, professionals are rightly expected to be loyal to the interests of their clients, to remain independent and objective in their judgment, and to avoid even potential conflicts of interest. Professionals must also keep the private affairs of clients confidential. This is central to preserving trust between client and professional. Professionals should also be discreet in discussing their clients, even when the information is a matter of public record and, thus, discussion of it does not violate the client's right to privacy. Most people would be distressed to learn that a professional whom they consult gossips about them.[45] Professionals are well advised to follow the simple procedure of putting themselves in the shoes of their client and asking what *they* would want the professional representing them to do.

Obligations to Third Parties

Professionals have special obligations to their clients, obligations growing out of the professional relationship itself. Just as parents are not only permitted but obligated to provide a greater level of care to their children than they do to other children who may be equally or greater in need, so professionals are justified, indeed required, to do things for their clients that they are not called upon to do for nonclients.

Nevertheless, elementary moral obligations limit that which professionals are permitted to do on behalf of their clients. Professionals, like everyone else, must respect the rights of third parties and strive to deal honestly and fairly with others. They cannot, for example, collude with clients to defraud their insurance companies, to falsify records or official submissions, or to mislead or lie to government inspectors. Professionals are not morally permitted to do in the name of a client what it would be wrong for clients to do for themselves.

These points seem obvious, but lawyers have often contended that their professional loyalty to clients exempts them from other moral obligations. Put this way, the claim is simply untrue. However, in "Lawyers' Ethics in an Adversary System," reprinted on page 511, professor of law Monroe H. Freedman defends actions by lawyers that strike many nonlawyers as immoral: for example, cross-examining a truthful witness in a way that undermines his or her credibility. But Freedman defends such unsavory actions as a necessary part of our adversarial criminal justice system, which is itself morally justifiable.

In other words, there are actions that are morally permissible within the framework of our adversary system that would not be permissible on the outside (just as football players can do things on the playing field—like knock other people down—that it would be wrong of them to do off the field). Thus Freedman is not saying that a lawyer's professional role, in particular, the duty to advocate the client's cause, excuses the lawyer from moral assessment. His position also leaves open the possibility that the rules governing our adversary system might be improved upon.

The legal profession has long recognized that lawyers have duties to the court and to the legal system as well as to their clients. In particular, lawyers cannot act illegally. This still leaves the question of whether they are morally justified in doing on behalf of their clients anything whatsoever that the law permits. On this point there is controversy, and lawyers disagree among themselves. In the defense of clients in serious criminal cases, most lawyers would say yes: The lawyer's job is not to judge the client, but to find the strongest legal defense available. But fewer people inside or outside the profession would endorse the principle when it comes to harassing people with legal suits, using technically legal but otherwise excessive delaying tactics in civil cases, or negotiating in an unscrupulous way.

Obligations to Colleagues and to the Profession

In addition to their moral obligations to third parties, professionals have obligations to their professional colleagues and to the profession itself. The Hippocratic Oath, for example, requires doctors to swear to "hold my teacher in this art as equal to my own parents . . . and to consider his family as my own brothers." And the World Health Organization reformulation of the Oath in 1948 states simply that "my colleagues will be as my brothers." Accordingly, doctors treat the family members of other doctors for free, they avoid overt competition for patients, and they protect each other from outside censure.[46]

Loyalty to colleagues can be carried too far, as when peer pressure on professionals prevents them from testifying against fellow professionals in malpractice cases. The obligation to support and assist one's professional colleagues does *not* require one to cover up their wrongdoings. On the contrary, reporting unethical conduct to the relevant professional authorities, thus helping the profession to monitor itself, is a clear and elementary duty to the profession. The ethical codes of both the legal and medical professions explicitly acknowledge this.

Moral dilemmas clearly arise, though, in numerous borderline cases—cases where colleagues are mediocre but not totally incompetent, where they have made a serious mistake that is not likely to recur, or where ill-equipped hospitals subject patients to greater risks than other hospitals. Clearly, no one likes being an informer or damaging the careers or reputations of others, and an atmosphere of mistrust can destroy a productive and professional work environment.[47] Nonetheless, professionals must balance loyalty to and sympathy for colleagues against the interests of the public and a general responsibility to the profession.

Earlier we discussed the responsibility of the professions and of professionals to the society that grants them their privileges and makes their professional life possible. This is the basis of the obligation of engineers to look after public safety and of accountants to certify financial statements honestly. These are among the obligations one assumes by joining a certain profession. They can, in a sense, be seen as obligations to the profession itself.

Joining a profession, like joining a club, may bring with it certain obligations to contribute to the ongoing development of the profession. Tasks such as reviewing contributions to professional journals, speaking to students undertaking professional training, or participating in basic committees are among the often thankless but necessary tasks for a profession to flourish. Given the nature and goals of the profession, individual professionals should also make an effort to improve, if necessary, the profession's code of ethics and its monitoring procedures and, in general, to strengthen its organizational structures in a way that enhances the profession's ability to serve the public.

An obligation to the profession definitely does not spell blind loyalty. A professional should not refrain from constructive criticism of the profession or its organizational structures. On the contrary, honest and candid discussion of problems can be for the profession's own good, and it should not occur only behind closed doors. Given the potential biases of any occupational group, public involvement in debates over professional goals, standards, and rules is to be welcomed. Finally, a duty to the profession does not oblige the professional to promote the economic interests of his or her profession to a greater extent than social justice demands.

SUMMARY

1. Socially and economically, the professions play an increasingly important role. Professionals (1) receive extensive training and (2) provide important social services; and (3) their training and distinctive skills are largely intellectual in character. Typically, professional practice is licensed; professionals have organizations representing their interests; and professionals enjoy significant control over the work they do.

2. Professionals have special obligations in virtue of their social role (their specialized knowledge and the services they provide) and the trust invested in them by society. Society invests heavily in the training of professionals, grants them a wide area of self-governance, and often permits them a monopoly over the provision of certain services. As a result society expects professionals to exercise their skills in a socially responsible way.

3. Professional codes of ethics, established procedures, and customary practices guide much of the day-to-day conduct of professionals. In addition, individual values, ideals, and professional self-understanding influence the moral choices of the members of a profession. Professional obligations do not replace one's general moral obligations; rather, they elaborate or extend them.

4. Professional organizations typically formulate codes of conduct. These are sometimes criticized as being window dressing or as being too vague and general. But these codes are an important basis of a profession's claim to be self-regulating. They deserve to be taken seriously, and the members of a profession should work to improve and refine them.

5. For a professional code to be effective, it must be specific and detailed. Precise rules for handling routine situations and general ethical guides for situations that are not black and white are both important. To retain credibility, a profession must also enforce its code.

6. Critics charge that the professions have not succeeded in enforcing their own norms and that they routinely sacrifice the public interest to professional advantage. The professions are also criticized for failing to guarantee the continuing competence of their members. Some

recommend more extensive layperson involvement in the formulation and enforcement of professional codes.

7. Professionals also have business or economic interests, which can conflict with the public good. Possible examples are the setting of minimum fees, discouragement of price competition, and resistance to advertising.

8. Occupational licensure has been criticized by Milton Friedman. Requiring people to obtain a license before engaging in an occupation restricts entry into the field (thus limiting individual freedom) and permits the occupational or professional group to enjoy a monopoly (thus keeping prices artificially high). Friedman would allow the marketplace, rather than the AMA, to distinguish between competent physicians and quacks.

9. Critics of Friedman fear that without licensing people will be victimized by the incompetent. A middle-of-the-road approach suggests that services be restricted to licensed and qualified professionals only when (1) no reasonable person would want the service provided by a less than fully trained professional or (2) permitting inadequately trained persons to provide such services would be a burden on the public.

10. The choice of clients and the acceptance of professional projects often pose difficult ethical decisions for professionals. The freedom of professionals to decide what work they do, and for whom, should be respected. But some professional services, like legal representation in felony criminal cases, can be so important that people may have a right to them.

11. The professional-client relationship is best seen as a fiduciary one. The professional has superior knowledge, which the client is dependent on, but the activities of the professional must ultimately be based on the consent of the client. Trust is at the heart of this relationship.

12. Professionals are obligated to work diligently and competently for their clients, to be honest and candid, and to ensure that consent is meaningful and informed. They must be loyal, remain independent and objective in their judgment, and avoid even potential conflicts of interest.

13. Professionals must also respect the rights of third parties and deal honestly and fairly with others. Loyalty to clients does not exempt professionals from other moral obligations.

14. Professionals have obligations to colleagues, but loyalty to them does not justify covering up wrongdoing. Professionals also have a responsibility to contribute to the ongoing development of their professions.

CASE 11.1
Victims of Confidentiality

A young man with a history of mental illness voluntarily commits himself to a state hospital in Michigan. After two weeks he asks to be released, and because the hospital psychiatrist can find no evidence of violent behavior to justify retaining him against his will, he is let go.

Two months later he kills his mother during a struggle over a shotgun. His mother's sister sues the psychiatrist for negligence in releasing the man and failing to warn his mother of possible danger. She wins, and the jury awards her $500,000 in damages.[48]

This 1983 case and dozens of others since the famous *Tarasoff* decision in California have put the mental health profession in a quandary. How are therapists to keep the thoughts of their clients confidential and also protect others against possible danger from them? In the *Tarasoff* case, Prosenjit Poddar was a voluntary outpatient at Cowell Memorial Hospital at the University of California at Berkeley. He told Dr. Lawrence Moore, his therapist, that he was going to kill an unnamed girl, readily identifiable as Tatiana Tarasoff, when she returned home from spending the summer in Brazil.

In consultation with two other doctors, Moore requested Poddar's commitment to a mental hospital for observation and asked the campus police for their assistance in securing Poddar's confinement. Three officers took Poddar into custody but, satisfied that he was rational, they released him on his promise to stay away from Tatiana. The director of the department of psychiatry, Moore's superior, then directed that no further action be taken. Shortly after Tatiana Tarasoff's return from Brazil, Poddar went to where she was living and killed her.

Tarasoff's parents sued the University of California on several grounds, including the failure of Moore and other university psychiatrists to warn Tatiana of any danger. The defendants denied that they had any such duty and argued that requiring psychiatrists to warn possible victims would force them to breach the trust of their patients and to reveal confidential communications. The case was fought to the California Supreme Court, which decided in favor of the Tarasoffs in 1976.[49]

Although under common law no one has a general duty to control the conduct of others or to warn those endangered by that conduct, there is an exception, the Court held, when someone stands in a special relationship either to the person whose conduct needs to be controlled or to the foreseeable victim of that conduct. The relationship between a patient and doctor or psychotherapist is just such a special relationship.

The Court accepted the testimony of the American Psychiatric Association and other professional societies that therapists are unable reliably to predict violent acts. They overpredict violence and are more often wrong than right. In this case, though, the Court said, the therapists had predicted that Poddar would kill, but were negligent in failing to warn Tatiana Tarasoff:

> Once a therapist does in fact determine, or under applicable professional standards reasonably should have determined, that a patient poses a serious danger of violence to others, he bears a duty to exercise reasonable care to protect the foreseeable victim of that danger.

In his dissent to the decision, Justice Clark argued that imposing such a duty on psychiatrists would violate the rights of patients and would destroy the confidentiality essential to effective treatment of the mentally ill. Without the assurance of confidentiality, patients will be deterred from assisting treatment; without it, they will be reluctant to disclose their innermost thoughts; and without it, the trust which is so necessary for successful treatment will not develop. He concluded: ''Given the importance of confidentiality to the practice of psychiatry, it becomes clear the duty to warn imposed by the majority will cripple the use and effectiveness of psychiatry.''

Discussion Questions

1. Doctors, and especially psychiatrists, have a professional obligation to respect the confidentiality of their patients. Do

they also have a duty to warn possible victims of their patients? If so, how are these apparently conflicting obligations to be reconciled?

2. What would you have done if you had been Dr. Moore? Were Moore and his colleagues negligent in failing to warn Tatiana Tarasoff or her parents of Poddar's threats? Was the Court's decision a just one?

3. Does the decision of the majority undermine doctor-patient confidentiality and trust as Justice Clark argues? Will the decision reduce the effectiveness of psychiatry?

4. What rule governing doctor-patient confidentiality would best serve the public interest?

5. If psychiatrists cannot predict violent behavior accurately, should they be held liable for determining when a threat is serious and when it is not?

CASE 11.2
Turning Away Patients

In the 1970s the song "Take This Job and Shove It" was a smash hit on the country and western charts. It also expressed with conviction what many working people see as a basic right. While most people are not able to do just the kind of work they want, they can at least quit a job they don't like. Professionals are more fortunate, however. They have much greater control over the kind of work they do because they are free to accept or reject clients. If they have ethical doubts about a potential client or a proposed project, they can normally decline to accept the client or the project without any great personal sacrifice.

This freedom is an important one, but in exercising it, can professionals interfere with the rights of potential clients? Do they risk letting their own values interfere with the choices of others? This question often comes up with abortion, when doctors or nurses at certain hospitals refuse to perform abortions on grounds of conscience. In these situations, there is usually an alternative open to the pregnant woman—other physicians or clinics that are not ethically opposed to abortion. But what if there is no such alternative readily

available to the patient? Consider the following two actual cases.[50]

A college student decided when he was eighteen that he did not want to be a father. Worried about overpopulation and other world problems, he resolved not to assume the responsibility of bringing any more children into an already overcrowded and troubled world. So he decided that a vasectomy would be the best choice for him. But all the physicians he contacted in the Boston area refused to perform this operation on him.

A poor twenty-three-year-old woman living in a small town faced a similar situation in the 1960s. She already had three children and had suffered two miscarriages. She sought a tubal ligation to prevent her from becoming pregnant again. Her physician refused, and she had no medical alternative readily available to her. She had two more children.

Discussion Questions

1. Why, in your view, did the physicians refuse to perform the vasectomy or tubal ligation? Did they do so on moral grounds?

2. Does a professional have an obligation to consider the consequences of refusing a client?

3. Granted that the physicians had a legal right to refuse, were they morally justified in exercising that right?

4. Professionals can decline potential clients because they have too much work already, because the project doesn't interest them, because it is outside their preferred areas of specialization, or because they think what they are being asked to do is unwise or unethical. Suppose refusal to accept a client works a hardship on the client. Are these reasons all equally legitimate reasons for refusing?

5. Suppose the professional and client disagree over some value judgment, about which reasonable people differ. Should the professional's decision be affected by this realization?

6. Does it make a difference whether it is a new client or an established client who is requesting the service that the professional thinks would be unwise or immoral?

CASE 11.3
Unprofessional Conduct?

Teaching retarded elementary school children requires skill, patience, and devotion, and those who undertake this task are among the unsung heroes of our society. Their hard and challenging work rarely brings the prestige or financial rewards it deserves. Mrs. Pettit was one of those dedicated professionals. Licensed to teach in California since 1957, she had been working with retarded children for over thirteen years when her career came to an end in 1973. Throughout that career, her competence was never questioned, and the evaluations of her school principal were always positive.

Teaching was not Mrs. Pettit's only interest, however. She and her husband viewed with favor various "nonconventional sexual lifestyles," including "wife swapping," and in 1966 they had discussed their ideas on two local television shows. Although they wore disguises, at least one fellow teacher recognized them and discussed Mrs. Pettit's views with colleagues. A year later in 1967, Pettit, then 48 years old, and her husband joined "The Swingers," a private club in Los Angeles that sponsored parties intended to promote diverse sexual activities among its members. An undercover police officer, Sergeant Berk, visited one of those parties at a private residence. Amid a welter of sexual activity, he observed Mrs. Pettit commit three separate acts of oral copulation with three different men in a one hour period.

Pettit was arrested and charged with oral copulation. After a plea bargain was arranged, she pleaded guilty to the misdemeanor of outraging public decency and paid a fine. The school district renewed her teaching contract the next academic year, but in February 1970, disciplinary proceedings were initiated against her. The State Board of Education found no reason to complain about her services as a teacher, and it conceded that she was unlikely to repeat her sexual misconduct. But the Board revoked her elementary school life diploma—that is, her license to teach—on the ground that by engaging in immoral and unprofessional conduct at the party, she had demonstrated that she was unfit to teach.

Pettit fought the loss of her license all the way to the California Supreme Court, which in 1973 upheld the decision of the Board of

Education.[51] In an earlier case, the Court had reversed the firing of a public schoolteacher for unspecified homosexual conduct, concluding that a teacher's actions could not constitute "immoral or unprofessional conduct" or "moral turpitude" unless there was clear evidence of unfitness to teach. But Pettit's case was different, the Court hastened to explain.

The conduct in the earlier case had not been criminal, oral copulation had not been involved, and it had been private. Further, in that case the Board had acted with insufficient evidence of unfitness to teach, while three school administrators had testified that in their opinion Pettit's conduct proved her unfit to teach. These experts worried that she would inject her views of sexual morality into the classroom, and they doubted that she could act as a moral example to the children she taught. Yet teachers, the Court reaffirmed, are supposed to serve as exemplars, and the Education Code makes it a statutory duty of teachers to "endeavor to impress upon the minds of the pupils the principles of morality . . . and to instruct them in manners and morals."

In a vigorous dissent, Justice Tobringer rejected the opinion of the majority, arguing that no evidence had established that Pettit was not fit to teach. The three experts didn't consider her record; they couldn't point to any past misconduct with students, nor did they suggest any reason to anticipate future problems. They simply assumed that the fact of her sexual acts at the "swingers'" party itself demonstrated that she would be unable to set a proper example or to teach her pupils moral principles.

Such an attitude is unrealistic, Tobringer argued, when studies show that 75 to 80 percent of the women of Pettit's educational level and age range engage in oral copulation. The majority opinion, "is blind to the reality of sexual behavior" and unrealistically assumes that "teachers in their private lives should exemplify Victorian principles of sexual morality." Her actions were private and could not have affected her teaching ability. Had there not been clandestine surveillance of the party, the whole issue would never have arisen.

Discussion Questions

1. Was Mrs. Pettit's behavior "unprofessional"? Was it "immoral"? Did it show a "lack of fitness" to teach? Explain how you understand the terms in quotation marks.

2. Should the Board of Education have revoked Mrs. Pettit's teaching license? Explain.

3. Was the Court's verdict consistent with its earlier handling of the case of the homosexual teacher?

4. If teachers perform competently in the classroom, should they also be required to be positive "moral examples" in their private lives? Are other professionals expected to provide a moral example—both on and off the job?

5. Which of the following would, in your view, show unprofessional conduct, immorality, or lack of fitness to teach: drunken driving, smoking marijuana, advocating the use of marijuana, forging a check, assaulting a police officer and resisting arrest, being discovered in a compromising position with a student, propositioning a student, cheating on income tax, leading an openly homosexual life?

CASE 11.4
Midwifery

In the past, female midwives were the only attendants at birth. That began changing in the eighteenth century, and the change was further assisted in the nineteenth century by the American Medical Association's success in passing licensing laws that reserved to doctors the right to practice medicine. By the 1930s physicians had managed to convince women to rely only on them to deliver their babies. Midwife deliveries, which dropped from 50 percent in 1900 to 12 percent in 1936, were successfully stigmatized as being the choice only of those who were too poor or too ignorant to get a doctor.[52]

Midwifery is now making a comeback. Despite controversy and frequent objections from the medical profession, it is once again legal in most states. In Robert McHugh's state, however, while midwifery is not illegal, there is no state-recognized licensing or certification procedure for midwives. McHugh is the lay administrator who chairs the governing board of Mid-County Hospital. He must decide whether the hospital grants staff privileges to midwives.

No other hospital in the area grants this privilege, although McHugh knows that some respected hospitals in other states do. Several pregnant women, seeking a more natural, less technologically oriented and less male-dominated birth process, have recently requested that Mid-County allow their babies to be delivered by midwives. McHugh is skeptical. Although not a physician himself, he is committed to providing the highest possible quality of medical care and thinks that in the case of childbirth only physicians can guarantee that quality.

Kathleen Robbins's presentation to Mid-County's board on behalf of the local association of midwives puts a dent in McHugh's skepticism. She points to studies that show that a midwife-attended birth is as safe as one attended by a physician.[53] Robbins contends that in light of this, the hospital should respect the choice of those pregnant women who do not wish their babies delivered at home but who nevertheless want the experience of a midwife-attended birth. Robbins also alludes to the fact that in some states hospitals have been successfully sued for refusing to permit midwives to practice.

The three physicians on the board, two men and one woman, are unmoved by Robbins and remain adamantly opposed to midwives. They stress the lack of any state certification procedures as a major obstacle. Without that, how can the hospital maintain quality control? Robbins counters that the hospital itself can develop its own procedures for examining midwives prior to granting them hospital privileges, and she adds that there are already some physicians at the hospital who would be willing to work with midwives. The meeting ends inconclusively.

McHugh later talks with the hospital's attorney, who advises him that the legal situation is unclear. The legal victories of midwives in other states will probably have no precedent value in their state. McHugh's insurance broker, however, tells him that the hospital could have real difficulties with its insurance coverage if midwives begin practicing there. The hospital's existing policy will be terminated, and new coverage could be much more expensive.

As he drives home from the hospital that evening, McHugh is still undecided.

Discussion Questions

1. What do you think McHugh should decide? Explain your reasoning.

2. What principles, values, and interests are at stake?

3. Given that midwifery cuts into the business of doctors, do you think the three physicians on the board are capable of being completely objective?

4. If McHugh accepts Robbins's arguments about safety and freedom of choice, what weight should he put on the fact that the vast majority of the hospital's physicians are strongly opposed to midwives delivering babies? Without their cooperation and support, the hospital cannot run. How should McHugh balance the possible economic loss to the hospital as a result of a changing insurance picture?

4. Suppose that it were safer for women to have doctors deliver their babies. Could some women still reasonably prefer to have midwife delivery? Would it be wrong to obstruct their decision to do so by not allowing midwives to deliver babies in the hospital?

NOTES

1. Martha McMullen, "State Law Acknowledges 'Patient Dumping' a Crime," *Guardian* (New York), October 28, 1987, 9.

2. David Braybrooke, *Ethics in the World of Business* (Totowa, N.J.: Rowman and Allanheld, 1983), 445–446.

3. Peter F. Drucker, "The Rise and Fall of the Blue-Collar Worker," *The Wall Street Journal*, April 22, 1987.

4. Michael D. Bayles, *Professional Ethics* (Belmont, Calif.: Wadsworth, 1981), 4.

5. Ibid., 7–9. See also William B. Griffith, "Ethics and the Academic Professional: Some Open Problems and a New Approach," *Business and Professional Ethics Journal* 1 (Spring 1982): 78.

6. William W. Lowrance, "Of Acceptable Risk," in Tom L. Beauchamp and Norman E. Bowie, eds., *Ethical Theory and Business*, 2nd ed. (Englewood Cliffs, N.J.: Prentice-Hall, 1983), 194.

7. Ibid.

8. Griffith, "Ethics and the Academic Professional," 77.

9. See his essay "In Defense of Whistle Blowing," reprinted on page 337.

10. Richard T. DeGeorge, *Business Ethics*, 2nd ed. (New York: Macmillan, 1986), 336.

11. Quoted in Heinz C. Luegenbiehl, "Codes of Ethics and the Moral Education of Engineers," *Business and Professional Ethics Journal* 2 (Summer 1983): 41.

12. DeGeorge, *Business Ethics*, 343.

13. Heinz C. Luegenbiehl, "Codes of Ethics and the Moral Education of Engineers."

14. John Kultgen, "The Ideological Use of Professional Codes," *Business and Professional Ethics Journal* 1 (Spring 1982): 67.

15. DeGeorge, *Business Ethics*, 342–343.

16. Bayles, *Professional Ethics*, 141.

17. Bayles (*Professional Ethics*, 143) suggests the names of professionals be withheld until preliminary investigation determines that there is sufficient evidence to proceed to a hearing.

18. Ibid., 132.

19. Sissela Bok, *Lying: Moral Choice in Public and Private Life* (New York: Pantheon, 1978), 154.

20. Bayles, *Professional Ethics*, 130.

21. Ibid., 133–134.

22. See Kultgen, "The Ideological Use of Professional Codes," 66.

23. Bayles, *Professional Ethics*, 134.

24. Ibid., 138–139.

25. Ibid.

26. *Goldfarb v. Virginia State Bar*, 421 U.S. 733 (1975).

27. Bayles, *Professional Ethics*, 34.

28. Ibid., 41.

29. "Growing Pains for Shrinks," *Newsweek* (international edition), December 14, 1987.

30. DeGeorge, *Business Ethics*, 351; and Doug Bandon, "Doctors Operate to Cut Out Competition," *Business and Society Review* 58 (Spring 1986).

31. See the Chapter on "Occupational Licensure" in Milton Friedman, *Capitalism and Freedom* (Chicago: University of Chicago Press, 1962), in particular page 149.

32. Richard L. Abel, "The Transformation of the American Legal Profession," *Law & Society Review* 20, no. 1 (1986): 11.

33. TRB, "Doctors Overdose," *The New Republic*, July 7, 1986, 4.

34. Ibid.

35. Bernard Gert, "Licensing Professions: Preliminary Considerations," *Business and Professional Ethics Journal* 1 (Summer 1982): 52.

36. Donald Weinert, "Commentary," *Business and Professional Ethics Journal* 1 (Summer 1982): 62.

37. "Preying on AIDS Patients," *Newsweek*, June 1, 1987.

38. Bayles, *Professional Ethics*, 31.

39. Ibid., 32.

40. Ibid.

41. Albert Speer, *Inside the Third Reich* (New York: Macmillan, 1981).

42. Charles Fried, "The Lawyer as Friend: The Moral Foundations of the Lawyer-Client Relation," *Yale Law Journal* 85 (1976): 1060.

43. See Joseph S. Ellin, "Special Professional Morality and the Duty of Veracity," *Business and Professional Ethics Journal* 1 (Winter 1982): 83; and Bayles, *Professional Ethics*, 68–69.

44. See Bayles, *Professional Ethics*, 70–85.

45. Ibid., 83.

46. Bok, *Lying*, 152.

47. Ibid., 156.

48. Alan L. Otten, "More Psychotherapists Held Liable for the Actions of Violent Patients," *The Wall Street Journal*, March 2, 1987.

49. *Tarasoff v. Regents of the University of California et al.*,17 Cal. 3d 425, 131 Cal. Rptr. 14 (1976).

50. From Bayles, *Professional Ethics*, 51.

51. 10 C.3d 29; 109 Cal. Rptr. 665.

52. Gail A. Robinson, "Midwifery and Malpractice Insurance: A Profession Fights for Survival," *University of Pennsylvania Law Review* 134 (April 1986): 1005.

53. Ibid., 1013.

Engineers' Duty To Speak Out

Dave Lindorff

Author Dave Lindorff reviews several recent cases in which engineers have been aware of life-threatening problems but have not pushed hard enough to prevent them. He maintains that corporate and organizational culture inhibits the exercise of professional autonomy by engineers. Among other factors working against their asserting an independent and professional concern for the public interest, he cites the fact that few schools of engineering stress ethics and that the profession itself has not done enough to make safety a priority and to protect whistle blowers.

For eight years before the space shuttle Challenger's seventy-three-second flight, on January 28, [1986], engineers at the National Aeronautics and Space Administration and at Morton Thiokol knew that its huge solid-fuel booster rockets were badly designed. And the night before the fatal launch, when the temperature dropped below freezing at Cape Canaveral many of them feared the infamous O-rings would fail.

A number of those engineers voiced their concerns, sometimes vigorously, to their superiors in the corporate hierarchy and the NASA bureaucracy. They were ignored, and no one went to the press or to a member of Congress. No one tried to reach the astronauts themselves. Instead, high-level engineers at Thiokol reportedly donned their "management hats" and acted in what were considered the best interests of the firm, telling NASA what it wanted to hear. And low-level engineers "held their breath"—as they told colleagues—and went back to work.

Now a presidential commission investigating the explosion has released its report, concluding that "serious flaws" in NASA's decision-making process helped cause the disaster. The problems highlighted by the commission are hardly unique to NASA; rather, they reflect a deeper malaise in corporate America, where hushing up, and punishing, Cassandras is often the rule.

NASA's rush to launch in the face of engineering objections is, in the view of some, typical of American corporate behavior. Although NASA is a government agency, not a business, by trying to make the shuttle commercially viable, NASA subjected its operations to business considerations almost from the outset. Furthermore, the agency is essentially a coordinator of the work of a large number of private corporations, where most of the engineers and technicians in question are employed.

"If somebody saw something going on that was unsafe, they'd probably say something about it to their supervisor, but in this company, not many people would go outside with that information if their complaints were ignored." The speaker is not from Morton Thiokol. He's a chemical engineer at Union Carbide, the multinational chemical company notorious for its giant toxic gas leak in Bhopal, India. In light of the evidence that company officials were warned in advance about problems at the Bhopal facility and went ahead with operations until there was a disaster which killed some 2,000, his words are ominous.

"Most of the engineers at Union Carbide think of themselves as part of the company," he confides. "They refer to Union Carbide as Uncle Charlie, and they'd have a hard time going to the press about a problem. Besides, if you were identified, that would be the end of your career."

Such a view is all too common among the hands-on experts involved in most companies. "What happened to the shuttle is just like what happened a few years ago with the Ford Pinto," says Seymour Melman, an industrial engineer at Columbia University, referring to the car's propensity for blowing up when bumped from the rear by another vehicle. "You had plenty of engineers inside Ford warning executives that they had this problem with the gas tank, but even though correcting the problem would have cost only a few dollars a car, the company ignored the warnings and continued with the design."

As in the case of the shuttle, the engineers wrote memorandums to management. But when their pleas were ignored, they fell silent. As a result, about forty people died in explosions before Ford, facing lawsuits for millions of dollars in damages, moved to correct the problem. But even as it was recalling the Pintos to make alterations, Ford was producing Mustang IIs with the same generic flaw.

How can it be that people know about a life-threatening problem and let it pass? For corporate management the answer is easy. As testimony in the Ford Pinto product liability cases demonstrated, judgments are made by considering potential liability versus the cost of rectifying a problem. It's called a cost-benefit study, and if the potential cost in legal damages from not correcting a design flaw seems less than the cost of fixing it, no correction is made. The long list of such decisions, and the resulting disasters, have involved Ford transmissions that jump from park to reverse without

warning, Babcock & Wilcox nuclear reactors prone to catastrophic failure, DC-10 jets with too few backup hydraulic systems, drugs and pesticides that are carcinogenic or cause birth defects, and intrauterine devices that cause infections and sterility. But what about the engineers and production people who design and maintain today's technological products—people who are supposed to take a professional view of their work?

The shuttle explosion is "another example of the accelerating degradation of the status of the engineer in the American corporation," says Ralph Nader. "The profit motive is overriding engineering concerns at exactly the time when engineers' views are becoming crucially important. What happened [at NASA and Morton Thiokol] is instructive: not only were the engineers overruled by management; they were so afraid of retaliation that they didn't go outside the chain of command." They had good reason to be, too. Morton Thiokol's first reaction to the disaster was to punish Allan McDonald and Roger Boisjoly, the engineers who testified before the presidential commission, by reassigning them and reducing their responsibilities. In the glare of publicity, the company eventually transferred three executives responsible for approving the launch (a fourth retired) and reinstated the two men, putting McDonald in charge of the redesign of the booster.

The nuclear industry is probably even tougher on employees who complain about safety hazards, according to Louis Clark, executive director of the Government Accountability Project (GAP), a whistleblower support organization in Washington. "They fire anybody who goes outside the company, even to the N.R.C., which an engineer is required to do by law when nuclear safety issues are involved. And the N.R.C. itself always turns the names of whistleblowers over to the companies, which means they're finished. There is also an industry blacklist—we've proved it in some firing cases we've fought."

Although intimidation no doubt plays a big role in the problem, there may be a deeper explanation. Says Melman:

> The problem is that the engineers, at least here in the United States, don't organize independently. They have no kind of protection—even the engineering societies don't come to the aid of someone who protests. There's

even a name for those who do stand up: "whistleblower." Think about it. What does that imply: a lone guy making noise! Engineers, and people in production in general, willingly subordinate themselves to management, totally, and this is the kind of thing that happens. In the Soviet Union it's called democratic centralism—you argue and debate until the leadership reaches a decision, and then you shut up and go along. Here in the United States it's just called putting on your management cap. In the end, they're the same thing. The only difference is that here, after a disaster, you learn about it because we have a tradition of independent institutions, like the *The New York Times* or National Public Radio.

"The code of ethics of engineers says if you are overruled on a matter of safety by management you *shall* go to the proper authority," says Dan Pletta, professor emeritus at Virginia Polytechnic Institute and State University, an engineer who has spent much of his life trying to get professional engineering societies to act more forcefully in defense of whistleblowing members of the profession, and trying to raise the issue of ethics more generally among his colleagues. "But where is the 'proper authority'? They don't say. The problem is that, for the most part, when people raise complaints they get fired."

Pletta says several of the engineering societies have safety committees that are supposed to investigate members' complaints independently, but he says the systems aren't working. The reason? "People don't know they exist, for one thing. I did a survey and found that 59 percent of the members of the National Society of Professional Engineers [the organization that represents most engineers in corporate employment] didn't even know such a committee existed, and the society doesn't really want to support such activity or publicize it, for fear of liability suits, etc."

Certainly the attitude among future engineers, the students at major universities and technical institutes, doesn't bode well. Louis Guy, president-elect of the American Academy of Environmental Engineers, says that few departments of engineering even offer ethics courses, adding: "I was recently interviewing an applicant for membership in our academy, and I asked him at one point, in discussing his career, whether he considered himself a job holder or a professional. He just gave me this blank stare. The concept never occurred to him, and that's scary!"

The argument is echoed by Ralph Nader: "This should lead to a big debate in engineering circles, but it probably won't. There's no interest. Engineers see themselves as technicians, not professionals, for the most part."

After McDonald, the ranking engineer on the solid-fuel rocket project at Morton Thiokol, testified before the presidential commission, the reaction of several engineering students at the Polytechnic Institute of New York in Brooklyn was probably all too typical. "I hope he's looking for a job in academia. Nobody's going to hire him in industry now!" one student remarked, to a chorus of agreement from other engineering students riding to classes in an elevator with him.

The students' grim view of the corporate culture in which they hope eventually to work is not unwarranted. "There are lots of companies that say they have whistleblower programs," says Clark, at GAP's office in the Institute for Policy Studies. "Then it turns out that these just exist to isolate and identify the whistleblowers, and get rid of them."

The current merger trend in corporate America has further undermined the position of engineers. With each merger another complex industrial process comes under the management and control of a group of corporate executives who have little or no technical knowledge of what is being done. The top management at Morton Thiokol hails from Morton-Norwich Products, a specialty chemical firm best known for making Morton Salt, which gobbled up Thiokol in 1982. Says Guy:

> Mergers do present an added problem. You have the M.B.A. syndrome of making short-term profits, with blinders where consequences five years later are concerned. With takeovers, you can have the milking of a company for whatever you can get out of it becoming the end justification. And the business schools preach that management is an art, almost a mystique. Once you have it you can manage anything. So the M.B.A. doesn't need any engineering expertise to run a technical system.

Add to that what Guy says is a tendency among engineers who move into management to say, "I don't do engineering anymore," and you have the makings of a disaster.

Some states have responded to the problem by passing statutes protecting people who go public with information about safety hazards, but few have proved effective either in protecting jobs or in encouraging civic-minded behavior. Russell Mokhiber of the Center for the Study of Responsive Law thinks the answer is to encourage stiff prosecution of key individuals in companies when warnings are ignored. "If you personalize the crime, people will start holding management to the kind of moral standards the larger society has," he suggests, adding that perhaps the principle of limited liability which is the legal basis of corporations is fundamentally flawed. "The philosophy of limited liability has spread through the whole management hierarchy of the American corporation," he says, "and if you can't have a lawful or ethical corporation, maybe you shouldn't have corporations in the first place."

In the meantime, engineering societies and technical schools had better start pushing the idea of professional behavior and social responsibility on members and students. Few schools offer ethics courses; even at the Massachusetts Institute of Technology, the nation's premier school for engineers, there is no required course in ethics, although several are offered as electives. But courses alone may not be the answer; when they exist, they are sparsely attended. However, some students do question the prevailing corporate morality, as the annual student-organized alternative jobs fair at M.I.T. demonstrates.

On the professional side there have been some positive developments, as evidenced by the efforts of the Institute of Electrical and Electronics Engineers, a leading engineering society. Most recently it presented an award for outstanding public service to Richard Parks, a nuclear engineer who lost his job with the Bechtel Group for questioning the safety of some clean-up operations he was involved in at Three Mile Island.

But these are small steps. As technology advances, the consequences of managers ignoring engineering and production workers become increasingly awesome, as the shuttle explosion, the T.M.I. accident and the Chernobyl meltdown amply demonstrate. Society cannot afford to have those who can spot developing problems just "doing their job." Perhaps the best near-term solution is for engineers and other white-collar technical workers to follow the example of industrial colleagues in Europe and Australia and form trade unions, to give them some protection and independence from the whims of bosses who put private profits before the public's safety.

Review and Discussion Questions

1. Why do engineers in organizations sometimes remain silent about life-threatening problems?

2. Is Ralph Nader correct in maintaining that the professional status of corporate engineers has been degraded?

3. What steps can be taken to increase professional responsibility among engineers?

Lawyers' Ethics in an Adversary System

Monroe H. Freedman

In this selection from his book Lawyers' Ethics in an Adversary System, *Monroe H. Freedman, Professor of Law and Dean of the Hofstra University School of Law, examines the obligations of criminal defense lawyers in three difficult, morally troubling cases: whether to keep knowledge of a client's crime confidential, whether to allow a client to present perjured testimony, and whether to destroy a truthful witness through tough cross-examination. Freedman notes the conflicting obligations facing the conscientious attorney, but he defends zealous and aggressive advocacy in these cases as a necessary part of our adversarial criminal justice system.*

From Monroe H. Freedman, *Lawyers' Ethics in an Adversary System* (Indianapolis: Bobbs-Merrill Company, 1975). Reprinted by permission of the author. Professor Freedman has elaborated on his views in several articles, including "Personal Responsibility in a Professional System," 27 *Catholic Univ. Law Rev.* 191 (1978) [Pope John XXIII Lecture], and "Legal Ethics and the Suffering Client," 36 *Catholic Univ. Law Rev.* 331 (1987). His book, which is excerpted here, received the American Bar Association's Gavel Award Certificate of Merit in 1976.

Where the Bodies Are Buried: The Adversary System and the Obligation of Confidentiality

In a recent case in Lake Pleasant, New York, a defendant in a murder case told his lawyers about two other people he had killed and where their bodies had been hidden. The lawyers went there, observed the bodies, and took photographs of them. They did not, however, inform the authorities about the bodies until several months later, when their client had confessed to those crimes. In addition to withholding the information from police and prosecutors, one of the attorneys denied information to one of the victims' parents, who came to him in the course of seeking his missing daughter.

There were interesting reactions to that dramatic event. Members of the public were generally shocked at the apparent callousness on the part of the lawyers, whose conduct was considered typical of an unhealthy lack of concern by lawyers with the public interest and with simple decency. That attitude was encouraged by public statements by the local prosecutor, who sought to indict the lawyers for failing to reveal knowledge of a crime and for failing to see that dead bodies were properly buried. In addition, the reactions of lawyers and law professors who were questioned by the press were ambivalent and confused, indicating that few members of the legal profession had given serious thought to the fundamental questions of administration of justice and of professional responsibility that were raised by the case.

One can certainly understand the sense of moral compulsion to assist the parents and to give the dignity of proper burial to the victims. What seems to be less readily understood—but which, to my mind, throws the moral balance in the other direction—is the obligation of the lawyers to their client and, in a larger sense, to a system of administering justice which is itself essential to maintaining human dignity. In short, not only did the two lawyers behave properly, but they would have committed a serious breach of professional responsibility if they had divulged the information contrary to their client's interest. The explanation to that answer takes us to the very nature of our system of criminal justice and, indeed, to the fundamentals of our system of government. . . .

A trial is, in part, a search for truth. Accordingly, those basic rights are most often characterized as procedural safeguards against error in the search for truth. Actually, however, a trial is far more than a search for truth, and the constitutional rights that are provided by our system of justice may well outweigh the truth-seeking value—a fact which is manifest when we consider that those rights and others guaranteed by the Constitution may well impede the search for truth rather than further it. What more effective way is there, for example, to expose a defendant's guilt than to require self-incrimination, at least to the extent of compelling the defendant to take the stand and respond to interrogation before the jury? The defendant, however, is presumed innocent; the burden is on the prosecution to prove guilt beyond a reasonable doubt, and even the guilty accused has an "absolute constitutional right" to remain silent and to put the government to its proof.

Thus, the defense lawyer's professional obligation may well be to advise the client to withhold the truth. As Justice Jackson said: "Any lawyer worth his salt will tell the suspect in no uncertain terms to make no statement to police under any circumstances." Similarly, the defense lawyer is obligated to prevent the introduction of evidence that may be wholly reliable, such as a murder weapon seized in violation of the Fourth Amendment, or a truthful but involuntary confession. Justice White has observed that although law enforcement officials must be dedicated to using only truthful evidence, "defense counsel has no comparable obligation to ascertain or present the truth. Our system assigns him a different mission. . . . [W]e . . . insist that he defend his client whether he is innocent or guilty." . . .

Before we will permit the state to deprive any person of life, liberty, or property, we require that certain processes be duly followed which ensure regard for the dignity of the individual, irrespective of the impact of those processes upon the determination of truth.

By emphasizing that the adversary process has its foundations in respect for human dignity, even at the expense of the search for truth, I do not mean to deprecate the search for truth or to suggest that the adversary system is not concerned with it. On the contrary, truth is a basic value, and the adversary system is one of the most efficient and fair methods designed for determining it. That system proceeds on the assumption that the best way to ascertain the truth is to present to an impartial judge or jury a confrontation between the proponents of conflicting views, assigning to each the task of marshalling and presenting the evidence in as thorough and persuasive a way as possible. The truth-seeking techniques used by the advocates on each side include investigation, pretrial discovery, cross-examination of opposing witnesses, and a marshalling of the evidence in summation. Thus, the judge or jury is given the strongest possible view of each side, and is put in the best possible position to make an accurate and fair judgment. Nevertheless, the point that I now emphasize is that in a society that honors the dignity of the individual, the high value that we assign to truth-seeking is not an absolute, but may on occasion be subordinated to even higher values.

The concept of a right to counsel is one of the most significant manifestations of our regard for the dignity of the individual. No person is required to stand alone against the awesome power of the People of New York or the Government of the United States of America. Rather, every criminal defendant is guaranteed an advocate—a "champion" against a "hostile world," the "single voice on which he must rely with confidence that his interests will be protected to the fullest extent consistent with the rules of procedure and the standards of professional conduct." In addition, the attorney serves in significant part to assure equality before the law. Thus, the lawyer has been referred to as "the equalizer," who "places each litigant as nearly as possible on an equal footing under the substantive and procedural law under which he is tried."

The lawyer can serve effectively as advocate, however, "only if he knows all that his client knows" concerning the facts of the case. Nor is the client ordinarily competent to evaluate the relevance or significance of particular facts. What may seem incriminating to the client, may actually be exculpatory. For example, one client was reluctant to tell her lawyer that her husband had attacked her with a knife, because it tended to confirm that she had in fact shot him (contrary to what she had at first maintained). Having been persuaded by her attorney's insistence upon complete and candid disclosure, she finally "confessed all"—which permitted the lawyer to defend her properly and successfully on grounds of self-defense.

Obviously, however, the client cannot be expected to reveal to the lawyer all information that is potentially relevant, including that which may well be incriminating, unless the client can be assured that the lawyer will maintain all such information in the strictest confidence. "The purposes and necessities of the relation between a client and his attorney" require "the fullest and freest disclosures" of the client's "objects, motives and acts." If the attorney were permitted to reveal such disclosures, it would be "not only a gross violation of a sacred trust upon his part," but it would "utterly destroy and prevent the usefulness and benefits to be derived from professional assistance." That "sacred trust" of confidentiality must "upon all occasions be inviolable," or else the client could not feel free "to repose [confidence] in the attorney to whom he resorts for legal advise and assistance." Destroy that confidence, and "a man would not venture to consult any skillful person, or would only dare to tell his counselor half his case." The result would be impairment of the "perfect freedom of consultation by client with attorney," which is "essential to the administration of justice." Accordingly, the new Code of Professional Responsibility provides that a lawyer shall not knowingly reveal a confidence or secret of the client, nor use a confidence or secret to the disadvantage of the client, or to the advantage of a third person, without the client's consent. . . .

That is not to say, of course, that the attorney is privileged to go beyond the needs of confidentiality imposed by the adversary system, and actively participate in concealment of evidence or obstruction of justice. For example, in the *Ryder* case, which arose in Virginia several years ago, the attorney removed from his client's safe deposit box a sawed-off shotgun and the money from a bank robbery and put them, for greater safety, into the lawyers's own safe deposit box. The attorney, quite properly, was suspended from practice for 18 months. (The penalty might well have been heavier, except for the fact that Ryder sought advice from senior members of the bench and bar, and apparently acted more in ignorance than in venality.) The important difference between the *Ryder* case and the one in Lake Pleasant lies in the active role played by the attorney in *Ryder* to conceal evidence. There is no indication, for example, that the attorneys in Lake Pleasant attempted to hide the bodies more effectively. If they had done so, they would have gone beyond maintaining confidentiality and into active participation in the concealment of evidence.

The distinction should also be noted between the attorney's knowledge of a past crime (which is what we have been discussing so far) and knowledge of a crime to be committed in the future. Thus, a major exception to the strict rule of confidentiality is the "intention of his client to commit a crime, and information necessary to prevent the crime." Significantly, however, even in that exceptional circumstance, disclosure of the confidence is only permissible, not mandatory. Moreover, a footnote in the Code suggests that the exception is applicable only when the attorney knows "beyond a reasonable doubt" that a crime will be committed. There is little guidance as to how the lawyer is to exercise the discretion to report future crimes. At one extreme, it seems clear that the lawyer should reveal information necessary to save a life. On the other hand, as will be discussed [further], the lawyer should not reveal the intention of a client in a criminal case to commit perjury in his or her own defense.

It has been suggested that the information regarding the two bodies in the Lake Pleasant case was not relevant to the crime for which the defendant was being prosecuted, and that, therefore, that knowledge was outside the scope of confidentiality. That point lacks merit for three reasons. First, an unsophisticated lay person should not be required to anticipate which disclosures might fall outside the scope of confidentiality because of insufficient legal relevance. Second, the information in question might well have been highly relevant to the defense of insanity. Third, a lawyer has an obligation to merge other, unrelated crimes into the bargained plea, if it is possible to do so. Accordingly, the information about the other murders was clearly within the protection of confidentiality.

The suggestion has also been made . . . that the attorneys in Lake Pleasant were not bound by confidentiality once they had undertaken to corroborate the client's information through their own investigation. It is the duty of the lawyer, however, to conduct a thorough investigation of all aspects of the case, and that duty "exists regardless of the

accused's admissions or statements to the lawyer of facts constituting guilt. . . ." For example, upon investigation, the attorneys in the Lake Pleasant case might have discovered that the client's belief that he had killed other people was false, which would have had important bearing on an insanity defense.[1]

In summary, the Constitution has committed us to an adversary system for the administration of criminal justice. The essentially humanitarian reason for such a system is that it preserves the dignity of the individual, even though that may occasionally require significant frustration of the search for truth and the will of the state. An essential element of that system is the right to counsel, a right that would be meaningless if the defendant were not able to communicate freely and fully with the attorney.

In order to protect the communication—and, ultimately, the adversary system itself—we impose upon attorneys what has been called the "sacred trust" of confidentiality. It was pursuant to that high trust that the lawyers acted in Lake Pleasant, New York, when they refrained from divulging their knowledge of where the bodies were buried. . . .

Perjury: The Criminal Defense Lawyer's Trilemma

Is it ever proper for a criminal defense lawyer to present perjured testimony? . . . That question cannot be answered properly without an appreciation of the fact that the attorney functions in an adversary system of criminal justice which . . . imposes special responsibilities upon the advocate.

First, the lawyer is required to determine "all relevant facts known to the accused," because "counsel cannot properly perform their duties without knowing the truth." The lawyer who is ignorant of any potentially relevant fact "incapacitates himself to serve his client effectively," because "an adequate defense cannot be framed if the lawyer does not know what is likely to develop at trial."[2]

Second, the lawyer must hold in strictest confidence the disclosures made by the client in the course of the professional relationship. "Nothing is more fundamental to the lawyer-client relationship than the establishment of trust and confidence." The "first duty" of an attorney is "to keep the secrets of his clients." If this were not so, the client would not feel free to confide fully, and the lawyer would not be able to fulfill the obligation to ascertain all relevant facts. Accordingly, defense counsel is required to establish "a relationship of trust and confidence" with the accused, to explain "the necessity of full disclosure of all facts," and to explain to the client "the obligation of confidentiality which makes privileged the accused's disclosures."

Third, the lawyer is an officer of the court, and his or her conduct before the court "should be characterized by candor."

As soon as one begins to think about those responsibilities, it becomes apparent that the conscientious attorney is faced with what we may call a trilemma—that is, the lawyer is required to know everything, to keep it in confidence, and to reveal it to the court. Moreover, the difficulties presented by those conflicting obligations are particularly acute in the criminal defense area because of the presumption of innocence, the burden upon the state to prove its case beyond a reasonable doubt, and the right to put the prosecution to its proof.

Before addressing the issue of the criminal defense lawyer's responsibilities when the client indicates to the lawyer the intention to commit perjury in the future, we might note the somewhat less difficult question of what the lawyer should do when knowledge of the perjury comes after its commission rather than before it. Although there is some ambiguity in the most recent authorities, the rules appear to require that the criminal defense lawyer should urge the client to correct the perjury, but beyond that, the obligation of confidentiality precludes the lawyer from revealing the truth. . . .

If we recognize that professional responsibility requires that an advocate have full knowledge of every pertinent fact, then the lawyer must seek the truth from the client, not shun it. That means that the attorney will have to dig and pry and cajole, and, even then, the lawyer will not be successful without convincing the client that full disclosure to the lawyer will never result in prejudice to the client by any word or action of the attorney. That is particularly true in the case of the indigent defendant, who meets the lawyer for the first time in the cell block or the rotunda of the jail. The client did not choose the lawyer, who comes as a stranger sent by the judge, and who therefore appears to be

part of the system that is attempting to punish the defendant. It is no easy task to persuade that client to talk freely without fear of harm. . . .

Assume the following situation. Your client has been falsely accused of a robbery committed at 16th and P Streets at 11:00 P.M. He tells you at first that at no time on the evening of the crime was he within six blocks of that location. However, you are able to persuade him that he must tell you the truth and that doing so will in no way prejudice him. He then reveals to you that he was at 15th and P Streets at 10:55 that evening, but that he was walking east, away from the scene of the crime, and that, by 11:00 P.M., he was six blocks away. At the trial, there are two prosecution witnesses. The first mistakenly, but with some degree of persuasiveness, identifies your client as the criminal. At that point the prosecution's case depends upon that single witness, who might or might not be believed. The second prosecution witness is an elderly woman who is somewhat nervous and who wears glasses. She testifies truthfully and accurately that she saw your client at 15th and P Streets at 10:55 P.M. She has corroborated the erroneous testimony of the first witness and made conviction extremely likely. However, on cross-examination her reliability is thrown into doubt through demonstration that she is easily confused and has poor eyesight. Thus, the corroboration has been eliminated, and doubt has been established in the minds of the jurors as to the prosecution's entire case.

The client then insists upon taking the stand in his own defense, not only to deny the erroneous evidence identifying him as the criminal, but also to deny the truthful, but highly damaging, testimony of the corroborating witness who placed him one block away from the intersection five minutes prior to the crime. Of course, if he tells the truth and thus verifies the corroborating witness, the jury will be more inclined to accept the inaccurate testimony of the principal witness, who specifically identified him as the criminal.

In my opinion, the attorney's obligation in such a situation would be to advise the client that the proposed testimony is unlawful, but to proceed in the normal fashion in presenting the testimony and arguing the case to the jury if the client makes the decision to go forward. Any other course would be a betrayal of the assurances of confidentiality given by the attorney in order to induce the client to reveal everything, however damaging it might appear. . . .

For example, how would [one] resolve the following case? The prosecution witness testified that the robbery had taken place at 10:15, and identified the defendant as the criminal. However, the defendant had a convincing alibi for 10:00 to 10:30. The attorney presented the alibi, and the client was acquitted. The alibi was truthful, but the attorney knew that the prosecution witness had been confused about the time, and that his client had in fact committed the crime at 10:45. (Ironically, that same attorney considers it clearly unethical for a lawyer to present the false testimony on behalf of the innocent defendant in the case of the robbery at 16th and P Streets.) Should the lawyer have refused to present the honest alibi? How could he possibly have avoided doing so? Was he contributing to wise and informed judgment when he did present it?

The most obvious way to avoid the ethical difficulty is for the lawyer to withdraw from the case, at least if there is sufficient time before trial for the client to retain another attorney. The client will then go to the nearest law office, realizing that the obligation of confidentiality is not what it has been represented to be, and withhold incriminating information or the fact of guilt from the new attorney. In terms of professional ethics, the practice of withdrawing from a case under such circumstances is difficult to defend, since the identical perjured testimony will ultimately be presented. Moveover, the new attorney will be ignorant of the perjury and therefore will be in no position to attempt to discourage the client from presenting it. Only the original attorney, who knows the truth, has that opportunity, but loses it in the very act of evading the ethical problem.

The difficulty is all the more severe when the client is indigent. In that event, the client cannot retain other counsel, and in many jurisdictions it is impossible for appointed counsel or a public defender to withdraw from a case except for extraordinary reasons. Thus, the attorney can successfully withdraw only by revealing to the judge that the attorney has received knowledge of the client's guilt, or by giving the judge a false or misleading reason for moving for leave to withdraw. However, for the attorney to reveal knowledge of the client's guilt would be a gross violation of the obligation of

confidentiality, particularly since it is entirely possible in many jurisdictions that the same judge who permits the attorney to withdraw will subsequently hear the case and sentence the defendant. Not only will the judge then have personal knowledge of the defendant's guilt before the trial begins, but it will be knowledge of which the newly appointed counsel for the defendant will very likely be ignorant.

Even where counsel is retained, withdrawal may not be a practical solution either because trial has begun or it is so close to trial that withdrawal would leave the client without counsel, or because the court for other reasons denies leave to withdraw. Judges are most reluctant to grant leave to withdraw during the trial or even shortly before it because of the power that that would give to defendants to delay the trial date or even to cause a series of mistrials. . . .

Another unsuccessful effort to deal with the problem appears in the ABA Standards Relating to the Defense Function. The Standards first attempt to solve the problem by a rhetorical attack, unsupported by practical analysis or verifiable research, upon those who are concerned with maintaining confidentiality. Thus, the Standards state that it has been "universally rejected by the legal profession" that a lawyer may be excused for acquiescing in the use of known perjured testimony on the "transparently spurious thesis" that the principle of confidentiality requires it. While "no honorable lawyer" would accept that view and "every experienced advocate can see its basic fallacy as a matter of tactics apart from morality and law," the "mere advocacy" of such an idea "demeans the profession and tends to drag it to the level of gangsters and their 'mouthpiece' lawyers in the public eye." The Standards conclude that that concept is "universally repudiated by ethical lawyers," although that fact does not fully repair the "gross disservice" done by the few who are "unscrupulous" enough to practice it.

One hundred thirty-two pages later, however, the Standards express a very different assessment of lawyers' attitudes regarding perjury by the client. Although "some lawyers" are said to favor disclosure of the perjury, the Standards recognize that other attorneys (not characterized in the pejorative terms of the earlier passage) hold that the obligation of confidentiality does not permit disclosure of the facts learned from the client. To disclose the perjury, it is noted, "would be inconsistent with the assurances of confidentiality which counsel gave at the outset of the lawyer-client relationship." Thus, the Standards acknowledge a genuine "dilemma" in the forced choice between candor and confidentiality.

Since there are actually three obligations that create the difficulty—the third being the attorney's duty to learn all the facts—there is, of course, another way to resolve the difficulty. That is, by "selective ignorance." The attorney can make it clear to the client from the outset that the attorney does not want to hear an admission of guilt or incriminating information from the client. That view, however, puts an unreasonable burden on the unsophisticated client to select what to tell and what to hold back, and it can seriously impair the attorney's effectiveness in counselling the client and in trying the case.

For example, one leading attorney, who favors selective ignorance to avoid the trilemma, told me about one of his own cases in which the defendant assumed that the attorney would prefer to be ignorant of the fact that the defendant had been having sexual relations with the chief defense witness. As a result of the lawyer's ignorance of that fact, he was unable to minimize its impact by raising it with potential jurors during jury selection and by having the defendant and the defense witness admit it freely on direct examination. Instead, the first time the lawyer learned about the illicit sexual relationship was when the prosecutor dramatically obtained a reluctant admission from the defense witness on cross-examination. The defense attorney is convinced that the client was innocent of the robbery with which he had been charged, but the defendant was nevertheless found guilty by the jury—in the attorney's own opinion because the defendant was guilty of fornication, a far less serious offense for which he had not been charged.

The question remains: what should the lawyer do when faced with the client's insistence upon taking the stand and committing perjury? It is in response to that question that the Standards present a most extraordinary solution. If the lawyer knows that the client is going to commit perjury, Section 7.7 of the Standards requires that the lawyer "must confine his examination to identifying the witness as the defendant and permitting him to make his statement." That is, the lawyer "may not engage in direct examination of the defendant . . . in the conventional manner." Thus, the client's story will become part of the record, although without the attorney's assistance through direct examination. The general rule, of course, is that in closing argument to the jury "the lawyer may argue all reasonable inferences from the evidence in the record." Section 7.7 also provides, however, that the defense lawyer is forbidden to make any reference in closing argument to the client's testimony.

There are at least two critical flaws in that proposal. The first is purely practical: The prosecutor might well object to testimony from the defendant in narrative form rather than in the conventional manner, because it would give the prosecutor no opportunity to object to inadmissible evidence prior to the jury's hearing it. The Standards provide no guidance as to what the defense attorney should do if the objection is sustained.

More importantly, experienced trial attorneys have often noted that jurors assume that the defendant's lawyer knows the truth about the case, and that the jury will frequently judge the defendant by drawing inferences from the attorney's conduct in the case. There is, of course, only one inference that can be drawn if the defendant's own attorney turns his or her back on the defendant at the most critical point in the trial, and then, in closing argument, sums up the case with no reference to the fact that the defendant has given exculpatory testimony. . . .

It would appear that the ABA Standards have chosen to resolve the trilemma by maintaining the requirements of complete knowledge and of candor to the court, and sacrificing confidentiality. Interestingly, however, that may not in fact be the case. I say that because the Standards fail to answer a critically important question: Should the client be told about the obligation imposed by Section 7.7? That is, the Standards ignore the issue of whether the lawyer should say to the client at the outset of their relationship: "I think it's only fair that I warn you: If you should tell me anything incriminating and subsequently decide to deny the incriminating facts at trial, I would not be able to examine you in the ordinary manner or to argue your untrue testimony to the jury." The Canadian Bar Association, for example, takes an extremely hard line against the presentation of perjury by the client, but it also explicitly requires that the client be put on notice of that fact. Obviously, any other course would be a betrayal of the client's trust, since everything else said by the attorney in attempting to obtain complete information about the case would indicate to the client that no information thus obtained would be used to the client's disadvantage.

On the other hand, the inevitable result of the position taken by the Canadian Bar Association would be to caution the client not to be completely candid with the attorney. That, of course, returns us to resolving the trilemma by maintaining confidentiality and candor, but sacrificing complete knowledge—a solution which, as we have already seen, is denounced by the Standards as "unscrupulous," "most egregious," and "professional impropriety."

Thus, the Standards, by failing to face up to the question of whether to put the client on notice, take us out of the trilemma by one door only to lead us back by another. . . .

Taking into account, therefore, the lack of practical guidance in the Code, the practical and constitutional difficulties encountered by any of the alternatives to strict maintenance of confidentiality, the consensus and the practice of the Bar, and the implications of *Carroll*, *Hinds* and *Johns*, which are the three key cases cited in the notes to Canon 7, I continue to stand with those lawyers who hold that "the lawyer's obligation of confidentiality does not permit him to disclose the facts he has learned from his client which form the basis for his conclusion that the client intends to perjure himself." What that means—necessarily, it seems to me—is that the criminal defense attorney, however unwillingly in terms of personal morality, has a professional responsibility as an advocate in an adversary system to examine the perjurious client in the ordinary way and to argue to the jury, as evidence in the case, the testimony presented by the defendant. . . .

Cross-Examination: Destroying the Truthful Witness

More difficult than the question of whether the criminal defense lawyer should present known perjury, is the question of whether the attorney should cross-examine a witness who is testifying accurately and truthfully, in order to make the witness appear to be mistaken or lying. The issue was raised effectively in a symposium on legal ethics through the following hypothetical case.

The accused is a drifter who sometimes works as a filling station attendant. He is charged with rape, a capital crime. You are his court-appointed defense counsel. The alleged victim is the twenty-two-year-old daughter of a local bank president. She is engaged to a promising young minister in town. The alleged rape occurred in the early morning hours at a service station some distance from town, where the accused was employed as an attendant. That is all you know about the case when you have your first interview with your client.

At first the accused will not talk at all. You assure him that you cannot help him unless you know the truth and that he can trust you to treat what he says as confidential. He then says that he had intercourse with the young woman, but that she "consented in every way." He says that he had seen her two or three times before when he was working the day shift at the station, and that she had seemed "very friendly" and had talked with him in a "flirting way." He says that on the night in question she came in for gas; they talked; and she invited him into the car. One thing led to another and, finally, to sexual intercourse. They were interrupted by the lights of an approaching vehicle which pulled into the station. The accused relates that he got out of the young woman's car and waited on the customer. The young woman hurriedly drove off.

The accused tells you he was tried for rape in California four years ago and acquitted. He has no previous convictions.

At the grand jury proceedings the victim testifies that she was returning to her father's house in town from the church camp, where her fiancé was a counselor, when she noticed that her fuel gauge registered empty. She stopped at the first station along the road that was open. The attendant, who seemed to be in sole charge of the station, forced his way into her car, terrified her with threats, and forcibly had sexual intercourse with her. She says he was compelled to stop when an approaching car turned into the station. The alleged victim's father testified as to her timely complaint. No other testimony is presented. The grand jury returns a true bill.

You learn that the victim has had affairs with two local men from good families. Smith, one of these young men, admits that the victim and he went together for some time, but refuses to say whether he had sexual intercourse with her and indicates he has a low opinion of you for asking. The other, Jones, apparently a bitterly disappointed and jealous suitor, readily states that he frequently had intercourse with the victim, and describes her behavior toward strange men as scandalous. He once took her to a fraternity dance, he says, and, having noticed she had been gone for some time, discovered her upstairs with Smith, a fraternity brother, on a bed in a state of semi-undress. He appears eager to testify and he states that the girl got what she'd always been asking for. You believe Jones, but are somewhat repelled by the disappointed suitor's apparent willingness to smear the young woman's reputation.

Suppose the accused, after you press him, admits that he forced himself on the victim and admits that his first story was a lie. He refuses to plead guilty to the charge or any lesser charge. He says that he can get away with his story, because he did once before in California.

Should the defense lawyer use the information supplied by Jones to impeach the young woman and, if necessary, call Jones as a witness? . . .

That case takes us to the heart of my disagreement with the traditional approach to dealing with difficult questions of professional responsibility. That approach has two characteristics. First, in a rhetorical flourish, the profession is committed in general terms to all that is good and true. Then, specific questions are answered by uncritical reliance upon legalistic norms, regardless of the context in which the lawyer may be acting, and regardless of the motive and the consequences of the act. Perjury is wrong, and therefore no lawyer, in any circumstance, should knowingly present perjury. Cross-examination, however, is good, and therefore any lawyer, under any circumstances and regardless of the consequences, can properly impeach a witness through cross-examination. The system of professional responsibility that I have been advancing, on the other hand, is one that attempts to deal with ethical problems in context— that is, as part of a functional sociopolitical system concerned with the administration of justice in a free society—and giving due regard both to motive and to consequences. In that respect, the debate returns us to some fundamental philosophical questions that have not been adequately developed in the literature of professional responsibility. . . .

One of the major flaws in the traditional approach to legal ethics is that it seeks to answer the difficult questions in a legalistic fashion at the personal level, but begs completely the critical questions raised at the systemic level. Thus, if you say to a lawyer: "Lawyers are under a moral duty not to participate in the presentation of perjury, and therefore you are required to act in a way contrary to your client's interest if the client insists upon committing perjury," the lawyer is entitled to respond: "Let us consider your maxim. If it is embodied into the system as a universal law to be applied to all lawyers in all circumstances, would the maxim destroy itself and be destructive of the system?"

As we have seen [previously], the system requires the attorney to know everything that the client knows that is relevant to the case. In order to enable the lawyer to obtain that information, the system provides for an obligation of confidentiality, designed to protect the client from being prejudiced by disclosures to the attorney. In addition, the attorney is required to impress upon the client the obligation of confidentiality in order to induce the client to confide freely and fully.

Let us return, then, to the case involving the street robbery at 16th and P Streets, in which the defendant has been wrongly identified as the criminal, but correctly identified by the nervous, elderly woman who wears eyeglasses, as having been only a block away five minutes before the crime took place. If the woman is not cross-examined vigorously and her testimony shaken, it will serve to corroborate the erroneous evidence of guilt. On the other hand, the lawyer could take the position that since the woman is testifying truthfully and accurately, she should not be made to appear to be mistaken or lying. But if a similar course were to be adopted by every lawyer who learned the truth through confidential disclosures from the client, such disclosures would soon cease to be made. The result, for practical purposes, would be identical with the practice, disapproved in the ABA Standards, of "selective ignorance," in which the client is warned not to reveal to the lawyer anything that might prove embarrassing and prevent the lawyer from doing a vigorous job of presenting evidence and cross-examining. Of course, if that is the result we want, it would be far better that lawyers take a direct and honest approach with their clients, telling them to be less than candid, rather than lying to their clients by impressing upon them a bond of trust that the lawyers do not intend to maintain. Thus, when we examine the problem in a systemic context, we reach the conclusion that Chief Justice Burger was correct, although for the wrong reason, in supporting cross-examination of the prosecutrix in the rape case.

Obviously, however, the rape case is a much harder one, because the injury done to the prosecutrix is far more severe than the more limited humiliation of the public-spirited and truthful witness in the case of the street robbery. In addition, in the rape case, the lawyer is acting pursuant to a manifestly irrational rule, that is, one that permits the defense to argue that the prosecutrix is the kind of person who would have sexual intercourse with a stranger because she has had sexual relations with two men whom she knew in wholly different social circumstances. Irrational or not, however, in those jurisdictions in which the defense of unchastity is still the law, the attorney is bound to provide it on the client's behalf. For the lawyer who finds the presentation of that defense, and perhaps others in rape cases, to go beyond what he or she can in good conscience do, there are two courses that should be followed. The first is to be active in efforts to reform the law in that regard; the second is to decline to accept the defense of rape cases, on the grounds of a conflict of interest (a strong personal view) that would interfere with providing the defendant with his constitutional rights to effective assistance of counsel.

Notes

1. The suggestion has also been made that the attorneys might have revealed the information through an anonymous telephone call. I do not believe that the proposal merits serious discussion—that a breach of the client's trust can be legitimated by carrying out the breach in a surreptitious manner.
2. *American Bar Association Canons of Professional Ethics,* 15.

Review and Discussion Questions

1. Explain how Freedman appeals to our adversary system in order to defend confidentiality. What are the limits to what an attorney may do to assist a client?
2. What does Freedman mean by the "lawyer's trilemma"?
3. Should an attorney allow a client to present perjured testimony to the court? Is the Canadian Bar Association's rule an improvement over the system that Freedman defends?
4. How would you handle the cross-examination of the truthful witness?
5. Does Freedman's defense of the adversary system tip the balance too much in the favor of criminal defendants?

Investigative Journalism

Sissela Bok

In this chapter from her book Secrets, *Professor Sissela Bok explores some of the ethical dilemmas facing the journalism profession. The press and other media, she argues, have a clear public mandate to probe and to expose secrets, but there are moral limits on what they can probe and on their means of doing so. Information of legitimate importance to the public must be distinguished from reporting that only caters to public curiosity. Here greater respect for privacy is demanded. Bok also argues that only under very limited circumstances are reporters justified in the use of disguise or deception.*

Exposing Private Lives

In 1937 James Thurber unwittingly set in motion what he later described as the most important legal case in the history of the *New Yorker* magazine and its only conflict ever to reach the Supreme Court.[1] Using the pseudonym Jared L. Manley, he published an essay entitled "April Fool!" about a man once famous as a child prodigy who now shunned every mention of his former feats.[2] The essay brought out the contrast between the brilliant but exploited childhood of William James Sidis and what seemed an undistinguished, indeed shabby and ludicrous, later life.

Almost from birth, the boy was subjected to training sessions, hypnosis, and psychological experimentation by his father, Boris Sidis, a psychologist bent on producing a genius. William learned to read and write both English and French in his earliest years. At five, he had written a treatise on anatomy, and at eight he proposed a new table of logarithms. Boris Sidis reported on each new feat to the press. He wrote a book entitled *Philistine and Genius* to promote his methods of education.[3] Conventional education, he insisted, turns children into uncritical philistines and willing cannon fodder. By stimulating early development, on the other hand, one will "not only prevent vice, crime, and disease, but will strengthen the individual along all lines, physical, mental, and moral." He claimed to be able to speak with authority, "from my own experience with child-life."

When William was nine, his parents began taking him to nearby Tufts College. At eleven, having transferred to Harvard, the boy gave a stunning lecture before students and faculty on "four-dimensional bodies." The national press gave front-page coverage to this event, and editorialists gave favorable notice to the educational theories of Boris Sidis.[4] But in the ensuing years, William refused to cater to his father's hopes. Although he completed his college studies, he rejected the future his father had mapped out for him. Finding publicity offensive and mathematical work increasingly distasteful, William turned down all further requests that he display his powers in public. He left graduate school without a degree.

After a brief stint at college teaching, he abandoned academic life for good, severed relations with his family, and took up one menial job after another, only to leave it each time someone discovered he was the same William Sidis who had been so famous as a child prodigy. His childhood feats could not be kept secret or wiped out. They were

public knowledge. But his *connection* to those feats—this he could try to conceal.

The *New Yorker* article cornered him. Drawing on the account of an unnamed woman who "recently succeeded in interviewing him," its author exposed Sidis at age thirty-nine, living alone in an untidy "hall bedroom of Boston's shabby south end." After recounting once again Sidis's childhood exploits, the article focused with ruthless detail on his quest for anonymity and his incongruous present behavior. "He seems to have difficulty in finding the right words to express himself," the author noted, "but when he does, he speaks rapidly, nodding his head jerkily to emphasize his points, gesturing with his left hand, uttering occasionally a curious, gasping laugh."[5]

Writing the piece may have had its pleasures of accurate depiction and condescending humor. Reading it may have served for many as a reminder of the downfall of the famous and as a warning against pressing children too far. But for Sidis himself, the article came as a blow where he was most vulnerable. His fragile defenses were penetrated. Not only did the essay shine a hated spotlight once more on the life he wanted to live in obscurity; it also held him up, he felt, to ridicule and shame. His response was to sue for invasion of privacy, claiming that the article "tended to expose, and did expose, the private life of the plaintiff to unwarranted and undesired publicity of a nature unfamiliar and harmful to the plaintiff, and tended to and did hold up the plaintiff to public scorn, ridicule, and contempt causing him grievous mental anguish, humiliation, and loss of reputation."[6]

After the case had gone to court, Thurber explained that he had wanted to "help curb the great American thrusting of talented children into the glare of fame and notoriety" by showing how these children suffer in later life.[7] This aim is not evident in the essay itself, the less so as its author did more than anyone else to renew the glare of notoriety for Sidis. What comes across, rather, is a distant and amused contempt for those judged to be doing less than they might, and living boring lives in one-room apartments.

Sidis lost his suit and lost again on appeal. Judge Clark, though characterizing the *New Yorker* article as "merciless," held that it did not constitute punishable invasion of privacy.[8] In the first place, much of what the article had revealed about Sidis's childhood was already public knowledge. People have no legal claim to erase their childhood fame, nor to remain unconnected with it in later life. In addition, courts have held that, once a public figure, one has fewer lawful claims to privacy than other persons. The health of public officials, for example, or their children's peccadilloes cannot legally be kept out of the press in the same way that such information about private individuals might be.

When the Supreme Court refused to hear the case, Sidis had no further recourse. The courts may well have been right to rule as they did. To have acceded to Sidis's claims could have endangered much reporting about matters of public importance; every shady venture could then try to hide behind similar claims to invasion of privacy.

Nevertheless, Sidis felt violated—and *was* violated. What for many might have seemed a tolerable exposure touched, for him, on aspects of his identity that he ached to veil in secrecy. Wishing above all to be forgotten, he was condemned to being remembered.[9] Much abused as a child, he had developed an exaggerated sense of vulnerability; he now had higher but also more fragile defenses than most. When they were broken down, he felt more injured than most. In 1944, Sidis—unemployed and destitute—was found unconscious in his apartment and died without regaining consciousness.[10]

Though unusually hurt by his exposure, Sidis is far from alone in being drawn into publicity against his wishes. Yet it would be wrong to conclude that journalists ought to write only about persons who have given their consent. As I have indicated in earlier chapters, those who use secrecy to cover up for abuses often resort to spurious claims of privacy, confidentiality, or national security. It is important for reporters not to take those claims at face value.

There is no clear line surrounding private life that can demarcate regions journalists ought not to explore. The serious illness of a political candidate or the paranoia of a government leader are surely matters for legitimate public concern. Health professionals should not conceal them, much less lie about them as has so often been done, nor should reporters help keep the public in the dark through misguided discretion. Such concealment helped disguise from the public the mental deterioration

suffered by Winston Churchill in his last years, and Hubert Humphrey's worsening cancer at the time when he announced he would campaign to be the Democratic candidate in the 1976 presidential election.

Those who take public positions cannot always complain if they receive scrutiny of a kind that would be intrusive for completely private citizens. Thus a reporter who wrote a story proving that a prominent member of the American Nazi Party was half Jewish was not overstepping the bounds of legitimate privacy. True, the information was of a kind that the Nazi wanted kept secret; but having taken a strong public stance of anti-Semitism, he could hardly hold the information irrelevant to the public's evaluation of his views. Nor did his death, in what seemed to be suicide, the day after the story appeared render it more invasive.[11]

The children of those who have sought public attention, on the other hand, often have a stronger claim to be left in peace. Some are pursued relentlessly, the victims of a system of probing and reporting that draws few lines with respect to the invasion of privacy.[12] The Sidis case is marginal from this point of view. On the one hand it was Sidis, and not only his parents, who had been in the public eye. On the other hand, Sidis might have argued that he could not, as a child, have put up sufficient resistance to his father's efforts to publicize his precocity, nor even have known how they would affect him. Should he have to acquiesce in continued scrutiny because his parents had sought to make him famous? The judge in the Sidis case thought so. He held that public interest in Sidis was legitimate because of his earlier brilliance and fame.

The public doubtless had an interest in Sidis; and its interest was legitimate, not only in the sense of attaching to someone already in the public eye but also more generally. It is not wrong to be interested in another person's life, no matter whether that person is famous or not. However, the public's interest in Sidis was not based on any *need* to know what had befallen him—unlike, for instance, the need to know the whereabouts and employment record of someone running for political office. This difference in need engenders a difference in the degree to which reporters should respect requests for anonymity and privacy.

Though readers might well have had a legitimate interest, based on curiosity, to know more about Sidis, they could hardly claim a right to acquire such knowledge against his wishes.

The confusing expression "the public's right to know" is often used to justify all that reporters do to cater to both need and interest on the part of the public, of whatever degree of legitimacy. Thus the 1973 Code of Ethics for journalists holds that "the public's right to know of events of public importance and interest is the overriding mission of the mass media," and states that "journalists must be free of obligations to any interest other than the public's right to know."[13]

To question what is done to satisfy such an all-inclusive right to know is to risk being accused of making dangerous inroads on the constitutionally guaranteed freedom of the press. We see here once again a rationale serving the double function of offering reasons and of warding off legitimate criticism. Yet questioning is surely needed.

The Public's Right to Know

. . . Some argue that the First Amendment presupposes the existence of the public's right to know. Were there no such right, they hold, there would be no need for the amendment. This view, however, merely states a conclusion without arguing for it. No evidence is offered for the link; and it is not clear why, even in the absence of an underlying right to know, the freedom of speech and of the press would not be thought indispensable. Others argue that the link is so close that it is one of mirroring: We cannot have freedom of the press without having it reflected in a public right to knowledge. Since we recognize the former, we must recognize the latter as well. Each presupposes the other, and justifies it in turn. Thus Laurence Tribe has held that at times the right to know "means nothing more than a mirror of such a right to speak, a listener's right that government not interfere with a willing speaker's liberty."[14]

Ronald Dworkin has argued, on the contrary, that the right to speak does not entail or mirror the right to know; at most, he holds, it may support a right to *listen*, and thus not to have the government interpose obstacles to that right between willing speakers and willing listeners. But such a right to listen is "very different from the right to know, because the latter, unlike the former, supposes that those who have the information have a duty not simply a right to publish it. The Supreme Court has not recognized a right to know as a constitutional right. No one could sue the *New York Times* for *not* publishing the Pentagon Papers."[15]

Dworkin's distinction is persuasive. We cannot legitimately argue from someone's right to disseminate a story to the public's right to the information it contains, much less to any obligation to disseminate it. The entailment by the First Amendment of the public's right to know, therefore, is not tenable, and cannot provide the justification for all that is done in the name of catering to such a right.

If we give up this foundation for the public's right to know, might it not be possible to say that the freedom of the press can, in itself, provide the needed justification for all that reporters do? This is certainly the assumption of many who have begun to doubt the solidity of the right to know. Whatever the errors and abuses by reporters, they argue, the freedom of the press and of speech more generally must be protected against every inroad. Yet this assumption is too hasty. Even in the law, certain excesses are prohibited. And a *legal* right to free expression cannot do away with the need for *moral* scruples in choosing what to publish. Consider a derisive and condescending newspaper article about rape victims, complete with photographs and addresses acquired against their will. A reporter might not go to jail for publishing it, but he should nevertheless consider the moral reasons against publication before going ahead. He could not reasonably argue that the public has a right to such information; nor could he legitimately ignore the effects of his story on those already violated. . . .

For a circumscribed category of information . . . we no longer speak of some indiscriminate and vague public right to know, but of a clear legal right. It is the statutory right of the public to know about its government, expressed by the United States Congress in establishing the Freedom of Information Act. . . . For the great majority of government records, Congress held, "the public as a whole has a right to know what its government is doing."[16]

Long before such a law was enacted, this right was advocated as a means of limiting executive and legislative secrecy. In 1747, at a time of complete legislative secrecy in England, the *London Magazine* stated: "Every subject not only has the right, but is duty bound, to inquire into the public measures pursued."[17] And in the American Colonies, where equal secretiveness prevailed, the issue was similarly joined as one of whether the people did or did not have a right to know about government.

Such a right to know does correspond to a duty to reveal: the government has the duty to reveal that which the public has a right to know. In the same way, doctors have the duty not to withhold the information to which their patients have a right. Just as it is wrong to keep certain secrets from individuals, so it is wrong to keep some information from the public—about the misconduct of a war, for example, or the use of taxpayers' money for an official's private gain. But neither physicians nor governments have a duty to provide indiscriminate disclosure of all possible information.

Unlike the patient's right to information, the public's right to know about government activities can rarely be satisfied directly. To be sure, some can have direct access to certain information, or request it in person; but most people must rely on the media as indispensable intermediaries. As a result, the public's right to know about government does require a free press and access by the press to congressional and other deliberations.

But the public clearly has an equally legitimate interest in matters far beyond the domain of government. Unsafe private housing developments are of public concern fully as much as unsafe public housing; and the marketing of automobiles that are firetraps matters as much to the public as if the government were responsible for them. Indeed, it has become increasingly hard to draw a clear line between government information and information about the private sector. Commercial secrecy and scientific secrecy now blend with military secrecy in ways hardly imaginable by the early advocates of the public's right to know about government. And administrative secrecy now covers agencies and categories of persons and information to an extent equally difficult to foretell.

In addition, many countries have no statutorily guaranteed *right* of knowledge about government affairs; yet the public in those countries clearly has as great, and as legitimate, an *interest* in government action as elsewhere, and the press,

therefore, as strong a mandate to inform the public. Indeed, quite apart from one's country of residence, societies are now so dependent upon one another's fortunes that the public in each has a legitimate interest in the affairs of all the others. Thus the publics in the many countries without nuclear weapons can hardly be said to have less to lose from the production of such weapons in other states than the inhabitants of these states themselves. When the governments of the United States, the Soviet Union, England, France, and China chose in secret to develop such weapons, not only were citizens in their countries deprived of their right to debate the choices that were to affect their future so profoundly; people the world over were equally deprived of an opportunity to influence their own fate.

For these reasons, it would be wrong merely to cling to a legalistic notion of a statutory right to know about the affairs of one's government. Rather, the role of the press should be to satisfy in the first place the public's legitimate interest in learning about matters—governmental or not—that affect its welfare. The reporting concerning such matters should be forceful; and it should not accede to all the claims we have examined: to privacy, confidentiality, or trade, scientific, administrative, and military secrecy. At times these shields are legitimate; but their legitimacy cannot be taken for granted. The inherent secretiveness of governments and all other institutions calls for the greatest vigilance on the part of the media.

Some hold that the vigilance must be of an adversary nature—that there can be no truce between politicians and the press.[18] This goes too far, since adversary relations engender so many biases of their own. They lead too easily, as I have shown, to the adoption of quasi-military rationales that blur moral choice. And the adversary posture of one side only intensifies that of the other. Rather than celebrate such a posture as a model, the media might strive for one of vigilant objectivity with respect both to government rationales and to their own. The co-optation that is an ever-present danger can come not only from establishment groups but from opposition groups, even from the journalistic fraternity itself.

To sum up: The public's right to know, even where protected by statute, cannot be a right to knowledge or truth, but at best to access to information; and not to all information, but only to some. The public has a legitimate interest, however, in all information about matters that might affect its welfare, quite apart from whether a right to this information can be established. If the press is to fulfill its public mandate, it should provide the greatest possible public access to this broad range of information. In addition, journalists also report on much that is of interest to the public, not because of any need for information, but rather to satisfy curiosity. Such reporting is equally legitimate, but it requires special attention to individual privacy. It is in this respect that the story about Sidis went too far; and though its publication did not violate any law, no public right or need gave moral warrant to carry it through without securing William Sidis's consent.

We cannot know whether Sidis was interviewed without being informed that there would be a *New Yorker* article about him. Perhaps he did not even know that the young woman from whose interview Thurber drew his details *was* interviewing him for publication. If so, Sidis had reason to complain, not just about having been made the subject of an article against his will, but about the underhanded means used to acquire the information about him. It is to questions about the means of journalistic investigation that I want to turn next.

Reporters in Disguise

The reporter's role, like all others, masks the individual within and signals caution to outsiders. Reporters know that their very presence at a meeting, if known, alters that meeting. Participants are on their guard; many play to the gallery, and consider how the public will respond to the interpretation of what they do or say. And all who have something to hide are doubly cautious when they talk to journalists. The desire is therefore strong for reporters not to appear as reporters in order to catch those they study off guard, to unmask them or see beneath the appearances, to reach to "real" individuals, plans, and activities.

One way for reporters to disguise their intentions is to appear merely as anonymous participants. Another is to assume a new and different role. This can be done through a quick lie, as when a reporter gives a false name to secure entry to a gathering of celebrities or to the signing of a peace treaty. It can also be done by means of the most elaborate webs of deceit. Thus a group of reporters

for the *Chicago Sun-Times* bought and operated a bar—the Mirage—in 1977, in order to try to expose some of the payoffs, tax fraud, bribery, and illegal gun and liquor sales plaguing Chicago. With reporters working as bartenders, and others listening in and taking photographs from a hidden room, they gathered so much evidence that the authorities could hardly cope with all the indictments and investigations that ensued.[19] The scandal helped to unseat city officials and brought out countless reports of similar pressures for kickbacks and bribes by police, vending-machine operators, fire inspectors, and others. In this scheme, reporters assumed the investigative role of the police and indeed worked closely with certain police officials. In justification, those who sponsored the project held that the police could not cope with the pervasive corruption in the city, that the public was injured by not knowing enough to try to stop it, and that the persons who were profiting unfairly from the corrupt practices should be brought to trial.

Perhaps the best-known and most versatile master of disguise and infiltration for purposes of exposure is the German publicist Günter Wallraff. He has used every means of deceit and concealment in order to enter and explore secret domains. He has tricked the police into employing him as an informer infiltrating radical student groups, impersonated a guard in an insurance company in Cologne, and acted the part of a right-wing emissary of Franz-Joseph Strauss offering to arm and finance General Spinola's plot for a coup in Portugal. His books documenting these and other probes have sold throughout the world.[20]

Born in Cologne during World War II, Wallraff approaches his tasks with military precision and carefully mapped strategy. The enemy, for him, is the German state, and the press and bureaucracies and corporations that support it and feed on it. He has, therefore, a much more extensive mission of battle against corruption and coercion than the reporters who manned the Mirage bar in Chicago. He could never, as they did, let police officials know from the beginning about his plans. And to a much greater extent than they, he presupposes plots by the establishment to bring him down and to silence him.

Wallraff's most celebrated foray was the infiltration of the German tabloid *Bild-Zeitung*. Having exchanged his glasses for contact lenses, changed his way of combing his hair, bought an expensive suit, and changed his body language to give the impression of an ingratiating but ruthless careerist, he presented himself as "Hans Esser" for an interview with the local editor in Hanover. Hired as a free-lance editor, he saw from within how stories were forced out of unwilling witnesses, exaggerated, given the right political slant, sometimes made up from whole cloth. The macabre, the monstrous, and the titillating were extracted from everyday occurrences; and neither employees nor those interviewed were spared in the pressure for sensational stories. Social criticism was edited out of his articles, sexual innuendo brought in. Wallraff entered so wholly into his role that he made rapid progress. In his diary, he wrote of his constant fear of discovery and expressed his anxiety that he might be turning into the kind of person he portrayed.

> What is it really that changes? One goes through something, and there is always a residue, one cannot act as though one escaped completely unharmed. . . . it is as with smoking: one needs at least as long a time of not smoking to return to normal. Here one is also infected in some manner. One needs a long time. But what is it that has changed? Perhaps one is somewhat more coldblooded from now on, more hardboiled, colder toward many, and can feel aloof from things more easily. Much that earlier would have caused horror does not touch one anymore. One says: I don't see the story.[21]

As if to set his books apart from all his dissembling toward others and from the falsified stories he wrote while working for the *Bild-Zeitung*, Wallraff has gone to unusual lengths to insist on the truthfulness of his reporting. "Of course," he wrote in the preface to the book describing that experience, "nothing is either invented or fabricated."[22]

Such assurances are not unusual among journalists who undertake infiltrative reporting; the stealthier their methods of probing, the more forcefully they proclaim honesty and accuracy in reporting. It is as if they asked to be judged solely by what they say in print, not by what they do to investigate. But when a reporter infiltrates a newspaper, as Wallraff did, and writes misleading stories in order to maintain his disguise, the difficulty is compounded. He can no longer draw the distinction

between honest writing and deceptive action. And, as his diary excerpt shows, he feared being changed by the false role he lived. Just as one looks at others differently once one knows them to be smooth and experienced liars, so one's view of oneself may alter. For purposes of self-respect, it may then become especially important to set aside some aspect of one's work or some relationships in which one holds oneself to the highest standards.

To escape from the pressure of impersonating Hans Esser, Wallraff would take a few days off now and then, and spend time with friends in whom he confided and with whom he could be himself. He knew, he wrote, that many of them conveyed the secret to still others in spite of promises of confidentiality, and was pleased that, "during four months, nothing came out to the other side, that no one betrayed me for money or advancement."[23]

Abruptly, his cover was broken. A friend warned him that a small left-wing magazine was about to publish the news that Günter Wallraff was working for the *Bild-Zeitung* under the name of Hans Esser. Wallraff failed to show up for work the next day, and the newspaper chain, accusing him of a warped personality and "crypto-Communism," brought suit for "false impersonation and unauthorized use of title." The suit was lost, but the debate over Wallraff's methods continued in the media. Were they justified? And did the justification depend in part on one's view of what Wallraff meant to expose?

Wallraff goes to unusual lengths in answering such questions in his book. To begin with, he dismisses criticism from his opponents, arguing that they have forfeited all credibility in complaining about his deceptive methods. They are themselves so steeped in deceit and coercion, he holds, that they can hardly object to his dissimulation without the most contemptible hypocrisy. But by itself, this argument does nothing to justify his methods; certain critics may have ruled themselves out as credible judges by their own behavior; but Wallraff must, if he is to justify his methods, confront also the standards of persons he would recognize as more objective.

A second argument is meant to do so; it points to the disparity between his own small deceits and the vast conspiracies of coercion and manipulation they are mustered to combat. "I decided to conspire in order to take a look over the wall of camouflage, denials, and lies. The method I adopted was only slightly illegal by comparison with the illegal deceptions and maneuvers that I unmasked," Wallraff argues.[24] His job was "to deceive in order not to be deceived—to break the rules of the game in order to disclose the secret rules of power."[25]

By itself, this argument is also insufficient. No matter how deceitful or lawless the powers that Wallraff hoped to unmask, he might well agree that ordinary reportorial means should be preferred whenever possible. A third argument comes to the support of the preceding two: it claims necessity. Because his opponents are so powerful and so closely linked in a vast conspiracy with state, industry, and the military, no alternative method, according to this argument, can succeed. Anyone who is serious about the mission of unmasking must therefore use disguise and deceit. A sense of urgency comes to underline the need for such methods. The social crisis requires rapid action, by whatever means.

This argument resembles those made for deceit in war. Ordinary channels of correction and control have broken down; law and morality cannot be counted upon; more primitive principles come into operation, justifying actions with claims such as "All is fair in love and war." Such an argument requires for its effectiveness a sure belief in the hostility of those one combats and in the depth of their evil. And it explains the constant use of military language even in schemes that are not otherwise of a military nature.

Arguments of this kind are sometimes to the point, but they are peculiarly likely to function as rationalization. They obscure reasoning and invite bias of every kind. They often exaggerate the crisis at hand and the conspiratorial nature of opponents, and they underestimate the adequacy of other methods of investigation. Wallraff could not, in effect, demonstrate either conspiracy or crisis in the newspaper he was investigating, nor show why the many shabby practices that he uncovered could be exposed only by means of infiltration. For journalists as for social scientists and other probers, the infiltrator is often seeking a shortcut for which the more experienced have no need.

There are nevertheless cases of abuse so serious, and kept so secret, that few methods short of deceptive ones would be capable of the exposure that is clearly needed. Exploitative migrant-labor camps or substandard homes for the aged may exclude all investigators save those who gain entry under false colors. Can reporters claim to be justified, at such times, in presenting false papers of employment and identity in order to witness the abuses from within?

Even in such cases, while it may be true that reporters have no open means of investigation, public authorities do. Because journalists lack means such as subpoenas or search warrants, they may be tempted more often to resort to deceit. As a *Los Angeles Times* reporter is said to have remarked after posing as an animal keeper in a zoo, an employee in a juvenile detention facility, an oil pipeline worker in Alaska, and a doctor in a hospital emergency room:

> I'm a great believer in the reporter as observer. First-hand observation is the ultimate documentation. A reporter doesn't have a badge or subpoena power or . . . wiretap authority. He has to use his . . . wits. That's what I try to do. . . . Almost every big story I've done, I've had to impersonate someone.[26]

So long as the police or other public authorities are coping with the problem, it is not enough for journalists merely to show that *they* do not have methods of entry as satisfactory as infiltration. If the police can investigate openly what journalists must ferret out in disguise, the former have to be preferred. And even police undercover agents—though their methods are dangerous in their own right—are subject to more stringent regulation than the swarms of other investigators engaged in similar pursuits.

At times, however, the police either cannot or will not take part in the investigation. The government itself may be corrupt, or the police inefficient or overworked, sometimes even prevented from investigating a problem. In the Watergate affair, for instance, it would have been useless for journalists to seek police cooperation. When the government itself is at fault, or high officials within it, the justification earlier inferred from the public's right to know comes into play once again; the press's role as intermediary must then give way to a degree of probing and of suspicion ordinarily excessive.

If a group of editors and reporters have concluded that they see no alternative means and no alternative agencies of investigation to whom the probing of a particular problem can safely be left, they must still weigh the moral arguments for and against deceptive infiltration or other surreptitious methods. Knowing that such means are morally questionable, they must then ask whether their goal warrants the use of such methods. This would not be the case with respect to minor infractions. But once again, in the case of the Watergate investigation by the *Washington Post*, the issue was obviously of the highest importance. The reporters in that case did not use infiltrative means, and it is doubtful whether these would have worked, but they did resort to deception at times. Their book reveals no soul-searching on this score, and we cannot know whether the deception was necessary to uncovering the story.[27] If such a necessity could be shown, then the case would offer persuasive grounds for using limited deception.

Another consideration that newspaper or television editors should take seriously before going ahead even with clandestine investigations they consider important has to do with the effect on their own credibility and that of the media in general. They know that public confidence in media reliability is already low, and they recognize the existing pressure for rushed stories, forever incomplete, all too often exaggerated or misinterpreted. If the public learns about an elaborate undercover operation such as that of the Mirage bar, many may ask why they should have confidence in the published stories based on information acquired through such an elaborate hoax. The press can hardly afford to saddle itself with more grounds for mistrust; and this consideration should form part of editorial decision-making, even if it leads to the curtailment of an otherwise dramatic cover story.

The press and other news media rightly stand for openness in public discourse. But until they give equally firm support to openness in their own practices, their stance will be inconsistent and lend credence to charges of unfairness. It is now a stance that challenges every collective rationale for secrecy save the media's own. Yet the media serve commercial and partisan interests in addition to public ones; and media practices of secrecy, selective disclosure, and probing should not be exempt from scrutiny.

Without such scrutiny, the routine invocation of the public's right to know will combine with the fierce competition in news reporting to deflect questions about limits to what reporters and editors can do in pursuing their professional goals. And without such scrutiny, we shall see perpetuated the media's uneasy alliance with other forms of institutional secrecy—the dependency by certain insiders on favors granted by corporate and government executives, the over-reliance on leaks and on secret sources, and the silence about politically or commercially "sensitive" topics. Because the task of reporting the news is both an indispensable public resource and big business, and because of the great power now wielded by the media, a commitment to openness and to accountability is more necessary than ever.

Notes

1. James Thurber, *The Years with Ross* (Boston: Little, Brown & Co., 1957), 28, 210–12.

2. Jared L. Manley, "April Fool!" *The New Yorker*, August 14, 1937, 22–26.

3. Boris Sidis, *Philistine and Genius* (Boston: R. G. Badger, 1917), 113. Sidis also wrote *The Source and Aim of Human Progress* (Boston: R. G. Badger, 1919), as well as experimental studies of sleep, of "nervous ills," and of the psychology of suggestion.

4. For a discussion of the role of publicity in William Sidis's life, and of the education he received, see Kathleen Montour, "William Sidis, the Broken Twig," *American Psychologist* 32 (April 1977):265–79.

5. Manley, "April Fool!" p. 25. (The title refers to Sidis's April 1 birthdate.) The reader is not told by what stratagem the unnamed young woman managed to interview Sidis; it cannot have been by requesting an interview for the magazine in the normal manner, since his lawsuit would have had to be differently framed if he had consented to such a request.

6. 34 F. Supp. 19, 20 (S.D.N.Y. 1938). Sidis also sued for libel on account of a small inaccuracy and was actually awarded a small sum in compensation for libel, even though he lost his suit for invasion of privacy. For a discussion of the cases and their background, see Emile Karafiol, "The Right to Privacy and the Sidis Case," *Georgia Law Review* 12 (1978):513–38.

7. Thurber, *The Years with Ross*, 212.

8. *Sidis* v. *F–R Publishing Corp.*, 113 F.2d 806 (2d Cir. 1940).

9. Emile Karafiol suggested this formulation in a personal communication.

10. Obituary, *New York Times*, July 18, 1944, 21. Some have asserted that Sidis took his own life, but there is no clear evidence for such an assertion.

11. *New York Times*, October 31, 1965, 1, and November 1, 1965, 1.

12. See Dennis F. Thompson, "The Private Lives of Public Officials," in Joel Fleishman, Lance Liebman, and Mark Moore, eds., *Public Duties: The Moral Obligations of Government Officials* (Cambridge, Mass.: Harvard University Press, 1981), 221–48.

13. Society of Professional Journalists, Sigma Delta Chi, Code of Ethics, adopted 1926 and revised 1973. For an account of the teaching of journalistic ethics, see Clifford G. Christians and Catherine L. Covert, *Teaching Ethics in Journalism Education* (Hastings-on-Hudson, N.Y.: Hastings Center, 1980).

14. Laurence Tribe, "Accommodating Rights to Know, Rights Not to Know, Open Minds, and Closed Communities," *American Constitutional Law* (Mineola, N.Y.: Foundation Press, 1978), p. 675. See also Louis Henkin, "The Right to Know and the Duty to Withhold: The Case of the Pentagon Papers," *University of Pennsylvania Law Review* 120 (1971):271–80.

15. Ronald Dworkin, "Does the Public Have a Right to Know?" in U.S., Department of Health and Human Services, Ethics Advisory Board, *Appendix: The Request of the National Institutes of Health for a Limited Exemption from the Freedom of Information Act*, 1979.

16. U.S., Congress, Senate, 89th Cong., 1st sess., 1965, S. Rept. 813, p. 5.

17. Cited in James Russell Wiggins, *Freedom of Secrecy* (New York: Oxford University Press, 1964), 7.

18. See William L. Rivers, *The Adversaries: Politics and the Press* (Boston: Beacon Press, 1970).

19. Zay N. Smith and Pamela Zekman, *The Mirage* (New York: Random House, 1979).

20. Günter Wallraff, *Wallraff the Undesirable Journalist*, trans. Steve Gooch and Paul Knight (London: Pluto Press, 1978); *"Wir Brauchen Dich"* (Munich: Rütten & Loening Verlag, (1966); *Von einem der auszog und das Fürchten lernte* (Munich: Willi Weisman Verlag, 1970); *Neue Reportagen, Untersuchungen und Lehrbeispiele*, 1972; *Die Reportagen*, 1976; *Aufdeckung einer Verschwoerung*, 1976; and *Der Aufmacher: Der Mann, der bei Bild Hans Esser war*, 1977 (the last four published at Cologne: Verlag Kiepenheuer & Witsch).

21. Wallraff, *Der Aufmacher*. p. 223 (my translation).

22. Ibid., 10.

23. Ibid., 224.

24. Quoted in *Wallraff the Undesirable Journalist*, p. 8 (from his testimony at an earlier trial).

25. Ibid. 2–3. It is not clear whether the author of this statement is Wallraff speaking in the third person about himself, or an unidentified other.

26. David Shaw, "Deception—Honest Tool of Reporting," *Los Angeles Times*, September 20, 1979, 29.

27. Bernstein and Woodward, *All the President's Men*. See also David Anderson and Peter Benjaminson, *Investigative Reporting* (Bloomington: Indiana University Press, 1976), chap. 2; John L. Hulteng, *The Messenger's Motives: Ethical Problems of the News Media* (Englewood Cliffs, N.J.: Prentice–Hall, 1976); Paul N. Williams, *Investigative Reporting and Editing* (Englewood Cliffs, N.J.: Prentice–Hall, 1978), chap. 5.

Review and Discussion Questions

1. Do you agree with the court's decision in the *Sidis* case? Was Thurber wrong to have written the article?

2. Does the public have a "right to know"? What, in Bok's view, is the legitimate social role of the press?

3. How would you assess the investigative journalism of Günter Wallraff? Do you agree with Bok that journalists should not use infiltration or disguise to investigate what the police or other public authorities are capable of dealing with?

4. Design a code of ethics for journalists.

For Further Reading

A good, general guide to the subject, and one on which this chapter has relied, is **Michael D. Bayles,** *Professional Ethics* (Belmont, Calif.: Wadsworth, 1981.) Another useful introduction is **Alan H. Goldman,** *The Moral Foundations of Professional Ethics* (Totowa, N.J.: Rowman and Littlefield, 1980), which has chapters on the different professions.

For more on the moral issues facing specific professions, the following collections of articles are recommended: **David Luban,** ed., *The Good Lawyer* (Totowa, N.J.: Rowman and Allanheld, 1983); **Samual Gorovitz,** et al., eds., *Moral Problems in Medicine* (Englewood Cliffs, N.J.: Prentice-Hall, 1976); **Robert J. Baum** and **Albert Flores,** eds., *Ethical Problems in Engineering*, 2nd ed., 2 vols. (Troy, N.Y.: Center for the Study of the Human Dimensions of Science and Technology, 1980); and **Martin Snoeyenbos, Robert Almeder,** and **James Humber,** eds., *Business Ethics* (Buffalo: Prometheus, 1983), chapter 6, "Ethics and the Accounting Profession."

INDEX